DYNAMIC HUMA

Patrick O'Dwyer, Barry Brunt & Charles Hayes

What you need to study for Leaving Certificate Geography:

Higher Level students must cover *six* sections of this book:

1.   The Physical Environment (chapters 1-17)
2.   Regional Geography (chapters 18-36)
3.   Maps and Photographs (chapters 37-38)
4.   The Human Environment (chapters 39-64)
5.a Culture and Identity (chapters 65-85)
     or
5.b Geoecology (chapters 86-91)
6.   Fieldwork Investigation (chapter 92)

Ordinary Level students must cover *five* sections of this book:

1.   The Physical Environment (chapters 1-17)
2.   Regional Geography (chapters 18-36)
3.   Maps and Photographs (chapters 37-38)
4.   The Human Environment (chapters 39-64)
5.   Fieldwork Investigation (chapter 92)

DYNAMIC HUMAN GEOGRAPHY

Patrick O'Dwyer,
Barry Brunt & Charles Hayes

GILL & MACMILLAN

Gill & Macmillan Ltd
Hume Avenue
Park West
Dublin 12
with associated companies throughout the world
www.gillmacmillan.ie

© Patrick O'Dwyer, Barry Brunt & Charles Hayes
Authors:
Patrick O'Dwyer: chapters 1-17, 37-85, and chapter 92.
Barry Brunt: chapters 18-36.
Charles Hayes: chapters 86-91.

Artwork by Design Image, Dublin

978 07171 41192 0

Colour reproduction by Typeform Repro, Dublin
Print origination in Ireland by Design Image, Dublin

The paper used in this book is made from the wood pulp of managed forests. For every tree felled,
at least one tree is planted, thereby renewing natural resources.

CONTENTS

Maps and Photographs

The Human Environment

Acknowledgments

The authors are especially appreciative of the many people who were directly involved in the preparation, design and publication of this book. Special thanks are due to Hubert Mahony, Aoileann O'Donnell and Helen Thompson of Gill & Macmillan, to Picot Cassidy who was a critical and effective editor and to Kristin Jensen for proofreading. Dara O'Doherty and her team at Design Image are thanked for their creative design of the book.

Thanks are also due to geography teachers from many schools throughout Ireland who offered valuable insights on and inputs to the text. In particular, the authors acknowledge the contributions of Ms Una Nation, St Mary's High School, Midleton, Co. Cork in revising the content and layout of this book.

Patrick O'Dwyer would like to thank the Department of Geography at Maynooth and Edel Carmody at St Joseph's Secondary School, Doon, Co. Limerick for their advice and support.

Charles Hayes would like to thank the members of the AGTI, whose advice and support have been invaluable. Sincere thanks also to Baby Milk Action, Jacinta Brack, Sandra Carroll, Christian Aid, Citizen Traveller, Comhlamh, Concern, Corporate Watch, Debt and Development Coalition (Ireland), *The Ecologist* (London), East Cork Area Development Ltd, Fairtrade Mark (Ireland), Eugene Fraser, *The Independent* (London), International Baby Food Action, *The Irish Examiner*, *The Irish Times*, Irish Traveller Movement, Catherine Joyce, Joe Kelly of IRD Kiltimach Ltd, Anne Kinsella, Tom McGrath, Marine Current Turbines, John Mulcahy, *Multinational Monitor* (Boston), *New Internationalist*, Finbarr O'Connell, Kevin O'Dwyer, Crissie O'Sullivan, Pavee Point, Kathleen Regan, Conor Ryan, Jill Ryan, Martyn Turner, Richard Wilson, *Time*, Traveller Visibility Group and Trócaire.

Barry Brunt wishes to thank his colleagues in the Department of Geography and the staff of the Official Publications Section of the Library at UCC for their advice and support in researching and writing this text.

In addition, many other individuals and institutions provided access to a range of essential data and information. Included in this are: Bord na Móna; Bord Iascaigh Mhara; Central Statistics Office; Coillte; Cork and Dublin City Councils; Departments of Agriculture and Food, Education and Science, Finance, Foreign Affairs, Justice, Marine and Natural Resources; Electricity Supply Board; Fáilte Ireland Tourism; Ford Ireland; Forfás and IDA Ireland; and Wyeth Medica (Ireland).

THE PHYSICAL ENVIRONMENT

CHAPTER 1
THE PLANET EARTH

KEY IDEA! The ability of the earth's crust to move about produces forces that create different rock layers within the earth.

The planet earth is some 4.6 billion years old. It formed from a cloud of dust that became molten from the impact of meteorites crashing into it. As the earth cooled, heavier materials sank and lighter materials stayed at the surface, forming the different layers of the earth's crust. **The earth is still cooling, and its molten rock continues to rise from its core to the crust.** This liquid rock brings heat to the surface to be released, so the earth does not overheat.

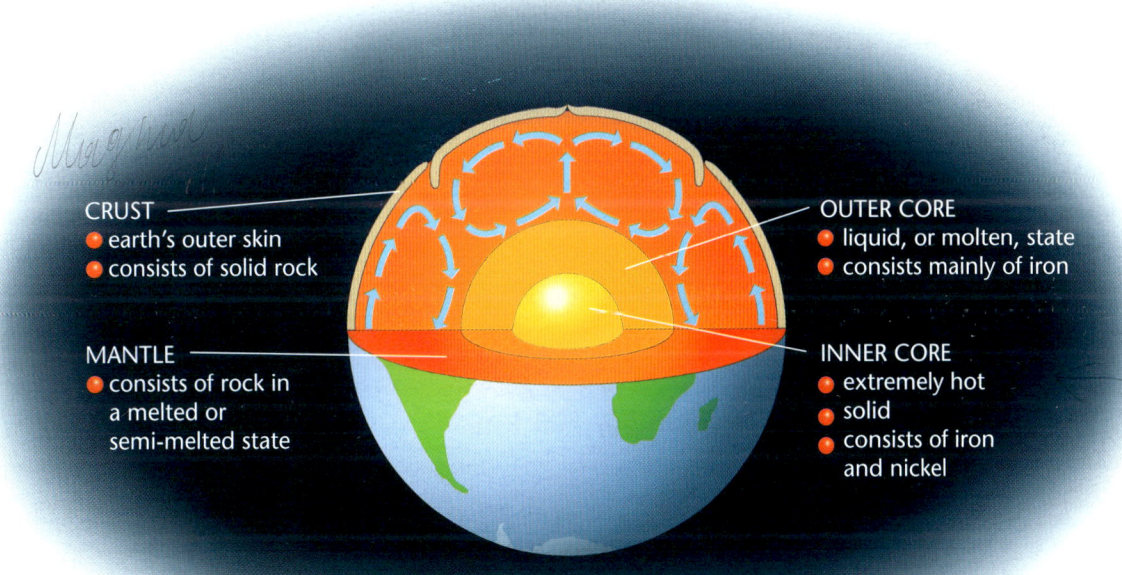

CRUST
- earth's outer skin
- consists of solid rock

MANTLE
- consists of rock in a melted or semi-melted state

OUTER CORE
- liquid, or molten, state
- consists mainly of iron

INNER CORE
- extremely hot
- solid
- consists of iron and nickel

Fig. 1.1 A section through the earth.

The rising molten rock forms **convection currents** that create earthquakes, volcanoes and mountain ranges that shape our lands and seas. Convection currents move slowly through the underlying mantle rock. Over millions of years, rock can flow like glacier ice, and it moves about as fast as our fingernails grow.

convection currents

Fig. 1.2 Convection currents in a heated pot.

1

The Earth's Crust

The earth's crust has two parts:

- The continental crust, which is formed of light rocks called sial.
- The ocean floor, which consists of basalt and is called sima.

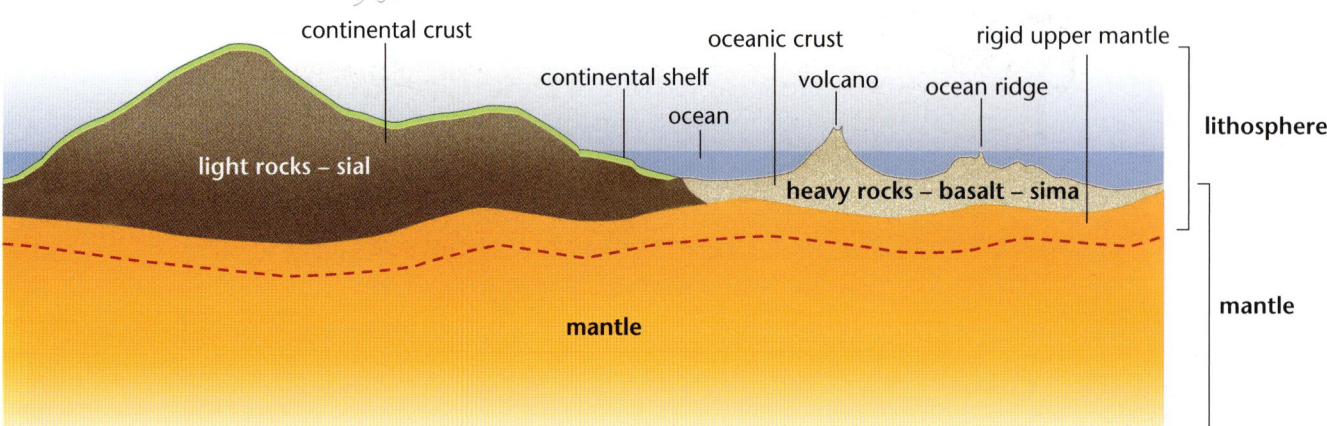

Fig. 1.3

Lithosphere

Crust 0–50 km

Continental Crust

The continental crust is **thick**. It averages between 35 and 40 km thick and is up to 70 km in thickness under the mountain ranges. The rocks that form the continental crust are **light** in weight.

Ocean Crust

The ocean crust is **thin**; it averages 8 km in thickness, but may be as thin as 3 km in some places. The rock forming the ocean crust is basalt, which is **heavy**.

Rigid Upper Mantle 50–100 km

The upper mantle is made up of rigid (inflexible) rocks. The continental crust + ocean crust + rigid upper mantle = lithosphere.

Mantle

Mantle 100–2,900 km

The mantle lies between the crust and the core. It consists of semi-molten (melted) rock that moves in convection currents. The plates of the earth's crust are carried about on these slow-moving convection currents.

Core

Core

At the centre of the earth is the heaviest of the three layers, the **core**. The core is composed mainly of **iron** with some **nickel**.

CHAPTER 2
GLOBAL CRUSTAL PLATE MOVEMENT

KEY IDEA!

The earth's crust is divided into plates, which are all in motion. Some plates are **moving apart** and some plates are **colliding**, while others are **sliding** past each other.

There are two types of plates:

- **Ocean plates,** which form the deep ocean floors.
- **Continental plates,** which form the continents and continental shelves.

These huge crustal plates of rock at the surface **float** on the layer of **heavier, 'plastic-like' rock underneath**, called the mantle. The plates on the surface move in relation to each other, carried along by **convection currents** within the mantle. To us, this movement may seem slow, but in terms of geological time it is fast. These movements cause **folding, faulting, volcanic activity** and **earthquakes**. This concept is known as plate tectonics and was first proposed by Alfred Wagner in 1915.

> What three parts form the lithosphere? Explain your answer.

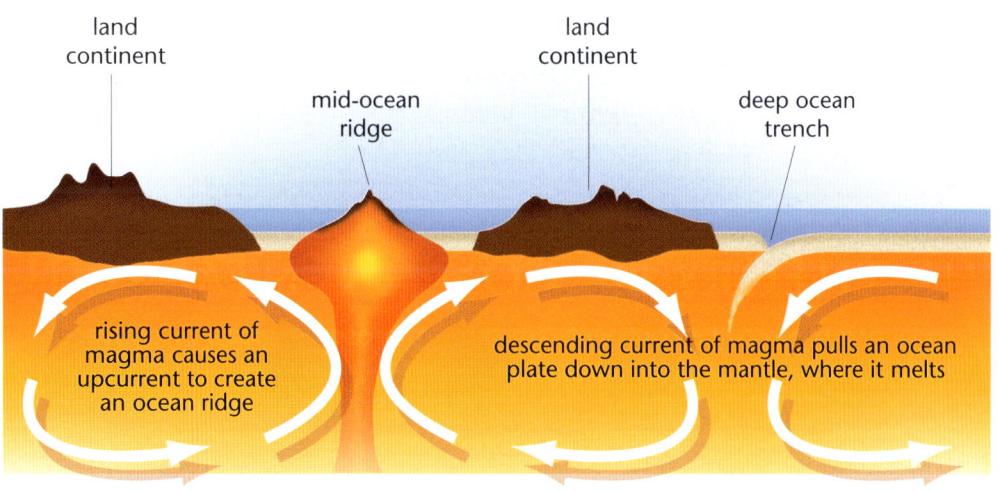

> On average, the ocean crust is about 8 km thick, while continents are between 35 and 40 km thick.

Fig. 2.1 Convection currents make the plates of the earth's crust move about.

Plate tectonics involves two theories:

- Sea floor spreading.
- Continental drift.

3

SEA FLOOR SPREADING

This suggests that ocean floors widen as **new rock** is formed at **mid-ocean ridges,** where continents were split apart originally. This new rock is then carried away from the ridge by **convection currents** within the mantle.

Fig. 2.2

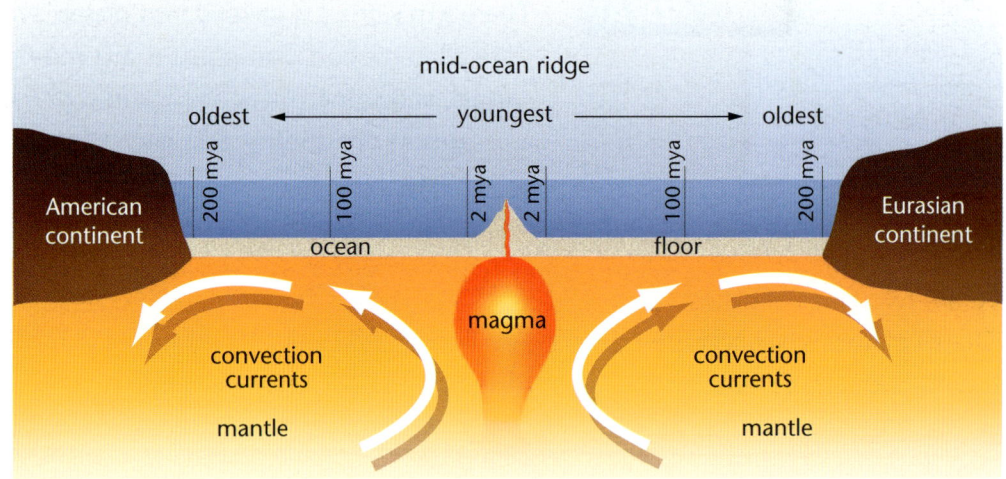

When hot magma cools on the sea floor at mid-ocean ridges, it adds new rock in equal proportions to both plates.

Some Proof of Sea Floor Spreading

- The existence of mid-ocean ridges.
- The varying ages of the sea floor – the age of the sea floor is youngest where new rock is formed along mid-ocean ridges and oldest along continental edges.
- Glacial deposits of similar types and ages are found in the areas where continents were attached before they drifted apart.
- Lasers and radio telescopes prove with unprecedented accuracy that continents are in motion.

THE THEORY OF CONTINENTAL DRIFT

Continental drift suggests the continents are carried **across the globe** by **convection currents** to locations where they **collide** with other continents. Here, the ocean floors in between are sucked into the mantle by the process of **subduction**. This allows the continents to collide.

Hot rock rises slowly from deep inside the earth and it cools, flows sideways and sinks. The rising hot rock and its sideways flow are believed to be the factors that control the positions of oceans and continents.

The Process of Subduction

Fig. 2.3

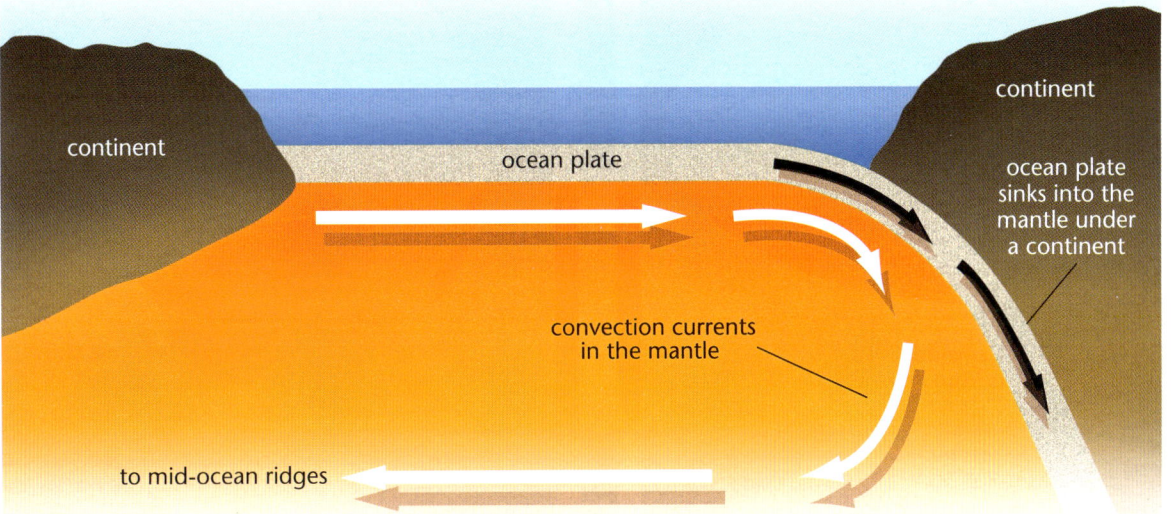

Proof of Continental Drift

- Matching rocks found on continents that are thousands of miles apart.
- Matching fossils that are found in precise locations in South America and Africa where the continents were once joined together.
- Matching edges of continents along the edges of the continental shelves that fit together like a jigsaw puzzle (for example, South America fits into West Africa).
- Mountains that were once part of the same mountain range are now found in North America, Greenland, Scandinavia, Britain and Ireland.

Fig. 2.4 Landmasses fit when they are placed in their pre-drift position.

The Movement of Continents and Ireland Over Time

The theory of continental drift suggests that the continents have moved great distances on the earth's surface and are still moving today. According to the theory, the continents once formed part of a single landmass, called Pangaea, which was surrounded by the world's single ocean, called Panthalassa. About 200 million years ago, Pangaea began to break apart. The formation of the present continents and their drift into their present positions took place gradually over millions of years (see Fig. 2.5).

Ireland's position on the globe has also changed over time. It was originally in two parts that eventually collided about 400 million years ago to form Britain and Ireland. Since then, it has migrated northwards from the southern hemisphere to its present location in the northern hemisphere.

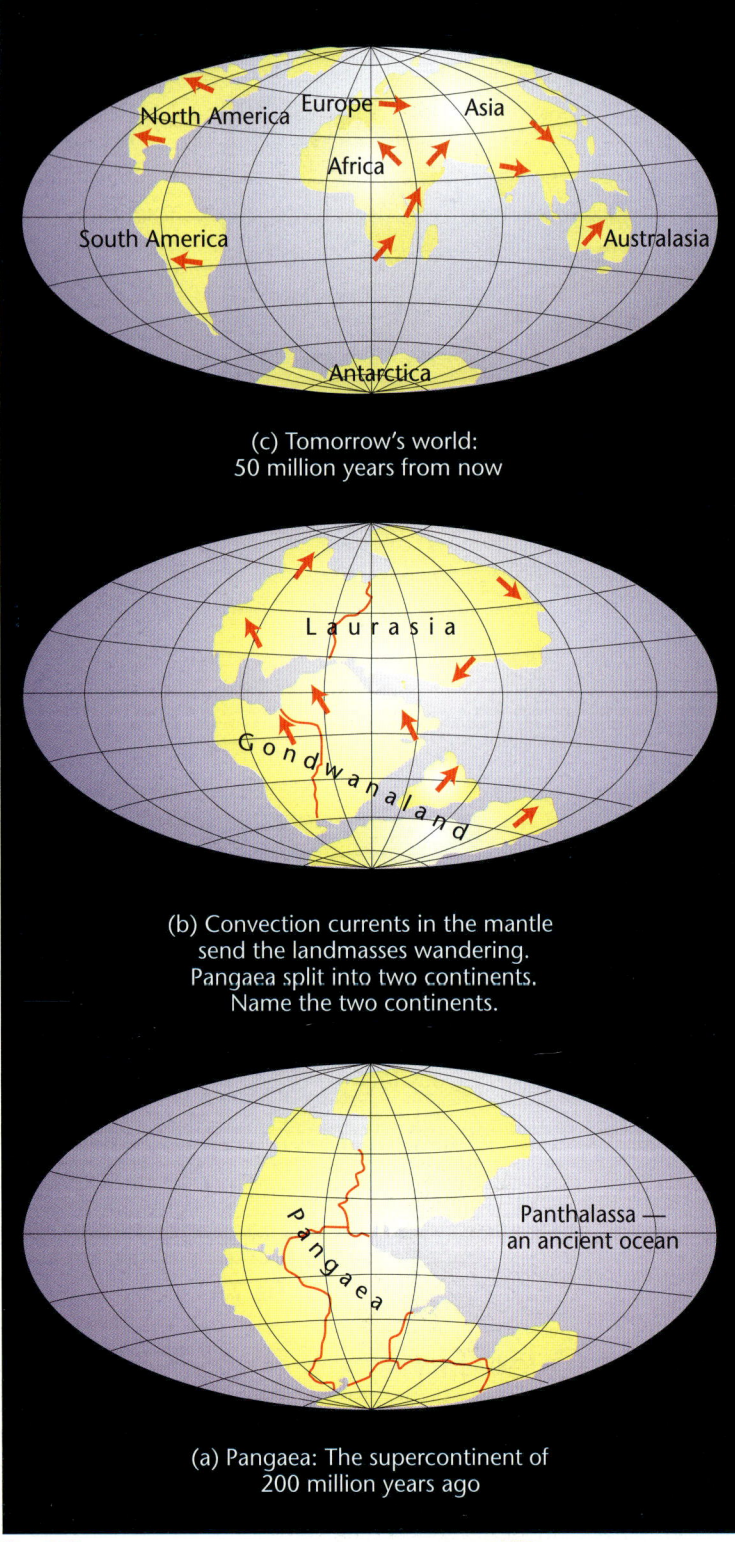

(c) Tomorrow's world:
50 million years from now

(b) Convection currents in the mantle
send the landmasses wandering.
Pangaea split into two continents.
Name the two continents.

(a) Pangaea: The supercontinent of
200 million years ago

Fig. 2.5

Ireland's present location

350 million years ago

west and northwest Ireland

south and east Ireland

500 million years ago

Fig. 2.6

Continents continue to
split apart today. Africa
is splitting apart along
the African Great Rift
Valley fault line.

The Global Distribution Of Plates

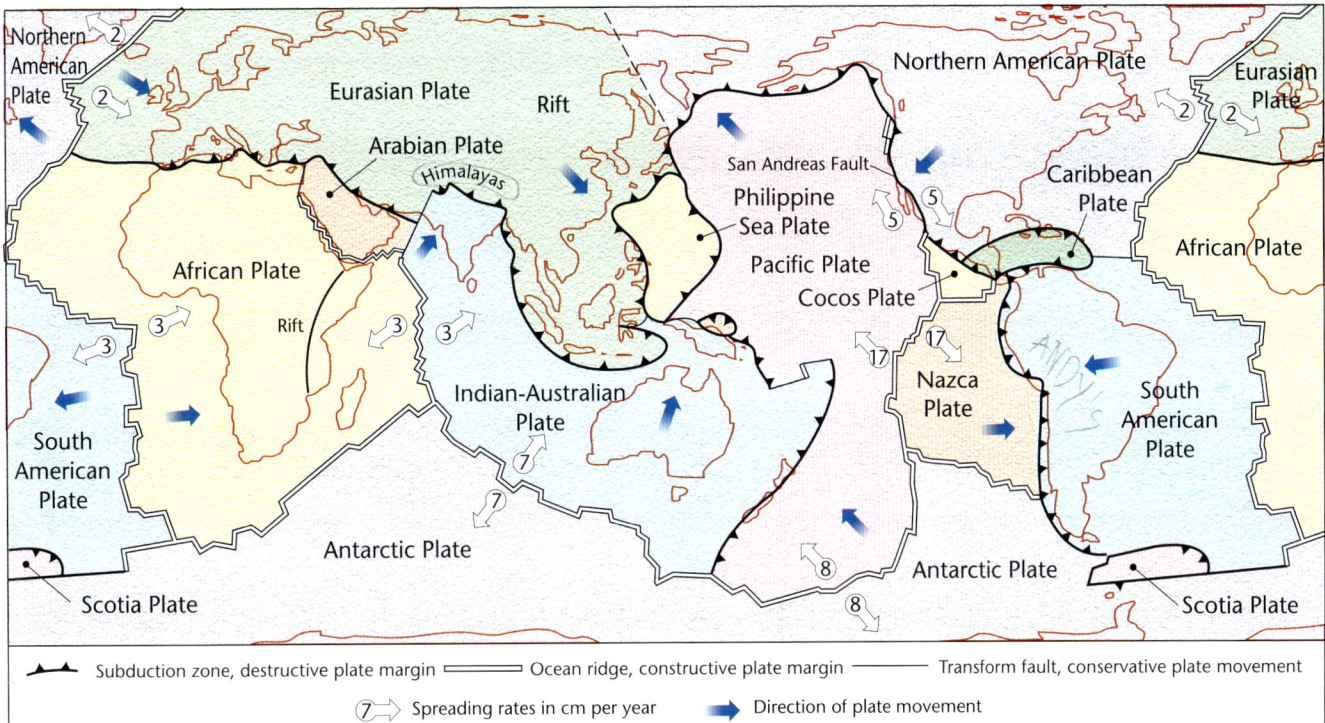

Fig. 2.7

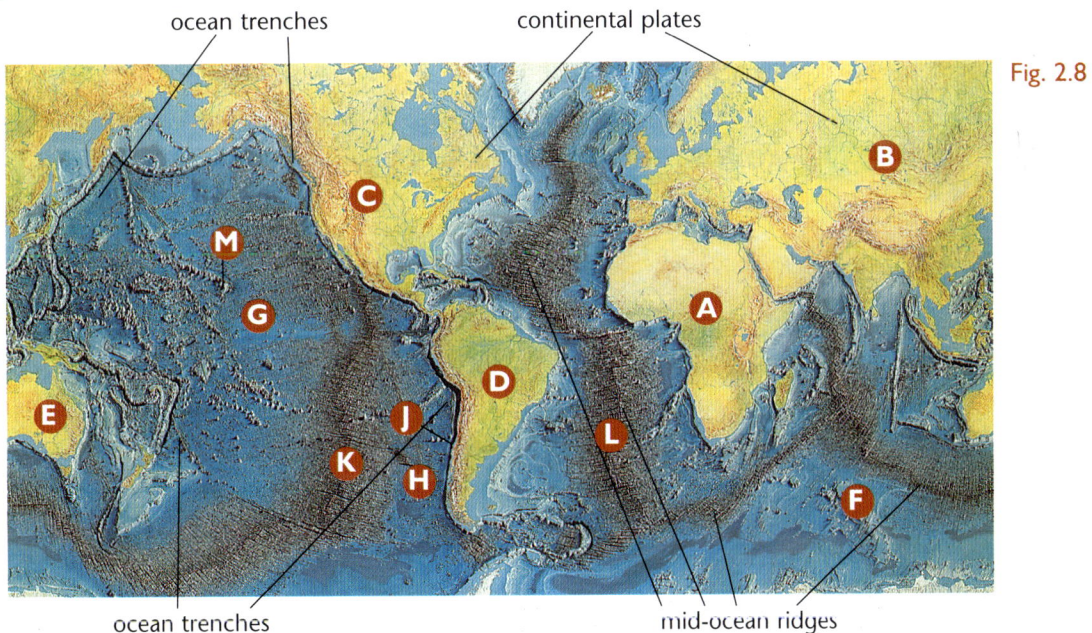

Fig. 2.8

CHAPTER 3
PLATE BOUNDARIES

 **KEY IDEA!**

Forces within the earth create, change and destroy rock and landforms where plates collide and separate.

See the school video *Written in Stone*.

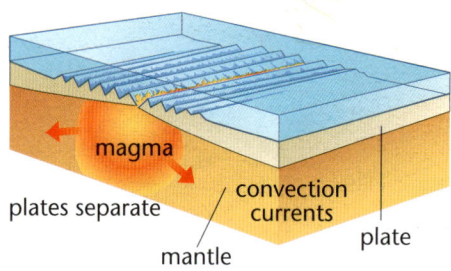

magma

plates separate

convection currents

mantle

plate

1. constructive

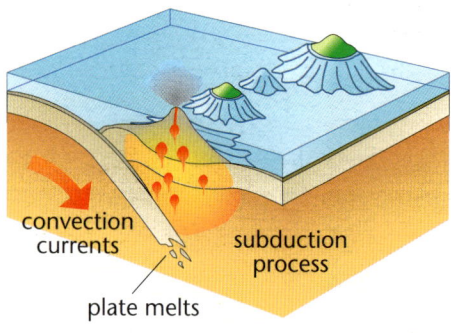

convection currents

subduction process

plate melts

2. destructive

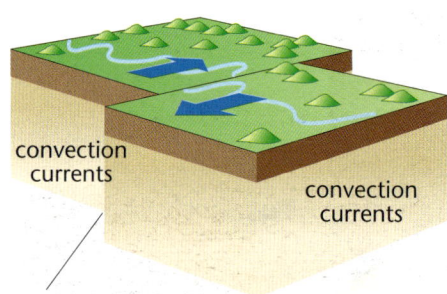

convection currents

convection currents

plates slide past each other along the transform fault

3. passive

Fig. 3.1

TYPES OF PLATE BOUNDARIES

At plate boundaries, rock and rock structures are formed, changed or destroyed. There are three types of plate boundaries.

Boundaries of Construction (Divergent Boundaries)

Here, new rock is formed to create mid-ocean ridges. Plates formed from this new rock separate and move away from each other. Example: The Mid Atlantic Ridge.

Boundaries of Destruction (Convergent Boundaries)

Here, rock is **destroyed** or **changed**. There are three types of destructive boundaries:

- Where two ocean plates collide, called **ocean-ocean**.
- Where an ocean plate and a continental plate collide, called **ocean-continent**.
- Where two continental plates collide, called **continent-continent**.

Where destruction occurs, an ocean plate sinks into the mantle beneath the other plate and melts. A deep **sea trench** is formed on the sea floor. This process is called **subduction**. Example: West coast of South America.

Passive Boundaries

Land is neither created nor destroyed at these boundaries. Plates simply **slide past each other.** Example: The San Andreas Fault.

Activity
1. With the aid of diagrams, explain why boundaries of construction are different from boundaries of destruction.
2. Explain why passive boundaries are different from both boundaries of construction and destruction.
3. Draw a labelled diagram to explain what happens when any two plates collide.

CONSTRUCTIVE PLATE BOUNDARIES
The Process of Rifting

The process of rifting includes continental break-up and the formation of mid-ocean ridges, new sea floor and new oceans.

A. A hot current of magma, called a plume, rises from the mantle towards the surface, stretches the crust of the continent and splits the continent. New volcanoes appear along the cracks at the surface. An example of this process in action is the East African Rift Valley, in eastern Africa.

B. Only two of the cracks widen and the continent splits into two new continental plates. Sea water floods into the new valley that forms in between. Hot magma rises from the mantle in the middle of the valley and cools quickly, forming basalt rock when it meets the cold sea water. This basalt forms the new sea floor, or ocean crust, and a mid-ocean ridge directly over the rising magma.

C. The plates continue to separate, widening the sea to form an ocean. As the continents move apart, their edges are no longer supported and they dip into the sea, forming shallow continental shelves.

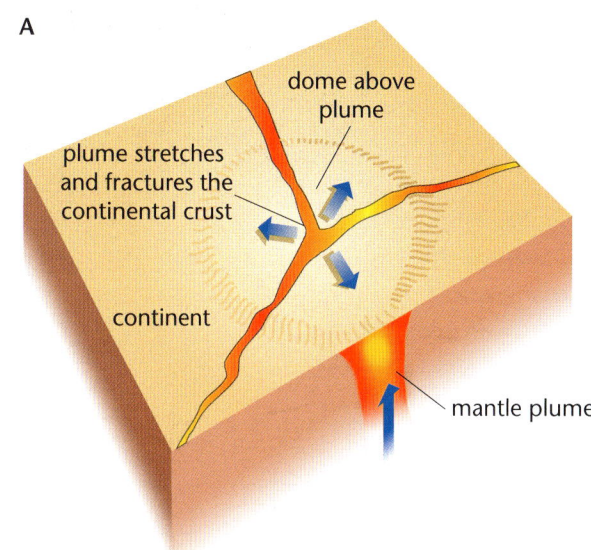

Fig. 3.2 Rifting of a continent.

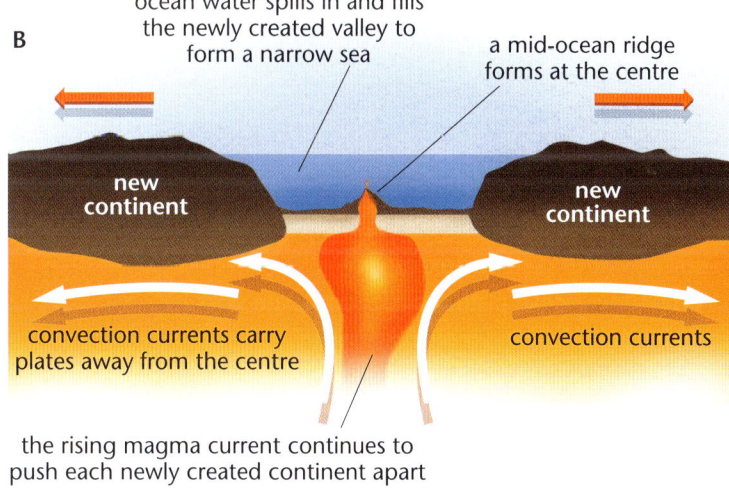

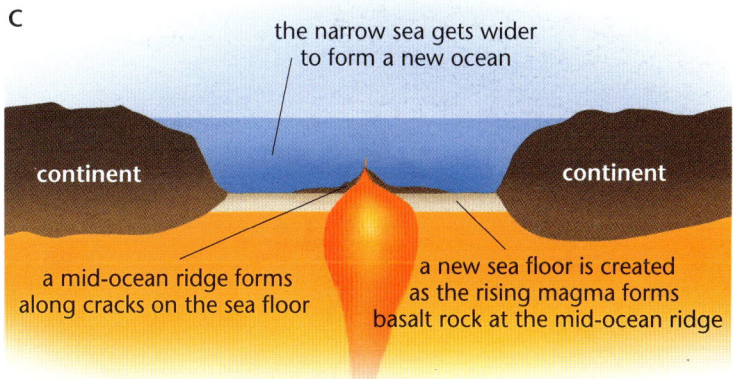

Fig. 3.3 Stages in the formation of a new sea floor, mid-ocean ridge and ocean.

Fig. 3.4 A mid-ocean ridge is not straight. It is offset by transform faults that allow newly created crust to adjust to the spherical (curved) shape of the earth.

9

DESTRUCTIVE PLATE BOUNDARIES
Ocean-Ocean Boundaries

Where two ocean plates collide, one plate is pulled under the other.

Volcanic island arcs form where two ocean plates meet. The Lipari Islands near Sicily, in Italy, also form an arc. The islands of Japan were formed when many volcanoes joined along an ocean-ocean boundary.

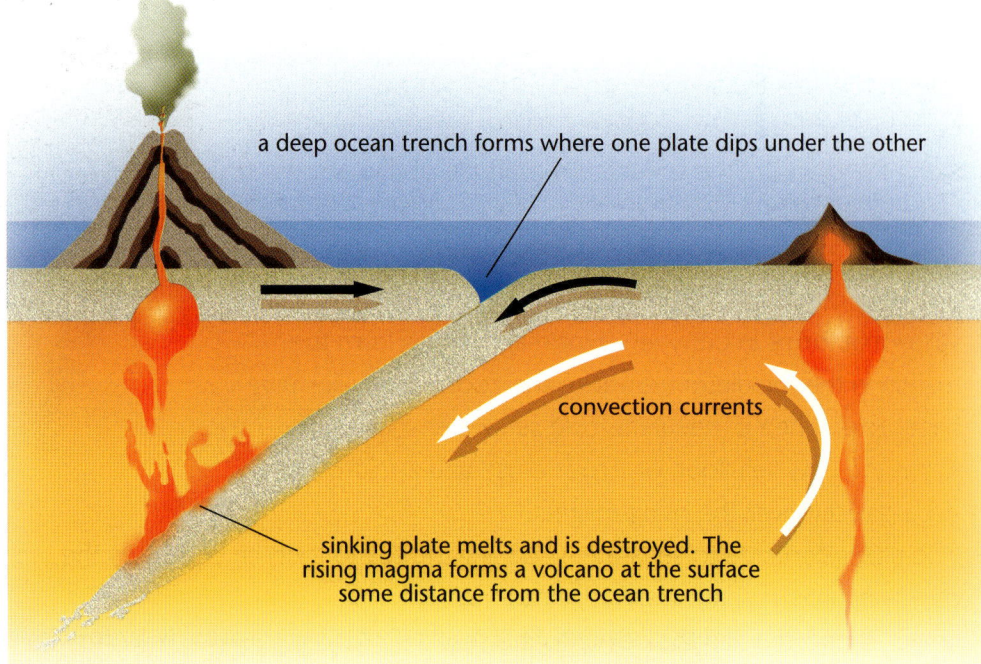

a deep ocean trench forms where one plate dips under the other

convection currents

sinking plate melts and is destroyed. The rising magma forms a volcano at the surface some distance from the ocean trench

Fig. 3.5

Student's Note:

Answers should always be written in the form of **significant relevant points (SRPs)**.

An **SRP** is a **significant relevant point,** or **statement of fact**. For example:
When two ocean plates collide, one plate sinks under the other and melts.

or

A deep ocean trench forms where one ocean plate sinks under another ocean plate.

- The descending plate bends downwards, forming a deep, curved ocean trench. As the plate descends, it melts because:
  – Heat radiates from the hot magma in the mantle.
  – Heat increases due to compression (being squeezed).
- Because the descending plate is saturated with water, it melts quickly.
- Magma then rises and forms volcanic cones on the ocean floor. Dry land eventually emerges from the ocean depths to form an island arc, a curved string of islands parallel to the ocean trench.

Activity

1. Explain what happens when one ocean plate is pulled under another ocean plate.
2. What landform develops because of this process?
3. There are many island arcs in the Pacific Ocean. Name them.
4. Write six SRPs to explain how volcanoes occur at this type of boundary.

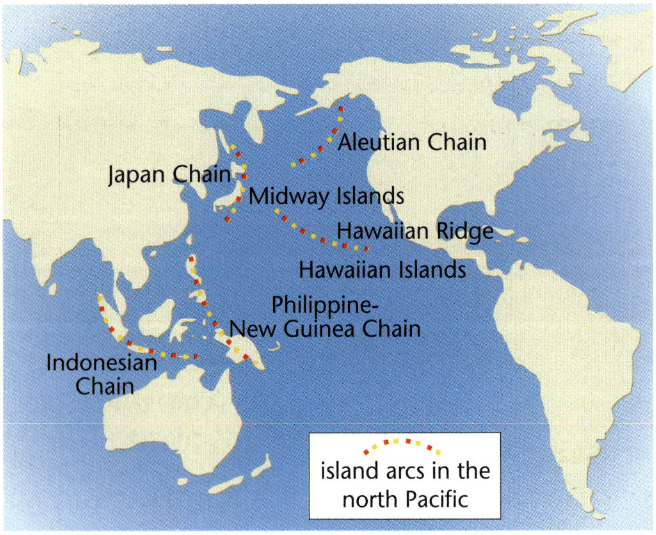

Aleutian Chain
Japan Chain
Midway Islands
Hawaiian Ridge
Hawaiian Islands
Philippine-New Guinea Chain
Indonesian Chain

island arcs in the north Pacific

Fig. 3.6 Island arcs in the Pacific Ocean.

Ocean-Continent Boundaries
Case Study: How the Rockies Were Formed

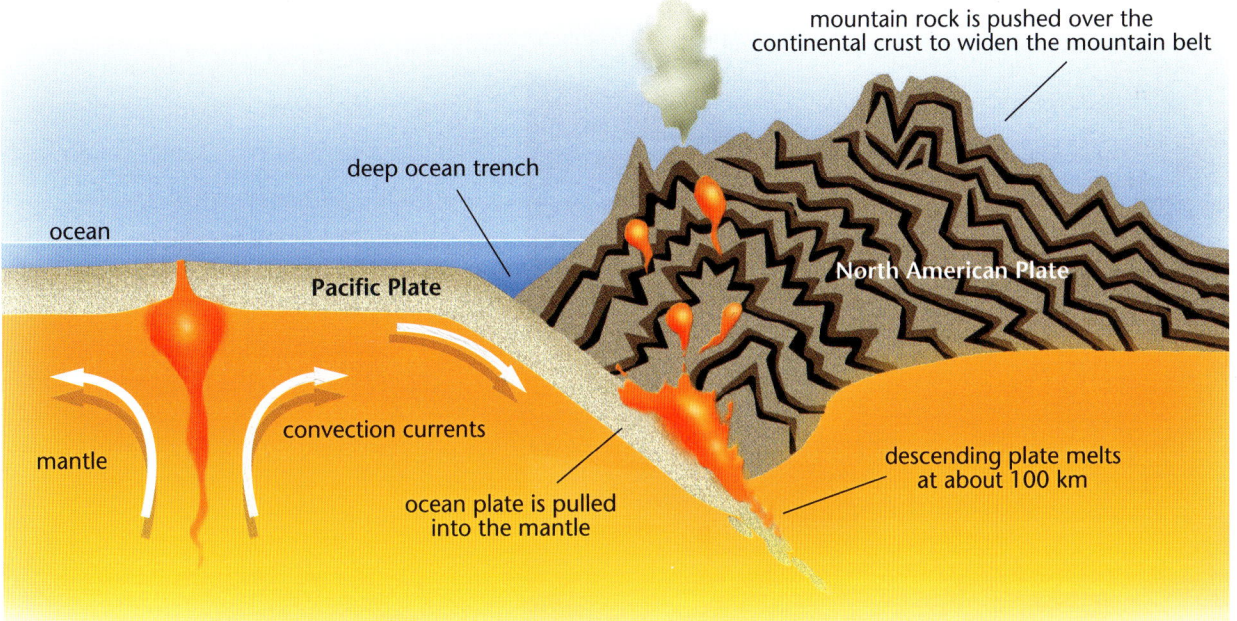

Fig. 3.7

mountain rock is pushed over the continental crust to widen the mountain belt

deep ocean trench

ocean

Pacific Plate

North American Plate

convection currents

mantle

descending plate melts at about 100 km

ocean plate is pulled into the mantle

When an ocean plate and a continental plate collide, the heavy ocean plate is pulled under the lighter continental plate. The ocean plate sinks into the **mantle** and **melts** at a depth of about 100 km. Magma rises to create volcanoes at the surface.

Meanwhile, the continental plate scrapes layers of sediment and islands off the descending ocean floor to form layers of rock along the seaward edge of the continent. Eventually these layers of rock are **compressed** (squeezed) and **folded** (buckled) to form fold mountains. In some places rock is **metamorphosed** (heated and changed). This has happened in the Rocky Mountains in North America, in the Andes in South America and in counties Donegal, Galway and Wicklow in Ireland.

Squeezing caused by the colliding plates causes **faulting**. Constant pressure over millions of years cracks the rock (faulting) and pushes some of it forward either horizontally or at a low angle for many kilometres, thus increasing the width and the thickness of the mountain belt. The faults created by this action are called **thrust faults** (see Chapter 8, page 50). Faults like these are found in the mountains of **Donegal**, such as the **Gweebarra Fault**, and the Rockies in North America.

MYA means millions of years ago.

intrusive
'Intrude' means 'enter by force'. Formed within the earth's crust.

Some ocean plates sink beneath other ocean plates.

Activity
1. Which two plates have collided to form:
   a. the Rockies
   b. the Andes?
2. What is a thrust fault?
3. How are some fold mountains formed? Explain using a labelled diagram.
4. Write six SRPs to explain the process that occurs at this type of boundary.

Continent-Continent Boundaries
Case Study: The Formation of Caledonian Fold Mountains 400 MYA

Stage 1

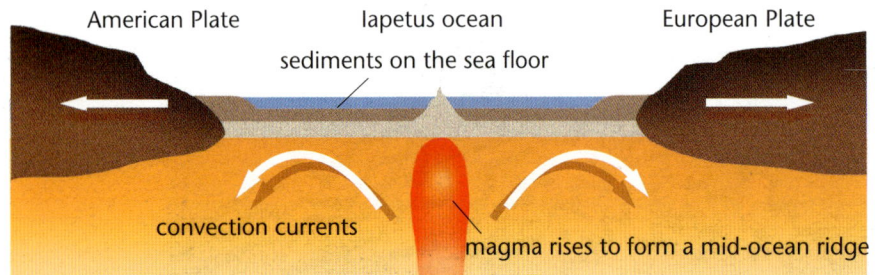

Stage 2

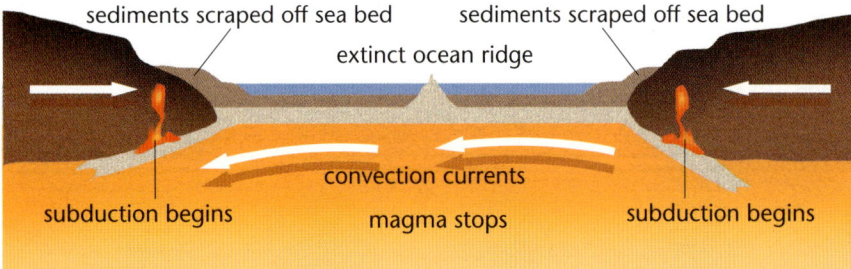

Stage 3

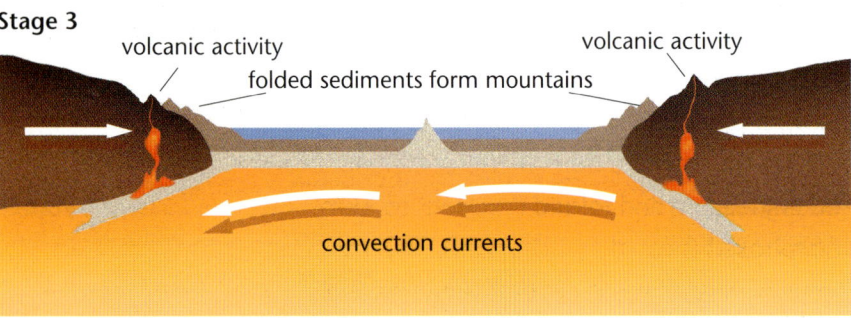

Stage 4

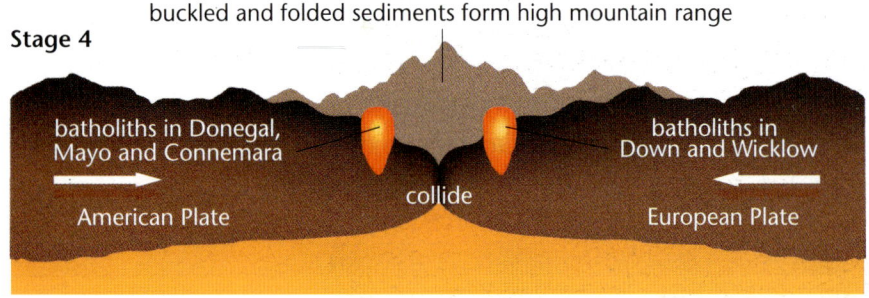

Fig. 3.8 The Iapetus Ocean disappeared and the Caledonian mountains were formed. These mountains included the mountains of Connemara, Mayo, Donegal, Down and Wicklow, the Scottish Highlands and the Scandinavian Highlands. These mountains tend to run north-east to south-west.

When two continental plates approach each other and collide, they will form a high fold mountain chain. Examples of fold mountains are the **Caledonian fold mountains of north-west Ireland, Scotland and Scandinavia** (see the activity on page 53.)

1. After the break-up of a continental landmass, seawater pours in to fill the area between the new continents and forms a new ocean. When this happens, new rock is created at a mid-ocean ridge to form an ocean floor, thus pushing the continents apart. Also, a thick wedge of sediment from erosion is deposited along each coastline.

2. For reasons not yet understood, at some stage the ocean basin begins to close. The continents approach each other and the ocean floor is pulled into the mantle. This starts a long period of volcanic activity and the creation of batholiths (see Fig. 5.9, page 29).

3. Eventually the continents collide. This event buckles, deforms or metamorphoses the rocks and trapped sediment washed in by rivers to form **fold mountains**. **Faulting and folding** of the trapped sediments occur in the fold mountains.

Activity
1. Explain what happens when continents approach each other.
2. Name two fold mountain chains that formed when continents collided.
3. Write eight SRPs explaining how the Caledonian fold mountains formed.

Passive Boundaries

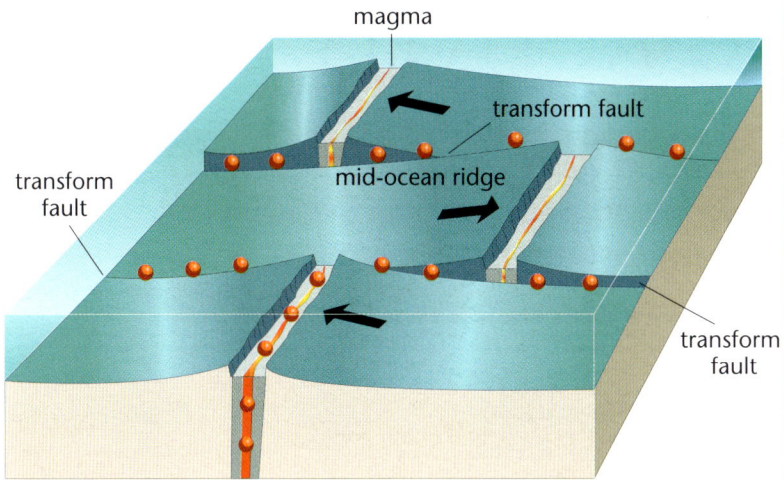

Fig. 3.9 Transform faults at a mid-ocean ridge allow the earth to retain its spherical shape.

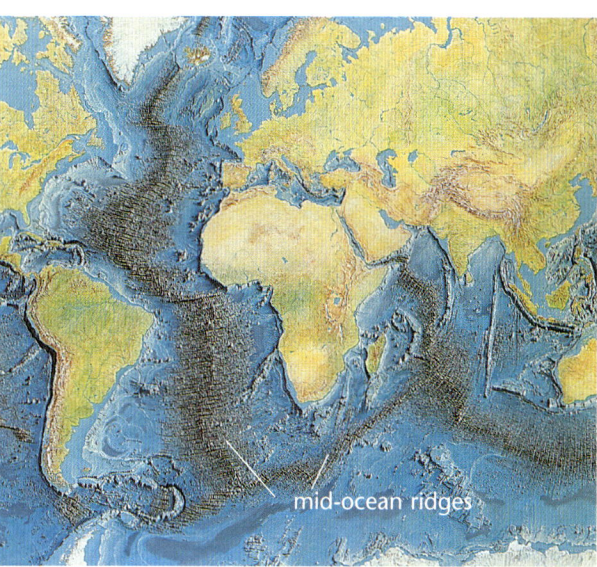

Fig. 3.10 A mid-ocean ridge and numerous transform faults in the Indian Ocean.
● *Can you identify the Mid Atlantic Ridge?*

Only earthquakes occur at passive boundaries. Passive boundaries occur where plates slide past each other without crust being created or destroyed, and there is no subduction. The line along which the plates slide is called a fault line.

These faults are called **transform faults** and they provide the means by which the ocean crust created at a mid-ocean ridge can be carried to a boundary of destruction. Most transform faults are located under the oceans, but a few, including the San Andreas Fault in California, are situated within continents.

A mid-ocean ridge is not straight. Many transform faults are offset and cross the mid-ocean ridge at right angles, so that new rock may fit on the curved surface of the earth (see Fig. 3.9).

Activity

1. Explain why there are no volcanoes along transform faults.
2. Name two regions of the world where transform faults are located.
3. Use a diagram to explain the purpose of transform faults at mid-ocean ridges.

The San Andreas Fault is clearly visible on a satellite photo of the earth's surface. Some rock is deformed along the San Andreas Fault.

13

CHAPTER 4
VOLCANIC ACTIVITY

KEY IDEA!

A volcano is a pipe-like outlet, called a vent, through which molten rock, gases, rock fragments and dust erupt and form a cone-shaped landform made of these materials.

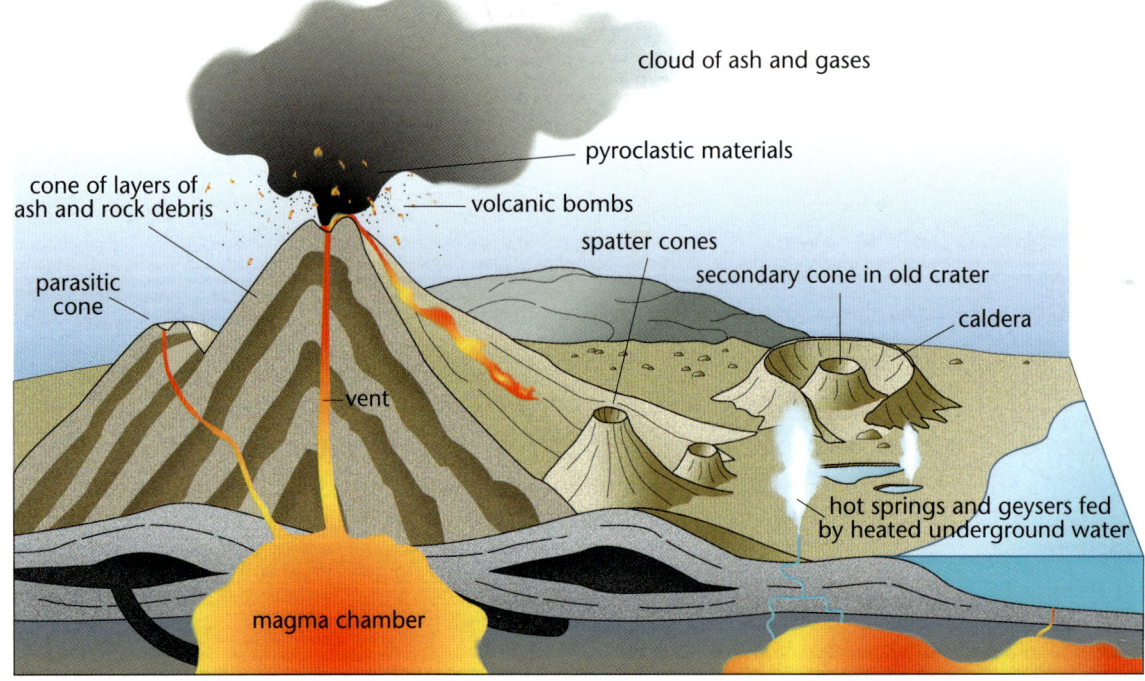

Fig. 4.1 A volcanic landscape (not to scale) showing some of the major features commonly associated with volcanic activity.

cloud of ash and gases

pyroclastic materials

cone of layers of ash and rock debris

volcanic bombs

spatter cones

secondary cone in old crater

caldera

parasitic cone

vent

hot springs and geysers fed by heated underground water

magma chamber

Volcanic activity occurs where plates **separate** and **collide,** but most volcanoes occur at **subduction zones** along the Pacific Ring of Fire where ocean plates are pulled into the mantle. They also occur at **hot spots.**

Fig. 4.2 Most volcanoes occur around the rim of the Pacific Ocean.

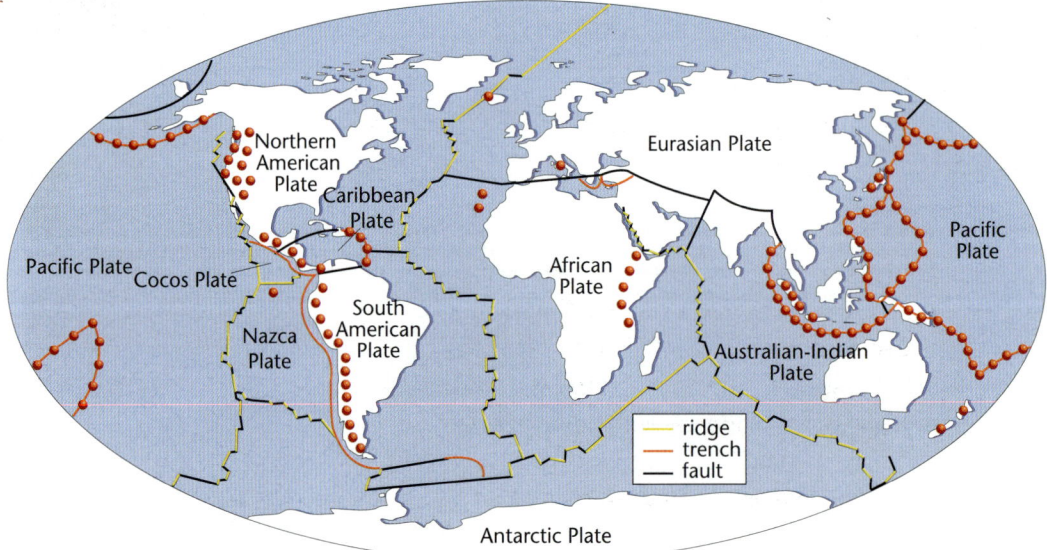

Northern American Plate

Caribbean Plate

Eurasian Plate

Pacific Plate

Pacific Plate

Cocos Plate

African Plate

Nazca Plate

South American Plate

Australian-Indian Plate

Antarctic Plate

ridge
trench
fault

Volcanoes are found at the following locations:
- At mid-ocean ridges.
- At subduction zones.
- At hot spots.

Magma also reaches the surface through long cracks called **fissures**. When magma reaches the surface, it is called **lava**. When lava and other volcanic materials reach the surface, they are called **extrusive** materials.

Materials that are pushed into the coast are called **intrusive** materials. Later, they may be exposed at the surface by erosion of the overlying rocks.

Both extrusive and intrusive materials are called **igneous rocks**.

There are three types of volcanoes:
- **Active:** Currently erupting, e.g. **Mt Etna**.
- **Dormant:** Has not erupted for some time, e.g. **Mt Vesuvius**.
- **Extinct:** Has not erupted for millions of years, e.g. **Slemish** mountain in Antrim.

WHY DO VOLCANOES EXPLODE?

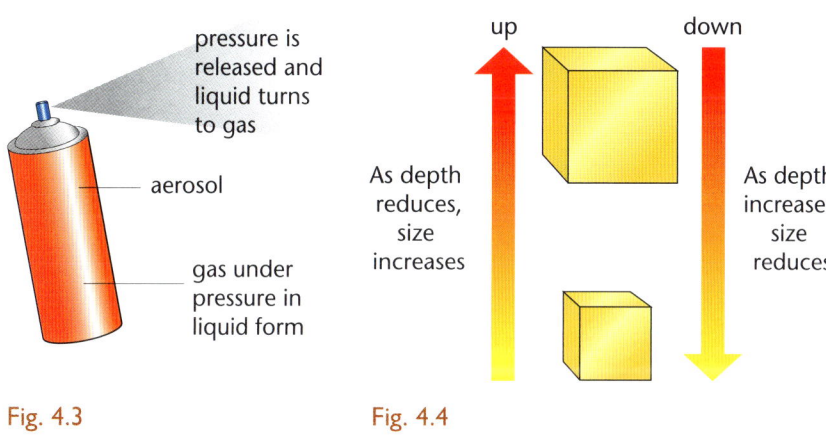

pressure is released and liquid turns to gas

aerosol

gas under pressure in liquid form

up   down

As depth reduces, size increases

As depth increases, size reduces

Fig. 4.3   Fig. 4.4

1. As magma rises, **gases** dissolved in the magma **expand** and bubble off, as water does when it is boiled. The resulting froth creates tremendous outward pressure that forces the magma upward.
2. As the magma meets groundwater near the surface, the volcano becomes like a **pressure cooker**.
3. The volcanic **mountain bulges**. Finally, the expanding gases push through cracks in the volcano. When they reach the surface, the pressures are suddenly released, the **bubbles expand dramatically** and the volcano erupts in an explosion of ash and molten rock.

Silica is a material formed from silicon and oxygen. It makes lava thick, or stiff. It **traps gases** within magma. The more silica in magma, the more gases it traps and the more likely the volcano will **explode violently**. Volcanoes at **subduction zones** contain a lot of silica, so they are **highly explosive** and dangerous.

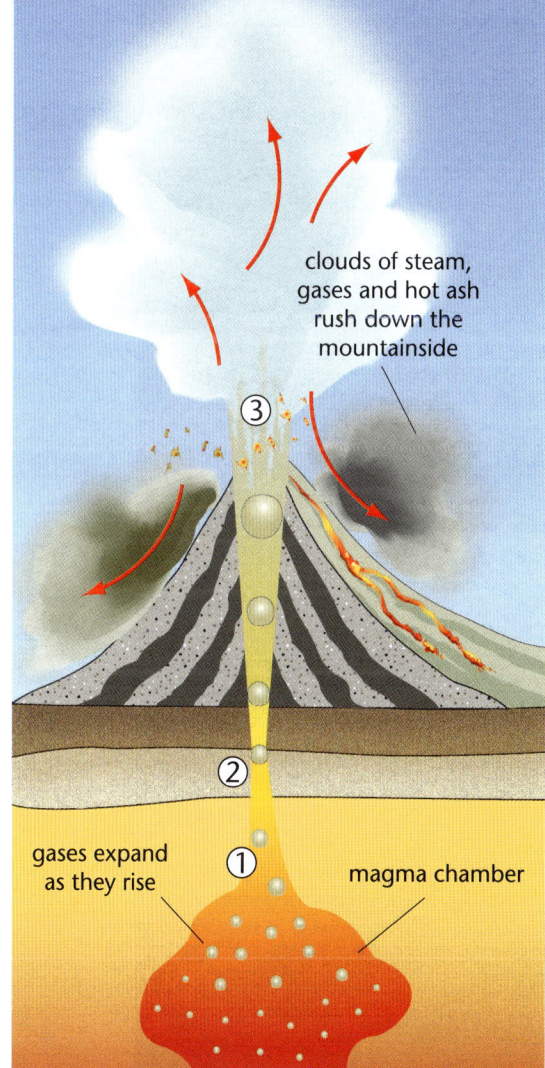

clouds of steam, gases and hot ash rush down the mountainside

gases expand as they rise   magma chamber

Fig. 4.5 Why a volcano explodes.

MATERIALS EJECTED FROM VOLCANOES

These include volcanic ash, which may be carried great distances from a volcano by the force of the eruption, by wind or both. Other materials, such as rock fragments, are called pyroclasts.

A lava fountain displays pyroclasts being blasted into the air.

Lava

There are two types of lava: acid and basic.

Acid Lava

When lava is high in silica (over 70 per cent), it is thick and does not flow far. Gases are trapped until the volcano explodes violently. It forms **steep cones** (see Fig. 5.3 on page 26).

Basic Lava

When lava is low in silica (45 to 55 per cent), it is very fluid (runny). Gases escape freely, and they push the lava forward, making it flow quickly. It forms **gently sloping cones**, such as Hawaii (see Fig. 5.2 on page 26).

Mobility of Lava

Gas helps lava flow. The mobility and cooling of lava depend on the **amount of gases** dissolved within the lava. In Hawaii, lava flows containing a lot of gas have remained mobile until they cooled at 850°C far from the volcano's vent. Other lavas with less gas have cooled at 1,200°C close to the vent.

When lava cools, it may take a number of forms. Some of these forms have Hawaiian names because of the research carried out there. **There are three main forms of lava.**

1. When lava is runny and has a **ropy texture**, it is called **pahoehoe lava.**
2. When lava has a **lumpy texture**, it is called **Aa lava.**
3. When lava appears under the sea, it comes out as rounded **blobs** and is called **pillow lava.**

Activity

Identify the types of lava in photos A, B and C and write the name in the box.

A		B		C	

HOT SPOTS

Some volcanic activity occurs **away from plate boundaries.** It is localised and confined to specific spots on the earth's crust, such as in Hawaii or the Canary Islands. These places are called hot spots. Some hot spots are located at plate boundaries, e.g. in Iceland.

Distribution of Hot Spots

Most evidence indicates that hot spots remain stationary. Only about twenty of the 120 hot spots that are believed to exist are near plate boundaries.

> The Pacific Ring of Fire, the largest earthquake and volcano zone, lies around the edge of the Pacific Ocean.

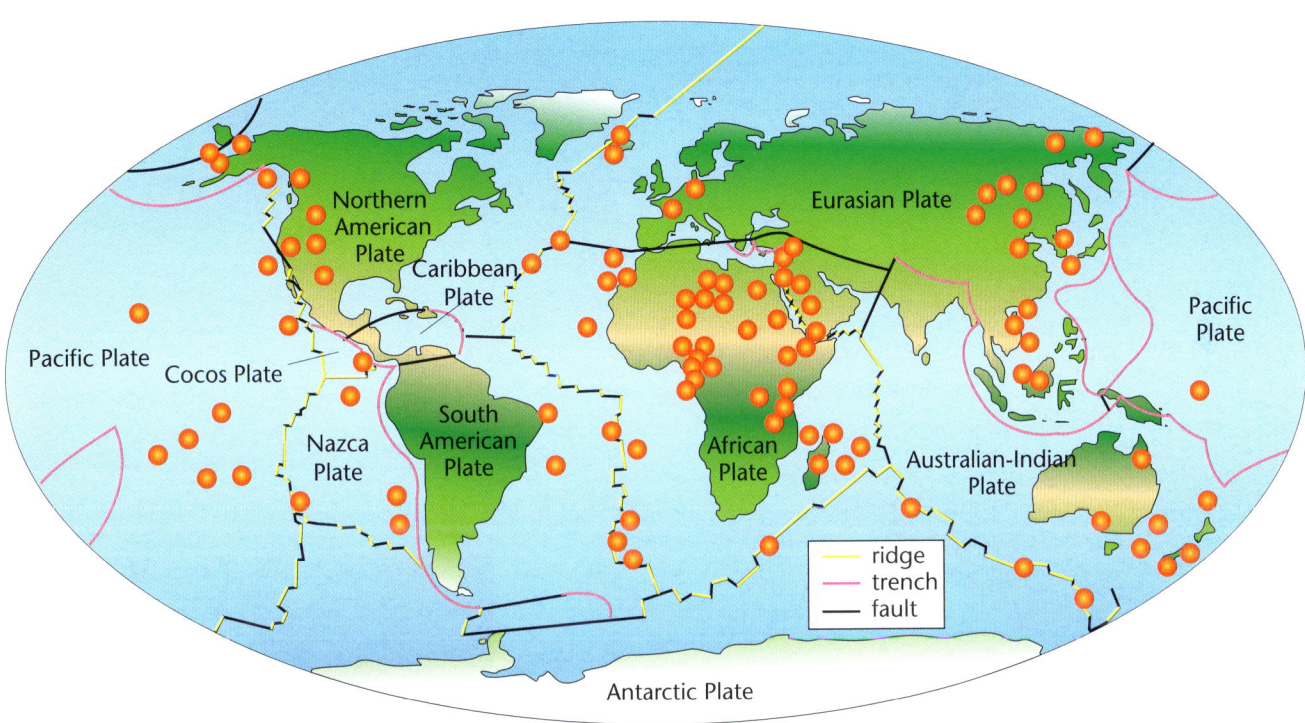

Fig. 4.6 Hot spots at the earth's surface; each is a centre of volcanic activity.
● *Which spot represents Hawaii?*

What Are Hot Spots?

Hot spots are unusually hot areas found deep within the earth's mantle. Some geologists believe that narrow columns of hot magma, called **plumes,** rise through the mantle to the surface in the way smoke rises through a chimney. These plumes can **split continents** (see page 9) or **create volcanoes,** as in Hawaii.

    A hot spot under Iceland is thought to be responsible for the regular volcanic activity on the island, which is sited on the Mid Atlantic Ridge. Another hot spot is believed to exist beneath the Canary Islands.

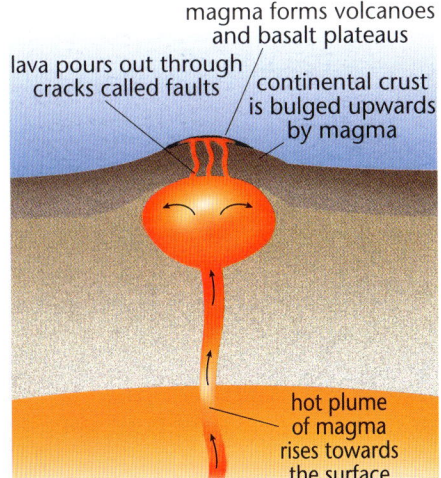

Fig. 4.7 A plume at a hot spot may cause rifting of a continent.

Activity
1. Why are volcanoes that form near deep ocean trenches the most dangerous?
2. Why are some volcanoes not as explosive as others?
3. Write six SRPs to explain how volcanoes occur at hot spots.

Fig. 4.8

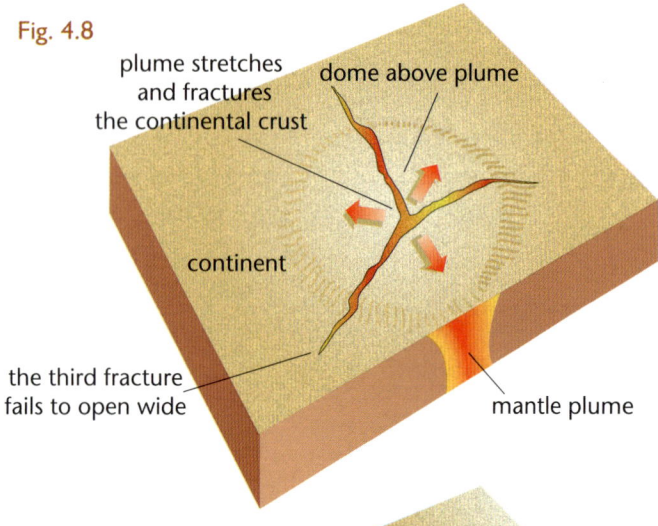

plume stretches and fractures the continental crust

dome above plume

continent

the third fracture fails to open wide

mantle plume

Hot Spots and the Process of Rifting

Scientists believe a continent may initially be split apart by rising magma at a hot spot. The rising magma creates a bulge that stretches the crust. This fractures the surface in a three-pronged, or Y-shaped, pattern.

Geologists suggest that rifting like this created the **Red Sea**, the **Gulf of Aden** and the **African Rift Valley.**

Fig. 4.9

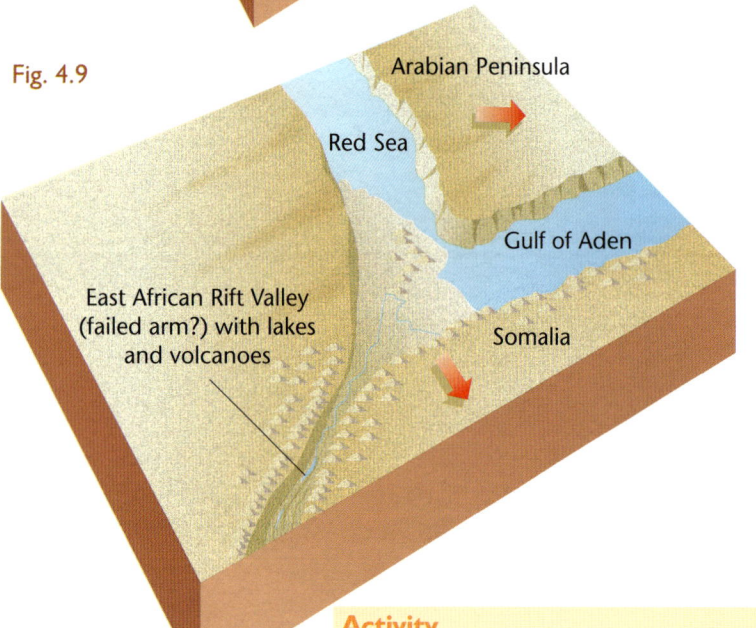

Arabian Peninsula

Red Sea

Gulf of Aden

East African Rift Valley (failed arm?) with lakes and volcanoes

Somalia

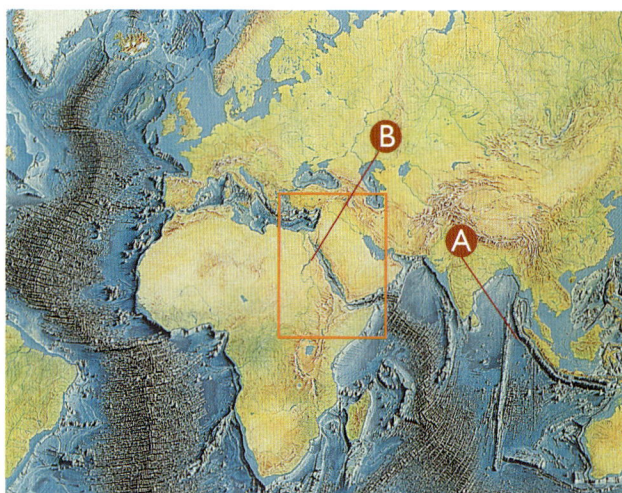

Fig. 4.10

Activity
1. In Fig. 4.10, identify:
   a. the Red Sea
   b. the Gulf of Aden
   c. India.
2. Identify the type of boundary at A and B.
3. Explain the process at one of these boundaries and name the plates involved (see Fig 2.7 on page 7 and Fig. 3.1, page 8).

Activity
Carefully examine the satellite image of the Middle East, then use your atlas to answer the following question.
1. Draw a sketch map of this region and on it mark and name the following.
   a. The Red Sea
   b. The Gulf of Aden
   c. The Gulf of Iran
   d. The Black Sea
   e. The Caspian Sea
   f. The Mediterranean Sea
   g. Saudi Arabia
   h. Yemen
   i. Egypt
   j. Sudan
   k. Eritrea
   l. Djibouti
   m. Somalia

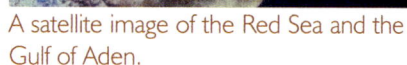

A satellite image of the Red Sea and the Gulf of Aden.

Case Study: Hawaiian Islands at a Hot Spot in the Pacific Ocean

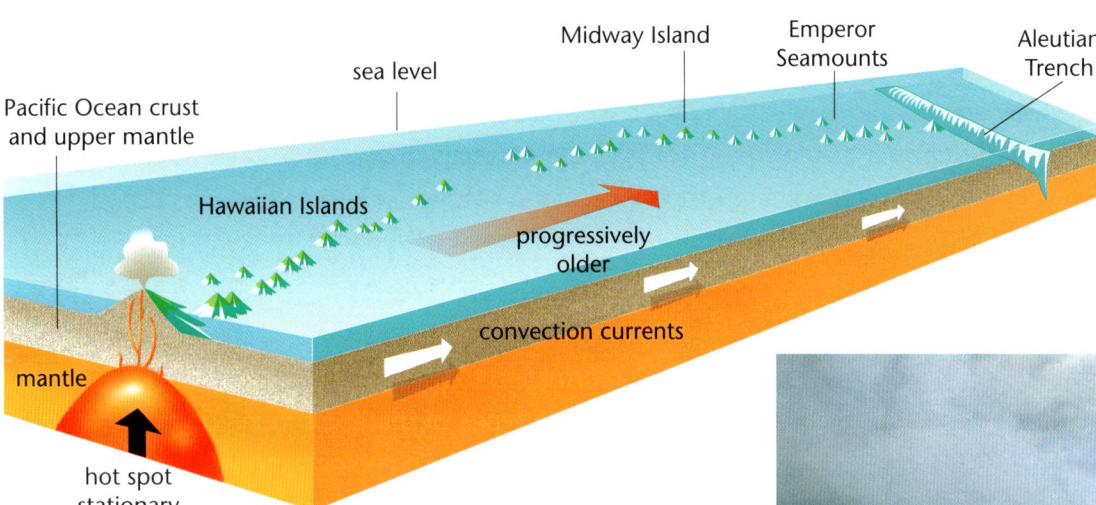

Fig. 4.11

Scientists discovered that the Hawaiian Islands in the Pacific Ocean are older the closer they are to Alaska. The probable explanation is that each volcano formed over the stationary hot spot over which Hawaii is now situated and then moved away from the hot spot as the sea floor spread to the north and then the north-west. As the ocean crust cooled, the sea floor deepened and the volcanic islands were submerged.

The Hawaiian Islands were created at a hot spot.

Other Forms of Volcanic Activity

Hydrothermal areas occur at sites of past volcanic activity where moisture is trapped and heated by the magma as it cools near the surface. These areas include geysers, hot springs and black smokers.

- **Geysers** are **jets of hot water** and **steam** that shoot into the air, often rising 30 to 60 m, at regular intervals. The most famous geyser in the world is Old Faithful in Yellowstone National Park in the US.
- **Hot springs** occur when groundwater circulates **at great depths** and becomes **heated**. If the water rises to the surface, it may emerge quietly as a hot spring. Hot springs are common in Iceland and Italy.
- **Black smokers** are **chimney-like openings** at mid-ocean ridges where super-hot water of **700°C** gushes out through vents on the new ocean floor from the mantle, and can be as tall as 30 m (see page 27).
- **Fumaroles** are small vents on the slope of a volcanic cone that emit steam or gas, such as sulphur.

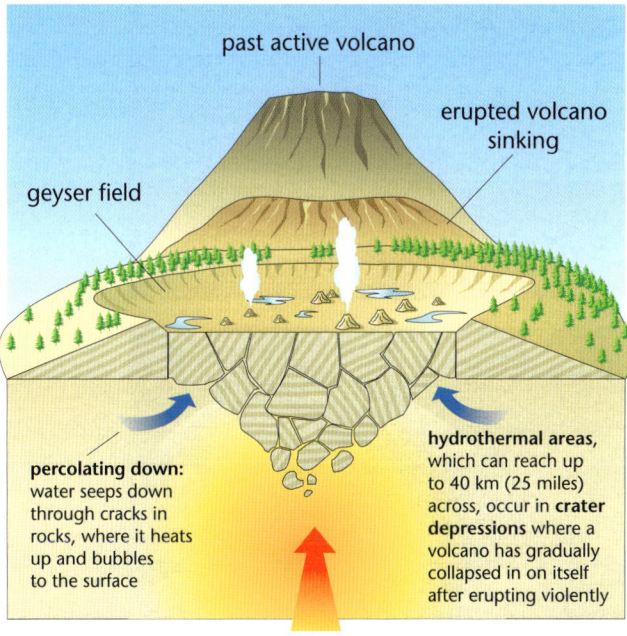

what is left of old magma chamber still produces a lot of energy

Fig. 4.12

How Volcanoes and Their Effects Can Be Predicted

Many steps are involved in forecasting volcanic eruptions and their effects. Firstly, geologists (people who study rock and rock structures) draw on their **background knowledge** of the way volcanoes are formed, how they are composed, the **type and date of deposits** that form the volcano, the **patterns of events** that have been associated with past volcanic eruptions and the **settings** in which volcanoes erupt.

Some geologists take great risks with their personal safety so that we can increase our knowledge of volcanoes and magma.

Geologists study rock samples around a volcano.

An erupting volcano. Column of ash, hot gases and pulverised rock.

A geologist installs a seismograph to detect earthquakes.

Patterns of Events

The type, date and patterns of deposits are useful information to geologists.

- The **types of materials** found on the sides of volcanoes help geologists to work out the power and explosive nature of past eruptions. **Dating** these deposits helps to establish a rhythm – whether the volcano erupts regularly, every 100 years, or once every 1,000 years.
- The **distribution of ejected material** and its relation to the local landscape is studied. This suggests where ejected material is likely to collect and helps geologists to **pinpoint the places most likely to be affected** by an eruption.

Minor Earthquakes

There is often an increase in the frequency of **minor earthquake tremors** (mild shaking of the ground) before a volcanic eruption.

- Having decided that a volcano may erupt in the foreseeable future, geologists set up a number of **seismographs** (instruments that measure earthquakes) around the sides of the summit of the volcano. These help to track the **location, strength and frequency** of earthquakes.
- Geologists also install **tiltmetres** to detect if there is ground swelling or other movements.

Activity
1. Why are volcanoes on some Hawaiian islands extinct, while on other islands they are active? Explain.
2. What are hydrothermal areas?
3. Identify three types of hydrothermal activity.

Other Patterns

Other signs that are monitored include:

- Changes in the quantity and type of gases escaping from the vent.
- Changes in the heat escaping from the crater.
- Changes in local groundwater.
- The appearance of geysers, hot springs or steam vents in the region.

By integrating this information, geologists hope to improve their forecasting abilities.

Past Volcanic Eruptions

Knowing the effects of volcanoes that erupted in the past in a certain area helps to **warn** people or to evacuate residents **who may be affected** if a new eruption is likely in that place. These effects include the following.

Lahars

Lahars are mud flows created by the sudden melting by hot ash and lava of ice on elevated, ice-capped volcanic cones. Earlier lahars may indicate where other lahars are most likely to occur again.

Poisonous gases, such as sulphur (which is yellow), escape from the sides of some volcanoes.

Nuée Ardente

When expanding hot, poisonous gases and glowing ash are ejected from a volcano, they may produce a heavy, fiery, grey cloud called a nuée ardente. Also referred to as glowing avalanches, these devastating clouds of steam, poisonous gases and ash flows, which are heavier than air, race down steep volcanic cones at speeds up to 200 km per hour and travel more than 100 km from their source.

Lahars cause great damage to towns and villages.

Activity

1. Explain the causes and effects of:
   a. a lahar
   b. a nuée ardente.
2. From your history studies at Junior Certificate, explain the type of volcanic processes that covered Pompeii in AD 79 and killed many of its citizens.

Nuée ardentes regularly cause loss off life during volcanic eruptions.

PEOPLE AND VOLCANIC ACTIVITY – OTHER NEGATIVE EFFECTS

Global Warming

Rising sea levels caused by global warming could trigger hundreds of volcanic eruptions around the world this century, wreaking havoc with the climate.

Deciding that the best way to predict the future behaviour of volcanoes was to study their distant past, scientists found that rises in sea levels caused by periods of global warming have almost all been followed by a surge in volcanic activity.

1 The present sea level is very low, caused by billions of tonnes of water being locked up in the ice caps. Global warming is melting the ice and experts predict a rise of up to a metre in sea levels over the next few decades.

3 These **landslides** weaken the outside rock. Eventually, the mountain becomes unable to withstand the internal pressure of the magma and erupts.

2 About 90 per cent of volcanoes are close to or surrounded by sea. As water rises, it begins to erode the lava. The rising water also causes landslides, triggering **tsunamis**.

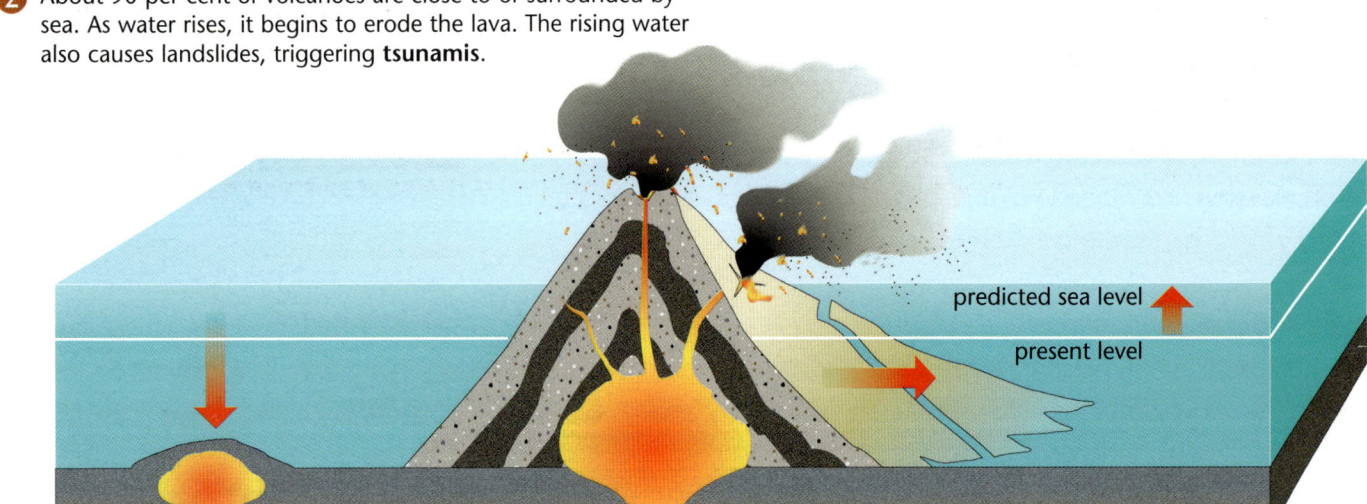

predicted sea level

present level

4 Huge magma reservoirs often lie close to the sea bed, held in check by the water pressure above. If levels change, the sea bed may crack, allowing the magma to come out and forming new volcanoes.

Fig. 4.13

PEOPLE AND VOLCANIC ACTIVITY – POSITIVE EFFECTS

Soils

Soil that forms from weathered lava in hot regions is called **laterite soil**. It is rich in minerals and is often called **terra rossa** (red soil). Cities such as Naples in southern Italy are surrounded by precious volcanic soils for growing vegetables. In Brazil and Central American countries, cash crops such as coffee are produced on terra rossa soils. Brazil is the largest exporter of coffee in the world.

Laterite soil developed in Antrim millions of years ago when lava was weathered during long intervals between lava flows. It was mined for:

- **Bauxite** (aluminium ore) during World War II. During this time, aluminium needed for aircraft manufacture was in short supply.
- **Iron** ore during the nineteenth century.

Tourism

Tourism is a major industry based directly on volcanic structures such as craters, volcanic cones or geysers. Every year, **Mt Vesuvius** attracts hundreds of thousands of tourists, who pay a fee to climb this dormant volcano. Nearby historical sites such as **Pompeii,** which was devastated when Vesuvius erupted in AD 79, also attract many visitors. Local spin-off industries, such as hotel and catering, souvenir manufacture and local guides and shops, all benefit from this kind of tourism.

Geothermal Energy

Geothermal energy is the use of natural steam to generate electricity. This type of energy source is available in areas where rock temperatures are high due to relatively recent volcanic activity.

Using water warmed by volcanic rocks, Icelanders heat their houses, grow tomatoes in hothouses and swim all year round in naturally heated pools, even though the temperatures outside may be below freezing. They also generate most of the electricity they need by using volcanically produced steam.

In Iceland, geysers are used to generate energy.

Geothermal Energy from Dry Rocks

Energy may also be generated where hot rocks lie close to the surface. Cold water pumped through fractures at the bottom of a deep well becomes heated, then flows back up to the geothermal power plant, where this energy is converted to electricity.

Mineral Deposits

Many mineral deposits form from mineral-rich fluids that escape from magma. These fluids are very hot and under tremendous pressure as they escape through cracks or faults in the crust. Some fluids cool along these cracks, or faults, and form **mineral veins**. Others are 'sweated' into rocks, where they form **mineral ores**, such as **copper ore** or **zinc ore**. Zinc ore is found at Lisheen in Co. Tipperary and at Navan in Co. Meath.

New Land

Volcanoes create new land in the sea. Many islands like this, as in Japan, are among the most densely populated regions on earth.

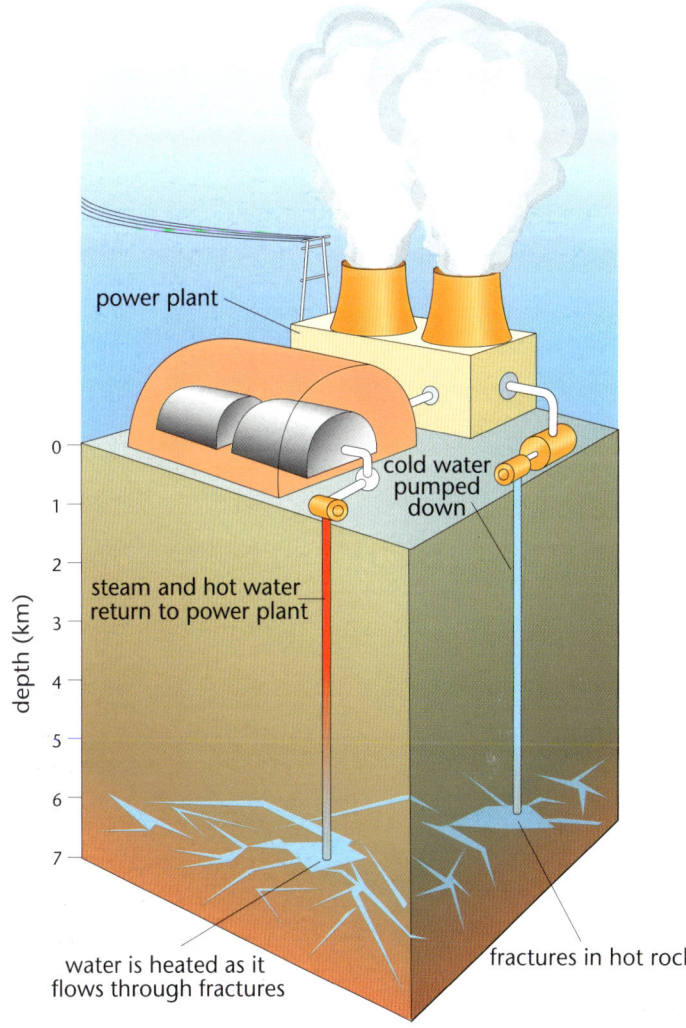

power plant

cold water pumped down

steam and hot water return to power plant

depth (km)

0
1
2
3
4
5
6
7

water is heated as it flows through fractures

fractures in hot rock

Fig. 4.14 The process of obtaining geothermal energy from dry rocks.

Activity

Short-answer Questions

1. Name the most volcanically active region in the world.
2. What is a volcanic arc?
3. What are pyroclasts?
4. Name four types of pyroclasts.
5. Name two types of lava based on silica content.
6. What is pahoehoe lava?
7. What is Aa lava?
8. Where would you locate new pillow lava?
9. What is the difference between magma and lava?
10. What is a hot spot?
11. Name one hot spot in the Pacific Ocean.
12. What is rifting?
13. Name one continent where rifting is splitting the crust.
14. Name one sea area that has only recently formed from rifting.
15. Identify one type of hydrothermal that occurs on the sea floor at mid-ocean ridges.
16. Name five signs that a volcanic eruption may be imminent.
17. What is laterite?
18. Name four ways that volcanic activity can be of benefit to people.

Multi-part Questions

1. Volcano, Mid-ocean ridge, Subduction zone.
   A. Select any **two** of the above features, and for each one you select:
      i. name **one** example in the world
      ii. describe and explain, with the aid of a diagram, how it was formed.   [20 marks]
   B. Describe one process that each of the above three features have in common.
                                                                                  [30 marks]
   C. Explain, with the aid of diagrams, the relationship between each of the above features and the theory of plate tectonics.   [30 marks]
2. A. Using a diagram, name and label the processes and landforms at any boundary of destruction.   [20 marks]
   B. Explain the processes involved in the formation of any mountain system that you have studied.   [30 marks]
   C. 'Many examples of island arcs are found in the Pacific Ocean.' Explain this statement.
                                                                                  [30 marks]
3. A. 'Ireland's location on the globe has changed over time.' Explain this statement.
                                                                                  [20 marks]
   B. Explain, with the aid of a labelled diagram or diagrams, the process of crustal plate movement as it is currently understood.   [30 marks]
   C. Explain why some volcanoes explode massively. In your answer, refer to one world example.   [30 marks]

CHAPTER 5
VOLCANIC AND PLUTONIC LANDFORMS

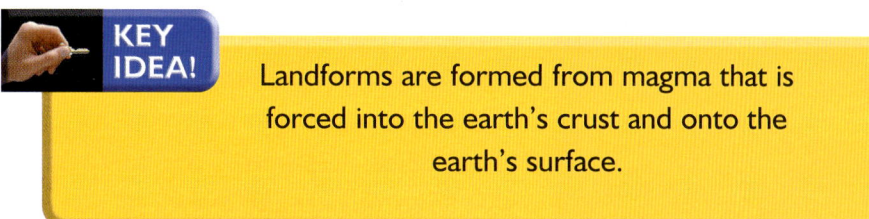

KEY IDEA!

Landforms are formed from magma that is forced into the earth's crust and onto the earth's surface.

Fig. 5.1 Volcanic and plutonic landforms.

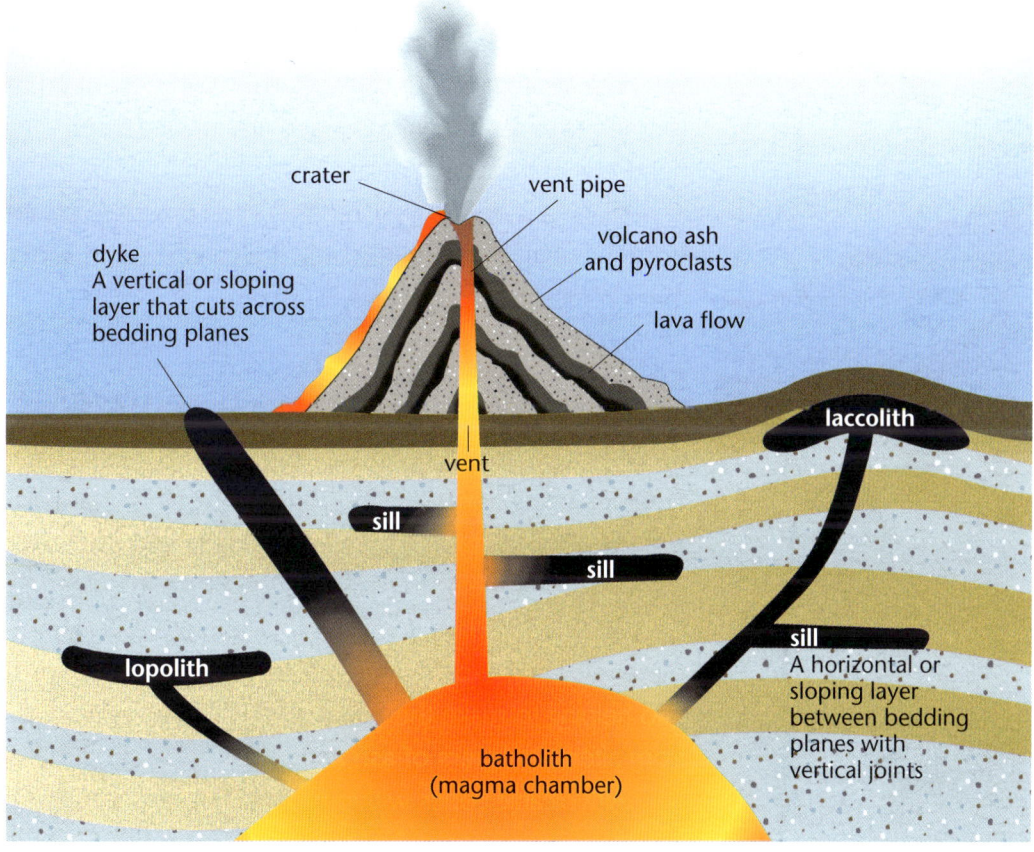

crater

vent pipe

volcano ash and pyroclasts

lava flow

dyke
A vertical or sloping layer that cuts across bedding planes

vent

laccolith

sill

sill

lopolith

sill
A horizontal or sloping layer between bedding planes with vertical joints

batholith (magma chamber)

Volcanic means 'formed on the earth's surface'. Plutonic means 'formed within the earth's crust'. Both may now be on the surface after millions of years of weathering and erosion.

Extrusive means 'formed outside the earth's crust'. Intrusive means 'formed within the crust'. Volcanic rocks are extrusive and plutonic rocks are intrusive.

VOLCANIC LANDFORMS

There are two types of opening through which magma reaches the crust and the earth's surface.

Vent

A vent is a pipe-like opening through which magma rises close to or onto the earth's surface. Vent eruptions create volcanic cones.

Fissure

A fissure is a long crack, or fault, through which sheets of lava pour out onto the surface. Fissure eruptions create basalt plateaus.

Pahoehoe lava is fluid and travels long distances.

Volcanic Cones

Examples: Mt Vesuvius in Italy
Mauna Loa in Hawaii

There are two types of volcanic cones: gently sloping and steeply sloping.

Gently Sloping Cones

Gently sloping cones are formed from **basic lava,** which is very **low in silica.** This type of lava is also very hot (about 1,000°C), so it **flows quickly and over long distances.** This lava has a smooth or ropy surface and is called **pahoehoe lava.**

Expanding **gas bubbles escape** rapidly and, as they do, they drive the lava forward, and it forms thin sheets of lava rock when it cools. These cones may be hundreds of kilometres wide at their bases and are formed from hundreds of thousands of lava flows.

Magma is driven high into the air as the gases escape from the vent. This is particularly dramatic at night, and these displays are called **lava fountains.**

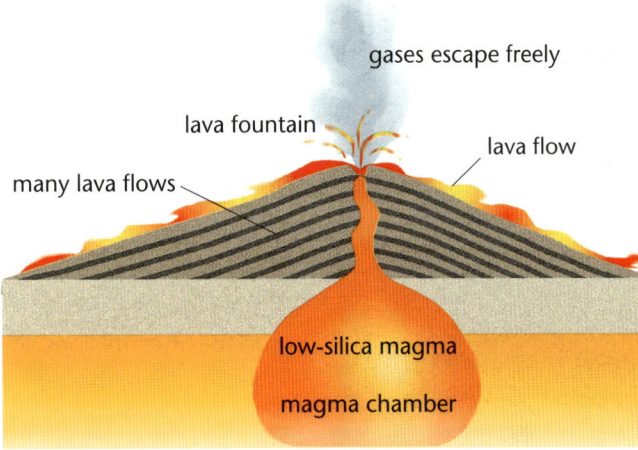

Fig. 5.2 These gently sloping cones form the Hawaiian Islands.

Steeply Sloping Cones

Example: Mount St Helens in the US

Steeply sloping cones are formed from viscous lava. It is **high in silica,** so it is stiff and **flows slowly and over short distances.** This helps to make the cones steep.

Because the lava is viscous, it is **explosive. Rock materials** from explosive volcanoes fall **around the vent,** also helping to make the cones steep. These cones form from alternate **layers of ash and lava.**

All volcanic cones within mountain ranges are steep and form from viscous lava and ash. They are located over subduction zones.

Rock fragments produced by volcanic explosions are called pyroclasts (from the Greek *pyro,* 'fire', and *clast,* 'broken'). Pyroclastic debris is also known as tephra.

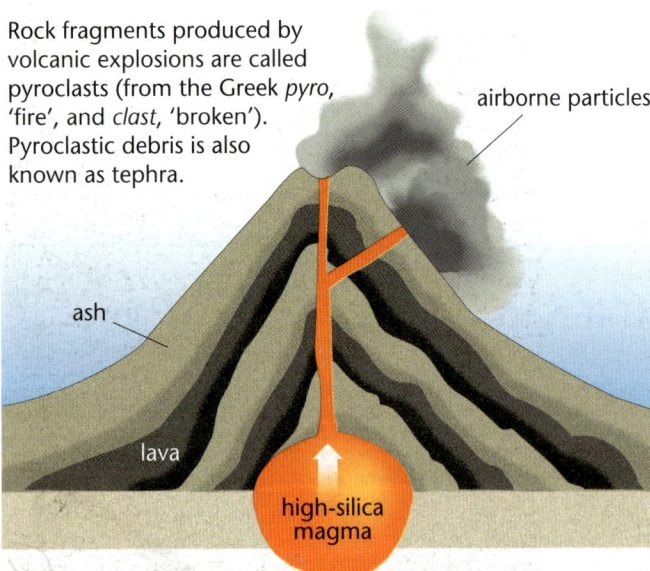

Fig. 5.3 Steeply sloping cones are formed from viscous lava.

This is a satellite image of an erupting, steep-sided cone in Japan formed from viscous lava.

Basalt Plateaus
Case Study: The Antrim Plateau
World example: The Deccan Plateau in India

About **65 million years ago** the American and European plates were still joined over what is now the Norwegian Sea. A new hot spot in this region caused **rifting**, and the Mid Atlantic Ridge extended northwards. The crust was stretched and lava poured out through this new mid-ocean ridge extension to form the Norwegian Sea region.

In Antrim, this stretching created **fissures** (cracks), and lava poured out red hot and liquid onto the surface. Each successive lava flow cooled quickly to form a layer of **basalt** rock. Eventually, the basalt layers built up to form a **high, flat-topped upland** called the **Antrim Plateau**.

Where there were long periods between lava flows, the surface basalt weathered to form **laterite** soil. This may be seen as a horizontal **red band** between the basalt layers in Antrim.

● *Can you identify the laterite soil layers on this cliff face in Antrim?*

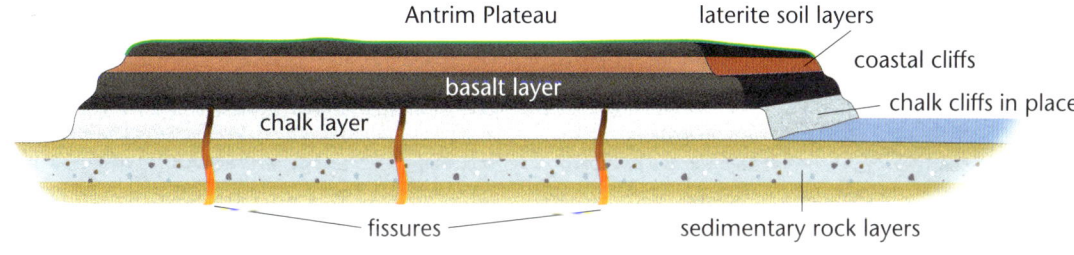

Antrim Plateau · laterite soil layers · coastal cliffs · basalt layer · chalk cliffs in places · chalk layer · fissures · sedimentary rock layers

Fig. 5.4 The formation of the Antrim Plateau.

Black Smokers

Black smokers are **chimney-like openings** at mid-ocean ridges, where super-hot water (**700°C**) with minerals dissolved in it gushes out from the mantle through vents on the new ocean floor. The **mineral-rich water** is highly toxic, but wildlife at the vent site has adapted uniquely by surviving on bacteria that flourish in this environment.

These smokers were first discovered in 1977 and can be as tall as **30 m**. The **minerals** dissolved in the super-hot water **solidify and build up a pipe-like chimney around the vent.**

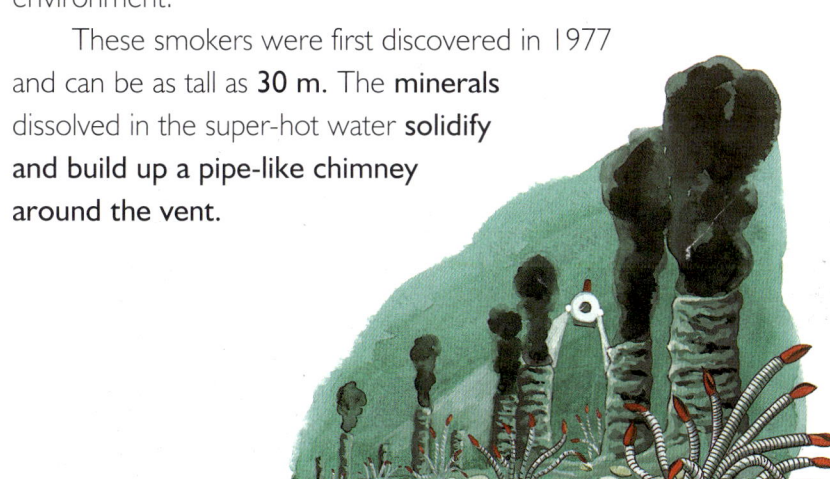

Fig. 5.5

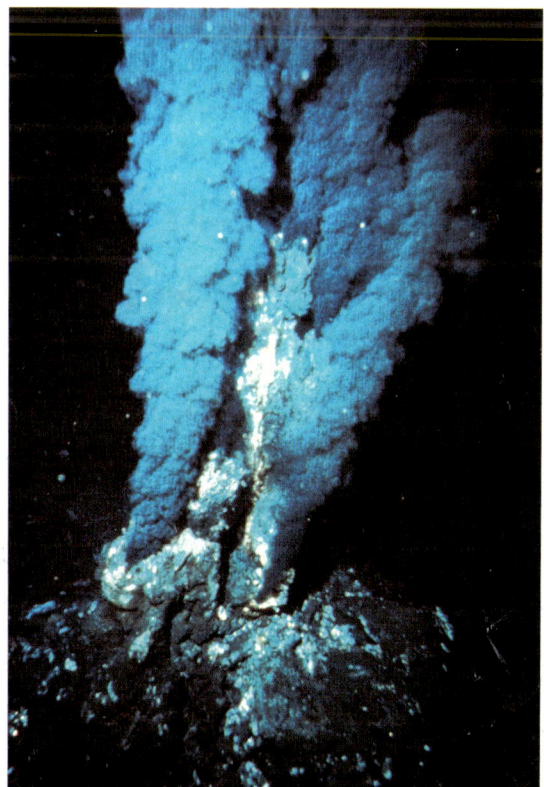

PLUTONIC LANDFORMS
Laccoliths, Sills and Dykes of Basalt Rock

In some places in Antrim, the magma was unable to find its way to the surface and so it squeezed its way into cracks (faults) and along bedding planes of sedimentary rock within the crust. Here it cooled to form **plutonic** landforms.

> When magma moves between bedding planes, it forms a sill. When magma cuts across bedding planes, it forms a dyke.

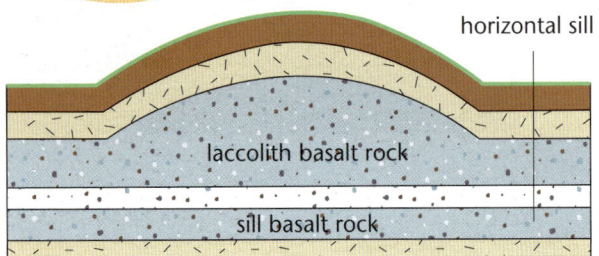

horizontal sill

laccolith basalt rock

sill basalt rock

Fig. 5.6

Laccolith

A laccolith is a small, **dome-shaped** mass of igneous rock **close to the surface.** It forms when a mass of magma forces the overlying layers of rock up into a dome, producing a low hill directly above the magma mass.

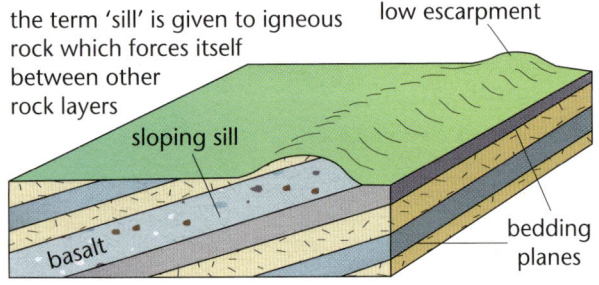

the term 'sill' is given to igneous rock which forces itself between other rock layers

low escarpment

sloping sill

basalt

bedding planes

Fig. 5.7

Sill
Example: The Grotto, Pallas Grean, Co. Limerick.

When a sheet of magma squeezes **along a bedding plane,** it hardens to form a sill. Some sills form **horizontal** layers, while others are **sloping** due to a tilt in the bedding planes.

This is an igneous dyke in rock in Thailand.

dyke

dykes cut across bedding planes

dyke resists erosion and forms a low ridge

Fig. 5.8

Dyke
Irish example: Site of Carrickfergus Castle, Co. Antrim

When a sheet of magma **cuts across bedding planes,** it hardens to form a dyke. Dykes form when magma rises through **vertical,** or near-vertical, fissures and cools to form igneous rock.

> **Activity**
> 1. Explain **how** and **why** the Antrim Plateau formed.
> 2. Explain, with the aid of diagrams, the difference between a laccolith and a sill.

Batholith
Case Study: The Leinster Batholith

A batholith is a dome-shaped mass of **granite** rock that cooled from magma deep within the earth's crust during a period of **mountain building**. Batholiths form from magma over **subduction zones**, where ocean plates sink under continents into the mantle and melt.

As in Leinster, the batholiths may also form from **continental crust** that has been buckled and **pushed down so deep** near the mantle that it melts to form magma. Magma is hot and lighter than surrounding rock, so it rises back up into the buckled continental crust. Here, it cools slowly to form huge masses of **granite**.

The Leinster Batholith formed within the **Caledonian mountains** when the American and European plates collided some **400 million years ago** (see the case study on page 12). This huge batholith stretches from Sandycove in Dublin through Wicklow to Thomastown in Co. Kilkenny. It includes the Dublin Mountains, the Wicklow Mountains and the Blackstairs Mountains.

This granite batholith is now exposed at the surface because weathering and erosion for over 400 million years have removed the overlying rock layers. Batholiths are also found in **Connemara,** in Co. Galway, and in Co. **Donegal** and Co. Down as well as in **Devon** and **Cornwall** in southern England.

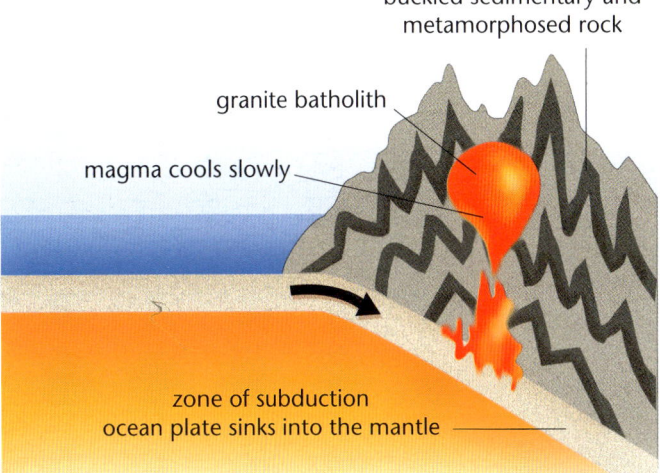

buckled sedimentary and metamorphosed rock

granite batholith

magma cools slowly

zone of subduction
ocean plate sinks into the mantle

Fig. 5.9

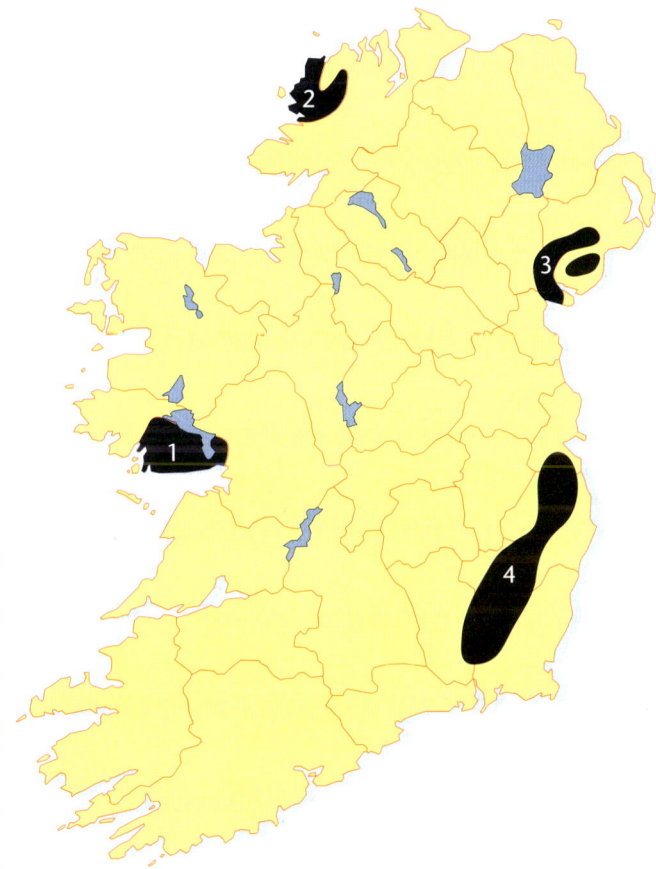

Fig. 5.10

Activity

1. Volcanic cone, Batholith, Basalt plateau, Dyke
   Select any **three** of the above landforms and for each one you select:
   i. Name one example of the landform.
   ii. Describe and explain, with the aid of a diagram, how it was formed.
2. Rifting in the northern region of the North Atlantic created major volcanic landforms in north-eastern Ireland. Select **one volcanic** and **one plutonic** landform in Antrim formed as a consequence of this rifting. For each one you select:
   i. Name one example of the landform.
   ii. Describe and explain, with the aid of a diagram, how it was formed.
3. Name the various counties where each batholith 1–4 or part of batholith is located on the map in Fig. 5.10.
4. What type of rock is found at each of these locations?

CHAPTER 6
EARTHQUAKES

KEY IDEA!

Earthquakes are caused by structures and processes that have resulted from the operation of the tectonic cycle.

The epicentres of over 99 per cent of the earthquakes that occur each year are confined to the boundaries of the earth's crustal plates. Ninety per cent of all earthquakes are shallow-focus quakes that occur close to the earth's surface.

DISTRIBUTION, CAUSES AND BOUNDARIES WHERE EARTHQUAKES OCCUR

Fig. 6.1

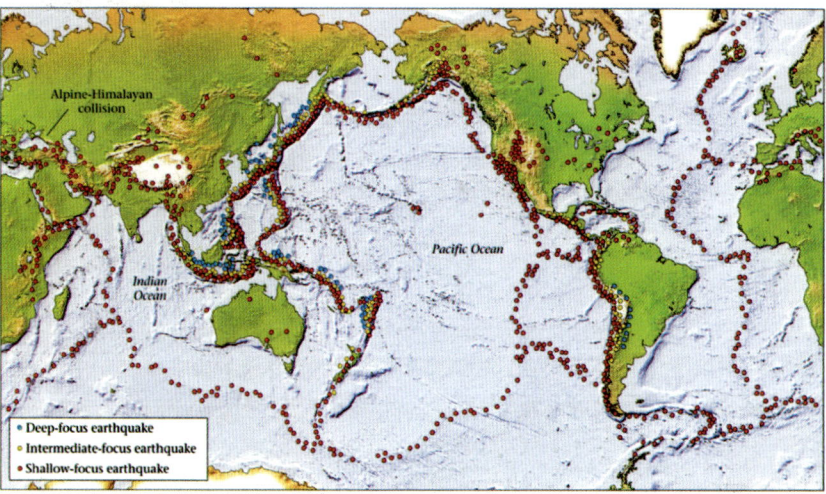

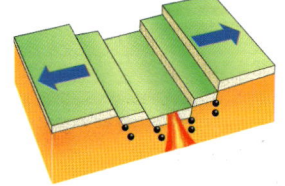

Fig. 6.2 Rifting.

Rifting over a hot spot splits a continent into new plates. As the plates separate, **tension cracks, or faults,** form. Rift valleys appear as **land drops** along parallel faults. Earthquakes occur **along the faults**.

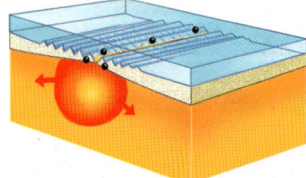

Fig. 6.3 Plates separate.

As plates separate, new **rock** at mid-ocean ridges **splits**. Most of these earthquakes occur under the oceans. **Transform faults** also create earthquakes here, as **new sea floor adjusts** to the curved shape of the earth.

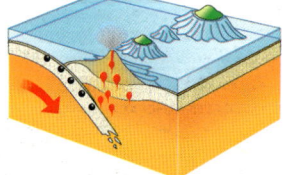

Fig. 6.4 Plates subduct.

• **Shallow quakes** occur because the sinking plate jams and then suddenly releases.

• **Intermediate quakes** occur when the plate melts.

• **Deep quakes occur** due to chemical changes and mineral changes.

• Earthquakes occur along the **Wadati-Benioff Zone**.

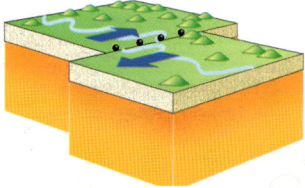

Fig. 6.5 Plates slide past.

As they **slide past** each other, **plates get stuck**. **Compression** builds up until the jammed plate suddenly frees and adjusts to its new position.

Other Causes of Earthquakes

Ice Age

Earthquakes may be associated with the melting of the great ice sheets that covered much of North America, Europe and Asia for over 2 million years. Melting relieved the load that pushed down the crust. This caused **rebounding of the crust** and strain on old faults created earthquakes.

Ancient Faults

Less than 1 per cent of all earthquakes occur away from plate boundaries, but some of these have caused great destruction to populated areas. Geologists believe that these devastating earthquakes may be related to a **renewal of ancient faults** that are buried deep in the earth's crust.

Case Study: Earthquakes on the San Andreas Fault Line

What is the **focus**?
What is the **epicentre**?

Activity
1. Identify the region of the world in this satellite image above.
2. Why is this region associated with earthquakes?

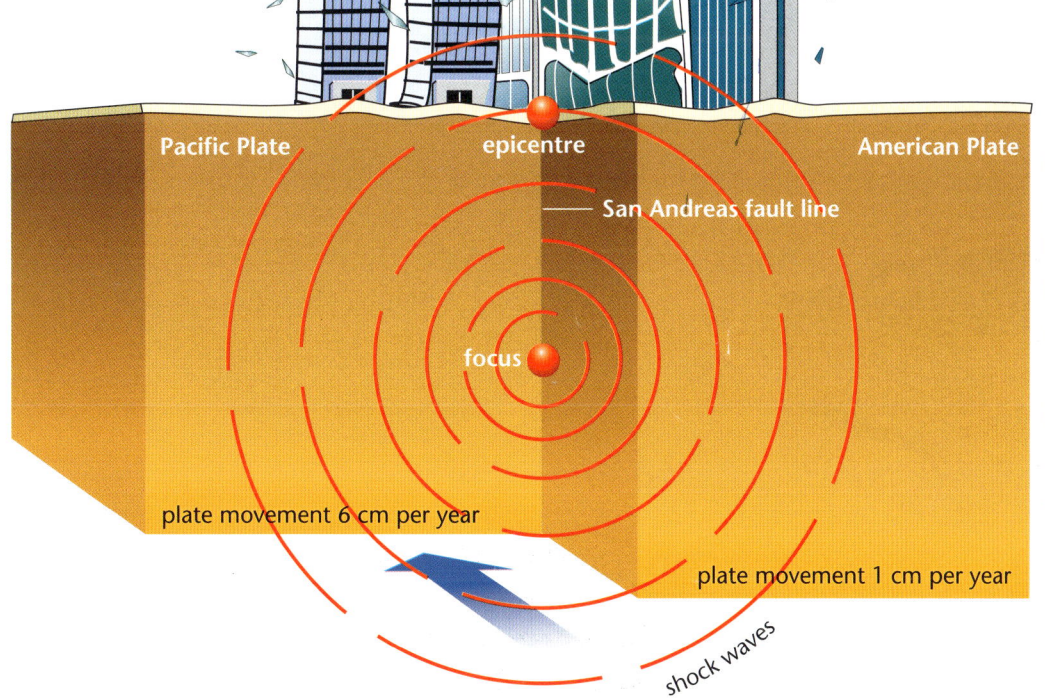

Pacific Plate   epicentre   American Plate

San Andreas fault line

focus

plate movement 6 cm per year

plate movement 1 cm per year

shock waves

The American Plate and the Pacific Plate slide past each other on the San Andreas Fault Line in California. Because the Pacific Plate is moving faster than the American Plate, it gives the impression that the plates are moving in opposite directions.

Fig. 6.6

31

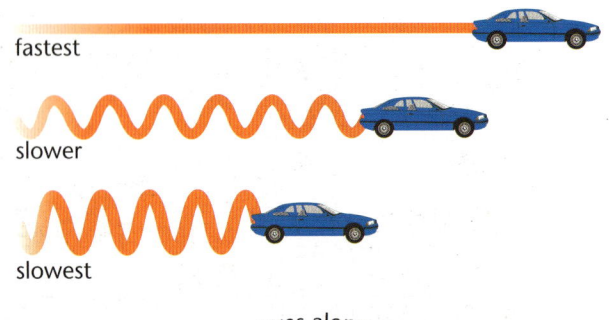

fastest

slower

slowest

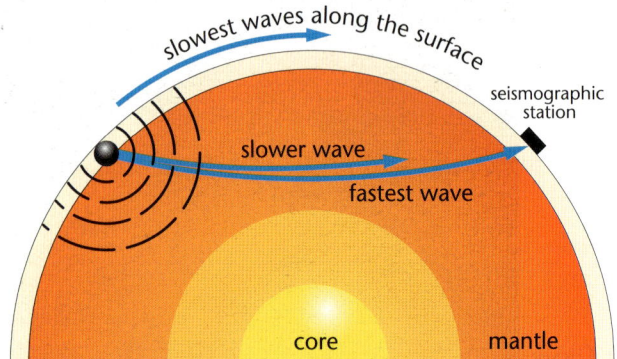

slowest waves along the surface

seismographic station

slower wave

fastest wave

core

mantle

Fig. 6.7 (a) Different seismic waves travel at varying velocities, like cars racing at different speeds. (b) Different waves arrive at different times at seismograph stations. P-waves arrive first, then S-waves, and finally surface waves. The difference in speed explains the seismograph in Fig. 6.9.

Wave-like

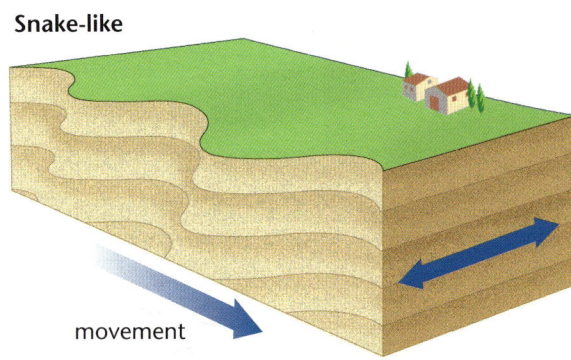

movement

Snake-like

movement

Fig. 6.8

Earthquake Waves

An earthquake releases two classes of vibrations, or seismic waves:

- **Body waves,** which travel through the interior of the earth. The body waves that travel through the interior of the earth are in turn divided into two types:
  - **Fastest waves.**
  - **Slower waves.**
- **Surface waves,** which travel close to the surface.

What Happens to the Crust During an Earthquake?

Some waves make the ground undulate in a rolling motion, like the surface of the sea. Other waves cause the ground to undulate laterally (sideways in a snake-like movement).

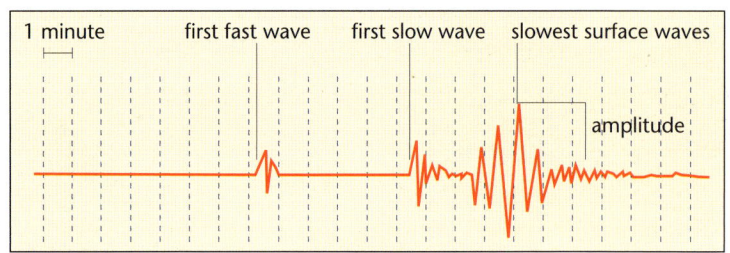

1 minute   first fast wave   first slow wave   slowest surface waves

amplitude

Fig. 6.9 Typical earthquake vibrations on a seismograph. The arrival times of shock waves from at least three recording stations are used to locate the quake's epicentre. See also Fig. 6.10.

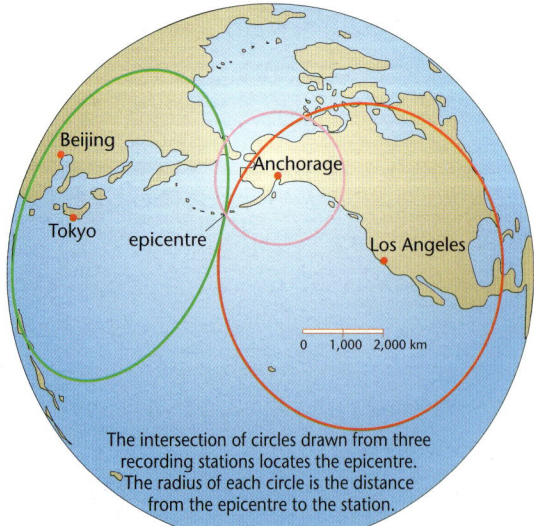

Beijing

Anchorage

Tokyo   epicentre

Los Angeles

0   1,000 2,000 km

The intersection of circles drawn from three recording stations locates the epicentre. The radius of each circle is the distance from the epicentre to the station.

Fig. 6.10 How epicentres are located.

Activity
1. Describe what is happening to the ground during an earthquake as shown in Fig. 6.7 and Fig. 6.8.
2. How do experts locate the epicentre of an earthquake at their recording stations? See Fig. 6.9 and Fig. 6.10.

Damage Caused by Earthquakes

The extent of the damage and loss of life caused by an individual earthquake depends on a number of factors:

- The magnitude (size) of an earthquake and its location.
- The depth of the focus.
- The types of rock and soil through which the waves travel.
- How close the epicentre is to cities.
- The buildings and utilities (water supply, gas pipes, etc.) affected.
- The time it happens, i.e. day or night, rush hour, etc.

An earthquake's **size** and its **location** indicate the potential damage that the earthquake will cause.

Estimating the Size of an Earthquake

The Richter Scale

The Richter Scale is an indication of the size, or magnitude, of an earthquake. A magnitude 2 is a mild quiver, undetectable by all but the most sensitive instruments. By contrast, a magnitude 7 is a major earthquake.

The size of an earthquake of 7 on the Richter scale is ten times more powerful than one of 6 and 100 times more powerful than one of 5. It is ten times less powerful than one of 8.

The Mercalli Scale

The Mercalli Scale measures earthquake damage on a 12-point scale: 1 means no damage, while 12 indicates complete devastation.

Finding the Location of an Earthquake

Once it has been established where an earthquake has occurred and what its magnitude (size) is, it is vital to estimate the damage created by an earthquake. For example, if an earthquake occurs in the middle of the Sahara Desert, it is unlikely to cause any great damage or loss of life because very few people live in this area. If the earthquake has occurred in a city in India, however, enormous damage and tens of thousands of deaths could have resulted. Locating and recording the size of an earthquake is vital to estimate potential damage and to arrange for **emergency aid** for the region. Local communications systems may be 'down' and there may be no way of contacting the population affected. The earlier help arrives, the greater the number of lives that may be saved.

A toppled train and burnt-out homes show some effects of an earthquake in Japan.

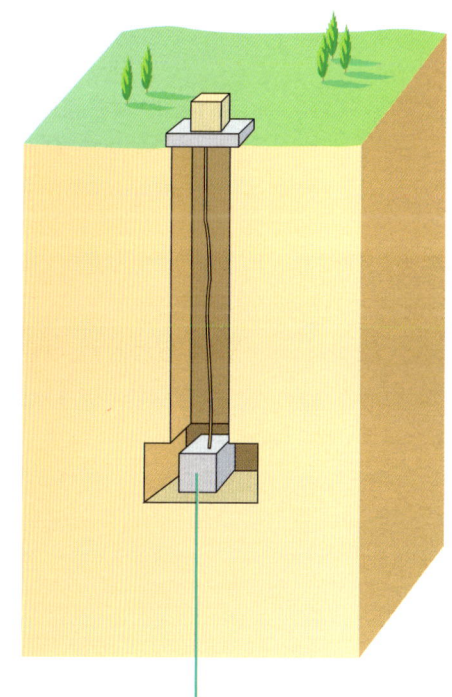

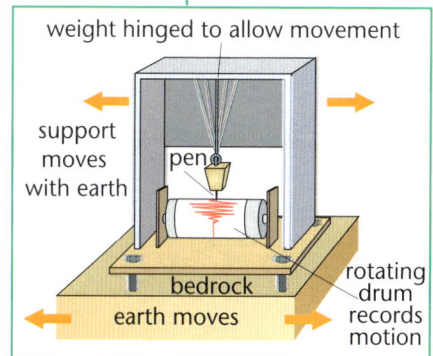

Fig. 6.11 A seismograph measures earth tremors.

How Earthquakes and Their Effects Can Be Predicted

What's the Difference between a Forecast and a Prediction?

- **Forecasts** are used for long-range planning, drawing up zoning and building regulations, setting up evacuation routes and emergency procedures.
- **Predictions** are used for immediate preparations, evacuating people, turning off gas pipelines, stopping trains, closing off bridges, etc.

Long-range earthquake forecasts are based on the idea that earthquakes are repetitive. As soon as one earthquake is over, the movement of the earth's plates builds strain until this is released by another quake along a fault line. This has led seismologists (scientists who study earthquakes) to study the history of earthquakes in an area and to search for patterns so that the occurrence of earthquakes might be predicted.

Seismic Gaps

Places along fault lines that have been '**quiet**' for a long time are called seismic gaps. According to recent studies, quiet segments of a fault bordered by the places (epicentres) of recent earthquake activity are the **most likely places** to look for the next great earthquake.

Dating

In order to forecast the future, it is important to know the past pattern of earthquakes in an area. For example, it was found in one region that there was an interval of 150 years between great earthquakes, and if the last one occurred about 120 years ago, the probability of a great earthquake occurring within the next thirty years is high, even higher within the next forty years and so on.

Other Methods

Small changes can warn us if **strain is building up** and close to snapping. These include:

- **Increased uplift of land:** Land levels are recorded over a long time. If there is a noticeable change in movement of the surface level, it is a sign of increased stress on rocks. This stress can be measured using **creep meters, bore-hole strain meters** and **tiltmeters.**
- **Movement of rocks: Lasers** can measure the slightest movement of rocks across a fault line. Again, this could indicate a build-up of strain in rocks on one or both sides of the fault.
- **Foreshocks:** Many **seismographs** are installed in an area to record **foreshocks** (tiny earthquakes that occur before a great earthquake). It has been observed that a pattern of numerous small quakes occurs over days, weeks or months before a major earthquake.

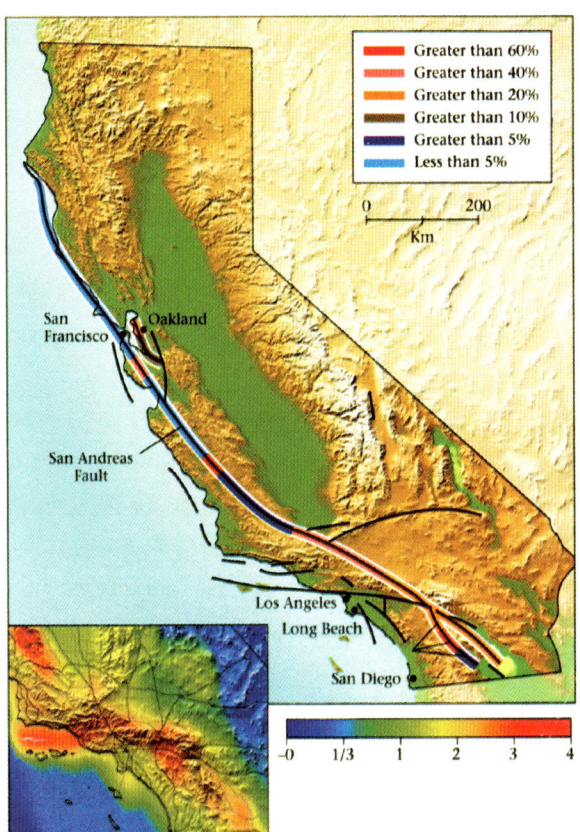

Greater than 60%
Greater than 40%
Greater than 20%
Greater than 10%
Greater than 5%
Less than 5%

0   200
Km

San Francisco Oakland

San Andreas Fault

Los Angeles
Long Beach

San Diego

-0   1/3   1   2   3   4

Fig. 6.12 This map forecasts the probability, as a percentage, of a strong to great earthquake occurring along segments of the San Andreas Fault during the next thirty years.

Activity

Carefully examine the earthquake forecast map in Fig. 6.12 and look in your atlas, then answer the following.

1. Name the American state in the map.
2. Identify the region of greatest earthquake probability.
3. Identify the region of least probability.
4. Which one of these regions you have named is a seismic gap? Explain.
5. Identify the fault line that creates these earthquakes in this region.
6. Explain the plate movements that create this fault line.
7. Identify the type of fault marked in the diagram.

Other Effects of Earthquakes

Liquefaction

Earthquakes can create a phenomenon called liquefaction which occurs when a great thickness of silt or sand is saturated with water. Under these conditions, for 15 seconds or so what had been a stable foundation soil turns into a thick liquid that is no longer able to support buildings. Buildings, especially multi-storey buildings, simply sink into the ground. Underground objects, such as storage tanks and sewer pipes, may float to the surface.

Because **Mexico City** has been built on a lake bed, it is likely that some parts of the city will suffer from liquefaction during an earthquake.

Landslides

The shaking of an earthquake can cause ground on steep slopes or ground with weak sediment underneath it to give way. This movement results in landslides, the tumbling and flow of soil and rock downslope. Landslides destroy everything in their path – buildings, trees and roads.

Landslides caused great damage in **Kashmir in 2005.** During an earthquake, roads on steep slopes through this mountainous region in the Himalayas were destroyed by landslides, cutting off access to isolated communities.

A building sinks due to liquefaction.

A landslide in action.

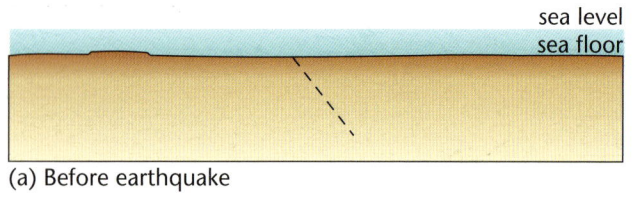

(a) Before earthquake

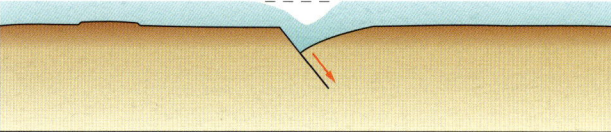

(b) Sudden displacement of sea floor by a normal fault causes sea level to drop

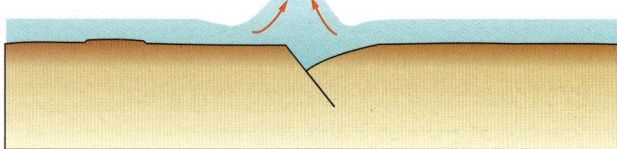

(c) Water rushes into depression and overcorrects, raising sea level slightly

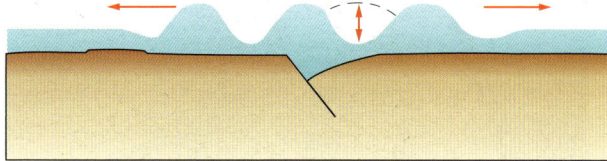

(d) Sea level fluctuates before coming to rest; long, low waves (tsunamis) are sent out over sea surface

Fig. 6.13 A similar effect is created if the sea floor suddenly rises due to a thrust fault movement set off by an earthquake.

Tsunamis

How a Tsunami Forms

If a **sea floor falls or rises suddenly** due to plate movement along a fault, it may generate a wave in the water above it. If it falls due to normal faulting, the water level above suddenly sinks, and water rushes in from the sides to fill the space. If the sea floor rises as a result of reverse, or thrust, faulting, the water level suddenly rises and water rushes off the uplifted area (see Fig. 6.13).

In either case, the sudden movement of the sea surface creates waves that radiate out from the epicentre across the ocean surface and may cause damage and loss of life even thousands of kilometres from where they originate.

Similar waves may be created by coastal landslides or by volcanic eruptions at sea. Such waves are called **tsunamis**, a Japanese word meaning 'harbour wave'. A wave like this may travel at speeds up to 80–100 km an hour. As the tsunami approaches the shore, it 'touches bottom' and the water builds up to form a monster wave up to **30 m high**. If the wave funnels into a narrow estuary or harbour, it may reach heights of 70 m.

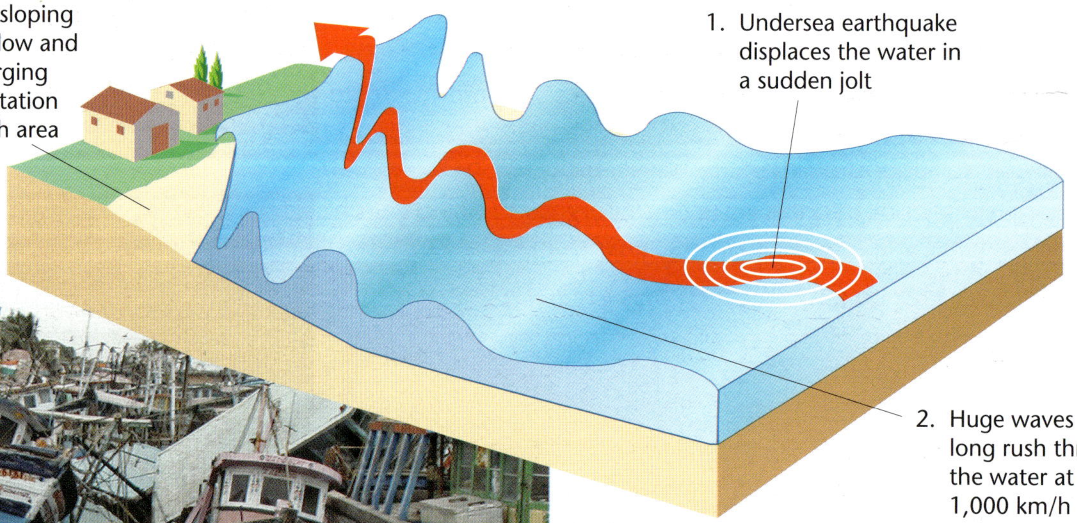

3. On reaching a gently sloping coastline, the waves slow and compress upward, surging ashore to cause devastation well beyond the beach area

1. Undersea earthquake displaces the water in a sudden jolt

2. Huge waves 160 km long rush through the water at up to 1,000 km/h

Fig. 6.14

These boats were crushed in a harbour by a tsunami in Thailand. The tsunami of December 2004 killed more than 250,000 people in Thailand.

Case Study: **The 2005 Earthquake in Kashmir**

The Kashmir earthquake in October 2005 measured 7.6 on the **Richter scale**, the same strength as the 1906 earthquake in San Francisco. Over 79,000 people died and more than 3.3 million people were left homeless, only weeks before the start of the winter snows.

The **epicentre** was located in the Pakistan-administered region of Kashmir, a territory disputed with India that is by far the most earthquake-prone region in the mountains. Kashmir lies in the area where the Eurasian and Indian **tectonic plates** are colliding. Out of this collision, the Himalayas began uplifting 50 million years ago, and continue to rise by about 3 mm per year. The **focus of the earthquake** was located at a depth of 26 km below the surface. About 50 million people are at risk from Himalayan quakes.

The earthquake caused widespread destruction in northern Pakistan, as well as damage in Afghanistan and the Kashmir valley in northern India. As the earthquake struck on a Saturday and this is a normal schoolday in the region, most students were at school at the time. Many were buried under collapsed school buildings. Many other people were trapped in their homes and, because it was also the month of Ramadan when most people were taking a nap after their pre-dawn meal, they did not have time to escape during the quake. Reports confirmed that entire towns and villages were completely wiped out in northern Pakistan, with other surrounding areas suffering severe damage.

Mountainsides collapsed, sweeping away houses and terraced fields. Some landslides collapsed into river valleys, creating mountains of rock and mud over 100 m high that changed the courses of some rivers. Thousands of people in villages were cut off from relief supplies by the landslides. There were multiple landslides on one road. The landslides were so big they had to be cleared by blasting them with explosives. Over much of the region, the only choice was to bring in supplies by air.

Some isolated communities suffered from outbreaks of diseases such as cholera. Blue canvas tents dotted the hillsides, where families camped beside their damaged homes. These tents and other supplies, such as blankets and food, formed part of the relief efforts by various agencies such as the Red Cross and the US, Indian and Pakistani armies.

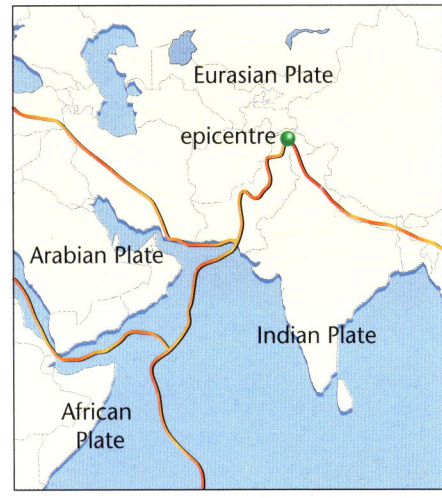

Fig. 6.15 The collision of the Indian and Eurasian plates creates earthquakes in the Himalayas.

Landslides block roads in mountainous regions such as the Himalayas.

Activity

1. Explain the terms Richter scale, epicentre, focus, tectonic plates.
2. Why is Kashmir an earthquake-prone region?
3. On Fig. 6.15, which shows the tectonic boundaries of this region, draw arrows showing the direction of the plates' movements (see Fig. 2.7 on page 7).
4. Landslides are part of which type of surface process? (see Fig. 11.1 on page 65.)
5. Using a diagram, explain how landslides occur (see page 70).
6. Why did so many landslides occur during the 2005 Kashmir earthquake?
7. Describe and explain the damage caused by the landslides.
8. Explain why so many buildings collapsed during the quake.
9. What type of aid was given to the people affected? Explain.
10. What is Ramadan? Explain.
11. Do all people of this region take part in Ramadan? (See Chapter 76 on religions of the world.)

37

Why Do Most Earthquakes and Volcanoes Occur Along the Pacific Ring of Fire?

Write four SRPs explaining the processes that occur in each of the diagrams in Fig. 6.16.

- The Atlantic Ocean, the Indian Ocean and the Pacific Ocean all have ocean ridges where new crust is being created. To balance this, there are corresponding locations where old crust is being recycled and sucked into the mantle.
- Most of this recycling, called subduction, occurs around the edges of the Pacific Ocean where ocean plates sink under continental plates and other ocean plates.
- Most earthquakes and volcanoes occur around the Pacific Rim at these **subduction** zones.
- These volcanoes are **highly explosive** because they have thick, **viscous magma,** high in silica, which traps gases.

What Happens at Subduction Zones Along the Pacific Rim?

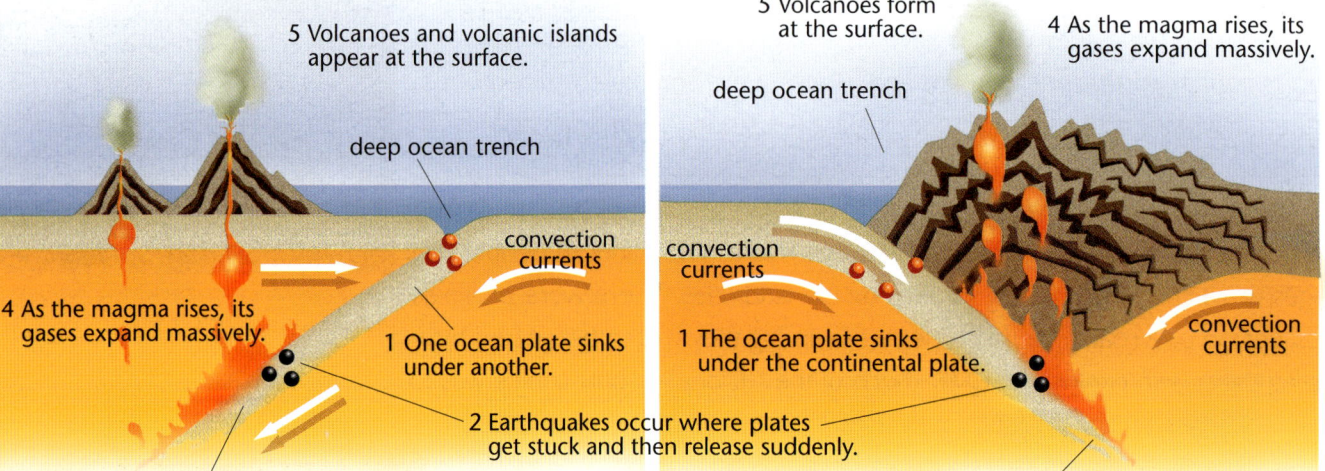

A. Ocean-ocean destructive boundary – example: Japan Islands and the Philippines

5 Volcanoes and volcanic islands appear at the surface.

deep ocean trench

convection currents

4 As the magma rises, its gases expand massively.

1 One ocean plate sinks under another.

2 Earthquakes occur where plates get stuck and then release suddenly.

3 Sinking plate melts at a depth of 100 km.

B. Ocean-continent destructive boundary – example: Rockies and Andes

5 Volcanoes form at the surface.

4 As the magma rises, its gases expand massively.

deep ocean trench

convection currents

convection currents

1 The ocean plate sinks under the continental plate.

3 Sinking plate melts at a depth of 100 km.

Fig. 6.16 Note that the intermediate and deep-focus earthquakes occur only within the sinking slab of the ocean plate. This is called the Wadatti-Benioff zone.

The earthquakes occur along the descending plates only. This is called the Wadatti-Benioff Zone. There are two types of subduction zones around the Pacific Rim:

- Diagram A represents an **ocean-ocean** boundary. This represents the **island arcs** of Japan, Indonesia and the Philippines in the western Pacific Ocean.
- Diagram B represents an **ocean-continent** boundary that matches the North American coast and the **Rockies,** and the South American coast and the **Andes** in the eastern Pacific Ocean.
- Each of these boundaries create **both earthquakes and volcanoes**.
- At each of these locations, an ocean plate is pulled into the mantle.
- These descending plates regularly get stuck, leading to earthquakes along their Wadatti-Benioff zones.
- All the descending plates eventually melt, creating volcanoes at the surface.

Sample Questions and Answers

Why Is Ireland Regarded as *Relatively* Safe from Destructive Earthquakes?

- Ireland is located far from its nearest existing plate boundaries. These are the Mid Atlantic Ridge to the west and the African-European Plate boundary to the south.

- Earthquake waves decrease in strength with distance from an epicentre. Most of the earthquake epicentres closest to Ireland are located on these distant plate boundaries.

- Ice sheets disappeared from the Irish landscape over 10,000 years ago. Most rebounding of the land that could cause earthquakes due to squeezing by overlying ice sheets has already occurred since the end of the Ice Age.

- When earthquakes have occurred over the past 300 years, they are generally small and are associated with rebounding rather than plate collision or transform boundaries, where most destructive earthquakes occur.

Why Are There No Active or Dormant Volcanoes in Ireland?

- Ireland is located far from its nearest existing plate boundaries. These are the Mid Atlantic Ridge to the west and the African-European Plate boundary to the south, where the closest volcanoes are located.

- Ireland lies on a passive margin where plate activity is absent. It lies on the stable continental shelf of the European Plate.

- Ireland has no hot spot activity beneath its surface. This creates a stable crust, free from volcanic activity.

- The most recent volcanic activity in Ireland occurred about 60 million years ago when rifting caused magma to pour out onto the surface to form the Antrim Plateau. No volcanic activity has occurred since that time.

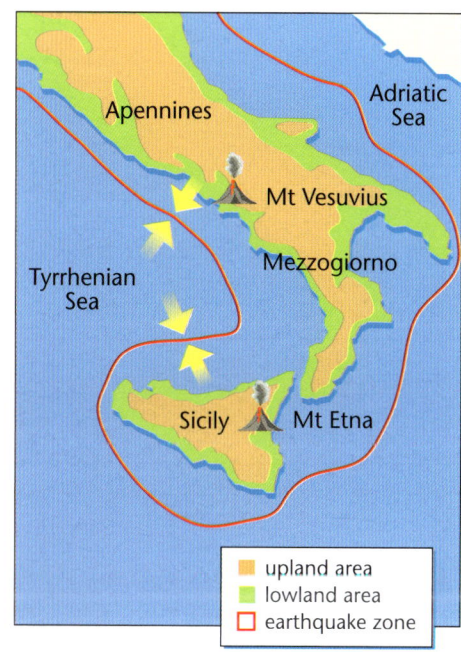

Fig. 6.17 Southern Italy is called the Mezzogiorno.

Why Do Earthquakes Occur in Southern Italy?

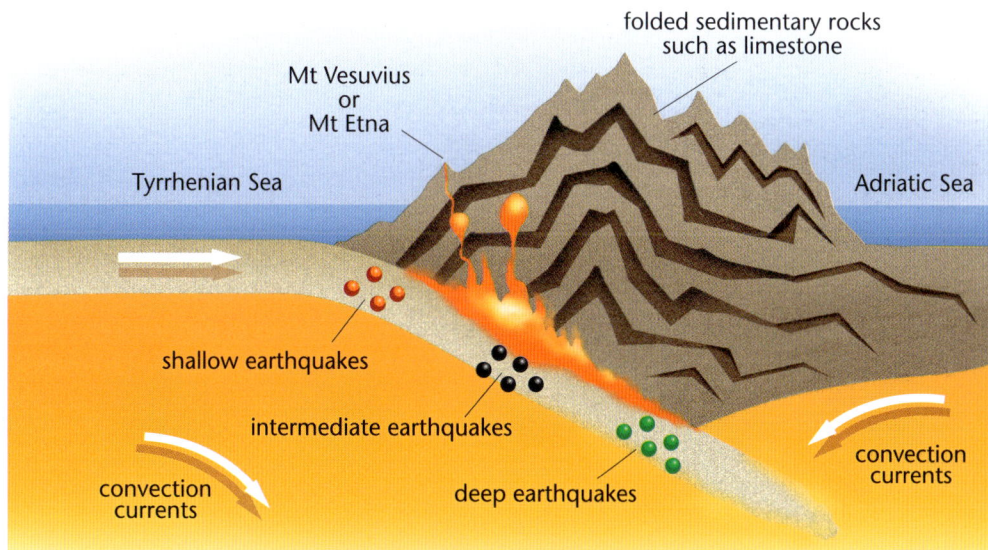

Fig. 6.18

The floor of the Tyrrhenian Sea slips under the toe of Italy. Earthquakes always **occur along the path of this descending plate**, as it dips into the mantle. In addition, limestone sediment from the sea floor is squeezed and buckled up to form the Apennines (fold mountains). This is why the land in southern Italy is steep. It is dry because any rain that falls on land quickly disappears through the limestone rock.

See Activities on Irish earthquakes in *Dynamic Geography Core Workbook*, pages 24–27.

Multi-part Questions

1. **A.** Name one active volcano and explain why it is active. [20 marks]
   B. 'Earthquakes and volcanoes occur in quite predictable locations on the globe.' Examine the theoretical basis for this statement. [30 marks]
   C. The frequency of occurrence of earthquakes and volcanic eruptions is much more difficult to predict than their location. Assess the accuracy of this statement with reference to examples you have studied. [30 marks]

2. **A.** Draw a map of the world and mark the names of regions of regular earthquake activity on it. [20 marks]
   B. With the aid of a diagram, describe the different types of seismic waves associated with earthquakes. [30 marks]
   C. Explain how loss of life and destruction of property differs between earthquake-prone regions of advanced and developing countries. [30 marks]

3. **A.** Explain the meaning of plate tectonics. [20 marks]
   B. Explain how plate tectonic theory has helped us to understand the world distribution of:
      i. fold mountains **AND**
      ii. volcanic island arcs. [30 marks]
   C. i. Another of the consequences of the movement of crustal plates is the occurrence of earthquakes. With reference to appropriate examples, describe the impact which a major earthquake can have on a human population.
      ii. Briefly examine attempts to lessen that impact.

4. **A.** Name and explain **one** example of each of the following:
      i. convergent margin
      ii. divergent margin
      iii. a transverse (transform) margin
      iv. a mid-plate volcanic island arc. [20 marks]
   B. Explain why most volcanoes and earthquakes occur around the Pacific Ring of Fire. [20 marks]
   C. Explain how people benefit from the occurrence of volcanic activity. [30 marks]

5. **A.** 'A study of patterns in the worldwide distribution of volcanoes and earthquake zones can help us to understand the causes of these events.' Examine this statement with reference to examples which you have studied. [50 marks]
   B. Describe two effects on human societies of the occurrence of: (a) a volcanic eruption (b) a major earthquake in populated areas. [20 marks]
   C. Explain how a tsunami forms. [30 marks]

6. Examine Fig. 6.19, which shows some of the landforms produced by volcanic activity, and answer the following questions.
   A. In the case of any **two** of these landforms, describe and explain the processes which shaped them. [20 marks]
   B. Briefly examine ways in which volcanic activity can be of economic benefit to people. [30 marks]
   C. Briefly explain three causes of earthquakes. [30 marks]

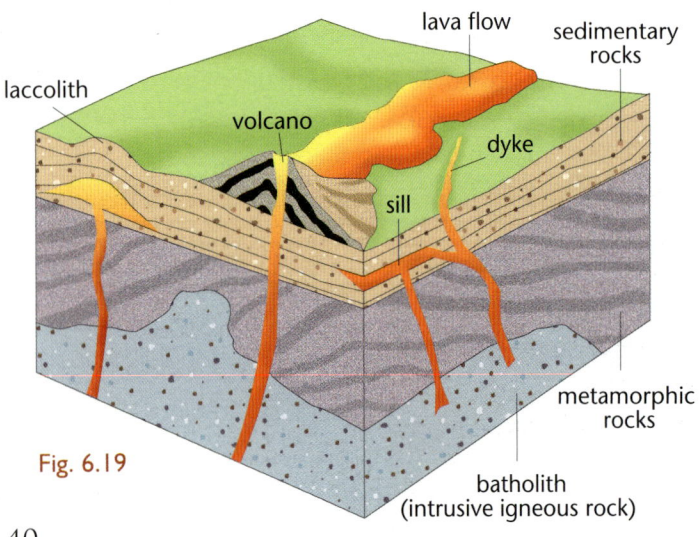

Fig. 6.19

laccolith

volcano

lava flow

sedimentary rocks

dyke

sill

metamorphic rocks

batholith (intrusive igneous rock)

CHAPTER 7
THE ROCK CYCLE

Rocks are continually formed, changed and destroyed by tectonic processes. They are also destroyed by weathering and erosion, and deposited to form sediments, which may in turn be changed or destroyed by tectonic processes.

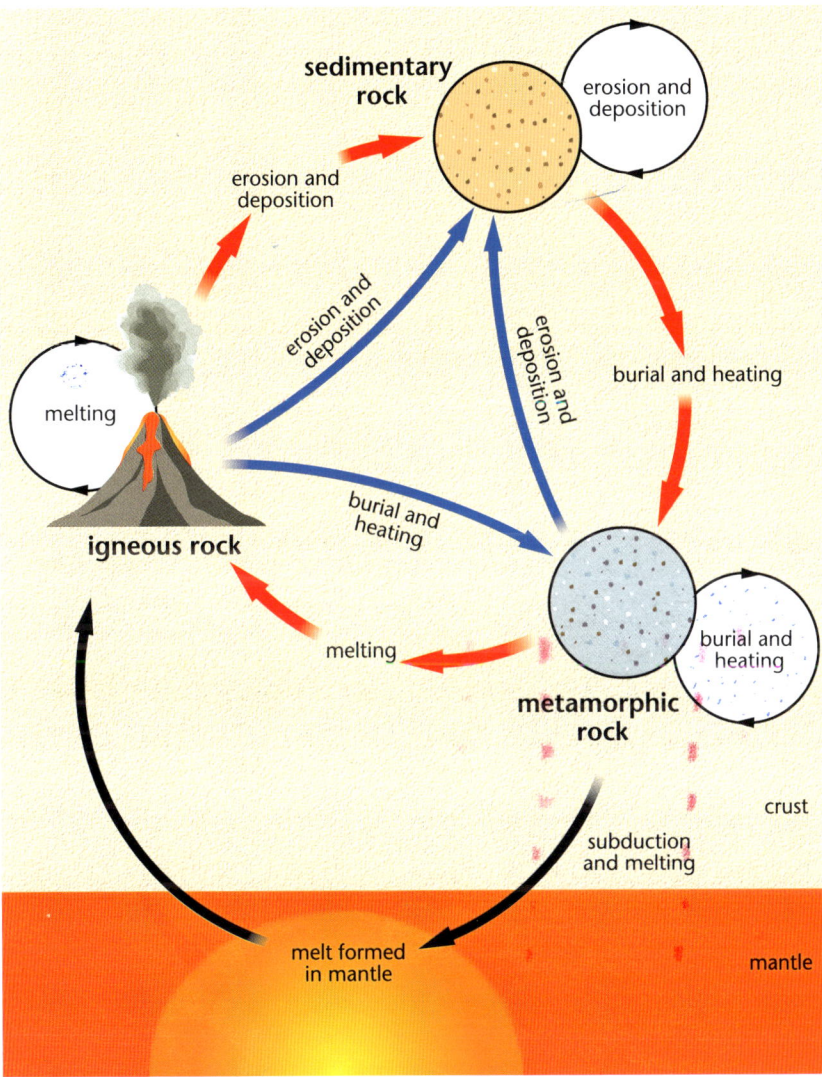

Fig. 7.1 The rock cycle.

Igneous activity and plate tectonics create mountain regions. Weathering breaks up the rock that forms these mountains, and erosion removes the rock particles to lowlands and seas where they form many types of sedimentary rock.

Plate tectonics may then buckle and raise some of these sedimentary rock layers to form mountains where denudation (weathering and erosion) repeats the cycle.

During new mountain-building periods, more of the sedimentary rock layers may be compressed, heated and then cooled to form metamorphic rock. Sometimes the cooled metamorphic rock may itself be changed by increased heat and pressure to form different types of metamorphic rock.

In some instances during mountain-building periods, the sedimentary rock layers may be pushed down into the crust so far that they melt to form magma. If this magma cools, it will form igneous rock within the crust. This is called plutonic rock. If instead the molten rock or magma rises, it may reach the surface to form volcanic rock, such as basalt, lava or pyroclastic rocks.

Activity
Carefully examine the diagram in Fig. 7.1 and use your studies so far to answer the following.
1. How does sedimentary rock become metamorphic rock?
2. How does metamorphic rock become (a) igneous rock (b) sedimentary rock?
3. What other type of rock can metamorphic rock become other than (a) and (b) above?
4. Explain the processes that cause igneous rock to change to other rock types.
5. List the various processes mentioned in this flow chart.

SETTINGS WHERE IGNEOUS, SEDIMENTARY AND METAMORPHIC ROCKS FORM

KEY IDEA!

Rocks are formed in different environments. Some are formed within the earth. Others are formed on the earth's surface, either on land or in water environments. These environments greatly affect the type of minerals that make up the rock.

Group	How Formed	Examples
IGNEOUS	They were formed when hot, molten rock matter cooled and became solid.	granite, basalt, lava, pyroclasts
SEDIMETARY	They were formed from the **crushed-together remains** (sediments) of animals, plants and other rocks	limestone, coal, sandstone, shale
METAMORPHIC	They were once igneous or sedimentary rocks, which were **changed by great heat or pressure.**	marble, quartzite, slate, schist

Activity

1. Using Fig. 7.2, identify the counties where the following rock types are located:
   a. granite
   b. basalt
   c. quartzite and some other metamorphics
   d. slates and shales
   e. sandstones only
   f. limestone only (four counties).
2. According to Fig. 7.2, which county has:
   a. only granite and quartzites and other metamorphics
   b. mostly basalt
   c. mostly sandstone
   d. only limestone at the surface?
3. Which region(s) has the most granite, quartzite and other metamorphics?

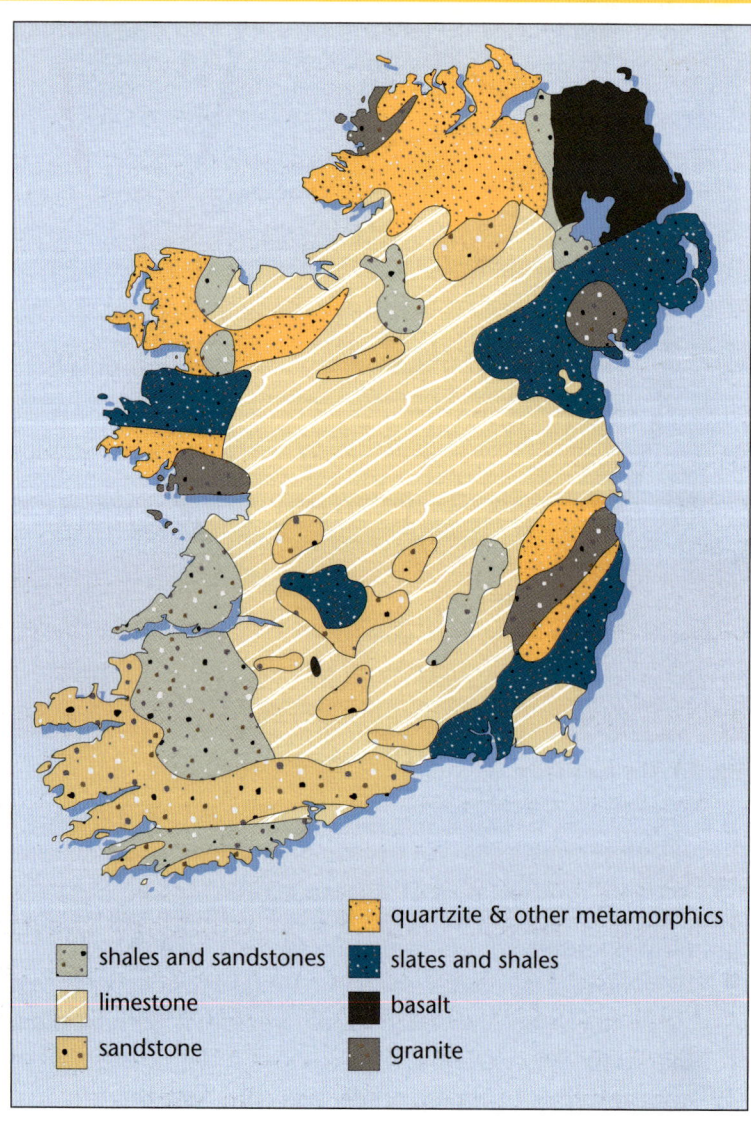

quartzite & other metamorphics
shales and sandstones
slates and shales
limestone
basalt
sandstone
granite

Fig. 7.2 Surface rock in Ireland.

IGNEOUS ROCKS

Igneous rocks were formed from magma either inside the earth's crust (called intrusive, or plutonic, rock) or on the earth's surface (called extrusive, or volcanic, rock).

All igneous rocks have crystals. The **largest crystals** are found in the rocks that cooled **slowly deepest** in the crust. The **smallest crystals** are found in the rocks that cooled **quickly on the surface.** Generally, crystal size in igneous rock decreases towards the surface.

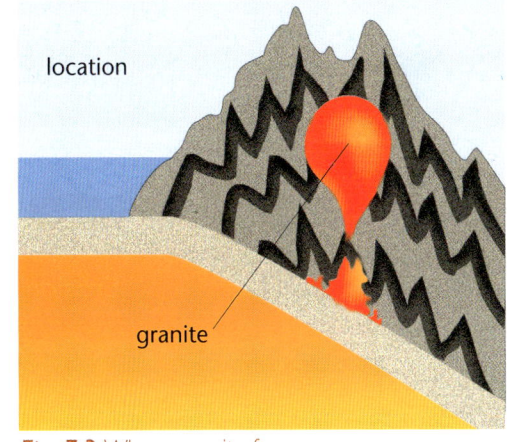

Fig. 7.3 Where granite forms.

Plutonic Rock

Plutonic rocks (also called intrusive rocks) are formed when magma cools within the earth's crust. The most common plutonic rock is granite.

Formation of Granite in Batholiths

Granite formed from masses of magma **deep within fold mountains.** These are destructive boundaries where the ocean crust is subducted into the mantle.

- Large masses of magma rise from the sinking plate into the buckled and folded rock to form **batholiths.**
- This magma **cools very slowly** over millions of years and creates **large crystals of mica, feldspar and quartz.** These three minerals form granite.
- The overall colour of granite can vary from pink with dark spots to black and white (looking something like a firelighter). The quartz grains are clear and glassy, the feldspars vary from white to pink, and crystals of mica are black or silvery.

Some varying colours of granite.

Volcanic Rock
Formation of Basalt

Basalt is a volcanic rock that cooled quickly **on or near the surface.** It has **tiny crystals** visible only under a microscope. It forms where magma **pours out quietly** from a crack, or **fissure,** on the surface and covers the surrounding landscape with a thick lava layer that cools quickly. These layers or sheets of basalt cover all humps and hollows and create a level surface. These flows are often 5 to 6 m thick.

- If the liquid lava is trapped to form **deep pools,** such as in a blocked river valley, the cooling rock cracks to form **five or six-sided columns** of basalt. Columns like these can be seen at the Giant's Causeway in Co. Antrim and at Linfield Quarry in Pallas Grean, in Co. Limerick.
- Basalt is a **dark heavy rock** when it forms. It may have **rusty spots** due to its high iron content. It may also have some **tiny holes** where gases escaped while cooling. If it is exposed at the surface, however, it may become coated with a whitish or other litchen that varies the appearance of the basalt.

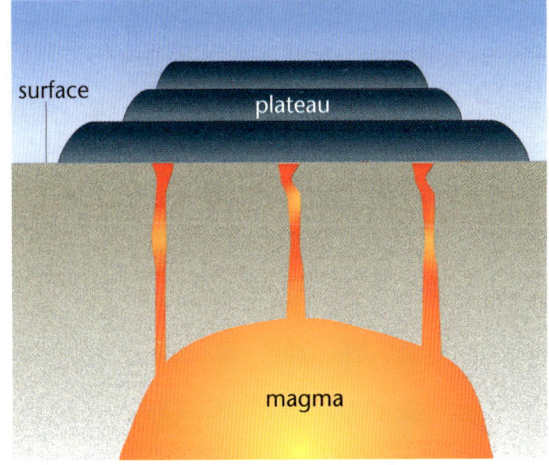

Fig. 7.4 Where basalt forms at the surface.

SEDIMENTARY ROCKS

Sandstone

> When granite weathers, the quartz grains are transported to form sandstone. The mica and feldspar weather to form clay and mud.

Sandstone is a hard rock that **resists erosion.** The most common type of sandstone is Old Red Sandstone. Approximately 350–400 million years ago, Ireland was located **20° south of the Equator.** The Kalahari Desert is at this latitude today, and it has the same **semi-arid climate** with seasonal rainfall as Ireland had at that time.

Erosion of the Caledonian mountains of Mayo, Connemara, Donegal and Wicklow **supplied sediments** carried in large rivers to huge deserts and lakes in lowland regions. The quartz grains from the eroding mountains were laid down in layers by the seasonal river waters to form thousands of metres of sandstone. The sandstone grains were compressed by the weight of overlying layers. They were **cemented together** by an iron cement, which was dissolved in groundwater that seeped through the rock. This iron cement also coloured the rock red, so it is called Old Red Sandstone.

The **mountains of Munster** are formed from this sandstone, which is over 6 km thick in places. (See page 51.)

Sandstone also formed from **delta deposits in river channels** and **floodplains**, and from **beach sand** and **sand dunes** at this time.

Many sandstones form from sand deposits in river channels.

Conglomerate

Conglomerate was formed from **gravel** in **alluvial fans** or **river channels** at the foot of steep slopes **within the Caledonian mountains.** The large particles, or clasts, were not eroded much because they were **not carried far** from their source in the mountains. These were deposited by **flash floods** in the same semi-desert conditions as the Old Red Sandstones. These may be seen on the **Devil's Bit** in Co. Tipperary.

Conglomerate forms from poorly sorted particles.

Shale

Shale forms in the sea from **fine particles of mud or clay.** These fine particles are so light they are carried far from their source in mountain regions. They are the last particles to be deposited by rivers that erode the mountains. This is why they are found on continental shelves and enclosed estuaries.

Shale is made up of numerous **thin layers** of sediment. Each layer represents a period of deposition that was separated from the next by a period of time when no deposition took place. Shale is easily broken and so is a **soft rock.**

Shale forms from the lightest rock particles (clay particles).

Limestone
The Setting When Ireland's Limestones Were Formed

1. Most of Ireland was submerged beneath a warm, equatorial sea. The Caledonian mountains of Connemara, Mayo, Donegal, Down and Wicklow stood as islands above the sea.

2. The great mass of Carboniferous rock that covers the plains of Ireland today must have originally been some thousands of metres thick.

3. The coalfields of Ireland, Britain and Europe were laid down in swamp-filled depressions at this time.

Fig. 7.5 Where limestone forms.

Activity
Look at Fig. 7.5. Why is there little limestone rock in Donegal, Galway, Mayo, Down and Wicklow?

Equator 0°

- dry land
- mountains
- warm seas
- coal swamps

Limestone is formed from the mineral calcium carbonate or calcite. It formed in two ways:

- **Calcium carbonate** from seawater collected around tiny sand grains floating in shallow lagoons near the Equator.
- **Billions of shells** and **skeletons** from tiny and large organisms, such as corals, which lived in the **tropical seas**.

Ireland's limestone formed when Ireland was **near the Equator 300–350 million years ago**. It is mostly composed of compressed shells, the remains of shellfish and coral skeletons that were abundant in the seas, so it has many **fossils**.

During this time there was an **explosion in new forms of sea life,** and many types of small, soft, slow-moving sea creatures **developed hard shells** to protect themselves from predators. They all lived in warm seas, coral reefs and shallow lagoons in the tropics. When they died, their shells and skeletons built up on the sea floor and were compressed by their own weight and the weight of later rocks to form solid limestone rock.

Because a lot of coal (which initially developed as peat in shallow swamps in delta areas at this time) became buried in the limestone, this period of time is called the **Carboniferous period**.

Ireland's limestone was formed in a setting of coral reefs similar to this photograph.

(Lithification)

45

METAMORPHIC ROCKS OF IRELAND

In a simple way, metamorphism is something like baking. When you bake, what you get to eat depends on what you start with and on the cooking conditions. It is the same with rocks: the end product is controlled by the initial make-up of the rock and by the metamorphic conditions (baking = the amount of heat).

Igneous and sedimentary rocks may change both in their **appearance** (physically) and in their **make-up** (chemically) as a consequence of heat or pressure, or both. This process of change is called **metamorphism**.

Factors that contribute to the end product include the **presence and amount of liquid** within the changing rock, the **length of time** a rock is subjected to **high temperature** or **high pressure**, and **whether** the changing rock is simply squeezed (**compressed**) or is **twisted**. These three basic factors all contribute to metamorphism: **heat**, **compression** and the **presence of liquids**.

Where Do Metamorphic Rocks Form?

Metamorphic rocks form **where plates collide**. In these places:

- Compression squeezes rock layers and they begin to heat and change.
- Rock layers come in contact with or are close to magma, which heats them intensely, causing change.
- Heating makes mineral atoms vibrate, and some break away. Liquids seeping through the heated rock carry the breakaway atoms to other locations, where they cluster to form new minerals.

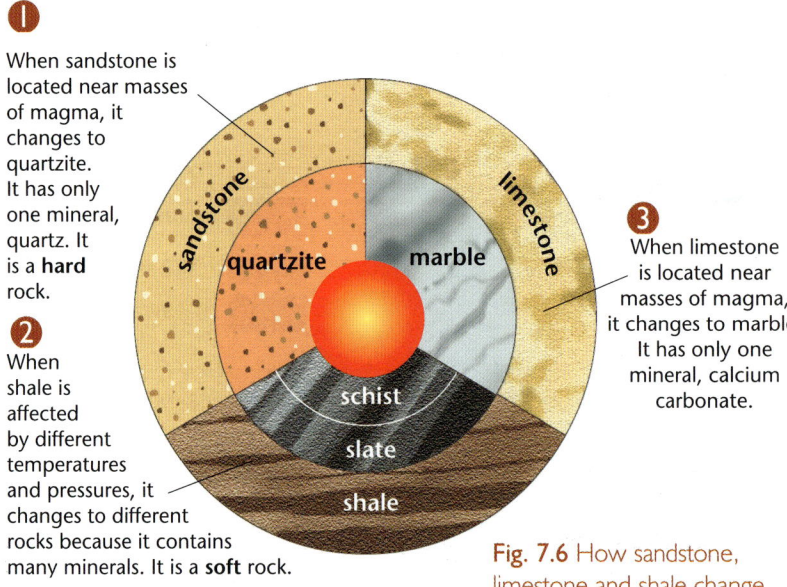

❶ When sandstone is located near masses of magma, it changes to quartzite. It has only one mineral, quartz. It is a **hard** rock.

❷ When shale is affected by different temperatures and pressures, it changes to different rocks because it contains many minerals. It is a **soft** rock.

❸ When limestone is located near masses of magma, it changes to marble. It has only one mineral, calcium carbonate.

Fig. **7.6** How sandstone, limestone and shale change.

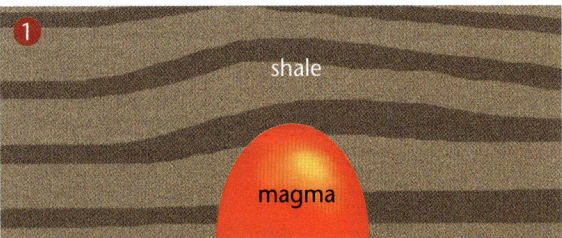

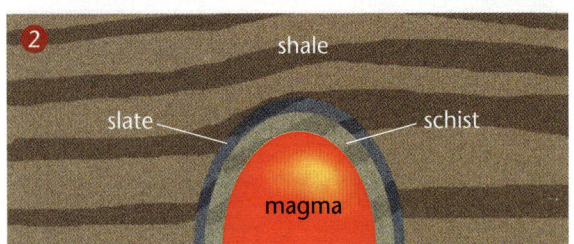

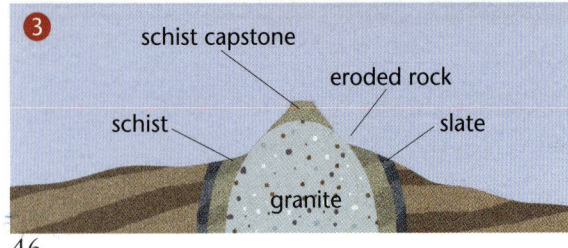

Case Study: Metamorphic Rocks in Leinster

The metamorphic rocks of Leinster formed when the European and American plates collided. Magma heated the buckled shale rock and changed it to schist or slate. In other places it changed sandstone rock to quartzite.

Fig. **7.7**

❶ Layers of shale were buckled and folded during collision. Then magma rose up into the shale.

❷ The magma heated and changed the shale. The hottest shale changed to schist. Farther out, with less heat, the shale changed to slate. The remaining shale was unchanged.

❸ After millions of years, most of the overlying schist, slate and shale has been removed by weathering and erosion. Because schist resists erosion, it still protects some peaks, such as Lugnaquilla.

ACTIVE AND TRAILING PLATE MARGINS

A continent's active margin occurs where an ocean plate sinks under the continental plate. On its western edge the American Plate is **colliding with or sliding past** plates such as the **Juan de Fuca Plate** and the **Pacific Plate**. This boundary is America's **active plate margin,** where faulting, earthquakes, volcanoes and high mountains are located. Because this plate margin is active, America's **newest igneous and metamorphic** rocks are forming here.

America's **east coast** has a wide **continental shelf**, just as Ireland has, where rivers from eroding mountains have built up **great depths of sedimentary rock**. This region is **not tectonically active**. No major earthquakes occur here and there are no active or dormant volcanoes. This is America's **passive, or trailing plate,** margin.

Which margin of the Eurasian Plate is:
a. an active margin?
b. a passive margin?

Fig. 7.8

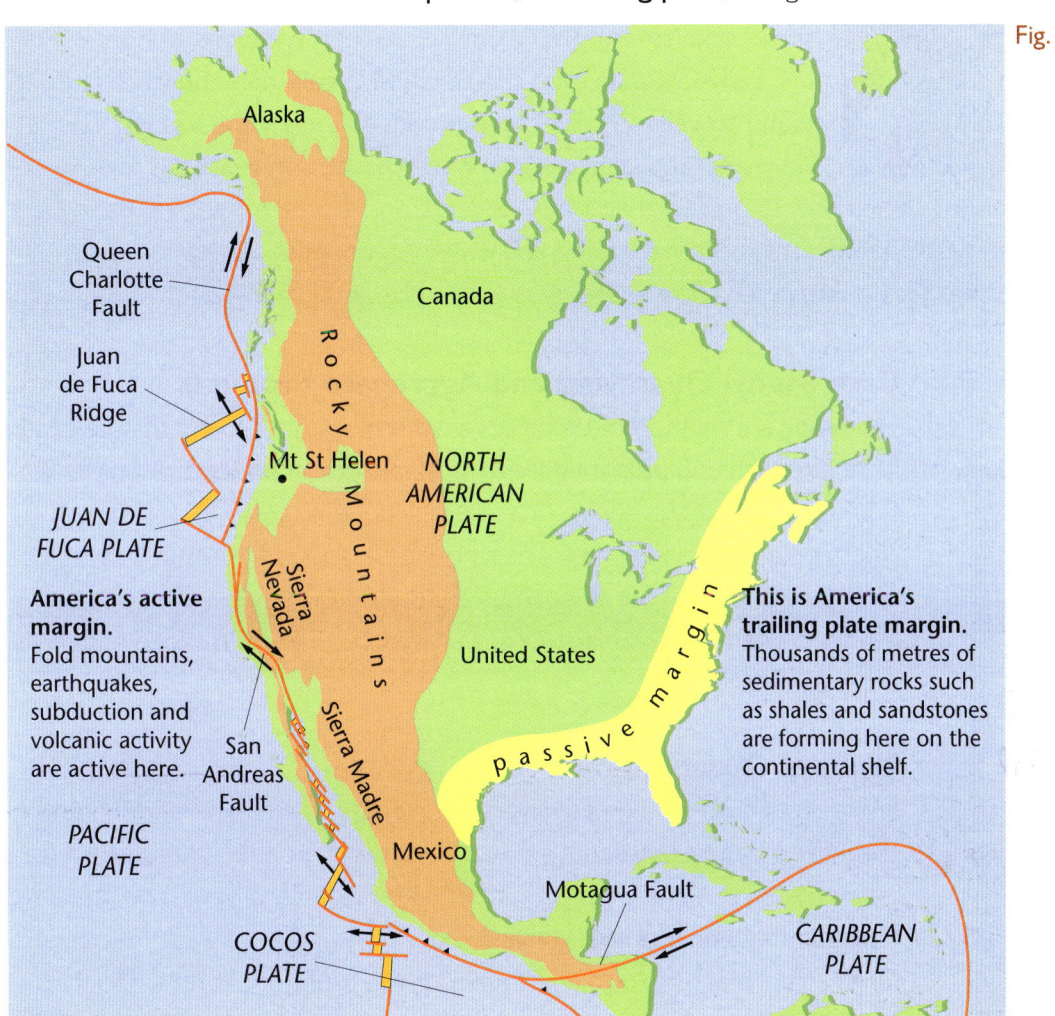

America's active margin.
Fold mountains, earthquakes, subduction and volcanic activity are active here.

This is America's trailing plate margin. Thousands of metres of sedimentary rocks such as shales and sandstones are forming here on the continental shelf.

Activity

Look at Fig. 7.8 and answer the following questions.
1. Which margin of the North American plate is (a) an active margin (b) a passive margin?
2. Name two major transform fault lines along the American west coast.
3. Name one ocean plate that is being subducted under the American Plate.
4. Name one active volcano along America's active margin.
5. Explain, with the aid of a diagram or diagrams, why this volcano is active.
6. Name one region that is regularly prone to earthquakes along this active margin.
7. Why is America's east coast a passive margin?

HOW PEOPLE INTERACT WITH THE ROCK CYCLE

Case Study: Extracting Building Materials

Most **buildings** are built from rock, such as **limestone, sandstone** or **granite**, or rock compounds, such as **concrete blocks** or **clay bricks**. To reinforce buildings or **pre-cast concrete** units, some metals, such as iron and steel, are included.

Stone Age people – Paleolithic, Mesolithic or Neolithic, as we now classify them – were so called because **tools** they used were made from stone. **Iron Age** people (Celts) used stone as a foundation for their forts and lake-side crannog settlements and extracted metal from stone (smelting) to manufacture their **weapons** of iron.

Early Christian monks built beehive **cells** and **churches** and **round towers** to protect them from attacks by the Vikings. The Normans, and later the Irish chieftains, built huge castles and defended settlements to protect their lands. Today, stone is used for road surfacing and in domestic house construction, for filling, foundations (concrete), blocks for **walls**, concrete **tiles** or **slates** for roofing, and gypsum for **plaster** in ceilings and walls.

Stone masons and sculptors create designs by working stone.

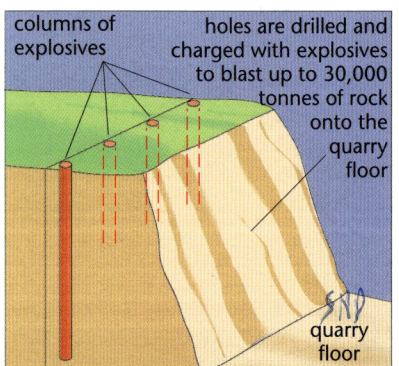

columns of explosives

holes are drilled and charged with explosives to blast up to 30,000 tonnes of rock onto the quarry floor

quarry floor

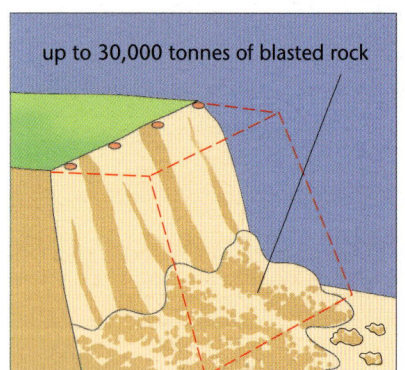

up to 30,000 tonnes of blasted rock

Fig. 7.9

Case Study: Quarrying and Aggregate Products

Quarrying is a method of taking large, solid blocks or broken masses of stone from the earth and preparing them for construction projects. A quarry is a large pit in the earth's surface from which stone is taken out (extracted). The types of stone taken from quarries include basalt, granite, limestone, marble, sandstone and slate. Some quarries are dug into the sides of mountains. Most are open at the surface. A quarry may be over 30 m deep and many times as wide as that.

Types of Quarrying

Stone is quarried by the plug and feather method, the explosive method or channelling by machinery.

Plug and Feather Method

Drill holes, wedges (plugs) and steel rods are used to split rock into thin slabs.

Explosive Method

The explosive method is used to break off huge masses of rock from a rock face.

Channelling by Machinery

Huge slices of rock are cut off a rock edge by a large rotating disc. These slices are taken away for cutting into various sizes.

The Economic Impact of Quarrying in Ireland

- Aggregates are an essential requirement for construction.
- About 90,000 people are employed in the construction industry.
- Over 40,000 housing units are built each year.
- About 7 tonnes of aggregates are used per 1,000 tonnes of building work.
- About 50,000 tonnes of aggregates are required each year.
- Ireland has over 200 active pits and quarries.

Two major quarrying companies in Ireland include **Roadstone** at Bunratty, Co. Clare and **Ready Mix** at Tullamore, Co. Offaly. Private quarrying companies include Kelly and Gleeson at Donohill, Co. Tipperary.

Carrara Marble Quarries In Tuscany, Italy

Carrara has been famous for its marble since Roman times. Stone from these quarries was used in Rome at the time of Emperor Augustus (27 BC–AD 14). Later, Carrara's finest pure white marble was made famous by the great sculptors, Leonardo da Vinci and Michelangelo. Marble quarries surround the town of Carrara and it is one of the world's major centres for marble production and export. The port of Marina di Carrara handles marble almost exclusively.

Marble is used extensively in the construction of buildings, especially in warm countries, such as Italy. It creates a **cool interior** atmosphere and so is used for **floors** in **airports** and other **public buildings**. Because it can be polished at quarries to produce a smooth surface, it is used for **walls and bathroom floors in domestic houses throughout the world**.

Negative Effects of Quarrying

Quarrying can have a negative impact on the landscape. Some impacts include:

- Airborne dust that can affect nearby homes and farmland.
- The generation of silt into rivers that affects water quality and fish spawning grounds.
- Noise and vibration from blasting and machinery.
- Damage to roads between the quarry and construction sites.
- Disused quarries scar the landscape and have regularly been reused as rubbish pits.

Carrara

About 60 hectares of land are used each year to extract 35 million tonnes of rock and 15 million tonnes of sand and gravel. This annual land usage by the whole Irish quarrying industry amounts to less than 0.001 per cent of the total land area of Ireland.

Quarrying for sand and gravel is carried out in almost every county in Ireland. Most of this material is found in esker ridges that were deposited as the ice sheets melted about 10,000 years ago.

Limestone rock in Ireland is a major economic resource. Explain three ways that limestone is used in the construction industry and farming.

- *How was marble formed?*
- *What are its uses today?*

CHAPTER 8
SEDIMENTARY LANDFORMS CREATED BY EARTH MOVEMENTS

 **KEY IDEA!**

Sedimentary landforms are created by earth movements.

The rocks of an anticline crack and open. This allows the forces of weathering and erosion to attack and erode the anticline quickly.

LANDFORMS CREATED BY FOLDING

Folding is caused by **compression**. It is associated with the **closing of an ocean**. On the ocean floor, thousands of metres of sediment are compressed by their own weight into solid rock. Once the ocean closes, these sedimentary rocks are crushed between the colliding continents. The **layers of sediments are compressed, folded and pushed up (and sometimes down) to form fold mountains**.

Fold Types	Formation	Fold Types	Formation
anticline syncline limb limb **Symmetrical fold (simple fold)**	Both limbs have similar slopes.	anticline limb limb **Over fold**	One limb is pushed over the other limb.
anticline limb limb **Asymmetrical fold**	One limb is steeper than the other.	thrust **Thrust fault**	When compression is great , a fracture (crack) occurs in the fold. One limb is then pushed forward over the other limb at a very low angle along the fault line. This limb may be displaced for a distance of a few kilometres.

Fig. 8.1

When bedding planes run parallel, as in Fig. 8.2, Diagram A, it indicates that all the rock layers were folded at the same time. It also indicates that the surface layers are younger than the lower layers. These layers are said to 'conform'.

Fig. 8.2

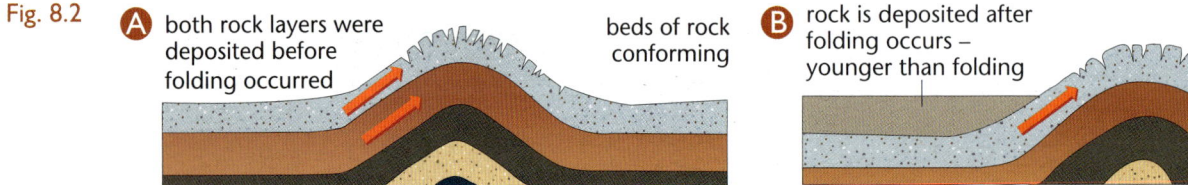

Ⓐ both rock layers were deposited before folding occurred — beds of rock conforming

Ⓑ rock is deposited after folding occurs – younger than folding — beds of rock not conforming

In Fig. 8.2, Diagram B, surface rock on the lowland does not follow the original folds, so it does not conform. It is clear, then, that this rock was deposited on the lowland after the folding took place.

THE ARMORICAN FOLDINGS IN MUNSTER 300 MYA

Sandstone and Limestone Rock Layers

Only 50 million years after their formation, the **Caledonian** mountains were worn down to sea level across the Irish **Midlands** and **Munster**. Their eroded materials were deposited in these regions to form layers of sandstone rock. At this time, Ireland had a hot, dry climate with seasonal rainfall.

Fig. 8.3

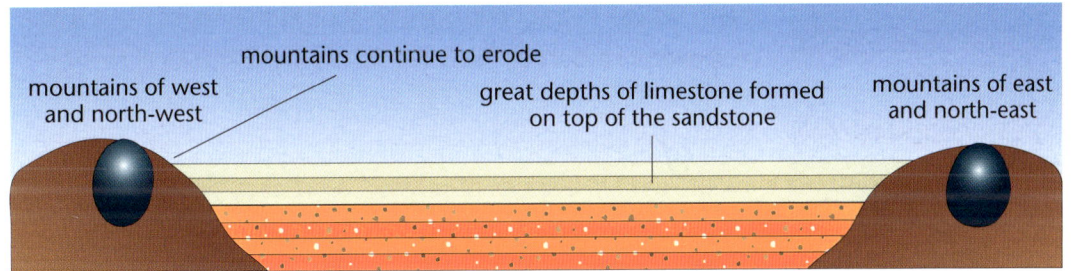

batholiths of Mayo, Connemara and Donegal

batholiths of Leinster and Co. Down

thousands of metres of sandstone rock

iron oxide coloured red

Then, about **350 million years ago,** Ireland and its level sandstone layers sank beneath a warm equatorial sea. Great depths of **limestone formed on top of the sandstones from the shells and skeletons of sea creatures.**

Fig. 8.4

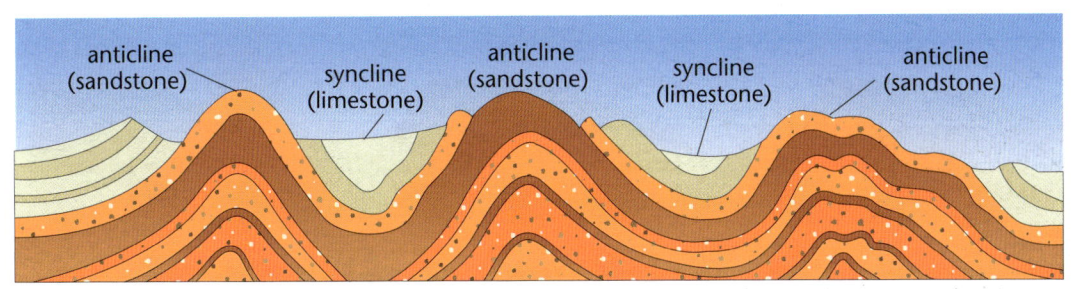

mountains continue to erode

mountains of west and north-west

great depths of limestone formed on top of the sandstone

mountains of east and north-east

Suddenly Africa crashed into Europe, and all the other continents were now welded into a single continent, Pangaea. The Appalachians in the US and the Pyrenees, the Urals and many mountains in Germany were buckled upwards.

Ireland was dry land once more, and its **limestone and sandstone rock layers were buckled and intensely folded in Munster,** forming **east-west ridges and valleys** because they were closest to the African-European boundary. They are the Armorican fold mountains.

Two types of rock were involved in the folding:

- **Old Red Sandstone**, the older rock, and so the lowest layer.
- **Limestone**, the younger rock, and so the surface layer.

Since then the **softer limestone** has **eroded faster** than the harder sandstone, so the **sandstone** stands out as **ridges,** while the limestone covers the valleys.

Some mountains have a distinctive **trend**. This means their ridges and valleys run in a definite direction.

Fig. 8.5 Munster's ridges and valleys.

anticline (sandstone)

syncline (limestone)

anticline (sandstone)

syncline (limestone)

anticline (sandstone)

51

LANDFORMS CREATED BY DOMING, SAGGING AND TILTING

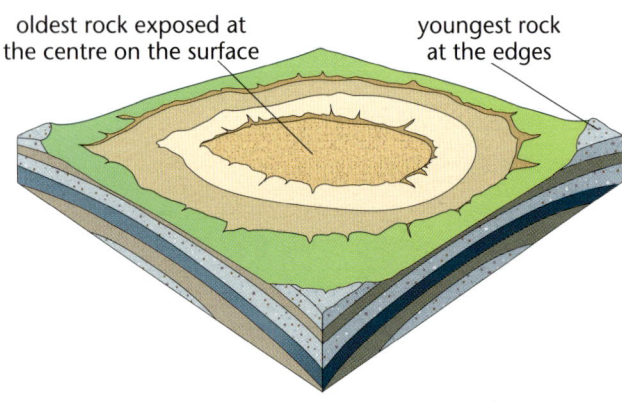

oldest rock exposed at the centre on the surface

youngest rock at the edges

Fig. 8.6 Dome landform in the Weald of southern England.

Doming

Example: The Weald in Sussex, in England, formed after the Alpine foldings

A dome is a structure in which the beds of rock dip away from a central point. The beds are like upturned saucers, one inside the other. A dome is formed by compression. Weathering and erosion attack the uplifted rock. Over time, wind, rain, frost and ice combine to expose the older rock layers in the centre. Thus, the **age** of the surface rock **increases towards the centre**.

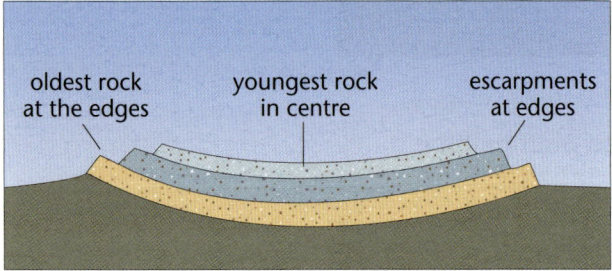

oldest rock at the edges

youngest rock in centre

escarpments at edges

Fig. 8.7 The Paris Basin is a dish-shaped structure.

Sagging

Example: The Paris Basin

When horizontal rock layers sag, they create a saucer-shaped basin, lower in the centre and higher at the edges. This is the opposite of a dome. The rock layers are first folded by compression. They then sag due to erosion. The higher edges are attacked by weathering and erosion, exposing the older rocks in a series of ridges, called **escarpments**. Thus, the **age** of rocks **reduces towards the centre**.

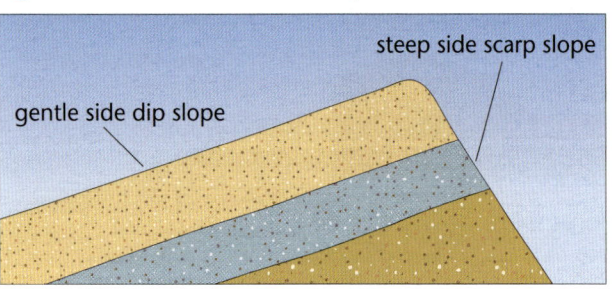

steep side scarp slope

gentle side dip slope

Fig. 8.8 An escarpment has dipping rock layers.

Tilting

Example: The Dartry-Cuilcagh Uplands

When horizontal rock layers are gently tilted by uplift or sagging, a structure with uneven slopes is formed. One slope, called the scarp slope, is steep. The other is gentle and is called the dip slope. This landform is called an **escarpment**. When the surface rock layer of the escarpment is sandstone, it will resist erosion and protect the underlying softer rock. Over time, surrounding rock may be eroded, leaving the escarpment to dominate the surrounding region.

LANDFORMS CREATED BY FAULTING

The following are some features that have been formed by vertical and horizontal rock movement.

Fig. 8.9 Landforms created by vertical movement.

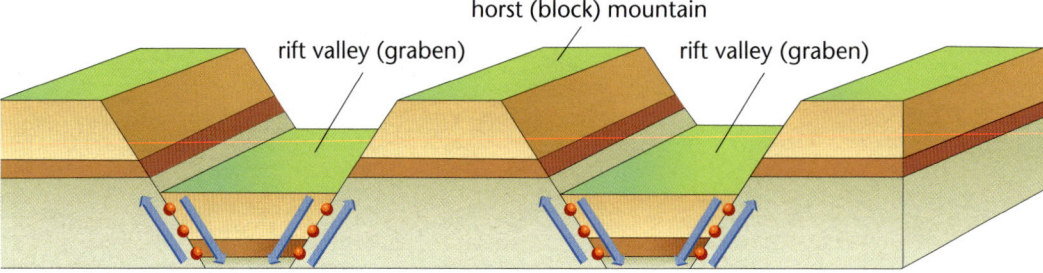

horst (block) mountain

rift valley (graben)

rift valley (graben)

 potential earthquake locations

Definitions of Faults and Landforms

Reverse Faults

Example: The Ox Mountains in Co. Sligo

A reverse fault occurs due to **compression** from destructive plate movement. Pressure causes the rock to fracture and there is an **upward** movement of land between parallel faults. Reverse faulting creates **block mountains.**

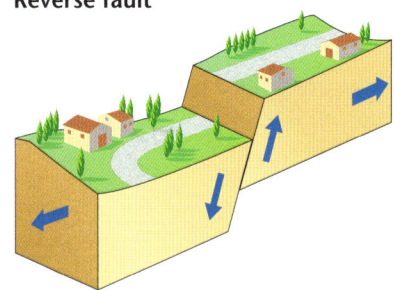

Reverse fault

Normal Faults

Example: The Rift Valley of Scotland

A normal fault occurs when bedrock is stretched due to tension until it fractures along a fault line. There is a **downward** movement of land between parallel faults. Normal faulting creates **rift valleys.**

Block Mountains (Horst)

Example: The Ox Mountains in Co. Sligo

Block mountains are upland regions that were pushed upward between parallel faults due to compression (bedrock being squashed from two opposite directions).

Rift Valleys (Graben)

Example: The Rift Valley of Scotland

Rift valleys are lowland regions that were dropped down between parallel faults due to tension (bedrock being stretched or pulled apart).

Normal fault
Fig. 8.10

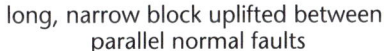

long, narrow block uplifted between parallel normal faults

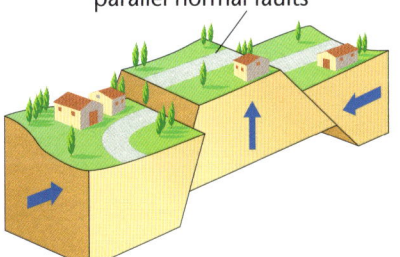

Block mountain (horst) – compression

Fig. 8.11

long, narrow sunken block between parallel normal faults

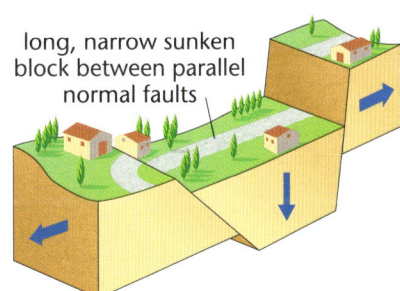

Rift valley (graben) – tension

The Victoria Falls in Zimbabwe are created by a fault line where the African Plate is being split apart. A rift valley has formed.

Activity
Carefully study the Ordnance Survey map of the Derryveagh Mountains in Co. Donegal on page 54, then answer the following.
1. What is the direction, or trend, of the Derryveagh Mountains?
2. Why do these mountain ridges run in this direction?
3. What influence does this trend have on the:
    a. local river pattern   b. local routeways?
4. What processes were responsible for the creation of this mountainous landscape? In your answer, refer to:
    a. internal forces (endogenic)   b. external forces (exogenic).

53

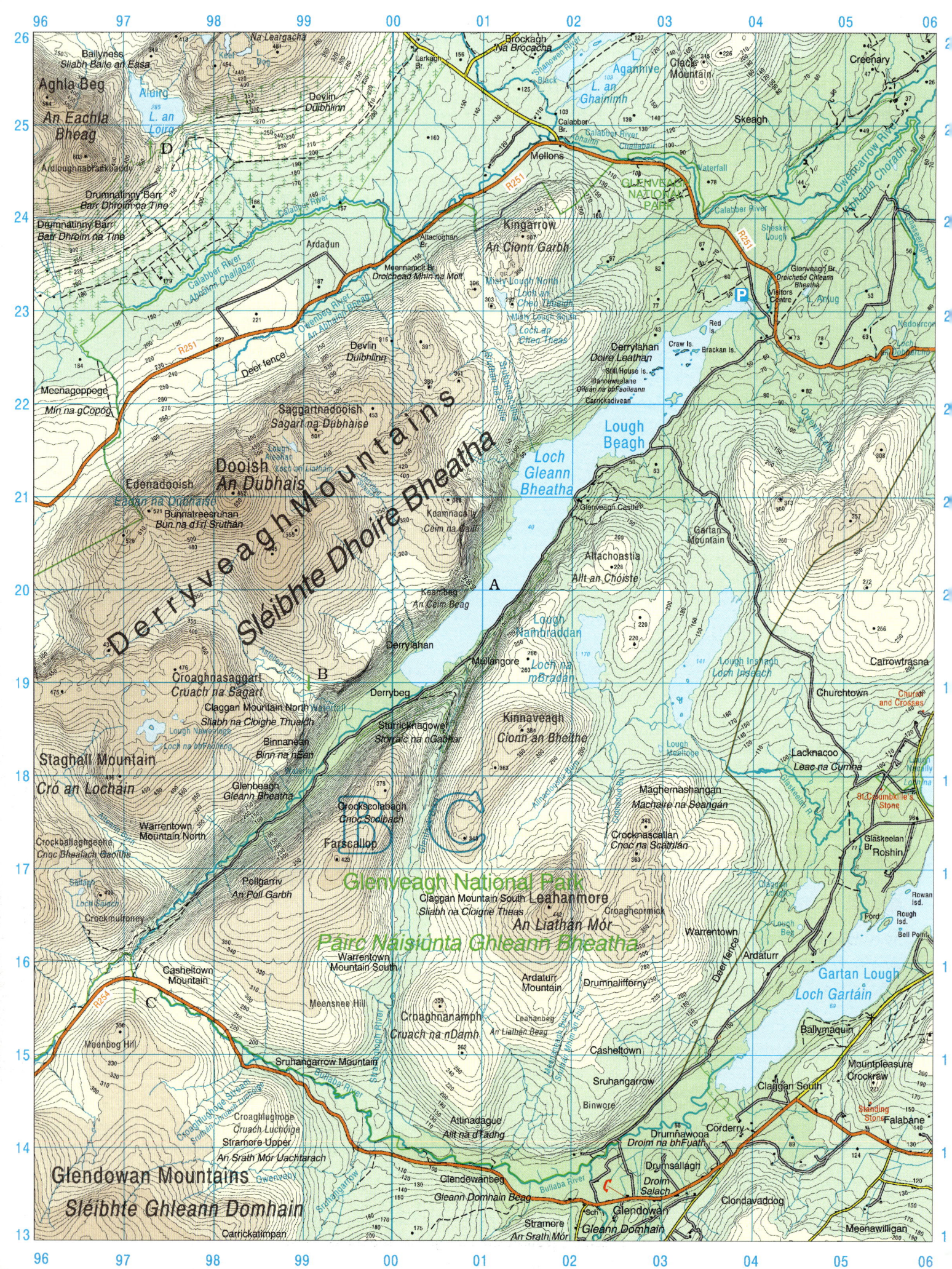

CHAPTER 9
WEATHERING PROCESSES AND LANDFORMS

KEY IDEA! When rock is placed in a different environment from which it formed originally, it becomes unstable and so is prone to rapid change by the elements of weathering and erosion.

Weathering is the breaking down or decay of rocks that lie on or near the earth's surface. There are two types of weathering: mechanical and chemical.

MECHANICAL WEATHERING

Mechanical weathering involves rocks breaking up into smaller fragments. Mechanical weathering in Ireland is caused by:

- Joint formation, onion weathering and exfoliation.
- Freeze-thaw action.
- Plants and animals.

Joint Formation (Jointing)

Rock buried deep beneath the ground surface is subjected to enormous confining pressure. This is **weight that squeezes the rock** from all sides. As **erosion** wears away the surface, the weight of the overlying rock and the **pressure is reduced.** This is called **pressure-release,** or **unloading. J**oints then form and these can break rocks into large or small rectangular blocks, or pillar-like columns.

Once formed, the joints act as passageways for rainwater to enter a rock. This increases the rate of further physical and chemical weathering.

Sheeting of Granite Batholiths

Typically, granite batholiths split into **onion-like sheets** along joints that lie parallel to the surface of the rock. This is due to **unloading** and is called **exfoliation**.

Fig. 9.1 Joints in rock aid the processes of weathering.

Well-jointed granite.

Sheeting of surface granite.

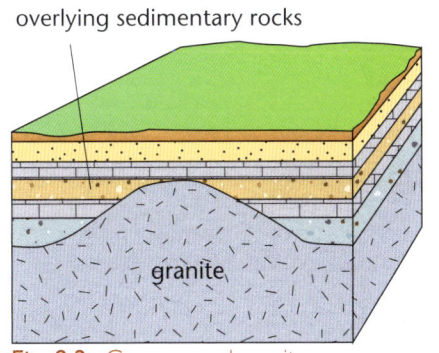

Fig. 9.2a Compressed granite.

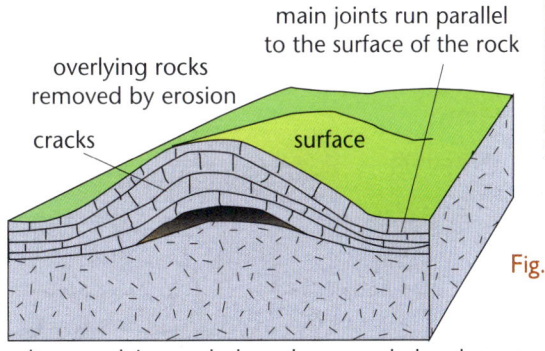

Fig. 9.2b Pressure removed from granite.

when overlying rocks have been eroded and removed, pressure is reduced from the granite and cracks appear

55

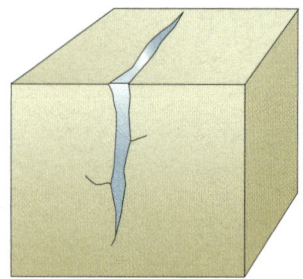

trapped water freezes during winter at night on high mountains

Fig. 9.3 Surface water fills cracks in rock.

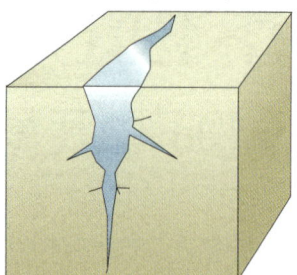

ice expands by about 9% and lengthens joints

Fig. 9.4 Freeze-thaw action shatters rock.

Freeze-Thaw Action

Freezing water bursts pipes and shatters bottles because water expands when it freezes and pushes the walls of the container apart. This also happens in rock. When the **water trapped** in a joint freezes, it **forces the joint open** and may cause the joint to lengthen. This is particularly active in temperate climates where water periodically **freezes and thaws**. This process shatters rock. The shattered rock collects at the foot of steep slopes, forming scree.

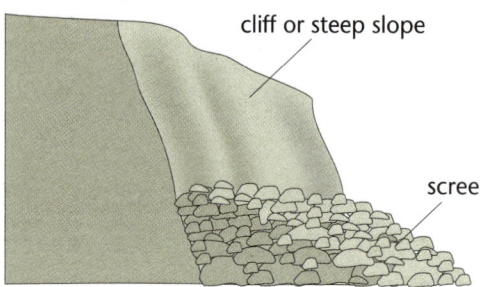

cliff or steep slope

scree

Fig. 9.5 The shattered rock at the foot of steep slopes forms scree.

scree

joints are opened by both frost action and expansion due to unloading

Fig. 9.6 Joints help rock disintegration.

Joints, Freeze-Thaw and Unloading

Some rocks break up into large rectangular-shaped blocks under the action of mechanical weathering. This is called block disintegration. It may be due partly to frost action and partly to expansion due to unloading and the creation of joints. This increases the surface area that is exposed to weathering.

Plant Roots

Seeds germinate in cracks in rock to produce plants. The plant roots then **penetrate into the cracks and crevices** in the rock, **widening these** as they grow larger and causing sections of rock to split apart.

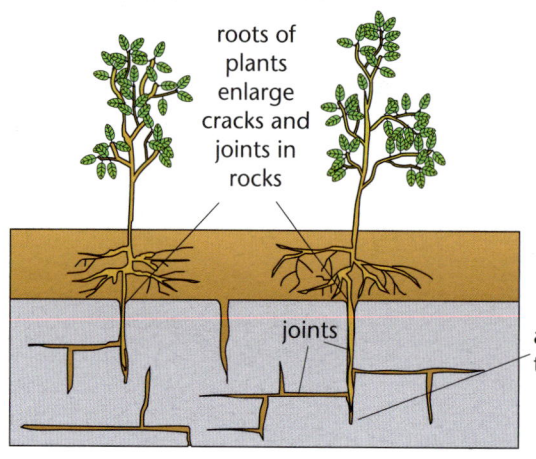

roots of plants enlarge cracks and joints in rocks

joints

Fig. 9.7 Plant roots enlarge joints in bedrock.

as the root grows, the joint is opened up

Surface Flaking

Water solutions containing minerals seep some distance into pores in some rocks like sandstone. The solutions dry out in hot weather and leave minerals behind that form crystals. Over time, this process helps the **crystals** to **grow**. These crystals **push out** neighbouring grains to form flaking at the surface.

CHEMICAL WEATHERING

Water and water solutions are the principal agents of chemical weathering. The effects of chemical weathering are greatest where the climate is **hot and wet**.

Most rocks are composed of two or more minerals. Exposure to chemical weathering weakens or breaks these bonds, causing disintegration of the rocks. The most important types of chemical weathering are:

- Carbonation.
- Oxidation.
- Hydration.
- Hydrolysis.

Carbonation

Rainwater falling through the air joins with small amounts of carbon dioxide to form a weak **carbonic acid**. As it reaches and trickles through limestone joints and bedding planes, it weathers the limestone. Weathering changes the calcium carbonate mineral that forms limestone into **calcium** and **bicarbonate minerals**. These are **soluble in water,** so they are carried away in solution.

Oxidation

This is simply the **rusting** of some minerals. Minerals, such as iron, become oxides in the presence of oxygen. This creates a **red** or **yellowish colouring** that is carried away by groundwater. When the mineral dries it becomes a cementing agent (a new mineral) in sedimentary rocks, such as sandstone. **Iron oxide** (haematite and magnetite) discoloured the quartz grains of sandstone to a brownish or reddish colour to form Old Red Sandstone.

Hydration

Some minerals **absorb water**. When they do, they expand. If a rock contains these kinds of mineral, the wet, expanding minerals **create stresses** within the rock and over time shatter the rock. 'Tiny' **freeze-thaw** within wet minerals also helps shatter rock particles, leading to them breaking up.

Hydrolysis

This is the most important chemical process in the break-up of rock. It involves a chemical reaction between some rock minerals and water.

In granite, for example, it joins with **feldspar** minerals to form **clay** minerals. But as the feldspar minerals were the **cement** that held the other minerals (the micas and quartz) together, the rock crumbles.

Surface flaking has damaged many urban buildings in recent decades.

Carbonation has increased and damaged many important monuments and buildings in recent decades.

Iron oxide tinted sandstone a reddish or yellow colour.

DISTINCTIVE LANDSCAPES AND LANDFORMS

KEY IDEA! When some rock types are weathered, they produce distinctive landscapes.

Granite tors on Dartmoor create a distinctive landscape.

Granite Landscapes

Granite rises to the surface when **overlying rock is removed** by weathering and erosion in fold mountain regions. The pressure of surrounding rock is no longer present and this **loss of weight** allows the granite to **expand**. This creates cracks, or **joints,** in the granite. Joints are enlarged through chemical weathering and this causes **the edges** of the blocks to **become rounded.** These rounded blocks of granite separated by joints are called **tors.**

Weathered granite forms gently sloping uplands. This combination of **gently sloping uplands** of fields for cattle and sheep grazing, **with tors on top,** creates a distinctive landscape. **Dartmoor,** in south-west England, has a distinctive granite landscape. The **Wicklow Mountains** have some tors on their summits (see **Mechanical Weathering and Chemical Weathering,** pages 55–7).

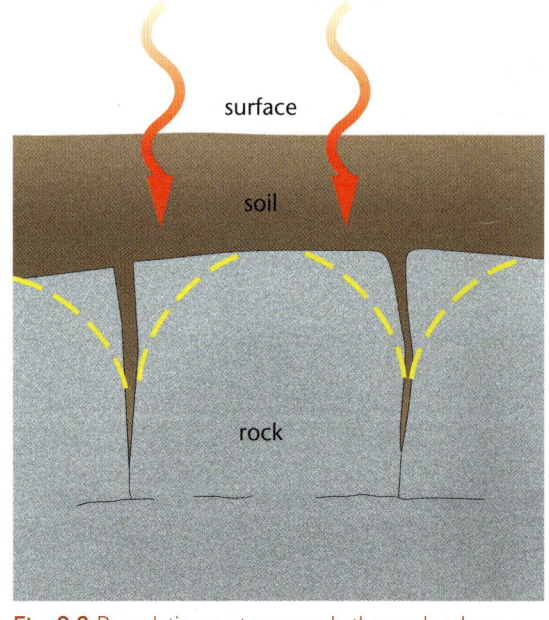

Fig. 9.8 Percolating water rounds the rock edges.

Quartzite Landscapes

Examples: The Great Sugar Loaf in Co. Wicklow
Croagh Patrick in Co. Mayo

Quartzite is found **near granite regions.** Unlike granite, quartzite is very resistant to chemical weathering, but it is **prone to frost action.** This **freeze-thaw** action breaks off long, angular slabs of the quartzite. This process creates the distinctive **pointed peaks** in quartzite regions.

Quartzite resists erosion and forms pointed peaks like Croagh Patrick in Mayo.

CHAPTER 10
DISTINCTIVE LIMESTONE LANDSCAPES AND LANDFORMS

KEY IDEA! The distinctive landscape and landforms of limestone regions are directly influenced by the mineral composition of the limestone rock.

The Burren, Co. Clare

Karst is a term used worldwide to describe the distinctive landforms that develop on limestone rock that is easily dissolved by water. Some Irish karst regions include the following:

Limestone Pavement

Irish examples: Near Black Head in the Burren, Co. Clare
Marble Arch Uplands in Co. Fermanagh

Formation

Limestone pavement forms in regions of medium to heavy rainfall with a warm to temperate climate. It also forms because limestone:

- Is composed of one mineral, calcium carbonate. This creates **even weathering** of the rock surface, so forming level land.
- Reacts with rainwater, so dissolving the rock.
- Has regular joints caused by unloading of overlying rock through erosion.
- Is pervious, which means rainwater is able to pass freely through its vertical joints and horizontal bedding planes.

Rainwater is a weak acid, called **carbonic acid**. This acid forms as rain falls through the air and absorbs **carbon dioxide**. When the rainwater lands on bare limestone rock, it creates a chemical reaction. The hydrogen in the carbonic acid separates the calcium carbonate of the limestone rock into separate **calcium** and **bicarbonate atoms,** which are both soluble in the groundwater. In this way the limestone is dissolved and removed, so the rock is worn away.

The parallel **vertical joints** in the limestone allow the water to trickle through the rock. These cracks are widened and deepened through solution. These widened cracks are called **grikes**. The wider the **grikes** become, the faster the water is able to sink through the limestone. In the **Burren** these grikes mostly run in a **north-south** direction.

The parallel grikes create **flat ridges of rock** between them, called **clints**. This combination of grikes and clints form a distinctive level surface that is only found in limestone regions.

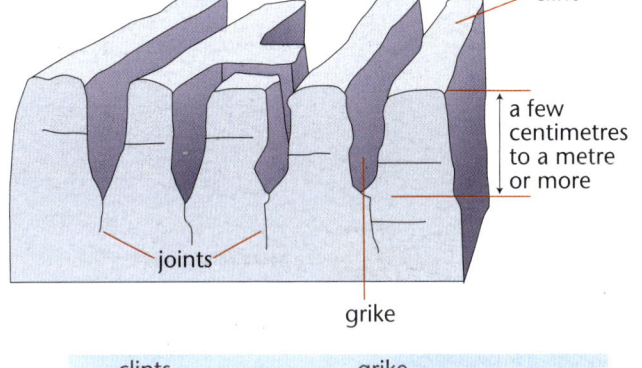

Fig. 10.1 The Burren in Co. Clare.

clint

a few centimetres to a metre or more

joints

grike

clints   grike

Limestone pavement in the Burren.

Limestone reacts with rainwater somewhat like the way soluble aspirin does when it is put in a glass of water.

59

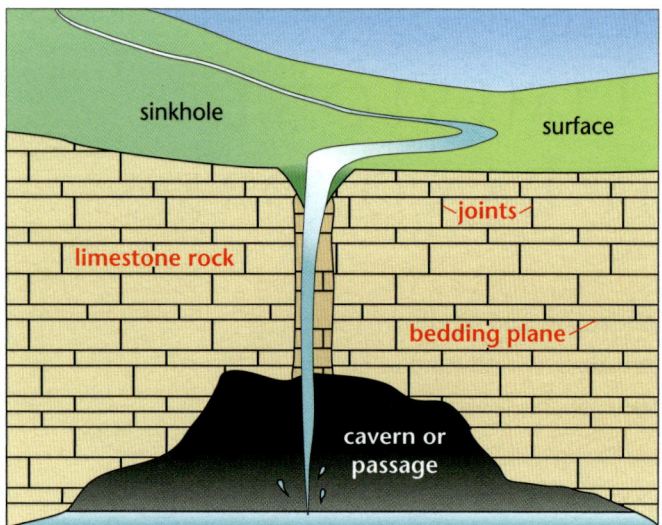

Fig. 10.2 Limestone pavement in the Burren.

Sinkholes

Example: Poulnabunny in Co. Mayo
The Cradle Hole in the Cuilcagh Uplands

A sinkhole is an opening in the bed of a river through which a river disappears underground in a limestone region. It is also called a swallow hole, a slugga or a sink.

Sinkholes may form at the surface where the roofs of underground caverns collapse, such as at Winter Garden in Florida, USA.

The opposite of a sinkhole is a **resurgence**. At a resurgence, a river appears from underground. It is not a spring; it is the location where a river that had gone underground at some upstream location **reappears on the surface.**

A **turlough** is a seasonal lake. It appears during long, wet spells when underground passages fill up. It dries out when the water table falls.

Formation

Rainwater is a weak acid, called **carbonic acid**. This forms as rain falls through the air and absorbs **carbon dioxide**. When the rainwater lands on bare limestone rock, it creates a chemical reaction. The hydrogen in the carbonic acid separates the calcium carbonate of the limestone rock into separate **calcium** and **bicarbonate atoms,** which are both soluble in the groundwater. In this way the limestone is dissolved and removed, so the rock is worn away.

As rivers flow across limestone regions, some of the rainwater trickles down through the joints and bedding planes on the riverbed. The joints and bedding planes are widened, also allowing more **surface water and any sediment** that the flowing water is carrying to go underground.

Underground, the flowing **groundwater dissolves** the limestone and the **sediment erodes** the rock through abrasion along these lines of weakness. These processes create underground **passages** that originate under the riverbed.

The joints and bedding planes divide limestone into blocks. These blocks become unstable where the rock beneath has been eroded. Where some **blocks fall** from the ceiling of the passages, this eventually leads to a collapse of the rock on the riverbed. This creates **an opening from the surface to the underground passage,** through which the river plunges vertically downwards.

The opening that swallows up the river is called a sinkhole. The remaining river valley downstream of the sinkhole becomes dry and so is called a **dry valley**. If the river floods, the underground passage may be unable to carry all of the river's volume. In this case, some water will pass through the dry valley again and temporarily occupy its original channel.

Caverns

Example: Marble Arch Cave in Co. Fermanagh
Mammoth Cave in Kentucky, USA

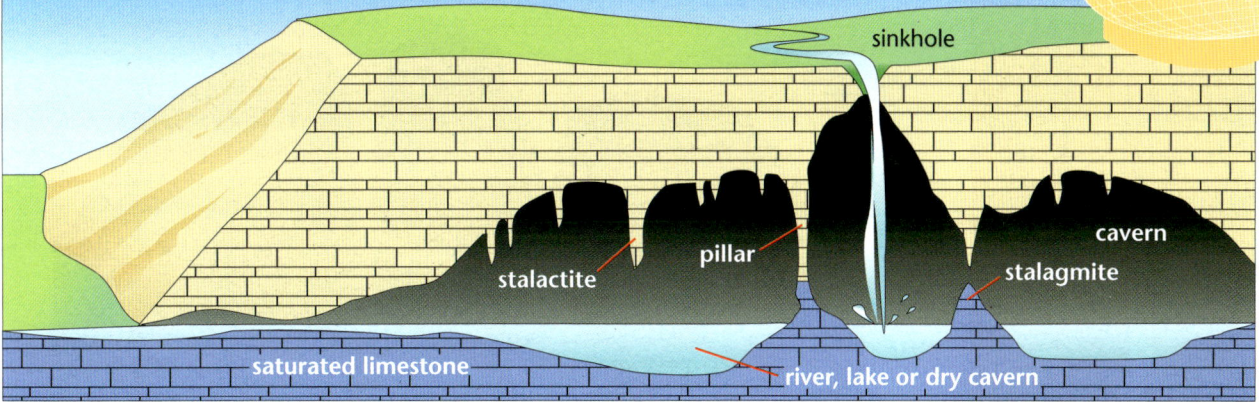

A cavern is a subsurface landform.

Fig. 10.3
A sinkhole.

Formation

The formation of most caverns takes place in the **zone of saturation**, at or below the water table in limestone regions. Some caverns, such as Marble Arch Caves, were formed by flowing water that came from the surface rivers.

When rain falls on the ground, it trickles through the soil and bedrock until it meets an **impermeable rock layer**. It cannot go down, so its level rises and it saturates the porous, or pervious, rock above so that all pore spaces between the rock grains and joints and bedding planes are filled with water.

This underground water is not stationary, as it constantly **seeps and flows through the bedrock**. This water is acidic because it dissolved carbon dioxide from the air and from organic matter as it trickled down through the soil. It is **carbonic acid** and it creates a chemical reaction with limestone. The hydrogen in the carbonic acid separates the calcium carbonate of the limestone rock into separate **calcium and bicarbonate atoms, which are both soluble in groundwater**. In this way the limestone is dissolved and removed, so the rock is worn away.

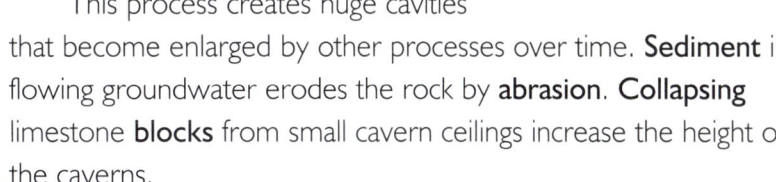

Mammoth Cave in Kentucky is world famous.
● *What features can you identify in this cavern?*

This process creates huge cavities that become enlarged by other processes over time. **Sediment** in flowing groundwater erodes the rock by **abrasion**. **Collapsing** limestone **blocks** from small cavern ceilings increase the height of the caverns.

Meltwater from melting ice sheets and glaciers at the end of the last Ice Age increased the flow of water through some underground passages and caverns. This vast release of meltwater carried sand, rocks and boulders into these underground channels through sinkholes and enlarged the channels into enormous caverns.

Many of these caverns are dry due to a fall in the water table or tectonic uplift.

Stalactites and stalagmites sometimes join to form pillars or columns.

Speleothems or Dripstone Formations

Examples: Marble Arch Caves in Co. Fermanagh
Mitchelstown Caves in Co. Tipperary

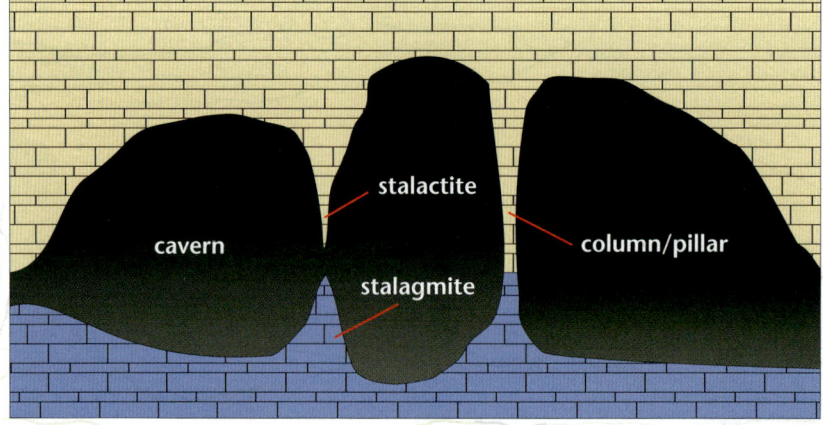

Fig. 10.4 A cavern.

Limestone caves are great tourist attractions. Can you name some?

Formation

Speleothems, or dripstone formations, include **stalactites, stalagmites, pillars or columns, and curtains.** They are all formed of the mineral **calcite.** Calcite is calcium carbonate and in its purest form it is white.

These landforms develop in caverns that are dry or partially dry due to a lowering of the water table by a stream or tectonic uplift. The drop in the water table exposes the underground chambers to the air, which in turn plays its part in the formation of the calcite landforms.

The calcite landforms form by the continuous deposition of calcite, where water drips from cavern ceilings. Some form on the ceiling, while stalagmites develop on the sides or floor of caverns. Groundwater in limestone regions is saturated in dissolved **calcium atoms** and **bicarbonate atoms.** It is also **supersaturated in carbon dioxide.** When the water that trickles down through vertical cracks reaches the cavern ceiling, the carbon dioxide escapes into the air and it **reverses the solution process.** Calcite is deposited where the water drops from the ceiling.

Initially, calcite builds around the outside of the drip, forming a delicate, hollow stalactite, called a **soda straw.** Eventually the hollow **fills up** or **gets blocked** with grit, and water seeps around the hanging stem to form a more massive solid **stalactite.**

Where the drip hits the floor, it splashes, and the resulting calcite builds up to form an upward-pointing cone, called a **stalagmite.** If this process continues over a very long time, the stalagmites and stalactites join to form limestone **columns, or pillars.**

If this process occurs along a crack in the ceiling, it builds a vertical **curtain-like** sheet of calcite that hangs from the cavern roof.

If the groundwater flows along the surface of a wall, it drapes the wall with **cloth-like** sheets of calcite called **flowstone.** Thin sheets of flowstone tend to be translucent when lit from behind.

Tower Karst Landscape

This dramatic landscape has inspired many Chinese artists and photographers.

Formation

Example: Guangxi, in south-west China, and north-east Vietnam

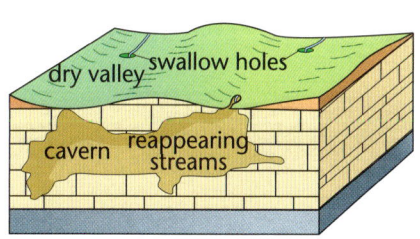

dry valley   swallow holes

cavern   reappearing streams

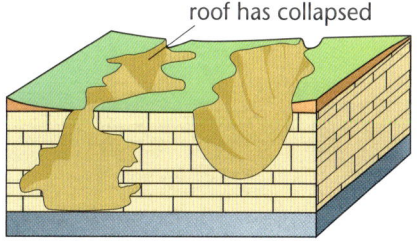

roof has collapsed

surface drainage returns as underground passages are filled with sediment

Fig. 10.5 Tower karst.

Tower karst consists of **isolated tower-like hills** separated by **flat areas of alluvium**. It represents the **late stage** of weathering of a limestone landscape.

- In the **early stage of karst formation**, weathering and erosion dissolve and erode away the surface limestone. **Joints and bedding planes** are widened, creating a limestone pavement of **grikes and clints**. Streams disappear through sinkholes into underground passages and caverns.

- The **middle stage** involves the **collapse of cavern and passage roofs,** creating large depressions, called **poljes**, surrounded by higher ground, as in the Burren in Co. Clare.

- In the **late stage** there is **large-scale collapse** of the underground landforms. This creates tower-like hills of limestone throughout the landscape. Sediment builds up in sinkholes and blocks underground drainage. **Surface rivers flow** once more, creating **flat floodplains of alluvial** soils between the towers.

In an exam, include the process of the chemical weathering of limestone as part of your answer. (See page 57.)

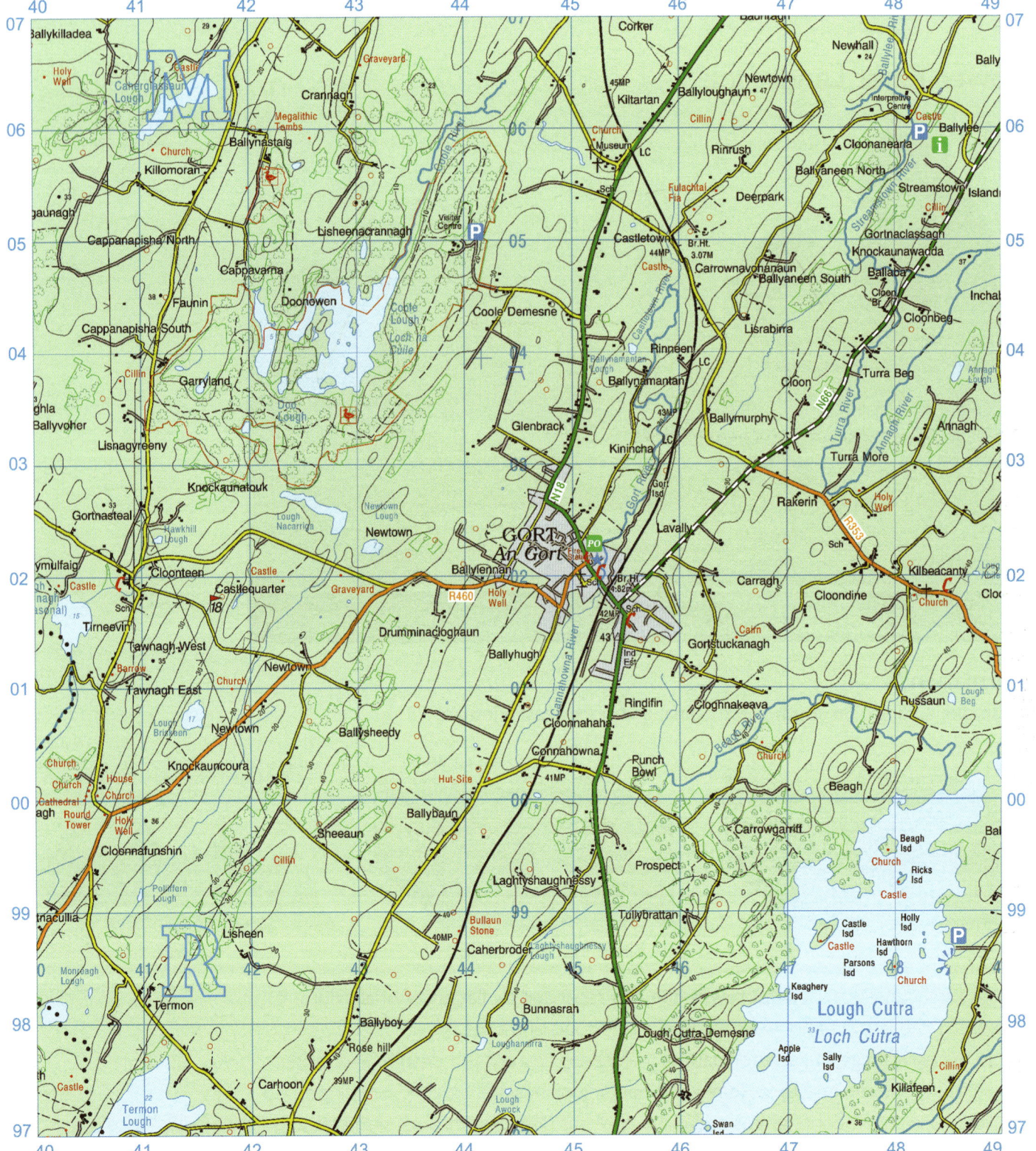

Activity

1. In which direction does the Beagh River flow?
2. Explain what happens to this river at the Punch Bowl at grid reference M 458 003.
3. Name and identify the type of lake at grid reference M 40 01. Explain.
4. Describe the course of the Gort River. Explain why the river ends at the town.
5. In which direction is the Coole River flowing? Explain fully.
6. There is a visitors centre at Coole Demesne, grid reference M 439 049. Explain the purpose of this centre. Explain your answer, using evidence from the map only.
7. From your rock and landform studies so far, classify this type of landscape. Use evidence from the map to explain your answer.
8. Is the landform at grid reference M 475 062 a sinkhole or a resurgence (see page 60)? Explain.

64

CHAPTER 11
MASS MOVEMENT, PROCESSES AND LANDFORMS

Mass movement describes all downhill movements of material (regolith), including soil, loose stones and rocks, in response to gravity. It excludes movements where the material is carried by water, ice or wind. The result of this movement is called mass wasting.

Although by definition mass movement does not include water, in reality, water is usually present and assists downhill movement. **Speed of movement and the amount of moisture present** are used as a basis to distinguish between the various types of mass movement.

Some mass movements are slow – almost impossible to notice – and continue over a long time. Others, usually on a large scale, act suddenly, rapidly and sometimes catastrophically. Some are caused by the results of weathering, others by erosion. Some rapid movements may be due to the influence of people's activity.

Study all the processes and landforms in chapters 11 to 14. Learn in detail the formation of landforms from ONE of these chapters.

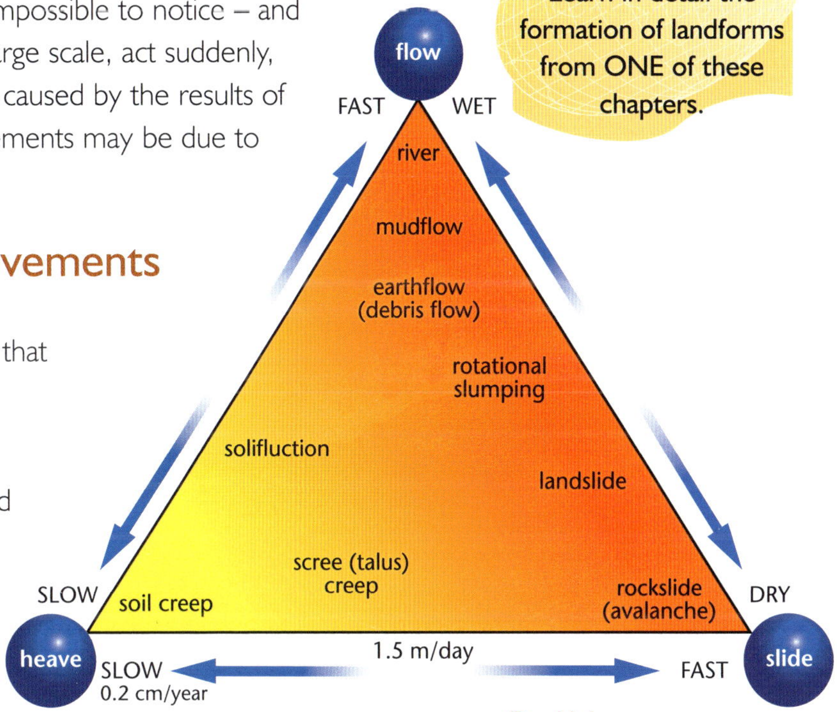

Factors that Influence Mass Movements

Angle of Slope (Gradient)
The steeper the slope, the faster and more likely that movement will occur.

Material
Loose material, rather than compacted or bonded material, is more prone to movement.

Water Content
The greater the water content, the greater the likelihood of movement. Porous bedrock and low rainfall reduce the risk of high water content at the surface.

flow
FAST   WET
river
mudflow
earthflow (debris flow)
rotational slumping
solifluction
landslide
scree (talus) creep
soil creep
rockslide (avalanche)
SLOW   DRY
heave
SLOW 0.2 cm/year
1.5 m/day
FAST
slide

Fig. 11.1

Vegetation Cover
Roots bind surface soil particles and so help to reduce movement, but bare regolith (bedrock) on gentle or steep slopes is prone to movement.

Tectonic Activity
Earthquake tremors and volcanic eruptions create many types of mass movements.

People's Activities
Road or trench construction as well as farming practices can lead to mass movements.

Activity
Use Fig. 11.1 to identify the following types of mass movement:
a. fast and wet
b. fast and dry
c. fast and moist
d. slow and moist
e. very slow.

TYPE AND SPEEDS OF MASS MOVEMENTS

Fig. 11.2

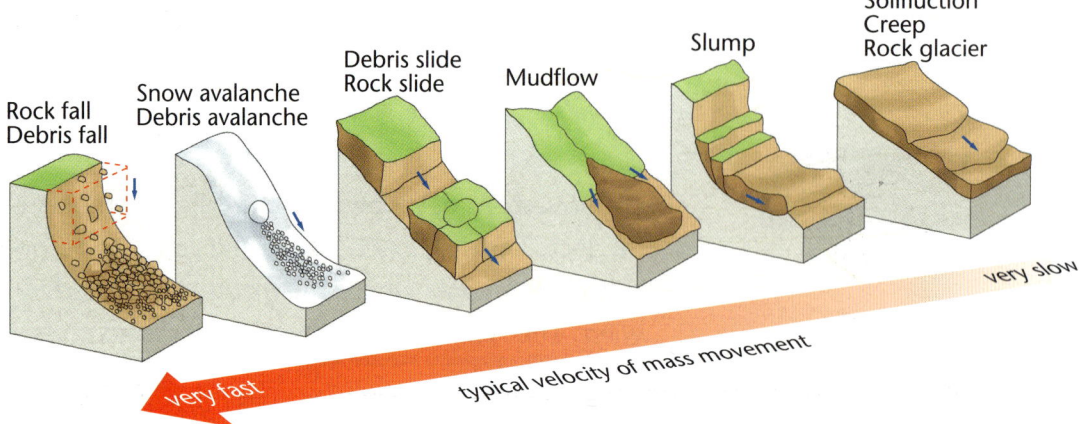

Slow Movements

Soil Creep

Examples: Steep slopes in Ireland

Solifluction on slopes in Alaska, USA

Soil creep is the slowest type of mass movement. We cannot see it happening, but we can see the effects of it on the landscape, especially on steep slopes.

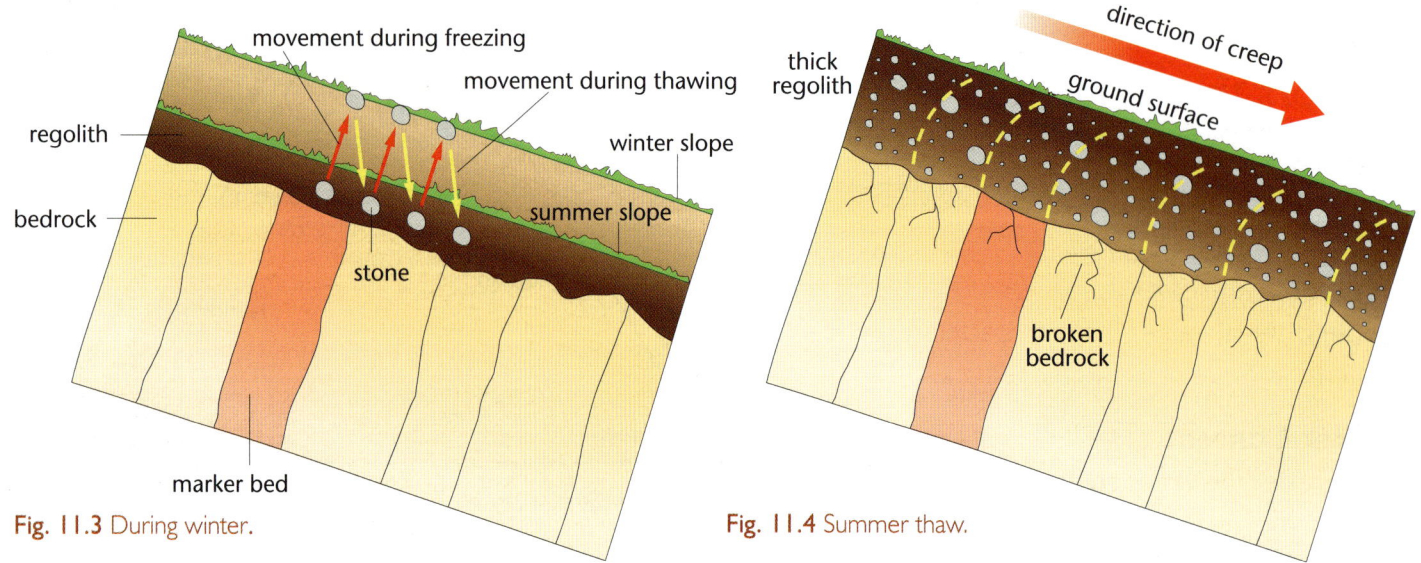

Fig. 11.3 During winter.

Fig. 11.4 Summer thaw.

Temperate Climates

Regions like Ireland have moist, cool winters. The upper few centimetres of ground freeze during very cold spells in winter, only to thaw again some days later. Because water expands by about 9 per cent when it freezes, the water-saturated soil and underlying fractured rock expand outward. Particles in the regolith **are pushed out at right angles to the slope**.

When the soil **thaws**, regolith ice changes back to water, and gravity makes the **particles sink vertically** and migrate downslope slightly. This gradual movement of regolith downslope is called creep. It creates a ribbed or stepped pattern that develops across the slope, called **terracettes**. The rate of movement is less than 1 cm per year.

Terracettes on the Galtees.

Solifluction flows in Alaska.

Arctic or High Mountain Climate

At high latitudes or in high mountains, **regolith freezes solid to a great depth** during the winter. During the short summer, only the uppermost 1 to 3 m of the ground thaws. Because the lower ground remains frozen (it is called the **permafrost layer**), the meltwater cannot seep downwards, and the uppermost, thawed **regolith** becomes **soggy** and weak and flows slowly downslope in **overlapping, tongue-like sheets**. This is called **solifluction**.

As well as adding to the weight of the material, water also causes some soil particles to swell. This swelling causes nearby particles to move and it lubricates the soil, making it more likely to move downslope.

Solifluction is slightly faster than creep and averages movement of between 5 cm and 1 m per year.

Slumping

Example: Slumps at Garron Point in Co. Antrim

A slump is a type of slide that occurs when blocks of rock that are intact or loose debris slide downwards **along curved planes** in response to **gravity**. The blocks tend to tilt backwards during the slump, so that rotation as well as downward movement take place.

Slumps generally occur on:

- Hills thickly covered with soil.
- Steep coastal cliffs made of loose or poorly cemented materials.
- River banks of incised meanders.

This happens because the forces that bind particles of soil together fail, causing a slump. This is called **shear failure**. As in all mass movement, slumps are most common on slopes that are over-steepened, water-saturated and undercut by rivers, ice, waves or human activities.

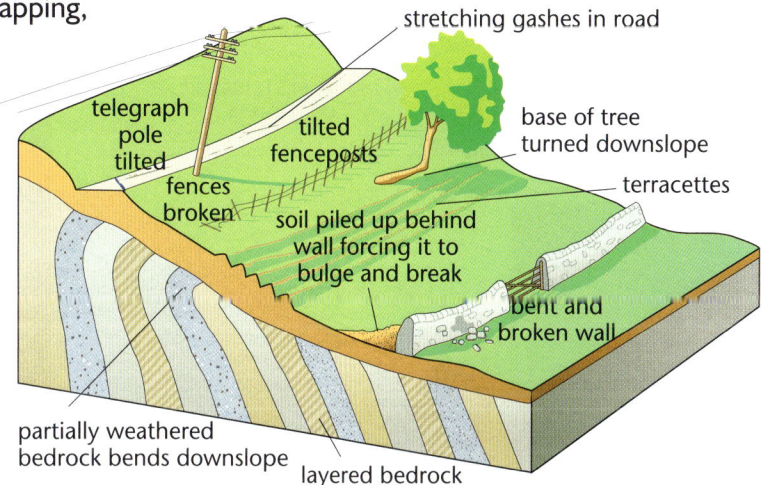

stretching gashes in road

telegraph pole tilted

tilted fenceposts

fences broken

base of tree turned downslope

terracettes

soil piled up behind wall forcing it to bulge and break

bent and broken wall

partially weathered bedrock bends downslope

layered bedrock

Fig. 11.5 The effects of soil creep.

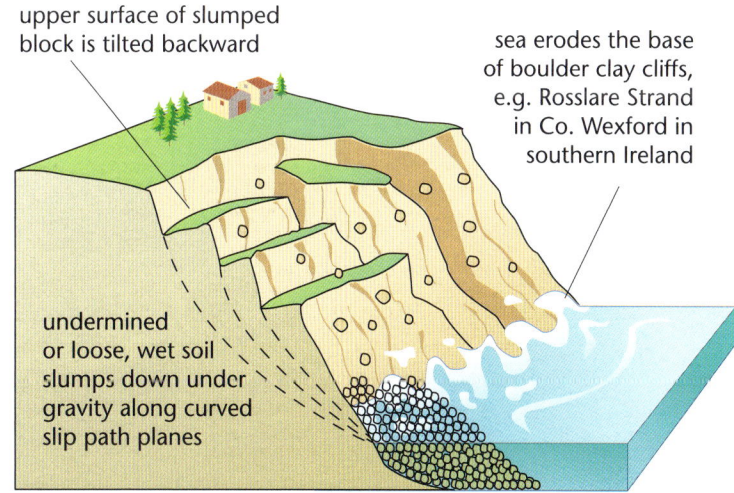

upper surface of slumped block is tilted backward

sea erodes the base of boulder clay cliffs, e.g. Rosslare Strand in Co. Wexford in southern Ireland

undermined or loose, wet soil slumps down under gravity along curved slip path planes

Fig. 11.6 The effect of slumping.

Case Study: Rotational Slumping on the Antrim Coast

The Glenariff Valley is a spectacular example of a glaciated U-shaped valley. The steep sides and its U-shape were created by the erosive action of a glacier. The valley floor is formed of soft mudstone, while the valley sides are made of chalk at the base, with basalt on top. Nearby at Garron Point, the same glaciers removed some of the mudstone and undermined the chalk. Consequently, when the ice melted, the **chalk and basalt cliffs** here slumped as large blocks shifted in a curved movement called rotational slumping.

In other places, the sea has undermined coastal cliffs, creating landslides and rock falls along the coast.

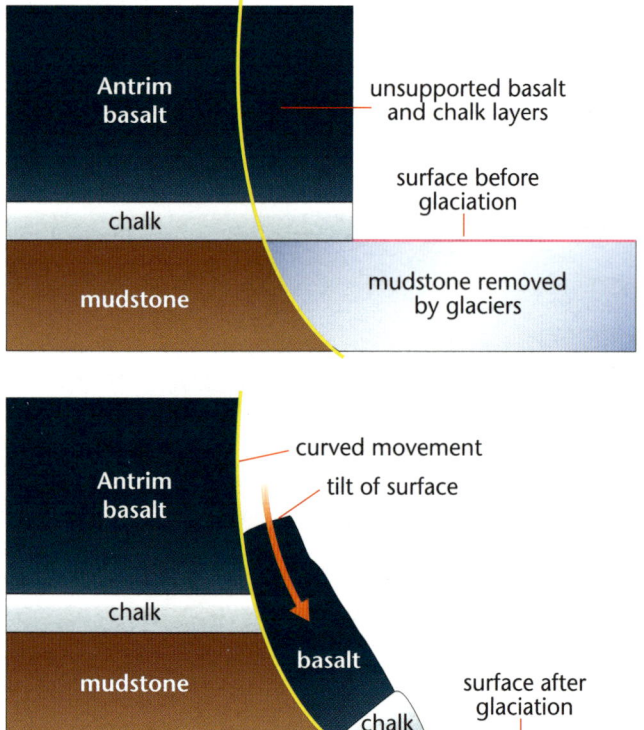

Sloping cliffs due to slumping at Garron Point, Co. Antrim.

Fig. 11.7 Slumping at Garron Point.

Slumping is also common on unconsolidated coastal cliffs. Expensive homes along the coast at **Malibu**, a region of steep coastal cliffs near Los Angeles **in southern California**, have been lost due to the collapse of unstable sediments. Here, slumping was caused by **earthquakes**. Slumping regularly occurs here because the San Andreas Fault is close by.

Slumping occurs regularly along the California coast near Malibu Beach due to erosion by the sea or earthquakes.

Bog Bursts

Example: Derrybrien in Co. Galway

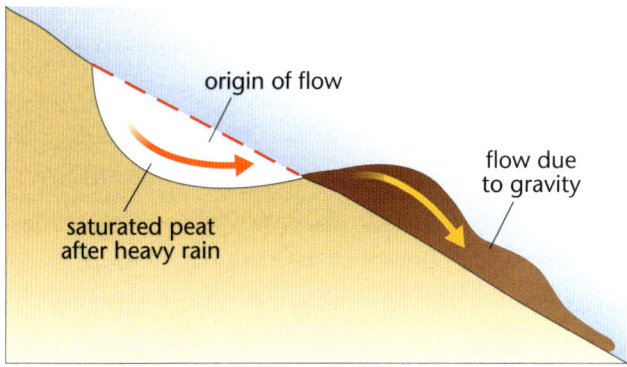

origin of flow

flow due to gravity

saturated peat after heavy rain

Fig. 11.8 Saturated peat may move downslope.

Bog bursts occur in upland regions of blanket bog.

A bog burst is a type of earthflow. Earthflows occur **on sloping ground** in regions of heavy rainfall where rock is deeply weathered. These deep soils become mobile when saturated with water and may suddenly slip downslope in response to **gravity.** This action leaves a curved-shaped scar where the slip begins and a bulge at the base of the slope.

The peat in bogs contains **95 per cent water** and **5 per cent solids,** so even in its normal state it may become unstable on steep slopes. This risk increases after periods of heavy rain. Some bog bursts may move slowly. Others that are completely saturated with water may move quickly. A slope of 4 degrees is sufficient for a burst to take place, but it may occur on a slope of as little as 2 degrees.

Whether the bedrock under the peat is **permeable or impermeable** will also affect the likelihood of flow. Impermeable bedrock will not soak up water, and the bog surface becomes saturated easily and quickly. The **quality and amount of vegetation** on the bog surface also has an important bearing on the eventual outcome. Roots from heathers, plants such as rhododendron and trees such as birch or pines help to prevent downslope movement of bog material.

Periods of very **heavy rain followed by** unseasonally long spells of **hot, dry weather** create the most risk of bog burst. During hot, dry spells, the intricate root system of the upper layer of bog, which under normal conditions acts as an anchor for the bog, starts to shrink and die back. With nothing left to anchor the bog, the peat mass may flow downslope.

- **Human activity** on the bog surface may also encourage a burst. Industrialised **peat harvesting, sheep grazing** and the removal of peat from hilltops for **wind farm construction** also encourage flow. This flow may take the form of a slow-moving mass or a free-flowing avalanche of soil that can often resemble a lava flow by the sheer force of its movement.

- Recent bog bursts include one at **Derrybrien**, in the Slieve Aughty Mountains, in Co. Galway in 2003. A bog burst in **Doon** in east Limerick in 1708 killed three families, twenty-one people in total. Their three dwellings were destroyed by a burst that was 7 m deep, 1.5 km long and 1 km wide. The bog burst travelled several kilometres, crossed several roads and demolished many bridges.

Gravity and saturation of peat causes a bog burst.

Peat contains 95 per cent water and 5 per cent solids.

69

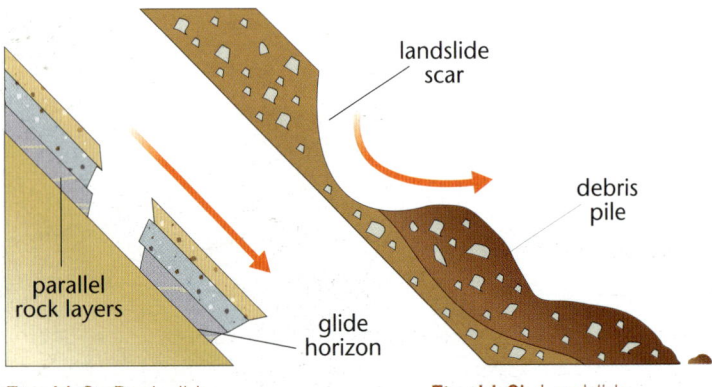

Fig. 11.9a Rock slide.   Fig. 11.9b Landslide.

Landslides

Geologists refer to a sudden movement of rock and debris down a non-vertical slope as a landslide. If the mass consists only of rock, it is called a **rock slide**. If it consists only of regolith, it is called a **debris slide**. Once a landslide has occurred, it leaves a **landslide scar** on the slope and forms a **debris pile** at the base of the slope.

Slides happen when bedrock, or regolith, breaks away from a slope and shoots downhill on a **glide horizon** (slope angle) roughly parallel to the slope surface. Slides may move at speeds up to 300 km an hour. They are particularly fast when a cushion of air gets trapped beneath the moving mass. In this case, there is hardly any contact between the moving mass and the ground surface, so the mass moves something like a hovercraft. Sometimes rock and debris slides move so fast they have sufficient energy to climb the opposite side of the valley.

Rock slides occur due to gravity on slopes where bedding planes of rock layers that lie parallel to the surface are undercut or become too heavy. The rock mass moves downslope when the weight of the surface layers is too great for the slope to support.

A landslide in Taiwan devestated the village of Wu Feng.

Landslides occur on a variety of scales. Most are small, involving blocks up to a few metres across. Some, however, are large enough to be catastrophic. **Earthquakes** in mountain regions cause **landslides**. Many such slides occurred in **Kashmir** in Pakistan in **2005** when an earthquake shook this region. They restricted access for getting emergency relief to the wounded and isolated communities in the mountainous region in the Himalayas.

Case Study: Vaiont Dam Disaster, Italy

The **Vaiont Dam** was **built** in the **Italian Alps in the 1960s**. It rose **260 m** above the valley floor, with a concrete wall as high as an **85-storey building** forming a large reservoir above the dam. The slopes of the reservoir lake were formed of **dipping limestone and shale layers** that lay parallel to the valley side and curved under the reservoir lake.

As the reservoir lake filled, the rock cracked, shook and rumbled. Several days of rain then added to the weight of rock on the slope. The mountain shook, but no one ordered the evacuation of the town of **Longarone** that was in the valley below the dam. That same day,

Destruction in the town of Longarone.

600 million tonnes of rock broke from the valley side and slid down into the reservoir. The displaced water poured over the dam, rushed down the valley and wiped out the town and its 1,500 inhabitants.

Lahars and Mudflows

Examples: Lahar: Armero in Colombia
               Mudflow: Sarno, near Naples in Italy

Mudflows

Mudflows occur when **deep soils become saturated with water** and move due to **gravity.** Soil particles expand rapidly and are separated by water molecules. **Grain-to-grain contact is lost,** and the saturated layer turns to slurry, which flows downhill. The steeper the slope and the greater the water and soil content, the greater the speed of the flow.

Gravity plays a major role in mudflows. Hot regions that often have **prolonged torrential downpours** are particularly prone to mudflows. In southern Italy, for example, the slopes of the Apennines are steep and have deep volcanic soils in some places. Vegetation is scarce because the original forest cover of pines has been cut down for farming activity. Grasses are scarce, and some surfaces have little vegetation cover. A lot of unrestricted construction has also disturbed the surface in places where buildings should not have been constructed.

- In 1998, at **Sarno near Naples**, forty-eight hours of torrential rain created mudflows on local hillsides. Rivers of mud burst into the town centre, tearing apart houses and bridges, covering people and cars, while other inhabitants were sent running for their lives. Over 100 people died. This region has experienced over 630 landslides over the past seventy years.

Lahars

Lahars are **mudflows caused by volcanic eruptions**. Many volcanic cones are so high that they are **permanently capped with snow**. The most dangerous lahars occur on volcanic cones in fold mountain regions that have been dormant for a long time. Over the years, great depths of snow and ice accumulate on the slopes of these cones. Their slopes are also composed of loose **ash and pyroclastic layers.**

When eruptions occur in these volcanoes, vast quantities of **hot ash** are **ejected** from the crater because the magma is **viscous** (thick). Viscous lava traps expanding gases. The hot ash lands on the surrounding ice fields and instantly melts the ice and snow. The vast quantities of water released rush downslope, gathering ash and pyroclasts as they go. This creates liquid mud that moves through the valleys at the base of the mountain, carrying along rocks, trees, houses and everything else it can root up on its journey.

- On 13 November 1985, a lahar descended the 5,400 m slope of **Nevado del Ruiz** in Colombia, in South America. It reached the town of **Armero**, which was 48 km from the summit, and approximately **20,000 residents** were buried alive in the mud. This disaster should never have happened. Soil studies later showed that many lahars had occurred there before in the distant past. Today, the authorities prevent people from building on that part of the valley.

A mudflow may cause great loss of life and destruction in built-up areas far from its origin.

- *Identify this type of mass movement.*

71

Multi-part Questions

1. Examine Fig. 11.10, which classifies mass movement, and answer the following questions.

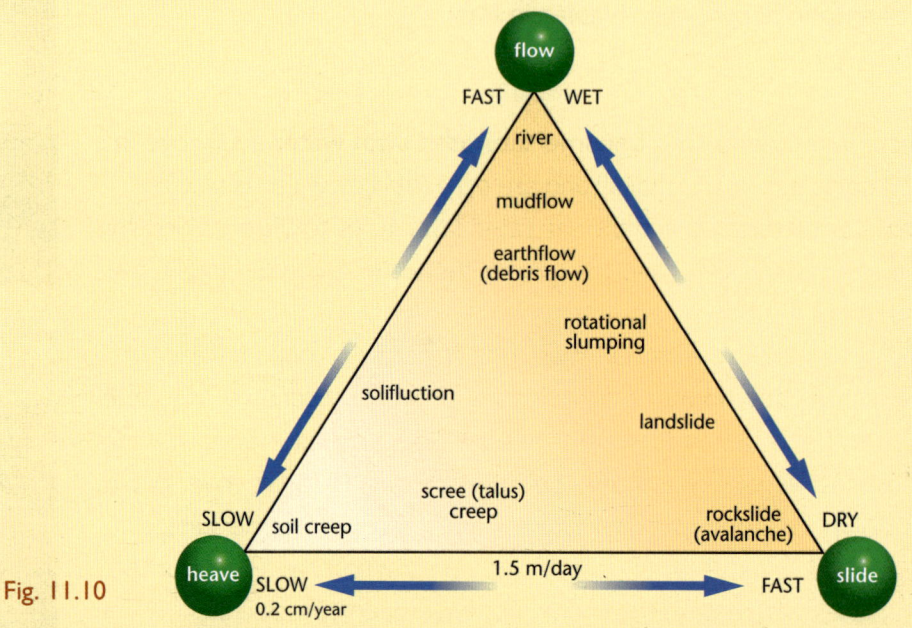

Fig. 11.10

    A. Identify **one** type of fast and **one** type of slow mass movement. In each case, name one Irish region where it occurs or occurred. [20 marks]

    B. With reference to examples that you have studied, fully explain **one** example of slow and **one** example of fast mass movements. [30 marks]

    C. Examine **two** ways in which human activities can accelerate mass movements. [30 marks]

2. Soluble limestone or karst regions, such as the Burren, contain a great variety of landscape features, both over and under the surface.

    A. Name any **three** of these features and in each case name an Irish example. [20 marks]

    B. For **two** of the features named above, describe and explain how they were formed. [30 marks]

    C. The Burren is Ireland's best-known soluble limestone region. Briefly explain its importance, referring to each of the following:
       i.   heritage
       ii. tourism. [30 marks]

3. Limestone pavements, Swallow holes, Limestone caves, Dry valleys.

    A. Limestone caves have interesting geographical features. Name any **four** features and identify the processes that formed them. [20 marks]

    B. Select **two** of the above features and, using a diagram, describe how they were formed. [20 marks]

    C. 'Weathering can be caused by physical **or** chemical action.' Explain this statemet, using one physical and one chemical process in detail. [30 marks]

4. As a result of pressure from tourism, karst regions have vulnerable environments.

    A. Examine **one** example of this vulnerability. [20 marks]

    B. 'The processes of weathering, together with gravity, are important factors in shaping landscapes.' Explain this statement, referring to **two** weathering processes. [30 marks]

    C. Examine how human activities can accelerate or intensify any **one** of the weathering processes referred to above. [30 marks]

CHAPTER 12
GLACIAL PROCESSES, PATTERNS AND LANDFORMS

KEY IDEA! Landforms are created by glacial processes.

During the last Ice Age that **began about 2 million years ago** and **ended about 10,000 years ago**, highland and lowland areas were covered by a layer of ice thousands of metres thick. Only some high mountain peaks, called **nunataks**, were exposed and subjected to severe frost action, so they became pointed. They are called pyramidal peaks. While ice increased in thickness in mountain areas, some ice moved down river valleys to form rivers of ice, called **glaciers**. When the glaciers reached the lowland, they joined to form **ice sheets** that completely blanketed the land.

Glaciers still exist today in Iceland, the Alps, the Rockies, the Andes and the Himalayas. By studying these glaciers and ice sheets, we can understand the various processes of ice action and how they created landforms of erosion and deposition.

Snowflakes are crystals of moisture. When they gather on the ground, they do not fit well together and so this snow contains about 90 per cent air and has a white colour. As snowflakes become buried, they are squeezed and change into grains of ice that fit together better. Only 25 per cent air remains trapped between the grains. This ice is called **firn**. With a little more pressure, it contains only about 20 per cent air trapped as air bubbles. This ice has a **bluish colour** and is called **glacier ice**.

The Matterhorn in Switzerland is a pyramidal peak that formed due to frost wedging (freeze-thaw action).

PROCESSES OF ICE ACTION
Processes of Ice Movement

Ice moves for one or a number of the following reasons.

Gravity

Ice moves downslope in response to gravity. The steeper the slope, the greater the pull of gravity and the faster the movement.

Basal Sliding

Meltwater exists at the base of some glaciers, and some sediment particles are also present. Together, these form a type of slush that the glacier slides on to move downslope.

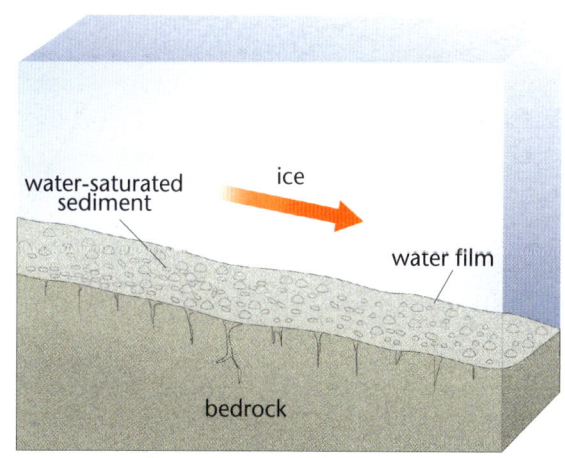

Fig. 12.1 Wet bottom (basal slidings).

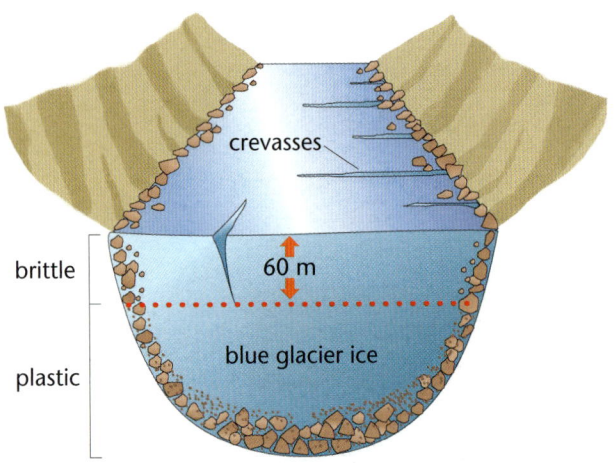

Fig. 12.2 Glacier ice.

Internal Flow

Below a depth of about 60 m, ice acts like plastic. It can **bend and twist** without cracking (a process called fracturing). Crystals of glacier ice **alternately melt and refreeze** to squeeze their way through valleys or around obstacles as the glacier moves along. The top 60 m of ice is brittle and cracks, forming deep chasms called **crevasses**.

The centre of a glacier moves about five times faster than its edges, and the top of a glacier moves faster than its base. Glaciers move at average speeds of tens of metres to hundreds of metres a year.

Plucking

The water slick between the bedrock and the ice regularly freezes. This causes freeze-thaw action in the bedrock surface. Once the ice starts to move, it **plucks** the loosened chunks of rock from the ground and carries them downslope. This process is especially effective where the rock is already jointed or faulted.

Abrasion

The plucked rocks become part of the base and sides of the glacier. As the glaciers or ice sheets move, these rocks **scour, polish and scrape** the surface over which they pass (much as rough sandpaper acts on wood), leaving deep grooves and scratches called **striations** on the rock landscape.

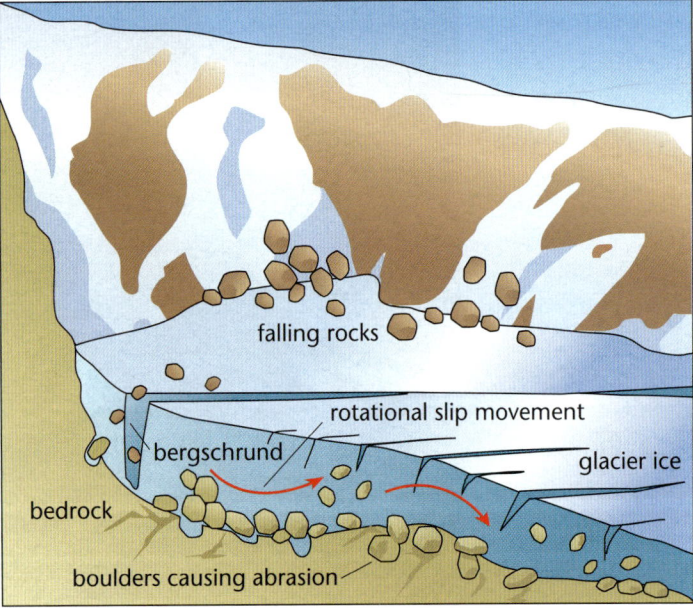

Fig. 12.3 Moving ice plucks and abrades the bedrock.

Other Factors

The amount of plucking and abrasion often depends on other factors.

- **The weight of ice:** Erosion increases with the weight of the overlying ice. Glaciers were often over 600 m thick in Ireland during the Ice Age.
- **The hardness of rock:** The softer the rock, the greater the amount of erosion and the more rounded the upland peaks. Evidence of rounded hilltops and mountaintops may be seen in the uplands of southern Ireland, such as the Slieve Felim Mountains in Co. Tipperary.

A glacier is a river of ice in a mountain valley.

Zones of Accumulation and Ablation

Ice gathers in high regions. This is the **zone of accumulation**. Ice melts in the zone of **ablation**. The **process of calving** occurs in the zone of ablation when large blocks of ice break off the edge of a glacier or ice sheet.

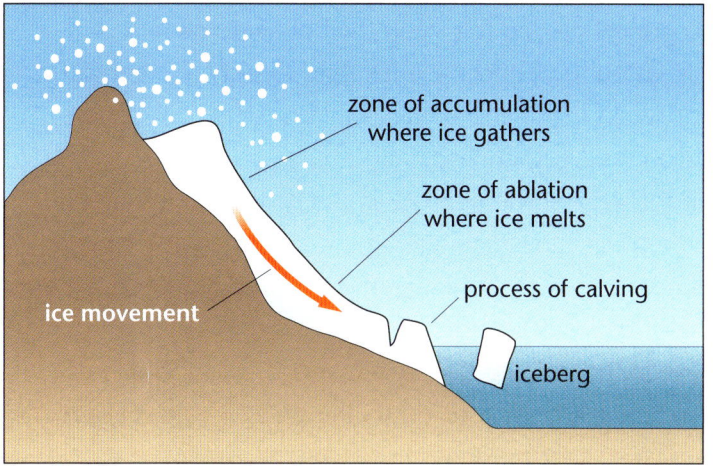

zone of accumulation where ice gathers

zone of ablation where ice melts

process of calving

ice movement

iceberg

Fig. 12.4 The process of calving.

Calving occurs where blocks of ice break off glaciers and ice sheets.

SOME LANDFORMS OF GLACIAL EROSION

Landform: Cirque

Example: Devil's Punch Bowl in the Macgillicuddy's Reeks

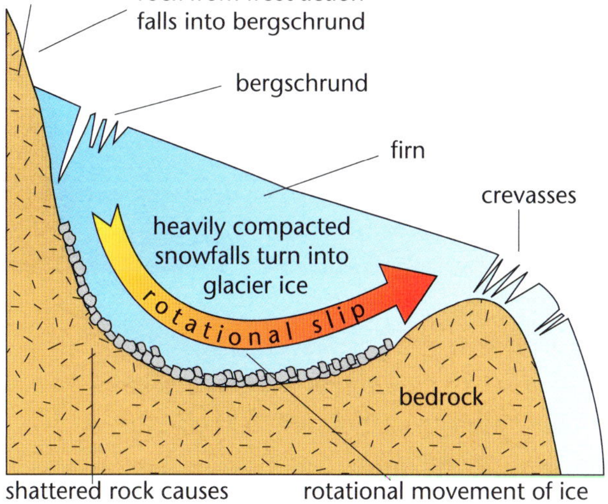

You must include the processes when you are writing out your landform feature.

plucking steepens back wall

rock from frost action falls into bergschrund

bergschrund

firn

crevasses

heavily compacted snowfalls turn into glacier ice

rotational slip

bedrock

shattered rock causes abrasion and deepening of cirque hollow

rotational movement of ice causes over-deepening of cirque

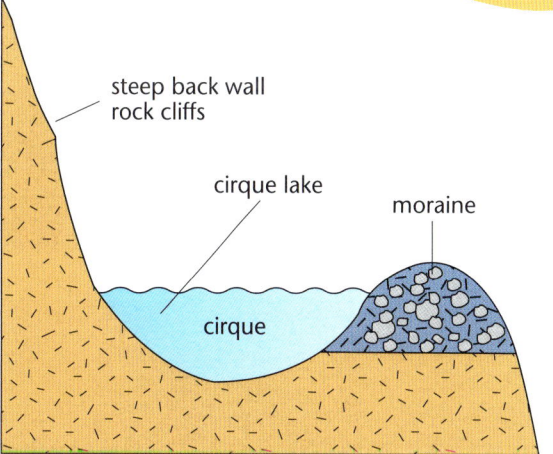

steep back wall rock cliffs

cirque lake

moraine

cirque

Fig. 12.5

Fig. 12.6 Cirques are regularly found on north-facing slopes.

Formation

Cirques began as slight hollows in mountain areas in the **zone of accumulation,** where snow gathered to form an **ice field**. Each snowfall added more weight so that the bottom snowflakes were squeezed to become **firn ice**. Great depths of ice built up until the hollow overflowed and ice began to move downslope.

This downslope pull due to **gravity** caused the ice in the hollow to **slide** in a process called **rotational slip** that lasted throughout the Ice Age. Gravity also caused the **ice** at the upslope side of the hollow **to crack** and break away from the rock surface. This created a deep **crevasse** called the **bergschrund**.

Meltwater seeped between the ice and the bedrock in the hollow. This water regularly froze, which shattered the rock surface beneath the ice. As the rock moved due to rotational slip, it **plucked** out large **rock boulders** and **abraded** the bedrock, thus **deepening** the hollow to form rock basins over time.

These basins are **amphitheatre-shaped** with three steep sides, and sometimes **vertical rock walls** on all sides except the one facing down the valley. Cirques are more common on **north-facing** and north-east-facing slopes.

At the end of the Ice Age many of these rock basins filled with water to form cirque lakes. These cirques are also called **corries, cooms, cums** and **tarns**.

Lakes with names beginning with 'coum' or 'coom' are cirque lakes.

Cirques are surrounded by cliff-like slopes on three sides.

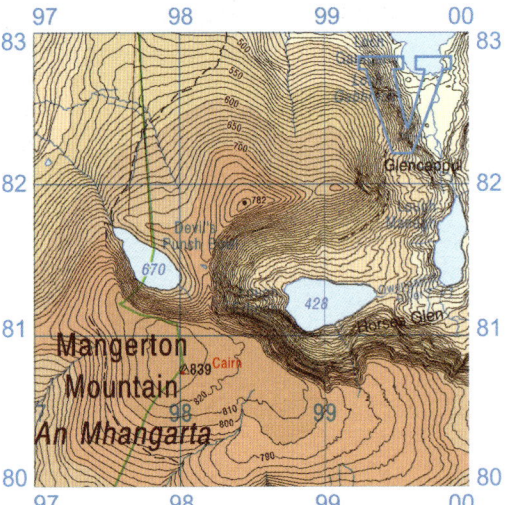

Activity

1. Use the contour pattern to describe the cirque hollows on Mangerton mountain.
2. Identify the glacial landform at grid reference V983 812.

Landform: U-Shaped Valley
Example: Glendalough in Co. Wicklow

Formation

From **snowfields** in the zone of accumulation high in the mountains, ice moved downslope under **gravity** through **river valleys**.

Meltwater seeped between the base of the ice and the bedrock, and mixed with sediment to form a type of slush. This allowed glaciers to slide downslope in a process called **basal sliding**. The meltwater regularly **froze** when the **ice stopped** moving. Freeze-thaw action then occurred, **shattering the rock** surface beneath the ice.

When the glacier moved again, it **plucked** large boulders and rocks from the bedrock surface and used them to **abrade** and **deepen** the valley. The **higher slopes** of the valley above the glacier were also exposed to frost wedging. **Shattered rock** fell onto the **glacier edges** and became **embedded** in the ice. Combined with other plucked rocks from the side of the valley, they **widened** and **straightened** the sides.

The processes of freeze-thaw and abrasion created **truncated spurs** by **eroding the interlocking spurs** of the original river valley through which the glacier travelled. These form **short cliff ledges** along glaciated valleys.

These processes also created **rock basins**, where shattered rock or patches of **soft rock** existed on the valley floor. These **long, deep hollows** later filled to form **ribbon lakes**. Where a stream joined the hollows together in a string, they are called **paternoster lakes**

Very deep glaciated valleys with vertical sides are called **glacial troughs**. If, after the Ice Age, the valleys were **flooded** by the sea, **fjords** were formed.

Hanging valleys formed where **smaller glaciers** entered the main valley. The **less erosive power** of these tributary glaciers caused them to 'hang' into the valley once the ice had gone.

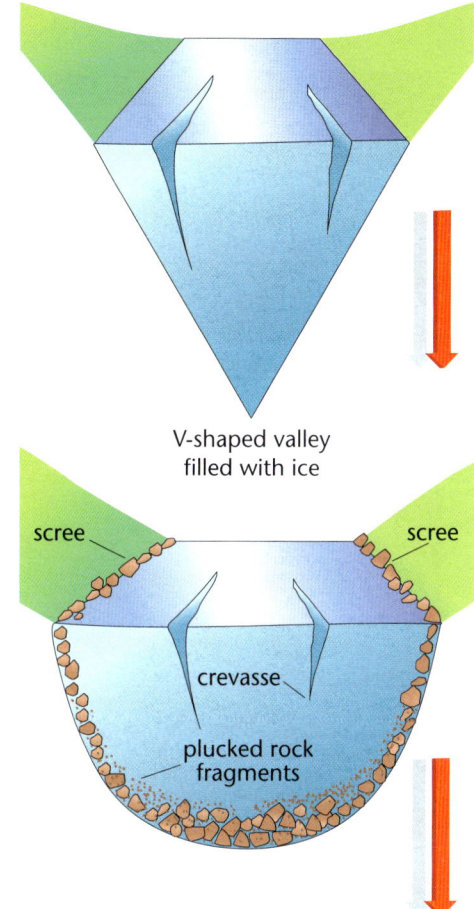

V-shaped valley filled with ice

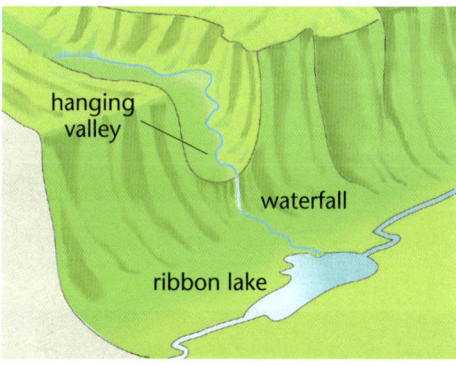

Fig. 12.7 Cirques are regularly found on north-facing slopes.

Activity

1. Use the contour pattern in the map to describe:
    a. the valley sides in Glendalough
    b. the valley floor in Glendalough.
2. Identify:
    a. The land use at T 115 977. Suggest one reason for the land use at this location.
    b. The tourist facility at T 122 968. Give two reasons for the facility in this area.

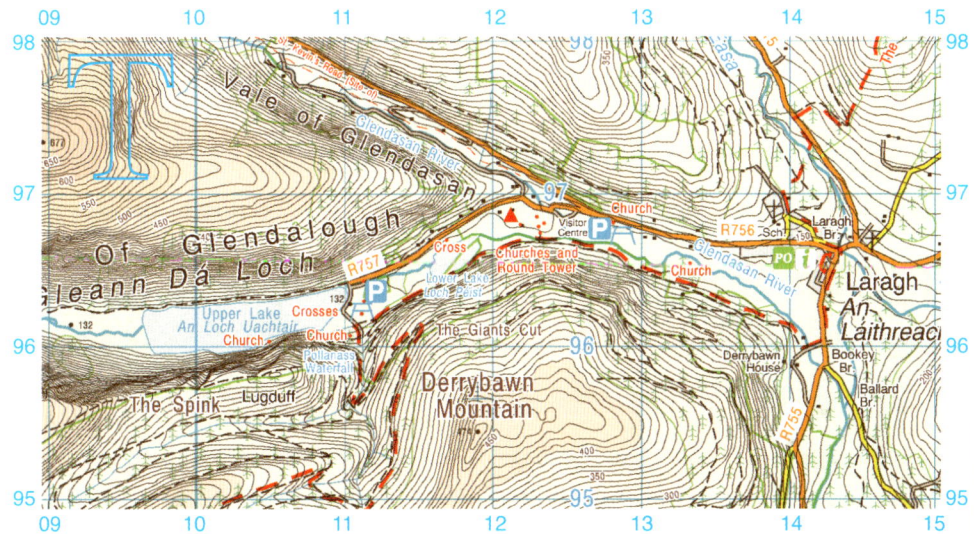

Fig. 12.8 V-shaped valley filled with ice.

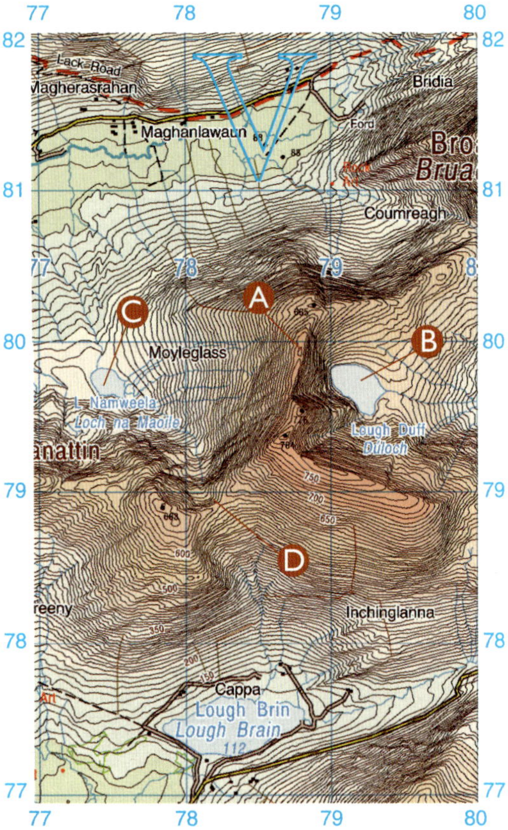

Fig. 12.9 Identify the landforms A–D.

OTHER LANDFORMS OF EROSION

Landform: Pyramidal Peaks
Example: Carrauntoohil in Co. Kerry

A mountain peak in the shape of a pyramid is a pyramidal peak. These peaks formed when mountaintops **stood above** the surrounding snowfields and **ice sheets**. They became pointed when:

- They were subjected to severe and continuous **freeze-thaw action** for a long time.
- Three or more cirques formed back to back in a process called **headwall recession**.

Landform: Arête
Example: The Devil's Punch Bowl on Mangerton Mountain

An arête is a **knife-edged ridge** between two cirques or two valleys. When two cirques erode back to back or side by side, they may create a very narrow, knife-edged ridge between them. This sharp ridge is an arête.

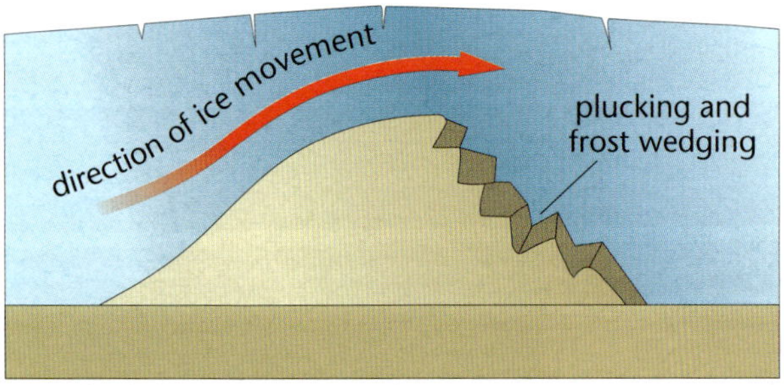

Landform: Roche Moutonnées
Example: Owenreagh Valley, near Killarney

Large rock outcrops on a valley floor or on plains were obstacles to the movement of valley glaciers. As the ice passed over the rock surface, it smoothed and polished the upstream side of the rock. **Plucking** occurred on the downstream side, leaving it irregular and angular.

Fig. 12.10 A roche moutonnée.

Rock Basins and Ribbon Lakes
Example: Lough Beagh in Co. Donegal

Rock basins formed by **freeze-thaw action** and **plucking**, where shattered rock or patches of soft rock existed on a valley floor. **Long, deep lakes called ribbon lakes** formed when the hollows later filled with meltwater. If a number of these lakes are linked by a stream, they are called **paternoster lakes**.

Deep rock basins form ribbon lakes.

Fjords
Example: Killary Harbour in Co. Galway

Some glacial valleys were over-deepened by erosion. When the Ice Age ended, **sea levels rose** again and some of the deep valleys that opened onto the sea became **flooded**. These **fjords** have **steeply sloping, parallel sides**. The Norwegian coast has many fjords.

- *What are the physical characteristics of these fjord inlets?*

SOME LANDFORMS OF GLACIAL DEPOSITION

The area where the ice melted and materials were deposited is called the **zone of ablation**. There are many landforms of deposition.

Drift is the term used to refer collectively to all glacial deposits. These deposits include boulders, gravels, sands and clays, and may be **subdivided** into **till**, which includes all material deposited directly by ice, and **fluvioglacial material**, which is the debris deposited by meltwater streams. **Till** consists of **unsorted material**, whereas **fluvioglacial** deposits have been **sorted**. Deposition occurs both in upland valleys and across lowland areas.

In this section, till is divided into separate landforms:

- Moraines.
- Boulder clay.
- Drumlins.

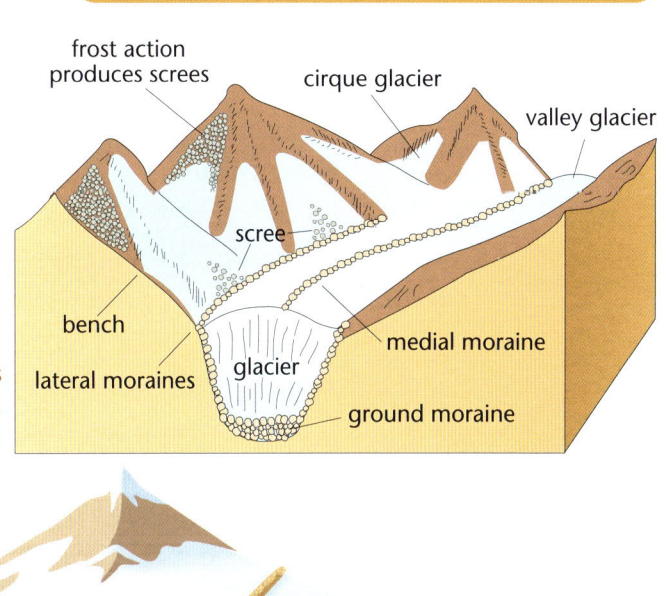

Fig. 12.11 The source of glacial material is generally in upland regions.

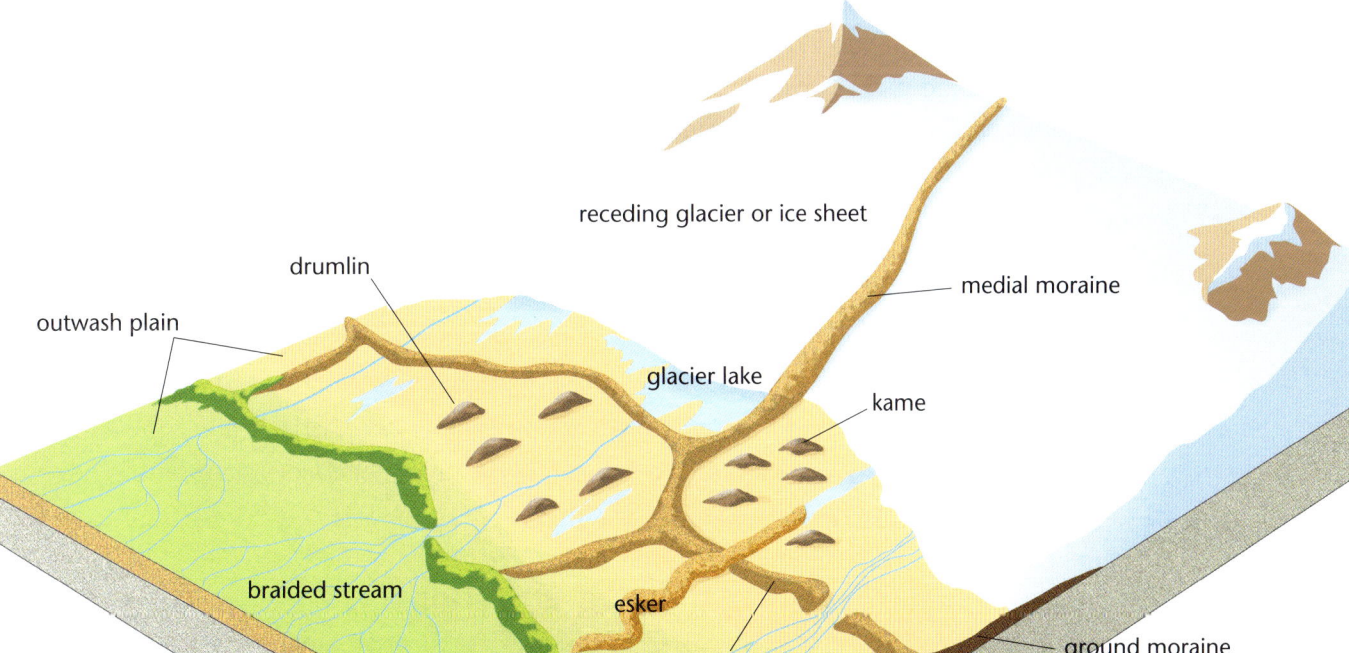

Fig. 12.12 The relationship of depositional features in a melting glacier or ice sheet.

79

Landform: Moraine

Example: In the Gap of Dunloe in Co. Kerry

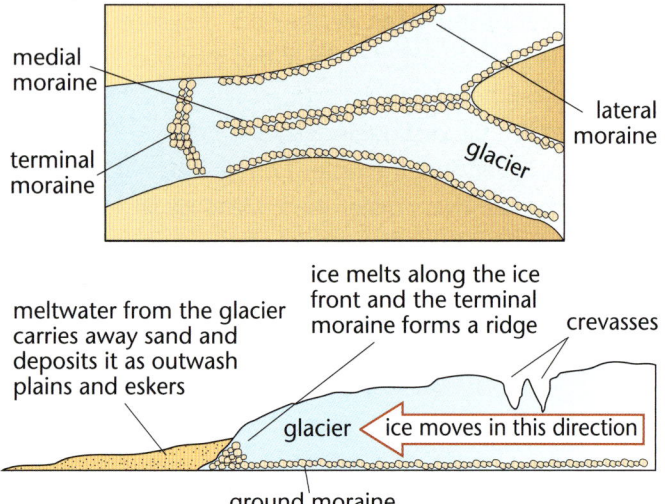

Fig. 12.13 Moraine deposits.

Unsorted material deposited by a glacier. Many of the rocks are angular.

Formation

Moraine consists of **unsorted debris** of rounded and angular boulders, stones, soil and sand deposited by glaciers. This material was **plucked** or **abraded** from the landscape over which the glaciers passed. It may be divided into three main types: **lateral moraine, medial moraine and terminal moraine.**

- **Lateral moraine** formed **long, sloping ridges** of material deposited along **valley sides. Freeze-thaw action** on the unglaciated **benches** above the ice caused angular rocks of all sizes to fall onto the glacier edges below. As the ice moved downslope, it became embedded in the glacier ice. As the glacier edges moved downslope, they **plucked** rocks from the valley sides. This removed the interlocking spurs and the valley sides were straightened and deepened by **abrasion.**

  Much of this eroded debris was deposited along the valley edge when all the ice had melted. It is recognisable as a **lesser slope** than the valley walls, or as a rocky, sloping surface.

- **Medial moraine** is an uneven, long ridge of similarly unsorted material that runs along the centre of valleys. It formed from the material of **two lateral moraines** when two glaciers **joined.** Large valleys may have had many medial moraines.

- **Terminal moraine** formed **crescent-shaped ridges** of unsorted debris across valleys and plains where glaciers or ice sheets stopped and melted for a long time. They represent the **farthest advance of the ice.**

Crag and Tail

Crag and tail formed when a **hard mass of rock**, called the **crag**, lay in the path of oncoming ice. The hard crag protected the softer rock in its lee from erosion by the ice that moved over and around the crag. On the downstream side, deposition by the ice created a **tapering ridge of moraine**. This is called the tail.

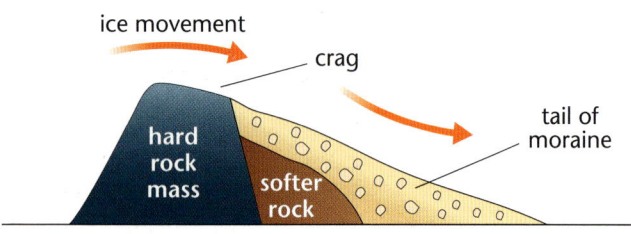

Fig. 12.14 Crag and tail.

Landform: Drumlins

Example: Hills in Cavan and Islands in Clew Bay

Formation

Drumlins are **rounded**, **oval-shaped hills** of ground moraine. They usually occur in clusters or swarms. They are especially well developed in Ireland, for example in **Clew Bay** in Co. Mayo.

Drumlins are mainly formed of **boulder clay**. This **unsorted material** consists of rocks, pebbles, gravel, sand and clay mixed up together. It represents the ground moraine of ice sheets. This debris came mainly from rocks that were **plucked** from the bedrock over which the ice passed and broken into stones, clay and sand.

Drumlins may have formed in a number of ways.

- The debris was deposited by moving ice sheets when they were **overladen** with material. As the ice moved over this material, it formed rounded hills with a **steep end facing the oncoming ice** and a low, tapered side in the direction of ice movement.

- When a glacier pushed forward over a terminal moraine, if the till was **dry**, it moulded the debris into long, streamlined hills. The **long axis** of a drumlin indicates the **direction of ice** movement. These hills range from small mounds just a few metres long to larger hills a few kilometres or more in length and as much as 100 m high.

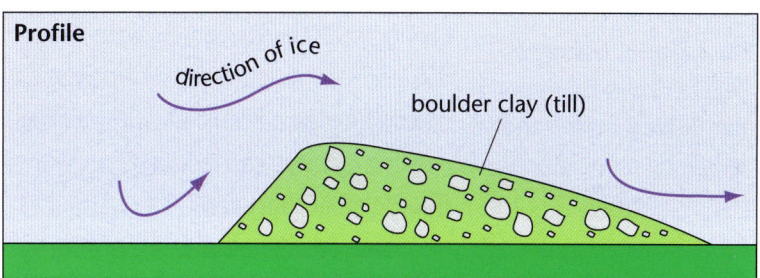

Profile

direction of ice

boulder clay (till)

Fig. 12.15 Drumlins are oval-shaped hills.

Drumlins form basket-of-egg scenery in Strangford Lough.

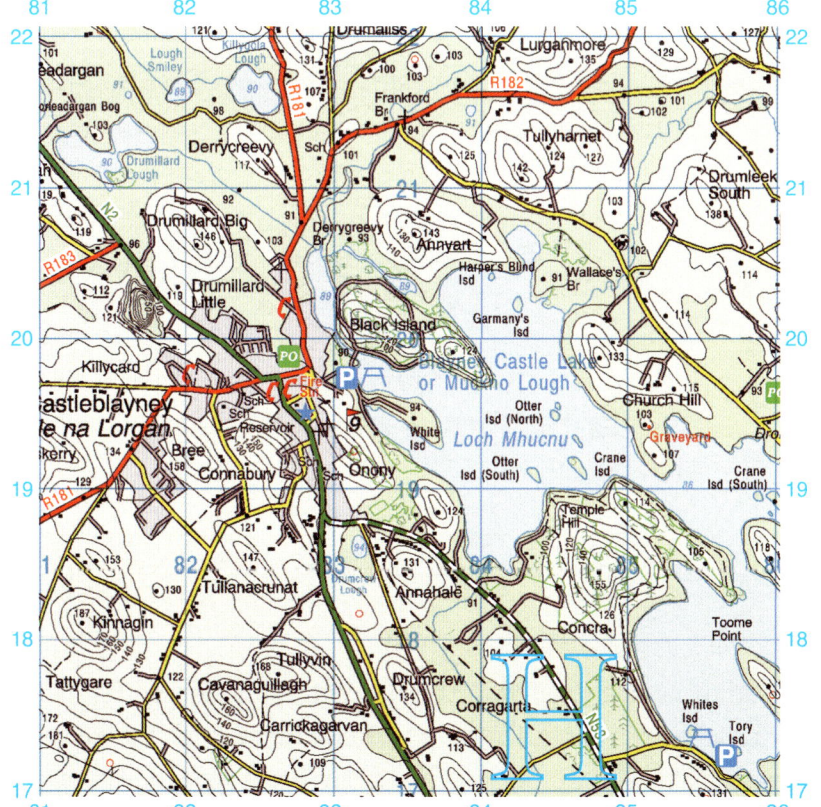

Fig. 12.16 Glacial deposits of Ireland's last ice advance.

Activity

Carefully study the Ordnance Survey map extract and answer the following questions.

1. Look at the island in Muckno Lough at grid reference H 847 192. Is this a drumlin? Explain your answer.

2. In which direction did the ice pass over this area? Was it:
   a. north-west to south-east
   b. south-east to north-west
   c. neither?

3. Have the drumlins in this area affected the shape of Castleblaney? Explain.

4. a. Where in Ireland are most drumlins located? (See page 82.)
   b. Explain, with the aid of a diagram, how drumlins form.

PATTERNS OF FLUVIOGLACIAL DEPOSITS

Fluvius is the Latin word for 'river'. Fluvioglacial materials are laid down by rivers that flowed under and from the front of ice sheets.

Fluvioglacial deposits include outwash plains and eskers. These features formed towards the end of the Ice Age, when vast quantities of meltwater were released from the melting ice as a result of rising temperatures. The many rivers that flowed from the melting glaciers carried large amounts of sand and gravel and deposited them to form **fluvioglacial features**.

Irish ice developed a number of ice domes, or ice caps. Ice sheets spread from these areas across the country, where they deposited moraine, drumlins, kames and eskers. The moraines, kames and eskers have since provided plentiful supplies of rocks, gravel and sand for the construction industry.

The two charts below show the location and direction of the ice that created these glacial deposits.

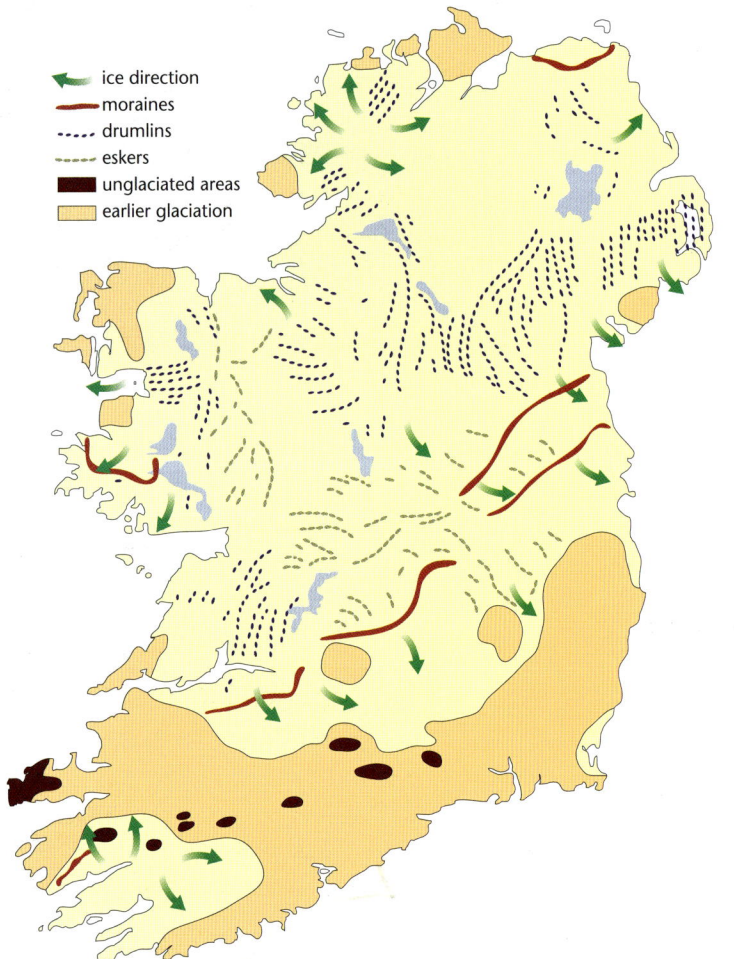

- → ice direction
- — moraines
- ····· drumlins
- ----- eskers
- ▮ unglaciated areas
- ▯ earlier glaciation

many moraine and esker deposits overlap in this area because ice sheets meet along a north-south line from just north of Galway through Mayo

many moraine and esker deposits overlap in this area because ice sheets meet along an east-west line from Galway towards Dublin

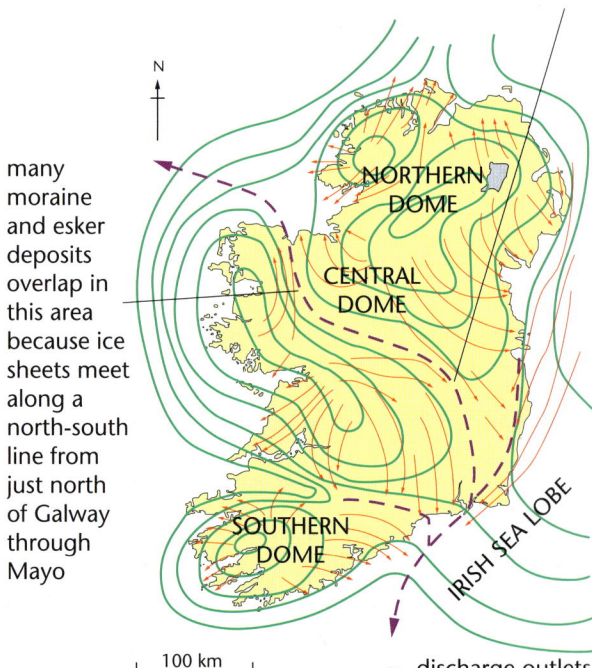

N

NORTHERN DOME

CENTRAL DOME

SOUTHERN DOME

IRISH SEA LOBE

|— 100 km —|

- - - → discharge outlets

Fig. 12.17 Domes of ice that created Ireland's ice sheets.

Outwash Plain

The melting ice sheet caused many rivers to flow from the front of the ice (see Fig. 12.12 on page 79). The meltwater flushed sand, gravel and clay through the terminal moraine to form an **outwash plain**. The Curragh in Co. Kildare is this type of feature.

Landform: Esker

Example: Eiscir Riada at Clonmacnoise, Co. Offaly

Fig. 12.18

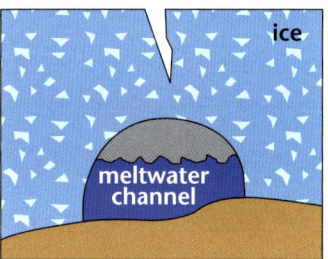

1. As ice melts, meltwater channels form under the ice.

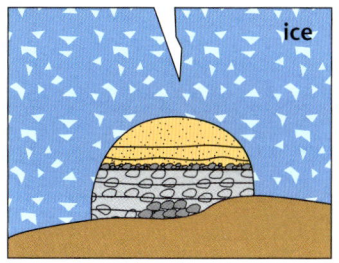

2. Sand, gravel and boulders are deposited, depending on the speed of meltwater flow.

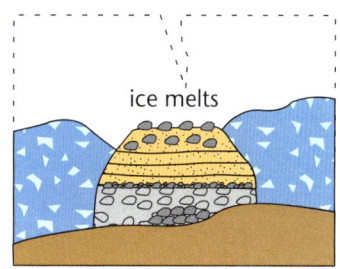

3. Meltwater channel fills with deposits as the ice melts.

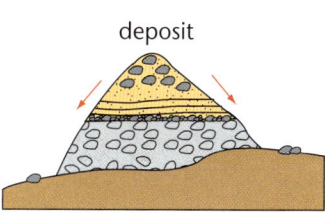

4. After the ice has melted, esker slopes stabilise, leaving a ridge of sand, gravel and boulders.

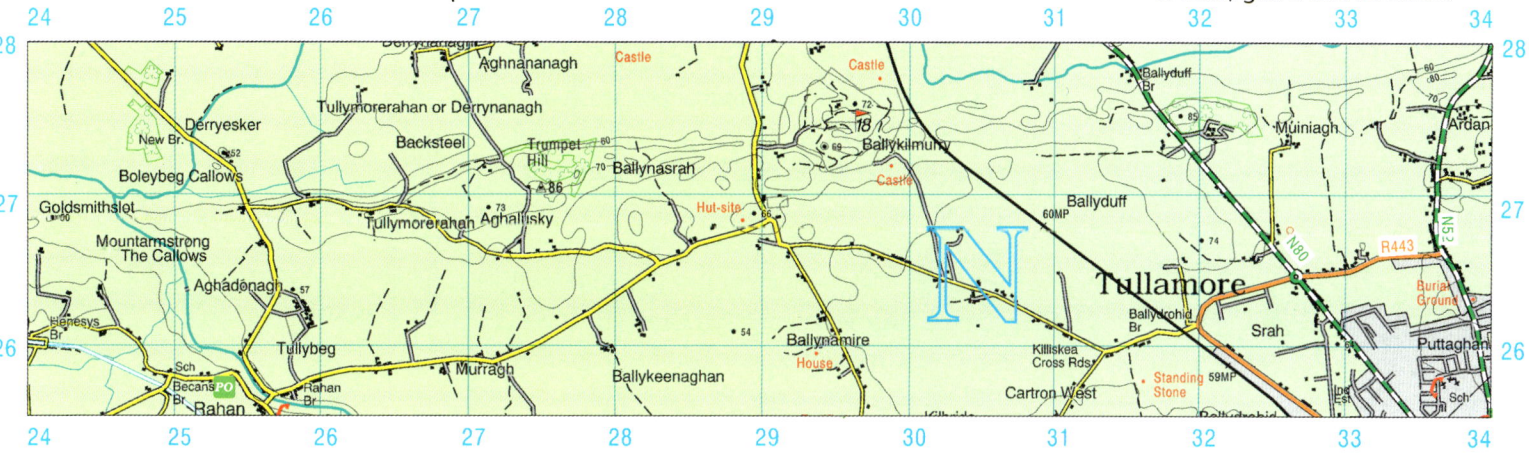

Fig. 12.19 The close irregular contours represent an esker located near Tullamore in Co. Offaly.

Formation

Melting ice sheets produced vast amounts of **meltwater**, some of which flowed through **tunnels** under the ice. The pressure of the water enclosed within the tunnels was considerable and caused the water to flow quickly.

The **fast flow** of the water allowed it to pick up **large quantities of sediment** from the ground moraine beneath the glacier. It washed and cleaned the sediment and carried it along, some in **suspension**, some by **saltation** and more by **traction** (see page 86). The **silt and clay particles** were carried far from their source to lakes or to the sea, while the **sand and gravel** particles were laid down in **alternate sorted layers** on the beds of the enclosed rivers and streams. Layers of fine sediment, such as **fine sand**, were deposited during times of **low water**, while **gravels** were laid down during periods of **rapid ice melt**, such as in summer.

These sub-glacial rivers formed a **winding course** across level plains beneath the ice, just as rivers do when they **meander** in their late stage of development. The deposits they made today form winding ridges of sand and gravel across lowland regions.

Once the esker ridges were exposed after the Ice Age, they were subjected to **weathering and erosion** forces. Parts of them may have **slumped** due to **gravity**, and over time they took on the more pointed ridge-like form they have today.

Esker ridges wind and twist across level lowland.

Transportation of Sediment
- Suspension – float
- Saltation – bounce
- Traction – roll

83

Multi-part Questions

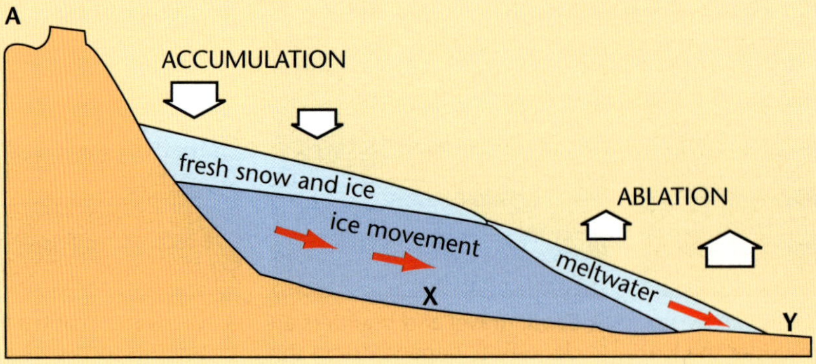

Fig. 12.20

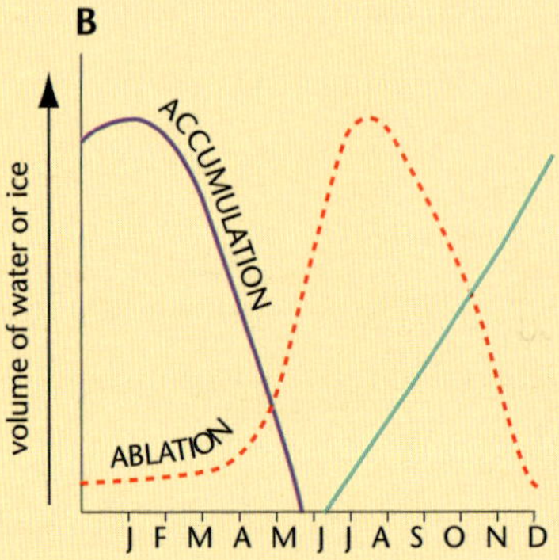

1. **A.** Examine Diagram A in Fig. 12.20, which illustrates the glacier system. Describe the different physical processes that are active at point X and point Y. [20 marks]

   B. Explain the formation of any **one** characteristic landform that would be produced at each point, with reference to the surface processes that formed it. [30 marks]

   C. Examine Diagram A, and also Graph B, which shows how rates of accumulation and ablation (melting) vary over a period of one year.
   Describe and explain what this information tells us about how the glacier system changes over time. [30 marks]

2. **A.** Identify **two** glacial landforms, one formed by glacial erosion and one by glacial deposition. In the case of **one** landform, describe and explain the processes involved in its formation. [20 marks]

   B. Explain how urban water supplies and tourism have been enhanced by glacial erosive action. [30 marks]

   C. The melting of ice masses at the end of the last glacial period released great quantities of meltwater that created landforms in lowland regions. With reference to **one** such landform, explain how it was formed [30 marks]

3. **A.** Cirque, Ribbon lake, Hanging valley, Fjord.
   With reference to any **one** of these landforms, explain how the processes of ice action led to its formation. [20 marks]

   B. Explain the basic conditions of climate and of topography that are necessary to bring about a period of widespread glaciation of a landscape. [30 marks]

   C. Explain the formation of any two landforms that were formed at or beyond the ice front. [30 marks]

4. Study the Ordnance Survey map of Ballyconnell in Co. Cavan on page 97, then answer the following questions.
   Drumlins are low, rounded hills of boulder clay created by glacial deposition. An example of a drumlin is at grid reference H 235 172. The low-lying areas around these hills have a coating of clay, also deposited by the ice. Carefully study similar contour shapes on the map that indicate drumlin hills. Explain how these hills:

   A. were formed

   B. have affected drainage on the map

   C. have affected land patterns in this region. [30 marks]

CHAPTER 13
RIVER PROCESSES, PATTERNS AND LANDFORMS

Rivers perform three basic functions: they erode, transport and deposit material. The energy of a river depends on its volume and its speed, or velocity.

The material that a river transports is called its **load**. Most of the river's energy is used up in transporting this load. **As a river's volume increases, so does its load**.

A river carries its greatest load, and its largest particles, when it is in flood after heavy rain. When in flood, a river's water turns brown due to the high content of soil particles that it carries in suspension. When a flood subsides and normal water levels return, the brown colour disappears and only tiny particles can be moved.

PROCESSES OF RIVER EROSION
Hydraulic Action

Hydraulic action is the force of moving water. By rushing into cracks, the force of moving water can sweep out loose material or help break up solid rock. Turbulent (very disturbed) and eddying (swirling) water may undermine (cut under) banks on the bend of a river. This process is called **bank caving** (see photo below).

Erosion also occurs because of **cavitation**. Cavitation takes place when **bubbles of air collapse** and form tiny **shock waves** against the banks. These tiny explosions loosen soil particles and are particularly effective on banks of clay, sand or gravel.

Torc Waterfall in Killarney.

Over time, hydraulic action breaks solid rock.

Abrasion

Abrasion is the way the river **uses its load to erode.** The greater the volume and speed of a river, the greater its load and the greater its power to erode. A river reaches its **greatest erosive power** during times of **flood,** when riverbanks are most likely to collapse.

Abrasion is seen most effectively where rivers flow over layers of rock. Pebbles are whirled round by eddies in hollows in the riverbed. This action forms potholes (deep pools), which are regularly found in mountain streams.

A river undercuts a bank when it is in flood, causing bank caving and slumping.

Pebbles and rocks become rounded as they hit off each other on the riverbed.
● *Name this process.*

Attrition

As a river carries its load, the **particles** are constantly **in collision** with each other and with the bed of the river. As these particles move downstream, they get progressively smaller. Boulders and pebbles in a river are always **rounded and smooth** to touch.

Solution

Solution is chemical erosion. **Rocks, such as limestone and chalk, dissolve** when water flows across their surface. As rainwater seeps through soil, it becomes more acid than rain. When it meets limestone or chalk, it reacts with them (it fizzes) and dissolves them. It then carries these dissolved particles away in solution.

PROCESSES OF TRANSPORTATION

The river's load is carried in the following ways (see Fig. 13.1).

Suspended Load

Most particles, including fine clay and silt, are carried in suspension by a river. Water action may initially cause fine particles to be lifted from the riverbed, but once in suspension the turbulence of the water keeps them up and the particles are transported downstream.

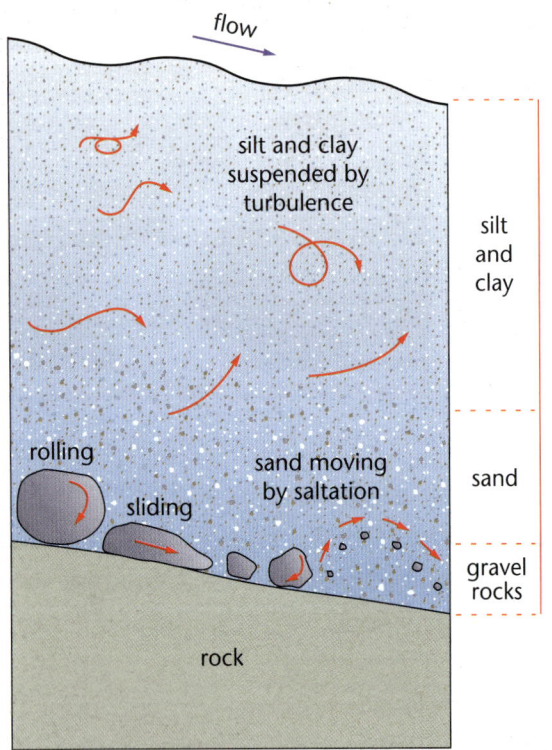

Fig. 13.1 Materials are moved along a river's course by processes of transportation.

Solution

Rivers that flow over soluble rock, such as limestone or chalk, will carry some matter in solution.

Saltation

Some particles are light enough to be bounced along the riverbed. They are lifted from the riverbed by **hydraulic action**. Because they are too heavy to form part of the suspended load, they fall back onto the riverbed to be picked up once more. This process is repeated and so the pattern of bouncing stones is achieved.

Traction (Bedload Drag)

The volume and speed of a river is greatly increased during times of flood. Pebbles, large stones and sometimes huge boulders are rolled along the riverbed during these periods of high water. This process is often referred to as **bedload drag**.

Drainage Basins

Rivers generally rise in mountain regions and flow downslope into the sea. On its journey, a river is joined by smaller streams, called tributaries. The area drained by a river and all its tributaries is called its **basin.** Each river basin is separated from neighbouring basins by areas of high ground called **watersheds**. All precipitation that falls within a drainage basin will eventually find its way into the main river. The name of the river gives its name to its drainage basin, e.g. the **Shannon Basin**.

Some drainage basins are small while others are large. The Amazon and the Mississippi basins are huge. The Mississippi Basin drains all the interior of the United States (except Alaska).

The Shannon Basin drains all the Midlands of Ireland, so it has many tributaries and lakes. As an exercise, use your atlas to draw a sketch map of the Shannon Basin and on it mark and name the River Shannon, its main tributaries and its main lakes.

Alluvial Fans

In mountain areas during periods of heavy rain or during **flash floods,** some water torrents pour over steep edges onto lower ground, or emerge from narrow valleys into more open ground. There, the water torrents deposit large and small broken rock particles, including pebbles and boulders in steeply sloping fan-shaped mounds. These landforms are called **alluvial fans**. This is where most **conglomerate rock** forms.

Alluvial fans form within mountain regions.

● *How many drainage basins are visible on this map extract?*

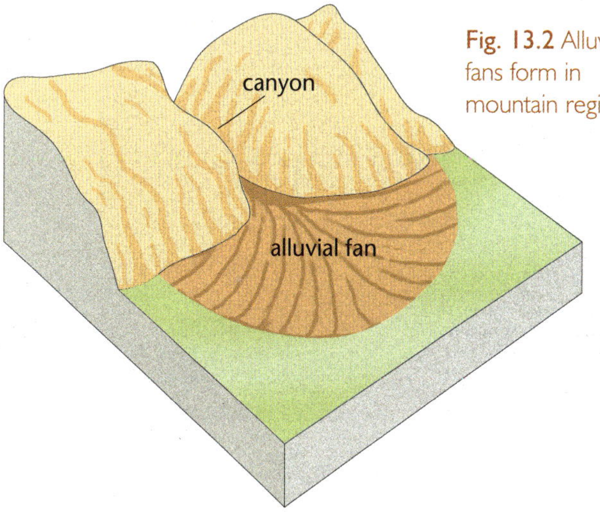

Fig. 13.2 Alluvial fans form in mountain regions.

canyon

alluvial fan

87

STAGES IN A RIVER'S COURSE

There are three stages in the course of a river: upper course, middle course and lower course.

(a) Upper course

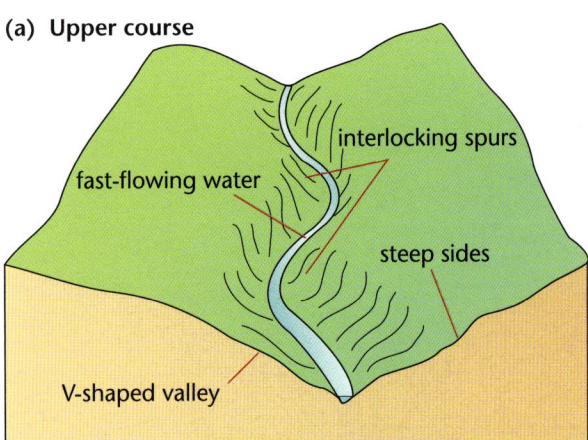

interlocking spurs

fast-flowing water

steep sides

V-shaped valley

The river flows around the interlocking spurs.

(b) Middle course

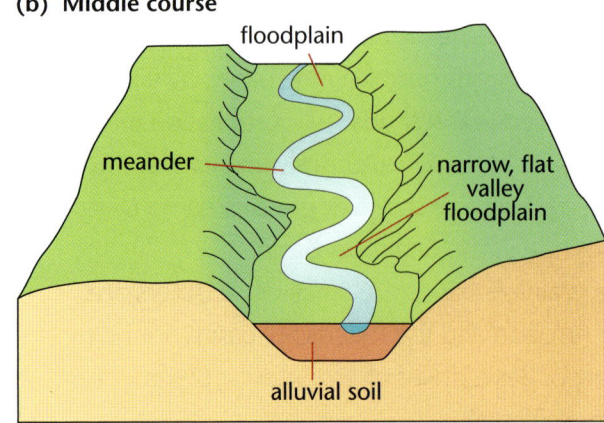

floodplain

meander

narrow, flat valley floodplain

alluvial soil

Interlocking spurs are cut away in a mature floodplain.

(c) Lower course

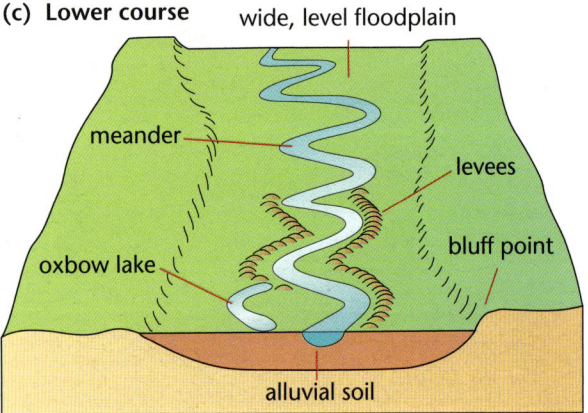

wide, level floodplain

meander

levees

oxbow lake

bluff point

alluvial soil

Oxbow lakes and levees are created in an old valley.

Fig. 13.3 The three stages in a river's course.

Rivers in their upper courses flow quickly within narrow, steep-sided V-shaped valleys.

Landform: V-Shaped Valley

Valley: Devil's Glen in Co. Wicklow

Formation

V-shaped valleys form on mountain slopes. The water from many **gullies** and streams joins to form substantial rivers in mountain regions. This water finds the easiest route downhill by **winding and twisting** its way around obstacles of **hard rock**.

The flowing water becomes a **current** that tends to flow **strongest** on the **outside** of the bends in the river. **Abrasion** by the river's load and the **hydraulic action** of the fast water at these locations make the bends more pronounced. The projections down the sides of the valley are called **interlocking spurs**.

Rainfall on the steep valley sides, the action of **freeze-thaw** in winter and **gravity** (creating soil creep) cause downhill movement of material into the river channel. Over time, the river moves this material to lowland areas.

Erosion is greatest in times of **flood**. The **increased speed** and **load** of the river allow the water to transport large rock particles by **traction** and **saltation**, as well as sand and pebbles, so increasing the river's erosive power. This erodes the riverbed and makes the **valley deeper**.

Landform: Waterfall

Example: Torc Waterfall near Killarney

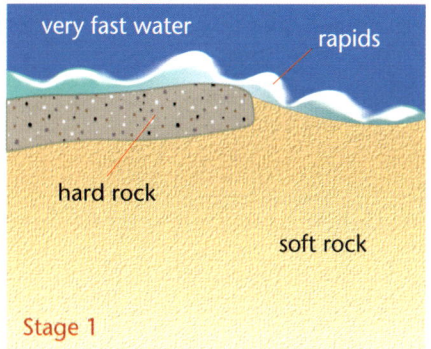
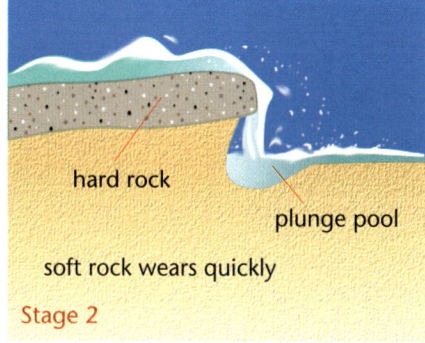
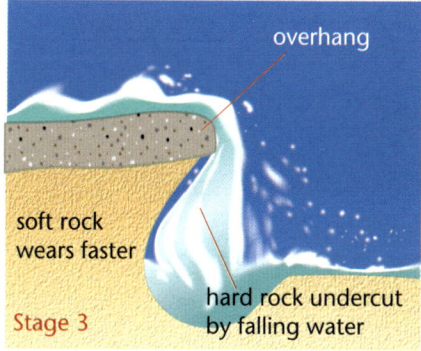

Fig. 13.4 The formation of a waterfall.

Formation

A waterfall usually occurs in the upper course of a river. It forms where a layer of **hard rock** that lies across the riverbed is **horizontal** or **tilted upwards**.

Uneven hardness of the bedrock leads to **differential erosion**. The softer rock is eroded at a faster rate than the hard rock layer. The river finds it difficult to remove the hard rock. Generally, this process is represented by a stretch of **rapids** above the hard rock. The rushing water forces its way into the **joints** in the hard rock, creating an uneven surface.

Directly downstream from the rapids, the softer rock undergoes severe erosion due to **hydraulic action** and **abrasion**. This causes a vertical drop on the riverbed, where the hard rock ends and the softer rock begins.

As the falling water strikes the soft rock on the riverbed, its erosive power gouges out a deep pool, called a **plunge pool**. This pool is gradually deepened with the **eddying** or swirling action of the water and its **load**, creating **abrasion** within the pool.

The mist created by the falling water rots the soft rock underneath the hard rock cap. This soft **rock crumbles** and the hard rock is undermined. Large **chunks** of the hard rock **break away** from the front of the waterfall and fall to the base of the waterfall as a result of undermining or opening up of its joints by hydraulic action.

In some regions where extremely cold conditions are experienced and the river **freezes** over, some freeze-thaw may result in these rock chunks being loosened. In this way the **waterfall retreats** upstream, leaving a deep, steep-sided narrow channel downstream from the waterfall. This landform is called a **gorge**.

Yosemite Falls in Yosemite National Park in California,
● *Suggest one reason why this waterfall formed here.*

Activity
1. Name one example of a waterfall in Ireland.
2. Explain, with the aid of diagrams, how a waterfall forms in a young river valley.
3. Explain, using examples, how waterfalls are used to encourage economic development.

Landform: Floodplain
Example: Blackwater Valley near Fermoy

Erosion occurs on the outside of a bend. Deposition occurs on the opposite side where water is slower-moving.

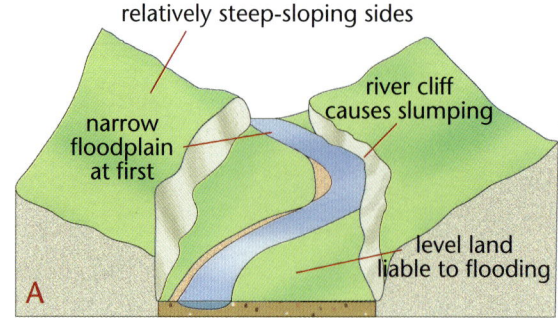

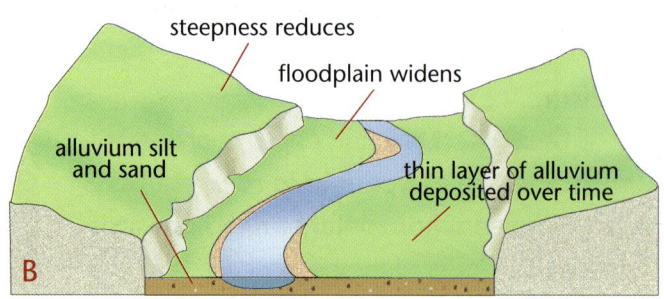

Fig. 13.5 A floodplain widens over time and the sides reduce in steepness.

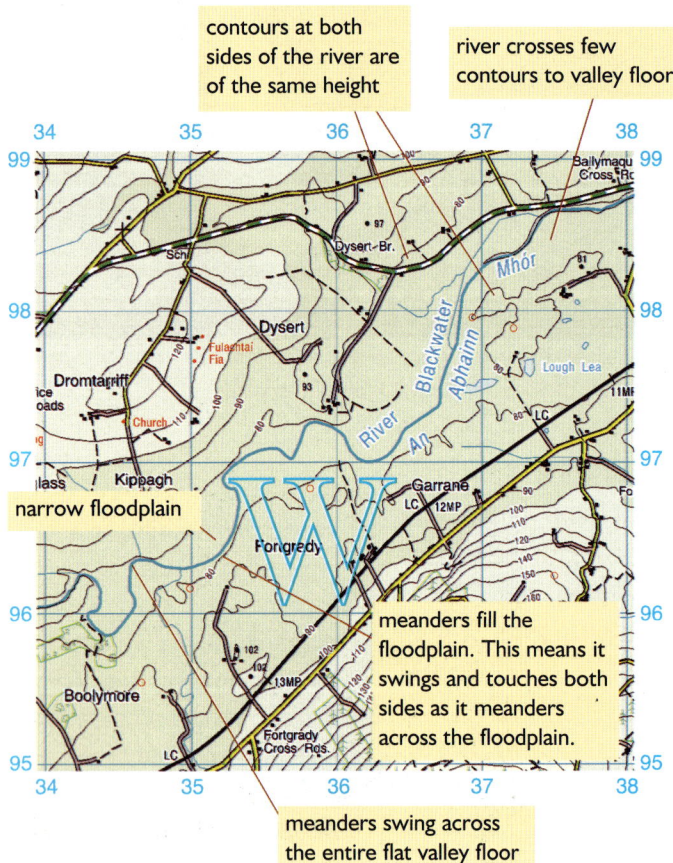

contours at both sides of the river are of the same height

river crosses few contours to valley floor

narrow floodplain

meanders fill the floodplain. This means it swings and touches both sides as it meanders across the floodplain.

meanders swing across the entire flat valley floor

Formation

When a river reaches lowland areas, it **slows down** and starts to swing from side to side. This creates **lateral erosion** and begins the process of removing the river's interlocking spurs. The processes of hydraulic action, cavitation and abrasion are very active at this stage.

As the river flows around a bend, it **erodes** most strongly on the **outside** of the bend, forming a **river cliff**. The bank is **undercut** and parts of it **slump** into the river.

Little erosion occurs on the inside of the bend, but there is often deposition, forming a gravel beach or a **point bar**. The lateral (side to side) wandering of the river is called **divagation**.

Over time, a wide and flat valley floor is created. During times of flood, the rivers **overflow** their channels and spread across the flat valley floor. Away from the river's channel, the floodwater is calm and it has lots of fine sediment, such as silt and fine sand, in suspension. This is deposited on the level surface of coarse deposits and is called **alluvium**. Over thousands of years each successive flow builds up a thick blanket of alluvium to form extremely fertile, level land, called a **floodplain**, suited to growing cereal or cattle grazing.

Landform: Oxbow Lake
Example: River Shannon at Leitrim town

Formation

Oxbow lakes are relic river channels where looping meanders were cut off from the main river and are no longer active. Their waters are stagnant and their levels rise and fall with the water table. Oxbow lakes form where a river makes huge sweeping or **looping meanders** as it flows across a wide, flat floodplain in the river's middle or especially in its **lower stage**.

Lateral erosion of a river's channel causes meanders to move across its floodplain and also to move downstream. This is called the process of **divagation**.

Constant **erosion** on the **outside** of a meander bend leads to a sweeping loop forming in the river's course. This process creates a '**peninsula**' of land with a narrow neck trapped by the looping river's channel. As the river sweeps around this looping bend, the zone of highest speed within the channel swings towards the outer bank. There is great water turbulence where the river strikes the bank, which is formed of sediment previously deposited by the river.

The **abrasive action** of the river's load, the collapsing of air bubbles (called **cavitation**), causing shock waves, and the **hydraulic** force of the water combine to cause **undercutting** of this soft material. The undercutting causes **slumping** of the bank into the river.

Meanwhile, along the inner side of each meander loop, where the water is shallow and slow-moving, coarse sediment (such as gravel and sand) builds up to form a beach, called a **point bar**. During a flood, the river cuts through the neck of land and continues on a straighter and easier route, leaving the cut-off to one side. **Deposition** occurs at **both ends** of this cut-off to form an oxbow lake. After a long time, the oxbows fill with silt from floodwater and eventually dry up. When this happens, they are called **meander scars**, or **mort lakes**.

Practise these drawings over and over again.

● *Can you identify the oxbow lakes in this satellite photograph of the Danube?*

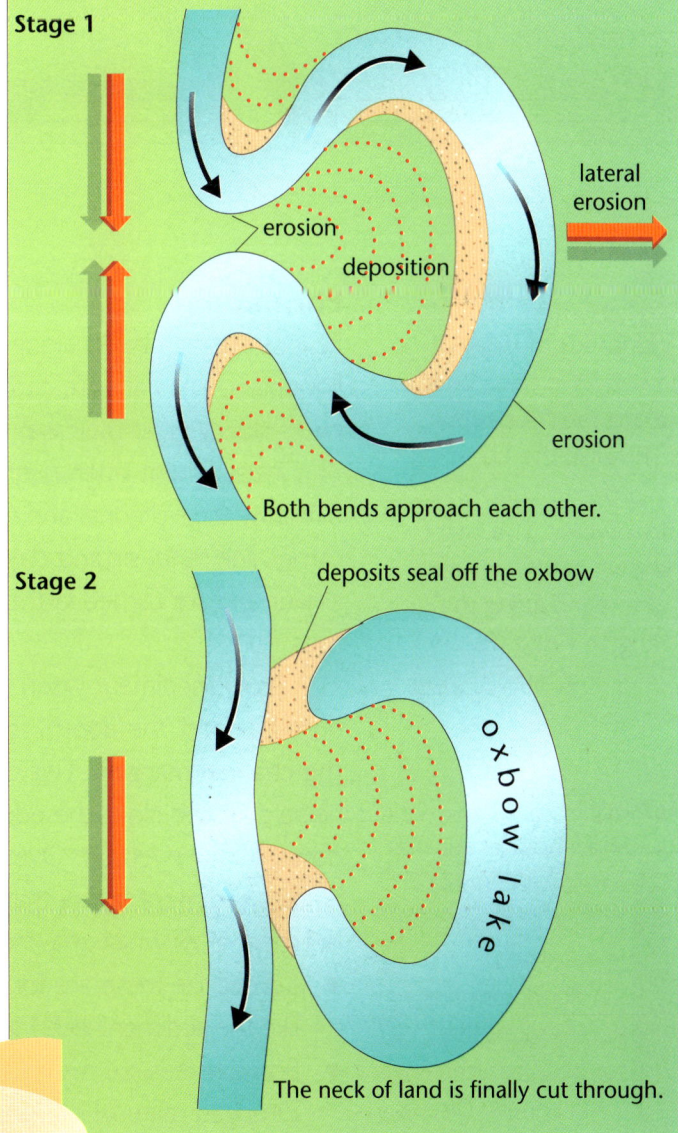

Stage 1

lateral erosion

erosion

deposition

erosion

Both bends approach each other.

Stage 2

deposits seal off the oxbow

oxbow lake

The neck of land is finally cut through.

Fig. 13.6 The formation of an oxbow lake.

Landform: Levee
Example: Mulkear River in Co. Limerick

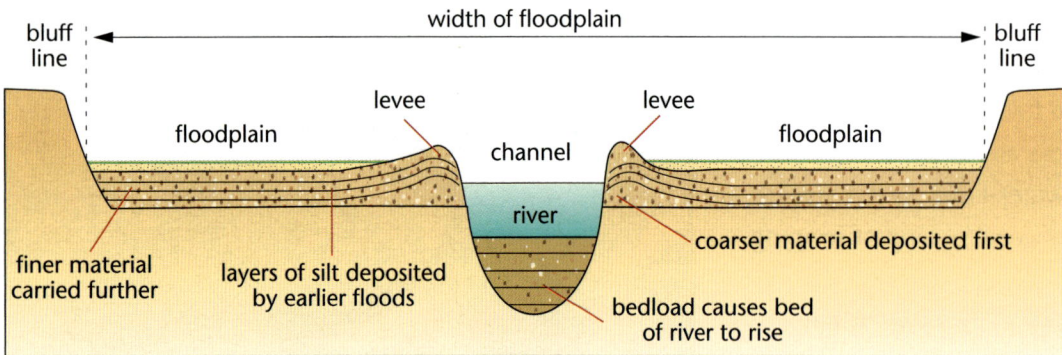

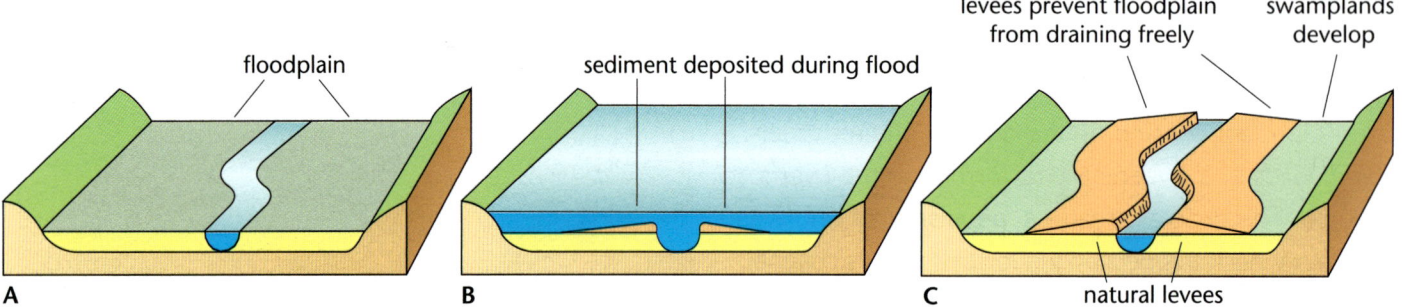

Fig. 13.7 The formation of levees.

Activity
1. Explain how levees may interact with people's activities, both positively and negatively.
2. River floodplains are natural regions that have been adapted for human benefit. Discuss.

Formation

Levees are high banks along the edges of a river's channel, raised above the floodplain. They are created naturally along the edges of **large, silt-laden rivers** as the rivers slowly wind their way across flat floodplains to the sea.

As sediment-laden rivers flood during prolonged spells of heavy rain, their waters overflow their channel and spread across the floodplain. At this lower stage the river carries fine sand, silt and clay particles in suspension. These are the lightest particles in a river and are carried farthest from their source in the mountains where the river rises.

As the sediment-laden waters flow out from their completely submerged channel during a flood, the **depth, force** and **turbulence** of the water **decreases sharply at the channel margins**. This decrease results in the fine sand and coarse silt suddenly being dropped along the edges of the channel. A thick sediment deposit is also laid down on the riverbed. Over hundreds of thousands of years, **repeated flooding** creates **sediment layers** that build up high banks parallel to the river's channel and a riverbed, all of which may be well above the level of the surrounding floodplain.

- Levees like these are found along delta distributaries, such as in a bird's foot delta like the sediment-rich Mississippi River estuary in the Gulf of Mexico.
- Some levees are man made to prevent flooding of farmland or an urban area. Dredged material is dumped along the channel edges by machines. These levees, however, are narrow and not as stable as naturally occurring ones.

Landform: Delta
Example: Clohoge River Delta in Lough Tay, Co. Wicklow

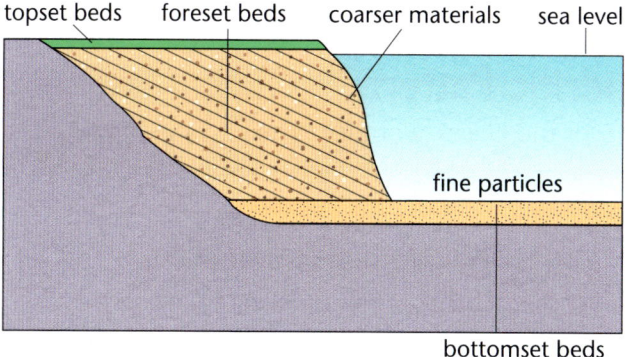

Fig. 13.8 Delta deposits.

This is a satellite image of the Mississippi Delta.
* *What type of delta does this river form? Explain.*

Formation

A delta forms at the **mouth of a river** if the river carries a heavy load as it enters calm waters in a lake or enclosed estuary. If the delta forms in a lake, it is a **lacustrine** delta. If it forms on the coast, it is a **marine delta**.

The materials that build up to form a delta are composed of **alternate layers** of **coarse and fine deposits** that reflect times of high and low water levels, respectively. On the coast the meeting of freshwater and salty seawater produces an electric charge that causes the silt and clay particles to '**clot**' and settle on the seabed.

These materials are classified into three categories:

* Fine particles, such as clay, are carried out to sea and deposited in advance of the main delta. These form the **bottomset beds**.
* Coarser materials, such as silt and very fine sand, form **sloping layers** over the bottomset beds and gradually build outwards, each one on front of and above the ones before, causing the delta to advance. These are the **foreset beds**.
* Sediments of various grain sizes, ranging from sand to fine silt, are deposited **between distributary channels**. These build out a flat surface, so extending the floodplain. These deposits are called the **topset beds**.

There are three types of marine deltas: arcuate, estuarine and bird's foot.

* An **arcuate delta** has a triangular shape, like the Greek letter 'delta'. The apex of the triangle points upstream. Arcuate deltas are formed mostly of coarse sands and gravels where coastal sea currents are relatively strong, e.g. the Nile Delta.
* **Estuarine deltas** form at the mouths of submerged river estuaries. The deposits form long, narrow, flat or sloping banks along both sides of the estuary, e.g. the Shannon Estuary.
* **Bird's foot deltas** form where rivers carry heavy loads of fine materials to the coast. These impermeable deposits cause the river to break up into a few large distributaries. Levees develop along these distributaries, so long 'fingers' project into the sea, making a shape like a bird's foot, e.g. the Mississippi Delta.

Activity

1. Deltas develop at various stages along the courses of some rivers.
   a. Identify two locations where deltas form.
   b. Explain how the sediments at each of these locations may differ considerably.
2. Use the diagram in Fig. 13.8 to explain three categories of sediments that are found in a delta.
3. Study the OS map extract on page 90. Explain the influence of the River Blackwater on settlement patterns in the area.

PATTERNS OF DRAINAGE

There are four patterns of drainage: **dendritic**, **trellised**, **radial** and **deranged**.

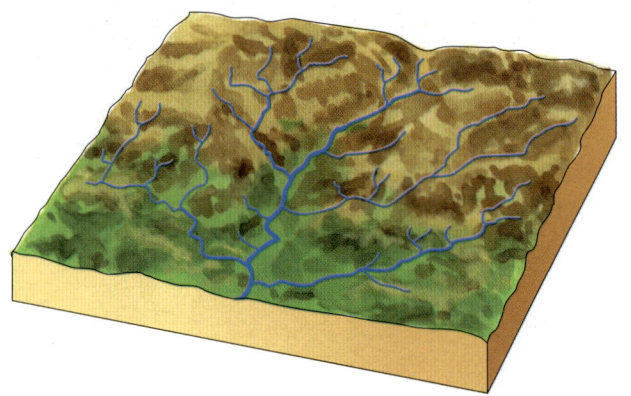

Fig. 13.9 Dendritic drainage pattern.

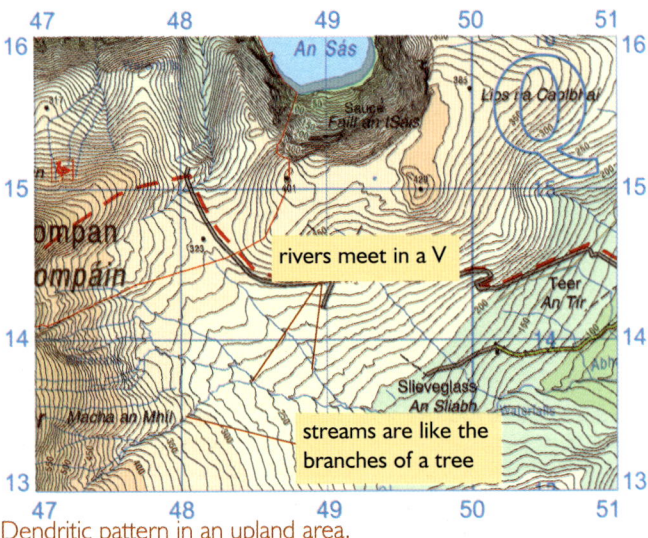

rivers meet in a V

streams are like the branches of a tree

Dendritic pattern in an upland area.

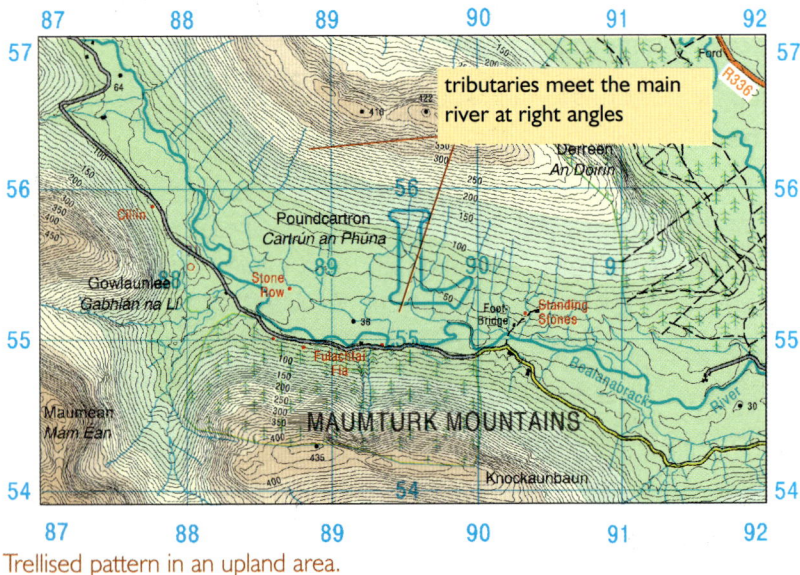

tributaries meet the main river at right angles

Trellised pattern in an upland area.

Dendritic Pattern

Dendros is the Greek word for 'tree', so a dendritic pattern is **tree-shaped**. In areas where the **bedrock** is of **equal hardness**, a river and its tributaries will erode evenly to provide a **tree-shaped river pattern**. The main river, because of its greater volume, will erode the most and so has the widest and deepest valley. The tributaries have less water, so their erosive power is less than the main river. Their valleys are therefore smaller and not as deep.

Each tributary **flows with the slope of the land** and meets the main river or other tributaries at an **acute angle** (an angle of less than 90°). This is why every tributary appears to consist of a main trunk, fed from a variety of branches, each one running into a valley proportional to the river's size.

Trellised Pattern

A trellised pattern forms when tributaries flow into the main river at right angles. This pattern forms when the bedrock of an area is of unequal hardness. Some areas have **soft rock**, while other adjoining areas have **hard rock**. The hard rock is resistant to erosion, while the soft rock erodes quickly.

In Munster, for example, the bedrock consists of alternate parallel layers of sandstone, which is hard, and limestone, which is soft. The limestone has eroded quickly and forms valleys. The more resistant sandstone stands out as parallel ridges that separate the valleys (see page 51).

Trellised patterns also develop in **steep-sided valleys**, such as glaciated U-shaped valleys. Tributary water rushes down the steep slopes of the sides and enters the main river at **right angles**.

Activity
Describe the patterns of drainage on each of the Ordnance Survey maps on this page.

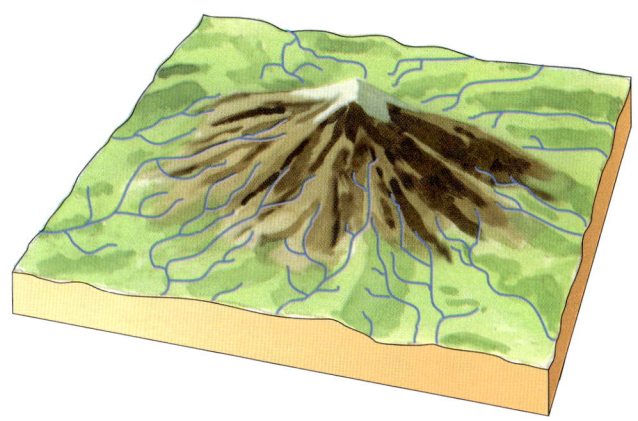

Fig. 13.10 Radial pattern in an upland area.

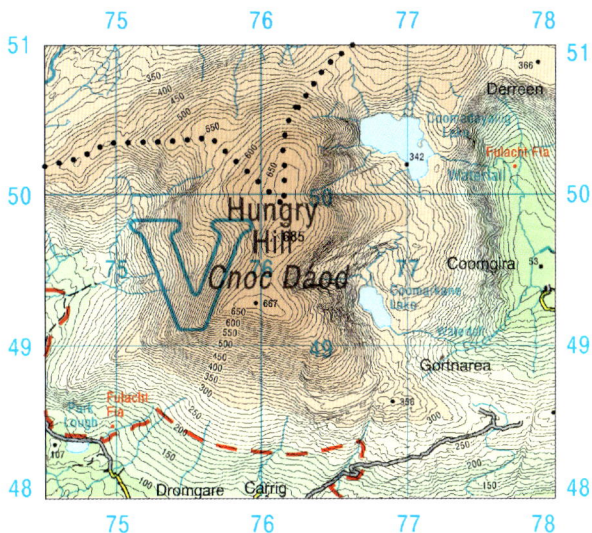

Radial pattern in an upland area. When several streams flow outwards (radiate) in all directions from a mountain or hill, they form a radial pattern of drainage.

Radial Pattern

Rivers which radiate outward from a mountain form a radial pattern. This is best displayed in well-defined circular or oval-shaped upland areas. Some of these rivers may in fact display a different drainage pattern from one another, but together they may radiate outward (north, south, east or west) from a central elevated area. They all share a common watershed at their highest source streams.

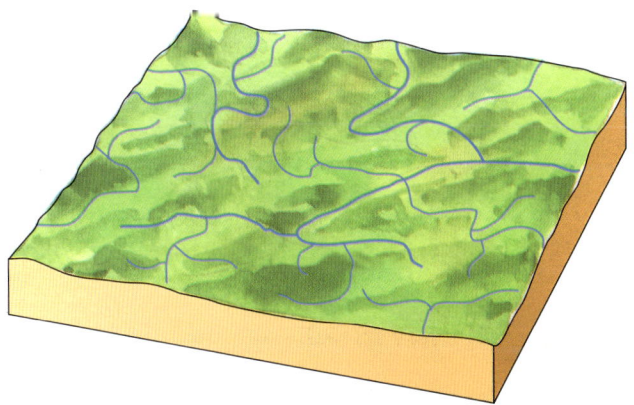

Fig. 13.11 Deranged pattern in a lowland area.

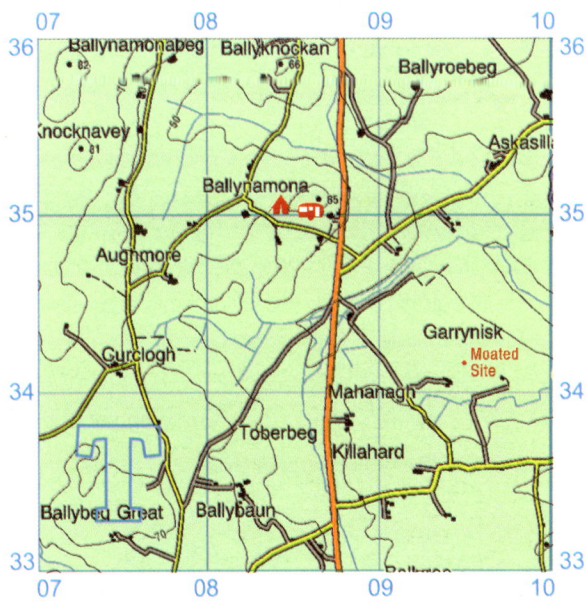

Deranged pattern in a lowland area. This is a river pattern which generally develops in a lowland area where glacial drift exists. The rivers have a chaotic appearance.

Deranged Pattern

Deranged drainage generally develops in a lowland area. Rivers have a chaotic appearance, with streams intersecting each other and flowing in no apparent direction. Deranged drainage usually develops as a result of widespread deposition of glacial material, through which post-glacial streams have had to find a route. An example of deranged drainage can be found on the coastal plain west of Cahore Point in Co. Wexford.

Multi-part Questions

Carefully study the Ordnance Survey map of Ballyconnell in Co. Cavan on page 97, then answer the following questions.

1. River processes have affected this region in Co. Cavan over time. Using evidence from the map, identify **two** landforms that have been created by these processes. In each case:
    A. i.   name the landform
        ii.   locate the landform on the map
        iii. give another Irish example.   [20 marks]
    B. Explain the processes that led to the formation of one of these landforms.   [30 marks]
    C. Explain two ways that people have attempted to manage or control the natural processes that operate in river valleys.   [30 marks]

2. Carefully study the Ordnance Survey map of Ballyconnell in Co. Cavan on page 97, then answer the following questions.
    A. Name and locate three types of drainage patterns. For any **two** of these patterns, describe how and why they formed.   [20 marks]
    B. Describe, using evidence from the map, the stage of formation of the Woodford River.   [30 marks]
    C. Draw a sketch map of the area on the map.
        i.   On it, mark and name two distinct physical regions.
        ii.   Explain how any one of these regions affects the development and pattern of routeways.   [30 marks]

3. V-shaped valley, Oxbow lake, Delta, Levees, Interlocking spurs, Waterfall.
    A. **Each** of the above features found along the course of a river, state whether it is formed by erosion or deposition.   [20 marks]
    B. Select any **two** of these features and, with the aid of a diagram, describe how each was formed.   [30 marks]
    C. 'Large-scale flooding by rivers has caused enormous problems for local communities.'
        Discuss this statement.   [30 marks]

4. Carefully examine the hydrograph showing a river's discharge after a downpour in Fig. 13.12, then answer the following questions.
    A. i.   At what time of day did the river's water level rise initially?
        ii.   What was the lag time, i.e. the length of time between maximum rainfall and peak discharge?   [20 marks]
    B. Did this river flood the surrounding landscape, i.e. did it overflow its banks? Explain.   [30 marks]
    C. How long did it take for the floodwaters to recede?
    D. Give one reason why the lag time is so fast.
    E. Would you think the falling limb suggests a heavily vegetated drainage basin that has a less rapid run-off rate? Explain.   [30 marks]

> The lag time varies according to conditions within the drainage basin, e.g. slope and size of the basin, number of tributaries, type and amount of vegetation and water already in storage.

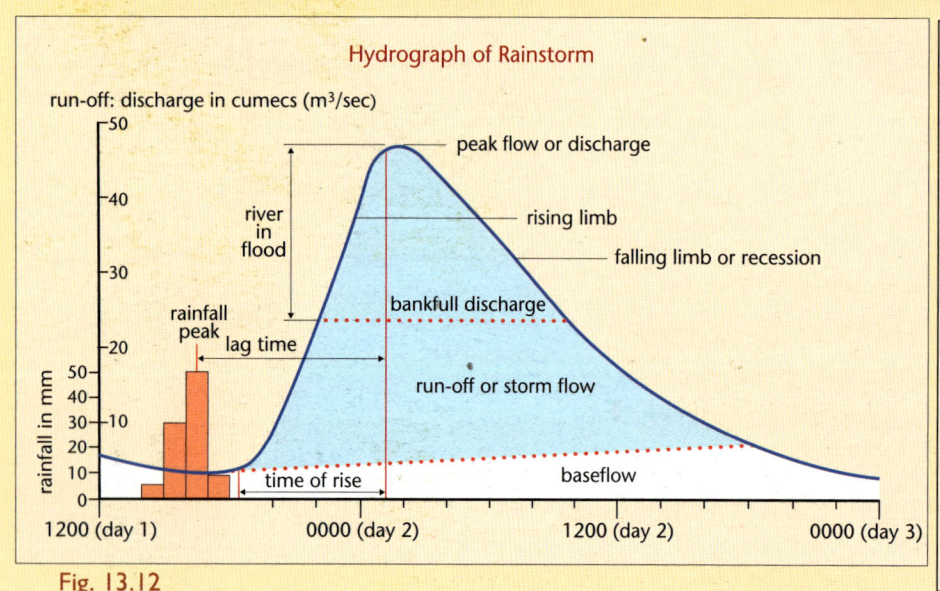

KEY TO DIAGRAM
- **Approach segment** shows the discharge of the river before the storm.
- **Rising limb** shows the rapid increase in discharge in response to rainfall. (The steeper the rising limb, the faster the water flows off the landscape into the river.)
- **Peak discharge** shows when the river reaches its highest level.
- **Lag time** is the period between the maximum rainfall and peak discharge.
- **Falling limb** shows when discharge is decreasing. Dense vegetation reduces run-off rate.
- **Bankfull discharge** occurs when a river's water level reaches the top of the river bank. Any further increase results in flooding of surrounding land.
- **Base flow** is the normal water level released by the ground surface.

Fig. 13.12

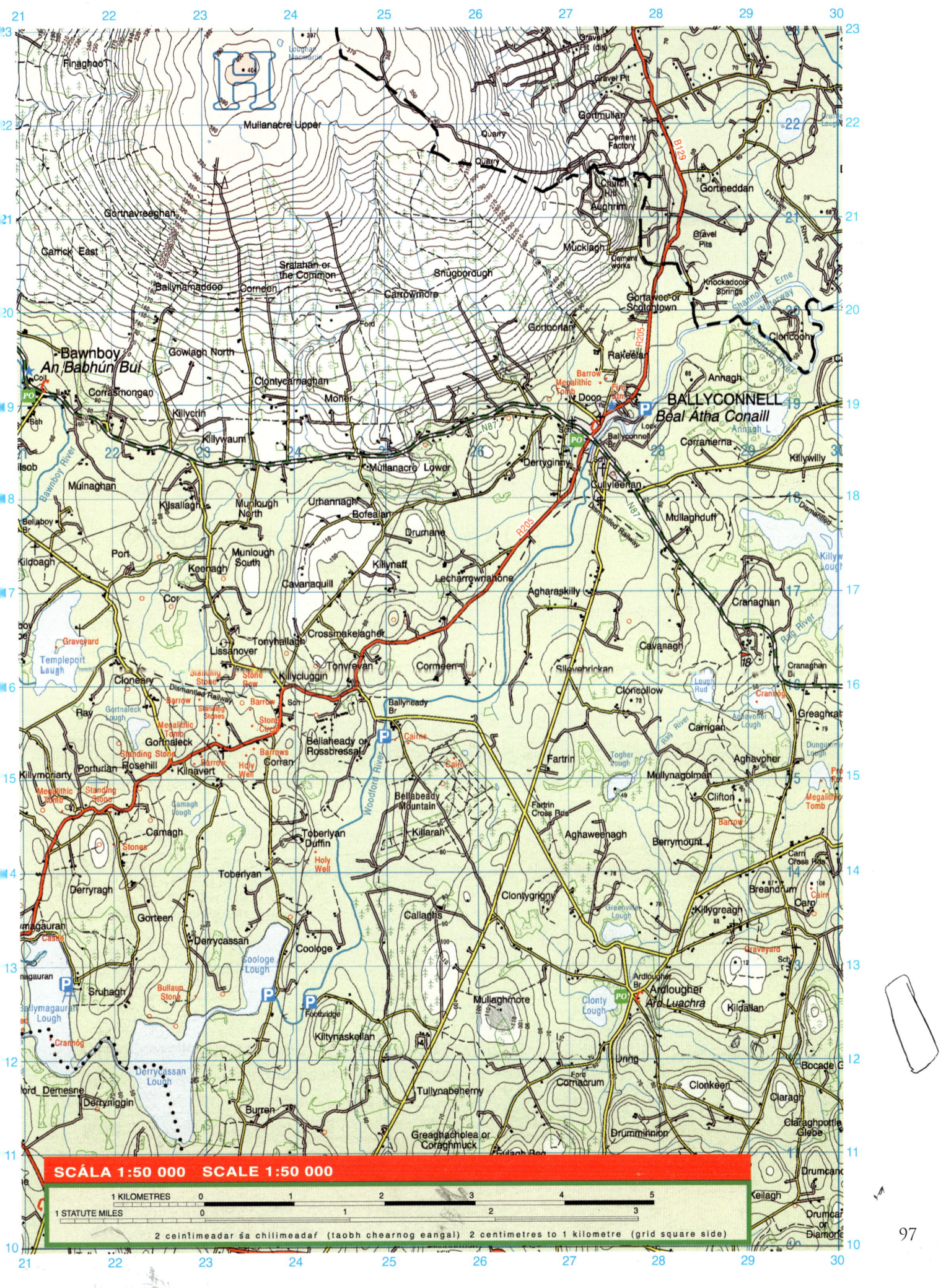

SCÁLA 1:50 000   SCALE 1:50 000

1 KILOMETRES   0   1   2   3   4   5

1 STATUTE MILES   0   1   2   3

2 ceintiméadar sa chilíméadar (taobh chearnóg eangal)   2 centimetres to 1 kilometre (grid square side)

97

CHAPTER 14

COASTAL PROCESSES, PATTERNS AND LANDFORMS

 **KEY IDEA!** Landforms are created by coastal processes.

The character of any coastline depends on a number of factors. These include:

- The **work of waves, tides and currents**, which erode, transport and deposit materials.
- The **nature of the coastline**: whether the coastal rock is resistant or not; whether it is varied or even in character and the type of coastline – highland or lowland, even straight or indented.
- The **changes** in the relative **levels** of land and sea.
- **Human interference**: the dredging of estuaries; the creation of ports; the reclamation of coastal marshes; the construction of coastal defences against erosion, such as groynes, dykes and breakwaters; and the building of piers and promenades.

FACTORS THAT AID EROSION

Destructive Waves

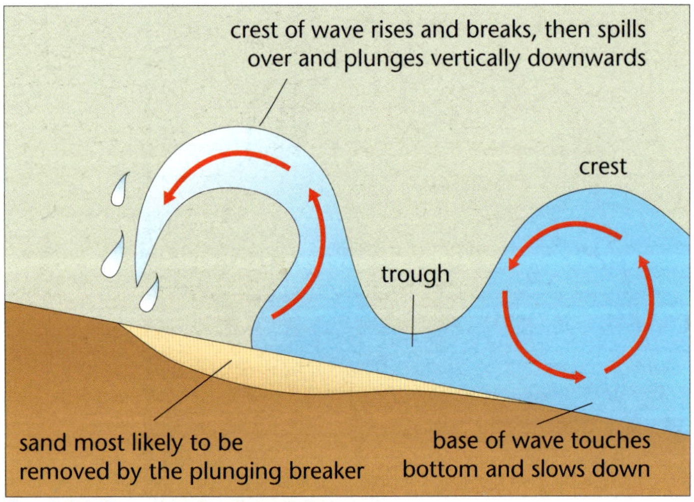

The power and size of a wave depends on the speed of the wind and the **fetch**. The fetch is the length of open water over which the wind blows. The stronger the wind and the longer the fetch, the stronger the waves will be and the greater their erosive power.

Destructive breakers that pound a coastline have their greatest effect during storms. Because of the frequency of the waves (twelve per minute) and because of the **vertical plunge** of the breakers (breaking waves), the backwash (when waves move back) is much more powerful than the swash (when water rushes onto the beach). Thus these destructive waves dig up beach material and carry it seaward or pick up loose material near a cliff and bash it against the cliff face.

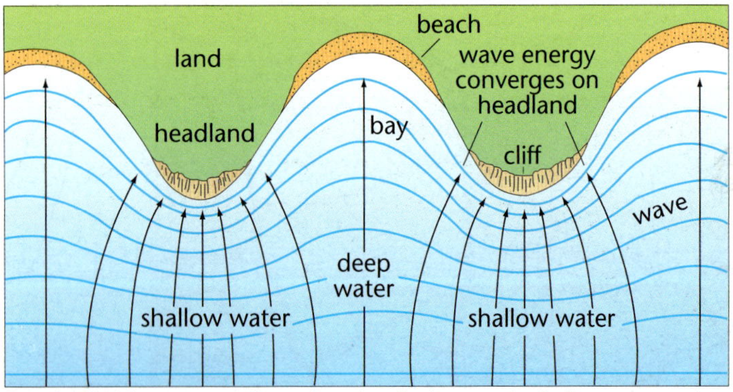

Refraction

The depth of water varies along shorelines that have promontories and bays. The water is **shallower** in front of the **promontory**, or **headland**, than in the bay. As waves approach the shore, the shallower water off the promontory causes the waves **to bend** towards the headland, thus increasing erosion there. This wave **refraction**, or bending, also occurs when waves pass the end of an obstacle, such as a spit, which create a **hook**. The process of refraction is involved in both erosion and deposition along a coastline.

Fig. 14.1 Process of a destructive wave.

crest of wave rises and breaks, then spills over and plunges vertically downwards

crest

trough

sand most likely to be removed by the plunging breaker

base of wave touches bottom and slows down

Fig. 14.2 Waves are deflected and pulled towards shallow water along headlands.

beach

land

wave energy converges on headland

headland

bay

cliff

wave

deep water

shallow water

shallow water

PROCESSES OF COASTAL EROSION

These processes include:

- Hydraulic action.
- Compression.
- Abrasion.
- Attrition.

Fig. 14.3 Hydraulic action.

Hydraulic Action

When strong waves crash against a coast, they have a **shattering effect** as they pound the rocks. Waves crashing against the base of a cliff **force rocks apart,** making them more prone to erosion. Cliffs of boulder clay are particularly affected, as loosened soil and rocks are washed away.

Compression

Air filters into joints, cracks and bedding planes in cliff faces. As incoming waves crash against the coast, the **air is trapped**. The trapped air is compressed by the waves squeezing their way into the air-filled cavities. When the wave retreats, it results in a **rapid expansion** of the compressed air, creating an **explosive effect** that widens the cracks (fissures) and shatters the rock face.

Abrasion

When boulders, pebbles and sand are pounded against the foot of a cliff by waves, fragments of rock are broken off and **undercutting** of the cliff takes place. The amount of abrasion depends on the ability of the waves to pick up rock fragments from the shore. Abrasion is most active during storms and at high tide, when **incoming waves throw water and suspended rock material** high up the cliff face and sometimes onto the cliff edge.

the seas load is pounded against the coast by the waves

Attrition

Fragments that are pounded by the sea against the cliff and **against each other** are themselves worn down by attrition, creating sand and shingle.

Rocks carried by the sea cause the knock of each other

The ability of waves to pick up rocks and lash them against a coast is many, many times greater than waves during periods of calm weather.

Wave action creates caves and inlets on Ireland's west coast.

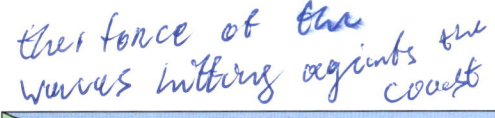
the force of the waves hitting against the coast

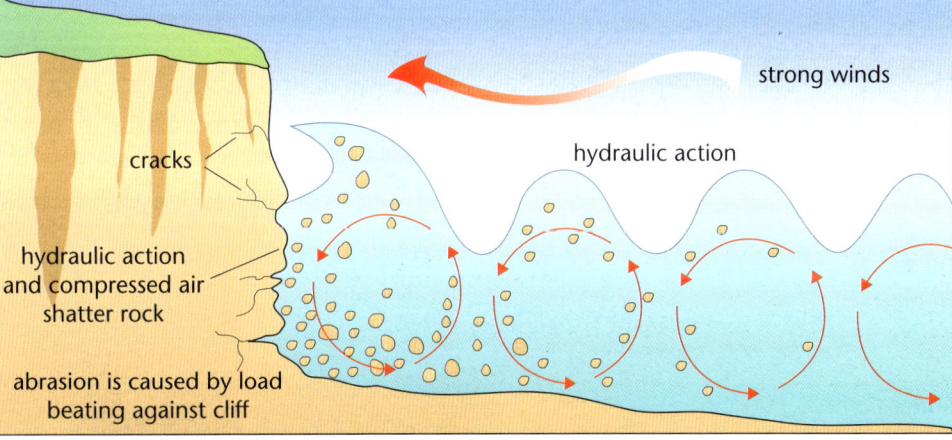

cracks

hydraulic action and compressed air shatter rock

abrasion is caused by load beating against cliff

strong winds

hydraulic action

Fig. 14.4 Storm waves bash rocks and boulders against a coast. These rocks are also reduced in size as they shatter upon hitting the cliff face.

air is trapped in the cracks when the air retreats thus shatters the rock

Water-rolled rocks are rounded and smoothed as they roll back and forth on top of each other.

LANDFORMS OF COASTAL EROSION
Landform: Cliff
Example: Cliffs of Moher in Co. Clare

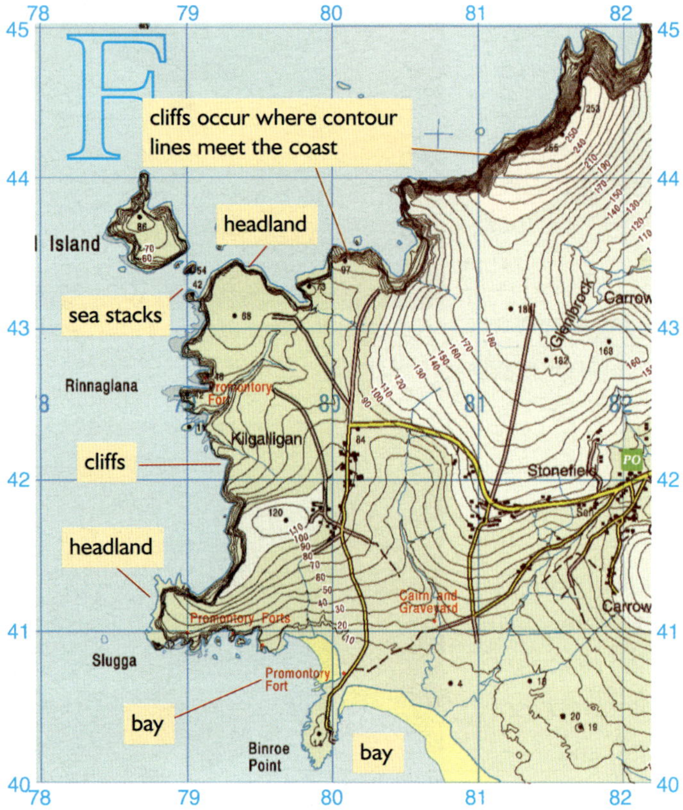

The map on the left shows the following labels:
- cliffs occur where contour lines meet the coast
- headland
- Island
- sea stacks
- Rinnaglana
- cliffs
- headland
- Kilgalligan
- Stonefield
- Carrow
- Carrow
- Glenbrock
- Promontory Forts
- Slugga
- Promontory Fort
- bay
- Binroe Point
- bay

Formation

Wave action cuts a **notch** on any new land surface that is exposed to the force of the sea. This notch is eroded by the processes of hydraulic action and abrasion. When joints and bedding planes in rock surfaces are exposed to wave action, air is forced into them. The **air is trapped** and **compressed** by the force of incoming waves. This is called **hydraulic action**. As each wave retreats, the air instantly expands and this **'explosive' expansion** enlarges the cracks and eventually **the rock shatters** into small and large blocks and boulders. The rock particles are removed by the crashing waves and fall to the seabed. **Strong waves** pick up these shattered rock particles and bash them off the coast. Most of this action takes place at or below high tide level. This process is called **abrasion**.

The combined processes of hydraulic action and abrasion eventually cut a notch in the coast that creates an **overhanging rock ledge**. When this notch lengthens, the overhanging rock mass becomes too heavy to be supported and **collapses** into the sea. This creates a vertical 'wall' of rock along the water's edge and it is called a cliff.

As the cliff 'retreats', a level rock surface is formed at the base of the cliff. This surface is called a **wave-cut platform**. This may be exposed at low tide in some places.

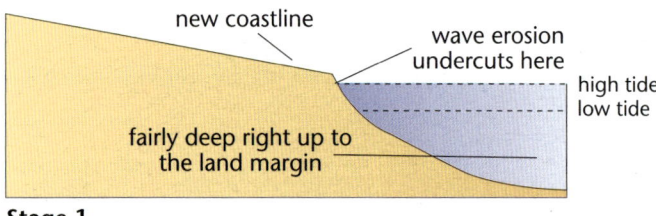

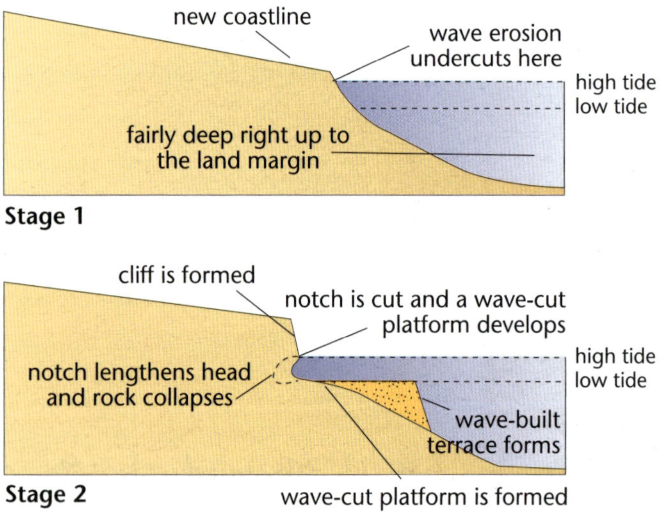

Stage 1
- new coastline
- wave erosion undercuts here
- high tide
- low tide
- fairly deep right up to the land margin

Stage 2
- cliff is formed
- notch is cut and a wave-cut platform develops
- notch lengthens head and rock collapses
- high tide
- low tide
- wave-built terrace forms
- wave-cut platform is formed

Fig. 14.5 A wave-cut platform.

● *What features indicate that this is a wave-cut platform?*

Landform: Sea Stack

Example: Sybil Point in Co. Kerry

Formation

Sea stacks form in areas of active erosion, where a **large joint** in a cliff or a **faulted zone** or a **soft rock area** may allow severe wave erosion at a particular spot on a promontory or headland. First a cave forms, then an arch and finally a stack.

Air is **forced into joints** and bedding planes in the rock surface. The air is trapped and compressed by the force of incoming waves. This is called **hydraulic action**. As each wave retreats, the escaping air instantly 'expands' and the **explosive expansion** enlarges the cracks and eventually the rock shatters into small and large rock particles and boulders. The rock particles are removed by the crashing waves and fall to the seabed. Strong waves pick up these rock particles and boulders and bash them off this same rock surface. This process is called **abrasion**. Eventually both processes create a **cave**.

The **force of the waves** themselves also erodes part of the cave surface. Over time all these processes **lengthen the cave** until it cuts through the promontory or headland. A **sea arch** then forms.

Continual erosion of hydraulic action and abrasion increases the width and height of the cave until the roof becomes too wide and heavy to be supported. The **roof collapses, cutting off** a part of the promontory or headland from the coast. This cut-off rock structure is called a **sea stack**.

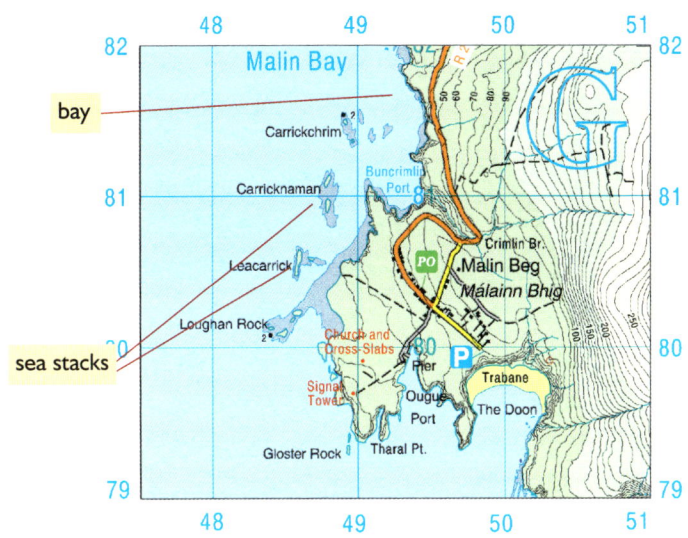

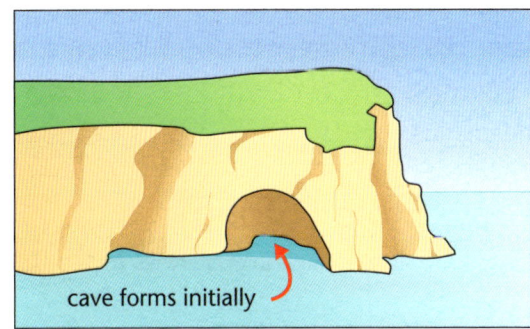
cave forms initially

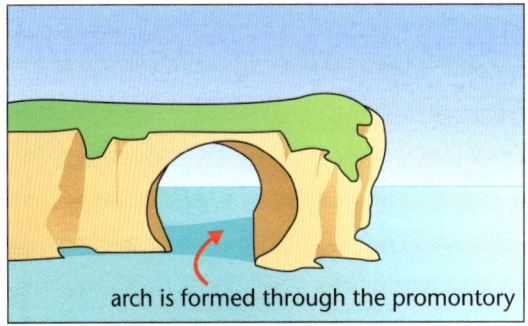
arch is formed through the promontory

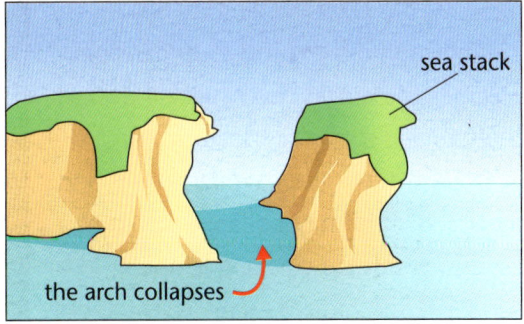
sea stack

the arch collapses

Fig. 14.6 Stages in the formation of a sea stack.

When this sea arch collapses it will leave a sea stack cut off from the coast.

Bays and Headlands

Examples: Clew Bay in Co. Mayo

Erris Head in Co. Mayo

Coasts are composed of **alternate bands** of rock that vary in hardness and structure. Some rock, such as shale, is **soft** and has many closely spaced bedding planes that are easily shattered by hydraulic action. It is eroded quickly by destructive waves. Boulder clay coasts are also quickly eroded and may retreat by as much as 1–2 m a year. Other coastal stretches may have **harder rock,** such as sandstone, that resists erosion.

The way in which coasts do not erode uniformly is called differential erosion. This is especially noticeable on coasts where areas of hard and softer rock lie side by side. The less resistant rock erodes more rapidly and forms **bays**. The harder rock resists erosion and forms **headlands**.

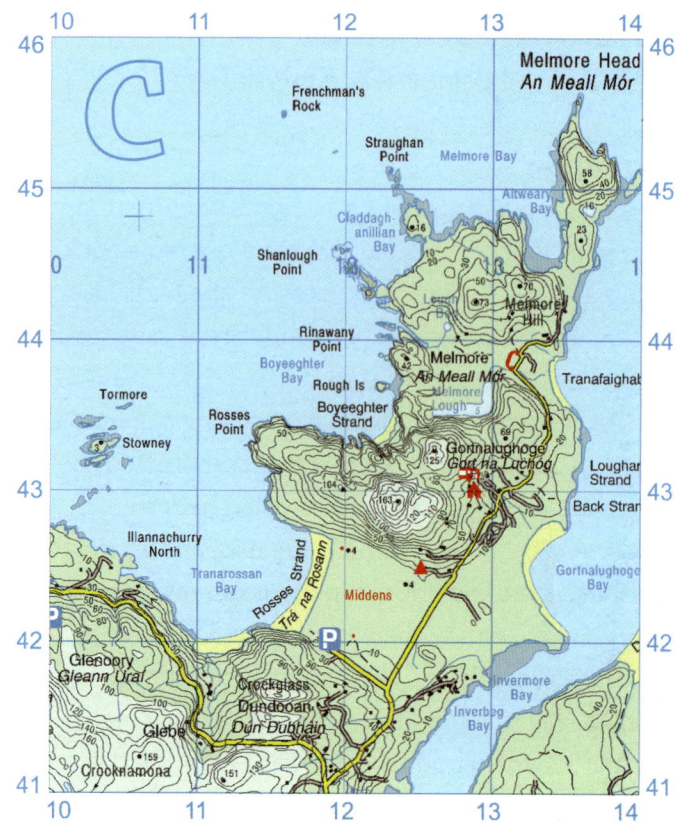

Blow Hole (Gloup)

Example: At the Bridges of Ross in Co. Clare

Blow holes form at weak points, or **faults,** in coastal rock along the coastline. They form in **wave-cut platforms** or on **cliff edges** directly above caves where the roofs have collapsed.

The force of waves acts on weak rock areas or fault lines in rock surfaces. As waves crash against the rock, **air is forced** into cracks, fault lines, bedding planes and joints. When each wave retreats, the escaping air expands instantly and the **explosive expansion** enlarges the cracks. Eventually the rock shatters and a cave is created.

Over time, the cave lengthens and part of its **roof may collapse** into the cave to create an opening to the surface some metres away from the cliff edge or water's edge. During storms, **surf and foam** may be forced upward to the surface through this opening.

Activity

Identify:

a. four bays and four headlands in the map extract above

b. the landforms A–E in the photo below.

PROCESSES OF COASTAL TRANSPORT AND DEPOSITION

These processes include:

- Longshore drift.
- Wind action.

Longshore Drift

Longshore drift refers to the movement of material, such as sand and shingle, along a shore. When waves break obliquely onto a beach, pebbles and sand are moved up the beach by the **swash** at the same angle as the waves. The **backwash** drags the material down the beach at right angles to the coast, only to meet another incoming wave. As the process of swash and backwash in longshore drift is repeated, material is moved along the shore in a zigzag way.

Wind Action

As beaches dry at low tide, some dry sand is blown up the beach, and it gathers above high tide level in large heaps or small hills that get more extensive over time. These hills are called sand dunes.

Breaking Waves and Surf

On reaching a shore, waves are said to **break**. The way this happens is of fundamental importance to coastal processes. Shallow water causes incoming waves to steepen, the crest spills over and the wave collapses. The turbulent water created by breaking waves is called **surf**. In the landward margin of the **surf zone**, the water rushing up the beach is the **swash**; water returning down the beach is the **backwash**. The swash moves material up the beach, and the backwash **may** carry it down again.

As well as destructive waves, there are **constructive waves**. They break slowly, and more material is left on the beach.

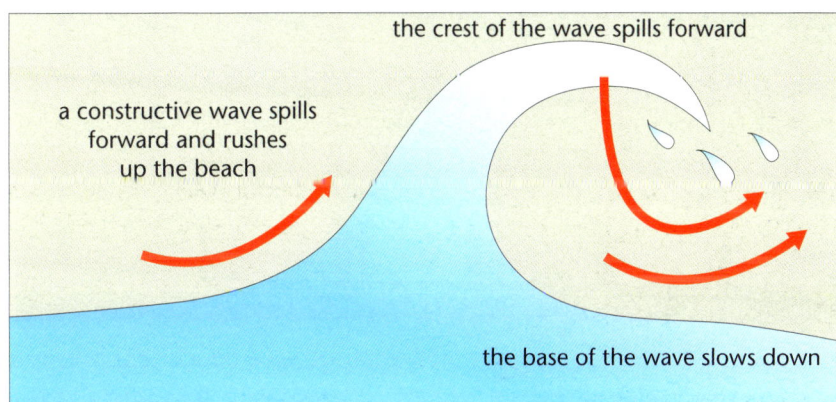

Fig. 14.7 The process of longshore drift.

Fig. 14.8 A constructive wave: spilling breaker.

Waves break as they approach a shore.

103

Landform: Beach
Example: Tramore Beach in Co. Waterford

Fig. 14.9 The profile of a beach.

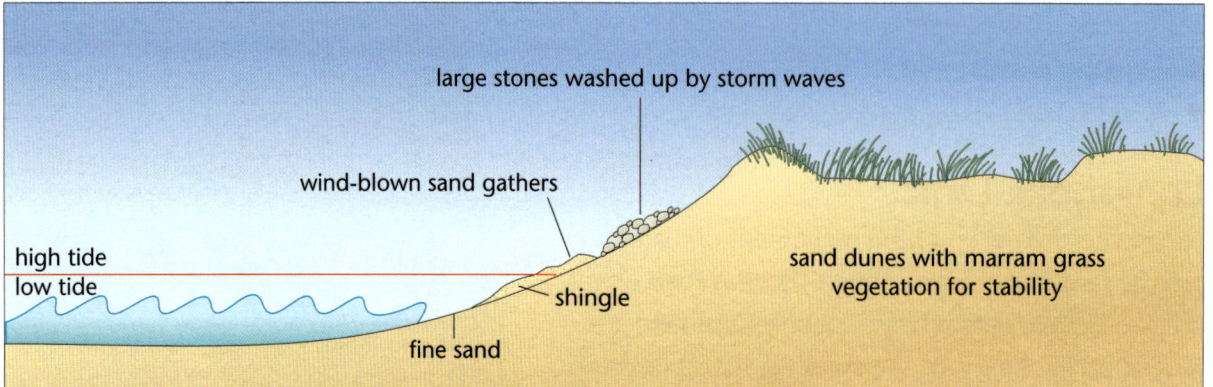

large stones washed up by storm waves

wind-blown sand gathers

high tide
low tide

shingle

fine sand

sand dunes with marram grass vegetation for stability

Groynes are sometimes built to create a beach and prevent erosion on the coastline.

yellow indicates a beach

Formation

A beach is formed by the process of **longshore drift**. This refers to the **zigzag movement** of beach material, such as sand and shingle, along a shore. Every constructive wave that approaches a shore carries some of this sand and shingle with it and will eventually deposit some of it on a beach.

As a constructive wave approaches a shore, part of the wave 'touches ground' and slows down, while the remainder of the wave in deeper water continues at a faster speed. This makes a wave tend to **bend** as it approaches a beach and breaks at an **oblique angle**.

Constructive waves are low waves and when they 'break' they are called **spilling breakers**. Because they commonly occur on **beaches with a low angle**, they have a wide area to cross and so their swash loses its energy quickly, leaving a weak backwash. In this way, sand and shingle are slowly but continually moved up the beach.

With constructive waves, little material is pulled down the beach by the **backwash**. The force of the backwash is called the **undertow.** Constructive waves have a gentle undertow and so are not dangerous to people.

During storms, sea level is higher than normal due to low atmospheric pressure. Waves are also stronger and they regularly throw **large rocks**, broken shells and driftwood up on the shore above normal high tide levels. This forms the **backshore**, or **storm beach**.

The **foreshore** is composed of **fine sand** and small shell particles. It has a gentle gradient and is covered regularly by the tide each day. Some beaches may be crescent-shaped in pocket bays or coves. Others are long and narrow and run parallel to the shore.

Landform: Sand Spit

Example: Inch Strand in Co. Kerry

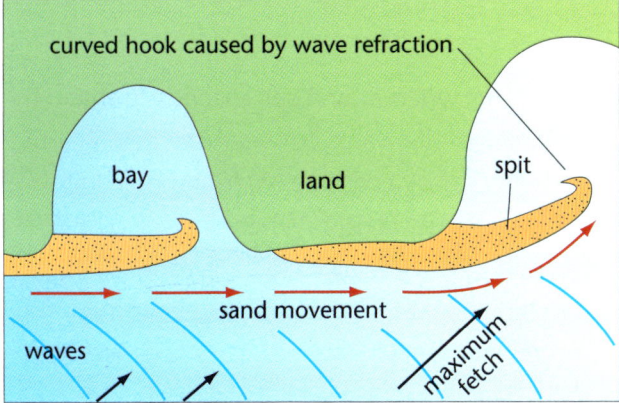

Fig. 14.10 Longshore drift of sand can form spits.

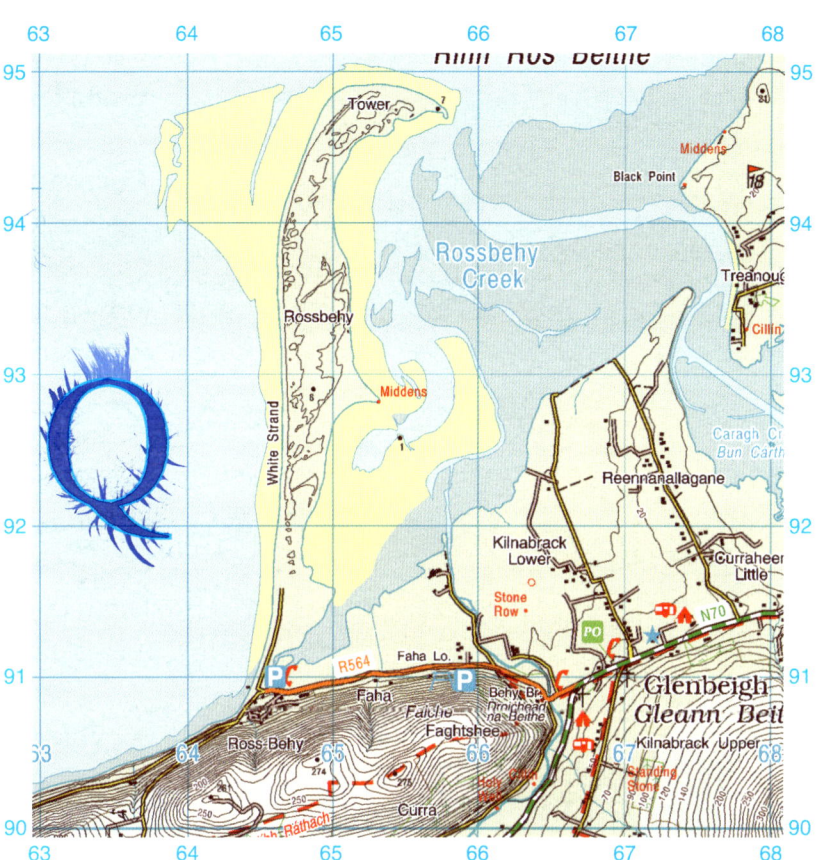

Formation

A sand spit is a beach that extends out across a bay or a river estuary. It is formed by the processes of **longshore drift** and **deposition**. A spit develops where a coastline **changes direction sharply** and longshore drift is unable to continue its zigzag movement of sediment along the shore.

Initially, **sand, shingle** and **pebbles** are deposited in the **slacker water** in the **lee of the headland** or the changing shoreline. These build up to the level of the sea surface, and this forms a foundation for deposits of finer material to be carried a little farther out into the bay by longshore drift.

As the spit continues to grow, incoming **constructive waves** pass over this extended shore, depositing fine sand and shingle on its base of coarser material. **Storm waves** throw some **larger material** above the high water mark, making the spit more permanent. Fine sand is added by **surface winds** blowing it from the beach to create **sand dunes** on the landward side of the spit. **Marram grass** then grows and its long roots stabilise the dunes.

Many spits develop a **hooked, or curved, end**. This is generally formed by wave refraction where waves bend around the end of the spit. A change in prevailing winds for an extended period or a storm may also aid the development of a spit.

Spits rarely join up with the opposite side of a bay where a **river estuary** keeps a channel open and free from sediment due to **scouring action** after high tide.

A sand spit projects into the bay at Glenbeigh in Co. Kerry.

Activity

1. Look at the Ordnance Survey map and photograph above. What human activities in this region relate directly to the natural processes at work in this coastal area? Explain.

2. Choose two coastal landforms and explain how the processes of erosion and/or deposition have formed them.

3. What do the irregular contours on the sand spit at Q 647 928 refer to?

when all sands Bar

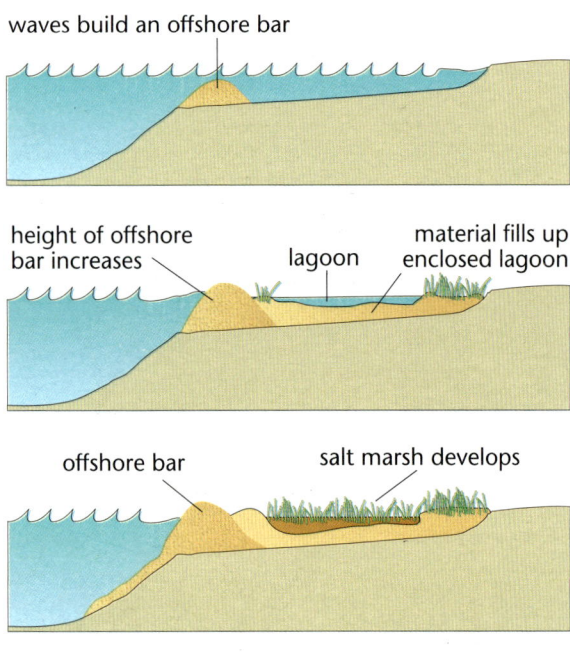

waves build an offshore bar

height of offshore bar increases

lagoon

material fills up enclosed lagoon

offshore bar

salt marsh develops

eventually the sand dunes move over the salt marsh

sand dunes

finally the marsh becomes an area of sand dunes

Fig. 14.11 The life cycle of a lagoon.

A baymouth bar cuts off Lady's Island Lake from the sea in Wexford.

Landform: Sand Bars and Lagoons

Example: Lady's Island Lake and sand bar in Co. Wexford

Formation

Generally, a sand bar forms when a sand spit extends to the opposite shore, trapping the bay water between the newly formed sand bar and the old bay coastline. As longshore drift forms sand spits, it also forms sand bars. When a bay is cut off from the sea, the **trapped seawater is called a lagoon**. In times of storm, waves sometimes wash sand and pebbles into the lagoon's seaward edge, and rivers and winds carry sediment into it. The lagoon eventually becomes a marsh, with reeds and coarse vegetation growing in the sediment. Finally, the combined forces of waves, wind and rivers turn the marsh into an extensive area of sand dunes.

There are two main types of sand bars:

- **Offshore bars** are ridges of sand or glacial till lying parallel to the shore and some distance out to sea. Sometimes these offshore bars are pushed along in front of the waves until finally they may lie across a bay to form a baymouth bar (see Fig. 14.12). Bartragh Island in Killala Bay is an offshore bar.
- **Baymouth bars** form from offshore bars, as mentioned above, but generally they form when sand spits grow across a bay to the far shore. In this way they cut off the original bay from the sea to form a lagoon.

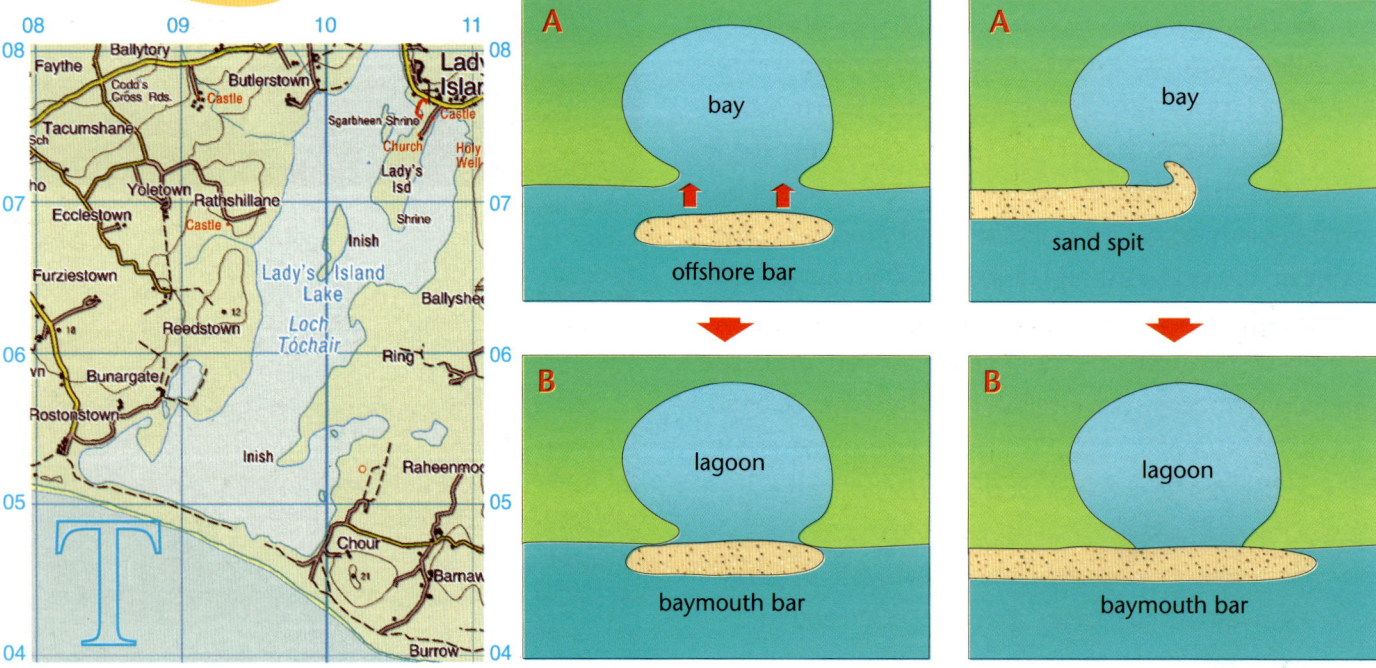

Fig. 14.12 Stages in the formation of a lagoon.

Landform: Tombolo
Example: Omey Strand in Co. Galway

[handwritten note: Its an Island connected to the main land by an ...]

Formation

This landform is created when either a spit or a bar links an island or a sea stack to the mainland. If two tombolos join an island from opposite directions, they may enclose seawater between them and create a lagoon. Tombolos are regularly formed along rugged coastlines, such as the west coast of Ireland.

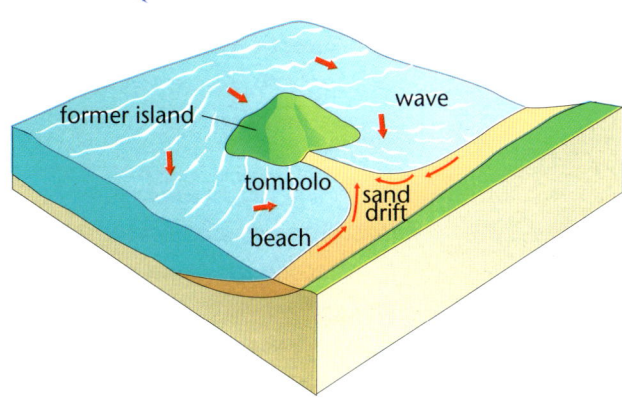

Fig. 14.13 A single tombolo may join an island to the mainland.

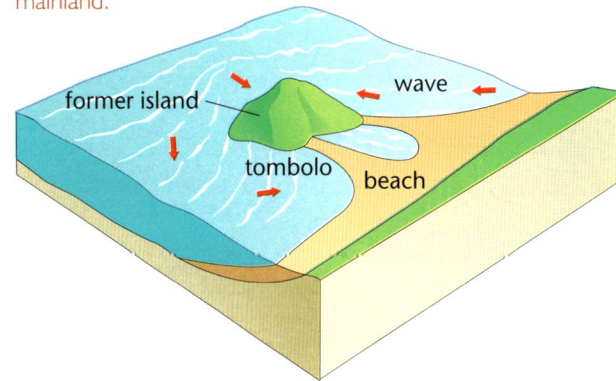

Fig. 14.14 Two tombolos may create a lake between them as they join an island to the coast.

A tombolo joins this island with Castle Tioram to the mainland in Scotland.

Activity

Study the OS map of the Omey Island region on the right, then answer the following questions.

1. Carefully examine the contour pattern in Omey Island, then suggest how Fahy Lough may have formed. Explain.
2. Omey Strand is a tombolo. Explain why this feature may have formed at this location.
3. The term 'midden' is marked at four locations on this map. Explain its significance to Ireland's history of human settlement and patterns (see Chapter 50).

Multi-part Questions

1. Sea cliff, Sea arch, Beach, Lagoon, Blow hole, Sand spit.
   A. In the case of **each** of the above coastal features, state whether it is the result of erosion or deposition.
   [20 marks]
   B. Select any **two** of the features listed above and in the case of **each**:
      i. name a specific location where the feature may be found
      ii. describe and explain, with the aid of a diagram, how it was formed. [30 marks]
   C. In recent years, coastal erosion has caused enormous damage to coastal areas. Describe **two** methods used to limit this damage. [30 marks]

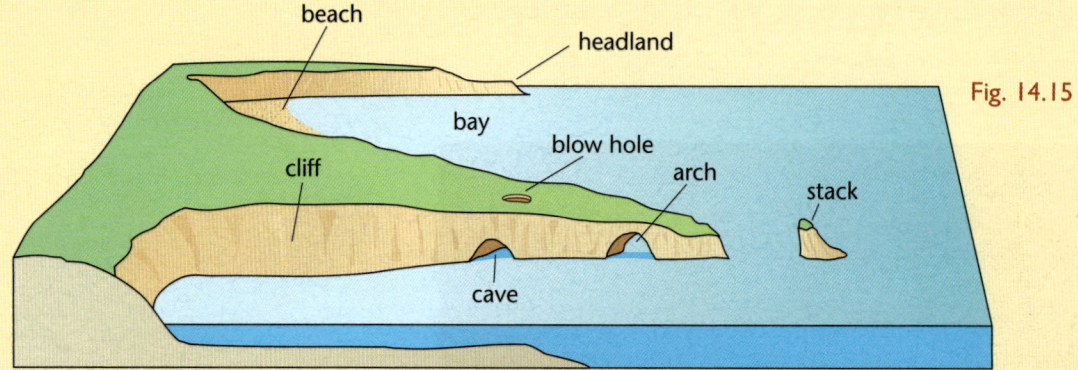

beach   headland

Fig. 14.15

bay

cliff   blow hole   arch   stack

cave

2. The diagram in Fig. 14.15 shows an area where marine erosion has been active.
   A. With reference to any **one** major landform which is evident in the diagram, describe and explain how marine erosion has shaped it. [20 marks]
   B. Identify any **two** landforms of marine deposition.
      i. In each case name **one** Irish example.
      ii. Explain the processes involved in the formation of any **one** of these landforms. [30 marks]
   C. 'Materials produced by erosion at one part of a coastline are transported to other parts and deposited. Human action is sometimes taken in order to interfere with these natural processes.' Explain this statement. [30 marks]
3. Examine the OS map on page 109, then answer the following quesitons.
   NB: DO NOT use tracing paper when answering this question.
   A. On a sketch map based on the map, mark and label:
      i. the coastline
      ii. the network of roads
      iii. **four** different coastal landforms. [20 marks]
   B. With reference to **one** landform mentioned above, describe and explain how the processes of erosion and/or of deposition affect coastlines. [30 marks]
   C. 'Conflict is inevitable between the different ways in which people make use of coastal areas like this.' Examine this statement. [30 marks]
4. The shaping of coastal landforms involves interaction between three forces: waves, currents and tides.
   A. Examine this statement with reference to **three** landforms that are typical of coastal regions. [20 marks]
   B. With reference to the map on page 109, describe fully how Keel Lough, the golf course and Trawmore Beach formed. [30 marks]
   C. Growth of urban settlement in coastal areas regularly changes the quality of the local environment over time. With reference to the map, explain how this might occur. [30 marks]

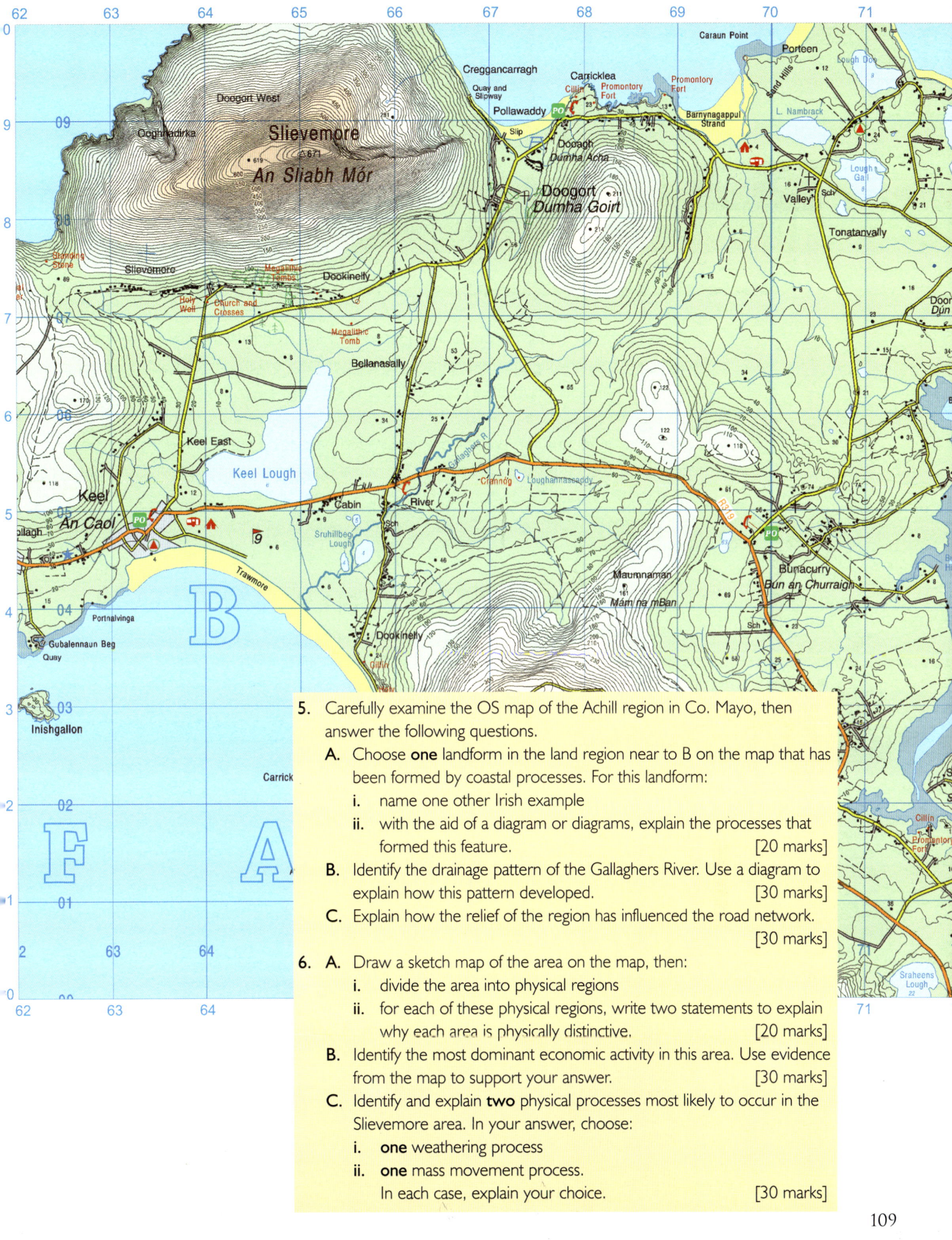

5. Carefully examine the OS map of the Achill region in Co. Mayo, then answer the following questions.
   A. Choose **one** landform in the land region near to B on the map that has been formed by coastal processes. For this landform:
      i. name one other Irish example
      ii. with the aid of a diagram or diagrams, explain the processes that formed this feature. [20 marks]
   B. Identify the drainage pattern of the Gallaghers River. Use a diagram to explain how this pattern developed. [30 marks]
   C. Explain how the relief of the region has influenced the road network. [30 marks]

6. A. Draw a sketch map of the area on the map, then:
      i. divide the area into physical regions
      ii. for each of these physical regions, write two statements to explain why each area is physically distinctive. [20 marks]
   B. Identify the most dominant economic activity in this area. Use evidence from the map to support your answer. [30 marks]
   C. Identify and explain **two** physical processes most likely to occur in the Slievemore area. In your answer, choose:
      i. **one** weathering process
      ii. **one** mass movement process.
         In each case, explain your choice. [30 marks]

CHAPTER 15
ISOSTASY

All landforms represent a balance between forces of erosion and deposition on the earth's surface and other forces within the earth's crust and mantle. From time to time, this balance changes.

The earth's crust 'floats' on the semi-liquid rock of the mantle. It acts like a weighing scales, with equal weight on both sides. When weight is transferred from one side to the other, the side that has lost weight rises and the side that gains weight falls.

Due to the surface processes of weathering and erosion, mountains are worn down over time, and the **weight** of their eroded particles **is transferred** from highland regions to lowland regions. In this way the lowland regions become heavier and push down more on the mantle and the highlands become lighter and rise to stay in balance. This transfer of weight keeps the earth's crust in perfect balance while it floats on the mantle.

ADJUSTING TO A NEW BASE LEVEL

When earth movements raise land, the rivers in that region will erode to create a new graded profile. This can also happen if sea levels fall. This process is called adjusting to base level.

The activity of a river concentrates on creating a slope from source to mouth, which will result in a river speed that keeps erosion and deposition exactly in balance. At this stage the river is said to be **graded** and to have achieved a **profile of equilibrium**. This kind of profile is rarely, if ever, achieved. Changes in volume, rising or falling sea level or unequal resistance of rocks all prevent a river from achieving a graded profile.

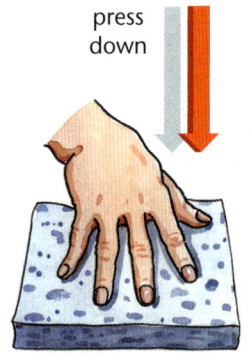

press down

squeezed

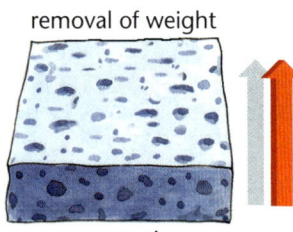

removal of weight

sponge rises

Fig. 15.1

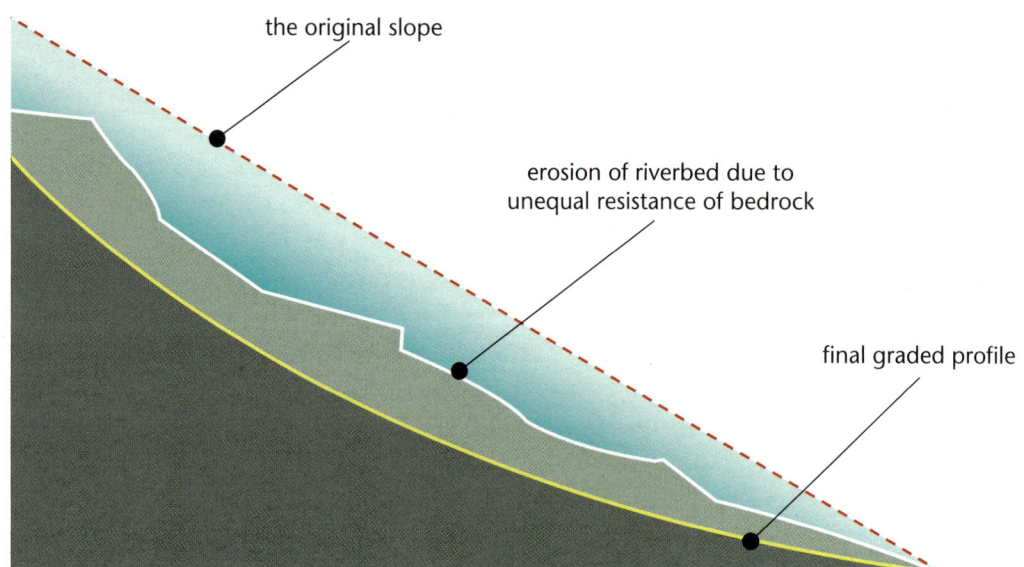

the original slope

erosion of riverbed due to unequal resistance of bedrock

final graded profile

Fig. 15.2

REJUVENATION

When land rises due to uplift, sea level falls and rivers get a new base level. Then the middle and lower courses of rivers begin a new phase of vertical erosion. This change is called **rejuvenation** (literally 'being made young again'). Many Irish river valleys display evidence of rejuvenation.

During the last Ice Age, Donegal in north-west Ireland had a cover in excess of a thousand metres of ice, pressing down on the land and 'squeezing' it like weight on a sponge. The loss of this weight about 10,000 years ago has allowed the land to rise, and the rivers now cut their way to the sea to create new river channels and new profiles.

Evidence of Rejuvenation in Ireland
Raised Beaches

Coastlines are particularly prone to changes of level. There is evidence that even since the end of the last Ice Age the level of the land in Ireland, relative to the sea level, has altered more than once. Traces of **old shore lines**, called raised beaches, are found along the coast some metres above high tide levels. Examples of these are found in Co. Donegal and Co. Antrim.

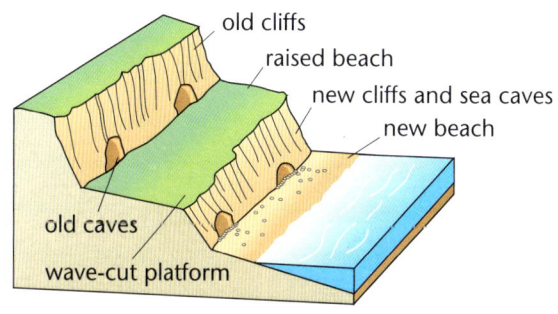

Fig. 15.3

Knick Point

When land rises relative to the sea, a rejuvenated river will cut upstream from its estuary. This creates a new base level. The change from the old to the new base level is marked by a sudden **change in the gradient** of the river. This is called the knick point and is represented by a waterfall or rapids. Over time, the knick point gradually moves upstream, until a completely new profile is achieved.

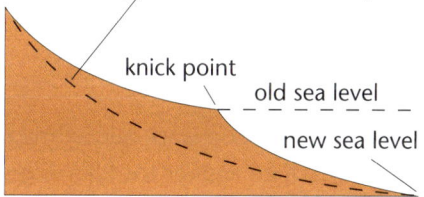

Fig. 15.4 The effect of rejuvenation on a river's profile.

Incised Meanders

On a rejuvenated river, vertical erosion begins again, so a meandering river that has been rejuvenated will cut deeply into its floodplain while maintaining its winding course. This process creates incised meanders. The River Nore has incised meanders in its valley.

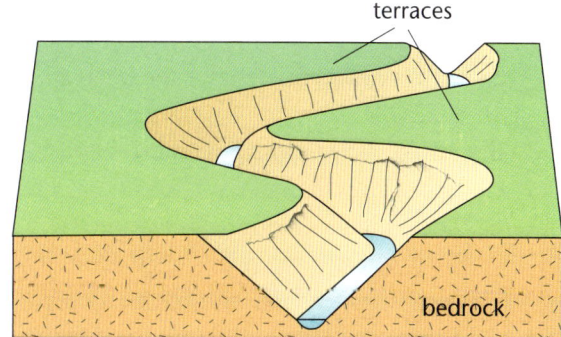

Fig. 15.5 Rivers cut into their floodplains to create incised meanders.

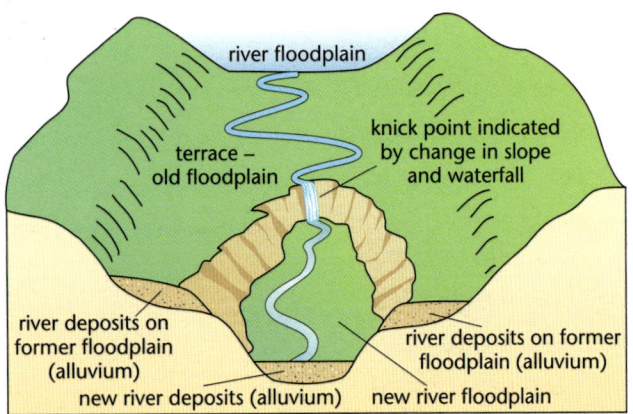

Terraces

Once incised meanders form, they begin to erode laterally and form a new floodplain at a lower level than the old one. The remnants of the old floodplain above the new level form terraces and are evidence that the river was rejuvenated.

Some river valleys display terraces at various levels. This suggests that the river was rejuvenated on a number of occasions in the past.

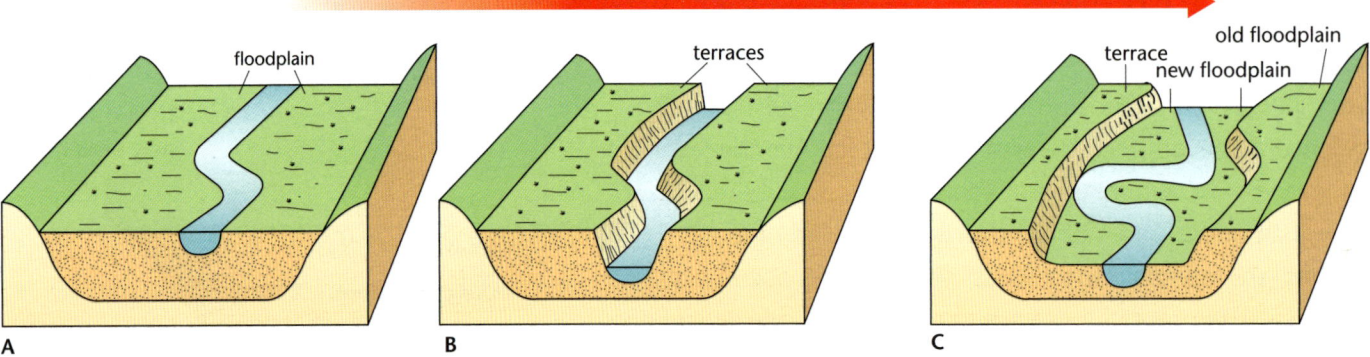

Fig. 15.6 The creation of terraces.

Activity

1. Explain the processes at work due to rejuvenation in diagrams A, B and C in Fig. 15.6.

2. Carefully examine the Ordnance Survey map on the next page, then answer the following questions.

   a. Does the River Barrow flow south through upland or lowland?

   b. Is the river following a straight or a meandering course?

   c. How would you describe the bend at S 72 35?

   d. At first glance, does this course suggest an upper, middle or lower stage of maturity?

   e. Look at the contour pattern at grid ref. S 73 36 along the river's edge. Does this suggest a V-shaped valley or a floodplain? Explain.

   f. From your studies of isostasy and adjustment to base level, explain possible reasons for the river's winding course and the contour pattern that borders the river.

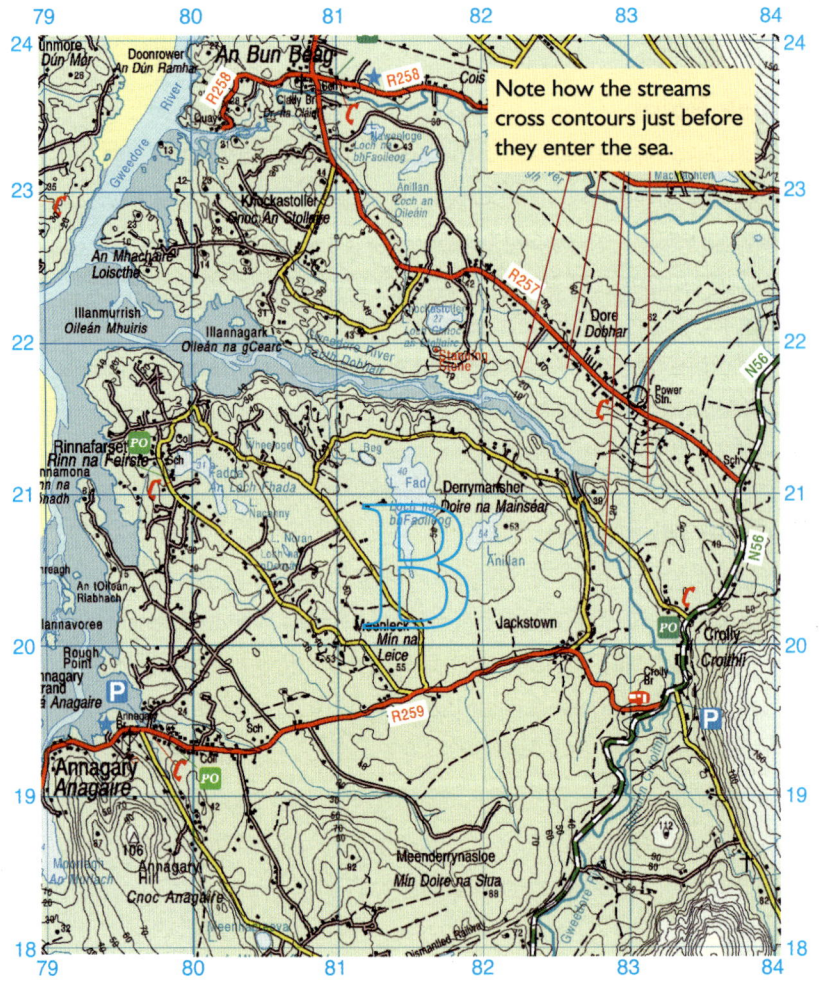

Note how the streams cross contours just before they enter the sea.

Evidence on maps of rejuvination in Co. Donegal. Rivers cross contours just before they enter the sea.

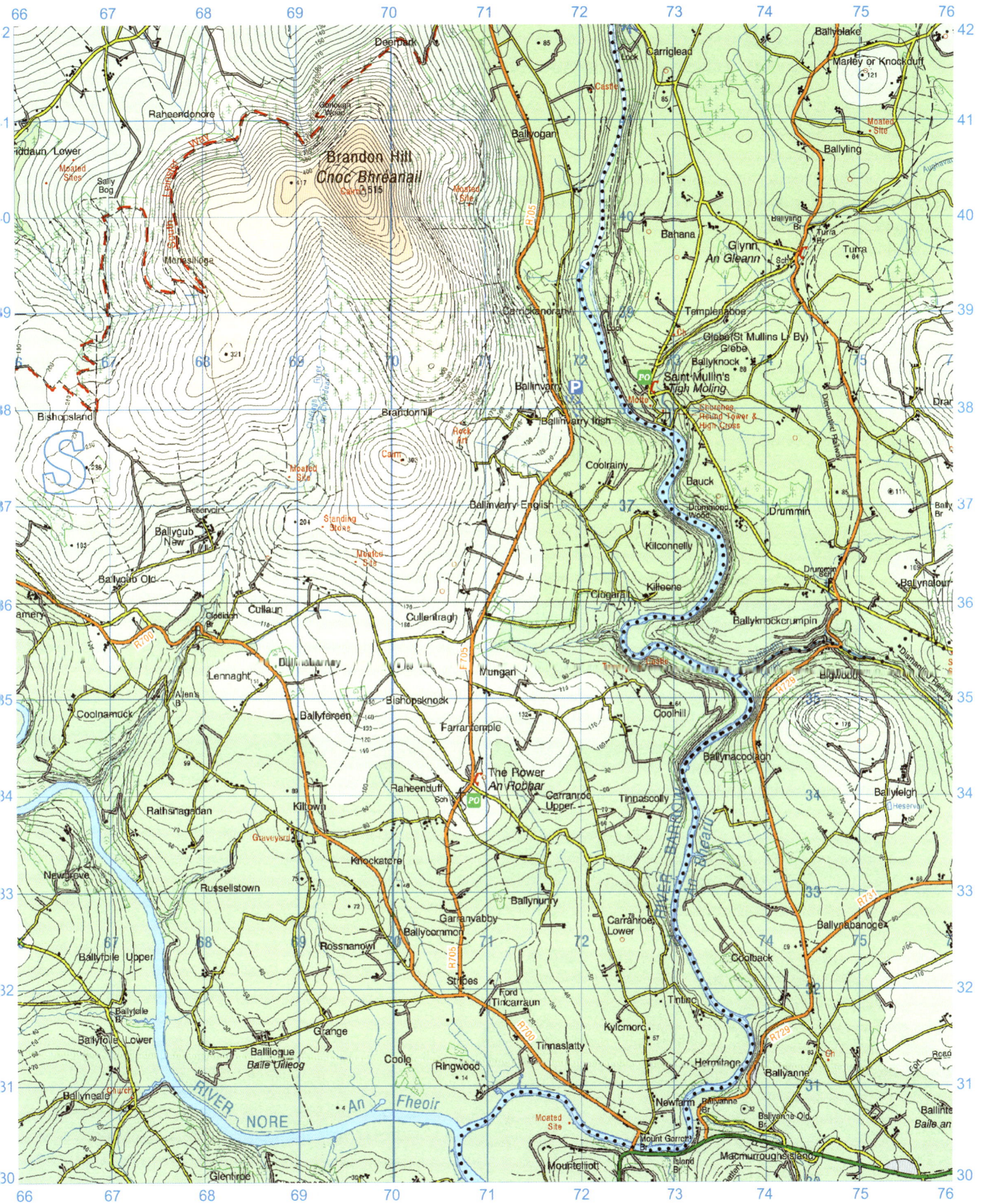

113

Cycle of Landscape Evolution

While streams are cutting their valleys, they are really sculpting the land. To describe this unending process, we have to visualise a beginning. For this, think of a relatively flat upland area with a wet climate, such as Ireland's. In this landscape, lakes and ponds will occupy any hollows that exist. As streams form and cut their valleys, they will eventually drain the lakes or fill them with sediment.

Early Stage

During the early stage, the landscape retains its **relatively flat surface**, interrupted only by narrow stream valleys.

Middle Stage

As vertical erosion (downcutting) continues, relief increases and the flat landscape is changed into one of **hills and valleys**. This is the middle stage. Eventually, some of the streams will approach base level. Downcutting will be replaced by lateral erosion, creating floodplains and lowering watersheds.

Later Stage

As the cycle nears the later stage, the effects of flooding, mass movement and lateral erosion and deposition by rivers will reduce the land to a **peneplain** (a gently undulating plain).

A simple cycle like this, however, rarely occurs because it could only happen if:

- The region was not affected by any additional local or global earth movements or climate change for tens of millions of years.
- The underlying rock layers had similar characteristics to the upper rock layers.
- No ice age occurred to:
  - Reduce sea levels, or for rivers to cut to new base levels.
  - Erode highlands and deposit materials on lowland.
  - Squeeze the land during glaciation and create uplift after glaciation.

We know, however, that change occurs regularly and over very short time spans, and a peneplain is rarely, if ever, achieved.

> A peneplain is the end result of an idealised cycle of landscape erosion that ends in a gently undulating plain almost at sea level, e.g. the Munster Peneplain.

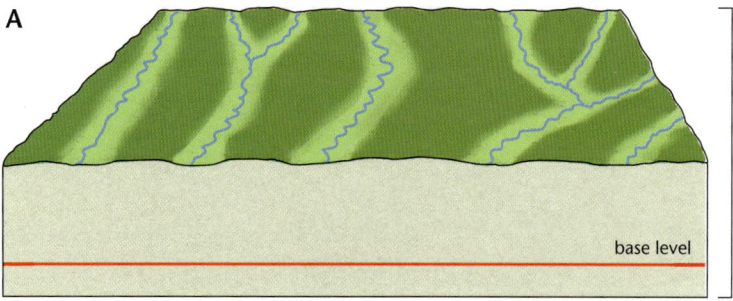

A

base level

B

base level

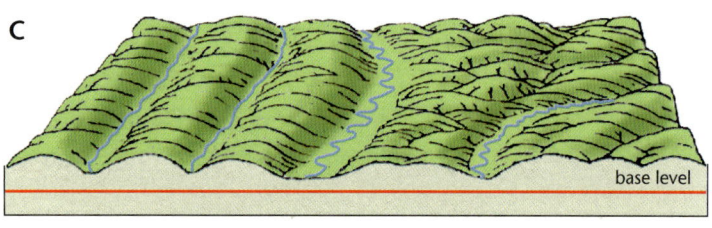

C

base level

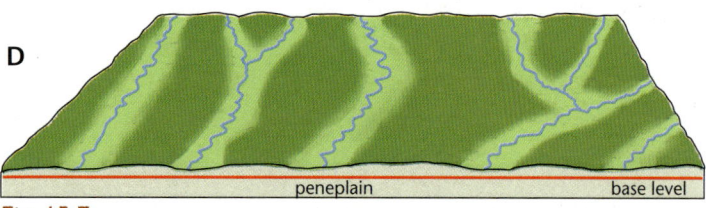

D

peneplain   base level

Fig. 15.7

Early

Middle

Later

CHAPTER 16
HOW PEOPLE INTERACT WITH SURFACE PROCESSES

 **KEY IDEA!**

People's activities can affect the process of mass movement.

MASS MOVEMENT AND PEOPLE'S IMPACT

The Impact of Overgrazing

At moderate densities, when farm animals graze land, they encourage plants to grow by manuring the soil and clipping off the tops of plants, just as pruning encourages new growth on fruit trees or roses. With a high density of animals, the **vegetation is eaten faster than it can grow,** plant cover is reduced and soil may be washed away or blown away by the wind.

The number of animals that can be supported on farmland varies from region to region. In areas with moderate to high rainfall evenly distributed throughout the year, such as Ireland, cattle can be maintained at high densities (about three cattle per hectare). For arid and semi-arid regions, the density drops greatly. In Arizona, in the US, it takes between 17 to 25 hectares to support one animal.

Over the past few hundred years throughout peninsular Italy, **sheep and goats have overgrazed the slopes of the Apennines.** Soils that once supported these animals were exposed to summer thunderstorms and winter rains and were washed downslope into rivers. Sediment **clogged the water channels,** and swamps and **marshes** were created. An example of this is the Pontine Marshes, south of Rome. Malarial mosquitoes bred in these warm swamplands, leading to widespread **malaria** among rural families and working conditions that made farming uneconomic.

Students need study only **one** of the following:
People's activities and their impact on:
- Mass movement processes.
- River processes.
- Coastal processes.

Overgrazing by too many sheep has led to severe soil erosion in the Galtee Mountains.

Erosion of Irish Mountainsides

Overgrazing has occurred on some Irish mountainsides. Two examples include the Galtee Mountains in Co. Tipperary and the Mweelrea Mountains in Co. Mayo. **Overgrazing by sheep** has been the main cause of this problem. Farm subsidies for sheep led to a rapid increase in sheep numbers on mountainsides. The land became overstocked, and the grasses and heather were overgrazed. Mountain **soil was exposed to heavy rains** and localised landslides became commonplace (see the photo of the Galtees on page 115).

The Dust Bowl in the US. The soil was literally blown away.

The Impact of Overcropping

One of the worst examples of overcropping occurred in the **Dust Bowl** region of North America between 1934 and 1936. The worst affected areas were parts of **western Kansas, Nebraska, Oklahoma** and **Texas**. Overcropping happened when wheat was planted in semi-arid grazing areas because grain was fetching high prices and the region appeared to be moist enough to produce crops. The years of sufficient rain were then followed by several years of very low rainfall. The tilled soil was exposed to the strong winds of these level lands and was literally blown away, leaving only sand and gravel particles.

Many **farmers abandoned their farms and their homes** and headed west with their belongings. They went to California to become penniless fruitpickers, like the people who were immortalised in *The Grapes of Wrath,* a novel by American writer John Steinbeck.

A family uses a raft made from banana shoots to reach their home in the state of Assam, in India, which borders Bangladesh.

The Impact of Deforestation

Deforestation has happened throughout the world and on every continent. Today, it continues where population numbers are increasing rapidly. Most of these regions are in the tropics.

Forests are a global resource, so cutting forests in one country may severely affect another. For example, **Nepal in the Himalayas**, one of the most mountainous countries in the world, lost more than half its forest cover between 1950 and 1980. Little forest cover now remains in Nepal, and the loss of it has increased flooding in Bangladesh.

Cutting down forests **removes the vegetation** (trees and plants) that protects the soil. Killing the **tree and plant roots** that **bind** the soil particles together **exposes the soil** to heavy monsoon rains, and the rate of **landslides increases**.

Large quantities of **soil** are **washed downhill** into streams and river channels that flow into India and Bangladesh. This sediment **clogs the river channels,** which in turn causes widespread flooding, bringing death and destruction to the delta lowlands.

Other reasons for felling trees include the use of wood for firewood and the sale of timber for construction and paper pulp. Slightly more than half of all wood used in a year is used for **firewood.** In developed countries, it forms less than 1 per cent of energy used, but in Africa it generates more than half.

Desertification in Rajasthan and Gujarat in India's North-West

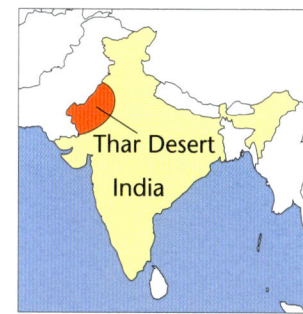

Fig. 16.1 The Thar Desert lands in India.

In India there are about 2.34 million square kilometres of hot desert called the **Thar**. It is an extremely arid region that receives only between **100 and 500 mm** of rain annually between July and September. Most of this rainfall filters quickly through the poor, sandy soils that are low in humus and mineral matter.

The Thar is a very hostile environment for living in, yet it is a densely populated tillage farming (crop-growing) region. The land is owned by **poor farmers** whose **traditional farming practices** restrict efficient conservation programmes.

Satellite images have proved that this region was once a rich agricultural area. The over-exploitation of land and water resources since earliest times has turned it into desert.

Problems

- The Thar desert suffers from **high winds, huge shifting sand dunes, high temperatures** by day and cold at night, **intense sunshine** and **high evaporation rates.**
- The cutting of wood for fuel and fodder production for cattle, the two basic necessities of life for the desert people, destroy the natural ground cover and aid desertification.
- Some regions have been grazed clean, and shrubs have been eaten down to extremely low levels.

Solutions

- The **Indira Ghandi Canal** was constructed to divert water from the Himalayan rivers to the desert region. This canal has dramatically changed the lands bordering the canal into an evergreen forest ecosystem.
- Because native trees in the region were few in number and also slow-growing, newer, **faster-growing species** were introduced from isoclimatic (similar) regions of the world. Each new species was chosen to suit individual environments, for example *Acacia tortilis* from Israel was ideal for stabilising sand dunes. Other species were chosen for biomass production and fodder.

Desertification has created major erosion problems in parts of India.

- **Shelter belts** and tree screens were grown as windbreaks to reduce wind speeds and to reduce erosion rates.
- **Seeding** from helicopters in association with the Indian military and manual seeding of dunes was also carried out.
- **Rooted grasses** were transplanted and **hedges** were established.

RIVER PROCESSES AND PEOPLE'S IMPACT ON THEM

The Impact of Hydroelectric Dams

Examples: Ardnacrusha on the River Shannon
Pollaphuca Dam on the River Liffey

KEY IDEA!

People's activities can interfere with the processes that operate in river valleys.

Dams are constructed across a river's channel to generate hydroelectric power. The dams **interrupt the natural flow of rivers and reduce the ability of rivers to carry sediment** from their upper valleys to their floodplains and their estuaries in lowland areas.

Hydroelectric dams are designed to block and use the flow of rivers. Water builds up behind the dams to form lakes, called **reservoirs**. The depth of a reservoir is regulated by allowing some water to flow through pipes in the dam, called penstocks, to generate **hydropower**.

Building hydroelectric dams may have **some positive results.** These include:

- Providing over 6 per cent of the world's energy needs.
- Providing reservoirs for irrigation and water supply.
- Regulating floodwaters to reduce flooding in lowland areas.

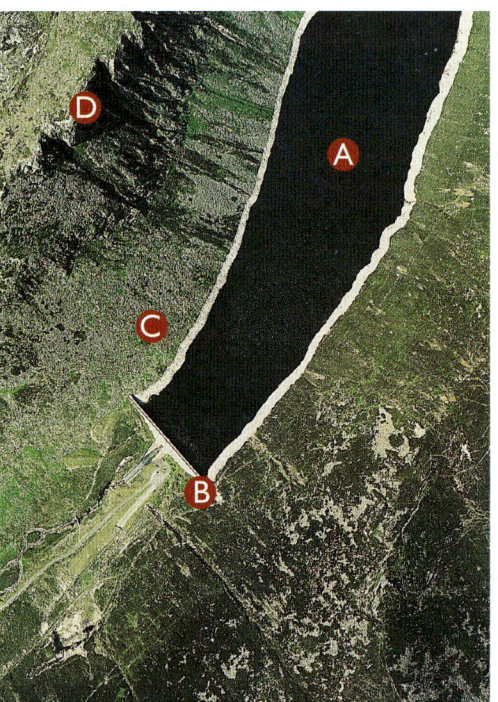

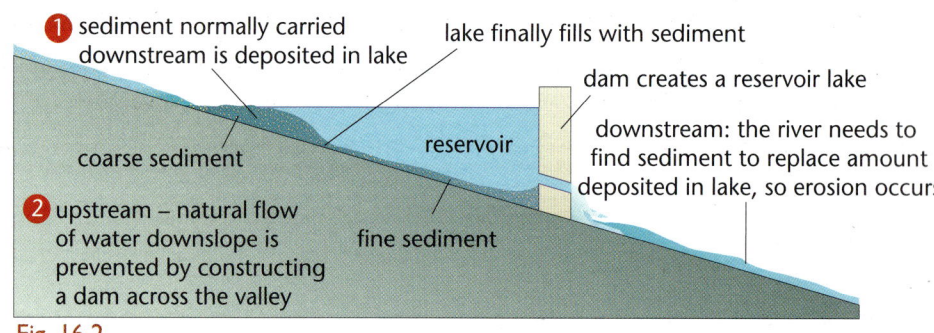

1 sediment normally carried downstream is deposited in lake

lake finally fills with sediment

dam creates a reservoir lake

coarse sediment

reservoir

downstream: the river needs to find sediment to replace amount deposited in lake, so erosion occurs

2 upstream – natural flow of water downslope is prevented by constructing a dam across the valley

fine sediment

Fig. 16.2

Dams are used to:

- Control floods.
- Store fresh water.
- Generate hydroelectricity.
- Supply water to industry and to people's homes, and for irrigation.

Activity

1. Carefully examine the aerial photograph on the left.
2. Identify the main landscape feature A.
3. Name the structure B.
4. Name the landforms C and D.

The way dams interfere with rivers' natural processes creates **some negative effects.**

Trapping of Sediment

The trapping of sediment in the reservoir lake reduces the silt and clay particles that are usually transported to the alluvial lowlands of floodplains and deltas. This reduces the fertility of the land and increases the need to apply expensive fertilizer.

As flowing water enters a reservoir, it drops its coarser sediment first, farthest from the dam. The finest material is dropped closest to the dam. The rapid build-up of coarse sediment may quickly build up a floodplain extending into the new lake and there may be flooding of settlements on the lake shores.

The fine silt may be removed at intervals to allow the dam to operate efficiently. This may lead to the reservoir having to be emptied and valuable water being lost as well as being a very costly operation.

The mass of the reservoir water may lead to faulting in regions prone to earthquakes. One fear of geologists for the new Kalabagh Dam in Pakistan is that this region is already tectonically active. This could lead to dam failure and a devastating outpouring of the lake waters from the dam.

Submergence of Land

Submergence of ecosystems, farmland and settlements occurs above dams. People are moved from their traditional homes and lands. As well as the **farmland** and **settlements, people's unique identity** is lost forever.

Reduced Volume

Reduced river flow out of dams proposed for the Indus in Pakistan could contribute to very low levels of water reaching the river's delta region. This would allow seawater to filter back into the delta lands and **poison the fragile freshwater ecosystem,** which includes wildlife, as well as turning fertile districts into waterlogged salt marshlands.

The Impact of Canalisation

Canalisation has been developed for:

- Improved water transportation.
- The transfer of water.

Improved Water Transportation

Canalisation may increase flooding. The River Rhine is Europe's most important navigable waterway. Ocean-going ships may go as far as Cologne, in Germany, and large barges may reach Basle, in Switzerland. Because of canalisation, however, meanders in the Rhineland have been straightened and floodwaters move too quickly downstream. This leads to flooding of towns and farmland in the lowlands of the Rhine.

The Transfer of Water

The need to transport water is growing as the world's population grows. But drawing water from source areas may have serious consequences if it is not managed carefully.

Activity

'The construction of the Three Gorges Dam is essential for the future development of economic activities in China.' Explain one point for and one point against this statement. Use the web to find out information on the Three Gorges Dam.

These consequences include the following.

Pore Collapse and Subsidence

When water fills the pore space of a rock in an aquifer (saturated rock layer below the water table), it holds the grains of the rock apart because water cannot be compressed. When too much water is taken for irrigation, air replaces the water. Air can be compressed, so the rock grains become packed more closely. This can have two effects:

- The ability of the rock to hold as much water as before may be reduced and so reduces its value as an aquifer.
- The surface level of the ground sinks. This is called subsidence and may cause the ground and the foundations of buildings to crack. Buildings may also tilt, such as the Leaning Tower of Pisa, or they may sink, such as happens in Venice.

Increased Salt Content

Groundwater contains dissolved minerals, called **salts.** Within normal limits these help crops to grow, but in regions of intensive irrigations practices, such as the San Joaquin Valley in California, the evaporation rates cause increased salt content that may poison land.

Destruction of Ecosystems

The reduction in outflow of the Sacramento River is due to diversion of water to the San Joaquin Valley. This has allowed seawater to replace freshwater along the river's estuary and to poison its ecosystem.

Case Study: The Aral Sea

The water of the two largest rivers, the **Amu** and **Syr,** which provide fresh water for the Aral Sea, were diverted through canals to irrigate 7 million hectares of cotton, rice and melons for the former Soviet Union. The loss of this water to the sea has had the following effects:

- The Aral Sea has greatly reduced in size. Some ships that once transported goods or fished its waters are now beached on a dry seabed.
- The salt content of the sea has increased from 10 per cent to 40 per cent. This has changed the sea from being a freshwater lake to a saltwater lake.
- Many fish species have been wiped out.
- Summer temperatures near the lake have risen at times up to 45°C. Winter temperatures have become colder.

> An aquifer is a body of permeable rock or regolith saturated with water and through which groundwater moves.

> The Aral Sea has been shrinking for the past thirty years because of the effects of canalisation.

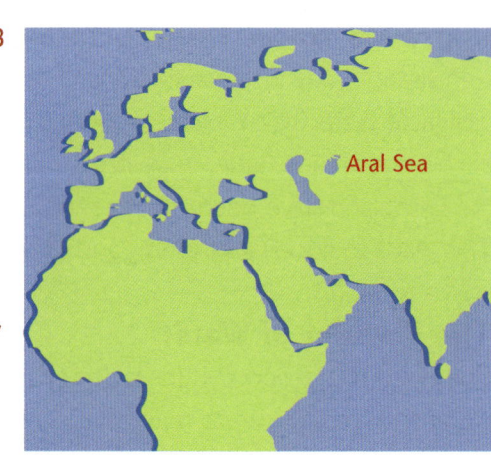

Fig. 16.3

Aral Sea

Fishing vessels now stranded on the dry seabed of the Aral Sea.

Flood Control Measures

Dam Construction

Dams are an efficient way to control floodwaters. The building of the Aswan High Dam in Egypt prevented annual flooding on the Nile downstream and allowed farmers to produce many crops in a single season.

Building Levees

Example: Mulcair River in Co. Limerick

Levee comes from the French word *'lever'*, which means 'to raise'. In the United States, the term is used to describe walls or dykes built along the southern part of the Mississippi River to retain floodwaters. The levees on the Mississippi are over 10 m high.

A river and its nearby flat floodplain together make up a natural system. In most untouched natural river valleys, the water flows over the riverbanks and onto the floodplain every year or so.

There are a number of natural processes that occur because of flooding:

- Water and nutrients are stored on the floodplain.
- Silt deposits on the floodplain increase the mineral content of the soil.
- Undeveloped land absorbs water and holds the excess until it can drain off naturally.
- Wetlands on the floodplain provide a natural habitat for many birds, animals, plants and other living organisms.

The construction of levees has a negative effect on all of these processes.

Floodplains are natural regions that absorb and store floodwaters until the water drains away naturally. Natural flooding is not a problem until people choose to build homes and other structures on floodplains. These structures are prone to damage and loss when flooded. People have chosen to build on so many floodplains that flooding is the **most universal natural hazard** in the world. The 1993 flood of the Mississippi took over fifty lives and caused over US$10 billion in damage when about 70 per cent of the levees failed. They simply were not designed to withstand a flood that lasted over two months.

The Mississippi floods vast regions of farmland and cities when its levees cannot retain its water.

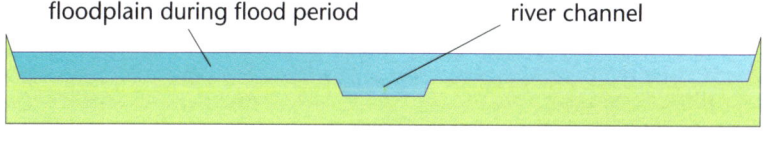

floodplain during flood period · river channel

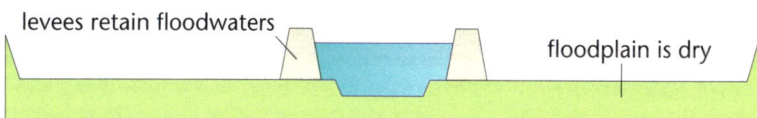

levees retain floodwaters · floodplain is dry

Fig. 16.4 Levees help retain floodwaters.

Levees retain floodwaters of the Mississippi River.

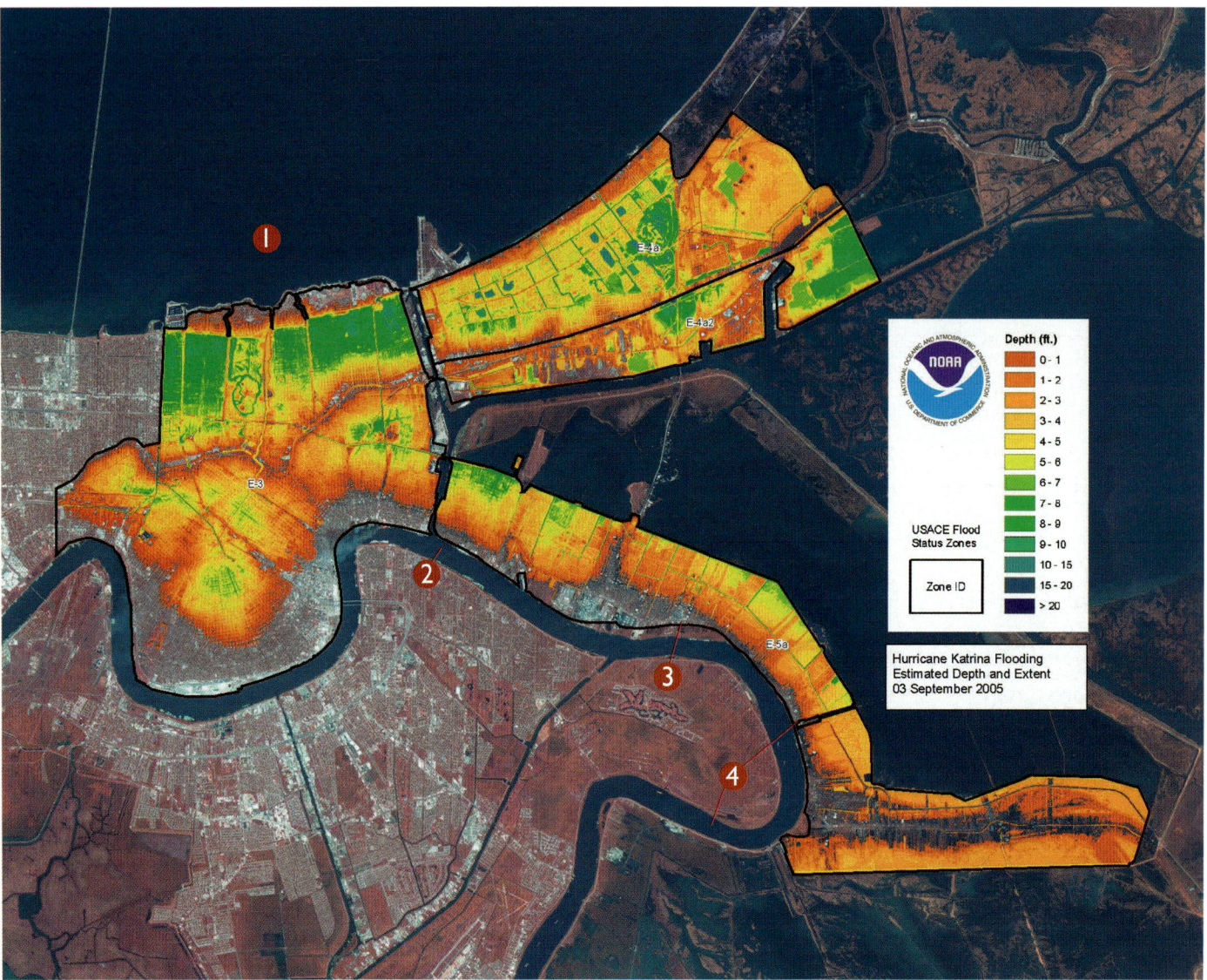

This is a satellite image of New Orleans in flood. Hurricane Katrina created such high water levels that its levees failed. New Orleans was flooded and many of its inhabitants died.

Activity

Carefully examine the satellite image, then answer the following questions.

1. Name:
    a. the sea area at 1
    b. the river at 2
    c. the landform at 3
    d. the landform at 4.
2. Identify the stage of maturity of this river in New Orleans. Explain.
3. What type of atmospheric pressure is associated with a hurricane?
4. What type of weather is associated with a hurricane? Explain.
5. What is the greatest depth of the floodwaters?
6. With the aid of diagrams, explain the formation of levees.
7. Explain why you think the levees may have failed.
8. Why do levees form along this part of the river?
9. Identify and explain the formation of the type of delta that is associated with this river.

COASTAL PROCESSES AND PEOPLE'S IMPACT ON THEM

 **KEY IDEA!**

People's activities can interfere with coastal process.

Recreational Pressures

Extensive construction of hotels, mobile home sites, golf courses, marinas and holiday homes along Irish and global coastal regions has increased pressure on fragile coastal environments in a number of ways.

In Ireland

- The **visual impact on the landscape** of hotels, mobile homes, golf courses and marinas has changed some regions dramatically. In addition, holiday homes, most of which are unoccupied for most of the year, have altered the character of some local communities.

- Increased tourism has created a difficulty with the **quality of coastal water** in seaside towns and with local sewage systems that struggle to cope with demand during the peak holiday season. Low funding from local authorities to improve these services adds to the difficulty. As settlements grow, their sewage discharges increase dramatically, especially during summer when towns that may have only 400 residents during winter swell to 25,000 in July and August.

- **The Environmental Protection Agency** and local authorities regularly monitor the quality of seawater and the maintenance of beaches at coastal resorts.

In Other Parts of the World

- **Access to beaches** has been restricted in places such as Malibu in California and around the Mediterranean where private dwellings and hotels form continuous development along the coast.

- The **location of coastal developments** on low-lying sand bars and spits make them vulnerable to storm damage. Coastal developments in the Caribbean and Florida have suffered severe damage during the hurricanes that regularly affect these regions.

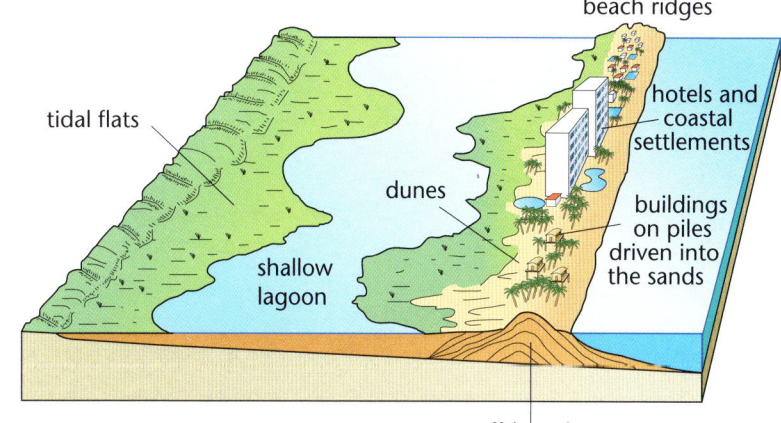

Fig. 16.5 Offshore barrier island bars are developed as coastal resorts, with hotels and holiday complexes along much of the east coast of the United States.

Coastal developments have altered many coastlines in warm regions.

The Impact of Coastal Defence Work

Sand dunes have suffered from severe erosion in some places in recent years. Here, **chestnut fencing** is used to trap sand and prevent erosion.

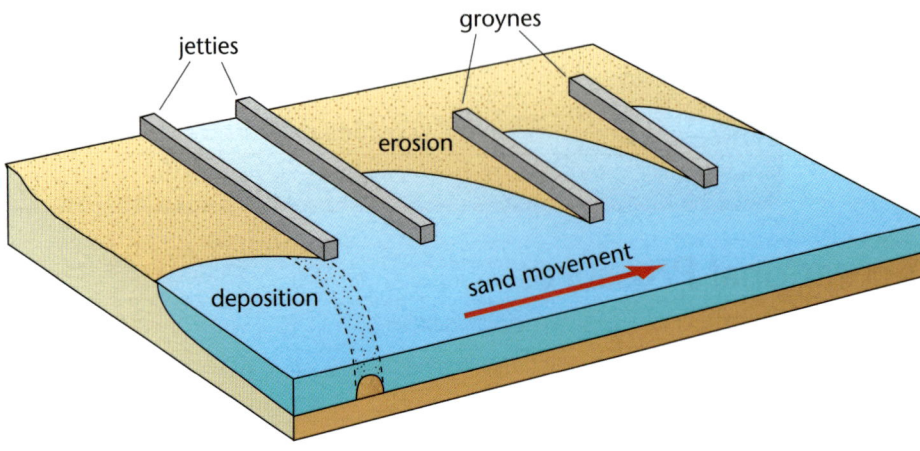

Fig. 16.6 Jetties, groynes and breakwaters interrupt the movement of sand by beach drift and longshore currents. Beach erosion often results downcurrent from the site of the structure.

Groynes

Groynes are **rock or wooden barriers placed at right angles** to the seashore to trap sand carried by longshore drift. This trapped sand eventually creates a beach that allows waves to lose their energy when they crash onshore. Groynes have to be carefully managed, as they reduce the amount of sediment carried further along the coast and this may lead to the erosion of other beaches.

The **location and spacing** of groynes is essential to make sure that the correct level of sediment is trapped by the groynes so that the need for protecting the area is balanced with the requirements of the zones further along the coast.

Breakwaters

Offshore breakwaters are **long, parallel mounds of rubble or rock that are built parallel to the shore to reduce erosive wave action.** Like groynes, breakwaters are designed to suit each individual site of coastal erosion.

Concrete sea walls and honeycomb rock are used to protect urban areas from erosion.

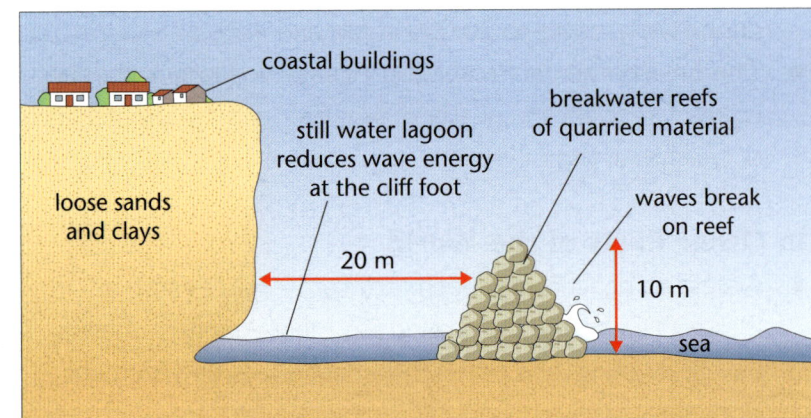

Fig. 16.7 There are many forms of breakwater.

The effect of wave change around the breakwater is to set up new currents that trap sediment in the sheltered side of the structure. The sediment deposited in the lee of the breakwater may result in either an increase in the beach width at the shoreline or a sandbar reaching to the breakwater in the form of a tombolo. The formation of the tombolo will depend on local factors, such as the tidal current, the storm frequency or the shape of breakwater.

Breakwaters are sometimes attached to the shore. These include long walls built across a harbour to protect fishing trawlers and ferries that are moored to a quayside. Leisure craft are sometimes moored away from industrial port areas and also need the protection of breakwaters from storm waves.

Fig. 16.8

(diagram labels: collapsing cliff, eroded rocks, original narrow beach, breakwater, new tombolo accumulations of sand)

Leisure craft, such as sailing boats, are often protected by breakwaters in coastal areas.

Conservation and Management Measures

In recent decades, it has been recognised that **a coastline is a valuable natural resource that needs careful and sensitive management.** This is especially so in the case of Ireland, where the shores are subjected to severe storm waves from the Atlantic every year and to human interference from the recent rapid developments of golf courses and coastal holiday homes and mobile home sites.

A code of practice for coastal management and conservation has been established on the **basis of pilot projects and by gathering expert knowledge** of individual coastal areas. The code of practice is called **ECOPRO – Environmentally Friendly Coastal Protection**. The objectives of ECOPRO are to:

- Develop monitoring methods suited to various types of coastline.
- Develop a sensitivity index to grade a coastline's susceptibility to erosion.
- Present an evaluation of various coastal protection and management methods.
- Present case histories of some of these methods.

Beach Management

The **principle** behind the code of practice **is to maintain** as far as possible **the protection created by the natural features** of the coast. For example, a beach is nature's way of reducing the energy of sea action. The objective should be to keep beaches in place. Beaches and sand dunes are valuable coastal resources that should be protected.

Straw bales and jute matting placed behind rocks to project beach sand from erosion.

Marram grass planted to stabilise sand dunes.

Concrete sea walls and rock armour are used to protect coastline areas from erosion.

Because the depth of sand on beaches may naturally fluctuate (increase or decrease) from season to season, the beach must be allowed to do this without interference. The dunes at the back of beaches form an integral part of the system, so they must also be allowed to fulfil their function. While sand dunes are valuable for leisure activities, it is necessary to regulate how they are used. It is important to note that a valuable resource may be easily and permanently destroyed by inappropriate management.

Where there is erosion, the new management policy must first:

- Deal with an assessment of the erosion problem. The aim is to determine the nature of the problem: whether there is continuous erosion, or erosion caused by a single storm or a few storms over a short period, such as a month or two. The aim is also to identify the causes, whether they were natural or man-made.
- Identify suitable solutions and assess how these solutions have worked in other areas.

Beach Nourishment

Beaches sometimes lose their sand covering during storms. Beach nourishment is simply **pumping new sand** onto eroded beaches to change wave movement from being destructive to being constructive. The presence of a renewed beach allows the swash to filter into the sand, while at the same time, depositing new sand in the process. The additional sand is usually obtained by offshore dredging, although in certain cases sand quarries are used for small schemes. Great care is taken in choosing **sand grain size** and its **distribution** so that it suits the site.

A beach nourishment programme was undertaken in Rosslare Strand from October 1994 to January 1995. Over a quarter of a million cubic metres of sand was dredged from a site 6 km offshore and pumped onto the beach. A rock groyne system helps to retain sand on the beach. In this case, beach nourishment was carried out for coastal defence work as well as for recreational use.

Causes of Erosion

Coastlines are constantly receding because they are being worn away by the forces of nature. The causes of erosion may be classified into two groups:

- Erosion caused by people.
- Erosion caused by nature.

Erosion Caused by People

Human interference includes removing sand directly (for building and other uses), or indirectly by interfering with natural processes such as longshore drift.

The coastal engineer must aim to strike a balance between preventing erosion and interference with natural processes that may destabilise the coastline.

Erosion Caused by Nature

Natural causes include:

- The erosion-deposition balance, which may be affected by climatic change (such as increased storm frequency).
- The rise or fall of sea level due to earth movements.
- Natural changes in sediment supply.

Sand Dune Management

Recreational activites, such as pedestrian traffic, cars, caravan parks, horse riding and motorbike scrambling, can seriously damage dune vegetation and increase the rate of sand loss through wind erosion. This loss of sand could directly affect the amount of sand on the beach and the size of the sand dunes.

Some Effects of Recreational Activities

- The trampling of vegetation by pedestrian traffic is the most widespread form of damage to sand dunes by people. This occurs where human activity is concentrated in small areas and a fan-shaped network of paths and tracks develop leading from caravan parks, car parks and other areas of public access to the coast. As vegetation is damaged, erosion begins and the wind attacks the exposed sand, eventually forming gullies and gaps called blow-outs. Paths across the tops of dunes are most at risk, as wind speeds are greater there and path slopes are often steeper. Gullies created in cliffs of boulder clay can lead to cliff slumping.
- Ideally, vehicles, horse riding and motorbike scrambling should be banned from beach areas because they can devastate sand dune systems. If 200 vehicles per year pass over sand dunes, it can reduce vegetation cover by 50 per cent. Where these activities are allowed on dunes, paths for them should run at right angles to the direction of the prevailing winds.

Protection of Natural Wildlife Habitats

Sandflats and **mudflats** in tidal areas, such as river estuaries, hold dense populations of marine worms, shellfish and other invertebrate life. These are the foods that attract large numbers of wintering migrant birds. Some of these birds include the oystercatcher, curlew, redshank, ducks (such as teal), waders and geese. **Salt marsh areas** attract birds to hatch and rear their young. One of the best-known wildlife habitats is in Dublin Bay, off **Dollymount Strand**. Usually, the greatest abundance of life is close to land and so is under constant threat of pollution and habitat destruction. Careless dredging, dumping of waste or coastal defences could pollute these areas or remove them due to changes in coastal currents. To protect these areas, some inshore areas are designated as **Natural Heritage Areas**.

Migrating birds seek tidal flats for their food supply.

Activity

1. Why are beaches important for controlling coastal processes?
2. Explain why evaluating and recording natural coastal processes is essential for balanced human interaction in coastal areas.
3. Describe the positive and negative effects of some engineering structures designed to reduce erosion.
4. Beaches are natural regions that are essential for coastal and human processes. Discuss.

CHAPTER 17
WEATHER CHARTS AND SATELLITE IMAGES

 **KEY IDEA!**

Changes in atmospheric pressure create different weather patterns.

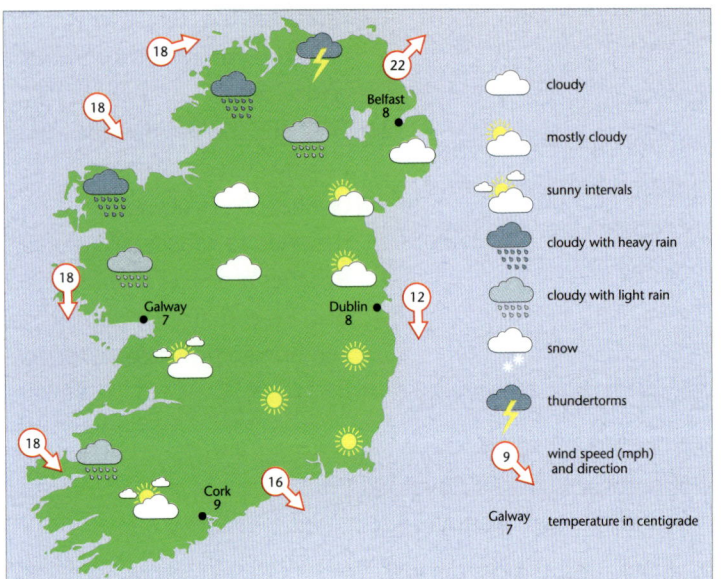

Fig. 17.1

A weather map is also called a **synoptic chart**. It shows weather for a particular area at one specific time. It is the result of collecting and sorting a considerable amount of information at numerous weather stations. This information is then refined by computers and plotted on a map, using internationally accepted **weather symbols**.

Weather maps are produced for different purposes and at various scales:

- The **daily weather map** as seen on TV or in the newspaper. This gives a clear but very simplified impression of the weather.
- At a higher level, a synoptic chart shows certain weather characteristics for specific weather stations. These characteristics generally include six elements: temperature, pressure, cloud cover, present weather (type of precipitation), wind direction and wind speed.
- At **the highest level,** weather maps show trends of pressure change, types of cloud at various levels and the dew point.

Forecasters now use satellite images that show a **simulated three-dimensional model** including present weather conditions and a short forecast.

The most typical weather patterns that develop over the north Atlantic Ocean include high pressure systems called **anticyclones** and low pressure systems called **cyclones**, or **depressions**.

Fig. 17.2

CLOUD		WEATHER		WIND SPEED			
Symbol	**Cloud amount (eighths)**	**Symbol**	**Weather**	**Symbol**	**Speed (knots)**	**Force**	3°Celsius
○	0	═	mist		calm	0	
	1/8 or less or 1 octa	≡	fog		5	2	Pressure is shown by isobars and is measured in millibars
	2/8 or less or 2 octas	,	drizzle				
	3/8 or less or 3 octas	;	rain and drizzle		10	3	
	4/8 or less or 4 octas	•	rain		15	4	——1012——
	5/8 or less or 5 octas	✳	rain and snow				
	6/8 or less or 6 octas	✱	snow	For each additional half-feather add 5 knots			mean sea level pressure
	7/8 or less or 7 octas	▽̇	rain shower				L = centre of an area of low pressure
●	8 octas or overcast	✳̽	snow shower	**WIND DIRECTION**			
⊗	sky obscured by fog	△̇	hail shower		Indicates a north-westerly wind direction at 15 knots		H = centre of an area of high pressure
⊗	missing or doubtful data	⃥	thunderstorm				

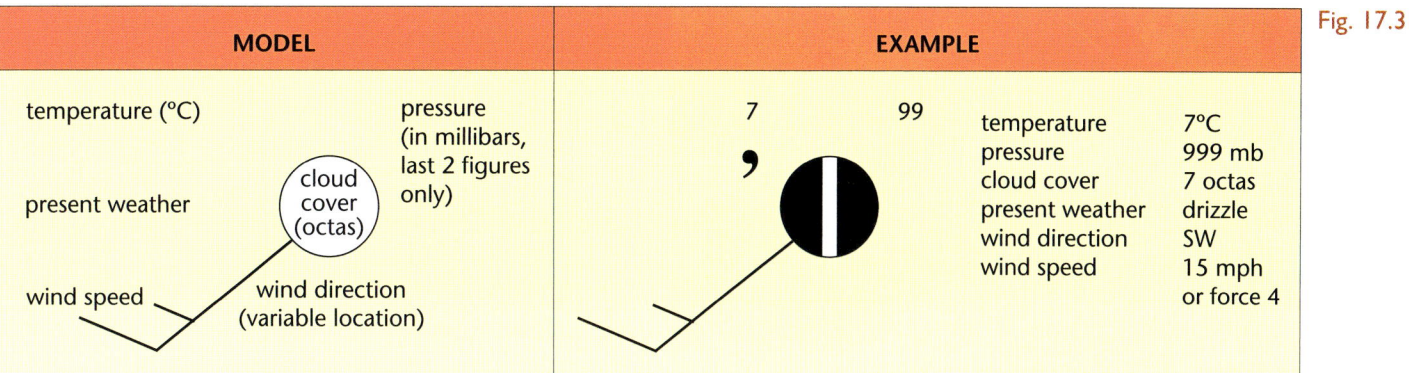

MODEL	EXAMPLE
temperature (°C) ... pressure (in millibars, last 2 figures only) / cloud cover (octas) / present weather / wind speed ... wind direction (variable location)	7 ... 99 ... temperature 7°C / pressure 999 mb / cloud cover 7 octas / present weather drizzle / wind direction SW / wind speed 15 mph or force 4

Fig. 17.3

During a Depression or Cyclone

- Warm air is forced to rise into the atmosphere, so creating low pressure.
- This creates **cooling** of the warm air, and cloud forms along the boundary of the warm and cold air masses.
- These boundaries are called **fronts**.

Within a depression there are two fronts:
- A warm front represented by this symbol ●●● on a weather map.
- A cold front represented by this symbol ▲▲▲ on a weather map.

Further cooling creates precipitation. The cloud or mist particles join to form water droplets. When the rising air is unable to suspend the droplets in the air, they fall as precipitation.

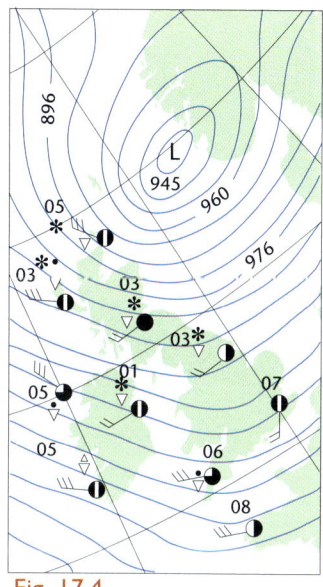

Fig. 17.4

OVERALL MOVEMENT OF DEPRESSION

① cold front
② warm front
③ warm front

warm air

cold air

cold air

A wedge of cold air cuts under the warm, humid, tropical air. The warm air is forced to rise, so it cools, condenses and clouds form along the cold front. Precipitation falls, mostly in the form of heavy rain. **Strong winds blow.**

The warm air continues to rise slowly until the cold wedges of air finally meet. Broken stratus clouds fill the sky. Some sunny spells occur. Drizzle sometimes falls. Gentle winds blow.

The warm tropical air is forced up over the cold polar air. Cooling and condensation of the rising air creates clouds along the warm front. Precipitation forms mostly as showers. **Strong winds blow.**

Fig. 17.5

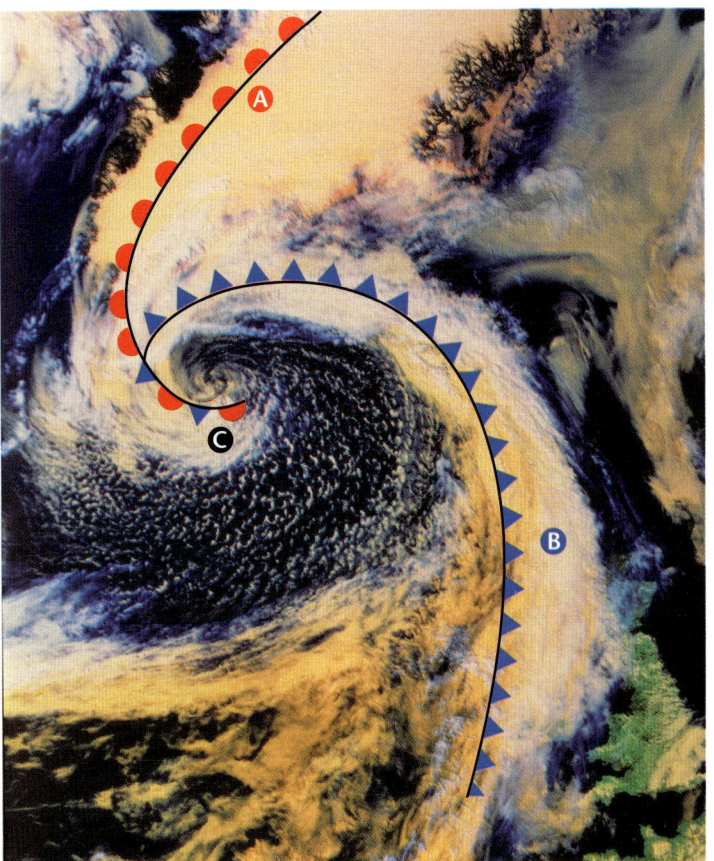

North Atlantic depression. Ireland and the UK are located in the bottom right. At top centre is the ice cap of Greenland. The frontal system is the swirling mass of cloud to the left of centre, with a low pressure area at the centre of the spiral. Low-level clouds are shown as yellow or pink. High-level clouds are white.

Activity

1. Over which region is the warm front located?
2. Over which country is the cold front located?
3. Describe the general weather conditions at A, B and C.
4. Look at the weather chart on page 128, then answer the following questions.
    a. Describe the weather conditions over the north Kerry/Dingle region.
    b. Does this type of weather system bring stable or unstable conditions? Explain.
    c. Is this weather system a cyclone or an anticyclone?

Activity

Examine the satellite image of a weather system below, then answer the following.
1. Identify this type of weather system.
2. Identify the land region on the top left and centre left.
3. Describe the weather conditions associated with such a weather system in this region.
4. At what time of year are these weather systems most frequent in this region? Explain.

Activity

This is a satellite image of a cyclone, or hurricane, in the tropics. Use the internet to learn about hurricanes that strike the Florida and Gulf coastal states in the US.

During an Anticyclone

- Heavy, cold air high in the atmosphere falls towards the earth's surface. It presses down, **squeezing** the air near the ground and creating **high pressure.**
- Winds blow outwards from the centre of the high pressure.
- Due to the **Coriolis force,** these winds blow in a **clockwise** movement.
- Increasing pressure heats the air, so it is able to hold more moisture. The air has little or no cloud, so it is **sunny** and **dry.**

Slack Winds

Anticyclones bring **light winds, or calm** conditions. When wind does exist, it will blow outwards in a **clockwise** movement due to the **Coriolis force. Isobars** are **widely spaced** to represent light or calm conditions.

Less Cloud

Descending air increases pressure, which has the effect of **increasing air temperature.** Warming air is able to **hold more moisture** than cooling air, so it is **dry** and creates **little or no cloud.** Little or no cloud results in **sunny** weather.

Dry Weather

Descending air gets warmer and holds its moisture in the **form of gas.** Even though the air may have lots of **water vapour,** little condensation occurs and there is little cloud.

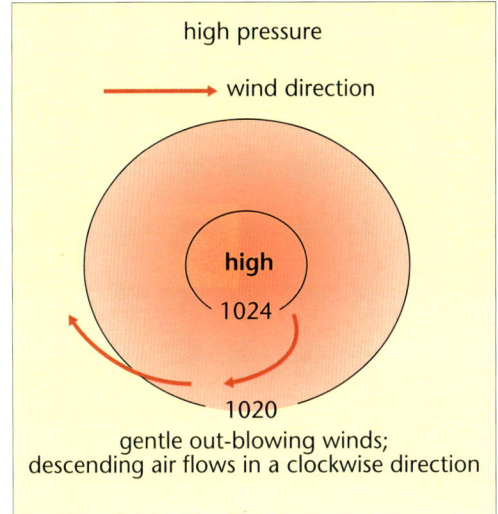

high pressure

wind direction

high
1024

1020

gentle out-blowing winds;
descending air flows in a clockwise direction

Fig. 17.6

Activity

Study the satellite image of weather systems over the north Atlantic in June, then answer the following questions.
1. Identify the type of weather system:
   a. over Ireland
   b. over north-east Canada and Greenland.
2. a. Describe the weather conditions over Ireland at this time.
   b. Explain the type of airflow one should expect during these atmospheric conditions.
   c. Is this type of weather over Ireland created by high or low atmospheric pressure? Explain.

CHAPTER 18

WHAT IS A REGION?

KEY IDEA!

A region is an area on the earth's surface that has a different identity from surrounding areas.

The Concept of a Region

What Is a Region?

A region is an area of the earth's surface that has human and/or physical characteristics that give it an identity and make it different from all the areas around it.

Table 18.1 illustrates some of the different types of region that we can study. These are highlighted and explained in the following chapters.

Table 18.1

Examples of Different Regions	
Region Type	**Example**
Climate region	Cool Temperate Oceanic (Chapter 19)
Physical region	The Burren (Chapter 20)
Administrative region	*Départments* in France (Chapter 21)
Cultural region	The Gaeltacht (Chapters 21; 33)
Core region	Paris region (Chapter 28)
Peripheral region	The Mezzogiorno (Chapter 27)
Industrial declining region	Sambre-Meuse Valley (Chapter 24)
Urban region	Dublin (Chapters 25; 34)

Activity

Study Table 18.1 and answer the following questions.
1. Suggest the main characteristic(s) which gives each regional example its distinctive identity.
2. Provide another example for each of the regional types.

Regions and Differences of Scale

There are many sizes of region. Some, such as the subcontinent of India, are huge, while others, such as the Gaeltacht regions in the West of Ireland, are small. The size of a region and **scale** of map used to define a region depend on the reason for studying it.

Figs. 18.1 and 18.2 show this with maps of two regions drawn at different scales. The first map, in Fig. 18.1, is drawn at a large scale to show the region of Europe. Not much detailed information can be shown at this scale. In contrast, Fig. 18.2 is drawn at a much smaller scale and allows for more detailed study of the Greater Cork Area.

Fig. 18.1 The countries of Europe.

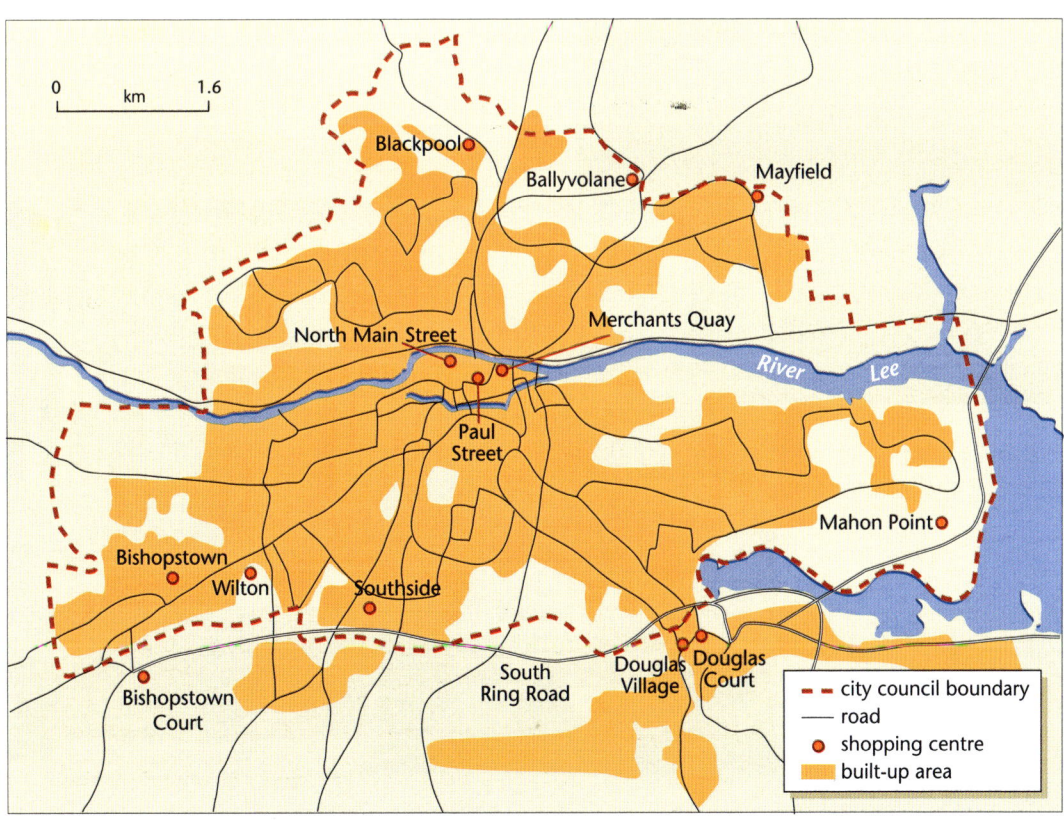

Fig. 18.2 Shopping centres in Cork city and suburbs.

General Characteristics of a Region

Although regions can be defined in different ways, some factors are the same for all regions:

- **Area:** Regions occupy an area of the earth's surface that can be identified as being different from surrounding areas.

- **Boundaries:** Regions are enclosed by boundaries that separate them from surrounding regions. Some boundaries are easily identified on the earth's surface, such as the crest of a mountain range or the course of a river. Most boundaries used by people, however, are not so easily recognised in the landscape, such as local government boundaries.

- **Image:** For most people, mentioning the name of a region often creates a perception or image of that region for them. These images are usually based on someone knowing about or being familiar with a region.

- **Change:** Regions change over time. At the start of the twentieth century, the Dublin urban region was quite small. Today, modernisation of transport systems has resulted in Dublin's urban region extending to 80 km or more from the city centre (see Chapter 34).

Different images of Ireland.
- *Which would be the image for a person living in Ireland as opposed to an American tourist planning a visit to Ireland?*

CHAPTER 19
CLIMATIC REGIONS

 **KEY IDEA!** A climatic region is an area with an identity that comes from regular weather patterns over a long period of time. These weather patterns affect vegetation and soils in a region.

Climatic regions are areas that have their own distinct climate and are separated from each other by boundaries. In some areas these boundaries are sharply defined, while in others they are not as well defined because one climate area blends into another. Within a climate region, the unique weather system and its temperature, precipitation, seasons, soil and vegetation make it completely different from all the surrounding regions.

Some climate regions are huge, for example the equatorial climate region that includes the Amazon Basin in South America, the Congo Basin in Africa and the Indonesian islands.

Remember from your Junior Certificate how climate affects soil. Cold boreal climate areas have **podzol** soils and hot climates have **laterite** soils.

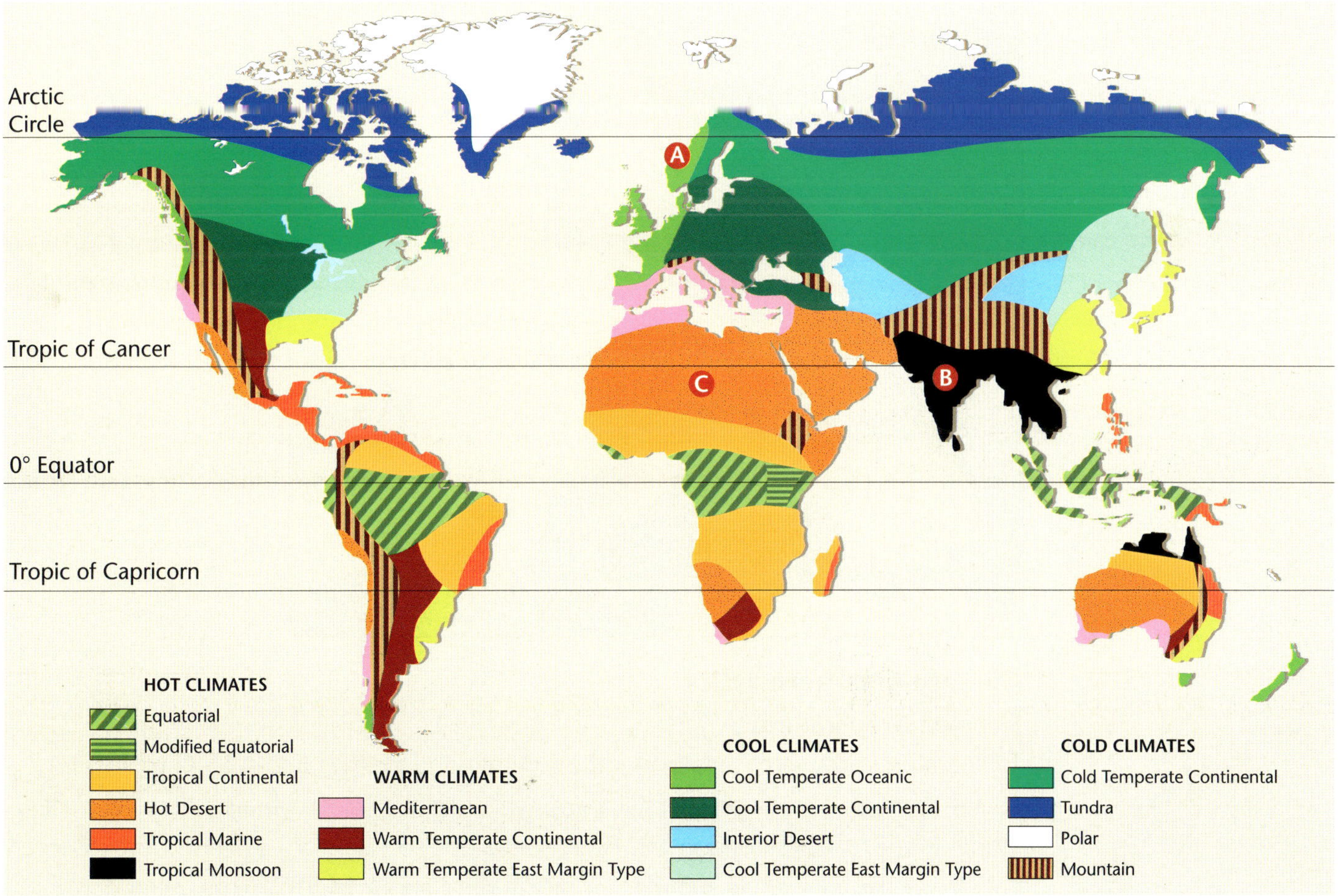

Arctic Circle

Tropic of Cancer

0° Equator

Tropic of Capricorn

HOT CLIMATES
- Equatorial
- Modified Equatorial
- Tropical Continental
- Hot Desert
- Tropical Marine
- Tropical Monsoon

WARM CLIMATES
- Mediterranean
- Warm Temperate Continental
- Warm Temperate East Margin Type

COOL CLIMATES
- Cool Temperate Oceanic
- Cool Temperate Continental
- Interior Desert
- Cool Temperate East Margin Type

COLD CLIMATES
- Cold Temperate Continental
- Tundra
- Polar
- Mountain

Fig. 19.1 These are the main climate regions of the world.
- *Identify the climates at A, B and C.*

135

Other climate regions are tiny. These are called **microclimates**. The physical presence of a city affects the local climate, and as a city changes, so does its climate. The bigger the city becomes, the more polluted the air is and the warmer its temperature. Buildings absorb and release heat, while the dust in the air traps and reflects heat back into the city, making the urban area warmer than its surrounding areas. This is called an urban microclimate. Microclimates may vary from one side of a rock to another, or from one side of a tree to another.

A cloud-covered Dingle Peninsula.
● *Suggest reasons for the high frequency of cloud cover and high rainfall experienced in such areas.*

Case Study: Climate of North-West Europe: Cool Temperate Oceanic Climate

This climate region occurs as a narrow coastal zone in Western Europe that stretches from northern Norway to north-west Spain. It includes the whole of Britain and Ireland.

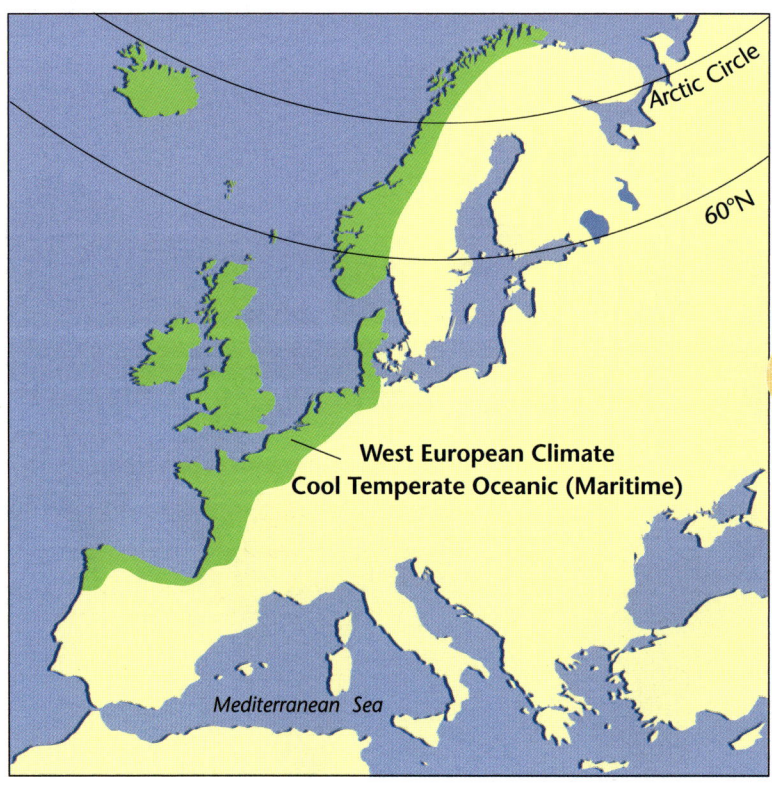

Fig. 19.2 Cool Temperate Oceanic climate in north-west Europe.
● *Name the countries on this map that have coastal areas with a Cool Temperate Oceanic climate.*

This climate is often called a Maritime or Oceanic Climate. Why do you think this is?

Climate Characteristics

Summer Temperature

Temperatures are warm throughout the summer and average about **15°C to 17°C**. Lower averages occur along coastal areas, while slightly higher averages occur in places further inland, such as London and Paris. Averages also vary from south to north. Bergen in Norway has an average summer temperature of about **14.5°C**, while Valentia in Co. Kerry averages about **15°C**. Daytime temperatures may reach **23°C** or more on hot days.

Winter Temperature

Temperatures are mild through winter months, and January temperatures may average about **4°C to 5°C**. The warm North Atlantic Drift that flows from the Gulf of Mexico to the west coast of Europe influences all the sea areas. Blowing over this warm water surface are the South-West Anti-Trade Winds that bring warm air to coastal areas throughout the year. This is most noticeable during winter, as temperatures are generally above **4°C** and so make the weather mild and moist.

Precipitation

The one certainty about precipitation (rainfall) in this climate region is that it may fall at any time of year. Most rain, however, falls in winter. It is mostly associated with depressions or cyclones that travel from a south-west to north-east direction across the North Atlantic and bring changeable weather to this coastal region.

Relief rain also occurs, and highland and upland areas, such as the mountains of the West of Ireland, the Scottish Highlands and the Scandinavian Highlands, receive more rain than lowland areas. Some precipitation falls as snow. The total rainfall can vary from as little as 500 millimetres (mm) in lowland areas to 2,500 mm in highland areas.

The Climate of Ireland

Ireland is located in north-west Europe and so has a Cool Temperate Oceanic or Maritime climate. Its prevailing winds are the South-West Anti-Trades that blow from the Atlantic Ocean. These winds and the presence of mountains along Ireland's coastline cause Ireland to be divided into **two climatic regions**. They are the wetter West of Ireland and the drier eastern Ireland.

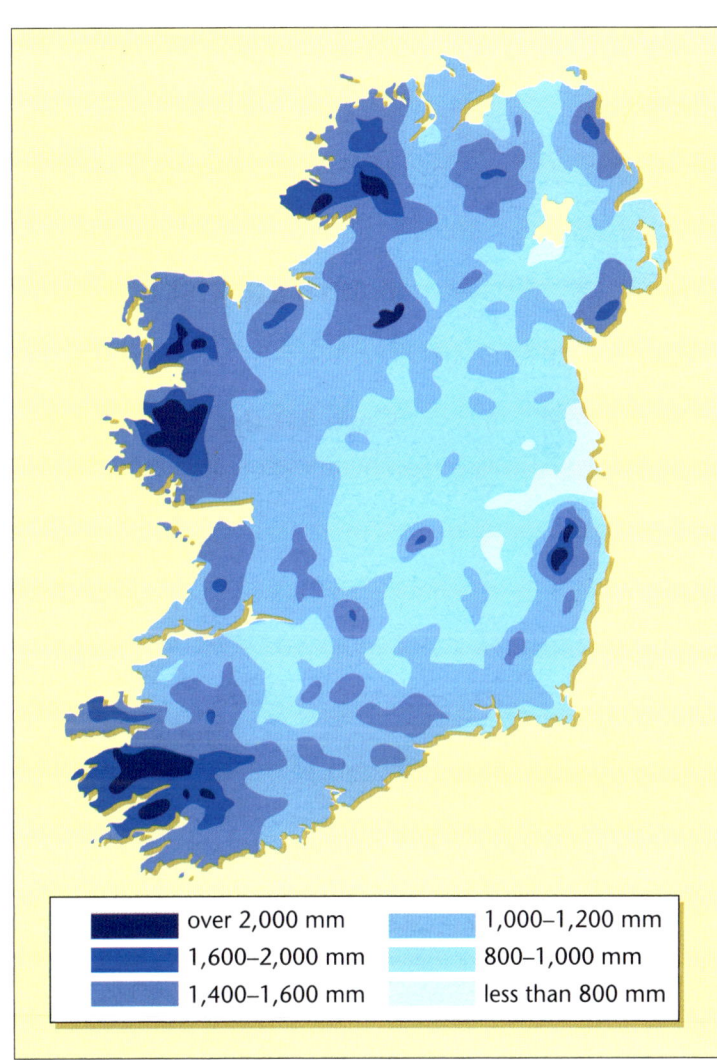

■ over 2,000 mm	■ 1,000–1,200 mm
■ 1,600–2,000 mm	■ 800–1,000 mm
■ 1,400–1,600 mm	■ less than 800 mm

Fig. 19.3 Annual rainfall totals in Ireland.

Activity

Look at Fig. 19.3 and answer the following.
1. Using a diagram, explain why Ireland's heaviest rainfall occurs along the western coast.
2. Explain why the Dublin region in the east of the country has the least rainfall. Think about relief rain and rain shadow.

CHAPTER 20
PHYSICAL REGIONS

Physical regions have surface characteristics that make them different from all the areas around them. The physical differences may be due to height and relief, the rock types, drainage pattern or internal rock structure, or a combination of these factors.

Karst Landscapes

Karst landscapes are regions formed by chemical weathering.

Remember how landforms of karst landscapes were explained in Chapter 10, page 59.

Case Study: The Burren in Co. Clare

The Burren is an upland, terraced limestone region in Co. Clare. The beds of rock dip gently to the south. In some places the limestone is covered by shale. Some of the soil cover was eroded by glaciers, while tilling the land by early farmers exposed the remaining soil to strong coastal winds.

Most of the Burren today has no soil cover and weathering has created a karst landscape. Large expanses of limestone pavement with grikes and clints dominate the area. There are few surface streams. Most disappear underground through sinkholes (swallow holes) and flow through underground passages and caverns.

Karst landscapes occur in many areas in Ireland, such as the Dartry-Cuilcagh Uplands in Co. Fermanagh and Co. Cavan (see Chapter 8, page 52). The best example in Ireland is the Burren in Co. Clare.

Formation

The Burren was formed when the African and European plates collided. This collision also formed a huge mountain chain across Europe, of which the Galtees, the Macgullicuddy's Reeks and the ridges of Munster are remnants.

● *What evidence in the photograph suggests that the Burren in Co. Clare is a karst region?*

Munster Ridge and Valley Region

This natural region is explained in Chapter 8, page 51.

The North European Plain Region

The North European Plain is a lowland region that extends from west to east across Europe from Ireland and Britain to the countries around the Black Sea, such as Romania and the Ukraine (see Fig. 20.1).

Formation

The forces that created the ridge and valley region of Munster and the Burren Upland in Co. Clare also rippled the seafloor that now forms the foundation of the North European Plain. Later, after the Alps and surrounding uplands were formed, sediments were washed down or blown by wind onto the plain from the weathered and eroded mountains and levelled it. The final result was the North European Plain. Slight warpings have made it undulating rather than flat.

During the last great Ice Age, an enormous ice sheet squeezed down this lowland region of north-west Europe. When the ice melted and raised the level of the sea, much of the land that had subsided was submerged beneath the North and Baltic Seas. In this way, Britain and Ireland were cut off from mainland Europe. Rivers flowed northwards and formed deltas along the coasts of the Netherlands, Belgium and northern Germany. As the great weight of ice was removed, the land started to rise again. This process continues today and is noticeable in the raised beaches found along the coast of Northern Ireland, Scotland and the Baltic coastline.

> Remember isostasy in Chapter 15 on page 110.

> The North and Baltic Seas are shallow because their floors were once part of the North European Plain.

Fig. 20.1 The North European Plain.

Activity

Look at Fig. 20.1 and name some of the countries that are in this lowland region.

CHAPTER 21

ADMINISTRATIVE REGIONS

KEY IDEA!

There are many types and sizes of administrative regions.

ADMINISTRATIVE REGIONS AT DIFFERENT SCALES

One of the most basic forms of region are administrative units such as county and city councils. Most governments divide their national space into a hierarchy of local and regional areas. This allows them to administer development more effectively.

Administrative areas need to be large enough to allow for providing services efficiently; an example of this is the Health Service Executive Areas (Fig. 21.5). The areas also need to be **small** enough to work effectively and reflect community interests, for example local school districts.

The links between various levels of administration generally take one of two forms (see Figs. 21.1 and 21.2).

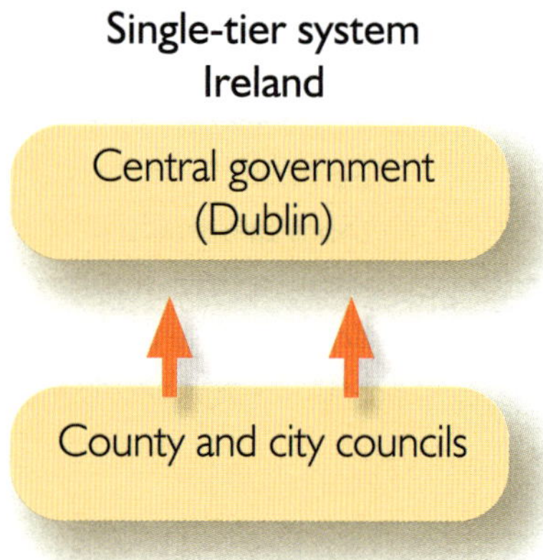

Why do communities prefer small and more localised forms of administration?

Multiple-tier system France

Central government (Paris)

↑

22 regional governments

↑

92 *départements* (local government)

Single-tier system Ireland

Central government (Dublin)

↑   ↑

County and city councils

- **Single-tier system:**
  Each administration area has direct access to central government, for example, Ireland.

- **Multiple-tier system:**
  Local authorities work with central government through a bureaucracy (system of government officials and departments) of one or more regional levels, e.g. France.

Fig. 21.1 A single-tier system of government.

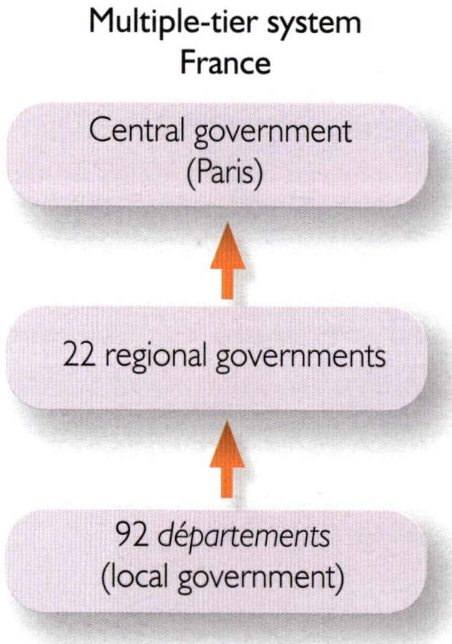

Fig. 21.2 A multiple-tier system of government.

ADMINISTRATIVE UNITS IN IRELAND
The Counties of Ireland

Following their invasion in 1169, the Anglo-Normans introduced new forms of administration or adapted existing forms to allow them to control the territory they conquered in Ireland. The **county** was the central part of this system.

By the mid-thirteenth century, the settled parts of Ireland had been divided into eight counties. The number of counties gradually increased, and from 1606 to 1994, twenty-six counties made up the Republic of Ireland (Fig. 21.3). In 1994, however, Co. Dublin was subdivided into three new counties – Dublin, Fingal and Dun Laoghaire-Rathdown – to reflect the complexity of this capital city region.

Many counties are defined by major physical features such as the River Shannon, or mountain ranges such as the Blackstairs Mountains. Counties also bring to mind powerful images of distinctive cultural and physical landscapes.

People identify strongly with their county and have a pride in and loyalty to their county. This is often expressed by the support and intense rivalries generated at GAA matches at county level and between neighbouring counties, such as Cork-Kerry, Dublin-Meath, Tipperary-Kilkenny.

● *While the landscape may not change dramatically when moving from one county to another, would you **feel** you were entering a different part of Ireland? Why?*

Urban-based Administrative Units

With the growing role of urbanisation in Ireland, three types of administrative units are based around urban centres:

● City councils.
● Borough councils.
● Town councils.

City Councils

There are city councils for the **five** most populous and important cities: Dublin, Cork, Limerick, Waterford and Galway (see Fig 21.3). These cities have played a major role in the development of the state, especially for their hinterlands (surrounding areas).

One of the critical problems for all city councils is that their administrative areas have not expanded enough to take account of suburbanisation (how large new housing estates or suburbs are built, allowing the population to spread outside historic city boundaries). Modern growth now occurs mainly outside town boundaries and in areas of neighbouring county councils, for example Limerick city spreading into Co. Clare.

Can you suggest any planning problems if a city expands into a different administrative region?

Limerick City Council offices and the River Shannon.

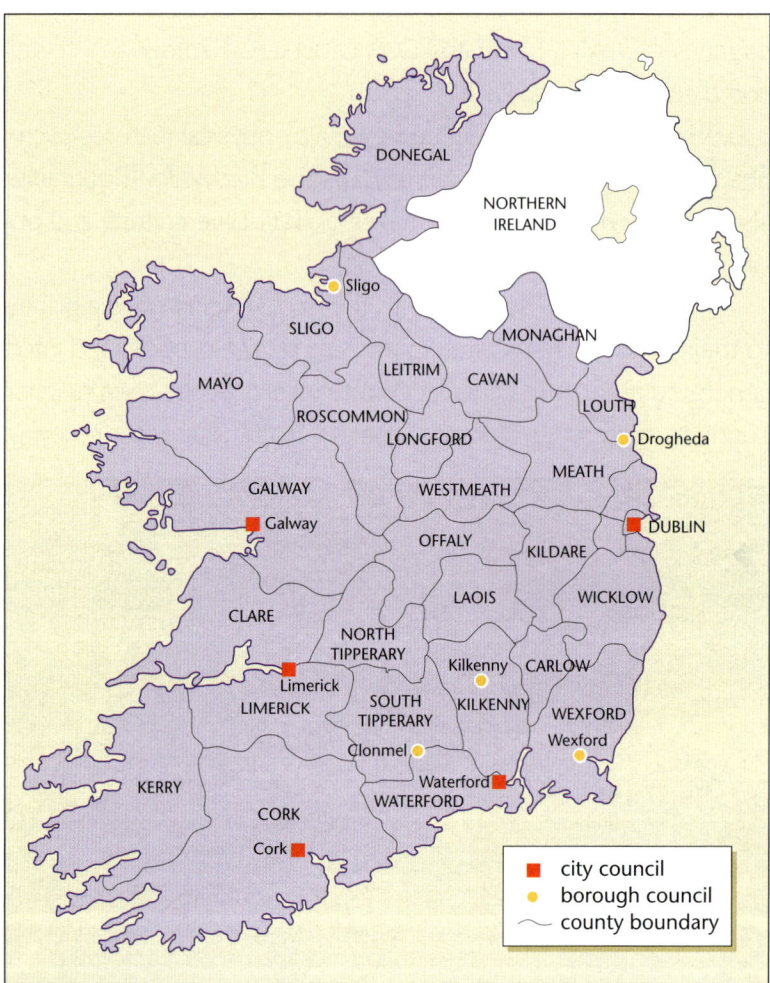
Fig. 21.3 Counties, city councils and borough councils in Ireland.

Borough and Town Councils

Borough councils administer the five medium-sized towns that come below the city councils in Ireland's urban hierarchy, for example Kilkenny.

The third type of urban-based administrative unit are the 75 **town councils**, which have their roots in the nineteenth century. These have some planning powers, but do not play a vital role in the administrative framework of modern Ireland.

Regional Administration

There is no effective regional level of administration in Ireland. From the 1960s, some efforts have been made to set up regional administration units to help planning within the state. Different types of regional authority areas relating to issues of public concern have been created, for example for regional development and health (see Figs. 21.4 and 21.5).

The central government does not give regional bodies important decision-making powers. Regional administrative units within Ireland are therefore not as important as in many other countries. In 1999, however, two new regions were created to more effectively administer Ireland's programme for national development and EU structural funds. These were the Border, Midland and West (BMW) and Southern and Eastern (S&E) regions (Fig. 21.4) and deal with local issues at a local level.

Fig. 21.4 Regional Authority Areas and two new planning regions for European Union (EU) funding.

Fig. 21.5 Health Service Executive Areas.

Activity
Look at Figs. 21.4 and 21.5 and suggest some problems that can arise for effective planning because of differences in regional authority areas.

Local Government in Ireland

There are over 100 local authorities in Ireland. They form the country's system of local government.

As well as providing the community with essential services, such as housing, water supply and sewerage, local authorities have also taken on a development role. Local authorities have to draw up strategic **development plans** to meet the development needs of their areas. These must be updated every six years and are key documents in zoning land for different uses. They help shape transport, industry and housing developments in local authority areas.

Activity
Access the development plan of your local authority area. What are the main features of the plan for your community?

143

Local planning operates under **three** key principles:

- **Subsidiarity:** Decision-making should allow people to have a major role in governing their own affairs. This encourages self-reliance rather than depending on outside organisations to promote development.
- **Appropriateness:** Services and administration should be provided as close to the people as possible. This emphasises, where practical, local rather than regional or national levels of government.
- **Partnership:** This encourages local people to take part in government.

Local authorities have provided over 350,000 houses for people in Ireland who otherwise could not afford a house of their own.

Do you think providing housing is an important role for local authorities?

The *Départements* of France

France is one of Europe's largest countries, with a surface area of 551,000 km², a population of over 62 million and a wide variety of human and physical landscapes. Despite its size and diversity, government is centralised on Paris, although by the late twentieth century, regional administrations had a stronger role.

Much of the present regional administration in France can be traced to the French Revolution of 1789. After the Revolution, a new pattern of local government was based on the *département*. These were designed to be approximately the same size in terms of area and total population and, where possible, with some special cultural feature. There are 92 *départements* in present-day France (see Fig. 21.6).

The *départements* are responsible for a number of functions, including social services and co-ordinating urban and regional planning in their areas. The central government in Paris still has a powerful role and influence on local administration because it appoints the key administrative officer, known as the *préfet*, for each *département*. Also, as local administration was centred on the main town in each *département*, no regional centres developed enough in size and function to rival the dominance of Paris.

After the Second World War, there was some administrative reform and twenty-two regions were created in 1955 (see Fig. 21.6). These were, however, little more

Fig. 21.6 The regions and *départements* of France.

Activity
Which French region in Fig. 21.6:
1. Is linked most to Celtic culture?
2. Produces high-quality sparkling wine?
3. Includes the capital of France?
4. Is the location of the EU Parliament?

Départements are the equivalent of counties in Ireland.

Map labels:
NORD-PAS-DE-CALAIS — Lille-Roubaix-Tourcoing
HAUTE-NORMANDIE
PICARDIE
BASSE-NORMANDIE
Metz-Nancy
Paris
ILE-DE-FRANCE
LORRAINE
Strasbourg
ALSACE
BRETAGNE
PAYS DE LA LOIRE
St. Nazaire
Nantes
CENTRE
CHAMPAGNE-ARDENNE
BOURGOGNE
FRANCHE-COMTÉ
POITOU-CHARENTES
LIMOUSIN
AUVERGNE
Lyons
St. Etienne
Grenoble
RHÔNE-ALPES
Bordeaux
AQUITAINE
MIDI-PYRÉNÉES
Toulouse
LANGUEDOC-ROUSSILLON
PROVENCE-ALPES-CÔTE-D'AZUR
Marseilles
CORSICA

0   150
km

Legend:
■ capital of France
● major regional centres to counteract the dominance of Paris
— regional boundary
— *département* boundary

than a collection of *départements* and had little authority. Pressure to decentralise (spread out) power from Paris increased in the 1970s, and a 1982 law gave the regions a new status.

French regions now have responsibilities for economic and cultural activities, such as job creation, tourism and heritage. They have become effective planning bodies and co-ordinate initiatives put forward by the *départements*. A region's population is also represented in regional assemblies through direct elections.

As each region is a large size and has a range of planning functions, some regional centres have now become more important. These include Lyons-St Étienne-Grenoble, Toulouse and Bordeaux. This is important to counterbalance the dominance of Paris.

The *départements* centred on Bordeaux have been linked to the production of high-quality wine for centuries.
● *In which ways would the wine industry have helped the growth of Bordeaux as an important regional centre?*

CHAPTER 22
CULTURAL REGIONS

KEY IDEA!

Language and religion are two major factors that are used to define culture regions.

Defining a Culture Region

In constructing regions based on human rather than physical factors, **culture** is the most fundamental factor. Yet culture is a difficult concept to define. It involves many features, such as behaviour, attitude, learning and knowledge, and how these are passed on from one generation to the next.

These values, however, have an impact on the landscape. This can be through the ways in which people organise and adapt to their resources. In farming, it could be building stone walls and the field patterns in Co. Galway, or in a city it might be its special architecture and street layout.

By mapping cultural features, geographers create **culture regions.** Identifying culture is complex, but **two key factors** are often used to map cultural regions. These factors are **language** and **religion.**

Three different cultural landscapes from Ireland, Italy and India.

Language Regions

Language is central to cultural identity, as it is the main way of passing knowledge and ideas between people. It is seen as a powerful symbol of cultural identity, and many cultures strongly resist outside pressures to reduce the vitality of 'their' language.

In many national territories, there are often strong passions about keeping minority regional languages, such as the Basques in Spain and Bretons in France. Yet there are also cases in which different language groups can co-exist with little sign of stress. In Switzerland there are four official languages: French, German, Italian and Romansch. This causes little or no problem for the Swiss.

Case Study: Ireland and the Gaeltacht

In the Republic of Ireland, the Irish language has an important role in expressing Irish culture and identity. In the 2002 Census, 1.57 million people (40 per cent) in the Republic claimed some ability to speak and understand Irish. This is almost three times the number of people who claimed this ability when the Free State was set up, reflecting the efforts of government and voluntary bodies to promote the Irish language, especially within the education system.

Although more people claim to have some knowledge of Irish, Irish is used in everyday life only in relatively small and peripheral parts of the country. These are the **Gaeltacht regions,** and are the heartland of the Irish language and culture (see Fig. 22.1).

The Gaeltacht was defined in 1925 by a Commission for Irish-Speaking Districts. To qualify as an Irish-speaking district (*Fíor Gaeltacht*), 80 per cent of the population had to speak Irish. Partly Irish-speaking districts (*Breac Gaeltacht*) were defined as areas where 25 to 79 per cent of the population spoke Irish. Using District Electoral Divisions as a basic area for analysis, the Commission was able to create distinctive cultural regions based on the Irish language (see Fig. 33.2 on page 241).

At the start of the twenty-first century, the Gaeltacht is composed of a number of relatively small areas scattered along the west and south coast of the country from Donegal to Waterford. The total population of the Gaeltacht in 2002 was about 86,500. Of this total, 61,150 people over the age of three years spoke Irish. Although these Gaeltacht areas are small and have peripheral locations, they have a special importance for the Irish people and are strongly supported by government grants and incentives (see Chapter 33).

Fig. 22.1 The Gaeltacht areas.

- less-developed western region
- Gaeltacht

How is Irish promoted as a language in the Irish education system? Is this a success?

In 2006, controversy arose over using only the official Irish place names for this important tourist centre in the Gaeltacht.

● *Why did many residents also want to keep the English version of the town's name?*

Activity

Look at Fig. 22.1 and answer the following.

1. In which counties are the Gaeltacht areas?
2. Why do you think the Gaeltacht is confined mainly to the less-developed West?

Belgium and Its Language Regions

Belgium was created as an independent state in 1830, following a revolution which led to this area separating from the Netherlands. Despite Belgium's relatively small size (30.5 million km², which is less than half the area of Ireland), the country has **three** official languages: Flemish, French and German (see Fig. 22.2). The Flemish language is a type of Dutch.

This Flemish-speaking area is culturally linked to the Netherlands. Historically, this was a poor region that lived from farming. Since the 1960s, this region has become more prosperous, attracting growth industries to places such as the port of Antwerp and its hinterland.

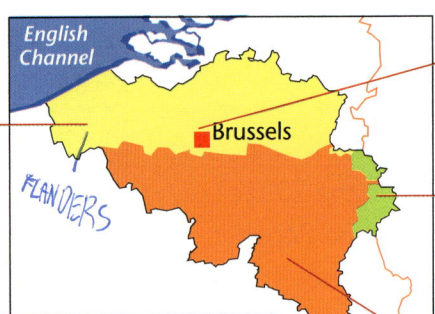

Fig. 22.2 The language regions of Belgium.

Brussels is the capital of Belgium. It is a bilingual city where French and Flemish are given the same status.

This small enclave of German speakers is territory ceded to Belgium by Germany after the First World War.

The southern part of Belgium is mainly French speaking because it is near France. During the 1800s, this region became prosperous, based on heavy industries that developed in the Sambre-Meuse and Liège coalfields. The collapse of these industries has seen the prosperity of Wallonia decline sharply.

This town near Brussels is located in Flanders, but has a majority of French-speaking people. Flemish language activists have crossed out the French place name, indicating the tensions between the two language groups.

Since the 1960s, tensions between the two main language-based communities (Flemish and French) have increased. Although Flanders has a majority of the national population and has attracted a lot of growth industries to become one of the EU's most prosperous regions, its Flemish-speaking community feels under threat from the more dominant international language of French.

As tensions grew and the different communities wanted to gain more autonomy (control) over their own affairs, fundamental reforms have been made to Belgium's constitution. There is now a federal-style government, which recognises three separate regions based mainly on language. These regions are Flanders, the Brussels-Capital Region and Wallonia (which is French speaking but includes a small German-speaking community).

The new political-cultural regionalisation has highlighted divisions within Belgium. The 'defensive' attitude of Flemish communities over the spread of the French language has led to the creation of a new political party called *Vlaams Belang*. This party is committed to protecting Flemish culture, with more extreme elements seeking an independent state. These language tensions make it difficult for Belgium to function as a single national state.

If you were going to live in Brussels, would you choose to learn French or Flemish? Explain your answer.

Regions and Religion

If cultural regions were based only on language, they would be relatively easy to define. Systems of belief, which are key elements in defining culture, can cut across language barriers. The Islamic world, for example, is made up of many different language groups. Sometimes similar language groups can be divided through religious conflict, as in Northern Ireland.

Each of the world's major religions has a distinctive geography (see Fig. 22.3) and has had a key role in shaping individual and group identities. These include aspects such as attitudes to women, birth control, the environment and diet.

For example, in some traditional Islamic societies, women generally play an inferior role to men in daily life. A large number may be uneducated.

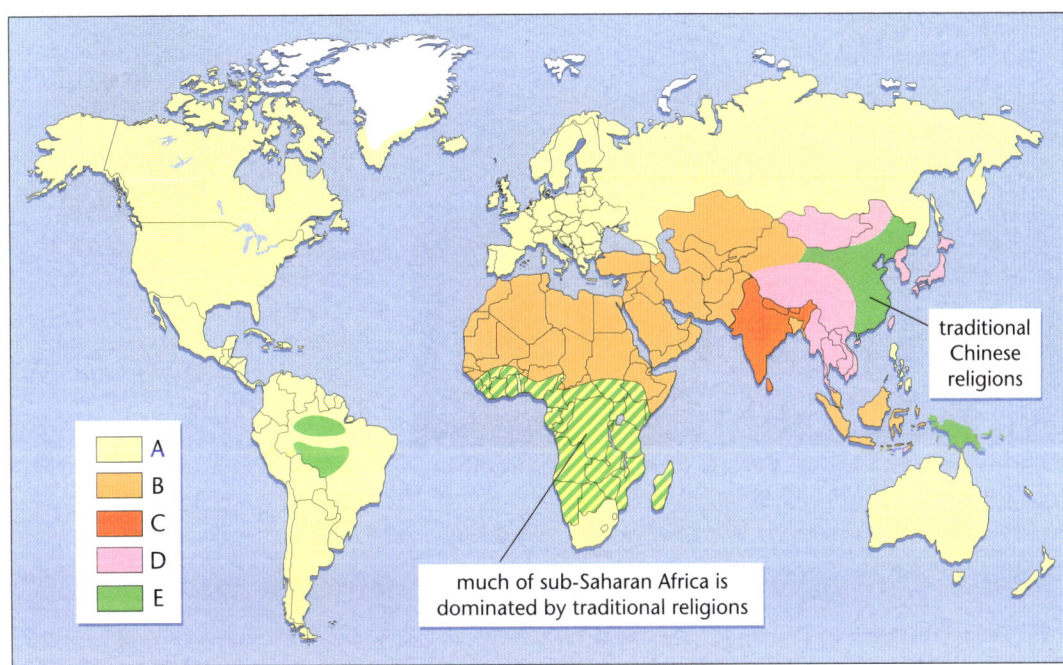

Fig. 22.3 The world's major religions.

traditional Chinese religions

much of sub-Saharan Africa is dominated by traditional religions

A
B
C
D
E

Activity

Look at Fig. 22.3 and say which of the major world religions matches A to E on the map.
Choose from:
- Hinduism
- Islam
- Christianity
- Buddhism
- Traditional/regional religions

Which two religious groups clash in Palestine and Kashmir?

Most religions wish to convert non-believers to their faith. As a result, boundaries that define religions change over time and for varying reasons, such as the work of Christian missionaries. The passion of some religious groups is so strong that conflict zones occur along boundaries between different religions. Present-day examples include Israel and the neighbouring Arab countries; Islamic Pakistan and Hindu-dominated India, especially in Kashmir; and Christian and Islamic communities in the Balkans following the break-up of Yugoslavia.

Two examples we shall look at are regions associated with religion but on very different scales:

- Northern Ireland.
- The Islamic world.

An estimated 200 million cows roam the streets in the towns and cities of India. Since cows are regarded as holy creatures in the Hindu faith, they cannot be killed or mistreated.
- *What problems could this create?*

In the middle of Rome is the Vatican City. It is the centre of the Roman Catholic Church, where the Pope lives.
- *What regions of the world are dominated by the Christian faith?*

A woman in Afghanistan dressed in traditional Islamic style.
- *How does gender inequality affect development in Islamic countries? (Think about employment and population growth.)*

Religious Divide in Northern Ireland

The Irish Free State set up in 1921 did not cover the whole island of Ireland. After a referendum, six counties in north-east Ireland chose to remain part of the United Kingdom. This decision was associated with British colonial rule when large numbers of English and Scottish Protestant communities had been settled there. In contrast, the rest of the island was, and remains, dominated by the Catholic faith. Northern Ireland emerged as a distinctive cultural region based around its majority Protestant population.

Despite many changes in the Protestant and Catholic populations in Northern Ireland, the political divide separating the region from the Republic has not changed. In Northern Ireland, however, Catholic and Protestant communities became increasingly segregated (e.g. Catholic and Protestant children attend different schools), especially after the outbreak of violence in the region in 1968. Generally, the Catholic population tends to form the majority in more rural areas, while Protestants dominate in the larger urban centres. At the start of the twenty-first century, approximately 55 per cent of Northern Ireland's population was Protestant.

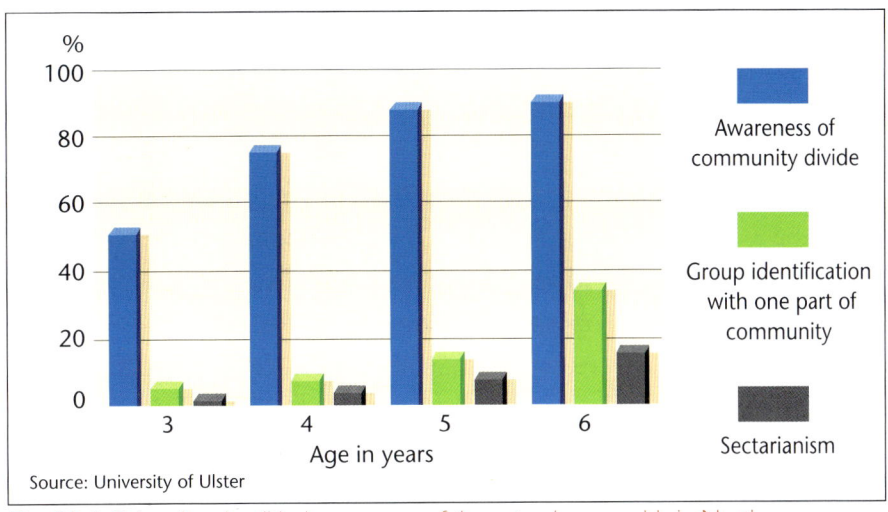

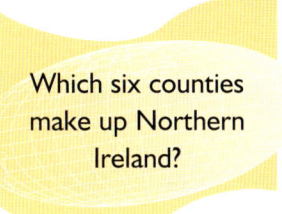
Which six counties make up Northern Ireland?

Fig. 22.4 Cultural and political awareness of three-to-six-year-olds in Northern Ireland (%).

● *What does this image and Figure 22.4 suggest about the cultural divide in Northern Ireland?*

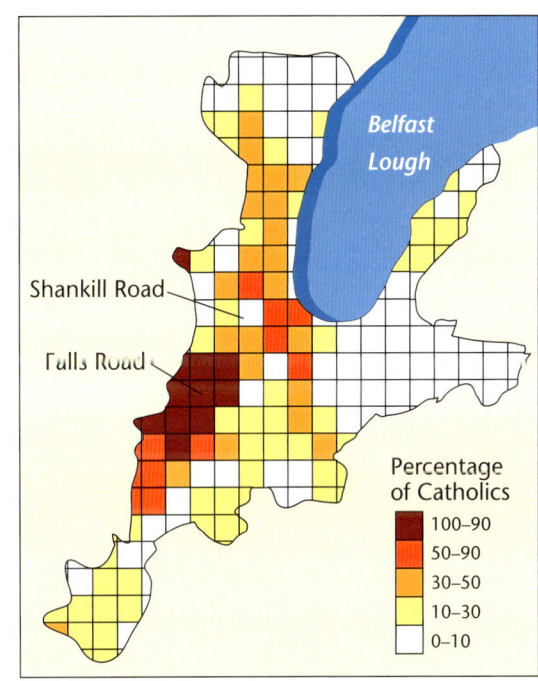

Fig. 22.5 Belfast Urban Area, 1981.

Within Belfast, there is religious segregation. After the outbreak of civil disorder in 1968, minorities of both religions who had chosen to live in a different majority community often had to retreat into their own communities. The result was Catholic-only and Protestant-only ghettos and a divided city.

A geographer named Paul Doherty drew up an interesting map of the Belfast urban area to show religious segregation in 1981 (Fig. 22.5). Using one-kilometre squares, Doherty shows that only nineteen out of 157 squares had a Catholic majority (for example, in the Falls Road). In contrast, there are large areas with a majority of Protestant residents (for example, in the Shankill Road).

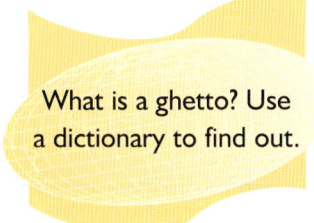
What is a ghetto? Use a dictionary to find out.

The Islamic World

Islam is one of the world's great religions, with more than 1 billion believers. It is a religion that is expanding its number of converts and the areas of the world in which it is practised.

The Islamic religion traces its origin to the prophet Muhammad (Mohammed), who was born at Mecca in the Arabian Peninsula in AD 571. Muhammad received revelations from Allah (God) and committed his life to teaching these divine revelations. At first there was opposition, but his teachings quickly became accepted in Arab society. After his death in AD 632, the Islamic religion, its teachings and cultural landscapes spread quickly from its source area in the Arabian Peninsula (its cultural hearth) to the surrounding regions.

Islam was spread by powerful conquering armies that invaded other parts of the Middle East and North Africa, Spain and the Balkans. Arab traders travelled to distant markets, such as the Indian subcontinent and the islands of South-East Asia, taking their faith with them and converting local populations to Islam (see Fig. 22.6).

Today, the global region of Islam occupies most of North Africa and south-west Asia, with important outlying areas in the densely populated islands of South-East Asia, such as Indonesia. In these regions, religion is still a powerful influence on the lives of people and in shaping distinctive cultural landscapes, such as the design of towns, palaces and mosques. Also, women generally have less control over their lives in this more male-dominated culture and are allocated the roles of wife and mother.

The Alhambra palace is in Granada, which became the capital of Moorish Spain from the eleventh century until 1492.

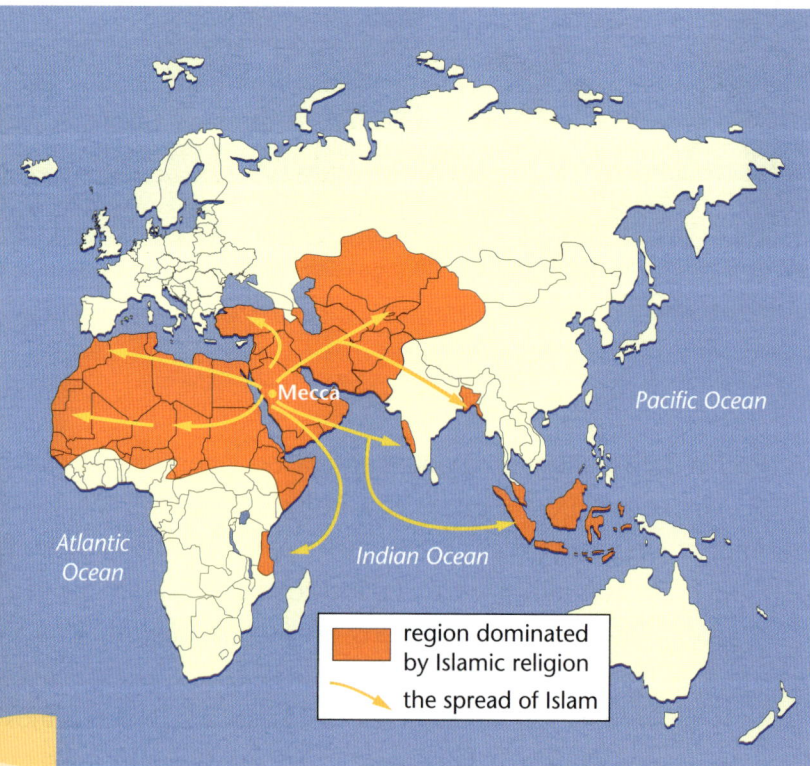

Fig. 22.6 Where Islam spread around the world.

Find the Arabian Peninsula on a map of the world.

Even in areas that were under the influence of Islam centuries ago, there are still impressions of the past in the present-day landscape, as in the case of **southern Spain.** When the Moors invaded Spain in 711, they spread the Islamic faith there. They were finally pushed out of Spain in 1492, but palaces like the Alhambra, in Granada, are a reminder of nearly 800 years of Moorish presence in Spain.

Mecca is the most sacred city in Islam. Up to 750,000 Muslims can gather to pray together at the Kaaba, or Sacred Mosque of Islam.

● *In which country is Mecca?*

Islam continues to expand as a global religion. For some, this is seen as a threat associated with **Islamic fundamentalism,** and conflict zones have emerged in places such as the Balkans and Kashmir. Yet Islam also expands along more peaceful avenues, often associated with migration into countries of the developed world. An increasing number of major cities in Western Europe, such as London, Paris and Amsterdam, and also in North America, now have mosques, reflecting their growing population of converts to Islam.

What do you know about Islamic fundamentalism? What is it?

For Muslims, making a pilgrimage to Mecca is one of the five pillars (or duties) of Islam.

153

Multi-part Questions

1. A. CONCEPT OF REGION

    i.   Define what is meant by the term 'region'.

    ii.   Explain some factors that are common to all regions.   [20 marks]

B. PHYSICAL REGIONS

    i.   Name one **Irish** physical region and one **European** physical region.

    ii.   In the case of one of the physical regions above, explain how it was formed.   [30 marks]

C. CLIMATIC REGION

Describe and explain the climate of north-west Europe.   [30 marks]

2. A. SKETCH MAP

Use your atlas to draw a sketch map of Ireland. On it, mark and name the following:

    i.   two major rivers

    ii.   two upland regions

    iii. one urban region.   [20 marks]

B. ADMINISTRATIVE REGIONS

'Administrative regions exist at a variety of scales.' Explain this statement using examples from Ireland and one other European country that you have studied.   [30 marks]

C. CULTURAL REGIONS

Explain the factors that define Gaeltacht areas as distinctive cultural regions.   [30 marks]

3. A. IRISH PHYSICAL REGIONS

    i.   **Identify** the physical region at **each** of the locations A, B and C.

    ii.   Name the counties in **each** case.   [20 marks]

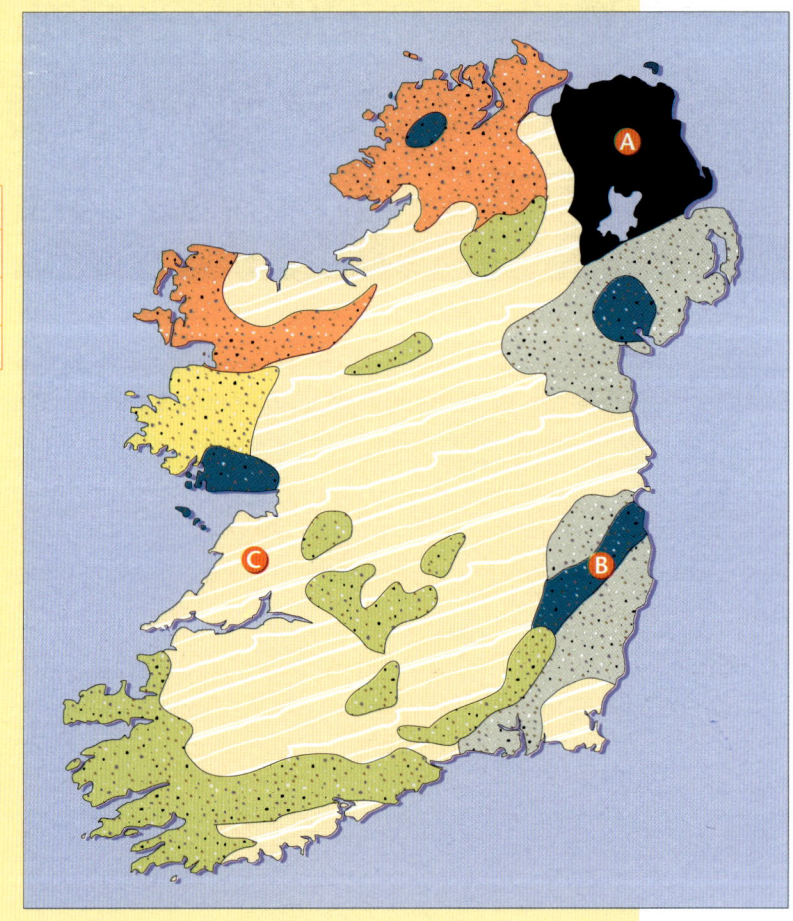

Physical Region	County
A:	
B:	
C:	

B. IRISH AND EUROPEAN REGIONS

With reference to one Irish language region and one European language region, explain the criteria that define these areas as distinctive cultural regions.

    [30 marks]

C. EUROPEAN OR NON-EUROPEAN REGIONS

With reference to one region you have studied, describe its regional extent and explain its growth over time.

    [30 marks]

CHAPTER 23
SOCIO-ECONOMIC REGIONS 1: CORES AND PERIPHERIES

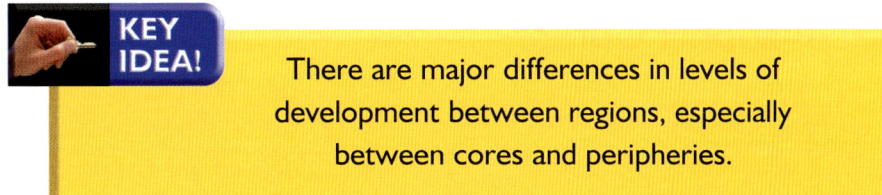

There are major differences in levels of development between regions, especially between cores and peripheries.

Economic development does not affect all areas in the same way. Some regions develop strongly because there is a good combination of factors, including what raw materials are available or being a strategic location for trade. In contrast, regions without enough resources, unfavourable environments and poor access to trade routes and market centres usually fail to develop prosperous communities.

It is important to note that less-developed regions can occur within countries that are prosperous. In this case, the status of these regions is relative to the more prosperous regions in that country. For example, the West of Ireland is less developed compared to the eastern region centred on Dublin.

The core-periphery model is a simple model that divides an area into two types:

- Core.
- Periphery.

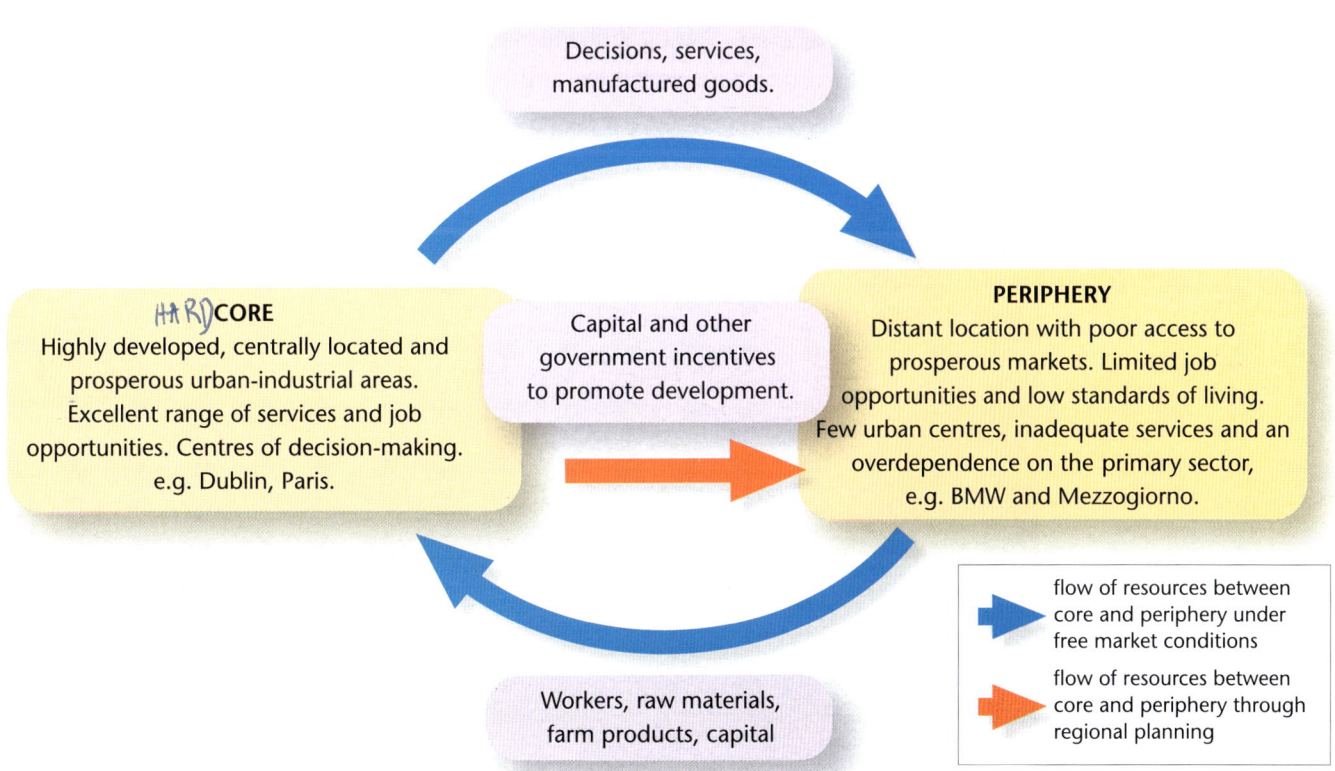

Fig. 23.1 The core-periphery model.

The difference between the core and periphery encourages resources to flow in a way that benefits the core, e.g. migration of young people. Some recent trends, however, have encouraged development in the periphery, but are linked directly to the flow of resources from the core: industrial investment, tourism and government incentives through regional planning. This is seen between the core region of northern Italy and the Mezzogiorno in southern Italy (see Chapter 27).

National Cores

All countries have a national core, which is the most important area for national development. Most national cores are centred on capital cities and have had a historic as well as a present-day role as core regions, for example London or Paris. Some important national cores, however, have evolved away from political capitals, such as the north-west region of Italy. Dublin is Ireland's national core.

The prosperity and growing economies of core regions create development in adjacent areas. This occurs through the overspill of jobs, people and investment via well-developed transport links, e.g. the expanding national cores of Paris (Chapter 28) and Dublin (Chapter 34).

An International Core in Western Europe

An international core has emerged in Western Europe as a number of national cores and growth regions have combined. They are usually located next to each other and are well connected through a variety of links. These links have become stronger throughout the last half of the twentieth century, as the European Union encouraged more international trade between its member states.

Fig. 23.2 shows the international core of the European Union, which has been given a variety of names, including 'European Dogleg' and the 'Hot Banana'. It also includes the four regions considered to be the 'motors' of the European Union. This is because of their powerful economies and their increasing role within the EU's single market.

Lyons on the River Rhône is one of four 'motors' of the European Union.

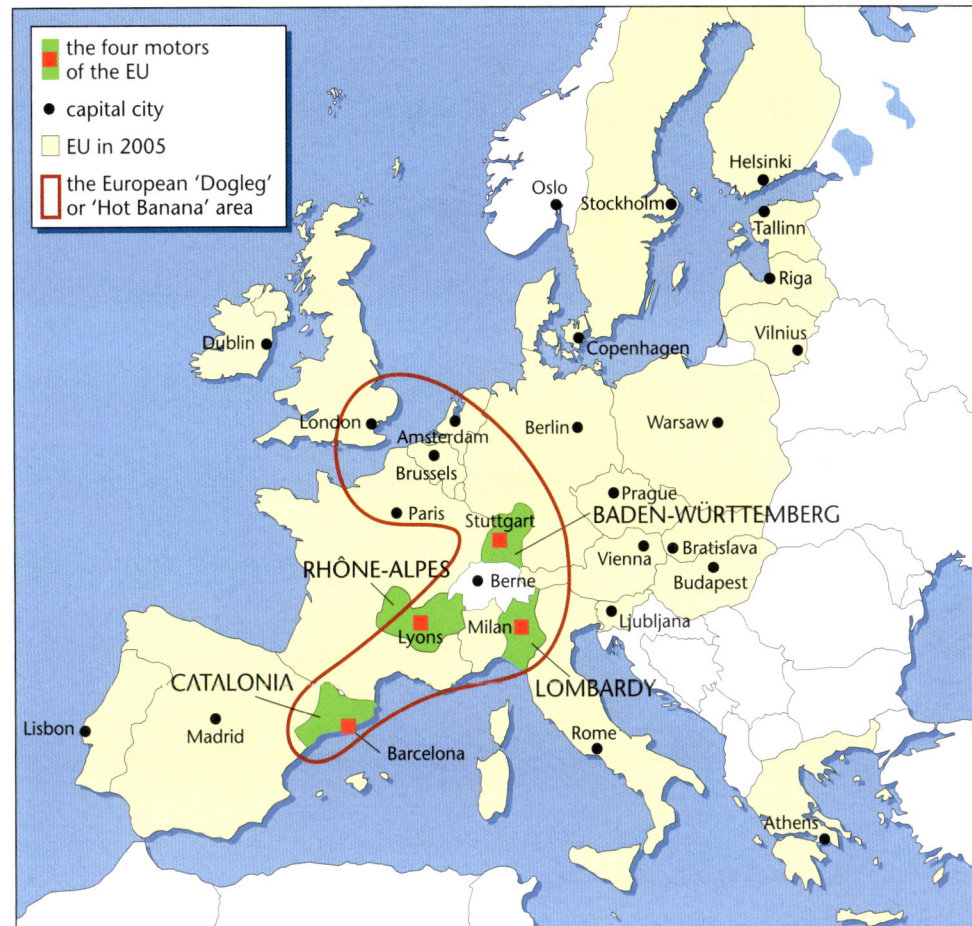

Fig. 23.2 The core region of the EU.

Why do you think the core of the EU has been given the name 'dogleg' or 'banana'?

Peripheral Regions

Although core areas have socio-economic problems such as congestion, high land values and inner city decline, regions with the greatest development problems are in peripheries. There are a variety of problem regions, but two types can be highlighted:

- Rural underdeveloped, e.g. the West of Ireland and the Mezzogiorno.
- Regions of industrial decline, e.g. the Sambre-Meuse Valley in Belgium.

Problem Regions in the European Union

Since 1988, the EU has had a well-defined Common Regional Policy. Under this policy, large and increasing amounts of money have been made available through **structural funds** to assist development of its many problem regions.

Most of the structural funds have been spent in the regions that experience the greatest problems, such as low income per person, high unemployment and poor transport links to core regions. Examples include Ireland, the Mezzogiorno and the countries from Central and Eastern Europe that joined the EU in 2004. Until 2007, these problem regions were called Objective 1 Regions (Fig 23.3).

A village in the Mezzogiorno.
- *What evidence suggests that this is part of Europe's periphery?*

157

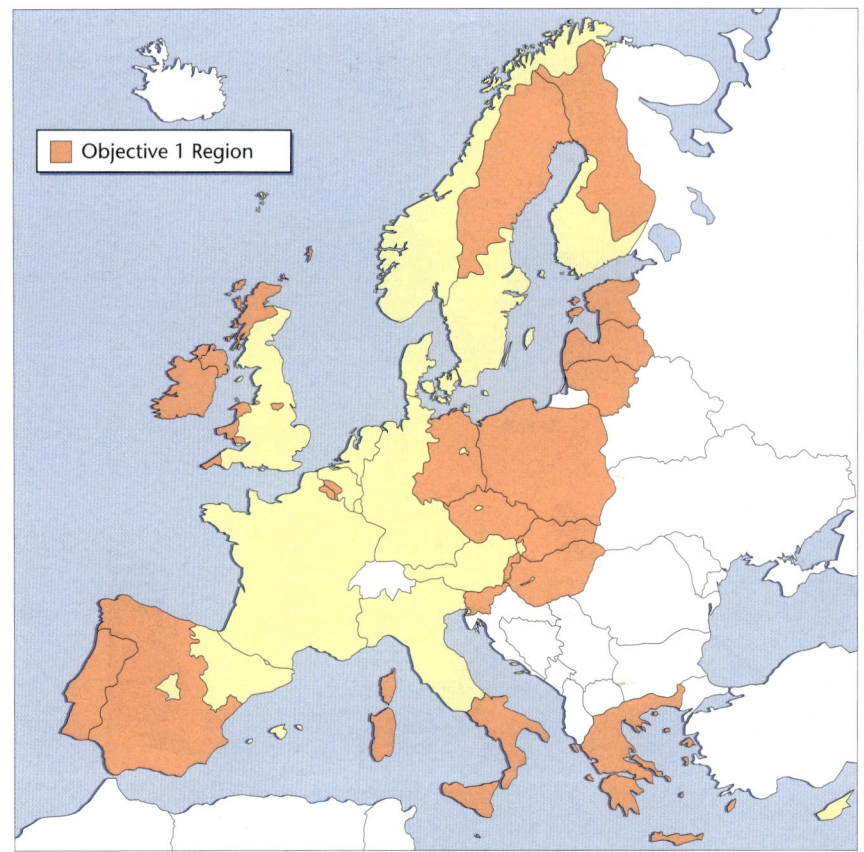

Fig. 23.3 Objective 1 Regions for the European Union, 2004–2006.

● *Do you think building new roads such as this in Spain is a good way to spend structural funds in Objective 1 Regions?*

Since 2007 the term 'Convergence Regions' has replaced Objective 1 Regions (see Fig 32.1 on page 237).

Up to 2007, structural funds were also available to help modernise the economies and environments of depressed and declining urban-industrial regions. These were called Objective 2 Regions and included declining coalfield economies such as the Sambre-Meuse area in Belgium (see Chapter 24).

● *Why is new international investment such as this modern chemical plant so important for depressed industrial regions such as Lorraine in north-eastern France?*

Ireland's Problem Region

Although the whole of Ireland was designated an Objective 1 Region in the EU, there were clear differences in levels of development between the east and the west of the country. This had been

● *Why is training or education so important for marginal groups?*

recognised as early as 1952 by the Irish government when it introduced the Undeveloped Areas Act. Under the Act, large areas of the West of Ireland received government funding to help promote this less developed 'half' of the country (see Fig 22.1 on page 147).

In 1999, the government adjusted this regional divide by creating two new regions. These are the Border, Midland and West (BMW) and the Southern and Eastern (S&E) regions (Fig 23.4). The BMW has major problems of rural underdevelopment and benefited least from the success of Ireland's 'Celtic Tiger' economy. As a result, this region continued to receive significant amounts of structural funding between 2000 and 2006. In contrast, the more prosperous Southern and Eastern Region was allocated a declining share of structural funds. By 2006, the S&E Region had lost its status as an Objective 1 Region.

Fig. 23.4 The BMW and S&E regions in Ireland.

● *Refer to Chapter 26 for a more detailed account of these two regions.*

*[handwritten:] Cyprus, (vis) check Bsju
Estonia, hungry, Latvia, Lithuania, Poland, Slovakia, Slovenia, [Ireland took 1973]*

159

CHAPTER 24
SOCIO-ECONOMIC REGIONS 2:
REGIONS OF INDUSTRIAL DECLINE

KEY IDEA!

Once-prosperous regions based on coal mining and heavy industries have declined and face major problems.

The Industrial Revolution started in Western Europe during the late eighteenth century. This led to a new regional pattern of industrial development, based around coalfields. These became the growth regions of the nineteenth and early twentieth centuries.

> For well over 100 years, coalfield areas were the growth regions of Western Europe.

Case Study: The Sambre-Meuse Coalfields

The Sambre-Meuse coalfields stretch about 150 km from the French border to Liège along the Sambre-Meuse Valley in Belgium (see Fig. 24.1). It was one of the first regions of continental Europe to experience large-scale industrialisation at the start of the nineteenth century. The region's development depended on reserves of coal, a location central to the major urban-industrial markets of north-west Europe and well-developed canal and railway networks.

The Sambre-Meuse coalfields are located in Wallonia. Rising levels of prosperity and jobs in coal mining and heavy industries, such as iron, steel, engineering and chemicals, attracted large numbers of migrants, especially from Flanders. This made Wallonia the dominant cultural and economic region in Belgium.

After the 1950s, the economy of the Sambre-Meuse coalfields declined. This was due to a number of factors:

- **Alternative sources of energy** to coal.
- **Costs of production** were high and the industries were less competitive in world trade.
- **Cheaper imports**, especially from less developed economies.
- **Alternative products** became available, for example plastics replaced metals.
- **New technologies** reduced the number of jobs available for people in these industries.
- **New plants** were built to replace older units, but these were often in different regional locations, such as coastal sites rather than inland coalfields, e.g. the modern steelworks at Zelzate.

Steelworks at Charleroi surrounded by old, working-class housing for its labour force. Note also the coal tips in the background linked to a large coal mining industry.

As the heavy industries declined, so did the regions that depended on them. There were huge job losses and high levels of unemployment, out-migration and economic depression in these once proud and prosperous communities. **Deindustrialisation** is the term used to describe a large-scale decline in the industrial base.

By 1984, the last colliery in the Sambre-Meuse coalfields had closed (Fig. 24.2). This left many mining communities with a high level of unemployment and a scarred landscape, which was not attractive to modern industries.

The decline of the heavy industrial base meant that the coalfields and Wallonia emerged as major problem regions. Out-migration increased from these economically depressed communities to more dynamic growth centres, such as Brussels, and Antwerp and Ghent in Flanders. Flemish-speaking Flanders replaced French-speaking Wallonia as the economic core of Belgium.

Government and EU support has been essential for promoting development in this declining industrial region. Most of the coalfields were designated as an Objective 2 Region in the EU.

Collieries such as this once had a dominant role in the landscape and economy of the Sambre-Meuse Valley.
● *What impact did their closure have for this region's economy and quality of environment?*

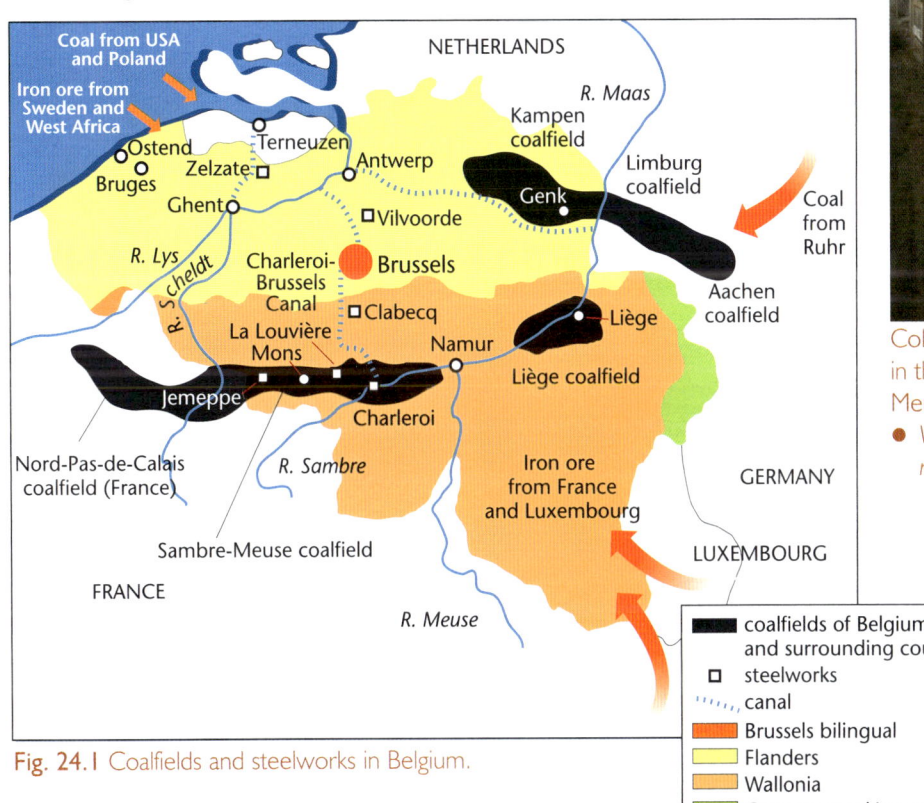

Fig. 24.1 Coalfields and steelworks in Belgium.

Which languages are spoken in Wallonia and Flanders? See Chapter 22.

Activity

Look at the map in Fig. 24.1 and answer the following.
1. In which Belgian region are the Sambre-Meuse coalfields?
2. Do you think rivers and canals have been an important factor influencing the location of Belgium's steelworks? Explain your answer.
3. How does the Belgian steel industry source its main raw material inputs even though the country now produces no coal or iron ore?
4. Is this a disadvantage for steelworks in the Sambre-Meuse area compared with Zelzate? Explain your answer.

Fig. 24.2 Whereas the coal industry of the Sambre-Meuse Valley ended in 1984, investment in the region's steel industry allowed for increased productivity.

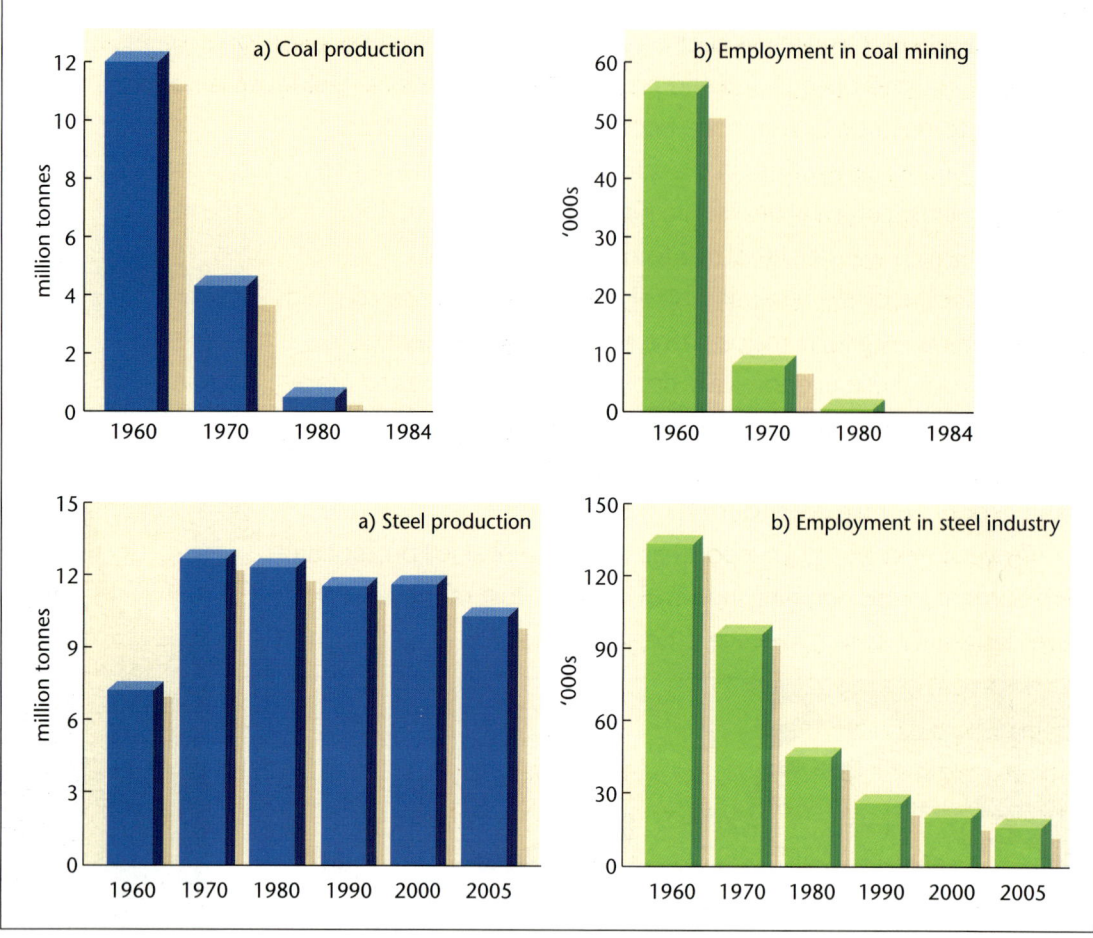

Activity

Look at Fig. 24.2 and study the caption to answer the following.

1. What is the trend for employment and production of coal from 1960 to 1984?
2. Why is the loss of jobs in mining an important problem for the Sambre-Meuse Valley?
3. Contrast the trends for steel production and employment from 1960 to 2005. Explain these different trends.

This Objective 2 Region has had a large amount of investment from the Belgian government and the EU to change its image and make it more attractive for private investment. Of special importance have been:

- Investment in transport infrastructure, especially new motorways that link the region to neighbouring growth regions, e.g. Paris, Ruhr, Randstad.
- New industrial estates located along the motorways and near larger urban centres such as Charleroi and La Louvière.
- Upgrading the airport at Charleroi, mainly for Ryanair, to improve international access.
- Cleaning up the derelict landscape to improve the image of the local environment and take away an impression of economic depression.

The results have been quite positive, and a large number of new industries, such as Caterpillar at Charleroi, have been attracted to the region. Despite this, the Sambre-Meuse area remains a problem region in Belgium and has a long way to go before it becomes as prosperous as it was in the early twentieth century.

Case Study: The Greater Cork Area

When Ireland joined the European Union in 1973, Cork was the country's dominant centre for large-scale, port-related industries. These included Ireland's only:

- Steelworks (Irish Steel).
- Shipyard (Verholme).
- Oil refinery (Irish Refining).
- Car assembly plant (Ford).

Cork also had a number of large chemical plants and a range of more traditional Irish industries, such as food processing, clothing and textiles.

These industries had been attracted to Cork by a combination of location factors linked to the city and its main physical asset: Cork Harbour (see Fig. 24.3).

Up to the 1980s, these industries provided the Greater Cork Area with good employment prospects. Cork was considered a **growth centre** for the national economy.

At the start of the 1980s, an international recession and growing competition in European and world markets caused major problems for Cork's industrial base. The local industrial plants were mostly small, relatively inefficient and high-cost producers by international standards. Decisions were taken to close or run down most of Cork's long-established industries.

> Before the 1980s, Cork had built its economy around a limited number of large but slow-growing or declining industries.

Cork Outer Harbour is an ideal location for a growing number of port-related industries, especially chemicals.

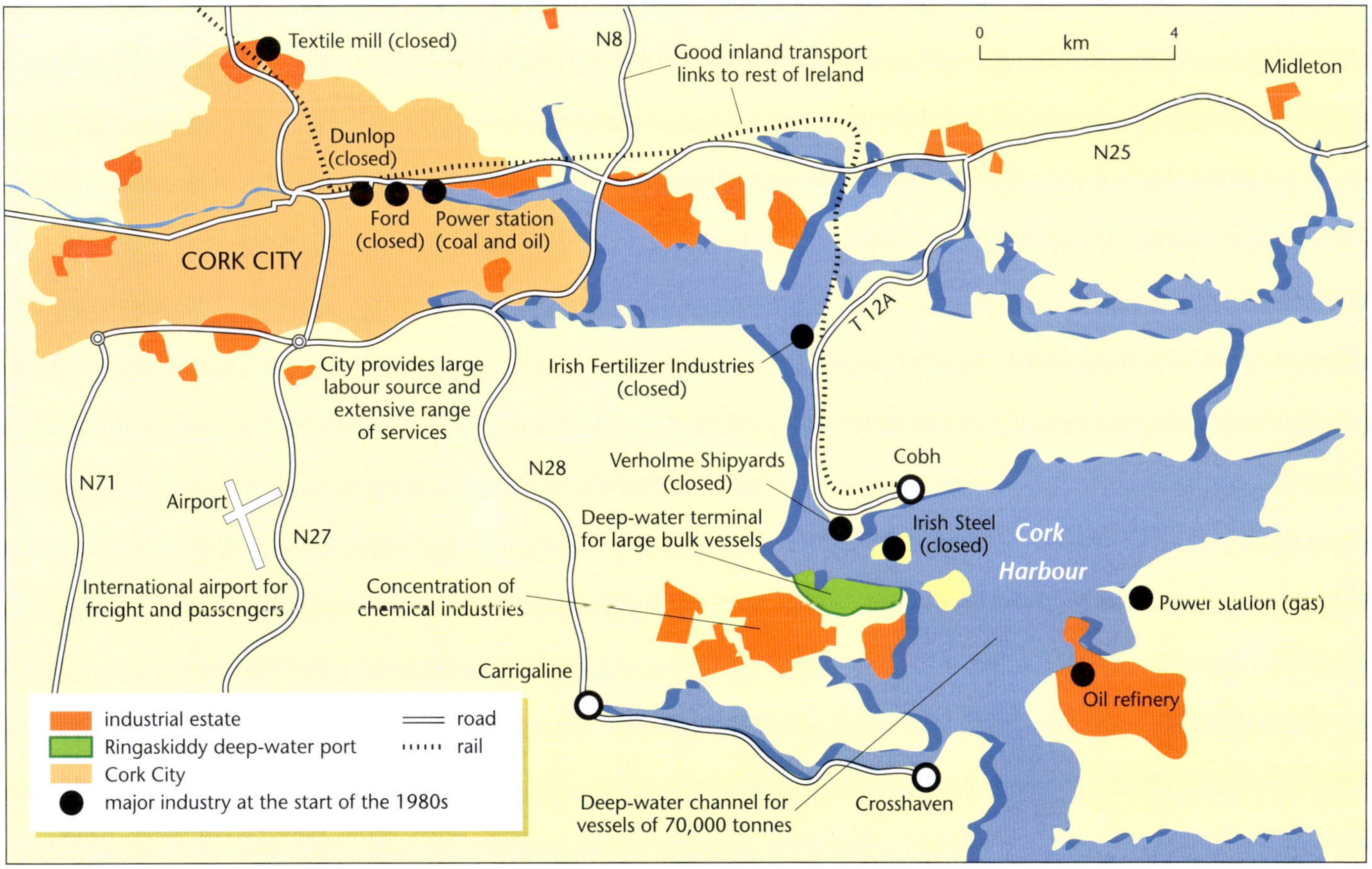

Fig. 24.3 Industrial development in the Greater Cork Area. Cork is the nearest port to continental Europe. This and access to shipping routes are important for import/export.

163

By 1985, the shipyards, Ford and Dunlop had been closed, with a loss of about 3,000 jobs. Cutbacks at other plants added another 2,500 job losses. Most of these jobs had been thought of as well paid and secure. Losing these jobs led to huge social problems for communities that had depended heavily on these industries. Cork had experienced **deindustrialisation,** becoming a region of industrial decline and a 'blackspot' for national unemployment.

> How many jobs in manufacturing did Cork lose from 1980 to 1985? Note that this was almost a third of the industrial base.

During the 1990s, Cork's industrial economy was revived, and a large number of new growth sectors were attracted to the city region.

- Chemical and pharmaceutical companies have located here, mainly around Cork's Outer Harbour and especially near the deep-water terminal at Ringaskiddy (see Fig. 24.3), e.g. Pfizer, Novartis. Cork is now regarded as the 'chemical capital of Ireland'.
- A growing number of electrical, IT (information technology) and health-related companies have set up in the 'necklace' of industrial estates that have been built around the edge of the city, e.g. Apple, Boston Scientific.

Government and regional planning have been vital in achieving this change of fortune for Cork. A large investment has been made in modernising the region's infrastructure, including education institutions, port facilities, airport, roads and urban renewal. This has changed the image and attractiveness of the region for growth industries.

At the start of the twenty-first century, Cork can no longer be described as a region of industrial decline. The change was not easy to achieve, but shows the importance of effective national and regional planning. In spite of this, the effects of a recent global recession have caused unemployment to rise from the low levels of 2000. It also shows the problem of depending too heavily on foreign investment.

The inner quays of Cork were the site of early industrial development in the city.
- *Do you think these areas remain attractive for manufacturing?*

Activity

Look at the chart in Fig. 24.4 and answer the following.
1. What were the years of lowest and highest unemployment?
2. Do the figures support the idea that unemployment became a major problem in the early 1980s?
3. Do trends for the late 1990s suggest that Cork benefited from a significant increase in new jobs?

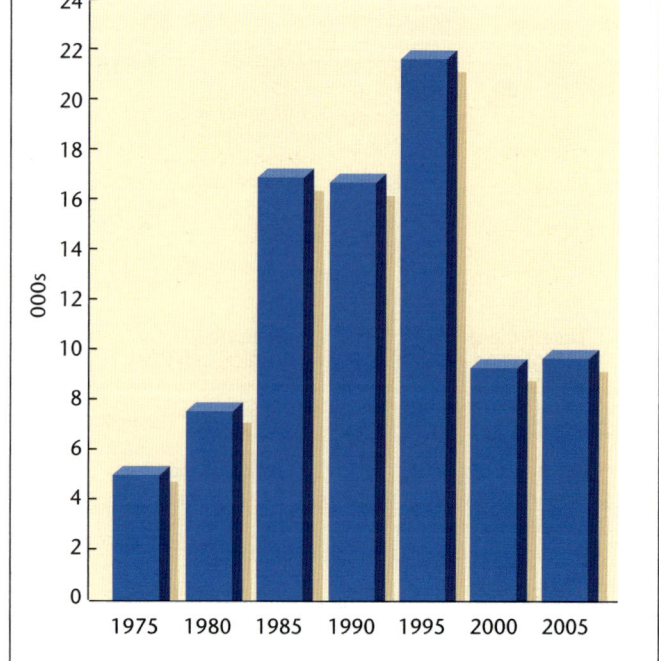

Fig. 24.4 Unemployment in the Greater Cork Area, 1975–2005.

CHAPTER 25

URBAN REGIONS

 **KEY IDEA!**

Urban regions (regions centred on urban areas) have become more important in modern development.

What Is an Urban Region?

An urban region is an area that surrounds a human settlement and is linked to it by interactions such as shopping, the journey to work and supplying farm produce. The area linked to the urban centre is called the **hinterland** of that centre. An urban region is also called a nodal or city region. It is important because:

* More and more of the world's population lives in towns and cities.
* The lives of people are increasingly organised by an urban-based environment.
* Urban areas can be seen clearly in the landscape. These built-up areas can be easily mapped.

European City Regions

By the start of the twenty-first century, about 80 per cent of the population of Western Europe was living in towns or cities.

The well-developed countries that border the North Sea have the highest levels of urbanisation. In Belgium, 95 per cent of the population lives in urban centres (Netherlands 89 per cent and Britain 87 per cent). Peripheral countries with underdeveloped economies usually have lower levels of urbanisation. In Portugal, for example, only 30 per cent of the population lives in towns and cities (Ireland 60 per cent).

Fig. 25.1 shows that there are three major zones of urban settlement in Western Europe:

* The **Manchester-Milan axis** is the most important area of concentrated urban development. It is based on the historic trading corridor of the **River Rhine** that links the North Sea lowlands and the Mediterranean.

Köln (Cologne) on the River Rhine has long been a major trade and religious centre.
* *What evidence in the photo supports this statement?*

Fig. 25.1 Major urban centres and axes where population is concentrated in the European Union.

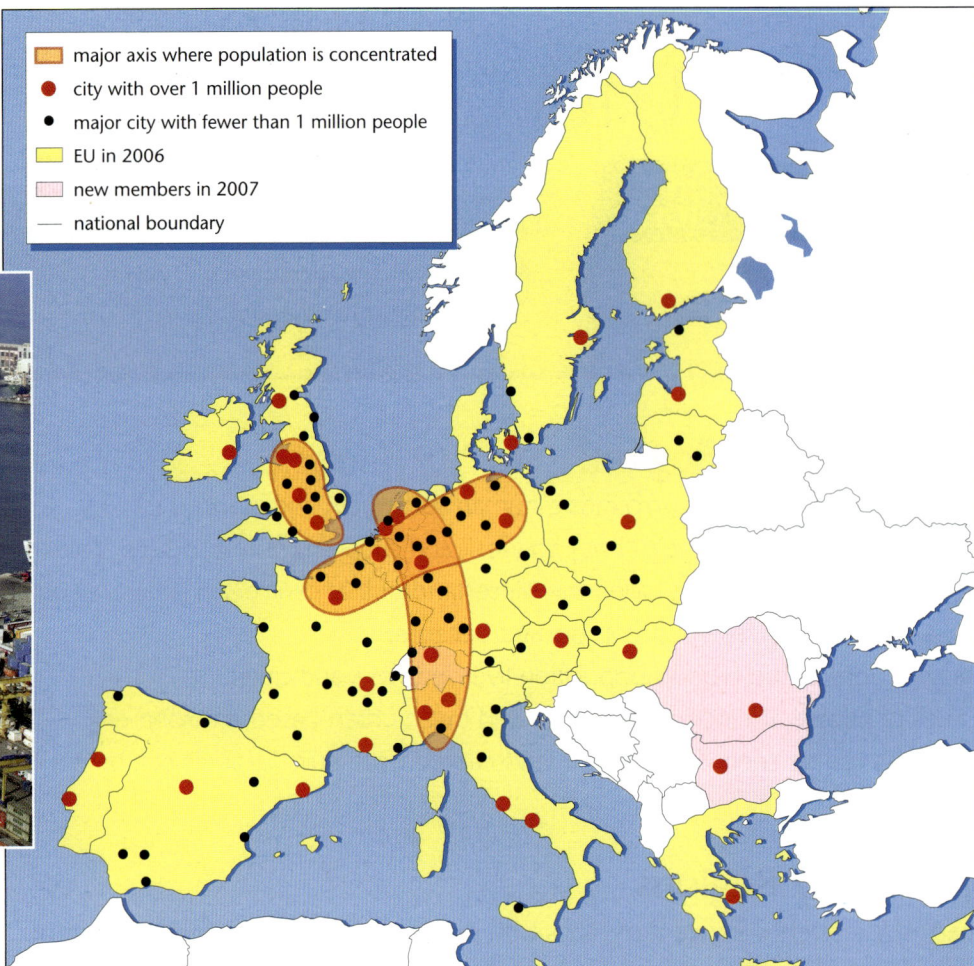

- major axis where population is concentrated
- • city with over 1 million people
- • major city with fewer than 1 million people
- EU in 2006
- new members in 2007
- — national boundary

Barcelona is one of the four 'motors' of the EU. Its prosperity is mainly due to its historic and present role as a major port.

- The **Paris-Berlin axis** links the capitals of France and Germany across the North European lowlands.
- The **coastline of Western Europe:** Many of Europe's largest cities are ports. This is linked to its long tradition of maritime (sea) trade and colonial empires of states such as France, Spain and Britain.

The **core** region for urban development in Europe occurs where the Manchester-Milan axis intersects with (crosses) the Paris-Berlin axis. Two **polycentred** urban regions have emerged here: Randstad Holland and the Rhine-Ruhr.

In Europe, it is more common for a single city to spread out to swallow up surrounding smaller settlements, as happened with London and Paris. These large areas of almost continuously built-up areas are called **conurbations**.

A polycentred urban region is made up of several closely located cities which interact strongly. No single city dominates.

Advantages for Urban Development in Europe's Core Region

- Centrality (central position).
- Access to major trade routes within Europe.
- Access to global markets through major ports and airports.
- Rich agricultural environment.
- Near coalfields and early industrialisation.

Ireland's Urban Regions

Ireland is one of the least urbanised societies in Western Europe. This reflects its past as a colony, its underdeveloped economy, peripheral location in Europe and its dependence on the primary sector. In 2002, 60 per cent of the country's population lived in urban centres.

Fig. 25.2 Cities and towns in Ireland by the size of population.

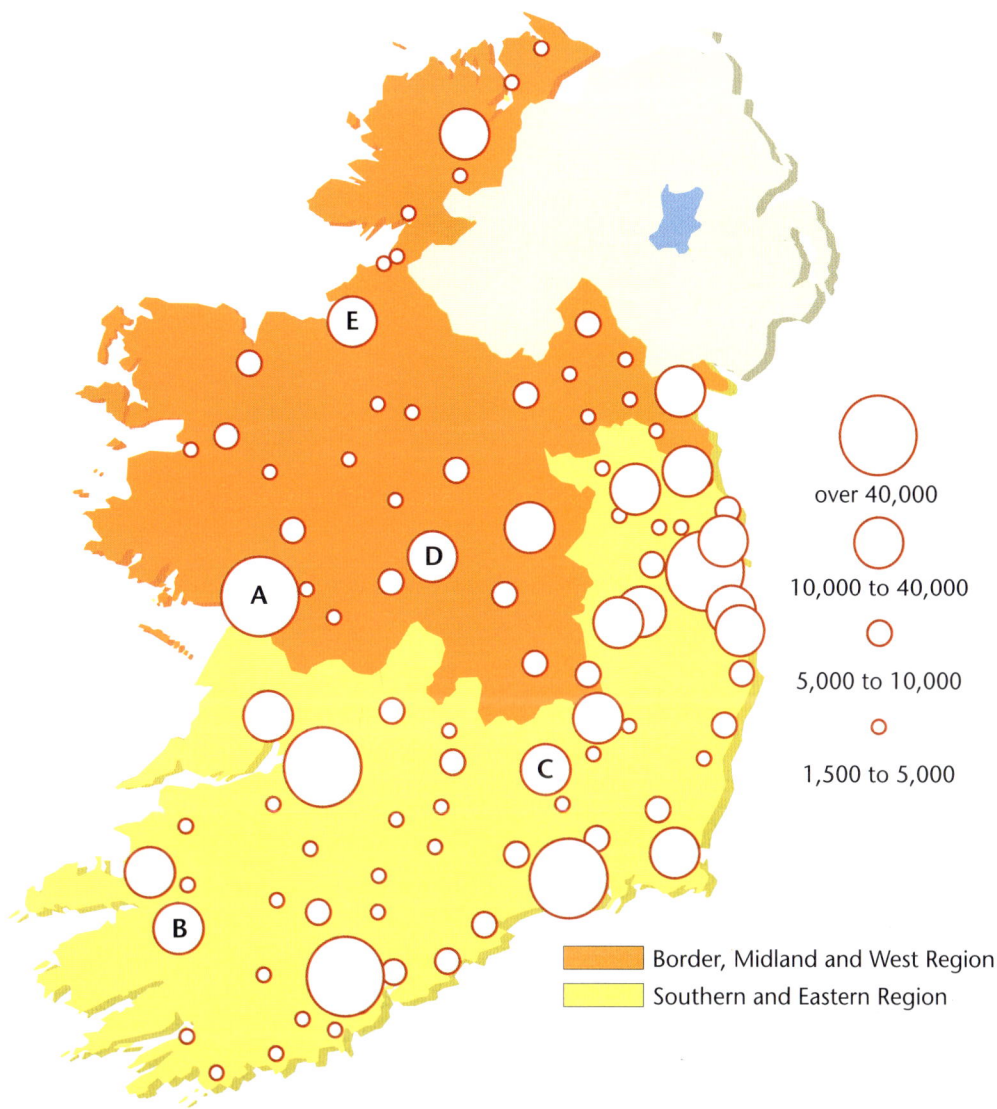

over 40,000

10,000 to 40,000

5,000 to 10,000

1,500 to 5,000

Border, Midland and West Region
Southern and Eastern Region

In Ireland, the eastern and southern parts of the country are the most urbanised. More market towns grew up on the richer agricultural land, while its ports were developed to trade with Britain. In contrast, the West of Ireland is in a more peripheral location and has difficult environmental conditions for productive farming. There are fewer towns and they are more dispersed across the region (see Fig. 25.2). In the Southern and Eastern (S&E) Region, almost 75 per cent of the population lives in urban areas (areas with a population larger than 1,500), while the Border, Midland and West (BMW) Region has only a third of its population in towns and cities.

Activity

Look at Fig. 25.2 and answer the following.
1. Name the towns marked A, B, C, D and E on the map.
2. Why are there so few towns in Connaught?
3. Why are the largest ports along the east and south coast?

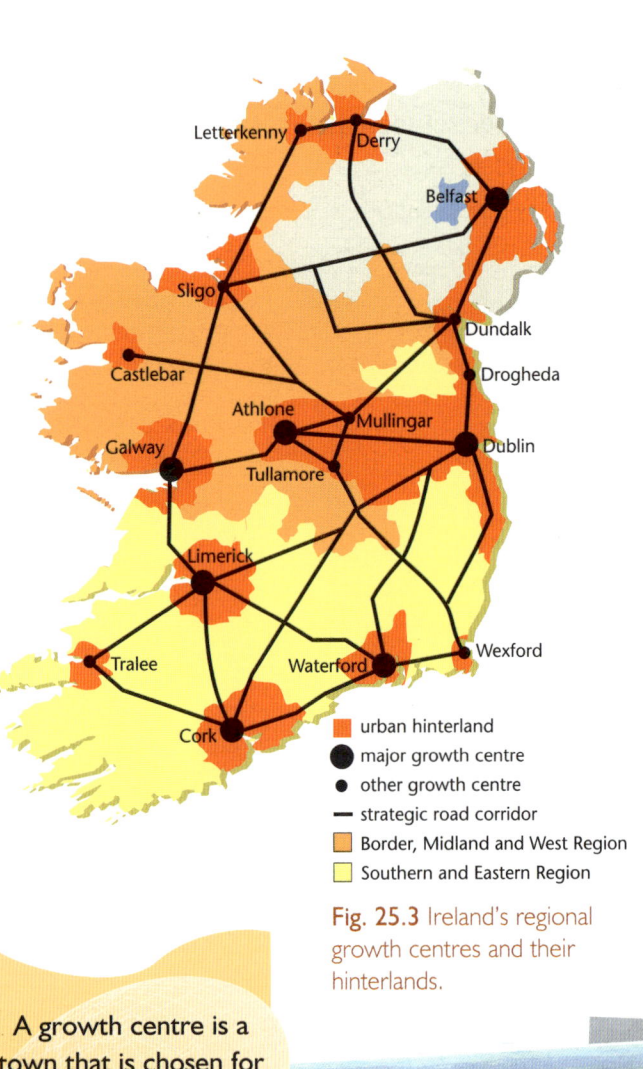

Fig. 25.3 shows the hinterlands of Irish cities and towns suggested by planners as growth centres for national development. It also highlights the large area influenced by Dublin. This stretches both north to south and east to west.

The north-south coastal corridor that links Dublin to Belfast is becoming an important area for economic development. To the west, Dublin's influence goes as far as Athlone. This leaves only a narrow strip of more rural space separating Dublin's hinterland from Galway, the main urban centre of the West of Ireland.

Apart from Dublin, you can see the important urban hinterlands of the other four main cities, which also have roles as regional centres. These cities supply a wide range of services and have improved transport links to their well-populated hinterlands.

The smaller an urban centre, the fewer services it offers and the smaller is its hinterland. Tralee, in Co. Kerry, and Castlebar, in Co. Mayo, are examples of reduced hinterland areas of smaller market towns in rural Ireland (Fig. 25.2).

■ urban hinterland
● major growth centre
• other growth centre
— strategic road corridor
■ Border, Midland and West Region
□ Southern and Eastern Region

Fig. 25.3 Ireland's regional growth centres and their hinterlands.

A growth centre is a town that is chosen for development, so that growth will spread out into its hinterland.

Explain the word 'hinterland'.

Apart from Dublin, what are Ireland's four other cities?

Kilkenny (left) and Clifden, Co. Galway (right) are examples of smaller urban centres that have developed in different physical environments.
● *Do these photographs suggest ways in which their locations influenced the scale and nature of their development?*

Case Study: Dublin

Ireland has one dominant city – Dublin. Since the foundation of the town by the Vikings in the ninth century, it has grown into a sprawling urban region. The population of the Greater Dublin Area is over 1.3 million, which is 35 per cent of Ireland's total population. It is therefore a primate city.

The growth and importance of Dublin is due to:

- **Site:** The original settlement occupies a low-lying site on either side of the River Liffey where it enters Dublin Bay. It is the lowest bridging point on the river and has a long tradition as a trade, administrative and military centre.

- **Situation:** The deep, sheltered waters of Dublin Bay allowed Dublin to become the most important harbour on the east coast. In addition, the valley of the River Liffey provides a natural route into the Central Lowlands (see Fig 26.1 on page 172). As a result, Dublin had easy connections to the rest of the country, while the short sea crossing to Britain enabled the city to dominate trade with Ireland's most important trading partner. These advantages are emphasised by the fact that Dublin is the focus of the country's road, rail and canal networks, and possesses the main airport and port facilities.

- **Capital:** Dublin is the capital city. Most of the national government and administration offices are located here, as well as the headquarters of many national and international companies.

- **Agriculture:** The hinterland of Dublin has some of the richest farmland in Ireland. Dublin became the main market for this region.

- **Industry:** The size of the market, efficient transport systems, labour force and a range of high-quality services, such as finance, education and legal, have attracted a large number of industries. This has been emphasised by the Celtic Tiger economy and the preference of high-tech growth industries to locate in this urban region. (See also Chapter 26, page 180.)

A primate city is one that contains a large proportion of a country's population. Other examples include Paris and London.

As the capital and primate city of Ireland, Dublin has expanded greatly from its original site on the River Liffey.

For further information on the expansion of the Dublin urban region, see Chapter 34, pages 245–9.

Chapter 28 provides a case study of the Paris urban region.

Multi-part Questions

1. **A.** SKETCH MAP

    Draw a sketch map to show the main physical characteristics of relief and drainage of a European region you have studied.

    [20 marks]

    B. MANUFACTURING

    Examine the development of manufacturing in one Irish region. [30 marks]

    C. CULTURAL DIVISION

    Examine two factors which have influenced the development of distinct cultural divisions within a European region.

    [30 marks]

2. **A.** EUROPEAN REGION

    'A region may be identified by one or more characteristics.' Draw a sketch map of a European region that you have studied to illustrate/explain this statement.

    [20 marks]

    B. SOCIO-ECONOMIC EUROPEAN REGION

    Describe one socio-economic region in Europe that has suffered economic difficulties over time. In your answer, refer to:

    i.   the causes of these difficulties
    ii. attempts to solve these difficulties. [30 marks]

    C. IRISH REGION

    Account for the distribution and growth of Ireland's urban regions. [30 marks]

3. **A.** EUROPEAN REGIONS

    Examine this map of Europe. In your answer book, associate each of these descriptions with the letters A, B, C, D:

    - an administrative region
    - a region defined by language
    - an economic core region
    - a geomorphological region.

    [20 marks]

    B. INDUSTRIAL DECLINE

    Explain, with reference to an example you have studied, the decline of one socio-economic core region in Europe.

    [30 marks]

    C. IRISH REGION

    Explain the factors that have led to the growth of Dublin's city region.

    [30 marks]

CHAPTER 26
REGIONAL CONTRASTS IN IRELAND

KEY IDEA!

The way human and physical processes interact gives rise to major contrasts between the east and west of Ireland.

Ireland is a relatively small island economy off the west coast of continental Europe. It forms part of the European Union's underdeveloped Atlantic periphery. Traditionally, there have been strong differences between the more prosperous eastern part of Ireland and the more marginalised western regions.

These differences are reviewed by contrasting the Border, Midland and West (BMW) Region and the Southern and Eastern (S&E) Region.

PHYSICAL PROCESSES

The relief, climate, soils and drainage of Ireland have a strong impact on the country's economic development and patterns of human activities, such as urban settlement. If you look at the **relief**, it is something like a saucer shape: a broad central lowland area surrounded by a broken rim of higher land (see Fig. 26.1).

The **climate** is influenced mainly by its island location and onshore south-westerly winds, which bring mild temperatures all year round and annual precipitation (rainfall) that is well distributed around the country. While these patterns are general to Ireland, there are important differences between the west and east of the country (see Table 26.1 on page 173).

Glacially eroded mountains in Connemara.
- *Do such areas provide a good basis for prosperous farming?*

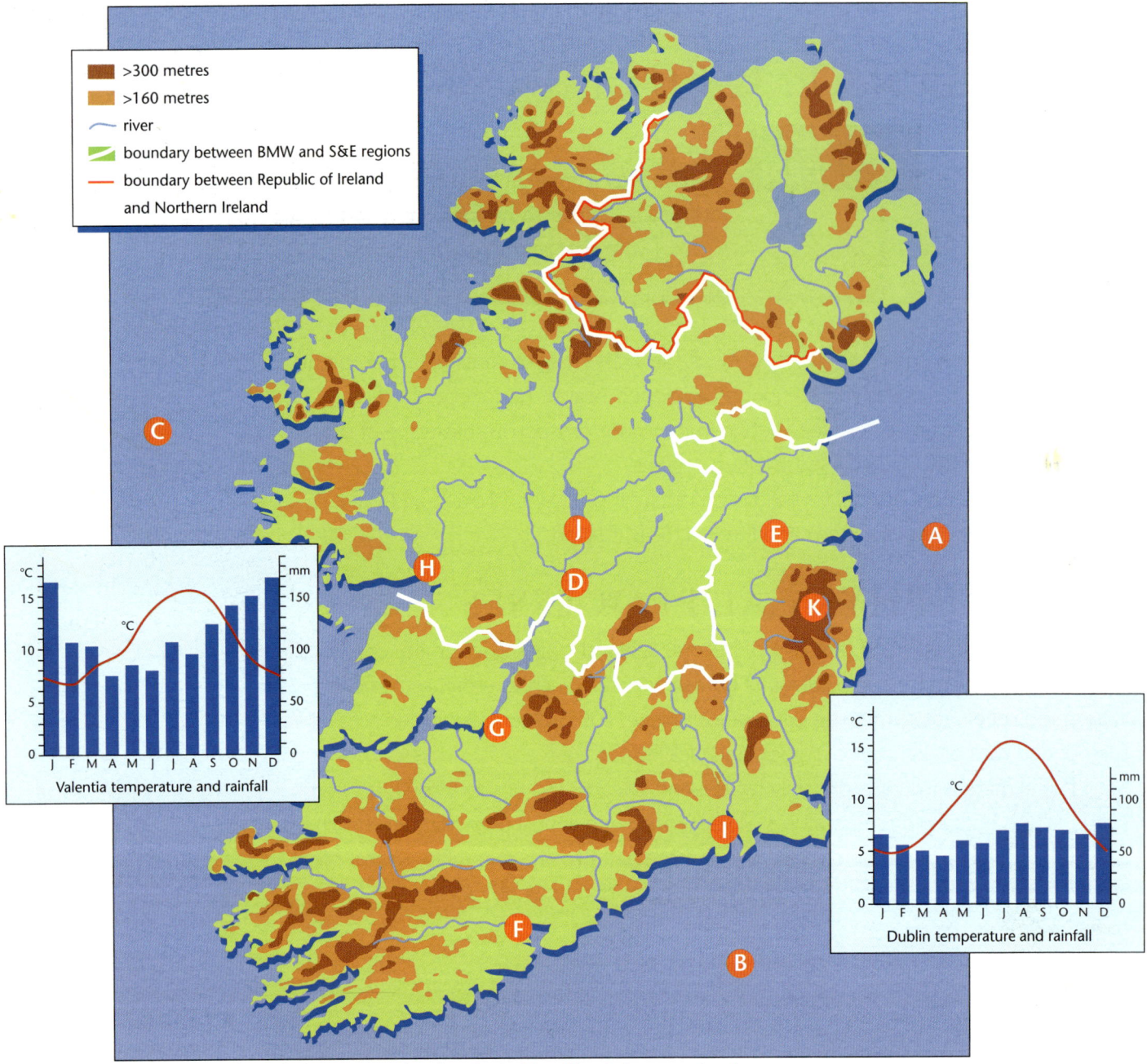

Fig. 26.1 Relief and drainage map, showing the height of land above sea level.

Activity

Look at the map in Fig. 26.1 and answer the following.

1. Name the:
   a. sea areas A, B and C
   b. rivers D and E
   c. towns F, G, H, I and J
   d. upland area K.
2. Why is 'saucer shape' a useful way to describe Ireland's physical relief?
3. Why is drainage so poor in the Central Lowlands?
4. Does Dublin have a greater temperature range than Valentia? Explain your answer.
5. Explain why Valentia has higher levels of rainfall than Dublin.

Relief, Climate, Soil and Drainage

Border, Midland and West Region	Southern and Eastern Region
Relief Much of the region has bleak, rugged upland areas, especially along the western seaboard where glacially eroded mountain ranges rise higher than 300 m. Inland areas form the western part of the undulating Central Lowlands (50–150 m). In general, the region has a submerged coastline that gives rise to a deeply indented coastal zone.	**Relief** The Central Lowlands generally have a larger area of low-lying and undulating landscapes. There is a mountainous area in the Leinster chain, centred on the Wicklow Mountains. The coastline tends to be less indented (jagged) and is more low-lying than the west coast.
Climate The climate is relatively mild, but very wet and windy. This is directly linked to the prevailing south-westerly winds and frontal depressions, which are forced to rise over the mountainous western coastline. Precipitation levels can be higher than 1,500 mm, with more than 250 days of rain in the year. The North Atlantic Drift has a moderating influence that keeps winter temperatures mild, while average summer temperatures do not rise much above 15°C.	**Climate** The lower relief and the rainshadow effect of the western mountains (when rain-bearing winds blow towards mountains and less rain falls on the other side of the mountains away from the wind) result in much lower levels of precipitation (less than 1,000 mm). Rainfall is also more evenly distributed through the year than in the West, where most rain falls in winter. The south-westerly winds have less of an effect. Winter temperatures are slightly colder, while summer temperatures and average amounts of sunshine per day are higher.
Soils The upland relief and high year-round precipitation give rise to large areas of peaty and waterlogged soils. These have low fertility, with blanket bog in many areas.	**Soils** Most of the region has brown soils, derived mostly from the limestone glacial drift that covers the Central Lowlands. These include some of the most fertile soils in the country.
Drainage Large areas of the West of Ireland have poor drainage. There are many lakes and poorly drained river floodplains, leading, for example, to flooding along the Shannon River. Apart from the Shannon, few major rivers reach the west coast.	**Drainage** This is a well-drained region with a number of large rivers that flow through the region into the Irish and Celtic Seas. These provide natural routeways and, at their mouths, important urban centres and ports have developed, e.g. Dublin, Waterford and Cork.

Table 26.1

ECONOMIC PROCESSES

The Industrial Revolution had little impact on Ireland, and its economy depended on the primary sector for much longer than most countries in Western Europe. During the 1960s, the country began its own industrial revolution based mainly on attracting a lot of foreign industries. This was a key factor in the take-off of the Celtic Tiger economy in the 1990s. Employment in services has also grown rapidly (see Fig. 26.2), although the level of development varies between the west and east of Ireland.

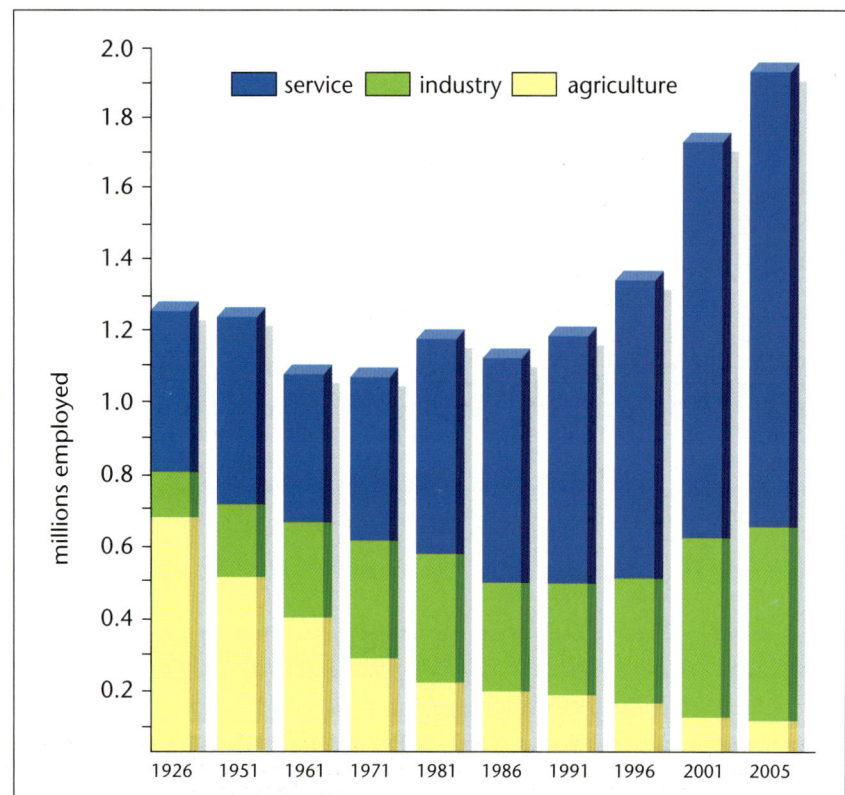

Fig. **26.2** Ireland's employment structure, 1926–2005.

Activity
Look at Fig. 26.2 and answer the following.
1. What was the most important sector in 1926?
2. What has been the trend for this sector since 1926?
3. Which sector was most important for employment in 2002?
4. Why has this sector grown so strongly since the 1960s?

The Primary Sector
Agriculture

Although agriculture is very important for Ireland, the trends and types of farming vary within the country. The way land is used highlights how physical factors can shape the agricultural geography of Ireland (see Fig. 26.3).

Traditional farming in the West of Ireland provides only low income to most farmers. This contrasts with intensive farming in eastern Ireland.
● *Do the photographs support this contrast?*

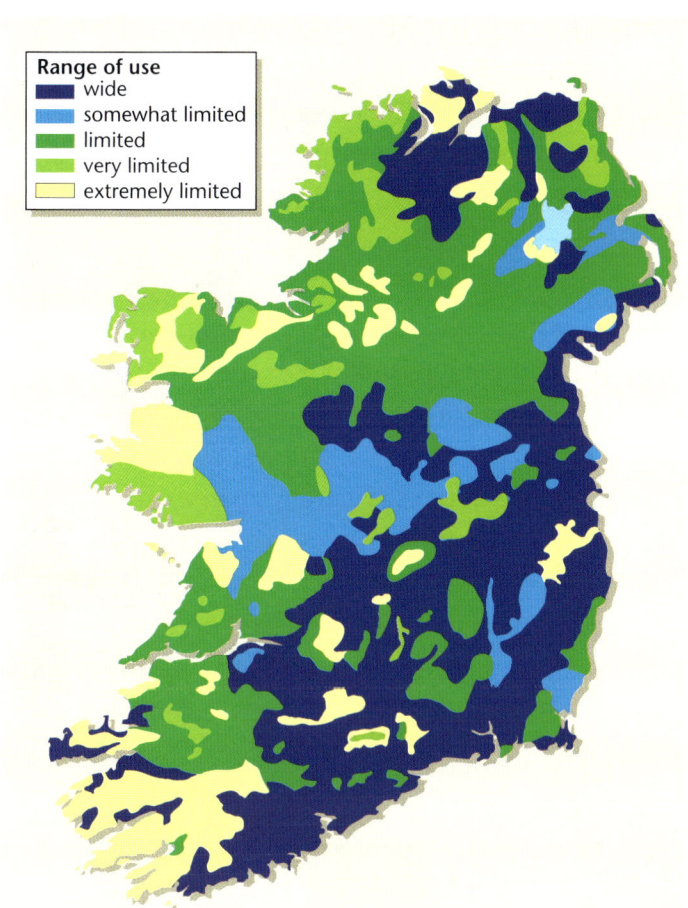

Range of use
- wide
- somewhat limited
- limited
- very limited
- extremely limited

Fig. 26.3 Land use capability in Ireland.
● *Which regions in general can support the widest choice and most productive farming?*

Activity

Look at Table 26.2 and Fig. 26.3 and answer the following.
1. What causes income levels to be so low in the West of Ireland?
2. Why is average income so high in eastern Ireland?
3. Why is the West of Ireland not suitable for arable farming?

What is the difference between intensive and extensive farming?

Agriculture in Western and Eastern Ireland	
Border, Midland and West Region	**Southern and Eastern Region**
● Difficult environmental conditions limit how productive the land can be for agriculture (see Fig. 26.3). Despite this, 63 per cent of Irish farms are located in the BMW Region.	● A favourable natural environment encourages a wide range of productive agriculture.
● The average farm size is small, levels of mechanisation are low and a high proportion of farmers are older.	● Although the region is more urbanised, farming remains an important economic activity.
● Tillage is not suitable for most of the region. Grazing is dominant, with beef cattle and sheep rearing.	● To be competitive, farms are more mechanised, larger and have a higher percentage of younger, more innovative farmers.
● Farming is widespread, but income levels are low. Poor prospects in the sector add to problems of rural depopulation and underdevelopment.	● Highly productive arable and pastoral activities occur throughout the region. Sheep and cattle reared in the West are often fattened on these lowland pastures.
● Average farm income is only 50 per cent of that of the eastern region, and only 14 per cent of farms can be considered viable, full-time units.	● Farming is intensive and specialised, giving better income levels and prospects for rural communities.
	● Average farm income is 40 per cent above the national level.

Table 26.2

175

Forestry

About 50 per cent of Ireland's land can be classified as marginal for agriculture. Environmental conditions are, however, more suitable for forestry. A long growing season, well-distributed rainfall and mild temperatures give an average growth rate of trees estimated at three to five times as high as in continental Europe.

Despite this favourable environment, only 10 per cent of the country is forested. The reasons for this are:

- Irish farms are generally small.
- In the past, farmers have not been keen to give up land for trees.
- Forestry involves high costs at first and requires a long-term view while trees are growing.

Since the 1980s, both state and private interests in forestry have increased. This has been aided by the EU, which sees forestry as a profitable, alternative enterprise for farmers, especially in more marginal agricultural areas. The environmental benefits of forestry (including drainage control, wildlife habitat and scenic qualities) have also been highlighted to help promote a stronger 'tree culture' within Ireland. State policy is to have 15 per cent of land under forestry, with most of the extra areas planted to be in the western regions.

New forested area in Connemara.
- *What benefits will new forest areas like this have? (Think about tourism, raw materials, jobs and environmental protection.)*

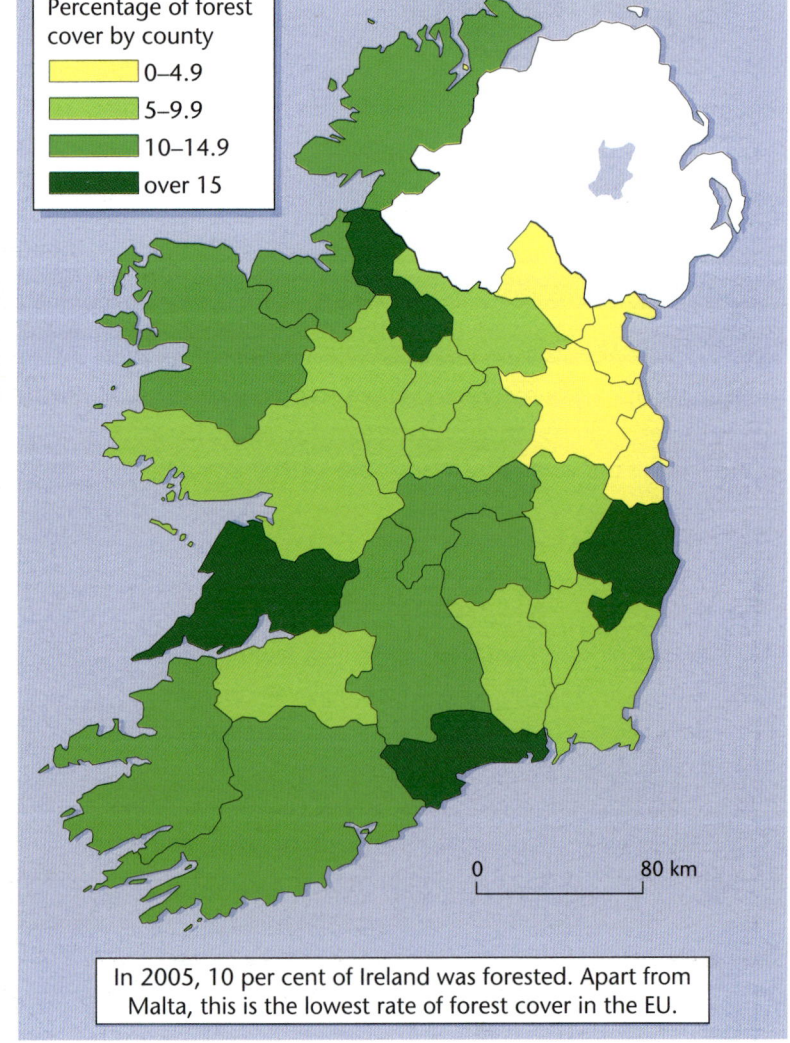

Percentage of forest cover by county

- 0–4.9
- 5–9.9
- 10–14.9
- over 15

0   80 km

In 2005, 10 per cent of Ireland was forested. Apart from Malta, this is the lowest rate of forest cover in the EU.

Fig. 26.4 Forest cover distribution in Ireland by county, 2005.
- *Why do you think forestry is a more important land use in the West of Ireland?*

Fishing

Although the continental shelf around Ireland is an extremely rich fishing area, the country's fishing industry is underdeveloped.

The importance of fishing as an industry that creates jobs and wealth for regional development has, however, increased recently with the growing market demand for fish products. Unfortunately, problems of overfishing and restrictions under the EU Common Fisheries Policy have reduced the opportunities for large-scale development of this industry in Ireland.

Despite problems of overfishing and EU fishing quotas, the quantity of fish landed at Irish ports has increased. There is also more aquaculture (fish and seafood farming) around Ireland's coastline, bringing more jobs and income from the fishing industry.

Do you remember how Ireland's continental shelf formed? These relatively shallow waters are a major fishing zone.

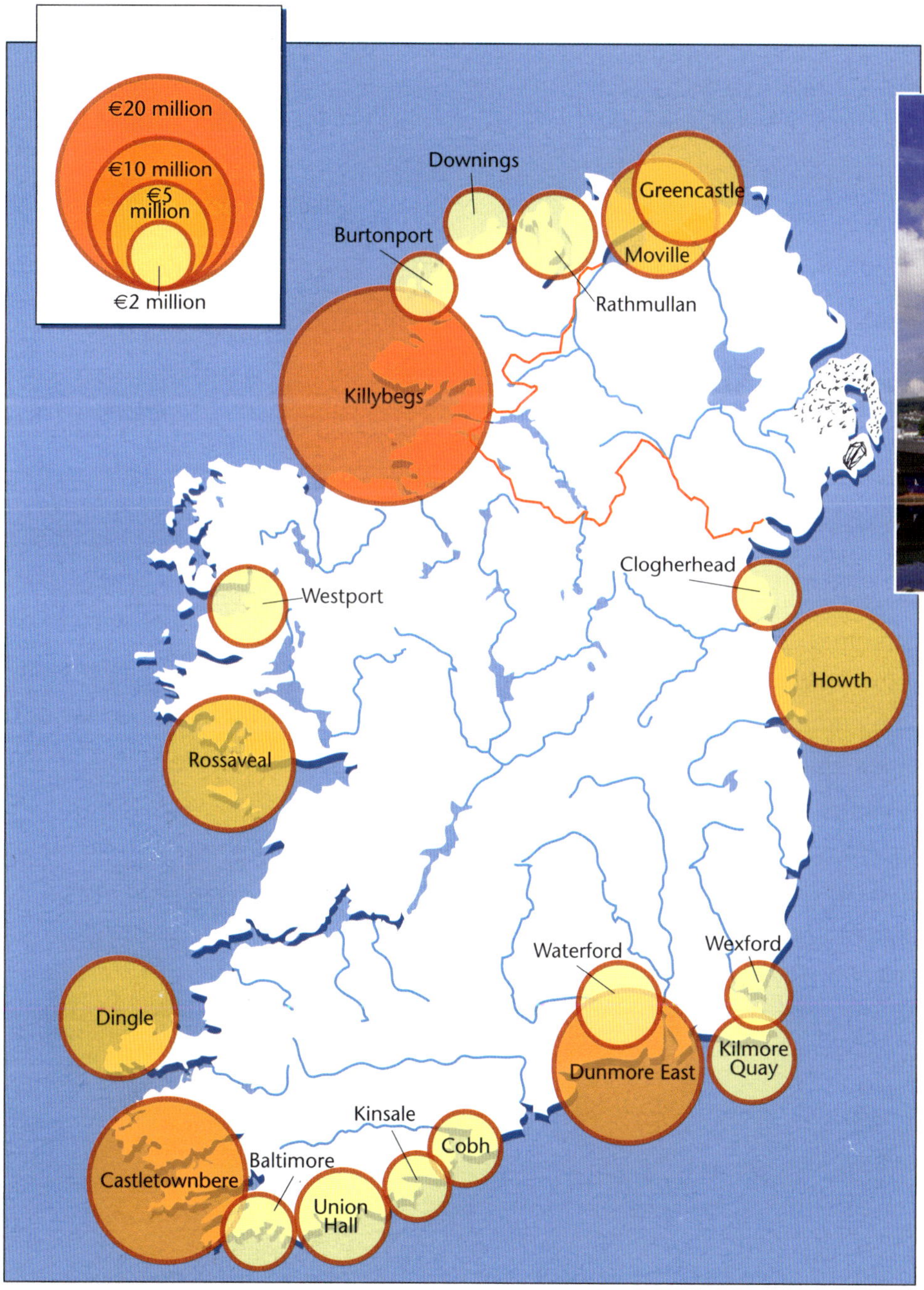

€20 million
€10 million
€5 million
€2 million

Downings
Burtonport
Greencastle
Moville
Rathmullan
Killybegs
Clogherhead
Westport
Howth
Rossaveal
Dingle
Waterford
Wexford
Kinsale
Cobh
Kilmore Quay
Dunmore East
Castletownbere
Baltimore
Union Hall

Modern fishing vessels in Killybegs, Ireland's largest port.

Activity

Look at Fig. 26.5 and answer the following.

1. Which is Ireland's most important fishing port?
2. How many of the top twenty fishing ports are on the west and south-west coast?
3. Why is the fishing industry concentrated along the western rather than the eastern coast of Ireland? (See Table 26.3.)

Fig. 26.5 The value of fish landings at Ireland's top twenty fishing ports in 2005.

Fishing in the Border, Midland and West and Southern and Eastern Regions	
Border, Midland and West Region	**Southern and Eastern Region**
• The deeply indented coastline provides sheltered harbours and faces onto the large fishing grounds of the North Atlantic. • Most of Ireland's fishing ports and fish processing plants are along the western seaboard. • 80 per cent by value of fish caught is landed at western ports. Killybegs is Ireland's largest fishing port by far, followed by Castletownbere. • Aquaculture is a growth industry. The deeply indented, sheltered and pollution-free waters along the western seaboard are an ideal environment for this industry, for example south-west Ireland and the Connemara coastline. • The lakes and rivers of western Ireland provide a good basis for inland fishing and add to the tourist potential of the region.	• Boats from ports on the Irish Sea have to travel further to access deep-water fishing grounds. • Smaller number of fishing ports as the industry concentrates on larger, specialised ports in the West. • Dunmore East and Howth are the two major fishing ports along the eastern seaboard. • The more polluted waters, especially along the coastline of the Irish Sea, limit opportunities for large-scale aquaculture. • Greater urbanisation and pollution along major rivers have had a negative impact on inland fishing. The clean-up of inland waters is helping to improve the tourism potential of these resources.

Table 26.3

Why are eastern waters more polluted than western coastal waters?

The Secondary Sector

Ireland's colonial history, peripheral location on the edge of Europe, lack of raw materials (such as iron ore) and a small population meant that the country was a late starter in the process of industrialisation. Most of the country's limited industry was located in major urban centres, such as Cork and Dublin, due to their large populations, infrastructure and access to ports for trade. **By 1961** over half of Ireland's manufacturing was in the east region, centred on Dublin.

During the 1960s, Ireland began its modern industrial revolution with a large increase in the number and range of manufacturing activities (see Fig. 26.6). The factors that account for the country's successful programme of industrialisation are:

- Membership of the EU (1973).
- Improved transport and communication systems.
- Larger and developing urban areas to provide a better range of essential services, such as banking, education and marketing.
- A growing and well-educated labour force.
- Government policy to attract, in particular, foreign companies to locate in Ireland, e.g low corporation tax.

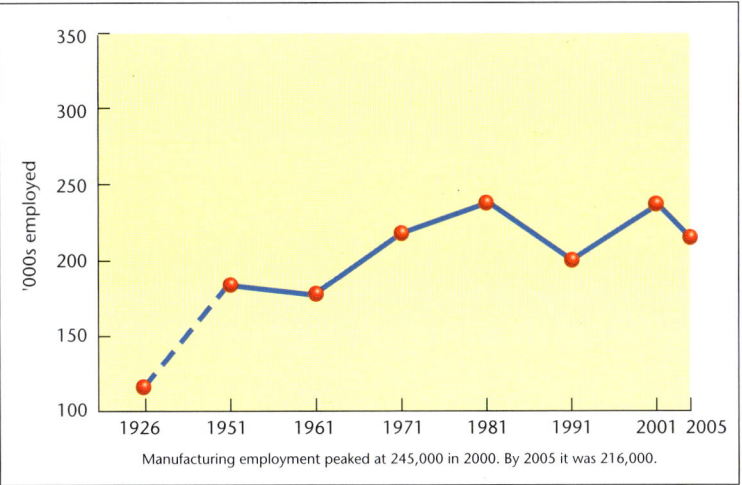

Fig. 26.6 Employment trends in Ireland's manufacturing industries, 1926–2005.

In the 1960s and 1970s there was rapid growth in manufacturing employment. Branch plants of foreign multinationals were attracted to rural areas in particular where the costs of land and labour were lower than in the more developed urban areas. Government policy also encouraged a dispersal of industry from the Dublin region to the underdeveloped western periphery. This resulted in significant gains for the BMW Region (see Fig 26.7).

Activity
Look at Fig. 26.6 and answer the following.
1. Estimate the total employment in manufacturing in Ireland in 1926. Compare this with 2005.
2. Was there growth in manufacturing employment throughout the period from 1926 to 2005?
3. Do the trends since 1991 justify Ireland being called the Celtic Tiger economy?

One of the first major foreign chemical companies attracted to Ireland was Pfizer. The US multinational established a large manufacturing plant in Cork Harbour in 1969.

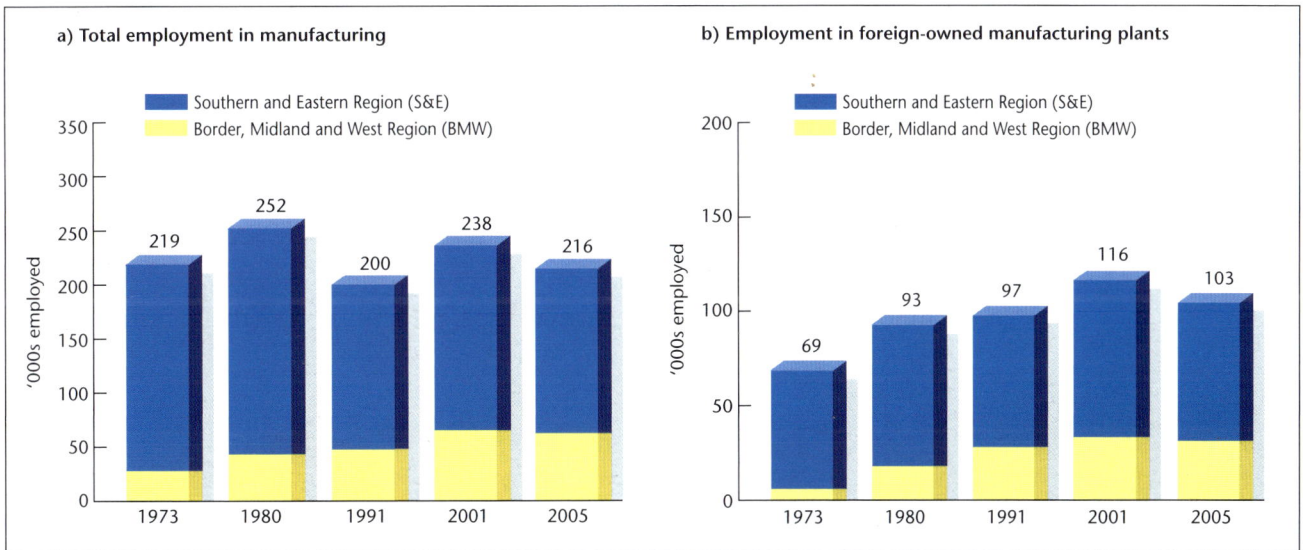

Fig. 26.7 Regional trends in manufacturing employment, 1973–2005.

Activity
Look at Fig. 26.7 and answer the following.
1. Which of the two regions is most important for manufacturing?
2. Have jobs in foreign industries increased?
3. What differences do you note between the two regions between 1980 and 1991?
4. Why did the S&E Region gain many more jobs than the BMW Region in the 1990s?
5. Can you suggest why employment in manufacturing has declined since 2001?

A branch plant is a factory set up by foreign multinationals to produce large quantities of a basic product.

Closure in 1984 of the Dunlop tyre factory in Cork led to the loss of almost 1,000 jobs. Derelict industrial sites, lost jobs and high unemployment were common features of Ireland's major cities in the 1980s.

During the 1980s, an international recession affected Ireland. Older and more traditional Irish industries, such as textiles and clothing, experienced heavy job losses. These industries were mainly located in the larger urban centres of the S&E Region. This, together with the relative failure to attract growth industries, meant that unemployment became a major problem for urban regions such as Dublin and Cork (see page 164). The BMW Region continued to grow, but at a much slower rate, as some branch plants were closed or reduced their workforce (Fig. 26.7).

From the early 1990s, employment growth has been impressive as many high-tech industries (especially electronics and pharmaceuticals) located and/or expanded production in Ireland. These include Dell, Intel, Boston Scientific and Wyeth. This is a vital factor for the Celtic Tiger economy, which changed Ireland from a peripheral and underdeveloped country to one of the most prosperous economies in the EU.

High-tech industries are strongly attracted to large urban centres. Good communications, access to universities and educated workers, international transport links and high-quality recreational facilities are key locational factors. The S&E Region, therefore, gained most from the Celtic Tiger economy. For the BMW Region to become more attractive for modern growth industries, access to EU structural funds and continued government support are vital to improve this region's infrastructure and urban services.

One problem common to both the BMW and S&E regions is the **high level of dependency on foreign companies.** Almost 50 per cent of Ireland's manufacturing employment is controlled by foreign companies. This leaves the country open to potential problems. For example, if there is a global or US recession, the headquarters of the foreign company may decide to close or run down the Irish plant. In addition, costs of production in Ireland have significantly increased, and some companies have **relocated** their production to cheaper countries, such as India and Poland. The result has been a **decline in employment in manufacturing** from the peak year of 2001 (Fig. 26.6).

In the 1990s, 60 per cent of Ireland's net growth in manufacturing was in the Dublin region.

Intel factory.
● Why do you think companies like this prefer to locate in the S&E Region rather than the BMW?

The Tertiary Sector

The tertiary sector is made up of activities that provide services rather than producing goods. Since the Second World War (1939–45), the service sector has become more important and now forms the main economic activity in all developed economies.

Growth in Ireland's service sector has been slower than in most other developed economies. This was linked to the country's underdeveloped economy and having many people with low income levels, which reduced the demand for services. Since the 1960s, however, Ireland's successful economic take-off and the higher living standards of a growing population have encouraged rapid growth in services. In 1981, for the first time, Ireland had more than half of its working population employed in the tertiary sector. By 2005, approximately 67 per cent of all employment was in services (Fig 26.8).

Developments in services have been different depending on the region. Service industries prefer major urban centres, which have good access to large and prosperous markets. The country's western regions have therefore benefited less than the more urbanised eastern regions in developments within the service sector (see Table 26.4).

> **Why are service industries located mostly in larger towns and cities?**

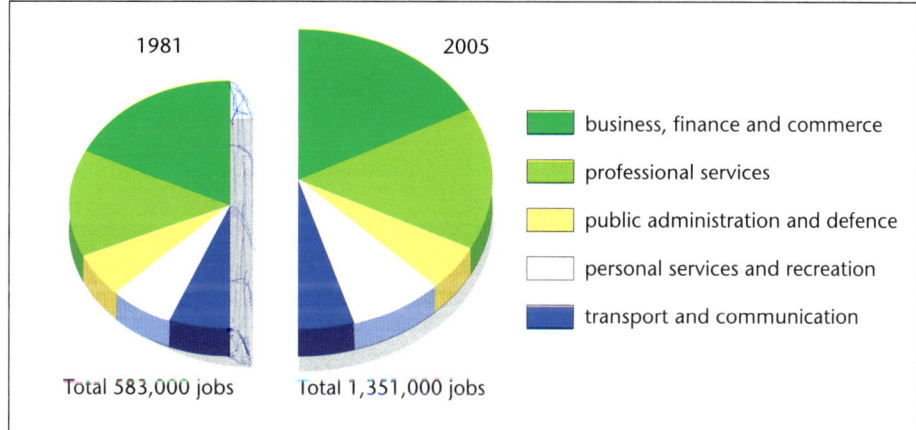

Fig. 26.8 Changes in Ireland's service sector, 1981–2005.

During the 1990s, 80 per cent of all new jobs were in services. This sector was therefore the main driving force behind the Celtic Tiger economy. Of particular importance was the growth of internationally traded services (ITS), which include:
- Computer software development.
- Data processing (including telesales).
- International financial services.

Since its development in the 1980s, the IFSC (International Financial Services Centre) has become a major employer and landmark of the modernisation of inner city Dublin.

Each of these sectors has received large inflows of foreign money. By 2005, over 71,000 jobs were available in ITS. This was an increase of almost eight times in twelve years. Ireland has also emerged as second only to the US in exporting computer software.

Greater Dublin has benefited most from ITS. One of its most notable developments has been the **International Financial Services Centre (IFSC)**, which has rejuvenated Dublin's inner city.

Although the capital has problems, do you think it is easy to get civil servants to leave Dublin and relocate to the West of Ireland? Explain your answer.

Services in the Border, Midland and West and Southern and Eastern Regions	
Border, Midland and West Region	**Southern and Eastern Region**
• Dependence on the service sector for employment (60 per cent) is less than the national average. • The more rural society, agricultural economy and lower average levels of prosperity are less attractive for large-scale developments in services. • Apart from Galway, most towns in the BMW Region do not provide a good range of high-quality services. Many people commute to cities such as Cork, Limerick and Dublin to access services. • Decentralising service jobs, especially in government departments, has aided growth in some regional centres, e.g. moving the Department of Education to Athlone. • The underdeveloped services sector is an important factor for future development. Improving quality of life for the region's population requires easier access to essential services.	• Almost three-quarters of Ireland's service jobs are in this region. Dependence on service employment is 70 per cent. • The region's well-developed urban areas and infrastructure and a large, relatively prosperous population are attractive for this high-growth sector. • Dublin is the key centre for many services. It is the country's capital and decision-making centre for many public and private enterprises. It is the dominant shopping centre, with a range of major education, health and recreational facilities, and is the hub of the country's transport system. • Planners have tried to decentralise service jobs from Dublin because of problems of higher costs and traffic congestion. In spite of this, the attractions of the capital city region mean it is still growing strongly. • The service economy of regional centres and larger market towns must be built up to act as more effective counter-poles to Dublin.

Table 26.4

Tourism

Tourism is part of the service sector and is one of Ireland's main growth industries. In 2005:

- 6.8 million foreign tourists visited Ireland.
- There were also 7.2 million trips by Irish tourists.
- Total foreign earnings were €4.8 billion.
- Total tourist revenue was €5.4 billion.
- Tourism provided the equivalent of 200,000 full-time jobs.

Some 75 per cent of tourist revenue is spent in the **Southern and Eastern Region.** This is linked to its international access (over 90 per cent of scheduled air flights to Ireland go to Dublin and all ferry ports are in this region). Dublin benefits from this gateway function, and with its cultural and historic attractions accounts for a quarter of all tourist revenue.

The **Border, Midland and West (BMW) Region** has many advantages for tourism: scenic landscapes, historic monuments and cultural tradition. Despite this, the industry remains underdeveloped and grew less in the 1990s than the Southern and Eastern Region. While the BMW Region has almost half of tourist bed capacity, it generates less than 40 per cent of the country's tourist revenue.

There are **two problems** for tourism in **the BMW Region:**

- **Direct access** to the region for foreign visitors is limited and more expensive than for the S&E Region.
- While **seasonality** of tourism in Ireland is high, it is especially strong in the BMW Region. Most visitors come in July and August.

Major efforts are needed to improve access to the BMW Region and provide facilities for tourists that would generate a greater year-round industry, for example conferences, leisure activities (golf, fishing) and cultural events.

- *Use this photo of Doolin in Co. Clare to suggest why tourists are attracted to the West of Ireland, and what benefits they might bring to the local economy.*

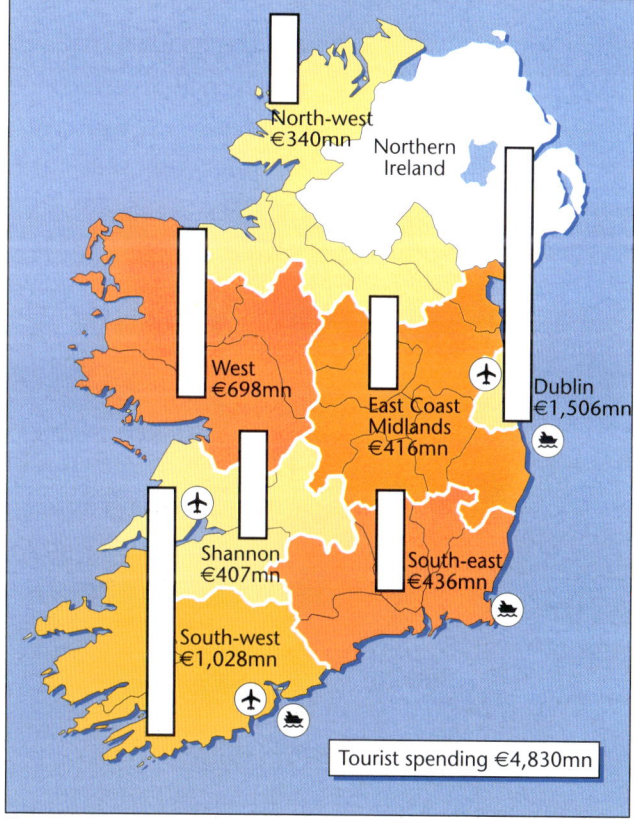

Fig. 26.9 Tourist revenue in Ireland by Bord Fáilte planning regions (in euros).

Activity

Look at Fig. 26.9 and answer the following:

1. Which region generates the most revenue from tourism? Why?
2. What advantages does the West of Ireland have for tourism?
3. Why is the tourism revenue so low in the north-west?

What is meant by seasonality? Why is it high in the BMW Region?

Transport

Successful socio-economic development depends, to a large extent, on an efficient transport system. Until the 1980s, Ireland's internal and external transport infrastructures were poorly developed. This added greatly to the country's problems of being a periphery and its difficulty in accessing EU and world markets. With the help of structural funds from the EU, the country's transport systems have been improved.

Ireland's National Development Plan (2000–06) allocated €10 billion to improve transport systems, while the more recent NDP (2007–13) proposes to spend a further €33 billion on transport. Strategic road corridors receive highest priority as they effectively link Dublin to all other major urban centres. In addition, a north-south Atlantic corridor from Derry to Cork and on to Waterford will provide better links within the West of Ireland.

The Southern and Eastern Region has more developed transport systems than the BMW Region (see Fig. 26.10):

- Apart from the Shannon Estuary, it has all of the country's major ports.
- It has two of the three major international airports.
- The national rail network converges on Dublin.
- The national road network and strategic corridors focus on Dublin.
- Despite severe congestion in Dublin's transport system, the S&E Region has a greater choice, a lower-cost and more efficient transport system than that which operates over most of the BMW Region.

The M50 ring road and the Red Cow interchange in Dublin.

- *Use the photo to suggest how such road improvements have assisted the development and expansion of the city. (Think of housing, industry and services.)*

Fig. 26.10 Transport in Ireland.

Legend:
- ☐ Border, Midland and West Region
- ☐ Southern and Eastern Region
- ● town
- ✈ major airport
- ✈ regional airport
- ⚓ port
- — strategic road corridor
- ···· passenger railway line

Human Processes

Differences in population dynamics, the rural-urban divide and levels of development occur within Ireland (see Table 26.5 and Fig. 26.11).

Table 26.5

Human Factors in the Border, Midland and West and Southern and Eastern Regions	
Border, Midland and West Region	**Southern and Eastern Region**
• Population has declined for most of the twentieth century. • Although it covers 47 per cent of the country, it has only 27 per cent of the country's population. • There are few large towns. Two-thirds of the population live in rural areas. Galway is the only urban centre with more than 50,000 people. It is the region's dominant town. • A lot of people have migrated from the region to the rest of Ireland and abroad. Since the 1990s, there has been a net inflow of migrants and retirees. • Only one of Ireland's seven universities is in the region. Most students have to leave for further education, and only 13 per cent of students graduating find a job in the region. This could be called a 'brain drain' and is an important problem for the BMW. • Low rates of natural increase (especially low birth rates) and an ageing population. • The region is the heartland of Irish culture, with most of the Gaeltacht areas located in the region (see Chapter 22, Fig. 22.1 on page 147).	• Throughout the twentieth century the region has increased its size and share of national population (see Fig. 26.11). • A densely settled region: the density of population is three times that of the BMW Region. • It has a well-developed and balanced distribution of urban centres. Almost three-quarters of people live in urban areas. Dublin is the dominant city, with 1.3 million people. Cork, Limerick and Waterford have populations over 50,000. • It receives a lot of migrants from the rest of the country and from abroad who are attracted by the job opportunities in Dublin. • An estimated 86 per cent of Ireland's third-level places are in the region. Almost all students wishing to enter further education can find a place in their home region. A variety of good-quality jobs also means that almost 90 per cent of graduates find employment in the Southern and Eastern Region. • Relatively high rates of natural increase (higher birth rates and inmigration) and a younger age profile are advantages for development. • A much more cosmopolitan society and culture shows more openness to outside influences.

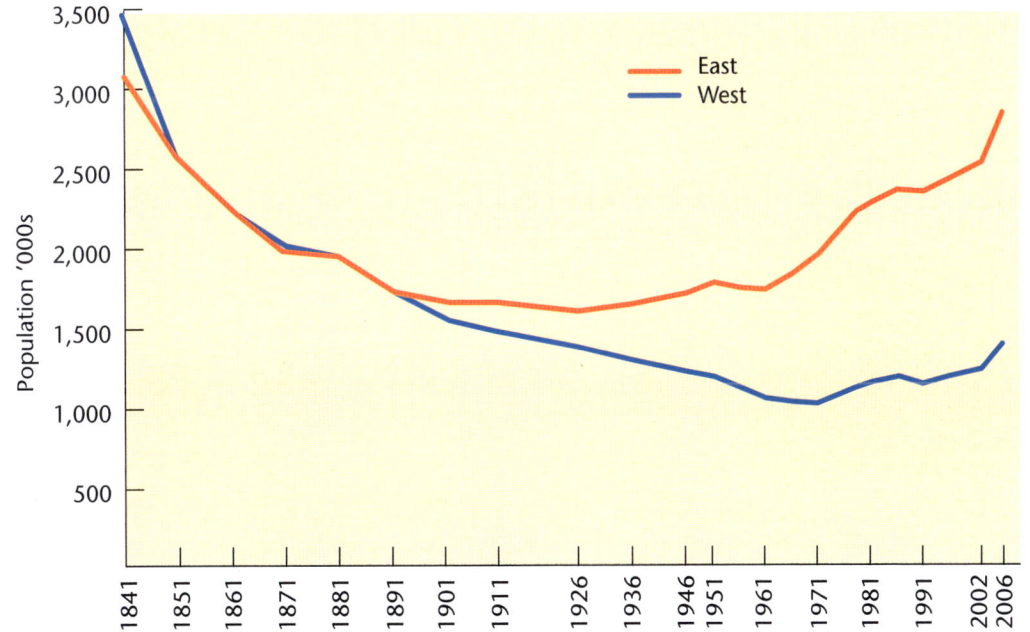

Fig. 26.11 Population changes in eastern and western Ireland, 1841–2006.

Activity

Look at Fig. 26.11 and answer the following.

1. Before the Famine, which region had the biggest population?
2. Contrast the trends for both regions before and after 1926.
3. Briefly explain these different trends and how they affect prospects for development.

CHAPTER 27
THE MEZZOGIORNO

The Mezzogiorno is one of the least developed regions in the EU.

Italy is a country of almost 60 million people and is one of the founding states of the EU. Today, it is one of the world's largest economies. It is also a country of great contrasts.

Some of Europe's most prosperous regions – centred on the cities of Milan, Turin and Genoa – are in northern Italy (see Fig. 27.1). Since the 1960s, growth has spilled over into nearby regions. The result has been a surge in prosperity and optimism in the centre of the country. The south of Italy, or the Mezzogiorno, however, is one of the poorest regions of the EU. It is an example of a **peripheral region**.

The Mezzogiorno (meaning 'land of the midday sun') is the part of the Italian peninsula south of Rome (see Fig. 27.1), and includes the islands of Sicily and Sardinia. This region has a long history of widespread poverty and underdevelopment and contrasts strongly with northern Italy.

Fig. 27.1 Italy's three main regions (The Three Italies).

The Mezzogiorno

- 40 per cent of Italy's territory.
- 36 per cent of the country's population.
- 25 per cent of its GDP (gross domestic product).
- 50 per cent of Italy's agricultural employment.

The Three Italies
- North
- Centre
- Mezzogiorno

Milan
Turin
Genoa
Corsica (France)
Rome
northern limit of the Mezzogiorno
Naples
Cagliari
Palermo

PHYSICAL PROCESSES

Relief, Drainage and Soils

Southern Italy is dominated by the steep slopes of the Apennines, the mountain chain that stretches 1,050 km down the Italian peninsula (Fig 27.2). About 40 per cent of the land in the Mezzogiorno is mountainous and too steep for crops to be grown. Another 45 per cent is hilly, and there are problems with soil erosion. The hilly soils have few nutrients.

The rich, fertile soils are mostly on narrow, coastal plains and valley floodplains that follow rivers flowing down from the Apennines to the coast. These include alluvial soils from river deposition and rich volcanic soils from weathered lava. Calabria, in the 'toe' of Italy, is mostly granite plateaus with poor-quality soils.

The largest river is the Tiber, which enters the sea south of Rome. The remaining rivers are small, fast-flowing streams from the Apennines that often reach the sea through narrow, gorge-like channels, especially in the west. To the east, along the Plain of Apulia, there are few rivers. The bedrock is porous limestone that allows little surface drainage. The high Apennines and some other uplands are karst landscapes, where no rivers flow on the surface. Where there are rivers, water levels can be very low during the hot, dry summers in June, July and August.

Climate

Summer

High pressure dominates in summer. Winds are hot and dry, and blow as north-easterly winds from the continent of Europe. These winds blowing off the land bring drought from June to September. Temperatures are high, with averages of between 28°C and 30°C throughout the summer (see Fig 27.3). Any summer rain usually falls in heavy downpours. This runs off the steep, sun-baked slopes, causing problems of gullying, soil erosion and mudflows.

Winter

Winters are mild, about 17°C, and moist. South-westerly winds that blow from the Atlantic and across the Mediterranean bring moisture that falls as relief rain over the Apennines. Amounts vary from 900 mm to 500 mm. The lower amounts fall along the Adriatic coast because it is in the rain shadow of the Apennines.

> Why does summer rain fall in heavy downpours? (Think about the type of rainfall.)

> Get to know the Mezzogiorno by learning the features of southern Italy on the map. Look at your atlas as well.

Fig. 27.2 The Mezzogiorno region of Italy.

Activity

Look at Fig. 27.2 and use an atlas to identify:

a. where the main lowland areas are located
b. sea areas A and B
c. island C
d. mountains D
e. river E
f. cities F to I.

187

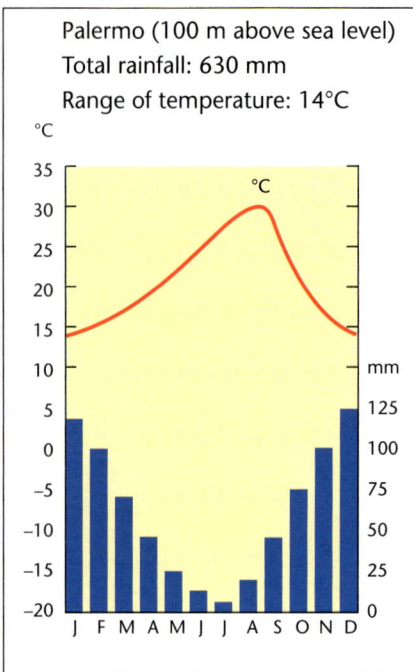

Palermo (100 m above sea level)
Total rainfall: 630 mm
Range of temperature: 14°C

Fig. 27.3 Temperature and rainfall in Palermo, Sicily.

Activity

Look at Fig. 27.3 and answer the following.
1. Which months have less than 25 mm of rain?
2. What is the temperature of the hottest month?
3. Contrast the climograph of Palermo with the one for Valentia (see Fig. 26.1, page 172).
4. Explain the reasons for the differences.

ECONOMIC PROCESSES
The Primary Sector

By the start of the 1950s, the Mezzogiorno was something like an underdeveloped country. Because people depended on a primary sector which was weak and in a difficult environment, most of the population was poor (see Fig 27.4)

Activity

Look at Fig. 27.4.
1. In which sector of the economy did most people work in 1950?
2. What have been the main changes in the Mezzogiorno economy since 1950?

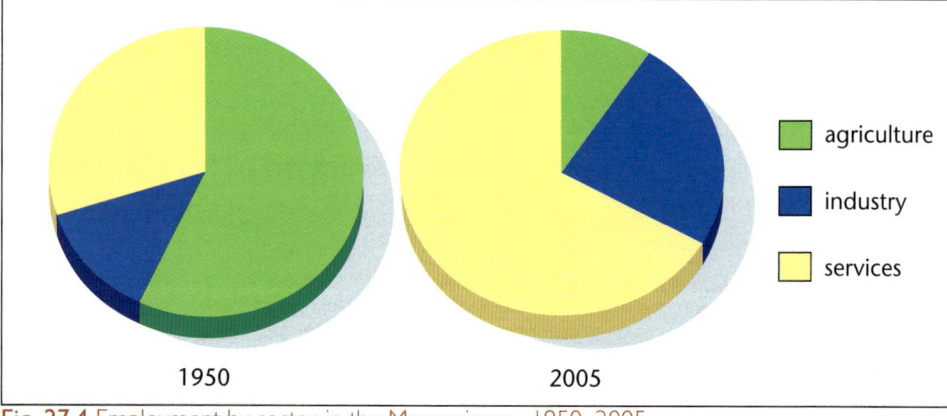

1950   2005

- agriculture
- industry
- services

Fig. 27.4 Employment by sector in the Mezzogiorno, 1950–2005.

Animals grazing on the poor and relatively arid landscape of the Apennines.
● *Would you describe this as subsistence farming?*

Agriculture

Until 1950, most of the land, and especially the more productive lowland areas, in the Mezzogiorno was owned by landlords, most of whom lived outside the region (absentee landlords). To work their large estates, large numbers of peasants were hired as day workers. Land was also leased to peasants for grazing animals (sheep or goats) or growing some cereals. Many peasants paid their rent with a share of their farm produce (this is called sharecropping).

This form of farming was extensive. Levels of productivity and total output were low, especially given the difficult natural environment, e.g. summer drought and mountainous relief. It was very inefficient and gave low income to the people. This system of land use is called *latifundia*.

With most land owned by landlords, there was not enough land available to make farms big enough to provide a reasonable income to the large rural population. In addition, since the average family size was large, farm holdings were usually subdivided between family members. By 1950, therefore, 70 per cent of land holdings in the Mezzogiorno were less than 3 hectares.

To support large families, these tiny holdings had to be worked intensively. This led to overgrazing and overcultivation, causing soil erosion and declining soil fertility. The result was even lower levels of output and increased levels of rural poverty.

By 1950, the Italian government realised that it was necessary to try to deal with the many problems of the Mezzogiorno's primary sector. To promote development, the Italian government introduced the **Cassa per il Mezzogiorno** (Fund for the South). This was also supported by the European Union. At first, about 80 per cent of funding went to modernise farming, and this had some success.

> **The Cassa per il Mezzogiorno operated until 1984. After that the Mezzogiorno received structural funds as an Objective 1 Region of the EU.**

Solutions to the Agricultural Problems

To introduce a more productive and intensive form of farming, a number of important changes were necessary.

- **Land reform** was vital to give the peasants access to their own land. Most of the large estates were bought by the state and the land redistributed to landless peasants. New holdings of approximately 5 hectares were created in the lowlands, but larger units (up to 50 hectares) were formed in the upland.

- On the new, family-owned farms, **farmers were trained** to use more intensive farm methods. This involved both growing **new cash crops,** such as citrus fruits and vegetables, and producing **traditional crops more intensively.** These traditional crops included olives, vines and cereals.

- The success of intensive farming in the region depends on a **regular supply of water** to compensate for summer droughts. Large amounts of money were spent on developing reservoirs, wells and **irrigation systems.**

- **Improved transport,** such as the *autostrada* (motorway) system, was needed to allow high-value but more perishable crops to gain access to major markets, such as north-west Italy and Germany.

- When the new family farms were created in the lowlands, many people moved from hilltop villages to **new farmhouses or villages,** which were built to act as new service centres. These villages had schools, health care, leisure facilities and other services, which helped raise the **quality of life** for people living in the countryside. Processing and packaging factories were also built in larger towns, and these provided more jobs.

A hilltop village in the Mezzogiorno. Note the scarcity of suitable farmland near the village to support the rural population. Farmers travelled to nearby lowland areas to work their small holdings.

> **What is quality of life? Why is it important for regional development?**

The most prosperous farming in the Mezzogiorno usually occurs in the coastal lowlands.
● *Use this photograph and the one on page 189 to contrast lowland and upland farming, e.g. relief, settlement type, land use and transport.*

Intensive growing of citrus fruits, such as oranges, provides a much higher income for family farms in the irrigated areas of the Mezzogiorno.

Present-day Farming Activities

Why has it been more difficult to change farming in the Apennines? (Think about environment and location.)

Dependence on agriculture has gone down dramatically. Today, only one in ten of the region's workforce works in farming (Fig 27.4). The move to more intensive farming has also increased rural prosperity. The Mezzogiorno is a now a major supplier of citrus fruits, vegetables and olives to European markets.

The successful transformation of farming in the South occured mainly in the coastal lowlands and river valleys, where irrigation is available. In the mountain areas inland, less successful traditional and extensive forms of farming are still used. Low incomes and continued out-migration from the region are typical of the more difficult conditions in Europe's most problematic farming regions.

The Secondary Sector
Industry

Briefly explain why each of these factors limits the development of industry.

By the early 1950s, only 17 per cent of Italy's industrial workforce and output were located in the Mezzogiorno. This was due to:
● Few sources of raw materials and energy supplies.
● Peripheral position and high transport costs.
● Unskilled and poorly educated labour force.
● A large but poor rural population.
● Few large towns to provide services, such as banking or legal services.

As with agriculture, government intervention was needed to encourage industrial take-off. From the 1960s, there was help from the Cassa per il Mezzogiorno and EU funding. Among the key incentives for promoting industrial growth in the South were:

- Generous grants and tax relief.
- Major improvements to the physical infrastructure, such as building an *autostrada* (motorway) system (see Fig. 27.5) and modernising key ports, such as Naples, Taranto and Siracusa.
- State-controlled companies had to make 80 per cent of new investment in the South.
- Across the South, a number of industrial development areas were created to act as a basis for regional growth.

Fig. 27.5 Industrial development areas in the Mezzogiorno.
- *Why are there almost no growth zones in the central spine of the Mezzogiorno?*

Industrial development in the Mezzogiorno has had successes and failures. Many new jobs have been created. Between 1960 and 2000, the region's industrial workforce almost tripled to 1.4 million. This has reduced dependence on agriculture and encouraged growth in the service sector. Overall, the region's economy became more diversified. Despite this, the economy of the Mezzogiorno remains less well developed than northern Italy (Fig 27.6).

Capital-intensive projects such as this coastal oil refinery in Sicily were the basis for economic development in the Mezzogiorno.

Fig. 27.6 Employment and prosperity contrasts between northern and southern Italy.

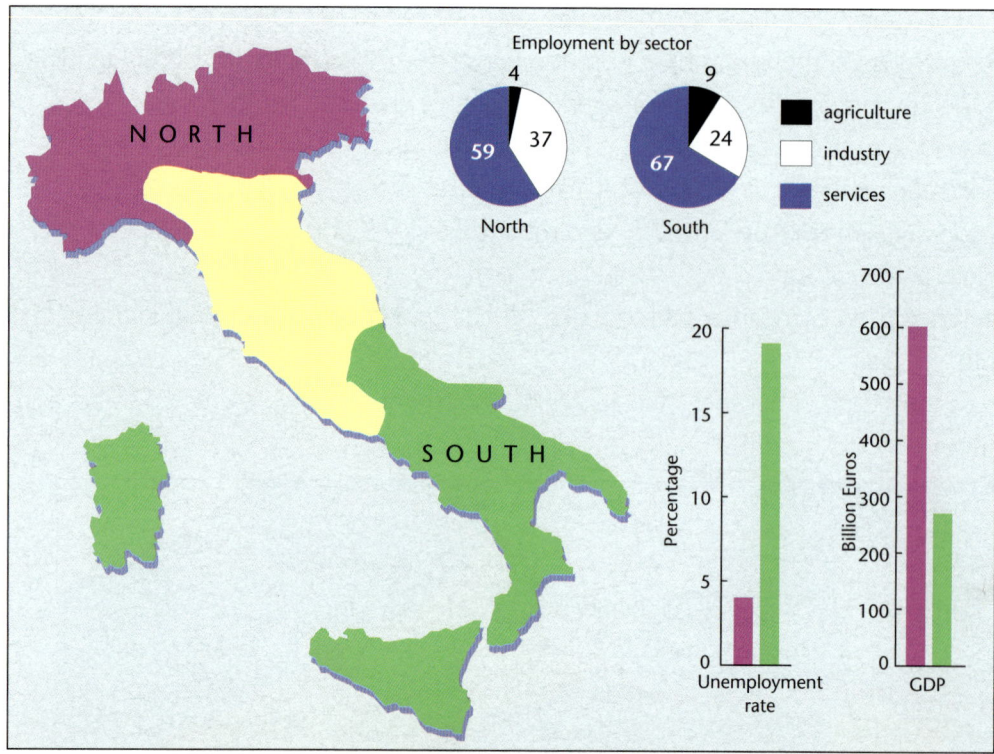

Activity

Look at Fig. 27.6 and answer the following.
1. Is the Mezzogiorno less dependent on industry? Suggest why.
2. Estimate the unemployment levels in the two regions.
3. Why do you think total wealth (GDP) is much lower in the Mezzogiorno?

Almost 75 per cent of all new industrial jobs have been in large, capital-intensive sectors such as steel, chemicals and engineering. Most of these are state controlled and need a lot of investment. While each project provides many jobs, in general they have failed to create many spin-off industries or jobs. This has led to the large-scale projects being called **'cathedrals in the sun'**.

While coastal zones have developed, inland areas remain depressed economically, so differences in levels of prosperity in the Mezzogiorno have increased. Some growth zones have been very successful in attracting industries. One of the best is the Bari-Brindisi-Taranto industrial triangle, where oil refining, chemicals and steel form the basis of a major industrial zone.

The Tertiary Sector
Transport

A key problem for the South is its peripheral location. To offset this, a major investment in transport infrastructure was needed to link the region to distant markets.

The *autostrada,* Italy's motorway system, was developed (Fig 27.7). The backbone of the system is the **Autostrada del Sole** ('sunshine motorway'). It starts near the Swiss border and runs along the western side of the country, ending in Calabria in the 'toe' of Italy. This, and another *autostrada* that runs along the east coast, provide fast, efficient links between northern and southern Italy.

Why are the giant new plants called 'cathedrals in the sun'?

Suggest why there is a difference in prosperity levels between the coast and inland areas.

As well as upgrading the road system, large investments were made to modernise key ports. Several of the ports have become a focus around which successful growth centres have developed. These include the deep-water port at Taranto (essential for the country's largest iron and steel plant) and port developments along the east coast of Sicily, which has one of the largest oil and chemical complexes in Western Europe.

Fig. 27.7 Italy's *autostrada* (motorway) system.
● *Why do you think the main routes are north to south in direction rather than east to west across the peninsula?*

The Autostrada del Sole was constructed through a very difficult landscape.
● *Why was this motorway vital for the development of the Mezzogiorno?*

See how the major cities are linked by the Autostrada del Sole.

Tourism

Located within the Mediterranean Basin, the Mezzogiorno has much to offer tourists, including a hot, sunny climate, beautiful scenery, beaches and historic cities. It also tends to be cheaper and less crowded than the more commercialised tourist resorts of northern Italy and southern France.

As tourism is an international growth industry, planners for the Mezzogiorno have made great efforts to promote tourism as a basis for economic development. To achieve this, transport has been improved for easier access to the region, and tourist facilities, such as hotels and recreation areas, have been upgraded.

This has been successful and the region has become more popular as a tourist destination. Over 12 million tourists visit the South, although three-quarters of these are from the rest of Italy. More has to be done to raise the profile of the region with international tourists.

Sorrento in the Bay of Naples is an important tourist centre in the Mezzogiorno.
● *What attractions does this area have for visitors?*

HUMAN PROCESSES

The Mezzogiorno is similar to the rest of Italy in its language and religion. Italian is the language people speak and almost all of them are Roman Catholic. Rome, the centre of the Catholic religion, is located between the Mezzogiorno and the more developed northern region.

The major differences in human processes between the North and South of Italy are in population trends.

Population Processes

In the 1960s, the population in northern Italy greatly increased, while people continued to leave the Mezzogiorno. From the 1980s, these roles began to be reversed. Five key factors that explain these trends are:

- Economic development.
- Natural increase in population.
- Internal migration.
- Emigration.
- Immigration.

Economic Development

Think of how the Cassa per il Mezzogiorno and economic planning helped the South.

Up until the 1980s, the underdeveloped and rural-based economy of the South did not experience population growth. This contrasted with the industrial region of northern Italy. In the 1980s, traditional industries, including textiles, vehicle assembly and shipbuilding in cities such as Milan, Turin and Genoa began to decline. This meant fewer job prospects and population growth rates in northern Italy were reduced. From this time, however, the South began to experience far more positive economic trends, linked to modernising agriculture and attracting new industries.

Natural Increase in Population

What does 'natural increase' mean?

For a long time, a high rate of natural increase was associated with Italy because the birth rate was high. The situation has changed, especially in northern Italy, where not enough babies are being born and the population is not replacing itself naturally. In the Mezzogiorno, however, birth rates continue to be higher than death rates. The result is a natural increase of population in the Mezzogiorno (Fig 27.8). If these trends continue, the region's total population will soon be greater than northern Italy.

Activity

Look at Fig. 27.8 and answer the following.

1. Why is the natural population change positive for the Mezzogiorno?
2. Is population growth higher in the North or South of Italy?
3. Does this provide advantages for the Mezzogiorno for economic development (think of labour force, market)?

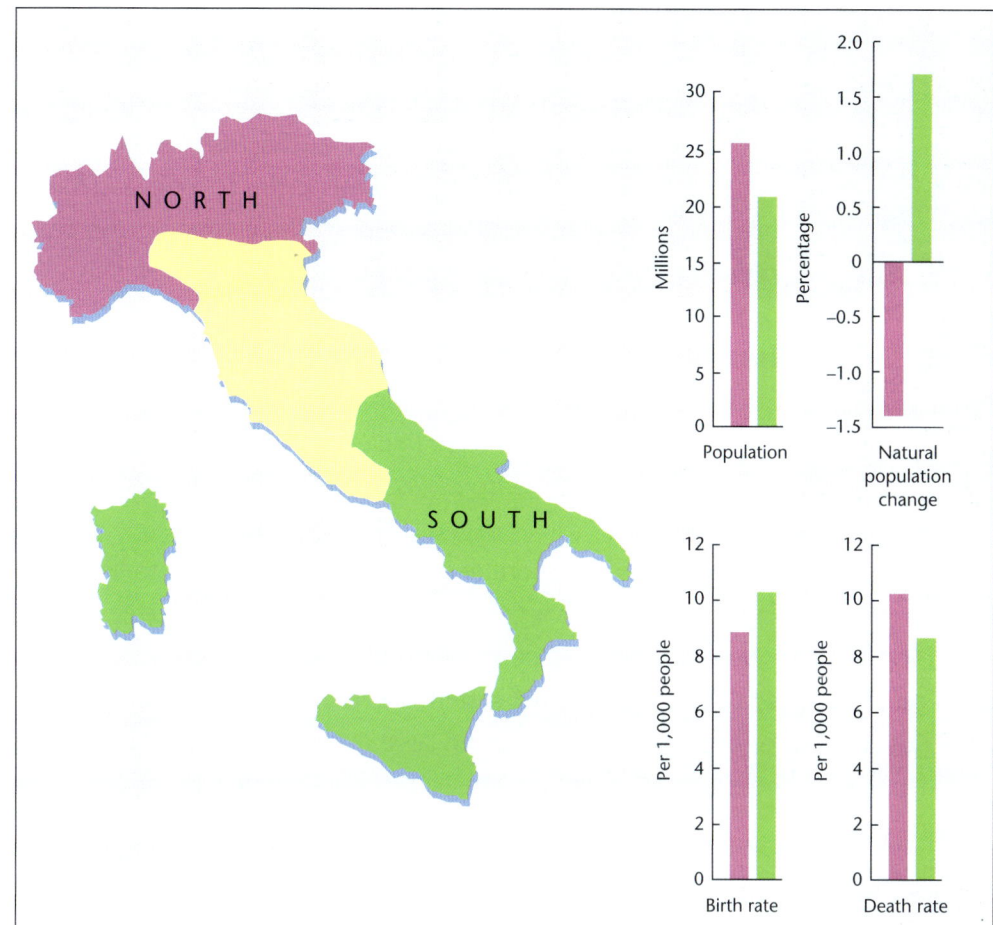

Population

Natural population change

Birth rate

Death rate

What are push and pull factors? List three push and three pull factors that influence migration from south to north in Italy.

Internal Migration

Internal migration has generally involved a flow of people from the countryside in the poor South to the richer cities of northern Italy. Between 1951 and 1981, over 4 million migrants left the South (**out-migration**) because of a number of **push factors**. Most of the people who left were attracted to cities (in-migration), such as Milan, Turin and Rome, by a variety of **pull factors**.

The out-migration to northern Italy continued up to the 1990s, with over 1 million people leaving the Mezzogiorno in the 1980s. The pull factors of northern cities have now been greatly reduced, while **modernisation of the South has reduced the push factors** that encourage people to leave. Better job prospects in growth zones of the Mezzogiorno have reduced out-migration. A 'trickle' of out-migration continues from the Mezzogiorno because unemployment levels are higher and prosperity is lower than in northern Italy.

The underdeveloped economy of the Mezzogiorno meant that large numbers of people migrated from overcrowded urban centres such as Palermo in Sicily.

195

Large numbers of refugees from Albania and other Balkan countries have tried to gain entry into the EU through Italian ports, such as Bari. Why?

Emigration

For a long time it was a tradition in Italy for people to go to other countries, such as the USA and Germany. Since the 1970s, fewer people have left Italy (including the Mezzogiorno) because there are better job prospects in the country, and Italy's rate of natural increase has declined. For Italian people, this has **reduced the importance of push factors.**

Immigration

Since the 1980s, an increasing number of migrants from other countries have been attracted (pulled) to Italy. At first, the majority of them came from less developed countries in Africa and Asia.

In the 1990s, more and more people migrated to Italy from nearby countries such as Albania and the former Yugoslavia. Most of them were trying to escape from the poor economies and devastation caused by the fall of the communist system and the outbreak of civil war in Bosnia and Kosovo. More recently, Italy has received large numbers of migrants from North Africa and Asia. These add significantly to the total population of Italy and the Mezzogiorno

It is difficult to patrol all of the Italian coastline to restrict the entry of refugees or migrants who are determined to get into the country. Many migrants see southern Italy as an easy way to enter the EU, believing that these coastal areas are less controlled than other parts of the EU. The east coast of the Mezzogiorno could be called the 'Achilles heel' for migration into the EU (Fig. 27.9).

In 2004, Italy received 560,000 migrants, which adds significantly to the country's total population.

Fig. 27.9 Migration into Italy through the Mezzogiorno.

As well as legal migration, up to 50,000 illegal migrants are estimated to enter Italy each year.

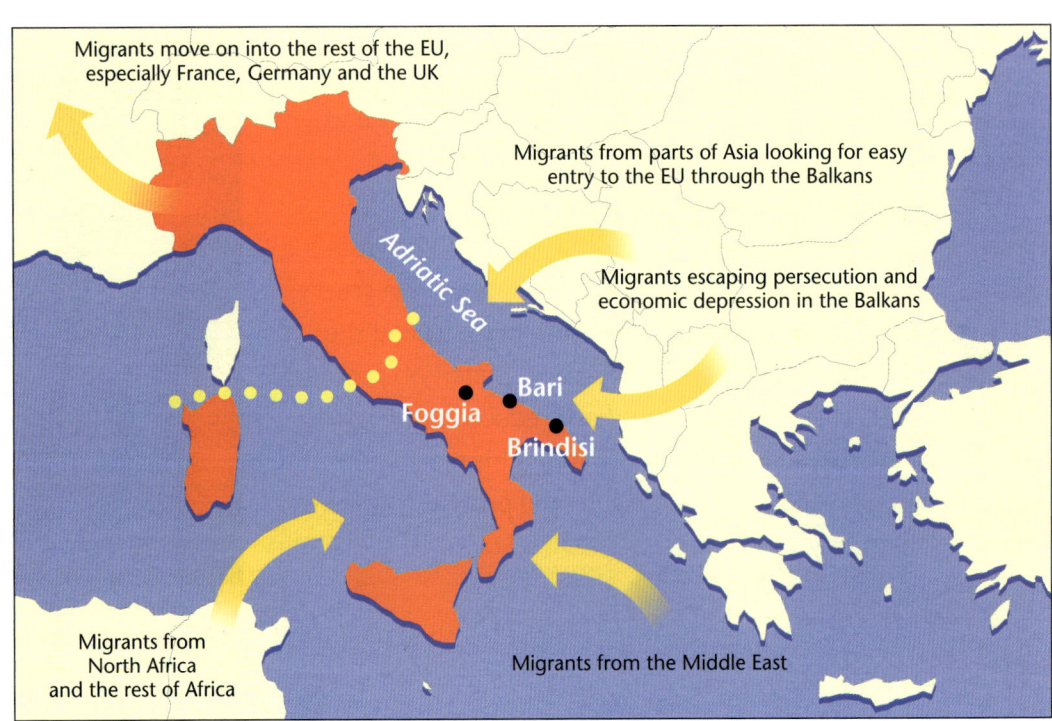

Migrants move on into the rest of the EU, especially France, Germany and the UK

Migrants from parts of Asia looking for easy entry to the EU through the Balkans

Migrants escaping persecution and economic depression in the Balkans

Adriatic Sea

Foggia

Bari

Brindisi

Migrants from North Africa and the rest of Africa

Migrants from the Middle East

CHAPTER 28
THE PARIS REGION

KEY IDEA!

The Paris Region is one of the most important core regions in Europe

France, one of the largest and most important countries in Europe, has a well-defined **core region.** This is the **Paris Region.** It is made up of the city of Paris, its sprawling suburbs and the four *départements* that surround the city (see Fig. 21.6 on page 145).

As is typical of cores, the Paris Region occupies only a small area of the country, but it dominates the economic, political and cultural life of France (Table 28.1). This dominance has caused many people to describe the rest of France as a periphery of this powerful national core.

There are several reasons why the Paris Region is such a powerful core region. These involve a combination of **both** physical and economic/human processes.

> The Paris Region is also referred to as the Ile de France.

Paris is one of Europe's most important cities.
● *Name the river on which it is located.*

Fig 28.1 France and the Paris Region.

2 per cent of area of France but:
● 19 per cent of population.
● 21 per cent of employment.
● 29 per cent of GDP.

Table 28.1. The economic importance of the Paris Region to France.

Activity
Review the core-periphery model on page 155 (Fig 23.1) to understand the dominant relationships between a core and its periphery.

> Remember what the meaning of a primate city and core region are.

PHYSICAL PROCESSES

Relief

The Paris Region is located at the heart of the much larger Paris Basin (Fig 28.2). This is an extensive, saucer-shaped depression, which is composed of a series of different landscapes where different sedimentary rocks reach the surface. The central area, or Ile de France, is a low-lying and gently undulating plateau which favours agricultural and urban development.

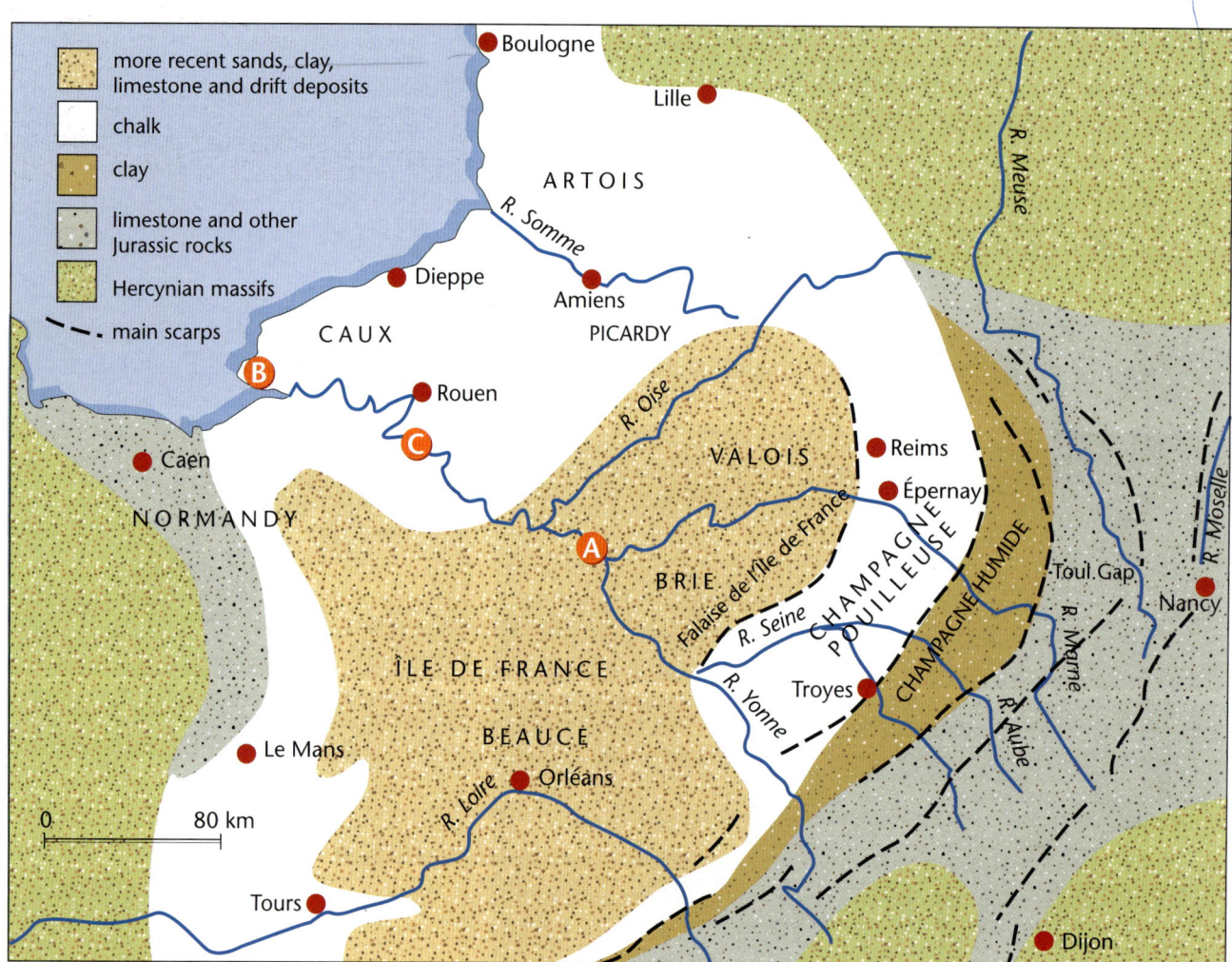

Fig. 28.2 The Paris Basin.

Activity
Study Fig 28.2 and answer the following.
1. Name urban centres A and B.
2. Name river C.
3. Why do rivers increase the centrality of Paris?

Soil

Most of the Ile de France region is covered by fertile **limon** (loess). This originated during and after the last Ice Age as windblown dust. Strong winds blowing south off the retreating ice sheets were able to pick up and transport large amounts of small, glacially eroded debris. These were then deposited in the Paris Basin, and elsewhere across the North European Plain, as deep layers of fertile and easily worked soil.

River System and Drainage

The Paris Region and Basin is drained by the **River Seine** and its tributaries. These form **natural routeways** which link Paris to other parts of France. The Seine also links Paris to the deep-water port of Le Havre.

> The Seine and its tributaries have helped Paris improve its accessibility to a large hinterland.

The broad valley of the Lower Seine provides Paris with a natural routeway to the ports of Rouen and Le Havre.

Climate

The climate of Paris is one of **transition** between Cool Temperate Oceanic and Cool Temperate Continental (see Fig 19.1 on page 135). Summer temperatures are quite high (25°C) and although rainfall is well distributed throughout the year, a maximum occurs in summer (Fig 28.3).

Onshore westerly winds maintain relatively high rainfall totals in winter, although temperatures fall to near freezing point. This can give rise to some winter snowfall.

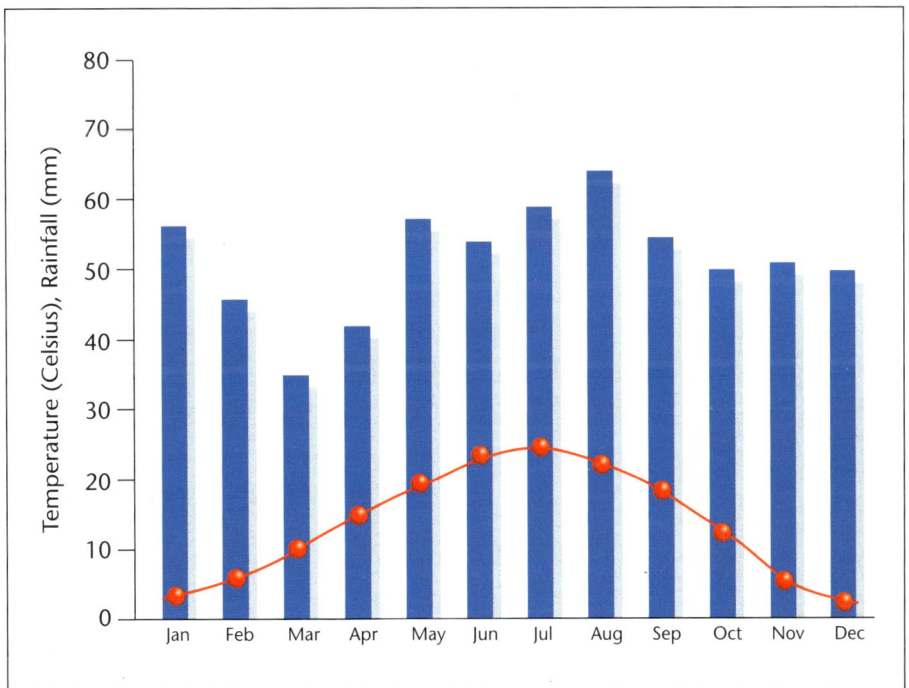

Fig. 28.3 Temperature and rainfall in Paris (Orly Airport).

Activity

Look at Fig 28.3 and answer the following.

1. What months have the highest temperature and rainfall?
2. Explain these observations (think about distance from area and type of rainfall).
3. Why is this climate suitable for intensive cereal farming?

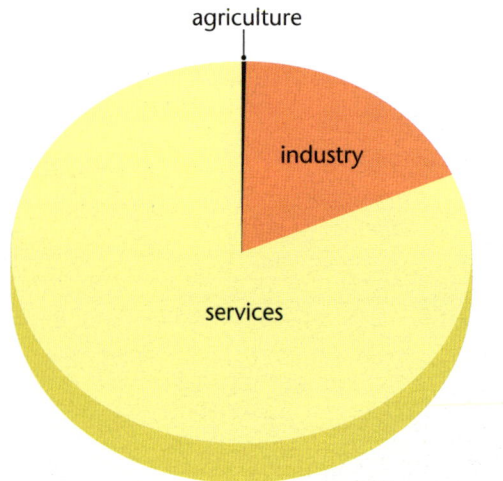

ECONOMIC AND HUMAN PROCESSES

The Paris Region is a highly dynamic and prosperous core region in terms of both France and the EU. Output from its diverse and modern industries (especially services) makes Paris the fifth-most prosperous city in the world, and one of the most competitive regions in the EU. In total, some 5.1 million people are employed in this region (Fig 28.4).

Activity

Look at Fig 28.4.
1. Which sector is dominant? Why?
2. Why would you expect core regions to have such a small primary sector?

The Primary Sector

Although dominated by the large urban landscape of Paris, the city's rural hinterland includes some of the most prosperous and productive farming in Europe (see Table 28.2).

Activity

Use Table 28.2 as a basis to contrast farming in a core region with that found in a periphery, e.g. the Mezzogiorno (Chapter 27) or West of Ireland (Chapter 26).

Physical and Human Factors Influence Farming in the Paris Region	
Physical	**Human**
• Relief: Low-lying/undulating and favours large, mechanised farms. • Soil: Fertile (limon). • Drainage: Good. • Climate: Seasonal temperature and rainfall patterns favour cereals.	• Market: Near the large Paris market (high demand). • Land prices: High due to competition from other land uses – intensive farming. • Food prices: High due to CAP and good market-high returns (profits) encourage investment in farms. • Farmers: Young and educated – farms operated as a business.

Table 28.2

Cereal farming in the Paris Basin.
• *Why does the rich agriculture of the Paris Basin add to the growth of Paris?*

A key characteristic of the region is that different areas **specialise** in different forms of intensive farming. Some examples include:

- The fertile (limon-covered) limestone plateau of **Beauce,** to the south of Paris, devotes 80 per cent of its land to large-scale, mechanical farming of **cereals** (especially wheat and maize). It produces some of the highest cereal yields in the EU.
- **Market gardening** is practised on many small plots of land **adjacent to large urban centres**. High-value products, such as vegetables and flowers, are produced for the regional market.
- **Dairying** occurs in areas of clay soils in **Brie,** to the east of Paris. These damp soils favour pasture, and farmers concentrate on supplying liquid milk and dairy produce, such as butter and cheese (Brie), to the Paris market.

The Secondary Sector

Industry

The development of Paris as a **core industrial region** is due to a number of factors:

- **Market:** The large and prosperous market of over 11 million people attracts a wide range of consumer industries, such as cosmetics, vehicles and electrical goods.
- **Centrality and excellent transport systems:** Paris is the hub of the country's transport system and has good links to other major markets in the EU (see Fig. 28.5). Navigable waterways also link Paris to the rivers Rhine and Rhone, and to the deepwater port of Le Havre. These allow for the efficient and low-cost import of raw materials and export of products.
- **Labour supply:** The Paris Region provides a large and varied supply of workers. This is vital, especially for labour-intensive industries, such as clothing.
- **Services:** A wide range of services, such as banks, legal and marketing, supports industrial development. A large number of high-quality universities and research centres also encourages research and development, which is essential for high-tech industries.
- **Environment:** The beauty of Paris and its cultural facilities attract investors.

> Within three hours from Paris, 380 million people are accessible by air or high-speed rail.

The modern design of the Paris City of Science and Industry Park illustrates the role of Paris as a major centre for scientific research and development.

Employment in vehicle assembly in Paris fell from 185,000 in 1975 to only 37,000 in 2005. This Renault factory on the banks of the Seine near Paris once employed 30,000 people. It closed in 1992.

From the 1970s, however, **deindustrialisation** has affected the core region. Employment in manufacturing was more than halved between 1975 and 2005 (see Table 28.3). By 2005, only one in eight jobs in the Paris Region was in manufacturing.

Manufacturing Employment in the Paris Region			
	Employment (000s)	% total Paris Region workforce	% of French industrial workforce
1955	1,370	29	25
1975	1,360	29	22
2005	600	12	12

Table 28.3

Activity

Study Table 28.3.

1. Describe the trend in industrial employment.
2. Has Paris become more or less important for industrial employment? Explain your answer.

Deindustrialisation in Paris, and most other core regions, has been due to several reasons:

Remember the meaning of deindustrialisation? See page 161.

- Increasing cost of labour.
- High cost of land for factories.
- Congestion, which increases the time and costs of transport.
- Cheaper sites and labour costs in peripheral regions.
- Government policy to decentralise industry to help develop peripheral regions.

Despite the decline in industrial employment, Paris remains important, especially for high-tech and high-value products, for example electronics and fashion goods. In addition, it has increased its role as a **decision-making centre for industry,** as most major French manufacturing companies have their headquarters in the city.

The Tertiary Sector

Paris is the **capital** of France and the seat of the country's government. This, together with its central location, large population, excellent transport systems and an attractive city environment, has encouraged the growth of a huge variety of high-quality services. Today, over 80 per cent of the region's workforce is in services (see Fig 28.4).

As a national and EU core, many French and other international organisations have located their headquarters in Paris. This makes Paris a major decision-making centre and one which influences development in the rest of the country, especially the periphery.

Paris is the headquarters location of:
- 38 per cent of all French companies.
- 96 per cent of French banks.
- 70 per cent of French insurance companies.
- A variety of international organisations, e.g. UNESCO, OECD.

The French multinational Renault is one of the world's major vehicle manufacturers and is headquartered in Paris.

Transport

A well-developed and modern transport system is essential for core regions. It allows core regions, such as Paris, to extend their influences over large areas of a country – and even across international boundaries.

Paris is the **focus of the national transport systems,** as well as being an important **international hub** for road, rail and air traffic. This emphasises the **centrality** of Paris and allows for the efficient movement of people and goods to and from other parts of France and Europe.

A good example of the centrality of Paris is its emergence as a major European hub for high-speed railways (HSR). The EU has put an increased emphasis on HSR because of:

- Its energy efficiency.
- More environmentally friendly than road or air.
- Fast and efficient transport of passengers from city centre to city centre.

France was the first European country to invest heavily in HSR. It now has a number of HSR lines connecting Paris to other regions of France and on to neighbouring countries (see Fig 28.5).

Paris has two international airports which process over 70 million passengers a year.

A modern high-speed train in one of the main railway stations in Paris. These trains provide an efficient link from Paris to many regional centres in France and elsewhere.

Tourism

Core regions are generally considered to be **sources** of tourists. Increasingly, however, they have also become **destinations**. Paris is no exception to this.

A HSR travels at over 250 km/hr. Travel time from Paris to Brussels is now only 1 hour 20 minutes and to London via the Channel Tunnel is only 2 hours 35 minutes.

Fig. 28.5 The high-speed rail network of France and the EU.

Activity

Study Fig 28.5 and answer the following.

1. Does the high-speed rail system highlight the centrality of Paris?
2. With what countries does it provide cross-border links?

Attractions of Paris for Tourists

- Beautiful and well-planned city, for example Eiffel Tower and parks.
- Rich array of historic churches, art galleries and museums, for example Notre Dame, the Louvre.
- Extensive range of high-quality shops and restaurants.
- Exciting night life and theatres.
- The 'atmosphere' of this historic city.

As a result of its attractions, Paris is the **most visited city in the world.** It receives over 30 million tourists a year, and 7 per cent of the city's workforce is involved in the tourist industry. This adds greatly to the wealth and international image of Paris.

The cathedral of Notre Dame is the top tourist attraction in Paris, receiving 13 million visitors each year.

Activity

Discuss the attractions of Paris for a holiday as opposed to the West of Ireland and the Mediterranean.

HUMAN PROCESSES

Population

The population of the Paris Region doubled between 1921 and 2004, and the area is now home to 11.3 million people (see Table 28.4). Such a large-scale increase could not be accommodated within the restricted administrative boundaries of the city of Paris. Huge suburban housing areas were built, and a series of new towns were planned to take the overspill of people (and jobs) from the city. The result is a sprawling urban region about 100 km in diameter.

> Almost 70 per cent of total employment in the region is located outside the city.

Table 28.4

Population Change in the Paris Region (000s)				
	1921	1975	1999	2004
City of Paris	2,907	2,317	2,125	2,145
Rest of Region	2,976	7,570	8,827	9,201
Total	5,883	9,887	10,952	11,346
% in city	49	23	19	19

> Refer to pages 205–206 to note the problems and plans that encouraged large-scale dispersal of people and jobs from the city.

Activity

Look at Table 28.4.

1. Describe population trends in the city.
2. Explain the growth of population in the city's hinterland.

Natural Increase in Population

Core regions are especially attractive for young adults. As a result, some 30 per cent of the Paris Region's population is aged between twenty and thirty-nine years, with a further one-quarter being under twenty. This helps explain the region's **high birth and low** death rate as compared with both national and EU averages (see Table 28.5). Natural change is now the major factor in the continued growth of population in Paris.

Migration

Core regions, such as Paris, have traditionally attracted large numbers of migrants who seek jobs and a better standard of living.

Although foreign migrants continue to be attracted by the pull factors of Paris, the **rate of immigration** has declined because of fewer job prospects and stricter laws on immigration. In addition, since the 1980s, there has been a **strong out-migration** of French people from Paris to other regions of France. This involves a large number of retirees, as well as younger people looking for cheaper housing and/or an improved quality of life. This form of **internal migration**, especially to nearby regions, greatly exceeds foreign in-migration to Paris. The result was a **net migration loss** of 490,000 in the 1990s.

Population Change in the Paris Region (000s)		
	Birth rate	Death rate
Paris Region	15.2	6.8
France	12.3	9.1
EU	10.2	10.0

Table 28.5

Some Facts on Migration to Paris
- 40 per cent of all foreign migrants in France live in the Paris Region.
- 13 per cent (1.5 million) of the region's population are migrants.
- The largest migrant groups are from Portugal and former colonies in North and West Africa.
- One-third of the migrant population is from the rest of France.

Planning for the Paris Region

Despite their growth and prosperity, core regions are also faced with **problems** that require careful planning. In Paris, these problems are generally due to the **scale and rapid growth** of the region. Its problems have effects at three spatial levels.

Out-migration from Paris is less likely to involve foreign populations. As a result, the number and importance of foreign populations will increase within the Paris Region. This may add to racial tensions.

1. Within the City

Planners in Paris have reacted to these problems by a variety of **urban renewal** projects, including demolishing poor-quality housing and replacing it with modern buildings, and improving transport systems.

Approximately 200,000 commuters come into the city of Paris each day.

Problems in the City
- Inner city housing is often old and in poor condition.
- Overcrowded living conditions.
- Traffic congestion linked to large-scale commuting.
- High costs of housing and property.
- Deindustrialisation and out-migration of people.

205

The main element of the plan, however, involved the creation of **eight large nodes** (centres) within Paris (Fig. 28.6). These include modern housing, employment opportunities and improved services. They are designed to reduce commuting and improve quality of life and therefore maintain people and employment **within the city.**

The La Défense node is located 6 km from the centre of Paris. This former undeveloped site of 640 ha now houses 200,000 residents and employs over 100,000 people in Europe's largest office complex.

2. Within the Paris Region

Problems for the Region
- Uncontrolled urban sprawl.
- Traffic problems as commuting levels increase.
- Environmental decline.
- Dominance of the city prevents other urban centres from providing a good range of services and jobs.

To help control the overspill of population and employment from the city, **five new towns** have been created along two axes to the north and south of the River Seine (see Fig. 28.6). These towns have been a success, and each has a population of over 100,000, as well as a good range of services and job opportunities.

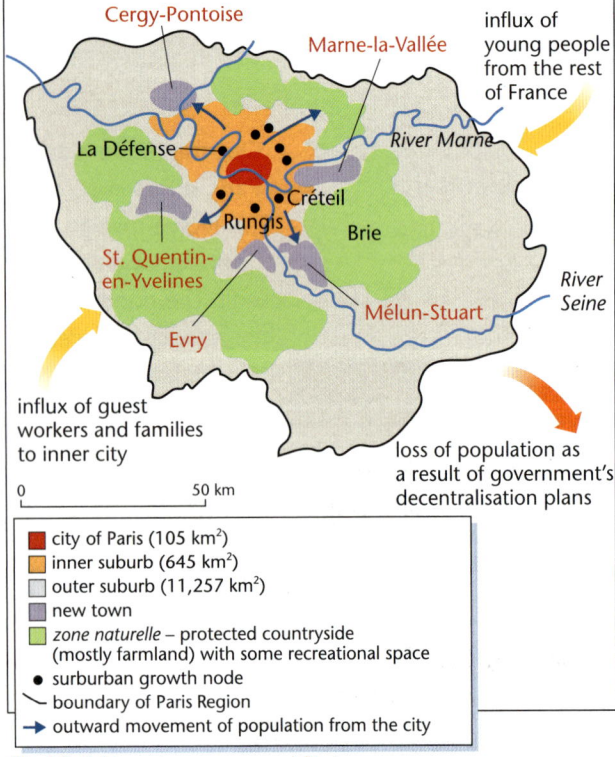

Cergy-Pontoise

Marne-la-Vallée

influx of young people from the rest of France

La Défense

River Marne

Créteil

Rungis

Brie

St. Quentin-en-Yvelines

Mélun-Stuart

River Seine

Evry

influx of guest workers and families to inner city

0   50 km

loss of population as a result of government's decentralisation plans

- city of Paris (105 km²)
- inner suburb (645 km²)
- outer suburb (11,257 km²)
- new town
- *zone naturelle* – protected countryside (mostly farmland) with some recreational space
- surburban growth node
- boundary of Paris Region
- outward movement of population from the city

Fig 28.6 New towns around Paris.

Modern urban layout at Marne-la-Vallée, one of the five new towns designed to accommodate dispersal of people and employment from the city of Paris.

3. Within the Rest of France

The dominance of Paris within French politics, culture and economics reduced the prospects for regional capitals to grow and to compete with Paris. French national planning has therefore selected a limited number of provincial cities, such as Lyons, Marseilles and Bordeaux, to act as **national growth centres**. A large amount of investment has been targeted on these centres to upgrade their infrastructure and make them more competitive for economic development.

Although this has had some success, Paris remains the dominant core region of France.

Multi-part Questions

1. State Examinations 2006 (Higher Level)
   A. NON-IRISH EUROPEAN REGIONS
   Examine the development of primary activities in one non-Irish European region of your choice. [20 marks]

   B. CONTINENTAL/SUBCONTINENTAL REGION
   Describe how any **two** of the following have influenced human activities in a continental/sub-continental region that you have studied:
   – climate
   – soil
   – relief
   – drainage. [30 marks]

   C. CULTURE
   'Culture is an important factor in defining some regions.' Examine this statement with reference to any region you have studied. [30 marks]

2. State Examinations 2006 (Higher Level)
   A. IRISH REGIONS
   Draw an outline map of Ireland. Show and name the following on it:
   i. any one Irish region that you have studied
   ii. any two physical features in the region
   iii. one urban centre in the region. [20 marks]

   B. EUROPEAN UNION EXPANSION
   Examine the impact of European Union expansion on Ireland's economy and/or culture. [30 marks]

   C. THE TERTIARY SECTOR
   Account for the development of tertiary activities in one non-Irish European region of your choice. [30 marks]

3. Example State Examination Paper 2005 (Higher Level)
   A. IRISH REGIONS
   Draw a sketch map of Ireland. On it, mark and name two contrasting regions. [20 marks]

   B. EUROPEAN REGION
   Select a non-Irish European region and explain how (i) relief and (ii) climate have influenced the development of its agriculture. [30 marks]

   C. NON-EUROPEAN REGION
   Examine **one** of the economic challenges facing a non-European region of your choice. [30 marks]

4. State Examinations 2006 (Ordinary Level)

The figures below show the tourist regions of Ireland visited by domestic tourists in 2004.

2004 – Regions Visited – Domestic Holidays (%)	
Dublin	13.9
Midlands-east	12.5
South-east	15.9
South-west	20.4
Shannon	11.3
West	17.9
North-west	8.1

A. IRELAND – DOMESTIC HOLIDAYS

Use graph paper to draw a graph that shows the data in the table above.

[30 marks]

B. EUROPEAN REGIONS

With reference to any **one** European region which you have studied, give and explain in detail **two** reasons why tourists might visit the region. [40 marks]

C. NON-EUROPEAN REGIONS

Describe the influence which **either** climate or the physical landscape has on the development of tourism in any non-European Continental or Sub-Continental region which you have studied. [30 marks]

5. State Examination 2006 (Ordinary Level)

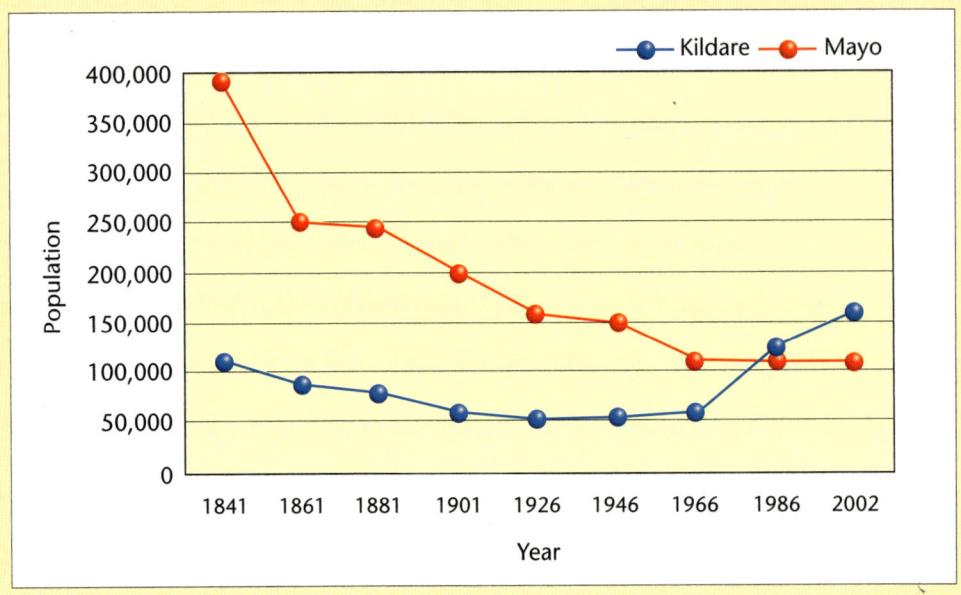

A. POPULATION TREND

Examine the above graph, which shows the populations of Mayo and Kildare since 1841.

i. After which census year did Kildare show a significant change in trend?

ii. In which census year did the population of Kildare first exceed that of Mayo?

iii. Explain briefly **two** causes of the rise in population in core areas such as Kildare.

[30 marks]

B. EUROPEAN REGIONS

With reference to **two** contrasting European regions, explain the differences between them under **one** of the following headings:

– climate
– population patterns
– energy sources
– manufacturing industry   [40 marks]

C. NON-EUROPEAN REGIONS

In the case of a non-European Continental or Sub-Continental region which you have studied, briefly describe **two** factors which have influenced the development of agriculture or industry in the region.   [30 marks]

6. State Examination 2006 (Ordinary Level)

A. IRELAND – REGIONS

Draw a sketch map of Ireland. On it mark and name:

i.   **two** contrasting regions
ii. **one** major city or town in each region.   [30 marks]

B. EUROPEAN REGIONS

Explain the importance of one of the primary industries listed below to the economy of any European region studied by you.

– Agriculture
– Forestry
– Fishing
– Mining/energy   [30 marks]

C. NON-EUROPEAN REGIONS

With reference to any non-European, Continental or Sub-Continental region you have studied, describe **two** factors which have influenced its industrial development.
                                                                           [40 marks]

CHAPTER 29
INDIA

KEY IDEA! India is part of the world's most populated and poorly developed global regions. Its human and physical geographies have a strong effect on each other.

The vast, triangular-shaped country of India stretches from approximately 36°N, along its mountainous northern borders, almost to the Equator. It divides the northern Indian Ocean into the Arabian Sea and the Bay of Bengal (see Fig. 29.1).

India is home to 17 per cent of the world's population. Its population exceeds 1 billion and will soon overtake China to become the most populous country in the world. India is a part of the less developed world and faces huge problems of poverty and underdevelopment. The average daily income per capita (per person) is only a little over US$1 (see Table 29.1). Despite this, India has recently developed strongly and has become a more important global economy (see pages 218–19).

Some Comparative Indicators of Development (2005)				
	Ireland	Italy	France	India
Area (000 km²)	70	301	552	3,287
Population (million)	4.1	58.5	62.3	1,015
Density (per km²)	58	194	113	324
Percentage of urban population	60	68	77	28
GNP (gross national product) per capita (US$)	40,150	30,010	34, 841	720

Table 29.1

Activity

Look at Table 29.1 and answer the following.
1. What percentage of the Indian population is rural?
2. In Europe, rural economies usually support only low densities of population. Is this true in India?
3. How prosperous is the average person in Ireland compared to India?

PHYSICAL PROCESSES

A country the size of India has a great variety of natural environments. This is a key factor in shaping the human geography of India, since almost three-quarters of the population live in rural communities and work mainly in agriculture.

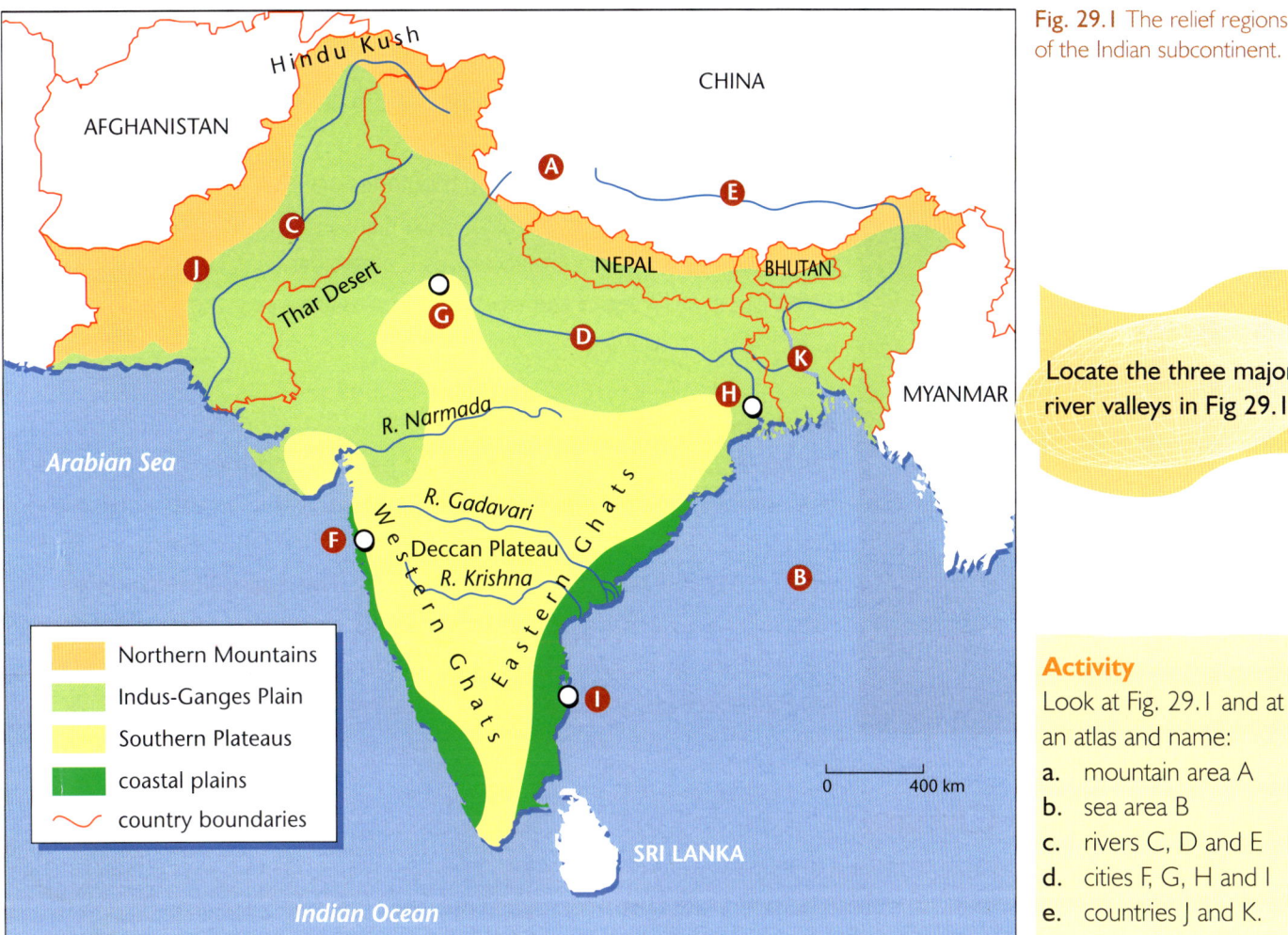

Fig. 29.1 The relief regions of the Indian subcontinent.

Locate the three major river valleys in Fig 29.1.

Activity

Look at Fig. 29.1 and at an atlas and name:

a.　mountain area A
b.　sea area B
c.　rivers C, D and E
d.　cities F, G, H and I
e.　countries J and K.

Relief and Drainage

There are three main landform regions in India (see Fig. 29.1):

- Northern Mountains.
- Indus-Ganges Plain.
- Southern Plateaus.

Northern Mountains

These towering mountains form India's northern boundary zone. They extend from the Hindu Kush in the north-west, through the Himalayas to the extreme north-east of the country. The world's highest mountain ranges (including Mt Everest) came from the collision of two great tectonic plates, which compressed the earth's crust and resulted in the uplift of these fold mountains. They form one of the earth's most dramatic physical features and are the source of many rivers that flow south into India.

Indus-Ganges Plain

The Indus-Ganges Plain follows the Indus River Valley from Pakistan through the Ganges Valley to end with the double delta of the Ganges and Brahmaputra rivers in Bangladesh. The earth movements that created the Himalayas also caused the Indus-Ganges Plain, a

Learn a simple sketch map that includes the major relief features and rivers of India.

major depression to the south of the mountains. The main drainage of northern India and the nearby states is directed to this depression. It includes India's three most important rivers (Indus, Ganges and Brahmaputra).

These rivers and their many tributaries are swollen by summer meltwaters from the surrounding mountains and, with monsoon rains, flood extensive areas of the lowlands. Large quantities of material eroded in the upper courses of the rivers are deposited along their lower courses as highly fertile alluvial soil.

Southern Plateaus

Peninsular India (the southern part that projects into the ocean) is made up of a number of plateaus. The **Deccan Plateau** is the largest of these and is tilted from west to east. Drainage flows from the higher elevations in the west across and out into the Bay of Bengal. The **coastal lowlands** are relatively narrow, rising abruptly along both west and east coasts to form the Western and Eastern Ghats. Both of these coastal mountain ranges have an effect on onshore winds and rainfall distribution for peninsular India.

The mountain ranges of the Himalayas form a northern boundary to the Indian subcontinent.

Climate

Most of India is in tropical latitudes. Only the mountainous zones of the north and north-west have frost. Temperatures year-round are relatively high, so the main climatic variable is precipitation and the **monsoon.** This shapes the patterns of development and livelihoods of the majority of people in India.

The monsoon is a reversal of winds over the Indian subcontinent and elsewhere in South-East Asia. The monsoon in India can be divided into **two** main seasons: **the dry and wet monsoon**.

Dry Monsoon

The dry monsoon occurs from October to June. It is caused by north-east winds that blow out from a high-pressure area in the continental interior, north of the Himalayas (see Fig. 29.2). From October to February, these are very cold winds that bring freezing temperatures and snow to the mountains of northern India. From March to June, the winds become warmer and, by June, temperatures in the Ganges Valley exceed 40°C. Coming from the continental interior, these winds are usually dry. Where these winds cross the Bay of Bengal and have to rise over the Eastern Ghats, this part of India receives a winter maximum of rainfall. The rest of India is dry.

> Why do these winds become warmer? (Think about the sun overhead.)

Wet Monsoon

From mid-June to September, warm ocean air is sucked into an intensive low-pressure area created in the continental interior (see Fig. 29.3). There are two branches to this monsoon.

One branch flows as a south-west monsoon across the Arabian Sea. Where these moist, warm winds are forced to rise over the Western Ghats, intense rain falls (more than 2,500 mm). A **second branch** crosses the Bay of Bengal and veers north to move along the Ganges. Torrential rain falls in the delta areas of the Ganges and Brahmaputra. In the hillier areas of north-east India, there can be more than 10,000 mm of rain in a period of six to eight weeks.

As these winds move westwards through the Ganges Valley, rainfall totals decline. In the extreme north-west of India there are areas not affected by the monsoon. Here desert conditions occur, as in the Thar Desert.

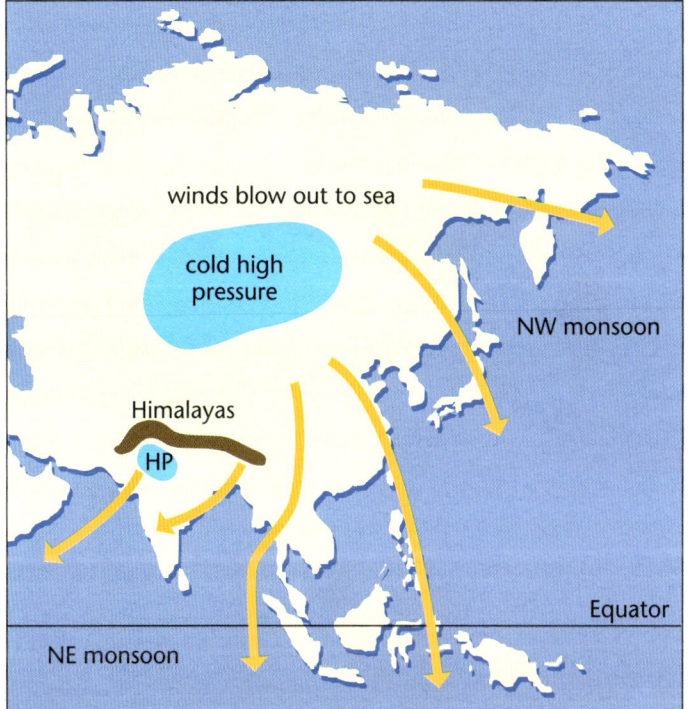

Fig. 29.2 October to June monsoon season.

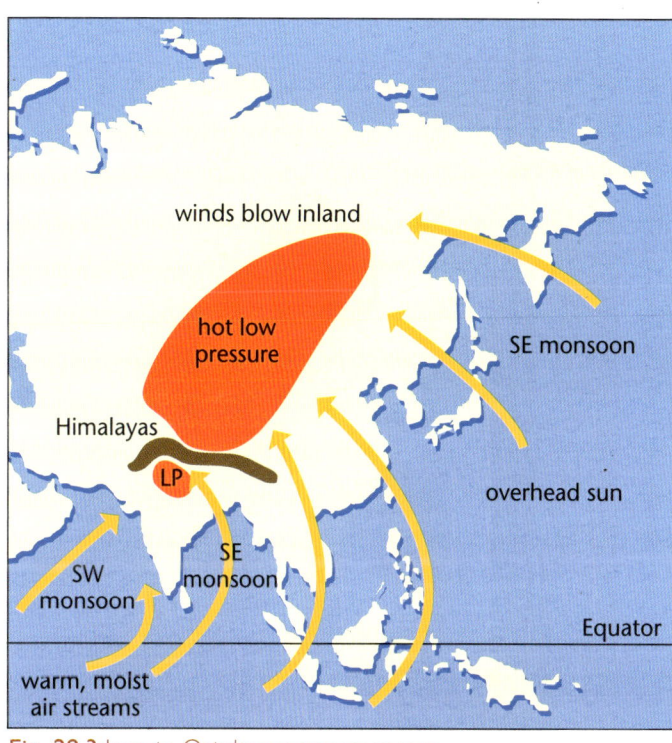

Fig. 29.3 June to October monsoon season.

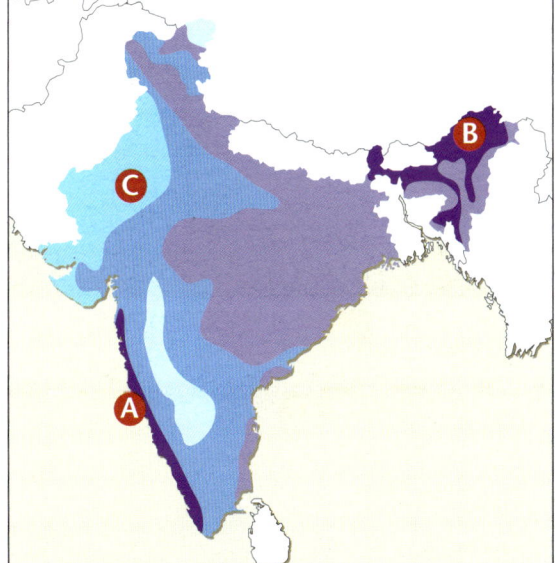

Fig. 29.4 Annual rainfall in India.

millimetres
- 200 to 600
- 600 to 1,000
- 1,000 to 2,000
- 2,000 to 3,000
- above 3,000

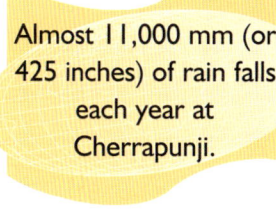

Almost 11,000 mm (or 425 inches) of rain falls each year at Cherrapunji.

213

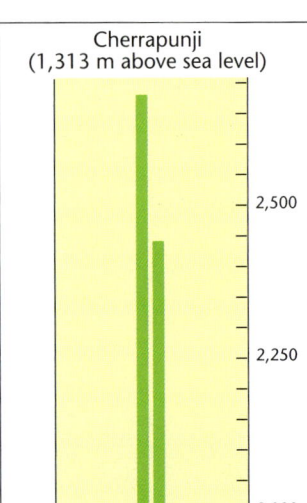

Cherrapunji
(1,313 m above sea level)

Activity

Look at Figs 29.1 to 29.5 and answer the following questions about the Indian monsoon.

1. Does Fig 29.2 or 29.3 illustrate the dry monsoon? Explain your choice.
2. Look at where Mangalore (A) is located on Fig. 29.4. Explain why its region is so wet and why there is a high summer rainfall.
3. Look at where Cherrapunji (B) is located on Fig. 29.4. Explain why this is one of the wettest places on the earth.
4. Give reasons for the desert region at C on Fig. 29.4.

While the monsoon rains are vital for agriculture in India, they also cause major problems and damage through flooding.

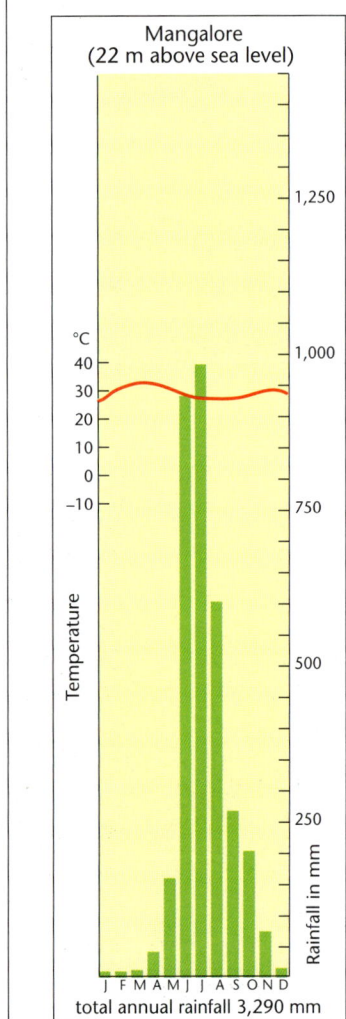

Mangalore
(22 m above sea level)

The regular monsoon rains provide for a rich vegetation cover on the Western Ghats, including tea plantations in the south.

total annual rainfall 10,800 mm

total annual rainfall 3,290 mm

Fig. 29.5 Annual rainfall in Cherrapunji and Mangalore.

Why Are Monsoon Rains Essential for India?

The people of the Indian subcontinent wait anxiously for the sudden burst of the summer monsoon. The timing and the intensity of the monsoon are very important for the livelihoods of hundreds of millions of people:

- **Delay in the monsoon's arrival** affects the planting of crops and the efficient use of irrigation systems. Harvesting can also be delayed.
- If the monsoon brings **low rainfall totals**, it has an adverse effect on growing crops such as rice, which needs waterlogged conditions. Low yields and poor harvests can lead to starvation for millions of farmers and their families who depend on the rice crop.
- When monsoon rains are **too heavy,** extreme flooding can occur and can wash away seeds, destroy villages and cause landslides.
- **A reliable, regular monsoon** is essential for India's agriculture and rural society. If the monsoon fails, it is disastrous for India. In 1987, a great famine followed the partial failure of the monsoon.

There is no social welfare system in India. What does this mean if there is a poor harvest?

ECONOMIC PROCESSES

India's economy is dominated by agriculture. To understand the country's problems, it is important to know about the nature and patterns of this sector.

The Primary Sector
Agriculture

The cultivated area of India (138 million hectares) almost equals the total area of land under cultivation in the European Union. A lot of the land has good agriculture potential, especially where water supplies are available. Only in the high mountains and dry areas, such as the Thar Desert along India's western border with Pakistan, are conditions too extreme for productive farming. Arable farming, especially cereals, is the main type of farming.

The Type of Farming

The dominant type of farming throughout much of India is intensive subsistence. It is used especially in rural areas with high population density, where people depend on being able to feed themselves. Rice is the chief crop for this type of farming, especially in the floodplains of the Indus and Ganges rivers. Other cereals, such as wheat and millet, are grown in drier parts of peninsular India (see Fig 29.6).

Almost all planting, weeding and harvesting is done by hand, with all family members being involved. Since plots of land are usually very small, no land is wasted. Roadways are narrow, and there are no field boundaries. Double cropping is also practised to make sure enough food is produced during the year to feed the farmer's family. While rice is grown in the wet monsoon season, alternative crops such as wheat and millet are grown in the drier months.

Trade in farm produce plays a vital role in the life of most rural communities. Most produce is usually sold locally. Why?

Plantation farming is important in some areas. The crops grown include tea, coconuts and cotton. Tea plantations of north-east India, especially in Assam, are major suppliers to the world tea trade. Coconuts are a speciality of the south-west coast, while cotton is important in parts of central India and north of Mumbai.

Wheat is the main crop in the drier north-west of India. Crop yields are quite high, especially where land can be irrigated. The Green Revolution has helped increase productivity levels. Corn (maize) and chick peas are also grown in some parts of this zone.

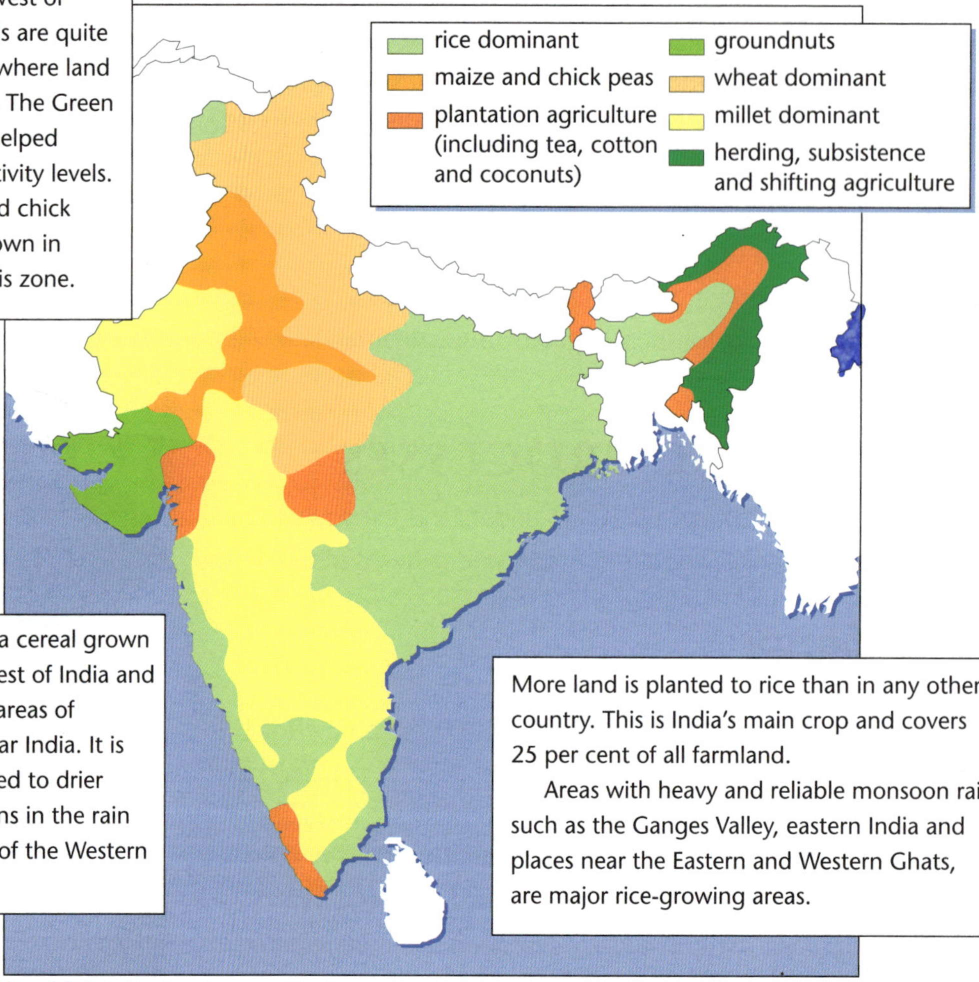

rice dominant	groundnuts
maize and chick peas	wheat dominant
plantation agriculture (including tea, cotton and coconuts)	millet dominant
	herding, subsistence and shifting agriculture

Millet is a cereal grown in the west of India and in large areas of peninsular India. It is well suited to drier conditions in the rain shadow of the Western Ghats.

More land is planted to rice than in any other country. This is India's main crop and covers 25 per cent of all farmland.

Areas with heavy and reliable monsoon rains, such as the Ganges Valley, eastern India and places near the Eastern and Western Ghats, are major rice-growing areas.

Fig. 29.6 Agricultural areas of India.

Preparing the land for growing rice.

Planting the rice.

Maintaining water levels for the rice crop.

Harvesting rice.

Activity
Do these photographs and those on page 216 support the view that the successful planting and cultivation of rice depend on the natural environment, and especially the wet monsoon?

Modernising Agriculture

India is a country that has benefited from the **Green Revolution.** This refers to the development and introduction of genetically modified, high-yield varieties of staple crops, such as rice and wheat. These 'miracle crops' produce high yields and are resistant to many diseases and pests. This has helped India meet its needs for food production, and by the late 1990s the country became a net exporter of food.

Yet there are **many problems** linked to the Green Revolution:

- It depends on large inputs of chemical fertilizers and pesticides.
- Labour is often replaced with machinery, so rural unemployment goes up and more people leave the land and go to towns, increasing rural-urban migration.
- Larger fields and farms are needed, so the number of farms is reduced.
- A well-educated farm population and capital (money) for investment are needed.
- It only benefits comparatively few, larger-scale farmers; large numbers of small-scale farmers are not able to participate in this process.
- There is environmental damage, for example water and ground pollution from chemicals.

For a large number of Indian farmers, a better solution to their problems involves a more effective programme of land reform. This would redistribute land from large estate owners to landless peasants.

In the 1990s, however, almost half of rural families had farms of less than 0.5 hectares, or no land at all. In contrast, a quarter of India's agricultural land was owned by less than 5 per cent of farm families. Most small farms are also broken up into tiny and scattered parcels of land. This reduces productivity even more and makes introducing modern farm practices, such as mechanisation, difficult. Land reform is therefore an urgent need.

Review the benefits and problems of the Green Revolution. Are you in favour of this approach? Explain your answer.

The failure to modernise India's agricultural sector and raise levels of productivity for many key crops remains an important issue. The country's growing population places more demand on the food supply. If the farming sector fails to meet this demand, it can lead to large-scale famine.

The Secondary Sector
Industry

When India became independent in 1947, it only had a limited range of industries, especially textiles and food processing. Only 2 per cent of the working population was employed in industry, which was concentrated mainly in the major cities: Bombay (now Mumbai), Calcutta (now Kolkata) and Madras (now Chennai).

On gaining independence, the new government was determined to encourage industrial development. The aim was to reduce India's dependence on imported industrial goods and to promote greater wealth and employment across the country.

Two key factors helped India's programme of industrialisation:

- The size of India's population provided a large home market.
- The country has some important natural resources, e.g. minerals such as coal and iron ore, a large and cheap labour force and outputs from agriculture (cotton, jute). Mineral resources encouraged the government to develop heavy industries, such as iron and steel, shipbuilding and chemicals.

Despite these advantages, progress was relatively slow and helped only a small number of preferred growth centres. In addition, by the 1980s, many heavy industries were in decline. Industrial policy has therefore been changed to emphasise:

- **Agri-industries:** These include fertilizers, machinery and food processing, which can benefit rural communities.
- **Consumer goods industries and small-scale craft industries:** These are more labour intensive than large-scale, heavy industries, so more jobs are created. They also benefit from low labour costs and traditional skills, which make them competitive in export markets. Examples include jewellery, clothing and leather goods.
- **Development in the countryside rather than the cities:** With more than 70 per cent of India's population living in rural areas, jobs need to be taken to these people, rather than encouraging migration to urban centres. This involves support for **community-based developments and self-help schemes** to improve facilities like basic health care and drinking water. Education schemes to improve skill levels are also important.

> Jute is used to make mats and rope.

Major deposits of iron ore and coal near Kolkata gave rise to an important iron and steel industry. This was important for national development.

> Do you think that small-scale industries and rural-based development are better for rural communities than trying to set up large branch plants owned by multinational corporations?

A rural family works together and uses traditional skills to make carpets which are mostly for export.
- *Do you think the development of such industries is important for India?*

Although large-scale industries have developed in India and provide employment, many workers are paid low wages and continue to live in poverty.

- **High-technology industries:** These are attracted to India by the country's growing population of skilled workers, low costs and improved communication systems. These high-value-added industries present a new and modern 'face' of India. They also suggest a brighter future for the country's industrial base.

India has emerged as a growing and significant manufacturer of computer software. Many major multinationals, such as IBM and Texas Instruments, have located in the country. Large numbers of locally owned companies have also been set up to supply software components to Western markets.

India's new policy of industrial development, its large and growing market and relatively cheap costs of production (especially labour) have attracted a lot of foreign investment. Many multinational companies have located factories and office activities in the country. **India is a newly industrialising country (NIC)** and has a growing share of world production and trade in industrial goods and services. In the new future, India (and China) will be a major competitor for the EU and USA in the world economy.

Where Industry is Located

Although the government has tried to spread industry across the country, this growing sector remains concentrated in a small number of key city regions (see Fig. 29.7). The most important are Kolkata, Mumbai and its hinterland in the state of Maharashtra, and Chennai-Bangalore.

> Give examples of high-technology industry.

> **India's Science Graduates**
> Although many people in the countryside are poorly educated, India has invested heavily in a well-developed education system, based largely in the cities. India now produces more university graduates than Canada and the USA combined, and 40 per cent of these are in science and engineering. A supply of skilled, English-speaking workers is attractive to international companies, especially as the cost of labour is low by Western standards. While a circuit board designer in California can earn between US$60–100,000, the salary in India averages about US$10,000.

> Note that the key city regions are the same as in 1947.

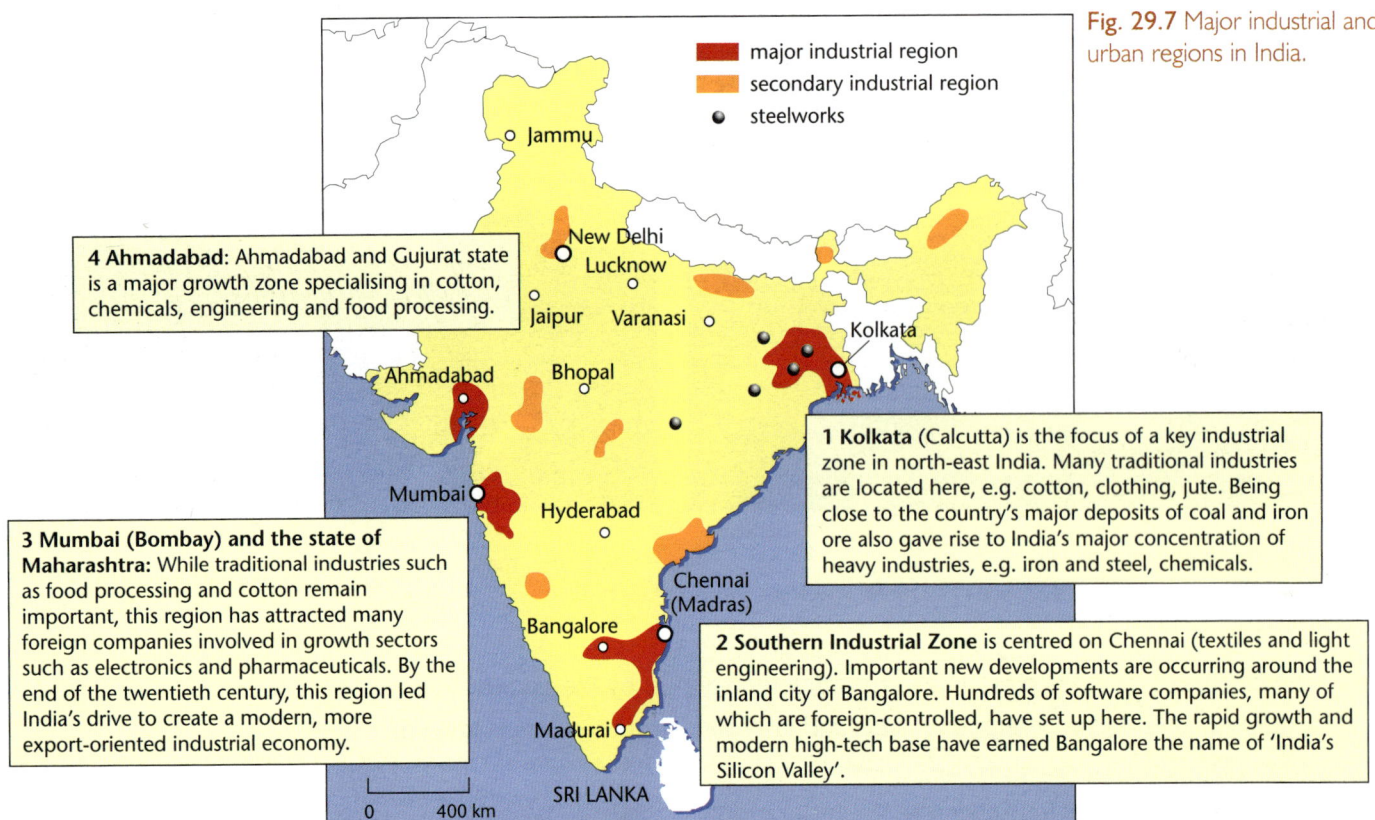

Fig. 29.7 Major industrial and urban regions in India.

4 Ahmadabad: Ahmadabad and Gujurat state is a major growth zone specialising in cotton, chemicals, engineering and food processing.

3 Mumbai (Bombay) and the state of Maharashtra: While traditional industries such as food processing and cotton remain important, this region has attracted many foreign companies involved in growth sectors such as electronics and pharmaceuticals. By the end of the twentieth century, this region led India's drive to create a modern, more export-oriented industrial economy.

1 Kolkata (Calcutta) is the focus of a key industrial zone in north-east India. Many traditional industries are located here, e.g. cotton, clothing, jute. Being close to the country's major deposits of coal and iron ore also gave rise to India's major concentration of heavy industries, e.g. iron and steel, chemicals.

2 Southern Industrial Zone is centred on Chennai (textiles and light engineering). Important new developments are occurring around the inland city of Bangalore. Hundreds of software companies, many of which are foreign-controlled, have set up here. The rapid growth and modern high-tech base have earned Bangalore the name of 'India's Silicon Valley'.

- major industrial region
- secondary industrial region
- steelworks

0   400 km

Modern textile factories provide opportunities for many workers, especially women.

One of an increasing number of high-technology parks in Bangalore which provides high-quality jobs for India's growing and educated workforce.

SERVICES

The Tertiary Sector

India's service sector remains underdeveloped. About 70 per cent of the country's population lives in rural areas. As so many people are poor and depend on a subsistence economy, they do not have the money for services. Many basic services are provided through self-help schemes and informal co-operation.

In India's cities, where most tertiary employment is located, there are **two types** of service activities.

- Large populations and more people with good incomes create demand for a full range of services. In the larger cities, there are increasing job opportunities in services, such as government administration, finance and banking, retailing and education.

- There is a second type of service activity in Indian and other cities of the less developed world. These services are in the **informal sector** (known before as the 'black economy'). Many people work as unlicensed sellers, offering a range of homemade goods and services. These services include street vendors, shoeshine boys and car repairs. Sometimes to survive, the urban poor are forced to take part in illegal activities such as drug dealing and prostitution.

Services in most urban centres remain underdeveloped, reflecting the poverty of the population. Here a woman's group has organised a co-operative bank to help improve the quality of life and development prospects for women.

Informal services are common throughout India. Here, a street typist works on a document for a customer.

Transport

Developing a country as large as India successfully needs an efficient transport system, but the government is not always able to find the money for improving transport. Transport systems in rural India are especially underdeveloped. One report suggested that by the late 1990s, half of the country's 600,000 villages did not have access to tarred roads suitable for motor vehicles. These communities use dirt-track roads and carts drawn by animals (usually oxen). It is unlikely that the transport networks in these areas will be modernised, especially in the short term.

Tourism

The size, history and variety of natural and cultural landscapes in India offer major attractions for the international tourist trade. International transport links to India have also improved in recent years, bringing more and more tourists to the country. For an underdeveloped economy, tourism offers many advantages, and the government actively promotes this industry.

Activity
What advantages does tourism have for a country like India, especially for its less developed regions?

The Taj Mahal is one of India's most famous tourist attractions. Over 3 million tourists visit this site each year.

Among India's attractions for tourists are:

- The spectacular mountain ranges of the Himalayas.
- The vast number of palaces and fortifications that reflect the history of India.
- Many religious temples, highlighting the variety of religions – Hindu, Buddhist, Sikh and Muslim.
- Cultural landscapes that are not familiar to many people from the developed world.
- The great rivers and varied physical landscapes.

To succeed in promoting tourism as a basis for development, a lot of investment has to be made in upgrading internal transport links and tourist facilities, such as accommodation. Another aspect to consider is that some tourists may be put off by the sheer pressure of population and the obvious poverty of many people in India.

HUMAN PROCESSES

Population

The size and especially the rate of population growth in India is the key factor behind many of the problems facing the country. At the start of the twenty-first century, the national population was more than 1 billion. India also has a comparatively high rate of natural increase (1.6 per cent a year) and its population could double to more than 2 billion by 2040.

The main reason for the rapid growth in India's population is natural increase (see Table 29.2 and Fig. 29.8). The country has only recently entered the third stage of the demographic transition model, whereas more developed countries, such as Ireland, Sweden and France, are in the fourth, or like Italy may have entered a fifth stage of this model. In India, while death rates have gone down a lot due to better health care, the birth rate remains high. The result is a high rate of population increase.

India has a large and rapidly growing population. In many rural areas children are often educated in open-air schools.

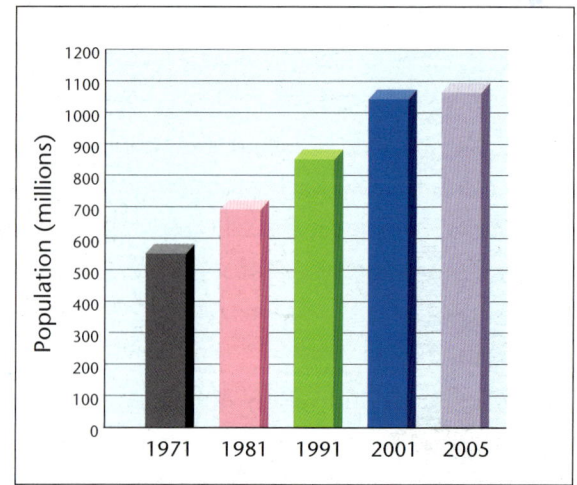

Fig. 29.8 Population growth in India from 1971 to 2005.

Some Demographic Indicators for India, Ireland, Italy and France				
	Birth rate (per 000)	Death rate (per 000)	Annual rate of natural increase (per 000)	Doubling time for population (years)
India	24	8	16	1.2
Ireland	16	7	9	1.9
Italy	9	10	–1	–0.4
France	13	9	4	0.3

Table 29.2

The Indian government recognises the problems caused by the country's large and expanding population. These include:

- Pressure on farmland.
- Making sure there is enough food.
- Rural-urban migration.
- Finding jobs for a growing labour force.

In the 1970s, the government started a campaign to reduce birth rates. They offered incentives to encourage people to use birth control (for example, a transistor radio for a vasectomy) and reduce average family size.

While the campaign had some success, it has been difficult to quickly educate large numbers of the population to the advantages of family planning. It is especially difficult in remoter rural communities, where large families are still seen in a positive way (for example, a sign of virility, help to work the land). Even with a slowdown in the rate of natural increase since the 1970s, the sheer size of the population and its young age profile have resulted in ever-greater numbers being added to India's total population. As urbanisation continues, it is thought that the birth rate will decline and help slow down the country's rate of natural increase.

Remember the demographic transition model shows the stages a country with high birth and death rates goes through until it has low birth and death rates.

Why will urbanisation cause birth rates to go down?

India has traditionally had a high birth rate. Here, a female health worker explains the importance of general health care and the use of contraceptives to women. Targeting women is thought to be especially important to reduce birth rates. Why?

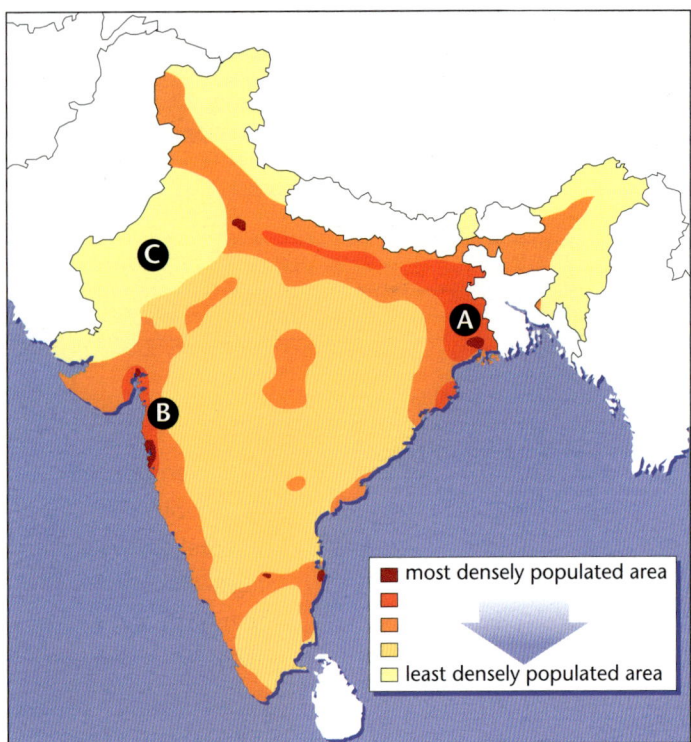

Fig. 29.9 Population density in India.

most densely populated area

least densely populated area

Population Distribution

India's population is not evenly distributed. There are many areas of very dense concentrations of people in the major river valleys, narrow coastal plains and hinterlands of major cities (see Fig. 29.9). These include:

- The major river valleys of the Indus, Ganges and Brahmaputra, where reliable water supplies and fertile alluvial soils provide the basis for intensive subsistence farming.
- The narrow coastal plains along the Eastern and Western Ghats also provide a rich agricultural environment. Areas of commercial farming mixed with intensive subsistence activities give a lower population density than in the major river valleys.
- The hinterlands of major cities, such as Kolkata (formerly Calcutta), Chennai (formerly Madras) and Mumbai (formerly Bombay). Growth of these and other large cities has attracted industrial development and a lot of immigrants.

- Less densely settled parts of India include the drier desert areas of north-west India, such as the Thar Desert, and the mountainous zones on the northern border.

Culture

India's large population is made up of many different culture groups. **Three major outside influences** have complicated India's cultural make-up, especially in language and religion:

- Early Indo-European influences.
- The spread of Islam.
- British colonialism.

Languages

The population of India does not speak a common language. A wide variety of different languages is spoken:

- The Constitution of India recognises eighteen languages.
- There are 1,600 minor languages and dialects.
- Schools teach in up to sixty languages.
- National newspapers are published in ninety languages.
- Radio programmes are broadcast in over seventy languages.

This creates communication problems between different language groups and for effective government in India.

Activity

Look at Fig. 29.9 and answer the following.

1. Why are population densities so high in the region marked A?
2. Why do coastal areas such as B have a high population density?
3. Why is the population density in area C so low?

What problems can be created by having many different languages in one country?

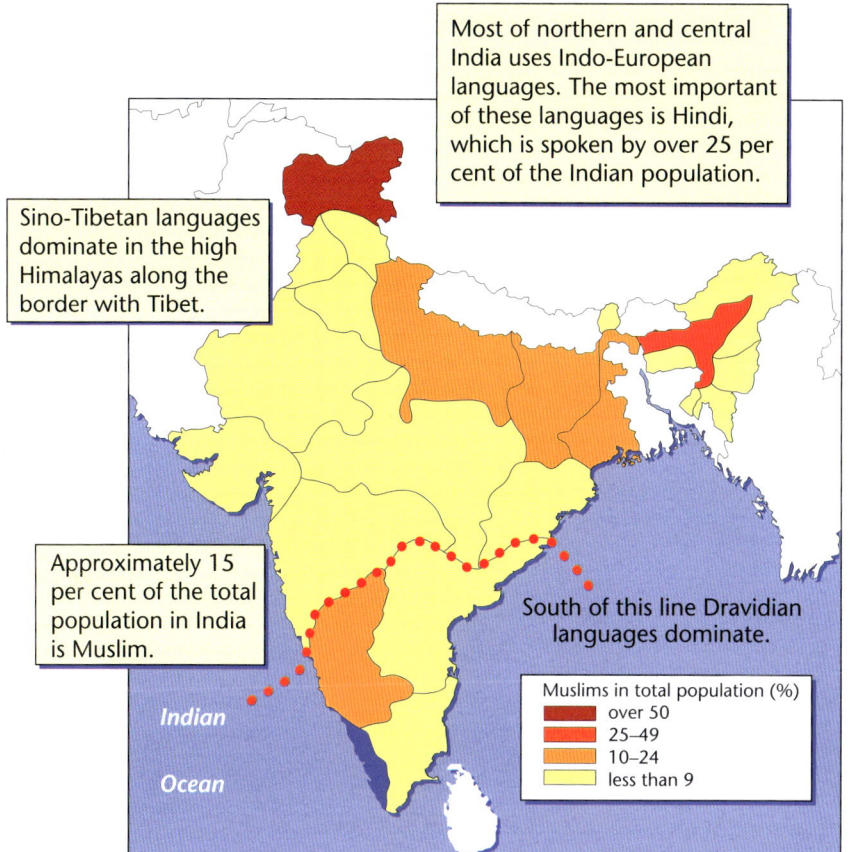

Most of northern and central India uses Indo-European languages. The most important of these languages is Hindi, which is spoken by over 25 per cent of the Indian population.

Sino-Tibetan languages dominate in the high Himalayas along the border with Tibet.

Approximately 15 per cent of the total population in India is Muslim.

South of this line Dravidian languages dominate.

Indian Ocean

Muslims in total population (%)
- over 50
- 25–49
- 10–24
- less than 9

Fig. 29.10 Language regions and main areas where Muslims live in India.

Activity

Look at Fig. 29.10 and answer the following.

1. What is the most-used language of India?
2. What is the main religion in most of India?
3. Does the high concentration of Muslims in the far north-west of India give rise to problems? (See Chapter 36.)
4. Can you suggest why a relatively high number of Muslims live in a zone going west to east across northern India? (Think about trade routes.)

The various languages of India are based on three language families. The **Indo-European language** group dominates in India. This can be traced to migrants who entered the north-west of India from Europe. **Hindi** is the largest and single most important language and is spoken by over 250 million people. It is the official language of India. **Dravidian** languages are spoken by about 200 million people, who live mainly in the south (see Fig. 29.10).

Although only 2 per cent of the population speaks **English,** it is an important language. Introduced under British colonial rule, it remains the language of business and the educated classes.

Although Hindi is the official state language, this is resented by many cultural groups. Bitter and often violent rivalries exist between language groups. Language is clearly a powerful expression of cultural differences and, as well as religion, often emphasises the divisions within India rather than the unity of the state. This is a major problem for the development of India.

Remember the language differences between Flanders and Wallonia in Belgium?

Hinduism

Indo-European influences also shaped the basis of **Hinduism.** This is the dominant religion in India and shapes much of the social and political life of the country and its people.

Hinduism introduced a multi-layered social system (or caste system). Individuals are grouped into a caste according to their job. At the top of the caste system are the priests (Brahmins) and other high-ranking officials or professions. At the bottom are the low castes that do menial and dirty tasks. They are said to be 'unclean' and 'untouchable'.

This street sweeper is one of the millions of 'untouchables' who live in extreme poverty in India.
● *Explain some of the reasons for this.*

Belonging to a caste is mainly decided by being born into the caste. This shapes the social prospects of an individual because members of a caste can only marry, associate or even eat within a narrow range of groups.

In urban centres, the caste system is breaking down and allowing for some social mobility, but it is still very strong in rural India. Many 'untouchables' are limited to a life of poverty and have little prospect for improving their status under the caste system of Hinduism.

For Hindus, the cow is a sacred animal, so it cannot be killed. While the cattle provide milk, dried dung for fuel and pull carts, they are an under-used resource. Many poorly bred, undernourished cattle roam the countryside. For many, these animals could be considered to be a parasite on the economy, rather than an advantage for development. This is a good example of the impact of culture on development.

Minority Religions in India

Although dominated by Hinduism, India also contains several important religious minorities, for example Islam. Many people living on the Indo-Ganges Plain were converted to Islam long ago. This was due mainly to Muslim traders who travelled to the area from Arabia (see Fig. 22.6 on page 152).

> People who practise the Islamic religion are Muslims.

There are now over 200 million Muslims in India, and most live in the north of the country. One of the major attractions of Islam for the low castes and 'untouchables' was that it rejects a rigid caste system and that all converts are considered equal.

Other examples of religious minorities are Buddhism, Sikhism and Christianity.

Muslim men at prayer in northern India, where this religion is concentrated.

Political-Religious Divides in India

India was a colony of Britain for centuries. After independence in 1947, two states were created. These were based on religious divides. India became a Hindu state, while Pakistan was Islamic.

Drawing political boundaries on the basis of a majority religion was very difficult, and large numbers of minority religious groups were left in both countries. This led to rioting and large-scale migration. More than 15 million people moved, as Muslims went from India to Pakistan, and Hindus from Pakistan to India.

Pakistan was based on the majority Muslim population living in the Indus and Ganges river systems. As a result, this state was split into two parts, separated by a long distance with northern India in between. This was not practical and, in 1971, Pakistan broke up into two distinctive states: Pakistan (around the Indus Valley) and Bangladesh (associated with the lower Ganges Valley – Fig. 29.1). Tensions between India and Pakistan remain high, especially over the disputed territory of Kashmir (see Chapter 36).

Hinduism is the dominant religion in India. Here, Hindus bathe in the holy river of the Ganges.

> Do you see any similarity over religious divides between India and Ireland?

Urban-Rural Development

The process of **urbanisation** is continuing strongly in India, especially because of large-scale rural to urban migration. Large numbers of people move (pushed) from poor rural communities by hope (pulled) of better prospects in growing cities.

While urbanisation has a long tradition in India, the present patterns of urban development are linked to **two processes:**

- **British colonialism:** This emphasised the development of key ports and centres of administration such as Mumbai, Kolkata and Chennai.
- **National planning:** Following independence, national planning recognised the importance of modern urban centres for promoting industrial development. Large-scale investment was made to upgrade the infrastructure (e.g. transport) of key centres. A new capital was also set up at New Delhi (near Delhi).

While towns and cities occur throughout India, there are **four main urban regions** (see Fig. 29.9):

- On the west coast around Mumbai (population 18.1 million).
- The southern tip of the peninsula linked to Chennai (6.6 million) and Bangalore (5.5 million).
- Kolkata (12.7 million) in the north-east.
- Delhi – New Delhi (11.7 million).

These four urban regions have grown rapidly and have attracted many manufacturing and service industries. They also have huge problems of **squalor and poverty** linked to large-scale in-migration. The government faces major challenges in dealing with the urban poor, including housing, employment, health and education.

Although urbanisation is growing, about 760 million people still live in **rural areas**. Studying the villages of rural India is important in understanding India's problems of development. Villages in rural India:

- Have a very conservative and traditional society; they resist change.
- Have a rigid caste system, which limits people's social and economic progress.
- Are very dependent on the natural environment (especially the monsoon rains) and can be exposed to problems of famine.
- Have a subsistence economy, which means a hand-to-mouth existence for the people living there.
- Are self-sufficient. They make goods and supply services for themselves, with little surplus for trade and interaction with outside areas.
- Are often overpopulated, especially as there is a limit to the amount of land available.
- Lack the money (capital) to invest in basic facilities.

Rural poverty and other related issues, such as rapid population growth and a reluctance to adopt more modern farming practices, are major issues for the government of India.

Over 275 million people live in India's urban centres.

World's apart. Prosperity in the modern centre of Mumbai contrasts with slum housing on the city's outskirts.

CHAPTER 30
ECONOMIC, POLITICAL AND CULTURAL ACTIVITIES IN REGIONS

KEY IDEA!

The study of regions highlights how complex the ways that economic, cultural and political processes act on each other are.

Regional identities are usually developed through **complex interactions** both within a region and between that region and its surrounding areas. In this chapter, the Republic of Ireland and Northern Ireland are used as an **example** to show how economic, cultural and political activities affect each other to make a region's special identity.

IRELAND'S CHANGING RELATIONSHIPS ON THE ISLAND OF IRELAND

At the start of the twentieth century, the two islands of Britain and Ireland were controlled by a powerful and centralised government in London. In 1922, Ireland gained political independence from Britain. Six north-eastern counties, however, remained part of Britain, and a new political boundary was created to separate what is now the Republic of Ireland from Northern Ireland (Fig. 30.1). This division of Ireland has strong historical roots and has had major implications on North-South relationships on the island of Ireland.

Ireland Before Independence and Partition

The population of the north-eastern part of Ireland had historically built up a culture and economy that was very different from the rest of the island. For example, large numbers of English and Scottish settlers were brought to the region during the **Ulster plantation** of the seventeenth century. These settlers had a different culture and religion to the local Catholic population.

The north-eastern region was also the only part of Ireland to experience large-scale industrialisation in the nineteenth century. At the time of partition in 1921:

- Two-thirds of Northern Ireland's population were Protestant, while the rest of Ireland was overwhelmingly Catholic.
- Northern Ireland was a prosperous industrial economy with strong trade links to Britain.
- The rest of Ireland was a depressed rural economy.
- The Protestant majority benefited from links with Britain, while the rest of Ireland associated British rule with poverty, migration and the suppression of Gaelic culture.

Activity

Look at Fig. 30.1 and at an atlas and answer the following.

1. Identify the six counties that form Northern Ireland.
2. Name the counties marked X, Y and Z that are part of the historic province of Ulster but not in Northern Ireland.
3. What effect do you think the border has had on towns like Dundalk and Derry?

The majority of Ireland's population saw political independence from Britain as essential for their economic and cultural development.

Fig. 30.1 The political divide in Ireland.

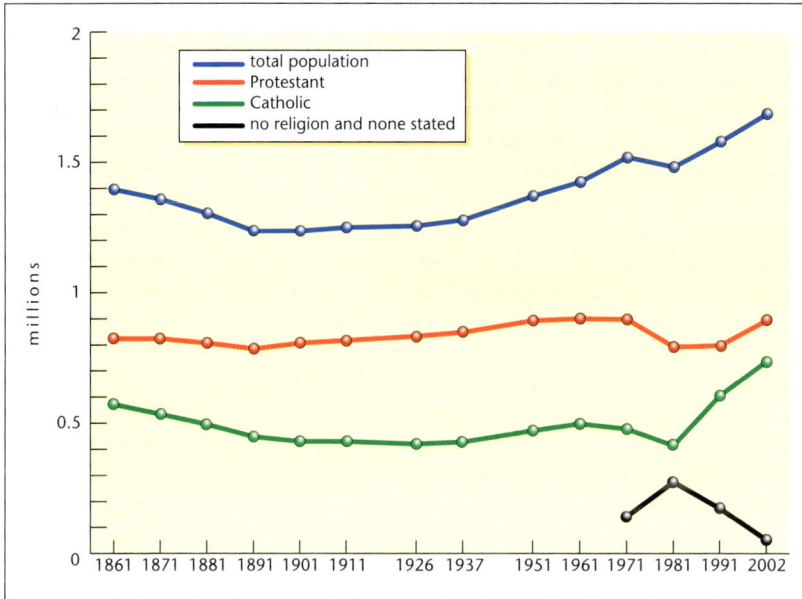

Fig. 30.2 Catholic and Protestant population trends in Northern Ireland.

Activity

Look at Fig. 30.2 and answer the following:

1. Estimate the proportion of Northern Ireland's population that was Catholic in 1926 and 2002.
2. What do you note about trends in Catholic and Protestant totals after 1981?
3. Why is this a concern for the Unionists?

Changing Relationships between the Republic and Northern Ireland

The creation of the political boundary between the Republic and Northern Ireland emphasised long-standing political, economic and cultural differences. Since the 1960s, however, these differences have been reduced. Much of this has been due to the **modernisation** of the Republic's economic, cultural and political systems.

Economic Trends

From the 1960s, the Republic has attracted many foreign industries and has built up a large and modern manufacturing economy (Chapter 26, pages 178–80). In contrast, most of Northern Ireland's old, traditional industries, such as textiles and shipbuilding, declined. Furthermore, the period of civil disturbances (the Troubles) that began in 1968 and continued into the 1990s discouraged foreign investors. The result was a depressed regional economy in the North as opposed to the prosperous Celtic Tiger economy of the South (Fig. 30.3 and Table 30.1). Since the Belfast Agreement of 1998, however, the economy of the North has improved.

Fig. 30.3 Manufacturing jobs in the Republic of Ireland and Northern Ireland.

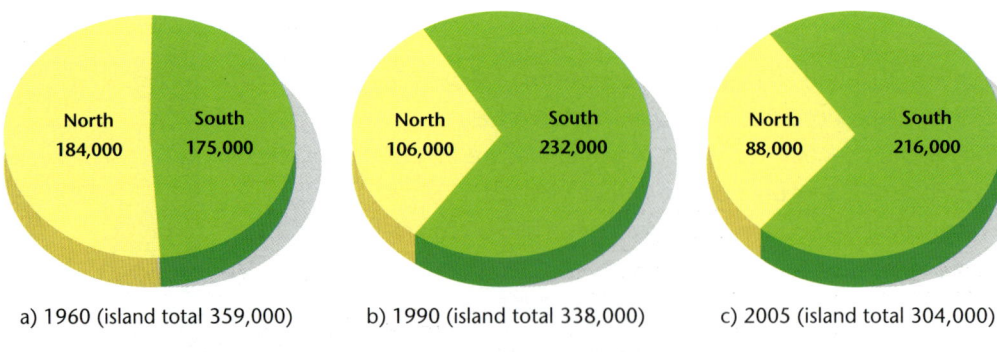

a) 1960 (island total 359,000)   b) 1990 (island total 338,000)   c) 2005 (island total 304,000)

	Republic of Ireland	Northern Ireland
1973	59	79
1980	63	62
1990	68	74
2000	126	82
2005	139	93

GDP per Capita in the Republic of Ireland and Northern Ireland as a Percentage of GDP in the EU

Table 30.1

Activity

Look at Fig. 30.3 and Table 30.1 and answer the following.
1. Describe the trends in manufacturing employment in the Republic and Northern Ireland from 1960 to 2005.
2. Estimate the proportion of manufacturing jobs in the Republic in 1960 and 2005. Explain the change.
3. When Ireland joined the EU in 1973, which part of the island was the most prosperous?
4. In terms of personal prosperity, is the Republic still 'the poor relation of the North'?

Cultural Changes

While there are still cultural differences between the North and South, they are now less marked. Much of this has been linked to changes to more modern attitudes and ways of life in Ireland, especially in the Republic.

Political Interaction on the Island of Ireland

Political tensions between the Republic, Northern Ireland and Britain have been harder to resolve. This was especially the case during the 'Troubles', when a state of almost civil war existed between extreme nationalist and unionist groups (see Chapter 22, pages 150–51).

During the 1990s, significant efforts were made to improve the political situation. In 1998, a major step forward occurred with the signing of the **Belfast Agreement** (also called the Good Friday Agreement). This created **three** new political bodies to act as the basis for what are called **strands** (see Fig. 30.4). These strands are designed to link together the political capitals of Belfast, Dublin and London. **In this way, inter-relationships are stressed rather than political division.**

How has greater prosperity and urbanisation, together with the Catholic Church having less influence in shaping people's lives in the Republic, helped reduce the sense of difference **between** North and South?

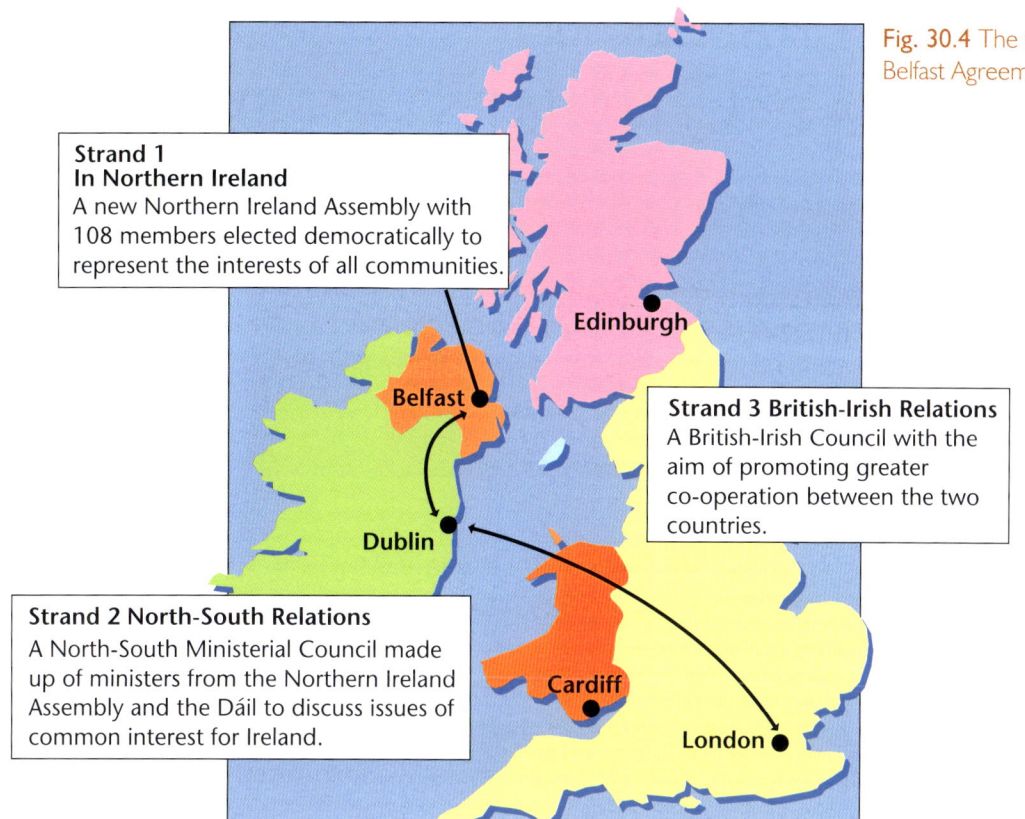

Fig. 30.4 The three strands of the Belfast Agreement.

Strand 1
In Northern Ireland
A new Northern Ireland Assembly with 108 members elected democratically to represent the interests of all communities.

Strand 3 British-Irish Relations
A British-Irish Council with the aim of promoting greater co-operation between the two countries.

Strand 2 North-South Relations
A North-South Ministerial Council made up of ministers from the Northern Ireland Assembly and the Dáil to discuss issues of common interest for Ireland.

Edinburgh

Belfast

Dublin

Cardiff

London

Do you think that an all-Ireland approach is the best way to address problems on the island of Ireland?

A street mural in the Republican Falls Road commemorating the 1916 Easter Rising. The current movements to integrate must combat deep historic and cultural divisions.

CHAPTER 31
CULTURAL GROUPS AND POLITICAL REGIONS

 **KEY IDEA!**

Cultural groups and regional identities are becoming more important in the political life of many countries.

A sovereign government is one with supreme power within its territory.

Europe is a patchwork of different cultural groups and political units. The interaction between these is essential for understanding Europe as a distinctive region. There are three terms that are important:

- **Nation state:** A country that has political boundaries containing a population with a high level of cultural sameness. It should also have a sovereign government.
- **State:** A state is a politically organised territory that is administered by a sovereign government.
- **Nation:** A group of tightly knit people who have a common culture – language, ethnicity, religion and other cultural values. Many nations have gained political recognition and have become nation states, for example the Irish Republic following independence from Britain. Other nations, however, have not yet established their own sovereignty, for example Wales and Scotland.

Although most of Europe's countries are considered to be nation states, they all have cultural minorities. Generally, these groups identify with the state they live in and add to the strength and character of the state; for example, Switzerland with its four language groups.

There are, however, some examples of minority culture groups, especially those with strong identities, who feel their interests are ignored or threatened by the dominant culture group. In such cases, the links that tie the state together become weakened. **Nationalist groups** can emerge to represent their interests and **begin to look for greater powers of self-government.**

Basques marching in San Sebastian in 2006 in support of an imprisioned leader of the ETA, the Basque separatist group.

The process by which regions within a state seek greater autonomy (political control) over their own affairs while reducing the powers of the central government is called **devolution**. A more extreme form of devolution is **separatism**. In some cases, national governments have accepted the demands for greater self-government and regions have been given more autonomy. Examples include Scotland and Wales in Britain.

In other cases, central governments cannot accept the levels of self-government some nationalist groups demand. This is especially the case where these groups demand independence and the break-up of an existing country. Where this happens, cultural and political relationships between a region and central government can become violent. The result may be extremist groups leading terror campaigns against the official government, as in the Basque Country in Spain.

Case Study: Cultural Groups and Devolution in Spain

In Spain, the government has been centred on the capital, Madrid, for centuries. Although the central government is still powerful, Spain has several well-defined cultural groups that have their own language. The best-known groups are probably in the Basque Country and Catalonia.

Each of these regions has been given powers by the central government to administer a range of key functions, such as cultural affairs, education, economic development and the environment. Both regions have their own parliaments. Their distinctive languages, Basque (called Euskera in the Basque language) and Catalan, are co-official languages with Spanish.

The Basque Country is perhaps the Spanish region that is best known for demanding independence from Spain. As a people, the Basques form a distinctive cultural group that occupies an area on each side of the Pyrenees in northern Spain and south-west France. The core of the Basque area is in northern Spain and has a population of 2 million. Bilbao is the largest city in the region (Fig. 31.1).

The Basques in northern Spain:

- Have lived in the area for about 10,000 years, so they have developed their own special cultural identity.
- Are a distinctive ethnic group.
- Speak a language (Euskera) that is not like any other European language.

Above all, it is **because the Basque language has survived that this is a distinctive cultural region.** Under past Spanish governments, the Euskera language was declared illegal, and large numbers of Basque nationalists were put in prison for calling for independence and for their cultural roots to be recognised.

One reaction to government repression was the extremist nationalist group called ETA (Euskadi ta Askatasuma), which declared war on the Spanish state. ETA became involved in a large number of bombings and assassinations in its drive to gain independence from Spain.

'Ethnicity' means belonging to a group that has certain common traits, e.g. race, language or religion.

Separatism sees devolution as a stepping stone to independence and the emergence of a new nation state.

Fig. 31.1 The location of the Basque Country and Catalonia in Spain.

In their attempts to gain independence from Spain, ETA has used violent tactics such as car bombs.

In 1979, the Basque Country in Spain was granted a high level of autonomy. This weakened public support for ETA because it seemed that democratic means were working to gain self-government for the region. Although the cultural strength of this region has been the basis for gaining the Basques a more equal relationship with the national government in Madrid, a weakened ETA continues to fight for independence.

Catalonia is another Spanish region that has gained a lot of regional autonomy because it has a distinct cultural identity. Centred on the major industrial and trading city of Barcelona, the Catalans have a strong sense of nationalism. They have their own language, Catalan, and have a very prosperous economy.

Although it has only 6 per cent of the Spanish population, Catalonia accounts for nearly 40 per cent of Spain's industrial exports. It attracts high-technology industry, has strong trading traditions, and Catalonia has emerged as one of the four motors of the EU (see Fig. 23.2, page 157).

With Catalonia's economic success, its pride in its cultural distinctiveness and the strength of feeling to achieve independence from Spain, it is not surprising that the Spanish government has devolved an increasing amount of political power to Catalonia to keep this important region within Spain.

> **Do you see any similarities between Ireland and the Basques in their efforts to achieve autonomy or independence?**

> **The Catalan demands for greater political autonomy are supported by a much stronger economic basis than in the Basque region.**

The modern cathedral of Sagrada Familia in Barcelona stands as a symbol of a strong and growing Catalan identity and culture.

CHAPTER 32
THE FUTURE OF THE EUROPEAN UNION

KEY IDEA!

Future developments in the European Union will have a major influence on the economies, politics and sovereignty within Europe.

In 1957, the Treaty of Rome brought together six countries to form an economic union to better promote development in Europe. The process was successful and, by 1995, the **European Union** had expanded to fifteen member states.

The process of enlargement was relatively easy because:

- Each enlargement involved no more than three countries.
- All new members were within Western Europe with similar cultural characteristics and were relatively well developed.

The enlargements in 2004 and 2007 were less easy. Proposals for further enlargement will also add to EU problems.

- **Ten countries** were admitted in 2004, and two more in 2007. Such a large number of new members has increased the **scale of impact** within the EU.
- Most new and proposed members are from **Central and Eastern Europe,** and were formerly part of a **communist system** dominated by the USSR. Their economies were less developed and the governments were not democratic. This made it hard to adjust to the EU.

The recent and ongoing process of enlargement will have major impacts on the future of the EU.

Look at Chapter 35 to learn more about how the European Union was formed and when different countries joined (enlargement).

Activity
Look at Table 32.1 and suggest some of the advantages and problems of the recent and future enlargements to the EU.

Table 32.1

Some Development Indicators of New and Proposed Member States of the EU				
	Area in sq. km (000s)	Population (million)	GDP per person (euros)	Unemployment (%)	Agriculture as % of total employment
EU (15)	1,317	380	24,250	7.8	4.0
Ten new states (2004)	736	74	9,550	14.9	13.2
EU (25)	2,053	454	22,300	9.0	5.4
New members (2007)					
Bulgaria	111	8	6,800	18.2	9.6
Romania	238	22	7,000	8.4	36.8
Applicant states					
Croatia	57	5	9,300	18.7	15.5
Turkey	780	70	5,600	10.1	36.0
Montenegro	14	0.6	2,850	28.0	2.0

Workers producing car engines for Audi in a major new investment in Hungary.

In Romania and Bulgaria, much farming remains underdeveloped.

Since Poland joined the EU in 2004, large numbers of Poles have migrated to countries such as Ireland to find work, e.g. in construction, agriculture and catering.

The Future of Economic Union

- **Prospects for economic development** have and will increase. This is linked to the increased population of the EU, which improves the market for goods and services (Table 32.1). The EU will become a larger and **more important power in world trade.**

- The **increasing area** of the EU provides more sources of raw materials and a **greater choice of location** for factories and offices. Newer member states have **lower costs of production** (especially labour) and this has and will encourage employers to **relocate production** to Central and Eastern Europe.

    Competition for foreign direct investment (FDI) is increasing. This has major implications for 'older' member states, such as Ireland, which rely heavily on FDI.

- New member states have a much **higher dependency on agriculture** than the EU of fifteen member states (see Table 32.1). The potential for increasing output by modernising their underdeveloped farming communities is huge. Reforms to the Common Agricultural Policy are therefore encouraging farmers to produce less but to **increase quality of production.** Farmers are also encouraged to **protect the environment** and to look for alternative sources of income, e.g. forestry, agritourism.

- Opportunities for international migration have and will increase in an enlarging EU. The **higher levels of unemployment** and **lower levels of prosperity** in newer member states create **push factors** than have caused many people to migrate to the countries of the EU 15.

    As the economies of newer member states improve, however, outward migration will be reduced.

- A **large new eastern periphery** will dominate EU regional policy and demands for structural funds. Most EU funding for 2007–13 is allocated to the problem regions (now called Convergence Regions) in Central and Eastern Europe (see Fig. 32.1). This means:
  - **Less money** will be available to aid development in long-established problem regions, such as the Mezzogiorno.
  - Some long-established **problem regions have been removed** from the list of regions that will receive significant support from structural funds. One example is Ireland, which is no longer classed as a problem (or convergence) region.

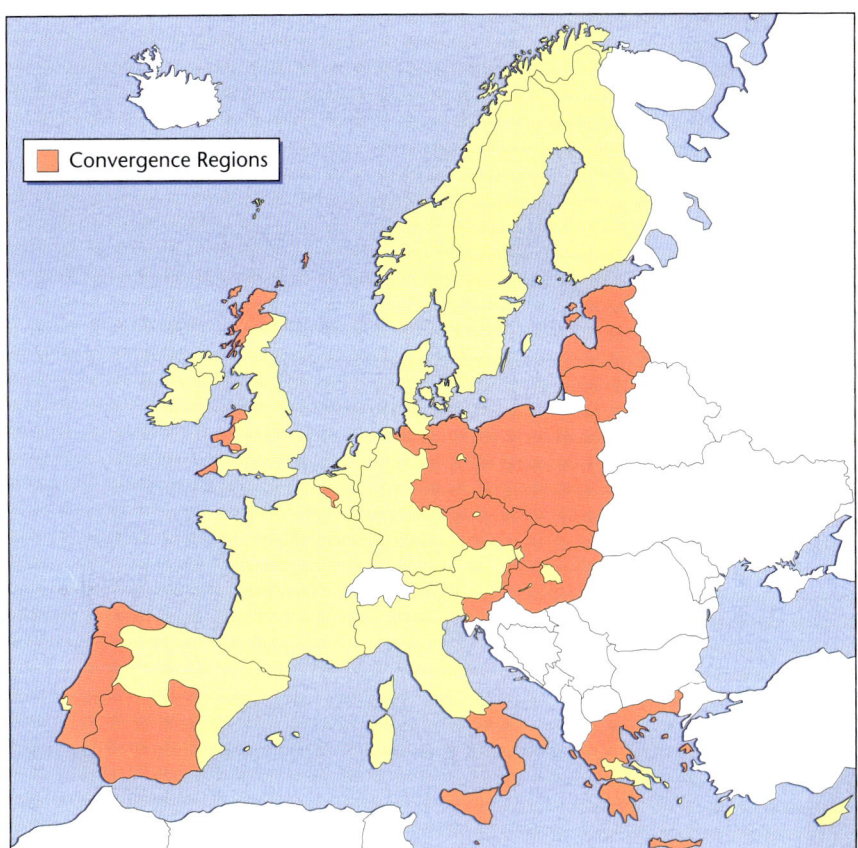

Fig. 32.1 Convergence Regions of the EU 25, 2007–13.

Convergence Regions

The Future of Political Union

In the 1990s, the EU became committed to **increasing political union** so it could play a stronger role in world affairs. This was prompted by the need for the EU to respond in a united way to events that were happening in nearby regions, for example the wars in (former) Yugoslavia and the Middle East.

Some progress has been made. The EU now has a **Foreign Minister**, who represents the views of member states at conferences that discuss important global issues, e.g. world trade and global warming. In addition, the EU has accepted a greater **peace-keeping role** in several conflict zones, e.g. Afghanistan, Bosnia.

Some key problems confront further political union:

- Persuading the populations of member states to accept an **EU constitution** to act as a political 'blueprint' to guide further development.
- Member states often have **different political agendas,** especially in foreign policy. As a result, states are reluctant to allow the EU to take policy decisions for them; an example of this is the different altitudes to the US invasion of Iraq in 2003.
- Neutral countries, such as Ireland, have major problems over suggestions of a **bigger military role** for the EU.

A lot of work has to be done before the EU can progress to a political union which matches what has been achieved for economic union.

The Future of Sovereignty

A key feature of the Treaty of Rome (1957) is that member states **have to give up some degree of sovereignty** (decision-making power) to this international organisation.

There are **three** main institutions that affect the sovereignty of member states.

237

European Commission

This is the main administrative body of the EU. Although it has no decision-making power, it is the only EU institution that can propose new legislation. It is located in Brussels and is divided into twenty-five directorate generals (government departments), each headed by a **commissioner.**

Currently, each of the twenty-five member states has a commissioner. It is proposed, however, to reduce this number to make administration more efficient. This will mean, especially with further enlargement, that **member states will lose their automatic right to have a commissioner.** For member states with no commissioner it will mean a loss of prestige and scope to shape developments in the EU.

The European Parliament building in Strasbourg.

European Parliament

This is the key forum for democratic debate. Since 1979, voters in all EU countries directly elect **members of the European Parliament** (MEPs) for five years. In 2007, there were 785 MEPs who represent 490 million people of the EU.

Although initially having limited powers, the parliament has increased its decision-making powers significantly. It now has joint decision-making power with the European Council in a growing number of policy areas.

It is proposed to reduce and cap the number of MEPs at 750 in the 2009 elections. This, and further enlargements, will reduce the number of MEPs allocated to individual countries (Ireland will lose one of its thirteen MEPs).

For small countries (such as Ireland) to be able to shape policy decisions in the European Parliament, it is essential that their MEPs **form effective political alliances** with other like-minded political parties from other member states.

Council of the European Union

This is the main decision-making institution in the EU. Each member state sends to the Council its minister responsible for the policy area to be discussed (for example, the minister for agriculture discusses agricultural policy).

To make decision-making more efficient, it is proposed that for a vote to pass in the Council, it must be supported by:

- 55 per cent of member states, and which represent
- 65 per cent of the total EU population.

To block a vote, at least four countries must support the block.

This proposal is designed to prevent a small number of large states dominating policy. It also means, however, that **smaller states that want to shape policy will have to form effective alliances with other member states.**

The EU has significantly increased its decision-making powers. As a result, member states have fewer decision-making powers. The issue of sovereignty will be an important element on any agenda for the future direction of the EU.

CHAPTER 33
CHANGING BOUNDARIES IN LANGUAGE REGIONS

KEY IDEA!

The size and shape of language regions can change over time.

The regional boundaries of human activities change a lot over time. This is due mainly to **two processes:**

- Push-pull forces of migration.
- The effect of strong external forces.

The **push-pull forces of migration** cause people to move from one region to another. When more people move into a region than leave it, the region usually expands its boundaries. For example, rural-urban migration (when people move from the country into towns) often creates population pressure in the urban area, which then expands outwards into suburbs and rural areas around the town.

On another scale, the widespread migration of Islamic people to areas outside the Middle East has resulted in a large increase in the regions influenced by the religion of Islam (see Fig. 22.3 on page 149).

Strong external forces affect a region's identity. Stronger and more aggressive cultural forces can work to reduce the importance and regional patterns of minority cultures. For example, modern communication systems (radio, television and the Internet) have allowed the importance of major world languages, especially English, to increase. This often reduces the status of minority languages.

The decline of Irish and Welsh are examples of how both processes have changed the regional boundaries of these ancient Celtic languages.

An emigrant family leaving Cobh for the USA in 1953.
- *Why did so many Irish people migrate for more than 100 years after the Famine?*

Boundary Changes of Gaeltacht Areas

In 1851, the census of Ireland recorded 1.5 million people as speaking Irish. Large areas along the southern and especially the western coastline kept Irish as their majority language (see Fig. 33.1).

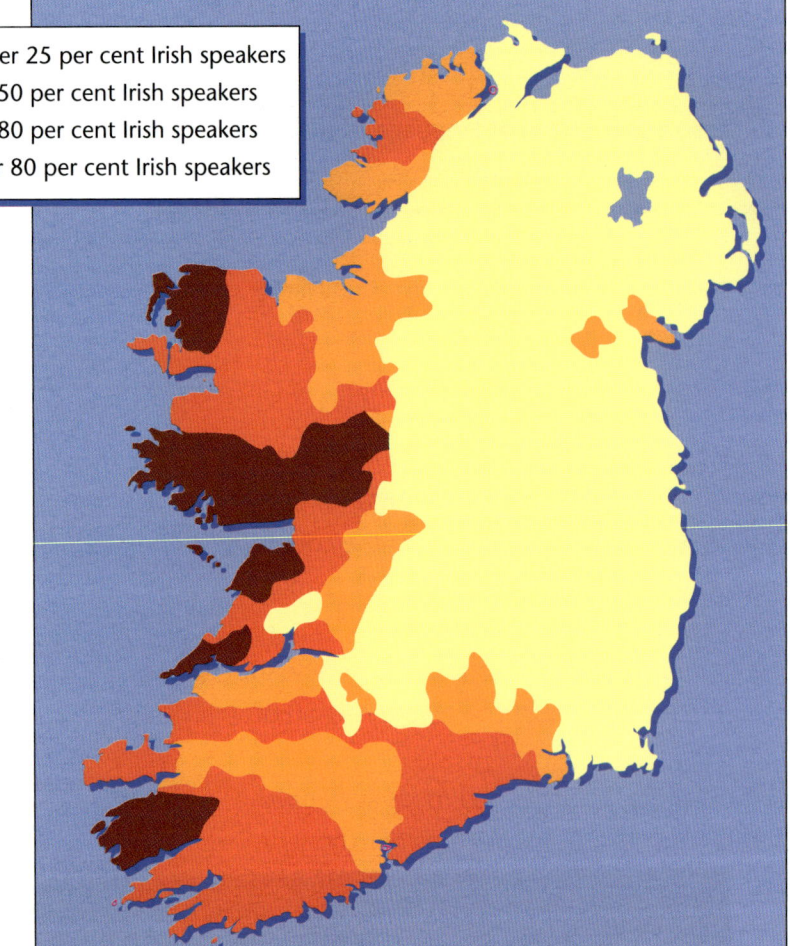

Fig. 33.1 The Irish-speaking population in 1851.

under 25 per cent Irish speakers

25–50 per cent Irish speakers

50–80 per cent Irish speakers

over 80 per cent Irish speakers

Activity

Look at Fig. 33.1 and answer the following questions.

1. Which parts of Ireland in 1851 show more than 50 per cent of the population speaking Irish?
2. Why was so little Irish spoken in eastern and northern Ireland?

The Irish Language from 1861 to 1926

In the period from 1861 to 1926, the number of Irish speakers declined to 544,000. The changes were greatest in Munster and Connaught, provinces that traditionally had the most Irish speakers (see Figs. 33.1 and 33.2). Decreases in these core regions for the Irish language were so strong that many people felt that the Irish language would become extinct in the twentieth century.

The decline in the area and numbers of Irish speakers was due to:

• Large-scale emigration.
• The growing dominance of English.

The Irish Language from 1926 Up to Now

On gaining independence from Britain, the new government committed itself to supporting the Irish language as an essential part of national identity. This support took several forms:

• Irish became the official language of the state, and being able to speak Irish was essential for many jobs, especially in government administration and public services.

- Irish was included as a compulsory subject in the school syllabus.
- An official Gaeltacht area, set up in 1926, has been strongly supported by the government.

These measures were aimed at reducing the dominance of the English language. Irish would be the majority language in the Gaeltacht and this would act as the core region to preserve and promote the Irish language.

At one level, the measures to support the Irish language appear to have been very successful. The numbers of people claiming to speak Irish in Ireland have increased from 589,000 in 1946 to some 1.57 million today. Interestingly, the largest numbers are located in Leinster. This reflects, perhaps, the fact that some knowledge of Irish is needed to work in government and administration, which is concentrated in Dublin.

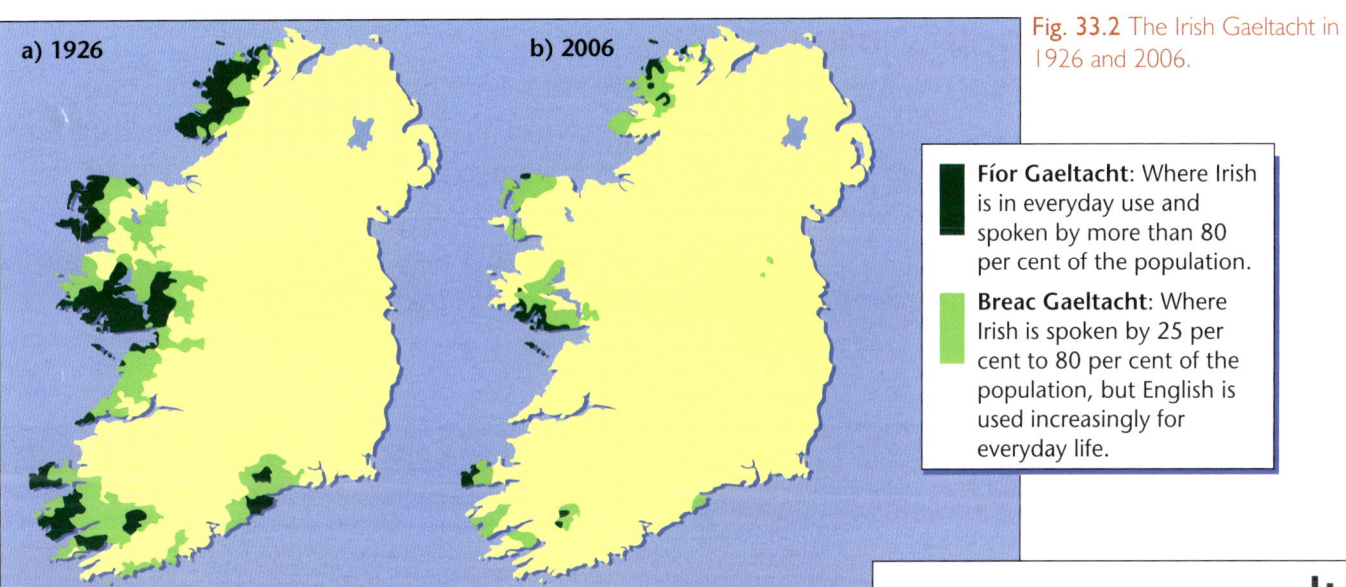

Fig. 33.2 The Irish Gaeltacht in 1926 and 2006.

a) 1926

b) 2006

Fíor Gaeltacht: Where Irish is in everyday use and spoken by more than 80 per cent of the population.

Breac Gaeltacht: Where Irish is spoken by 25 per cent to 80 per cent of the population, but English is used increasingly for everyday life.

Activity

Look at Fig. 33.2 and answer the following.
1. In 1926, which counties were identified most with the Fíor Gaeltacht?
2. What major changes took place to the boundaries of the Irish-speaking region from 1851 to 1926?
3. Where would you locate the core areas of the current Irish-speaking population?
4. In what ways are these different to 1926?

While a growing number of people in Ireland claim an ability to speak Irish, relatively few are fluent and use Irish on a daily basis. English is by far the dominant language of Ireland's population.

This is highlighted by the big change in the **boundaries of the Gaeltacht**, where Irish is the majority language (see Fig. 33.2). Compared to 1926, the present Gaeltacht has been reduced to relatively small and isolated areas that occupy the peninsulas of the west coast of Ireland (see also Chapter 22, page 147). Even these areas face an uncertain future because the English-language culture is so strong.

The boundaries of the Gaeltacht have changed. Various initiatives, such as the launch of the club SULT for young Irish speakers in Dublin, are being made to increase the use of Irish in non-Gaeltacht areas.
- *How effective do you think these will be in reviving the Irish language?*

CHAPTER 34
URBAN GROWTH AND CITY REGIONS

 **KEY IDEA!**

The growth of urban areas and the expansion of city regions are key features of development.

World Urbanisation

Urbanisation measures the proportion of a total population living in an urban area.

In 1950, only 6 per cent of the world's population lived in urban areas. Since then, however, there has been a massive increase in urbanisation. By 2000, this figure had risen to 48 per cent, and by 2025 it is expected to rise to 65 per cent.

Levels of urbanisation are highest in the more developed countries of the world (see Table 34.1). Urbanisation is growing fastest, however, in the less developed regions. **By 2025, some 80 per cent of the world's urban population will live in less developed regions of the world.**

Trends in Global Urbanisation 1970–2025						
Region	Urban Population (millions)			Urban Share (%)		
	1970	1995	2025	1970	1995	2025
More developed regions:	677	868	1,040	68	75	84
Europe	423	532	598	64	73	83
North America	167	221	313	74	76	85
Japan	74	97	313	71	78	85
Less developed regions:	676	1,653	4,025	25	37	57
Africa	84	240	804	23	33	54
Asia	428	1,062	2,615	21	32	54
Latin America	163	349	601	57	74	85

Table 34.1

Activity

Study Table 34.1 and the newspaper extract on the next page and answer the following.
1. In 1970, Europe and Asia had almost the same total urban population. Contrast the trends for these regions for 1970 to 2025.
2. Which continents will be dominated by conurbations (very large cities) in the future?
3. What problems will these large cities be exposed to?

Half the World Heads for Life in the Big City

Within six years more than half of humanity will live in cities for the first time in history. Increasing urbanisation will see growing concentration in the largest cities, with more than a quarter of people in settlements of more than 1 million by 2025.

The world will be increasingly dominated by vast conurbations in Asia and Africa. The populations of new giant cities such as Lagos (23.2 million) in Nigeria and Mumbai (26.1 million), plus twenty-five other cities, will pass 20 million. Such cities will prove increasingly difficult for poor countries to maintain. The poor will increasingly be concentrated in their own neighbourhoods characterised by high rates of crime, violence and social disaster.

Despite this, from 2015 the bulk of population growth will occur in urbanised areas, thus guaranteeing that the human future will be an urban one.

Sunday Times, 2 September 2002

Urbanisation in the European Union

The EU has many large and important cities, and 80 per cent of its population lives in urban areas (see Fig. 25.1 on page 166). Most of these cities continue to grow in population, and their built-up areas now extend well beyond their administrative boundaries. This is called **urban sprawl.**

In addition, modern transport and communication systems allow cities to have an important influence over an extensive area or hinterland (for example, travel to work and shop). This is called the **daily urban system.** For large cities like London, this can extend to about 150 km, while for Dublin it is some 80 km.

Two case studies are introduced to illustrate the growth and expansion of city regions in the EU:

- Randstad.
- Dublin.

Case Study: Randstad Holland

The western part of the Netherlands is one of the most urbanised regions in Europe. Most of the country's major cities are in this area, which has a radius of about 50 km. The growth and expansion of the towns and cities in this small area have resulted in a sprawling urban region called Randstad Holland.

The **Randstad** is shaped like a horseshoe, with an open end in the less populated east. It is a **polycentric city** region, which means it is made up of a number of major cities, with no single city being dominant. At its centre is an important agricultural and recreational area. This is the **Greenheart** of the Randstad (see Fig. 34.1).

Since the end of World War II, the Randstad has grown rapidly. This has been due to the region's strategic location within the core of the EU, its excellent transport systems and Rotterdam, the EU's largest port.

As this urban region developed, competition for land increased and caused urban sprawl to occur around the Randstad cities. In particular, it put huge pressure on the Greenheart.

> Car ownership has been a key factor in enabling large-scale urban sprawl to develop.

> **Activity**
> Look at Fig. 25.1 on page 166 and describe the patterns of urban development in the EU. Suggest reasons for the expansion of the urban axes in the directions shown.

> The Randstad contains 40 per cent (6 million) of the Dutch population living on only 17 per cent of the country's land area. Locate the Randstad on Fig. 34.1.

The town of Zoetermeer in the Randstadt is separated from other urban centres by the green belt in the background.

Planning for the Randstad

Planners face many difficulties in trying to overcome problems in the Randstad. The focus has mainly been placed on trying to limit urban sprawl.

At the **national level,** five regional centres have been designated for major investment in infrastructures such as transport and housing. Planners hope that these regional centres will become a stronger attraction for people and economic development, and reduce pressure on the Randstad (see Fig. 34.1).

In the **Randstad,** some high-density development will be allowed close to the major cities, but urban sprawl will be strongly controlled by using **buffer zones,** also called green belts. Urban developments will also be encouraged along the eastern edge of the Randstad to close off its 'open' edge.

Green belts are special areas where no new urban development is allowed. It therefore protects the existing natural environment and rural countryside.

Fig. 34.1 Planning for Randstad Holland.

Activity

Look at Fig. 34.1 and answer the following.

1. What planning tools are being used to reduce the amount of urban sprawl in the Randstad?
2. If there are no strict planning controls, which two major urban regions could spread and merge along the Rhine Valley?
3. Is urban sprawl putting pressure on the Greenheart?
4. Why is it important to ensure that the Greenheart remains as a significant area in the Randstad?

EU Concerns about Randstad Growth

For the EU, controlling the expansion of the Randstad is also important. If uncontrolled urban growth is allowed eastwards along the Rhine River, the Randstad could eventually join up with the expanding cities of the Rhine-Ruhr (see Fig. 34.1). To the south, unplanned expansion could link up with the Brussels-Antwerp-Ghent growth zone of Belgium.

The result would be a **West European megalopolis,** with a huge concentration of population and economic activities in one vast and almost continuous urban sprawl. This would be an environmental disaster and will require strong planning controls to keep open spaces between these expanding urban regions.

> **Increased demand for housing, industry, transport and recreation all contribute to the problems of congestion and urban sprawl.**

Case Study: Dublin

Ireland's urban system is dominated by Dublin, which is a **primate city.** Since the 1960s, its built-up area has expanded rapidly. In addition, Dublin's zone of influence has increased strongly to create an urban region (or daily urban system) that extends some 80 km from the city centre.

Three factors in particular have contributed to the expansion of Dublin's urban region:

- Focus of the country's transport network.
- Dominant employment centre.
- High cost of land in the city.

Before World War II, Dublin was a compact city. The built-up area did not extend more than 5 km from its centre (see Fig. 34.2a). In the 1960s a period of significant growth began. Most of this expansion occurred within 8 km of the centre. It involved the relocation of inner city populations to large new housing estates and apartment complexes, such as Ballymun. By the 1980s, this zone was almost entirely built up (see Fig. 34.2b).

Urban expansion continued in the 1970s into the zone 8 to 16 km from Dublin's centre. Most of the growth here was due to the development of three new towns: Blanchardstown, Clondalkin and Tallaght. About 40 per cent of the population of Dublin's urban region now lives in this zone.

As competition for land and the cost of living continues to rise in Dublin, more people are encouraged to look for homes further from the city. Many small towns and villages more than 16 km from the centre of Dublin have therefore increased in size, especially if they are located on or near a transport route to the city. For many people living in such places, **long-distance travel to work** to Dublin has become an accepted part of their daily routine (see Fig. 34.3). This has been an important factor in the way the boundaries of Dublin's urban region have been extended.

Expansion of the Dublin urban region has led to a great increase in journeys to work and therefore more traffic congestion at peak times.
- *Suggest how this problem can be resolved.*

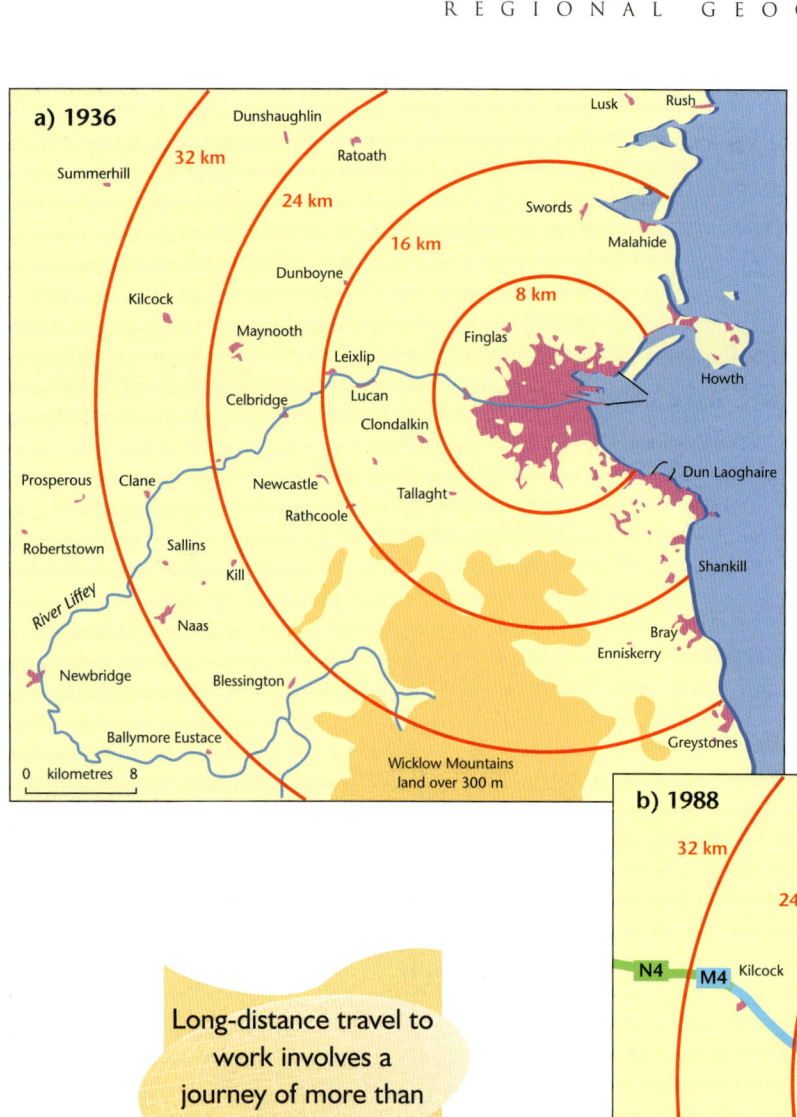

Fig. 34.2 Built-up areas in the Dublin region.

a) 1936

32 km · 24 km · 16 km · 8 km

Summerhill · Dunshaughlin · Ratoath · Lusk · Rush · Kilcock · Dunboyne · Swords · Malahide · Maynooth · Finglas · Howth · Leixlip · Celbridge · Lucan · Clondalkin · Prosperous · Clane · Newcastle · Tallaght · Dun Laoghaire · Rathcoole · Robertstown · Sallins · Kill · Shankill · River Liffey · Naas · Bray · Enniskerry · Newbridge · Blessington · Ballymore Eustace · Greystones

0 kilometres 8

Wicklow Mountains land over 300 m

Activity

Look at the two maps in Fig. 34.2 and answer the following.

1. In which direction has the urban area expanded the most? Why is further major expansion to the south of Dublin likely to be difficult?

2. Give examples of towns that have grown significantly because they are located on or near major roads that converge on Dublin.

3. Why are improved transport links important in extending Dublin's urban region?

> Long-distance travel to work involves a journey of more than 16 km.

b) 1988

32 km · 24 km · 16 km · 8 km

Dunshaughlin · Ashbourne · Rush · Lusk · Ratoath · N2 · N1 · N3 · Portrane · Swords · Dublin Airport · Malahide · N4 · M4 · Kilcock · Dunboyne · Portmarnock · Blanchardstown · Maynooth · Leixlip · Lucan · Phoenix Park · Howth · Celbridge · Clondalkin · Clane · Newcastle · Dun Laoghaire · Rathcoole · Tallaght · Prosperous · Sallins · N7 · Shankill · River Liffey · Kill · Naas · Bray · Enniskerry · Newbridge · Blessington · N11 · Ballymore Eustace · Greystones · Kilcoole

0 kilometres 8

Wicklow Mountains land over 300 m

Blanchardstown is one of the three new towns built in the 1970s to accommodate Dublin's increasing population.

● *What evidence do you see in this photo to suggest that it is a planned settlement?*

Fig. 34.3 Long-distance commuting from towns with a population of more than 5,000 in the Dublin urban region in 1981 and 2002.

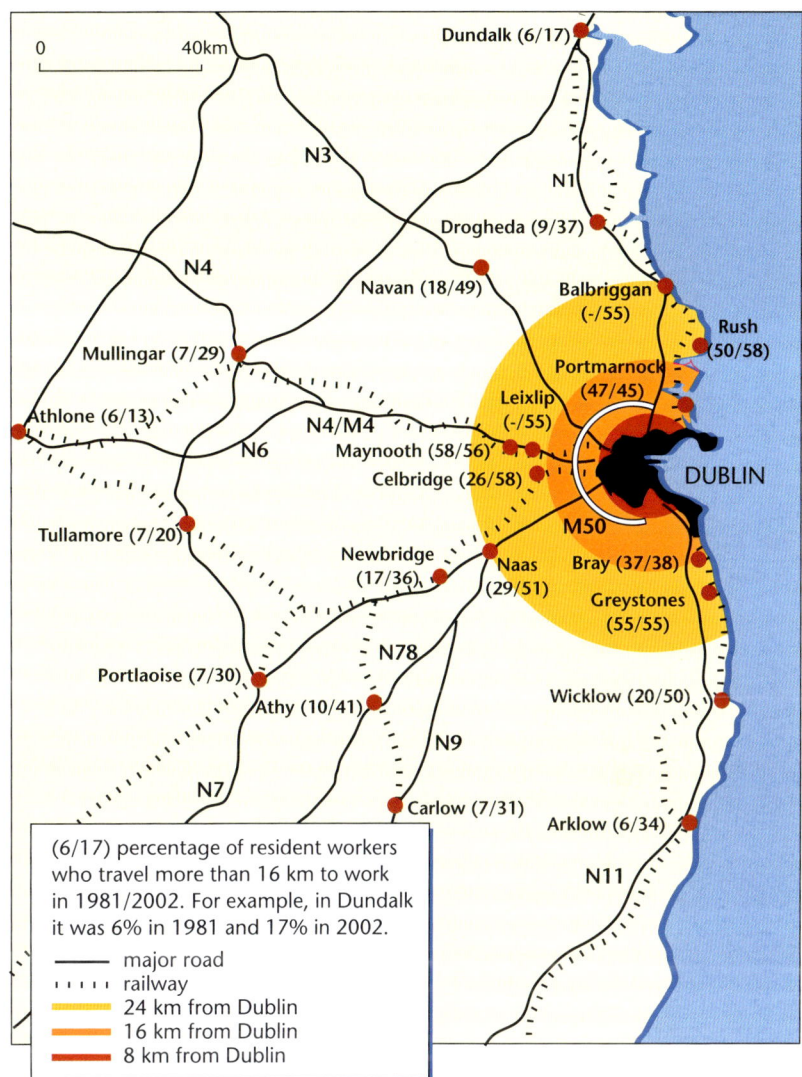

(6/17) percentage of resident workers who travel more than 16 km to work in 1981/2002. For example, in Dundalk it was 6% in 1981 and 17% in 2002.

— major road
ııııı railway
▬ 24 km from Dublin
▬ 16 km from Dublin
▬ 8 km from Dublin

Activity

Look at Fig. 34.3 and answer the following.

1. Which three towns in 1981 had 50 per cent or more of their resident workforce commuting long distance?

2. Compare the percentage figures for all towns for 1981 and 2002. What do they tell you about trends in long-distance commuting?

3. As you travel from Naas to Portlaoise along the N7, what do the percentages show about the relationship between levels of commuting and the distance from Dublin?

4. Do railways as well as roads have an influence on commuting and the growth of towns in Dublin's urban region? Explain your answer.

A Solution to Dublin's Continued Expansion?

The rapid and large-scale expansion of the Dublin urban region has raised concerns for both the city and country. These are highlighted in the following article.

Don't Let Isolated Rural Areas Become Ghost Towns

Dublin will continue to suck life out of major areas of the country unless there is a meaningful government intervention aimed at beefing up other regions.

It appears Ireland's lopsided development is destined to continue apace. Relentlessly, the population explosion of the capital and its sprawling hinterland along the east coast will accelerate unless urgent measures are introduced to redirect development from areas already mushrooming out of control.

The reality is that thousands of people in outlying regions have yet to hear the Celtic Tiger purring. While other cities and towns have benefited, the Tiger's economic impact is concentrated in and around Dublin.

Based on CSO figures, the population of the capital will tip 1,500,000 by 2020. That means traffic gridlock and a serious erosion of quality of life. The repercussions will reverberate right across the city, rippling outwards to greater Dublin and into the neighbouring counties already being turned into commuter dormitories.

Unless the trends are reversed, large areas of the country will be turned into reservations and stripped of people who are the lifeblood of Ireland's future.

Irish Examiner, 19 June 2001

A solution to the problems of Dublin's continued expansion appeared in the **National Spatial Strategy** (2002). This proposed large-scale developments in a series of **gateways and hubs** to encourage dispersal of population and employment out of the Dublin region (see Fig. 34.4).

- **Gateways:** Large urban centres with well-developed infrastructure that offer the best prospects for countering the dominance of Dublin.
- **Hubs:** Smaller urban centres that will help disperse development from gateways into their regions.
- **Strategic road corridors:** Important for providing efficient links between gateways, hubs and Dublin.

These developments will receive a significant amount of support from the government's €184 billion National Development Plan (2007–13).

Fig. 34.4 Ireland's National Spatial Strategy, 2002.

Activity
Do you think this system of gateways and hubs can produce more balanced urban and regional development?

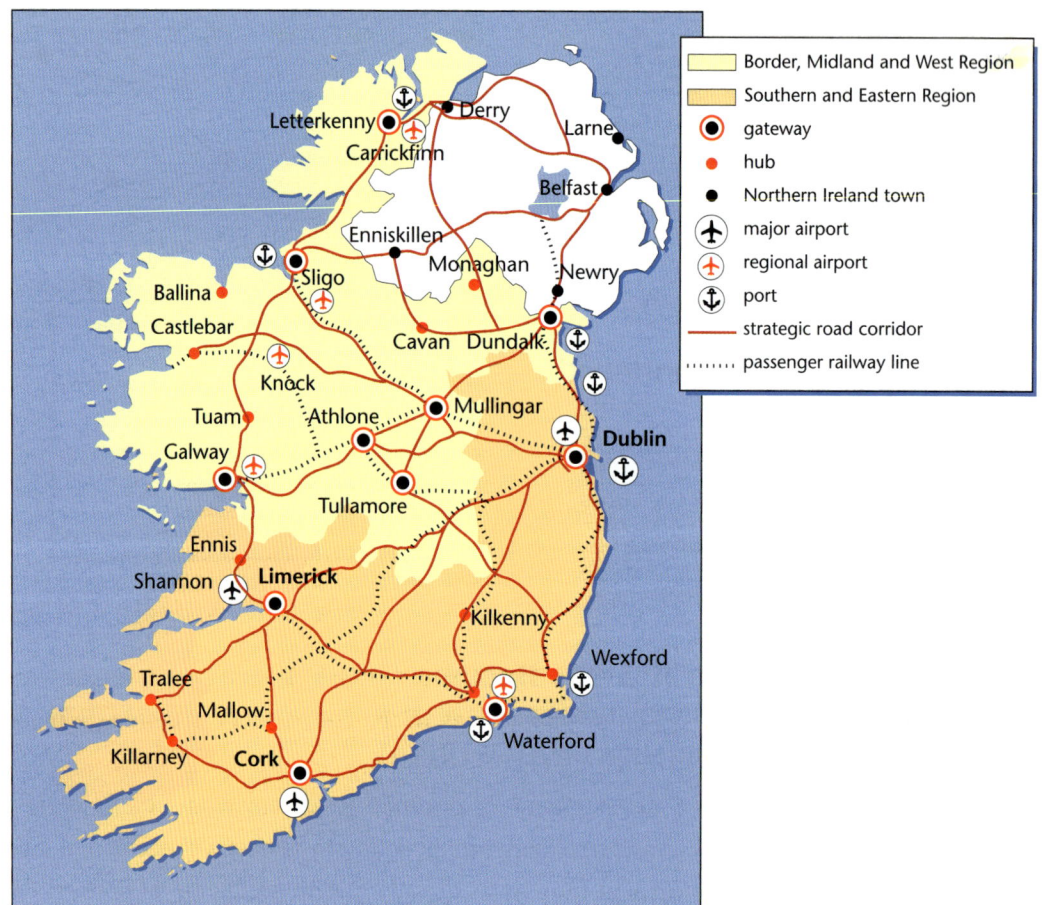

Administration Reform in Dublin

An important result of the increasing population and urbanisation within Dublin City and County has been the need to reform its local authority structure. Until 1994, the local authorities responsible for delivering essential services in Dublin were Dublin County Borough, Dun Laoghaire Corporation and Dublin County Council.

In 1971, two-thirds of the total population of Dublin City and County lived in the city (see Table 34.2). The dominance of the city declined as more of Dublin's population chose to live in the county's growing towns and rural communities. It proved increasingly difficult to serve the needs of such a large population growth, which was spread out across the county. As a result, it was decided to abolish Dublin County Council and Dun Laoghaire Corporation.

Three new counties were created: Fingal, South Dublin and Dun Laoghaire-Rathdown (see Fig. 34.5). These, together with the newly named Dublin Corporation, provide a more evenly distributed area and population for more efficient administration of Dublin's changing population patterns.

Population Trends in Dublin's Administrative Areas						Table 34.2
	1971 ('000s)	1981 ('000s)	1991 ('000s)	2002 ('000s)	2006 ('000s)	
Dublin County Borough/Corporation	568	545	478	496	506	
Dublin County	284	–	–	–	–	
South Dublin	–	165	208	239	246	
Fingal	–	115	153	196	240	
Dun Laoghaire-Rathdown	–	178	185	192	194	
Total	852	1,003	1,025	1,123	1,186	

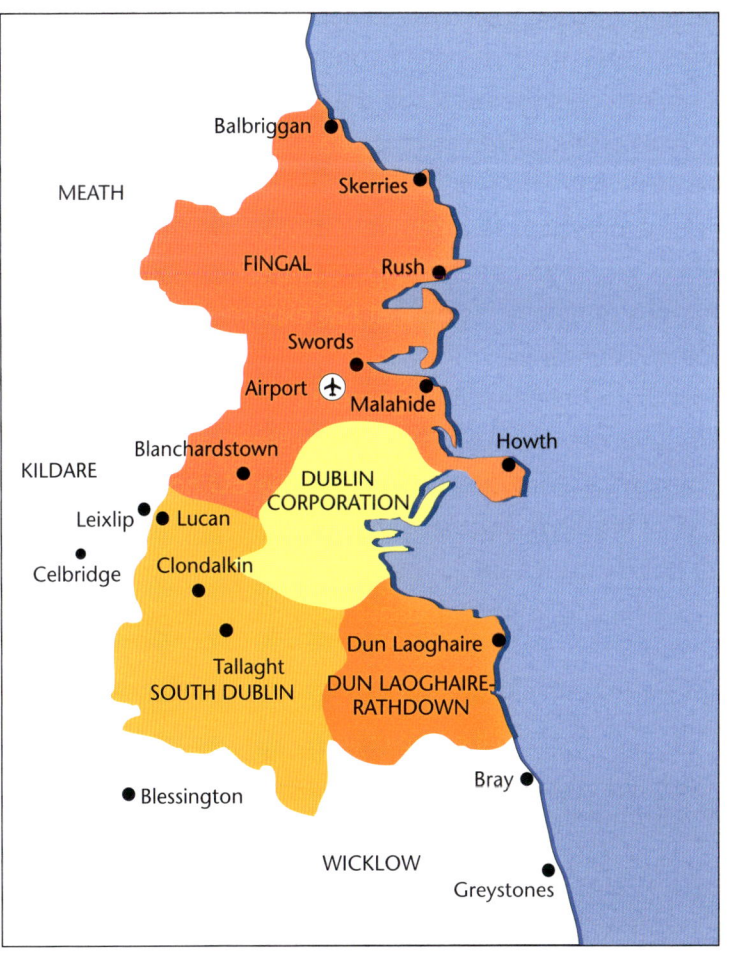

Fig. 34.5 Local government reform for County Dublin.

Between 1996 and 2002, Fingal was the fastest-growing county in Ireland.

Activity

Look at Table 34.2 and Fig. 34.5 and answer the following.
1. What share of the total population lived in the Dublin Corporation area in 2006 compared to 1971?
2. Do you think it was necessary to reorganise the local administration in Dublin? Explain your answer.
3. Which of the new counties has the largest and fastest-growing population? Explain your answer. (Think about new towns.)

CHAPTER 35
DEVELOPMENT AND EXPANSION OF THE EU

 **KEY IDEA!**

The European Union has expanded from six to twenty-seven member states and is now the world's largest trade bloc.

Following the destruction that occurred during World War II, prospects for development within Europe seemed limited.

- The economies of most countries were devastated.
- A new political boundary, called the Iron Curtain, divided a democratic Western Europe from a communist-dominated Eastern Europe.

From this uncertain time, a new, confident and prosperous Europe emerged. The basis for this began in Western Europe and involved a **process of economic integration.**

In 1957, the **Treaty of Rome** created the European Economic Community (EEC). This was a small, compact group of six countries located in the core region of north-west Europe (see Fig. 35.1a). Its main aims were to increase trade between member states and their level of economic development. This was successful and it encouraged other European countries to seek membership. As a result, the **European Union,** as it is now called, has become the world's largest and most prosperous trading bloc. It is an excellent case study of a region that has expanded its international boundaries.

> **The EEC has now become the EU.**

There have been **five enlargements** of the EU. As a result, the boundaries of the EU are now very different from those in 1957. Through a series of enlargements, **the EU now covers almost all of western, southern, northern and eastern Europe.** Its boundaries stretch from the Arctic to the Mediterranean, and from the Atlantic to the Russian border.

> In 1990, East Germany was reunited with West Germany (see Chapter 36). This did not increase the number of countries in the EU. It was seen only as an existing member increasing its territory. The reunification of Germany increased the population of the EU by 17 million.

Activity

Look at Fig. 35.1 and Tables 35.1 and 35.2, and with the help of an atlas answer the following.
1. Locate the member states listed in Table 35.1 on the maps of the EU in Fig. 35.1.
2. In the first enlargement, which new member state was responsible for the large increase in population and GDP?
3. Why did enlargements in the 1980s and in 1995 result in a decline in average population density for the EU? (Think about growth in area compared to population.)
4. Why do you think the enlargement in the 1980s was troublesome for the EU?
5. What evidence supports the view that the 2004 and 2007 expansions added to the problems of regional development in the EU?

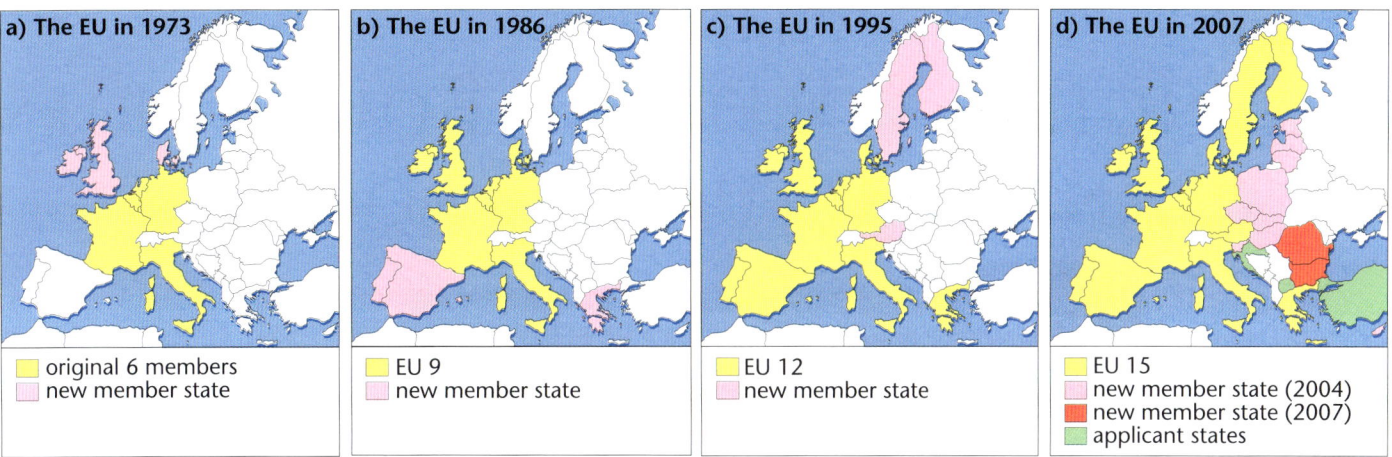

a) The EU in 1973

☐ original 6 members
☐ new member state

b) The EU in 1986

☐ EU 9
☐ new member state

c) The EU in 1995

☐ EU 12
☐ new member state

d) The EU in 2007

☐ EU 15
☐ new member state (2004)
☐ new member state (2007)
☐ applicant states

Fig. 35.1 Enlargements of the European Union.

Enlargements of the European Region		
1957	Belgium, France, (West) Germany, Italy, Luxembourg, Netherlands	The original six members, mainly from the **economic core** of north-west Europe.
1973	Britain, Denmark, Ireland	A **westward** enlargement of the economic core.
1981	Greece	These **southern** enlargements into Mediterranean Europe were considered to be troublesome due to their underdeveloped economies.
1986	Spain, Portugal	
1995	Austria, Finland, Sweden	Mostly a **northern** expansion into Scandanavia. It also included some of Alpine Europe. All were well-developed economies.
2004	Cyprus, Czech Republic, Estonia, Hungary, Latvia, Lithuania, Malta, Poland, Slovak Republic, Slovenia	The largest single expansion, involving ten countries. This **eastern** enlargement is difficult due to its scale and the underdeveloped economies of the new members.
2007	Bulgaria and Romania	This adds to the problems of an underdeveloped periphery.

Table 35.1

Selected Data for the Enlarging EU				
European Union	Increase in area (%)	Increase in population (%)	Increase in GDP (gross domestic product) (%)	Change in GDP per person (%)
EU 6 to EU 9 (First enlargement)	31	32	29	−3
EU 9 to EU 12 (Second and third enlargements)	48	22	15	−6
EU 12 to EU 15 (Fourth enlargement, including German reunification)	43	11	8	−3
EU 15 to EU 27	34	29	9	−16

Table 35.2

251

CHAPTER 36
CHANGING POLITICAL BOUNDARIES AND CULTURAL GROUPS

 **KEY IDEA!**

Changes in political boundaries can have an important effect on cultural groups.

How do you think the lives of people living in Northern Ireland have been affected by the creation of a border separating it from the Republic?

Changes in political boundaries often have major impacts for people who, as a result of boundary changes, find themselves living under a different political system. Their economic prospects, cultural experiences (language and religious beliefs) and human rights can all be affected by these changes.

This chapter will present **two case studies** to show how changing political boundaries affect cultural groups:

- **Kashmir:** An example of a violent clash of cultures after British India broke up and new political boundaries were drawn up.
- **A reunified Germany:** The peaceful reunification of East and West Germany.

Case Study: The Problem of Kashmir

In Chapter 29, important religious and other cultural differences in India were highlighted. These led to the partition of the subcontinent into three independent states, based primarily on religion: India, Pakistan and Bangladesh.

The differences are still strong and continue to give rise to tensions between different cultural groups. Nowhere is this more marked than in the Kashmir region, where India and Pakistan have fought three wars to settle their claims to this disputed border zone (see Fig. 36.1).

On gaining independence from Britain in 1947, the states of the Indian subcontinent had to choose whether to form part of Pakistan, dominated by Islam, or India, where Hindu was the majority religion.

In the Kashmir Valley, violent conflict broke out between the minority (25 per cent) Hindu population and the majority (75 per cent) Islamic population (see Fig. 29.10, page 225). The Hindu minority looked to India for support, while the Islamic population was supported by Pakistan. This resulted in war between the two newly independent states. Many civilians were killed and large numbers of people fled from areas where they were of the minority religion.

India is a country dominated by Hinduism, while Pakistan is an Islamic state.

The United Nations negotiated a ceasefire line to end the conflict. This **Line of Control** was to be temporary, but it has remained as the dividing line between the two cultural groups.

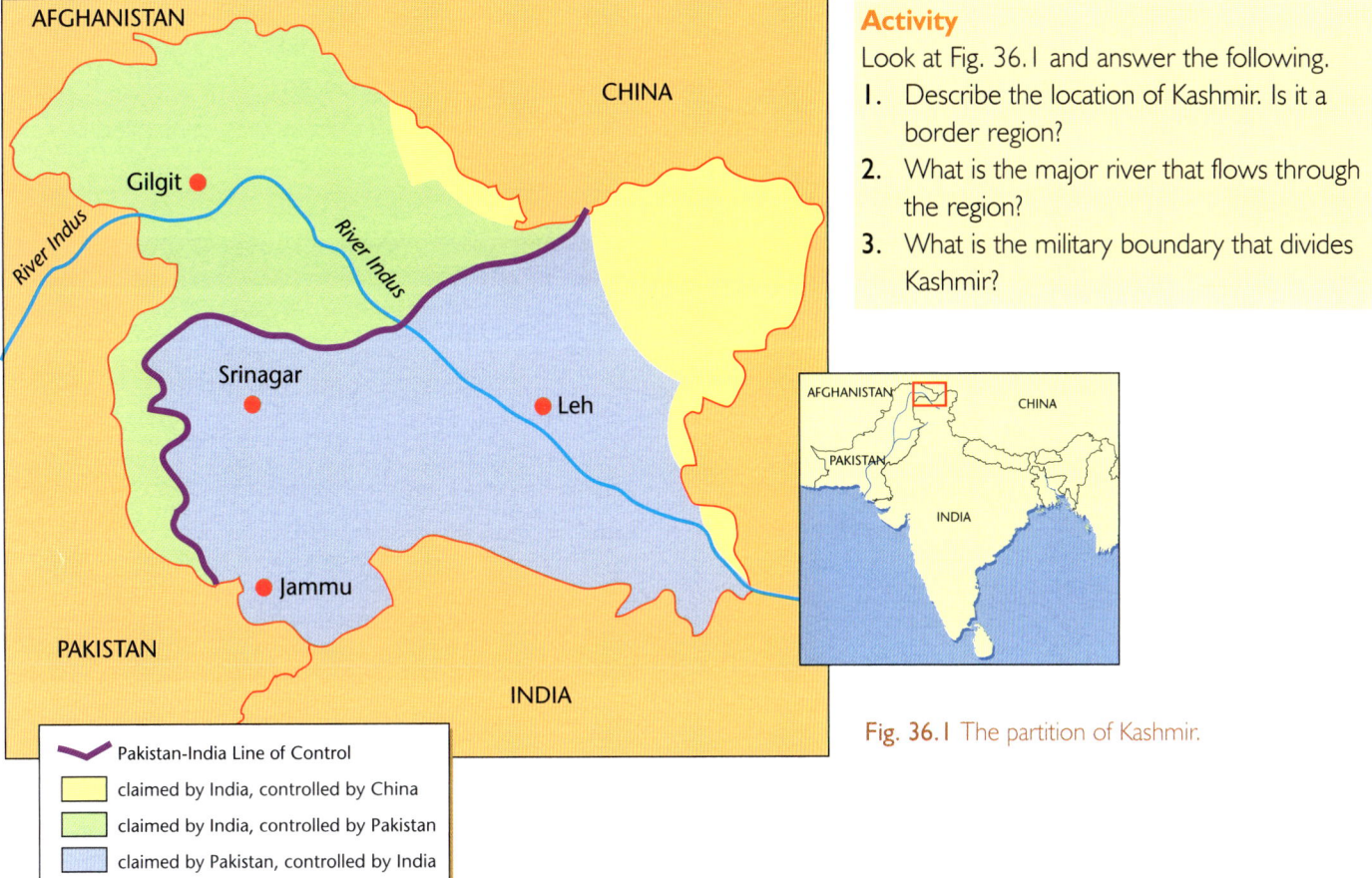

Activity
Look at Fig. 36.1 and answer the following.
1. Describe the location of Kashmir. Is it a border region?
2. What is the major river that flows through the region?
3. What is the military boundary that divides Kashmir?

Fig. 36.1 The partition of Kashmir.

The situation in the region remains sensitive because:

- India controls about 80 per cent of the Kashmir population, including large numbers of Islamic people.
- Pakistan and the majority Islamic population do not accept this. They want to integrate Kashmir into Pakistan.
- The Indus River and several of its large tributaries originate in Indian-controlled Kashmir. Pakistan wants to gain control over this essential water resource (for irrigation and industrial development).
- In the 1990s, an increase in Islamic fundamentalism has led to more fighting in the region.
- Both India and Pakistan have nuclear weapons. It is therefore a potentially dangerous situation when both countries come into conflict in this contested cultural and political border region.

Why is India more willing than Pakistan to make the Line of Control a permanent boundary?

Bill Clinton, a former US president, described Kashmir as 'the most dangerous place on earth'. Why?

Case Study: Reunified Germany

Changes in political boundaries not only have impacts on different cultural groups, such as in Kashmir and Northern Ireland. They can also create new conditions which affect a single cultural group. Germany is a good example of this with the changes in its political boundaries following World War II.

At the end of World War II, the victorious allies (USA, USSR, UK and France) were determined that a strong and united Germany would never again threaten the peace of Europe. As a result, a new political boundary was drawn which created **two Germanies** (Fig. 36.2).

These two new states operated under different political and economic systems, which had different effects on German people living in the two countries.

From 1949 to 1990, Germany was divided into two separate states.

- **West Germany** was a democracy and a free market economy.
- **East Germany** was a communist regime where the economy was controlled by centralised planning.

Comparison of Some Economic and Social Indicators for East and West Germany in 1989		
	East Germany	West Germany
Gross domestic product (billion Deutschmarks)*	353	2,111
Per capita GDP (Deutschmarks)*	21,500	33,700
% unemployment	–	6.9
% children under 3 years cared for in crèches	56	2
Doctors per 10,000 people	24	29
Hospital beds per 10,000 people	24	110

*The Deutschmark was the currency in Germany before it changed to the euro in 2002.

Table 36.1

Images of the two Germanies. Prior to reunification, drab state-built worker apartments and underdeveloped services in the east (top) contrast with the prosperity of cities in West Germany.

- *How did 'Ossies' react to such differences?*

West Germany's economy developed strongly and became the largest and most powerful in the EU. Its industries were very competitive and the population enjoyed a high standard of living. Population totals also increased from 50 million to 62 million between 1950 and 1989. Much of this increase was due to large numbers of migrants, from countries such as Turkey, who were attracted to this prosperous country (see Table 36.1).

In contrast, the East German economy was relatively inefficient, quality of life was poor and personal freedom was limited. Although the state provided its people with basic services, such as housing and health care, most East Germans looked with envy at those living in West Germany. Their population declined from almost 20 million to 17 million between 1950 and 1989.

Activity

Look at Table 36.1 and answer the following.

1. Which of the two Germanies was the largest and most prosperous economy?
2. Why did the East German population have relatively good access to a range of basic services?
3. Which of the two Germanies would migrant workers find more attractive?

A REUNITED GERMANY

In 1989, the communist government in East Germany collapsed, and in 1990 the political boundary that had separated the two Germanies was removed. Although now a single country, forty years of separate national identities had given rise to major differences between the **Ossies** (people from former East Germany and pronounced oss-sees) and **Wessies** (West Germans and pronounced vess-sees).

At first, there was considerable optimism that a reunited Germany would succeed in reducing east-west divisions. This has not occurred. In particular, the expectations of the Ossies that their standard of living and job prospects would rise quickly to those of the Wessies have not been met. Two main factors are responsible for this:

- **Free market forces** have meant that many of the older, less efficient industries located in East Germany were closed due to competition. Unemployment increased rapidly.
- **Freedom of movement** meant that large numbers of young East Germans migrated to Western Germany, leaving behind an ageing and economically depressed community.

East Germany became an Objective 1 Region in the EU and receives large amounts of financial support from structural funds and the German government. This contrasts with the prosperity of West Germany (see Fig 36.2). Therefore, rather than becoming equals within a united Germany, **Ossies felt that they were being treated as second-class citizens in their own country**. Meanwhile, many Wessies felt that Ossies were ungrateful given the high costs the West German government and citizens paid for reunification.

Ask your teacher about:

- Democracy.
- A free market economy.
- Communism.
- Centralised planning.

In 1990, Germany was reunited, with its capital in Berlin.

The upper photograph shows Berlin citizens protesting in November 1989 on top of the Berlin Wall, which symbolised the divisions in Germany. This was torn down in 1989. The lower photograph is of the same location today, showing free movement through the Brandenburg Gate. This symbolises the unity of Germany.

Fig. 36.2 East and West Germany before reunification.

Following reunification, an unprecedented consumer and construction boom, boosted by aid from the west, produced modern roads, sleek office buildings and shopping malls throughout East Germany. Easterners discovered the joys of fast cars and designer clothes. Their communist-era apartment blocks were given more colourful facades. For a while they seemed happy.

The merger, however, meant that western employment policies were extended to the east, where industries soon lost their competitive edge to Poland and the Czech Republic. Unemployment in eastern Germany has grown to 18 per cent, more than twice the western level and higher than in most of Eastern Europe.

'Just look out there,' said Manfred Geiger, behind the counter of his empty café in Reichenbach's central square. 'There are no young people here any more. They've gone. The east is dying.'

The German government has done nothing even while a 'brain drain' was depriving some eastern towns of doctors and dentists. Migration westwards, at more than 200,000 people a year, is greater now than in the years after the fall of the Wall.

'A collective depression has set in,' says Karen Retzel, the mayor of Cottbus, whose population is shrinking by 7 per cent a year. 'The promises of reunification have not been fulfilled.'

Sunday Times, 8 September 2002

Activity

Look at the newspaper extract and answer the following.

1. Is unemployment higher in eastern or western Germany? Suggest reasons why.
2. Is migration from eastern to western Germany a problem? Why?
3. If you were an Ossie, would you agree that the promises of reunification have not been met?

Multi-part Questions

1. A. EUROPEAN UNION UNEMPLOYMENT

Examine the table below, showing selected unemployment statistics for 2004.

Country	Unemployment Rate (% of Adult Population)
Austria	3.8%
Estonia	9.7%
France	9.5%
Latvia	14.6%
Poland	16.1%
Spain	10.5%

Using graph paper, draw a graph suitable to illustrate these data.

[20 marks]

B. MANUFACTURING INDUSTRY

Examine some of the factors that have influenced the development of one economic activity in a non-Irish region that you have studied.

[30 marks]

C. URBAN GROWTH

'The boundaries of city regions have expanded over time.' Discuss this statement, with reference to one example you have studied.

[30 marks]

2. A. EUROPEAN REGIONS

i.   Examine the map of Europe. In your answer book, associate each of these descriptions with the letters A, B, C.

  ● Peripheral economic region.
  ● Cultural (language) region.
  ● Climatic region

ii. Name **two** characteristics of the above climatic region. Explain **one** factor that influences the climate of the region.

[20 marks]

B. LANGUAGE REGIONS

Examine, with reference to an example or examples you have studied, the causes and consequences of changes in extent of language regions.

[30 marks]

C. URBAN REGIONS

With reference to one region you have studied, examine the growth in the extent of urban regions and the efforts to control this growth.

[30 marks]

257

3. A. EUROPEAN UNION
    Examine the map of Europe showing labelled political regions, then complete the
    following table, which refers to the European Union.

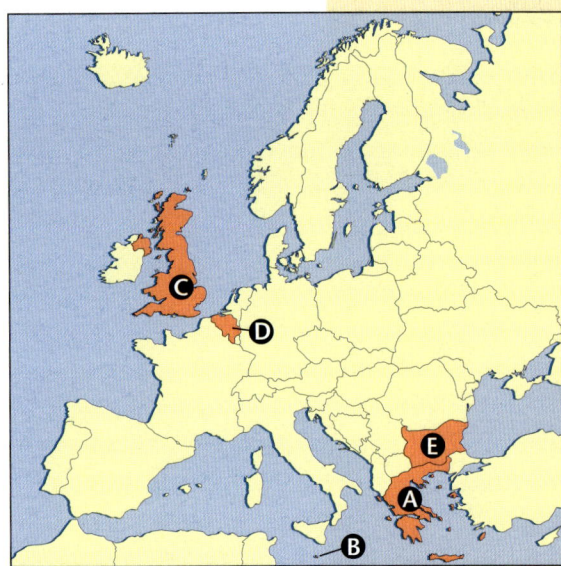

Description	Letter	Country
Member since 2007		
Member since 1981		
Member since 1957		
Member since 2004		
Member since 1973		

B. POLITICAL BOUNDARIES
    Examine, with reference to **one** example, the impact of changes in political boundaries
    on cultural groups.

[30 marks]

C. CULTURAL REGION
    Examine **two** factors which give rise to cultural identify or distinctiveness in a European
    or non-European region you have studied.

[30 marks]

4. A. REGIONS
    'A region is an area which may be identified by one or more characteristics.' Briefly
    explain this statement, using a sketch map to illustrate an example or examples.

[20 marks]

B. CULTURAL REGIONS
    Examine **two** factors which have influenced the development of distinct cultural
    divisions in a European region which you have studied.

[30 marks]

C. BOUNDARY CHANGES
    Explain, with reference to **one** example, the causes and consequences of change in the
    boundaries of a region over time.

[30 marks]

5. A. NON-IRISH EUROPEAN REGION
    Draw a sketch map of a non-European region you have studied. Mark the main relief
    and drainage features on the sketch map.

[20 marks]

B. IRISH REGION

'The physical environment affects human activities.' Examine this statement with reference to **one** primary activity in an Irish region you have studied.

[30 marks]

C. INDUSTRY

Examine the importance of the tertiary sector in a non-European country of your choice.

[30 marks]

6. A. AN IRISH REGION

Draw a sketch map to show the main physical characteristics of **one** Irish region you have studied.

[20 marks]

B. EU POLICY

Examine the influence of one EU policy on the development of a region you have studied.

[30 marks]

C. MANUFACTURING INDUSTRY

Select a non-European region and explain two factors that have influenced the development of manufacturing in the region.

[30 marks]

CHAPTER 37
ORDNANCE SURVEY MAPS

How to Locate Places on Ordnance Survey Maps

Can you remember how to locate a place on a map by a four-digit or six-digit grid reference? Remember **LATAS**: letter, across the top, then along the side.

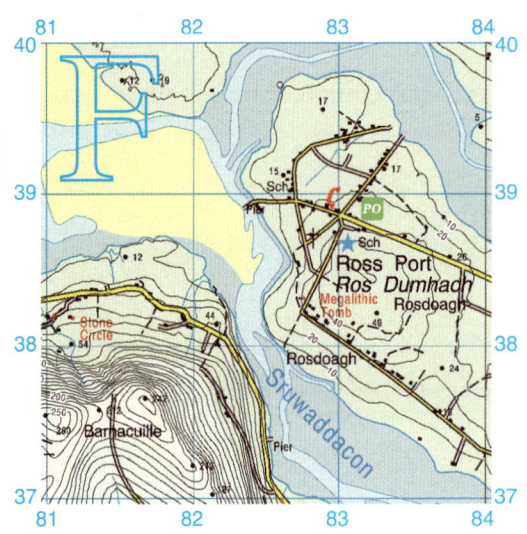

Activity
On the map extract, use:
a. a four-digit grid reference and
b. a six-digit grid reference to locate the post office.

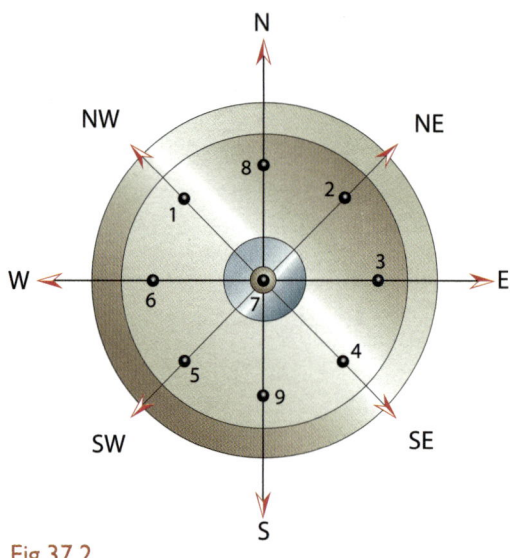

Fig.37.2

The National Grid

A	B	C	D	E
F	G	H	J	K
L	M	N	O	P
Q	R	S	T	U
V	W	X	Y	Z

Fig. 37.1 Remember, the national grid divides the whole country into twenty-five boxes, called sub-zones. Each sub-zone is identified by a letter of the alphabet.

How to Find Direction on Ordnance Survey Maps

Activity
1. Use Fig. 37.2 and look at the example given in (a), then answer the following:
   a. The number 3 is <u>east</u> of number 6.
   b. The number 2 is _____ of number 5.
   c. The number 8 is _____ of number 9.
   d. The number 7 is _____ of number 2.
   e. The number 1 is _____ of number 4.
   f. The number 7 is _____ of number 9.

2. In which direction would you travel when going from:
   a. 1 to 4   b. 5 to 2   c. 8 to 9   d. 7 to 1
   e. 7 to 3   f. 7 to 6   g. 9 to 3   h. 6 to 8

3. Carefully study the map extract at the top of this page.
   In which direction is:
   a. the megalithic tomb F 827 384 from the stone circle F 812 383
   b. the stone circle F 812 383 from the post office F 832 389
   c. the post office F 832 389 from the megalithic tomb F 827 384?

SCALE ON ORDNANCE SURVEY MAPS

Scale is the relationship between a distance on a map and its corresponding measurement on the ground. For example:

Remember what scale means. What does 1:50,000 mean?

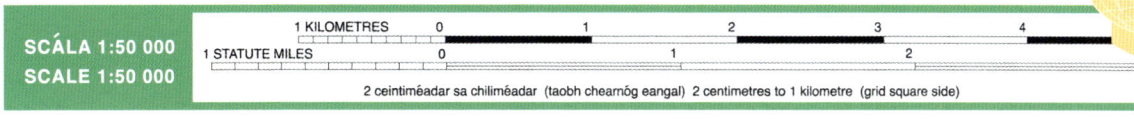

SCÁLA 1:50 000	
SCALE 1:50 000	

2 ceintiméadar sa chiliméadar (taobh chearnóg eangal) 2 centimetres to 1 kilometre (grid square side)

Fig. 37.3

Measuring Distance on a Map

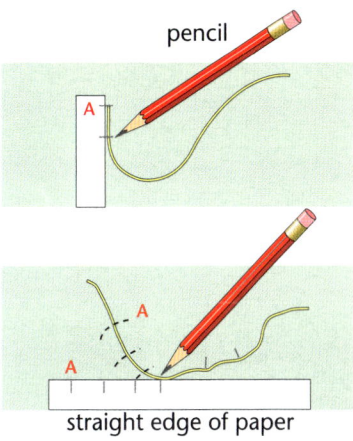

pencil

straight edge of paper

Fig. 37.4 Measuring a curved line.

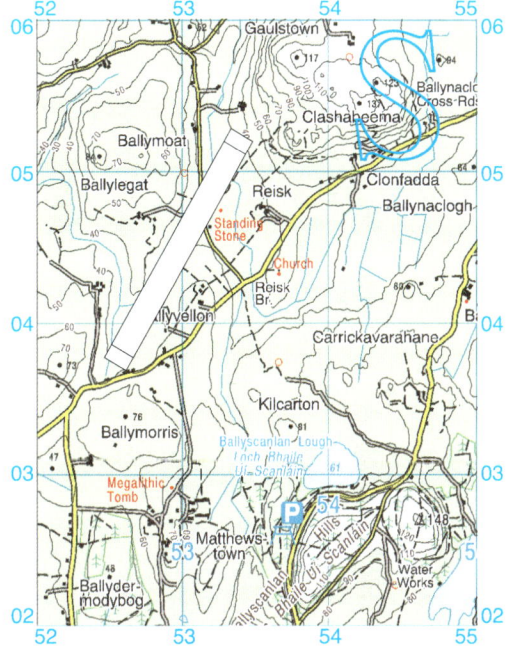

Measuring a straight line.

Activity

Find grid reference B 728 150 and measure the distance along the R259 between where the road enters the map at this point to where it meets the N56 at Dunglow. Then measure the distance between both places 'as the crow flies'. What is the difference in distance between these measurements?

- Small-scale maps show large areas in little detail.
- Large-scale maps show small areas in greater detail.

Some small and large-scale maps include:

Street map of a city for tourists	1:2,500
Rural place maps	1:15,000
National motoring map	1:250,000
World atlas map	1:100,000,000

261

Types of Slopes on Ordnance Survey Maps

Activity

Look at Fig. 37.5 and for A, B, C and D, find the numbers and descriptions that go together.

Fig. 37.5

Description:

- Concave
- Convex
- Stepped
- Even

A
B
C
D
1
2
3
4

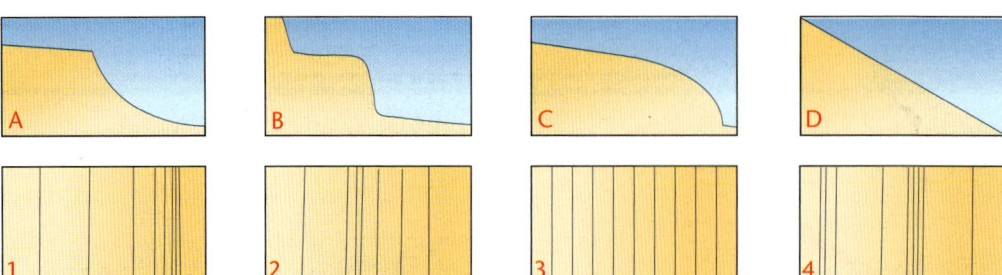

Case Study: Cross-Section

From spot height 397 m at grid reference T 012 730 to T 044 696 looking north-east.

397
380
350
300
250
200
150
120
Road
100
80
80
River
100
110
Road
120
120
130
Road
100
River
100
110
150
164
R749
R747
Coolross
Churchland
Lugduff
Kilcommon Br.
Mountpleasant
Boleybawn
Ballyraheen Cross Roads
Gorteen
Coolroe
Mill Land
Tomnafinnoge Wood
Tomnafinnoge
Coolafancy
Crosspatrick
Killaveny
Tobberpatrick Bridge
Barnadown
Loggan
Newtown
Holy Well
Dismantled Railway
River Doirioch
73
72
71
70
69
00
01
02
03
05
06
07
08

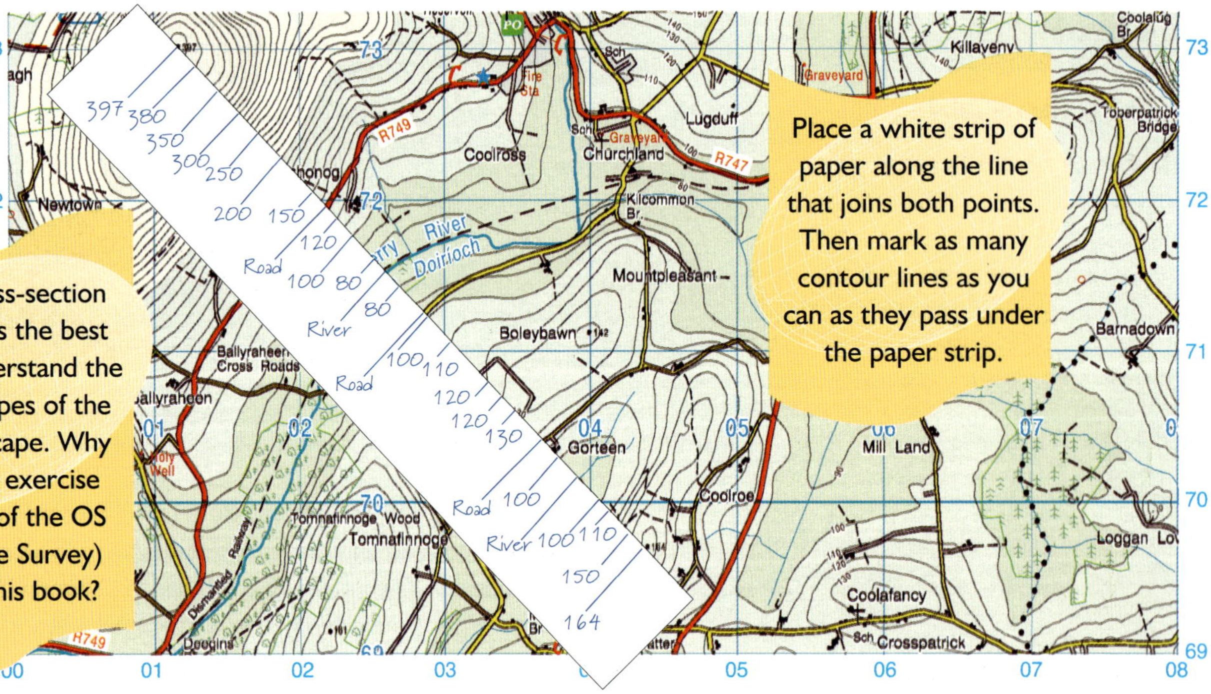

Place a white strip of paper along the line that joins both points. Then mark as many contour lines as you can as they pass under the paper strip.

Doing cross-section exercises is the best way to understand the various slopes of the Irish landscape. Why not do an exercise from one of the OS (Ordnance Survey) maps in this book?

spot height 397m
R749
Derry River
third class roads
river
spot height 164m
400
300
200
100
397
380
350
300
250
200
150
120
Road
100
80
River
80
Road
100
110
120
130
130
Road
100
River
100
110
150
164

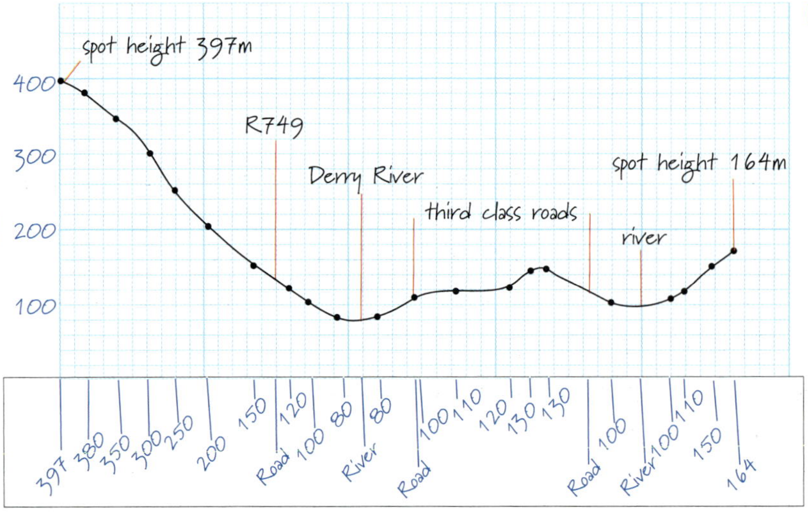

Fig. 37.6

Transfer marks and heights to graph paper. Then draw a cross-section.

Gradient

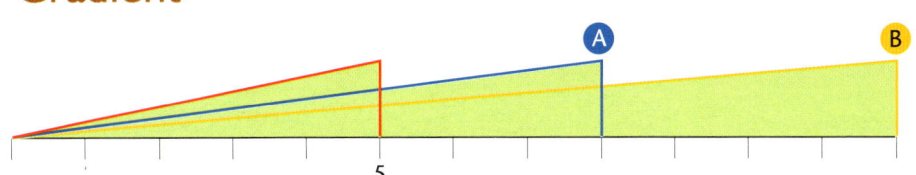

Activity

Look at Fig. 37.7. What are the gradients of slopes A and B?

Fig. 37.7

Gradient refers to a slope expressed as a ratio. A gradient of 1 in 5 means that the ground rises or falls one unit for every five units travelled horizontally.

Calculating Areas on Maps

To Calculate Regular Areas

1. Count the number of grid squares across the base of the area that you wish to calculate.
2. Count the number of grid squares up the side of the area.
3. Multiply the number across by the number up the side. This gives you the area in square kilometres (km²).

For example:

- The number of grid squares across the base = 7.
- The number of grid squares up the side = 3.
- Area = 7 x 3 = 21 km².

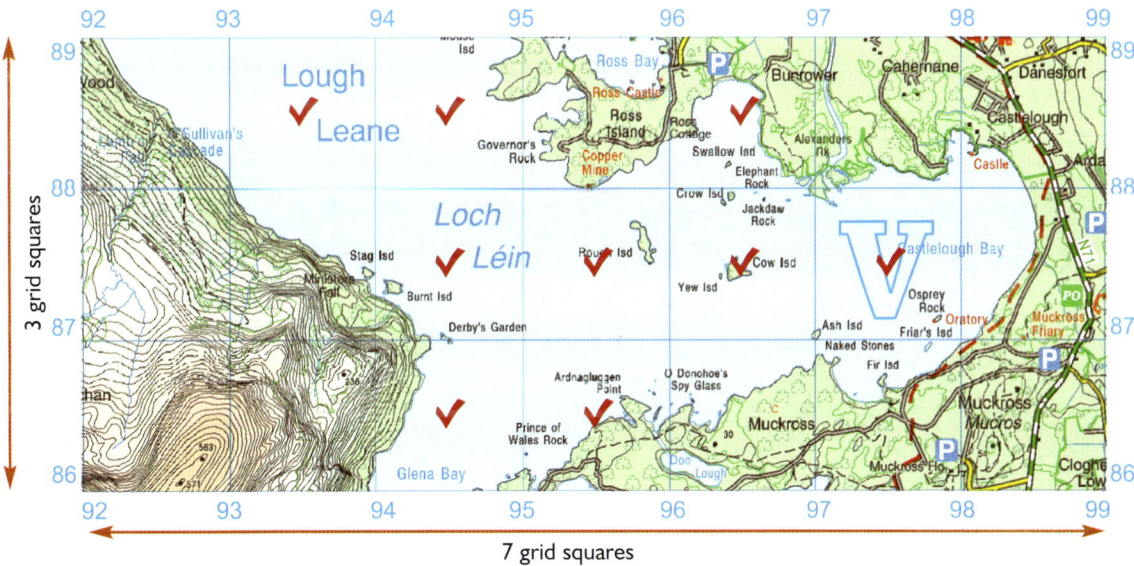

7 grid squares

To Calculate Irregularly Shaped Areas

Each grid square on a 1:50,000 map is one square kilometre. By using these grid squares, we can easily find the approximate area of an irregularly shaped region, such as a lake or sea region.

Count all the squares that are at least half-filled by the features that you wish to measure. This number is the approximate area of the feature in km². For example, to calculate the approximate area of Lough Leane:

- The number of squares at least half-filled with water = 9.
- Approximate area of lake = 9 km².

Multi-part Questions

Case Study: The Sligo Region

1. Carefully study the Ordnance Survey map of Sligo, then draw a sketch map of the region. Mark and label the following features on it:
   i. two upland regions
   ii. one urban region
   iii. a sea region
   iv. one recreation region.

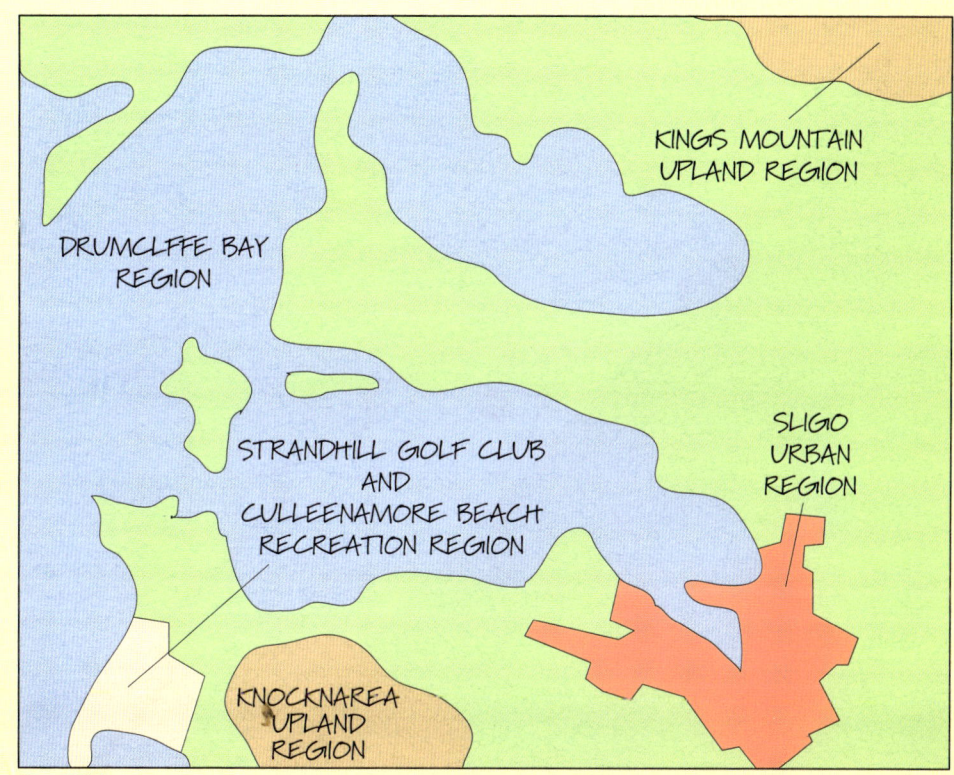

Fig. 37.8

2. **Class Activity 1**

   Draw a sketch map of the Sligo region. Mark and label the following features on it:
   i. the coastline
   ii. one upland region
   iii. one urban region (not Sligo town)
   iv. two national primary roads
   v. one regional road
   vi. one river.

3. **Class Activity 2**

   i. Calculate the area of the seawater region on the map.
   ii. Use the national grid map on page 260 to locate this region in Ireland.

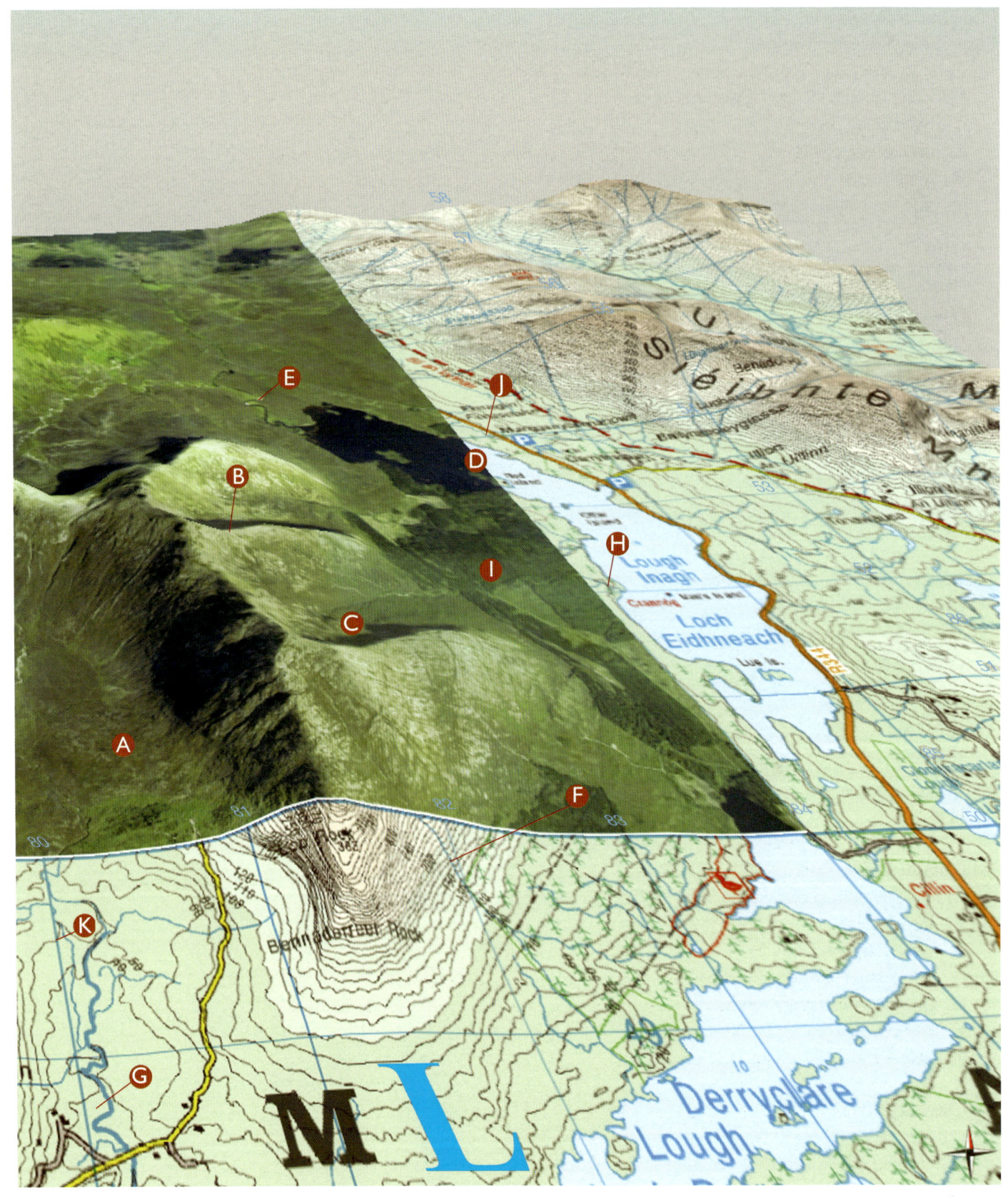

Trail Master Activities

Carefully study the Ordnance Survey map and photograph images of the Twelve Bens and Maumturk Mountains in Connemara, then answer the following questions.

1. **LANDFORMS**

    Identify the glacial landforms A to D and identify the process of erosion or deposition that formed them.

	Landform	Processes	Erosion/deposition
A			
B			
C			
D			

2. **LANDFORMS**

    Identify the river landforms E to H and identify the process of erosion or deposition that formed them.

	Landform	Processes	Erosion/deposition
E			
F			
G			
H			

3. **DIRECTION**

    i.   In which direction would you be travelling if moving from (use the gridlines to find direction):
         a. landform D to landform E
         b. landform C to landform H
         c. landform B to landform E?
    ii. In which direction would you be travelling if moving from the Cillín at L 843 496 to the Crannóg at L 845 519?
    iii. Identify the trend of Sléíbhte Mhár Tóirc.

4. **SCALE**

    i.   Is this image of the map and photograph 'true to scale'? Explain.
    ii. Use a paper strip and the gridlines to estimate the following distances:
         a. the distance from where the R344 enters the map in the south to the park and picnic site at L 845 538
         b. the distance between the letter K at L 800 496 and the Cillín at L 843 496.
         What does the comparison between both of these measurement methods tell you about scale on this image? Explain.

5. **LAND USES**

    Identify the land uses at:
    i.   I
    ii. J.

CHAPTER 38
UNDERSTANDING PHOTOGRAPHS

Types of Aerial Photograph

There are two types of aerial photograph:

- **Vertical photographs**, which are taken when the camera is pointing directly on the area being photographed.
- **Oblique photographs**, which are taken when the camera is pointing at an angle to the area being photographed. A **high** oblique shows **horizon**. A **low** oblique shows only **ground** surface.

Remember these few facts about aerial photographs:
- Scale.
- The nine divisions on an oblique photo.
- Direction.

Locating Places or Features on an Aerial Photograph

For easy reference, a photograph may be divided into nine areas, as shown below.

Vertical

Oblique

left   centre   right

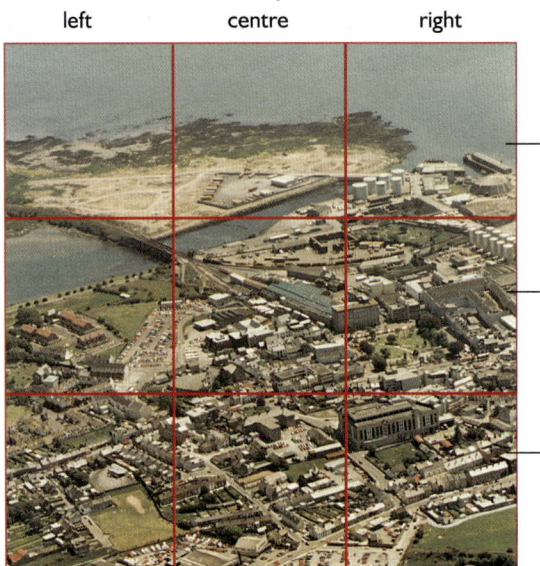

background covers a large area but background features appear small

middle

foreground covers a small area but features appear large

A north sign is given on a vertical photograph, so locations, such as the **north-west** or the **south-east** or the **east,** should be used.

For easy reference on an oblique photograph, nine divisions, such as **right background** and **left foreground,** should be used.

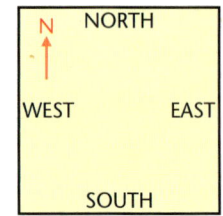

Fig. 38.1

Scale on aerial photographs

- All the features on a vertical photograph are in the same proportion to each other as they are on the ground. In other words, scale remains true throughout the photograph.

- Features which are located in the background of an oblique photograph appear small because they are far from the camera.
- Features which are located in the foreground of an oblique photograph appear large because they are nearer the camera.

When a direction arrow pointing north is given, turn the photo until the arrow faces upwards. Then write 'north' at the top, 'south' at the bottom, 'west' on the left and 'east' on the right.

Finding Direction on Oblique Photographs

An arrow indicating north is sometimes printed on a photograph. From this arrow we can find other directions. If an arrow is not given, we can find direction if we have an Ordnance Survey map of the same area.

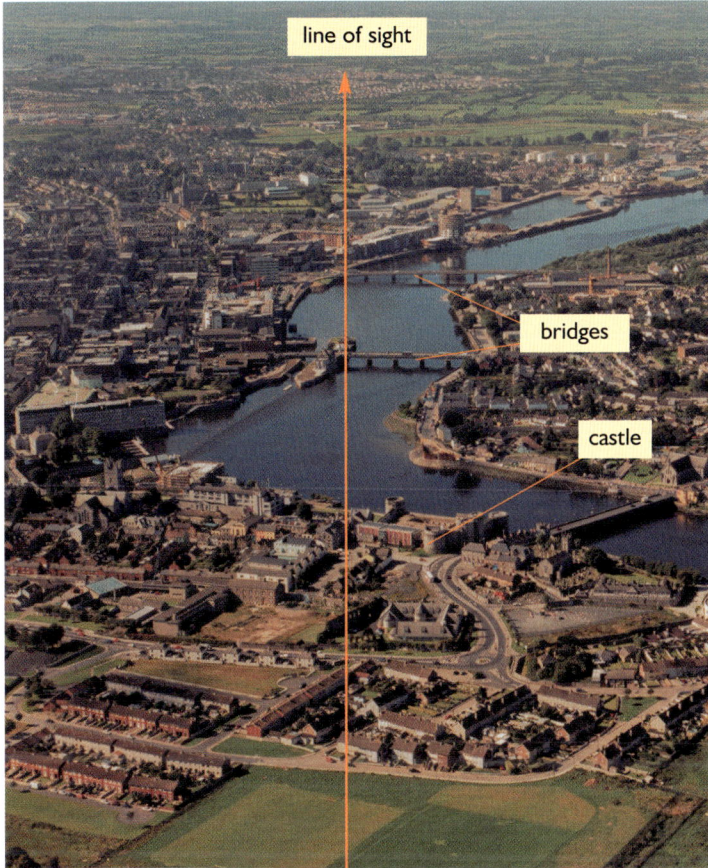

Aerial view showing Limerick city and the Shannon River.
● *Which direction was the camera lens pointing when this photograph was taken?*

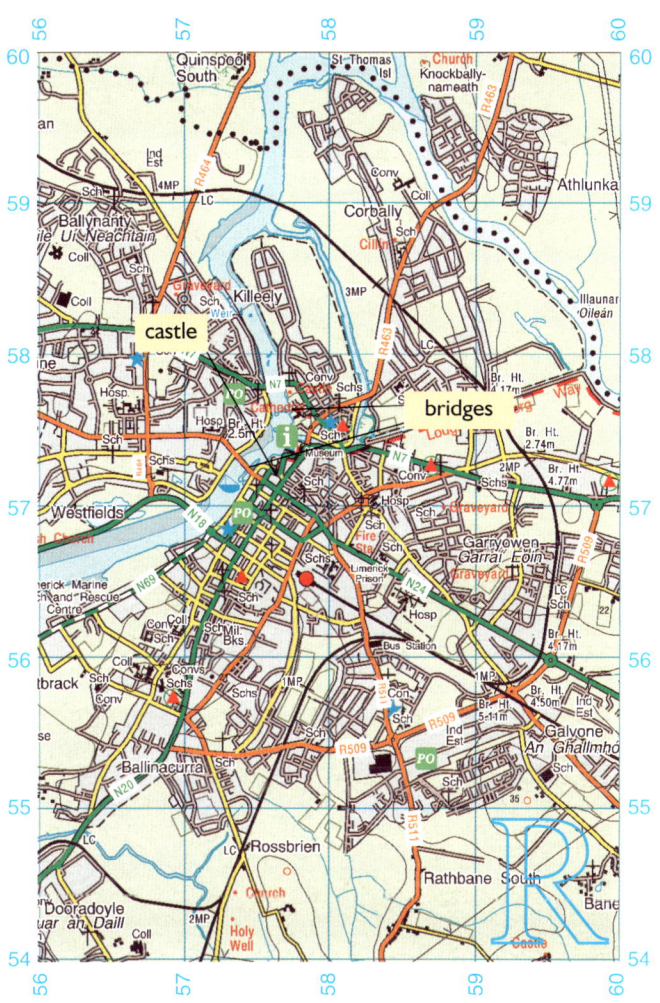

Finding Direction Using a Photograph and Map

Orientate Your Map or Photograph

1. Draw a line through the centre of the photograph from the foreground to the background (from the bottom to the top). This line represents the direction the camera was pointing when the photograph was taken.

2. Identify some important features through or near which your line passes, such as a church, a railway or a road.

3. Identify these same features on the Ordnance Survey map. Then draw a line on the map that corresponds to the line you drew on the photograph.

4. On the line, place an arrow near the feature on the map located in the background of your photograph.

5. Identify the direction of this line from the map. This represents the direction of the camera when the photograph was taken.

Match the features on the photograph with the ones marked on the map to find direction.

Time of year
Name all the features on a photo that may help identify the four seasons.

269

Sketch Maps from Photographs and Maps

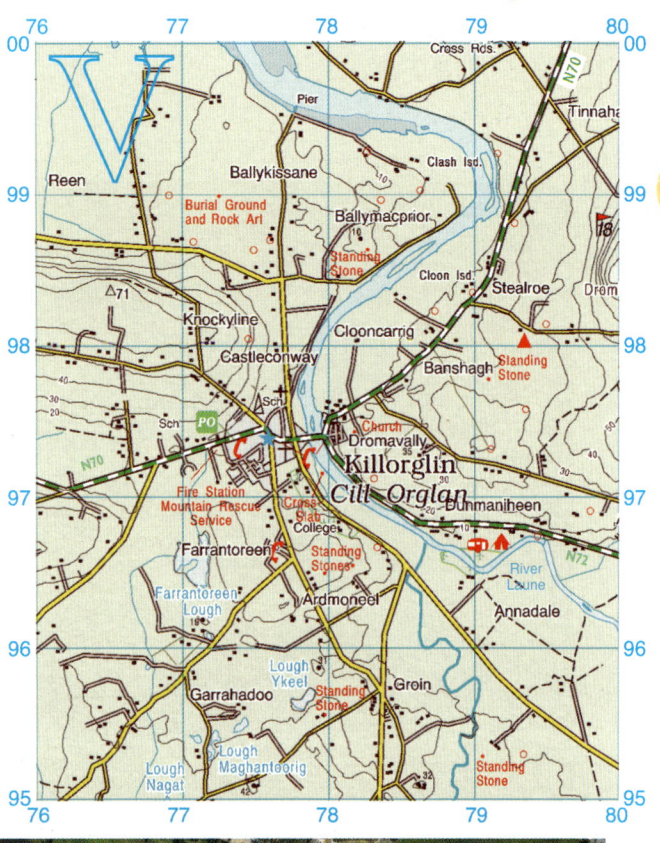

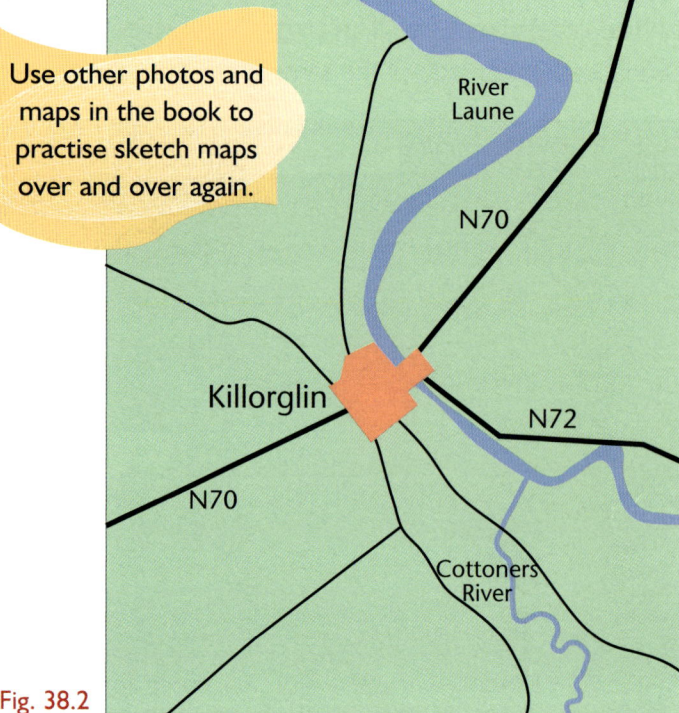

Use other photos and maps in the book to practise sketch maps over and over again.

Fig. 38.2

Roscommon town.

Mark in only those features that are asked for specifically.

Fig. 38.3

Activity

1. Draw a sketch map of the region shown on the Ordnance Survey map. Mark and name the following on it:
   a. Killorglin town
   b. two national secondary roads
   c. five third-class roads
   d. two rivers. (30 marks)

2. Draw a sketch map of the region shown in the photograph. Mark and name the following on it:
   a. a river
   b. the street pattern
   c. the main street
   d. a housing estate
   e. an area of on-street parking
   f. a church
   g. an industrial area. (30 marks)

GEOGRAPHIC INFORMATION SYSTEMS

A **geographic information system** (GIS) is a system for creating, storing, analysing and managing spatial data. In the strictest sense, it is a computer system capable of integrating, storing, editing, analysing, sharing and displaying geographically referenced information. In a more general sense, GIS is a tool that allows users to create interactive queries (user-created searches), analyse the spatial information and edit data.

Geographical information science is the science underlying the applications and systems.

Geographic information systems technology can be used for:

- Scientific investigations.
- Resource management.
- Asset management.
- Environmental impact assessment development planning.
- Cartography (map-making).
- Route planning or town planning.

For example, a GIS might allow emergency planners to calculate emergency response times in the event of a natural disaster, or a GIS might be used to find wetlands that need protection from pollution.

GIS is used in digital mapping of various kinds. Digital maps can hold lots of information about a particular region. All this information can be superimposed so that a greater understanding of a region may be achieved. This information is stored in digital form and can be updated or modified at any time.

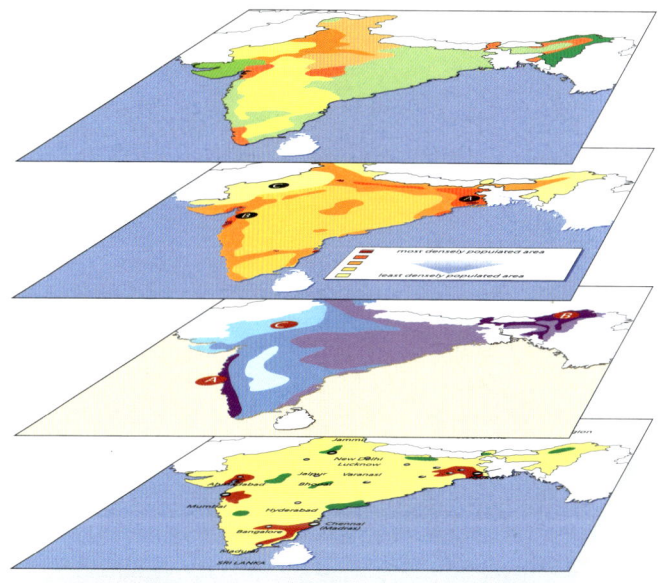

Fig. 38.4

Superimposition of information helps present maps in different layers. Each layer holds information about a particular topic, such as rainfall, hydrology (groundwater), housing, streets and drainage systems. Such related topics present a more complete three-dimensional understanding of pollution control, surface run-off and likely flooding points. The relevant information can be modified and projected outcomes can be viewed. For example, increased rainfall and waterlogging can be inserted to view likely outcomes.

GIS has been increasingly used by commercial bodies in recent years and this demand has funded the rapid growth of this new system of information. New urban developments, such as urban renewal projects, may use GIS to fully understand the factors involved in the building of large multi-storey structures that may house different commercial uses within a central business district in a major city. The manipulation of data allows for the interpretations of different outcomes or may highlight difficulties that may be faced during construction.

This is a three-dimensional computer map of Mt Shasta volcano in California, USA. The image was produced by the shuttle *Endeavor* mapping mission.

271

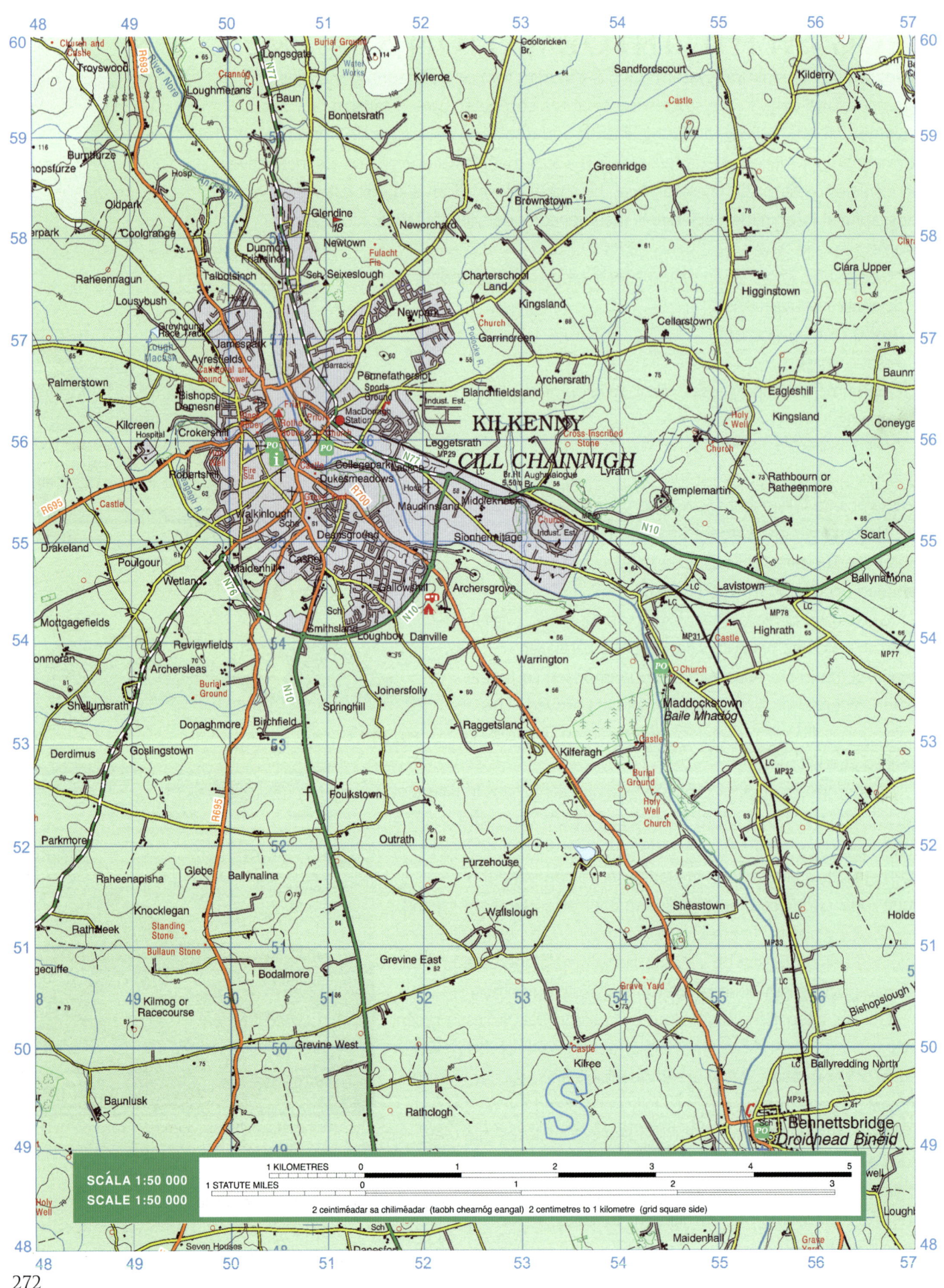

SCÁLA 1:50 000
SCALE 1:50 000

1 KILOMETRES   0   1   2   3   4   5
1 STATUTE MILES   0   1   2   3

2 ceintiméadar sa chiliméadar (taobh chearnóg eangal) 2 centimetres to 1 kilometre (grid square side)

Activity

Ordnance Survey Map

1. Identify by grid reference a suitable site for a major shopping centre. Using map evidence to support your answer, explain two reasons why you chose this site. [20 marks]

2. Describe:
   i. the location of Kilkenny (20 marks)
   ii. the location of Bennettsbridge. [20 marks]

3. The urban region of Kilkenny in the map extract shows evidence of historic development over time. Identify this evidence and explain its importance for the town's development. [30 marks]

4. 'The area shown on the map extract indicates evidence of a wide variety of historic settlement.' Examine this statement using map evidence, with reference to any three aspects of settlement. [30 marks]
   [Leaving Certificate 2006]

5. Draw a sketch map of the region shown on the Ordnance Survey map extract. On it, mark and name:
   i. one national primary route
   ii. one national secondary route
   iii. two regional routes
   iv. a railway
   v. the Nore River
   vi. the urban region of Kilkenny
   vii. one region of coniferous woodland. [20 marks)

Photograph: A Multi-part Question

A. Examine the aerial photograph **and** Ordnance Survey map of Kilkenny, then draw a sketch map of the photograph region. On it, mark and name:
   i. a large river
   ii. any five different land uses. [20 marks]

B. 'Much of Kilkenny's urban region was developed in the twentieth and twenty-first centuries.' Discuss this statement, using evidence from the photograph. [30 marks]

C. 'Kilkenny's urban street pattern poses many traffic problems for urban planners.' Discuss this statement, using evidence from the photograph. [30 marks]

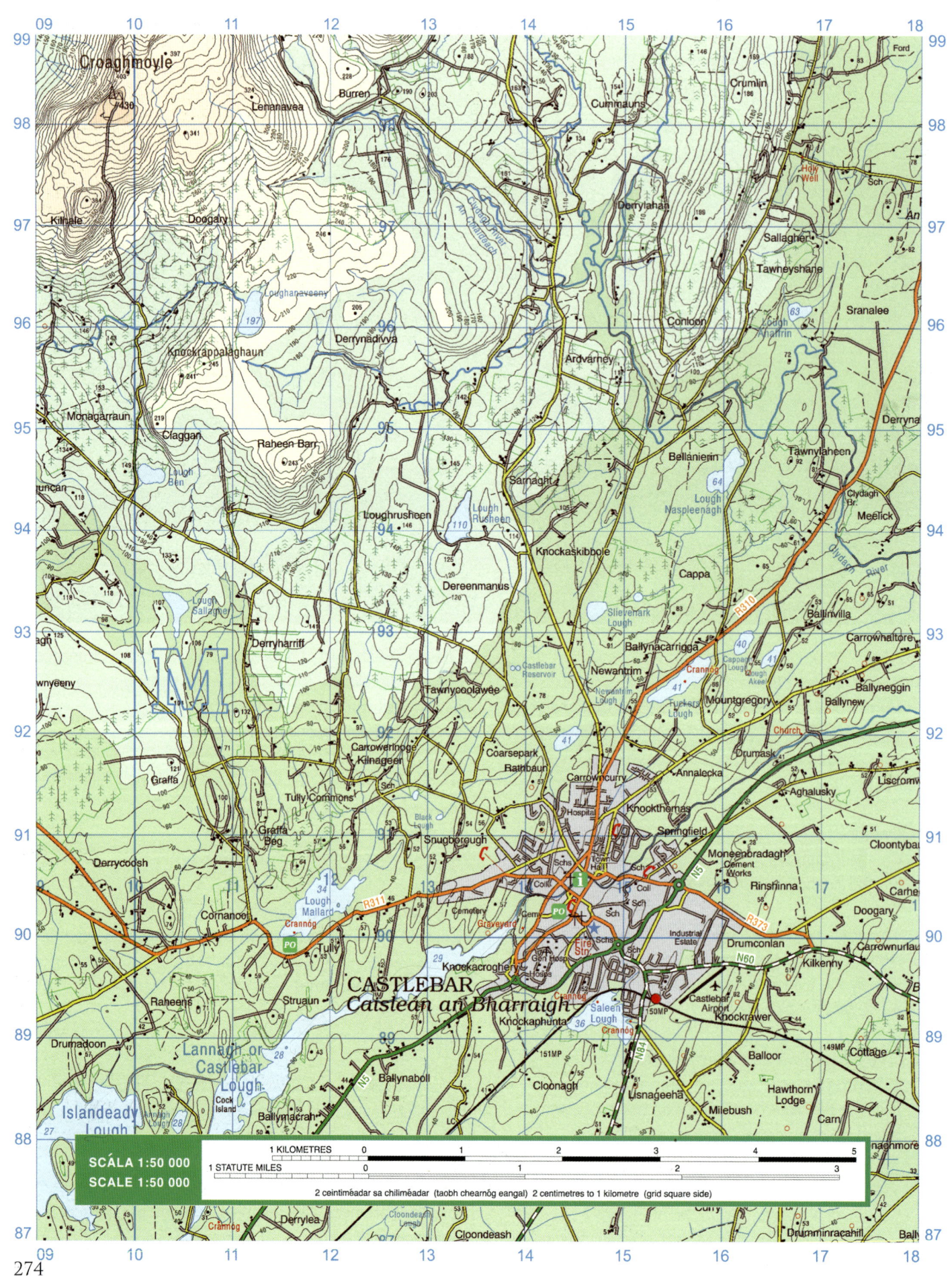

Ordnance Survey Map

A. Draw a sketch map and on it mark and name the following:
  i.   one major river
  II. two lakes
  iii. the urban region of Castlebar
  iv. a railway
  v.   one national primary route
  vi. one regional route.　　　　　　　[20 marks]

B. 'The urban region of Castlebar shows evidence of many types of services.' With reference to your studies of central place theory and evidence on the photograph, discuss this statement.　　　　　　　[30 marks]

C. The map region of Castlebar displays examples of a number of physical landforms. Name four of these landforms and state whether they are landforms of erosion or deposition.　　　　　　　[20 marks]

D. Use evidence from the map to identify, locate and explain any two types of drainage patterns.　[20 marks]

E. Draw a sketch map of the region. On it, mark and label the major drainage features of the area.　[20 marks]

Photograph and Map

A. Draw a sketch map. On it, mark and label:
  i.   a lake
  ii. a river
  iii. four main streets of Castlebar
  iv. regions of different urban land uses.　[20 marks]

B. Identify the following features on the photograph:
  i.   the lake in the left background
  ii. the route in the right background.　[20 marks]

C. In which direction was the camera pointing when this photograph was taken?　　　　　　　[5 marks]

D. What evidence in the photograph suggests that Castlebar was a planned town? Explain your answer.
　　　　　　　[30 marks]

E. 'The shape and height of many large urban buildings may suggest their functions.' Examine this statement using evidence from the photograph.　[30 marks]

Ordnance Survey Map: North Dublin Region

A. i. Calculate the approximate area of sea on this map. [10 marks]

ii. Calculate the distance from Lusk at O 217 544 to the post office at Skerries at O 255 606. [10 marks]

B. Draw a sketch map of the region. Mark and label (name) the following on it:
   i. the coastline
   ii. one region of coastal deposition
   iii. one region of coastal erosion
   iv. a nature reserve region
   v. one urban region
   vi. one motorway
   vii. one regional route. [30 marks]

C. Use evidence from the map to explain why housing development in rural environments needs to be restricted to prevent urban sprawl. [30 marks]

Photograph of Letterkenny

Carefully examine the photograph of Letterkenny, then do the following.

A. Draw a sketch map of Letterkenny's urban region. On it, mark and label:
   i. the street pattern
   ii. five different land uses. [20 marks]

B. 'Urban planners have carefully controlled the expansion and development of the town.' Discuss this statement with reference to the photograph. [30 marks]

C. Suppose the Irish Sports Council decided to build a large sports complex that would accommodate approximately 25,000 people. Choose a suitable site for this development and justify your choice of site using evidence from the photograph. [30 marks]

CHAPTER 39
POPULATION DISTRIBUTION CHANGES OVER TIME

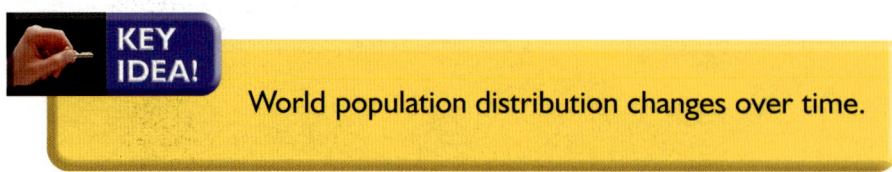

KEY IDEA!

World population distribution changes over time.

The distribution, density and number of people in the world is constantly changing over time and over the earth's surface. Population numbers vary throughout the world and between continents. They also vary between countries, within countries and within local areas, such as counties.

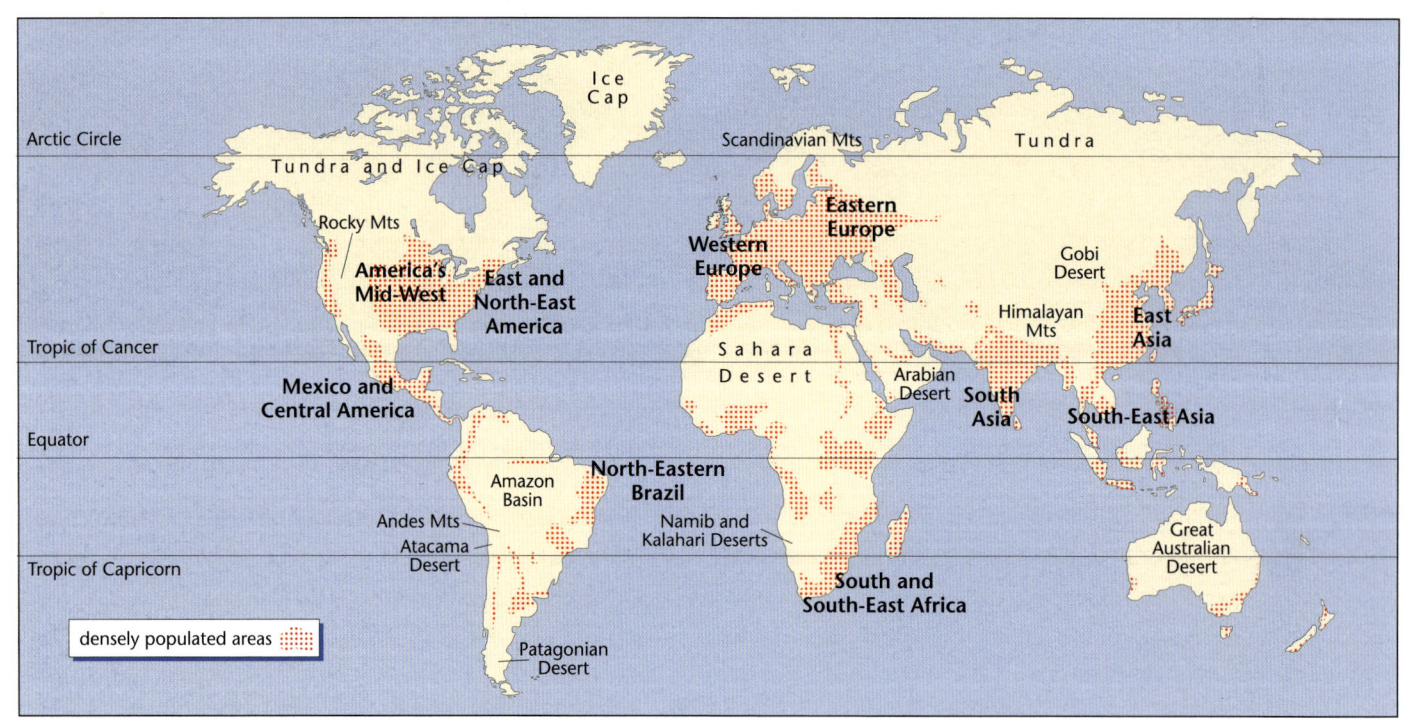

Fig. 39.1 World population distribution today.

> **World population distribution means the location and number of people who live in each continent.**

The world's population is very unevenly distributed. However, there are **four distinct areas** where most of the world's population is located:

- East and South-East Asia, including China, Korea, Japan, Malaysia, the Philippines and Indonesia.
- The Indian sub-continent, including Pakistan, India, Sri Lanka and Bangladesh.
- The eastern United States and south-eastern Canada.
- West and central Europe.

These areas are mostly in the **northern hemisphere** and mainly lie in **temperate** or **sub-tropical** latitudes. These highly populated locations are also lowland regions. They usually have deep fertile soils on river floodplains.

There are many areas, often of great size, which are very **thinly populated.** These are usually inaccessible places that may have thin, stony soils, are mountainous or too cold, too hot, too wet or too dry. These areas include:

- The **cold tundra** and ice cap regions of polar lands, e.g. northern Canada, Greenland, Siberia and Antarctica.
- **Mountainous lands**, e.g. the Himalayas, the plateau lands of central Asia, such as Tibet, and the Rocky Mountains in the USA and Canada.
- **Hot deserts** such as the Sahara, the Arabian and the Australian deserts.
- **Equatorial rainforests**, such as the Amazon, Borneo and the Congo.

Most megacities of the future will be in quickly developing countries.

Population distribution maps are an inaccurate way of representing population distribution. For example, in India, even though it has a very high population (over 1 billion people at present), many parts of the country are sparsely populated, while other areas are overpopulated. A better measure represents the ratio of people in a country per unit of area of agriculturally productive land. This is called the **physiologic density**. In India this index is about 650 per square kilometre (about 1,600 per square mile).

Water and food are two essential needs of people for survival, but owing to climactic change or other factors, some places that had large populations at one time are now thinly populated due to a loss of these resources. Other places, such as America, that were once thinly peopled are now heavily populated due to immigration of Europeans and Africans to the New World.

Today, over half the world's population lives in India, China and South-East Asia.

Cold regions are not attractive to humans.
- *Give three reasons why cold regions have low population densities.*

Fig. **39.2** Distribution of world cities with populations of over 1 million.

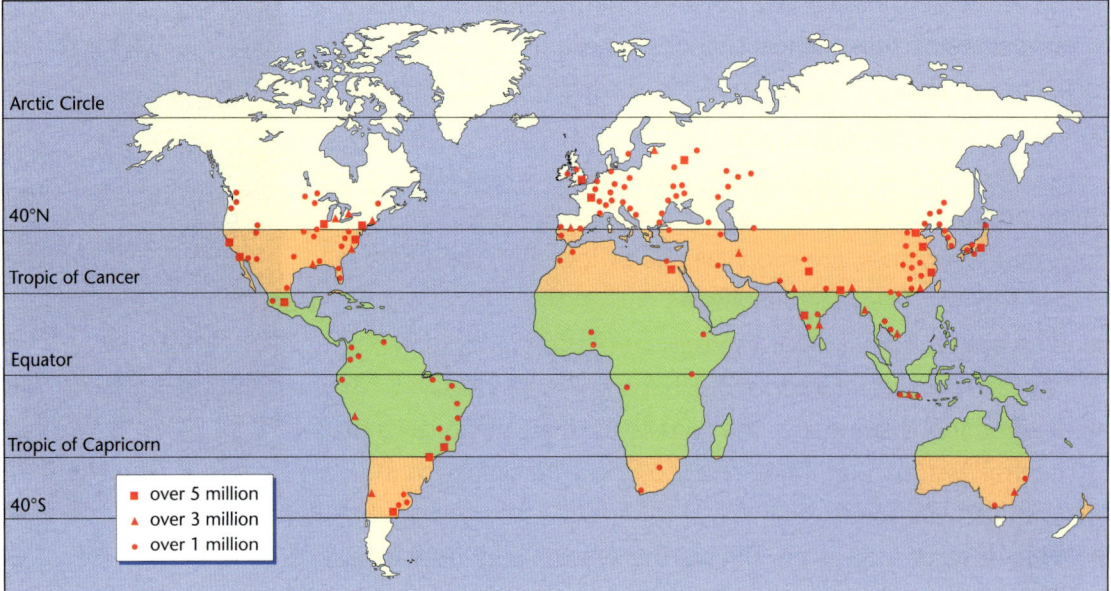

Fig. **39.3** Urban population growth. The increased urbanisation of the world's population has created changes in its distribution over time.

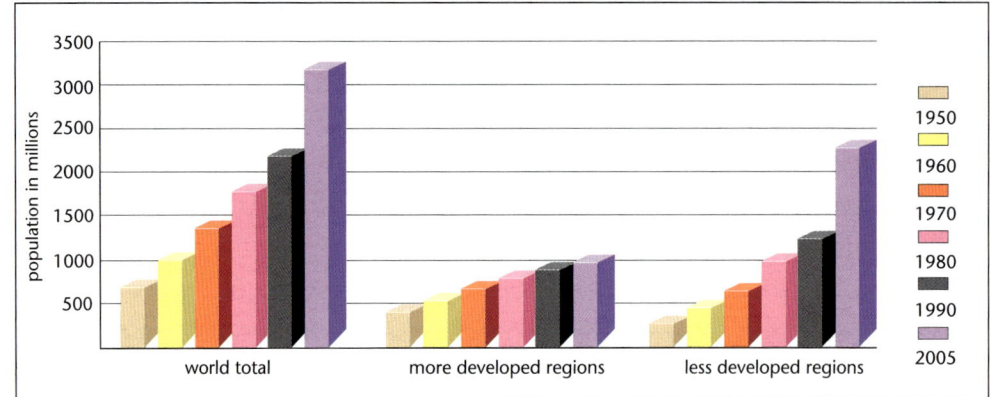

THE EFFECTS OF URBANISATION ON WORLD POPULATION DISTRIBUTION

The **growth of towns and cities** and industrialisation have changed the pattern of world population over the past 200 years, especially during the twentieth century. Large-scale migration of rural residents to towns and cities takes place as a country develops from an agricultural to an industrial economy. During this process, the growth rate of urban areas is typically double the pace of overall population increase. Thirty per cent of the world population lived in urban areas in 1950. This figure was 47 per cent in 2000 and 50 per cent in 2007.

Urbanisation eventually leads to a **severe decline in the number of people living in the countryside** with **negative population growth rates**. Cities are engines of social change; they continue to grow throughout the developing world. In 1960, one in three people lived in a city; today, half of all people do, and **it is predicted that by 2030 more than 60.8 per cent of the population will live in urban areas.** Forty-one of these urban areas are megacities with more than 5 million people. By 2015 this number will reach sixty, with forty-eight of these in less developed regions. All megacities lie within 500 km of a coastline.

CHAPTER 40
WORLD POPULATION DENSITY

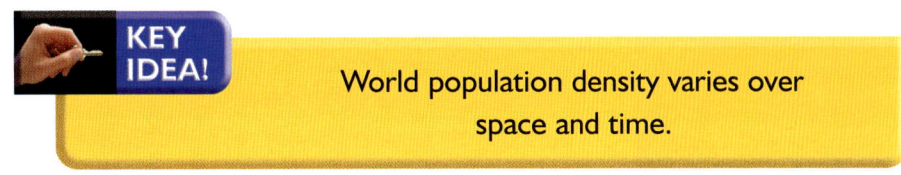

KEY IDEA!

World population density varies over space and time.

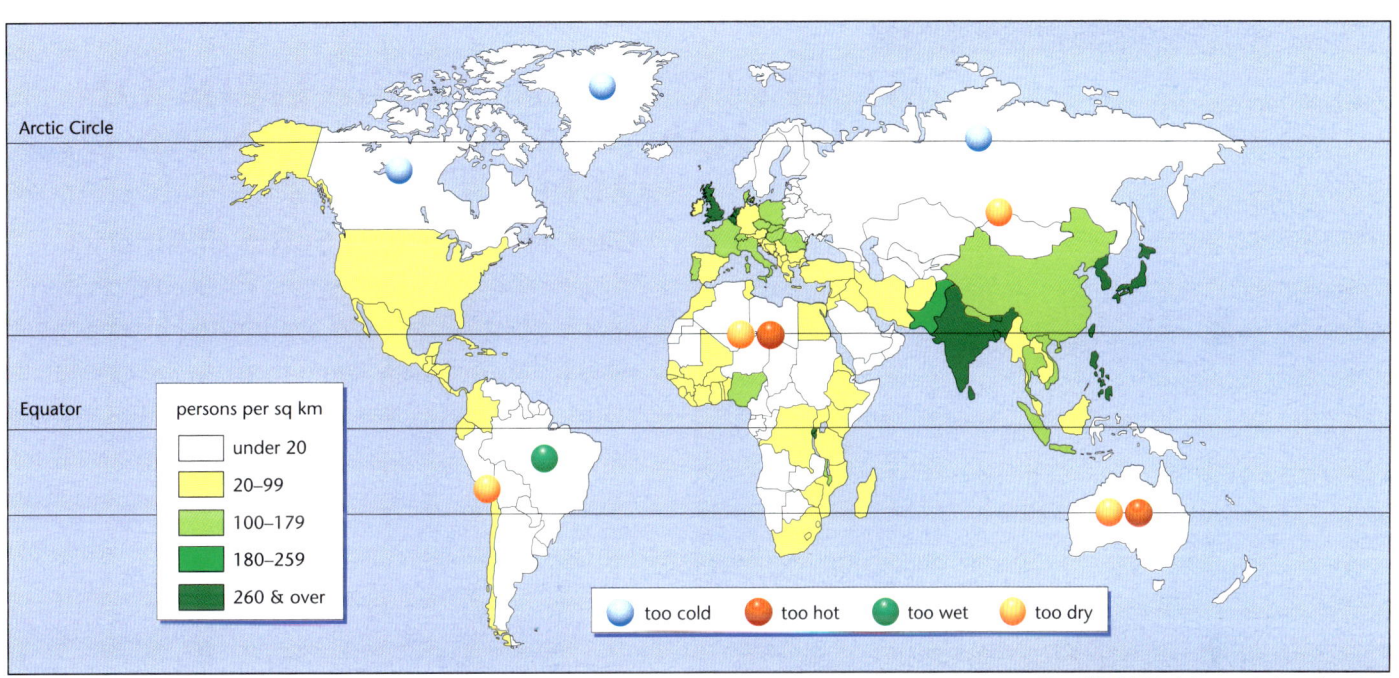

Fig. 40.1 World population density.

For most people:

- One-fifth of the earth is too cold.
- One-fifth of the earth is too hot.
- One-fifth of the earth is too wet.
- One-fifth of the earth is too dry.

Thus most of the world's people live on one-fifth of the world's surface, in areas which are scattered throughout the various continents.

To obtain population density, divide the total population of a country by the total area of that country. World population **distribution** means the location and number of people who live in each continent. Population **density** means the average number of people per square kilometre in a country.

The map in Fig. 40.1 displays present population densities throughout the world. It clearly shows that the greatest densities occur in South and South-East Asia, where over half of the world's population lives.

Activity
Carefully examine the world population densities in Fig. 40.1.
1. Name the countries with the highest densities.
2. Name one continent with a population density of twenty or fewer people per km².
3. Name one North American country with a population density of fewer than twenty persons per km².
4. With the aid of your atlas, give two reasons why South America has a low population density.

Migrations have dramatically changed world distribution and density over time.

A closer examination of these densities would indicate that the statistics hide irregularities. For example, India is shown with a density of at least 260 people per square kilometre. However, few people live in the Thar Desert in northern India or in the higher parts of the Deccan Plateau. In contrast, densities of over 2,000 per hectare may occur in parts of Kolkata (Calcutta) and Mumbai (Bombay).

Ireland, on the other hand, has a low population density of just 57 people per square kilometre, yet Dublin has a higher population density, while Connemara has a much lower one.

SOME EFFECTS OF MIGRATION ON POPULATION DISTRIBUTION AND DENSITY

Case Study: United States of America

In Junior Certificate Geography you studied that people's **first settlements are located in areas near where they originally came from**. In the United States, the north-east coast is where a large proportion of its population is located. Because the north-east coast is closest to Europe, emigrants from the European continent settled here. Over time this has led to a high population density in this region. The concentration of large cities, such as Washington, DC, Pittsburgh, New York, Albany and Boston, as well as numerous other cities and towns, forms a large urban region called a **megalopolis**.

There is a much lower population density in the Midwest (the Mississippi Basin) as it is away from the coast and is separated from it by the Appalachian mountain range, which initially formed a physical barrier to westward migration of new settlers.

Fig. 40.2 Population density in the USA.

Map labels:
- low population density Appalachian Mts
- low-density Midwest farming region
- very low Rocky Mountains
- high-density East Coast urban region

Case Study: Southern Italy

The migration of people from southern Italy (the Mezzogiorno) to northern Italy has led to a pattern of out-migration in the South and a corresponding pattern of in-migration in the North.

Over 4 million people left the Mezzogiorno between 1951 and 1971, and over 1.1 million people left between 1983 and 1993. Today, due to new investments in the region as a consequence of the Mezzogiorno being classed as Objective 1 status, employment prospects have been improved and out-migration is lower than before. However, out-migration still continues because growth in job prospects has failed to satisfy demands.

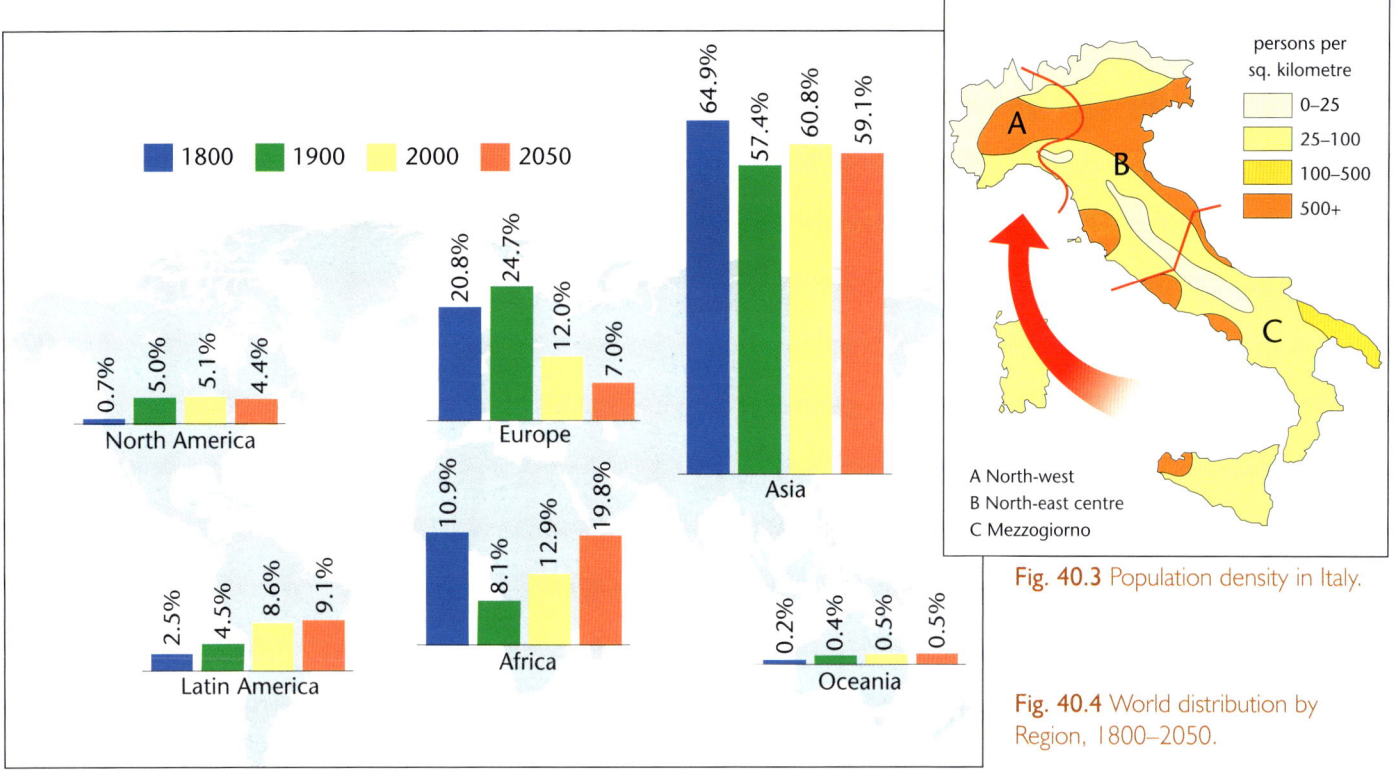

Fig. 40.3 Population density in Italy.

Fig. 40.4 World distribution by Region, 1800–2050.

Multi-part Questions

1. Carefully study this diagram of world population distribution over time, then answer the following.

   A. Explain why Europe's percentage of world population:

   i. rose from 20.8% to 24.7% between 1800 and 1900 (in your answer, refer to the influences of the Industrial Revolution and health improvements).

   ii. fell from 24.7% in 1900 to 12% in 2000. [20 marks]

   B. i. What change occurred in North America's and South America's percentage of world population from 1800 to 1900?

   ii. Explain the main cause of these changes. [30 marks]

   C. Suggest why:

   i. Australia's

   ii. Asia's

   percentage of world population have remained almost unchanged since 1800. (Refer to the location, relief and climate of Australia in your atlas as well as your general knowledge to answer this question. Refer to stage of development in Asia.) [30 marks]

2. A. Carefully study the population density distribution map of Italy in Fig. 40.3.

   i. Which region of Italy has the lowest density of population?

   ii. Which region has the highest density?

   iii. State the migration pattern illustrated in the map. [20 marks]

   B. With the help of your atlas and your studies in Regional Geography, explain:

   i. why south-eastern Italy has a greater density of population than most other parts of the Mezzogiorno

   ii. why the area around Naples has a high-density population. [30 marks]

   C. i. Name two world regions of high and low population density not mentioned in A and B above.

   ii. In each case, explain why some regions have high densities while other world regions have low densities. [30 marks]

CHAPTER 41
POPULATION GROWTH PATTERNS

 **KEY IDEA!**

Population growth rates are influenced by levels of economic development.

THE GROWTH IN WORLD POPULATION

The world's population has increased steadily over time. By the eighteenth century, population numbers in countries like Britain caused writers such as Thomas Malthus to believe that the world was becoming overpopulated. They believed that food supplies were not going to meet demand and that this was going to have catastrophic consequences for the human race.

Since then, population studies have identified a pattern of change over time. This is called the **population transition model/cycle**. Most countries of the **North** have gradually passed through this cycle over many generations, but newly expanding economies of the **South** are passing through the cycle over a much shorter timespan.

This population cycle suggests that **as the economy of a country develops, the population of that country goes through a series of predictable changes.** These changes have affected the pattern of population growth throughout the world.

Fig. 41.1 The population cycle.

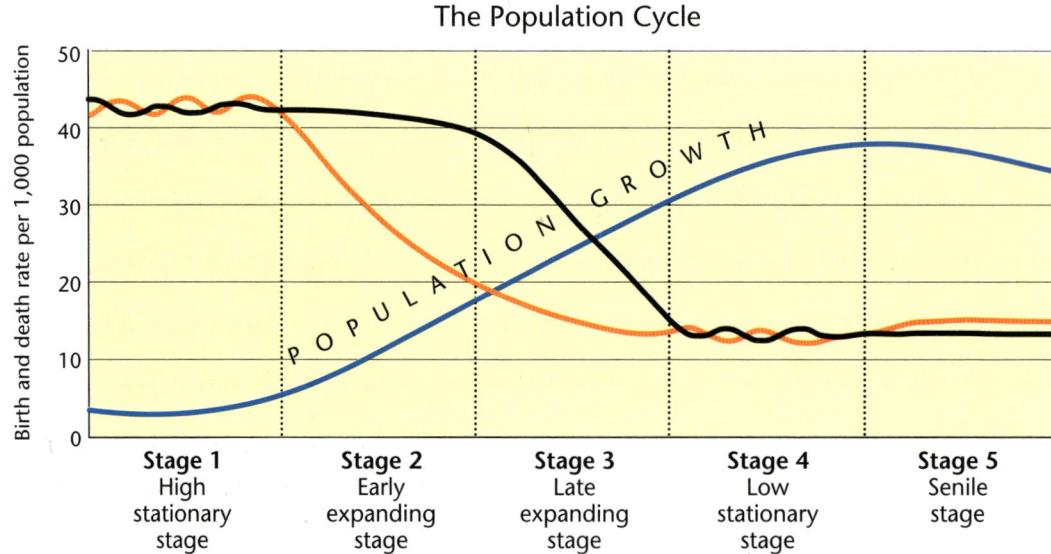

The Population Cycle

Advances in medicine and science have reduced death rates and led to increased population growth.

estimated population in 2025, by region (in millions)

rest of Asia 3,062

China 1,469

Africa 1,542

Latin America 865

North America 865

CIS 356

Europe 622

Oceania 36

1850: population of the developing world is estimated to have been three times that of the industrial world

1950: world total 2,500 million (double the 1850 figure)

1850 (1,200 million)

1900

1950

1960

1970

1980: world total 4,400 million

1980

1990 (5,300 million)

2000 (6,000 million)

1950–90: world total doubled (the developing world total doubled between 1960 and 1980)

2005 (6,500 million)

2005: world population = 6,500 million (compared with 1960 forecast of 7,500 million)

2020

2025 (8,300 million)

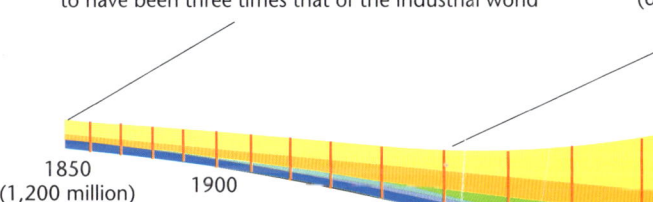

Fig. 41.2 World population growth.

Natural increase in a population occurs when **the birth rate is greater than the death rate**. When the death rate is greater than the birth rate, there is a **natural decrease**.

HIGH STATIONARY EARLY HISTORICAL TIMES

Before and during medieval times, population growth was slow. During this early period, population numbers **fluctuated** (went up and down). Birth and death rates were high.

This rise and fall of world population occurred because many wars, **plagues** (infectious diseases like the Black Death that devastated Europe's population), **tribal wars**, **famines**, **religious persecution** and **natural disasters** kept death rates high.

Regions were undeveloped and **food supply was undependable**. Most people depended on agriculture for a living. Medicine was primitive, mostly restricted to folk cures. Infant **mortality rates were high** and **life expectancy** was short.

EARLY EXPANDING THE INDUSTRIAL REVOLUTION

From 1750 onwards, the Industrial Revolution brought great social changes. Britain was the first industrialised country in the world.

- **New farming methods and improved technology led to increased food production.** These changes included:
  - The enclosure of land and the creation of farms.
  - Selective breeding and the use of new farm machines, such as the seed drill.
- **The invention of the steam engine** led to increased employment in coalfields and industrial textile mills. New housing for workers and the rapid growth of towns and cities led to improved living conditions.
- **Health improvements** including cleaner water supplies, urban sewage schemes and the control of infectious diseases led to a rapid fall in death rates and a corresponding rise in population. **Birth rates remained high.**

LATE EXPANDING 19TH AND EARLY 20TH CENTURIES

Death rates fell rapidly as urbanisation spread and living standards improved. This led to a rapid rise in production. As urbanisation spread throughout Europe, especially in Britain, Belgium and Germany, large families were regarded as an economic liability. With increased food supplies from the New World, family size became smaller as parents realised that their children would survive to become adults. Fewer children also meant improved living standards for parents, but **women still held a low status** and lacked decision-making powers.

LOW STATIONARY MID TO LATE 20TH CENTURY

At this stage society is industrialised and affluent and **women have reached a high social status**. Birth rates fall as women plan their family size – an average of 2.3 children per woman. This is called replacement level. Thus birth and death rates are almost equal and population growth ceases. However, immigration from surrounding countries may occur. **Increased demand for services** creates employment opportunities in rapidly expanding advanced economies. Ireland has reached this stage of development. This leads to population growth in those 'tiger' economies.

SENILE LATE 20TH AND EARLY 21ST CENTURIES

This fifth stage of the population cycle is called the senile stage. Birth rates are below replacement level. This creates a decline in population in those countries that have passed through the population cycle. Many European countries, such as Italy and Germany, have declining populations.

Recent Population Increase in Development Countries

Beginning about 1950, a new phase of population growth occurred in the underdeveloped nations of the South. New vaccines, antibiotics, insecticides and high-yielding varieties of seeds were introduced.

Life expectancy at birth in most developing countries increased from about thirty-five to forty years in 1950 to sixty-one years by 1990. The rapid decline in deaths among people who continued to have large families led to an annual population growth in developing nations that doubles population size in twenty-five years or less.

> **Birth Rate/Death Rate/Natural Increase**
> **Birth rate/death rate** refers to the number of births/deaths for every 1,000 people in a country for one year. The **natural increase** is found when the birth rate is measured against the number of deaths (death rate) for every 1,000 people in the same year.

> Population change may differ from the natural increase or decrease because it also takes into account migrants, which includes emigrants (out) and immigrants (in).

Case Study: Change over Time

Past and Present Population Trends for Britain

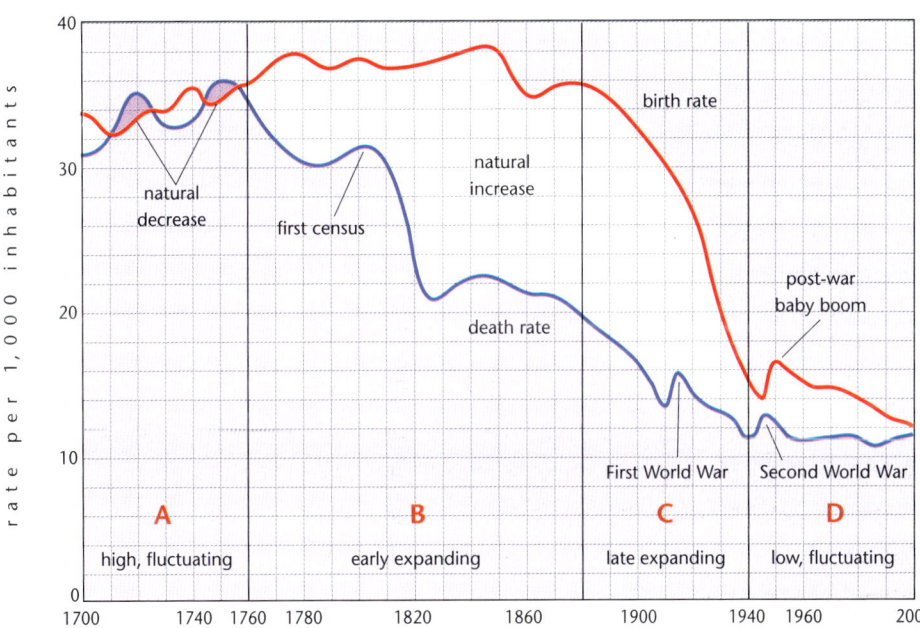

Fig. 41.3 Changes in Britain's population, 1700–2006.

Activity

Carefully examine the population model for Britain (Fig. 41.3).

1. Explain why Britain had high birth and death rates prior to 1760.
2. What factors caused the rapid fall in death rates between 1760 and 1940?
3. Explain why there has been a levelling off of birth and death rates with slight fluctuations since 1940.
4. Suggest what trend occurred in Britain's population between 1760 and 1960.
5. What effects did the First and Second World Wars have on Britain's:
   a. birth rates
   b. death rates?
6. Why is Britain's population growth an important one to compare to the demographic transition model? (Think of the Industrial Revolution.)

Britain was the first industrialised nation. Its early success was based on vast supplies of coal and local iron ore deposits.

Future Regional Growth Patterns

What statistics fail to show is the great variation in population growth between different areas in the world, especially between economically developed and economically developing continents.

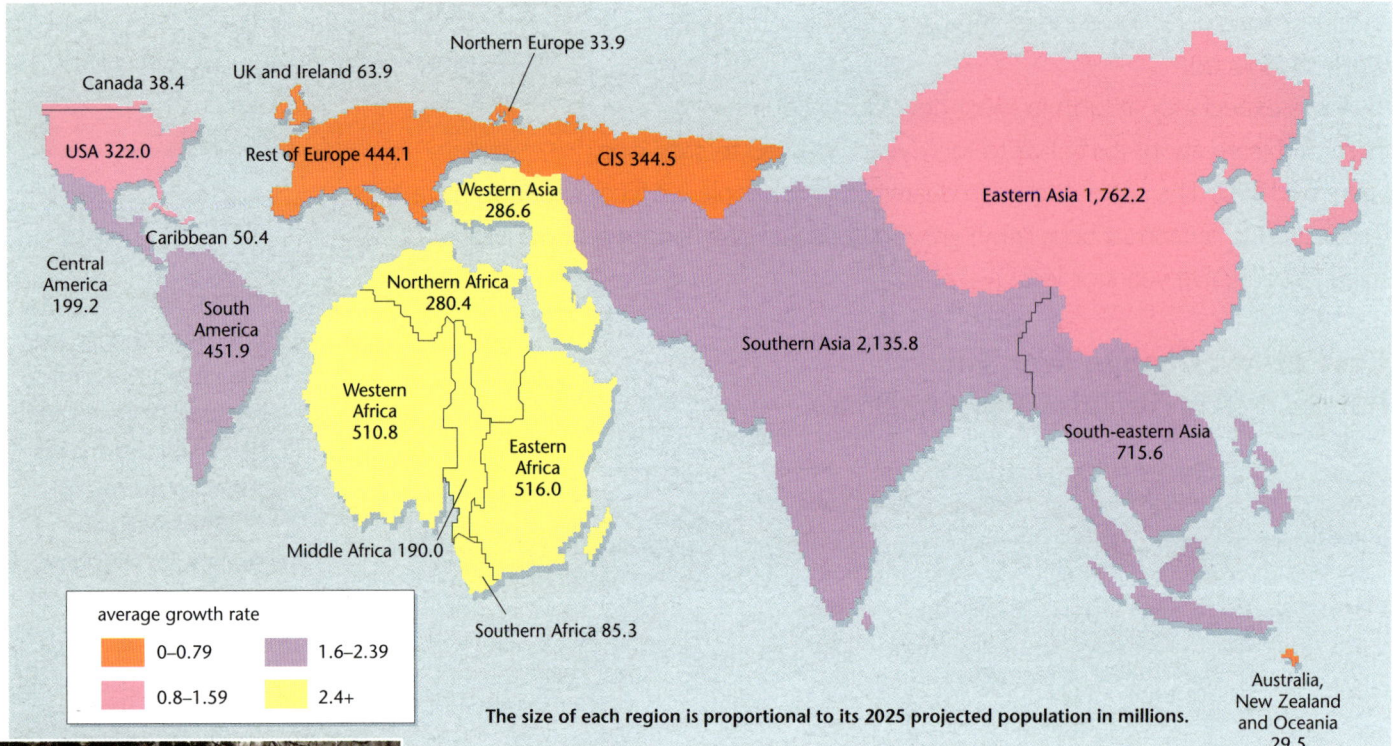

Canada 38.4

UK and Ireland 63.9

Northern Europe 33.9

USA 322.0

Rest of Europe 444.1

CIS 344.5

Eastern Asia 1,762.2

Caribbean 50.4

Western Asia 286.6

Central America 199.2

South America 451.9

Northern Africa 280.4

Western Africa 510.8

Eastern Africa 516.0

Southern Asia 2,135.8

South-eastern Asia 715.6

Middle Africa 190.0

average growth rate

■ 0–0.79	■ 1.6–2.39
■ 0.8–1.59	■ 2.4+

Southern Africa 85.3

The size of each region is proportional to its 2025 projected population in millions.

Australia, New Zealand and Oceania 29.5

Fig. 41.4 Future population growth patterns.

To achieve a stable world population, the average birth rate worldwide would have to be 2.1 children per woman.

In 2005 the world fertility rate was 2.65 children per woman. That is about half the level it was in 1950. This is expected to fall further to 2.05 children per woman within the next few decades.

Projected Growth Rates in the Developed World

Average fertility is currently 1.56 children per woman in developed countries. This is expected to increase to 1.84 children per woman by 2050, but this is still below the **replacement level of 2.1 children per woman**. The primary consequence of fertility decline, especially if combined with increases in life expectancy, is **population ageing**. This occurs when **the share of older persons in a population increases** relative to that of younger persons. Some developed countries have zero growth rates. The populations of fifty-one countries, including Germany, Italy, Japan and the newer states of the former USSR, are expected to be lower in 2050 than in 2007.

Life expectancy in the developed world is expected to increase from seventy-five years today to eighty-two years by 2050. However, life expectancy in Eastern Europe has fallen from 67.2 years in 1960 to 55.5 years in 2006. The most affected countries include the Russian Federation or Ukraine, partly because of the spread of HIV.

Many elderly Japanese enjoy healthy lifestyles.

Projected Growth Rates in the Developing World

World population growth is highly dependent on the course that future fertility takes.

- **Average fertility** remains above five children per woman in thirty-five of the 148 developing countries; of these countries, thirty are least developing countries. The pace of decline in several countries of sub-Saharan Africa and south-central Asia has been slower than expected. In contrast, fertility has reached below replacement levels in twenty-three developing countries that account for one-quarter of the world population. This group includes China, whose fertility during 2000–07 is estimated at 1.7 children per woman.

- **Life expectancy** among the least developed countries is just under fifty years and it is expected to rise to sixty-six years by 2050. This rise is dependent on the implementation of effective programmes to prevent and treat HIV infection. In the rest of the developing world that continue the same programmes, life expectancy should rise from sixty-six years today to seventy-six years by 2050.

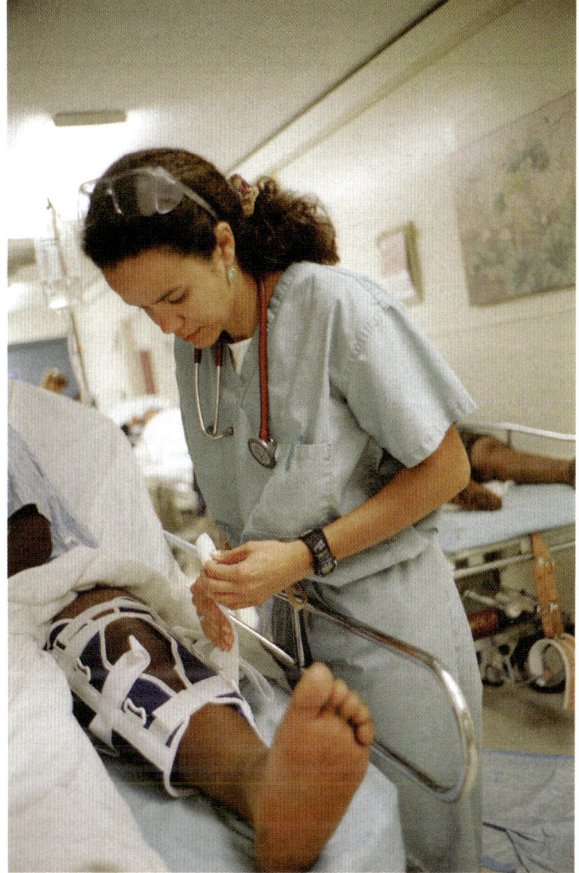

The Effects of the AIDS Virus

Africa is the continent most affected by AIDS (Acquired Immune Deficiency Syndrome); over 20 million people there suffer from the disease. **Life expectancy** in most countries of **sub-Saharan Africa** has fallen. In Zimbabwe and Botswana, for example, life expectancy has fallen by twenty years within the last decade. **Infant mortality** has risen in these countries by twenty per 1,000, many of the deaths also due to AIDS.

Many married women pursue careers to realise their potential and improve their living standards.

Activity

Carefully study the chart in Fig. 41.4 showing projected regional growth patterns in population worldwide for 2025 on page 288, then answer the following.

1. a. Identify the region with the largest population.
    b. Identify its average population growth rate.
    c. Name the largest country in this region. Use your atlas.
    d. Identify four other countries in this region.
    e. Calculate the total population for Eastern, South-East and Southern Asia.
    f. How does this figure compare to the total world population in 1970 of 3,500 million people?

2. Describe the effects of the population cycle on world population growth and distribution.

3. Explain how future regional population growth rates may differ between the developed and the developing world.

CHAPTER 42
CHANGING POPULATION CHARACTERISTICS

 **KEY IDEA!**

Population structure, fertility rates and mortality rates change over time throughout the world.

Three important basic characteristics of a population are:

- **Age structure**, which refers to the proportions of a population that belong to different age groups.
- **Sex structure,** which refers to the ratio between the number of males and females.
- **Dependency ratio**, which refers to the number of people who are **economically inactive** (under fifteen and over sixty-five), children and old-age pensioners compared to those who are **economically active** (fifteen to sixty-four years) and form the working population, which the economically inactive depend on to support them.

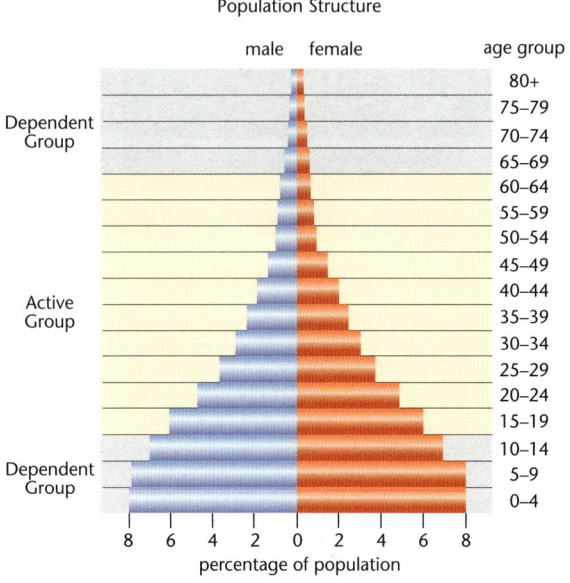

Fig. 42.1 A population pyramid.

POPULATION STRUCTURE

The best way to illustrate population structure and future trends is by a **population pyramid.** They divide the population into **five-year age** groups; for example, 0–4, 5–9, 10–14 and so on. As there are generally more young people than old, the diagram has the general shape of a pyramid. The differences in age, sex, birth rates and death rates create an irregular shape that indicates the structure of a population.

As well as showing **past changes,** population pyramids can predict short- and long-term **future changes** or **trends** in population. Population pyramids are used by governments to forecast **social needs** such as the number of schools, teachers, hospitals or community care nurses needed in any given area. These statistics can be applied at both **national** and **regional** levels; for example, a narrow base indicates that fewer schools and teachers will be needed. A wide top indicates more nursing homes may be needed. Population pyramids can also show the effects of migration, the age and sex of migrants and the effects of large-scale wars, famines and epidemics or disease.

The Basic Models or Stages of Population Pyramids

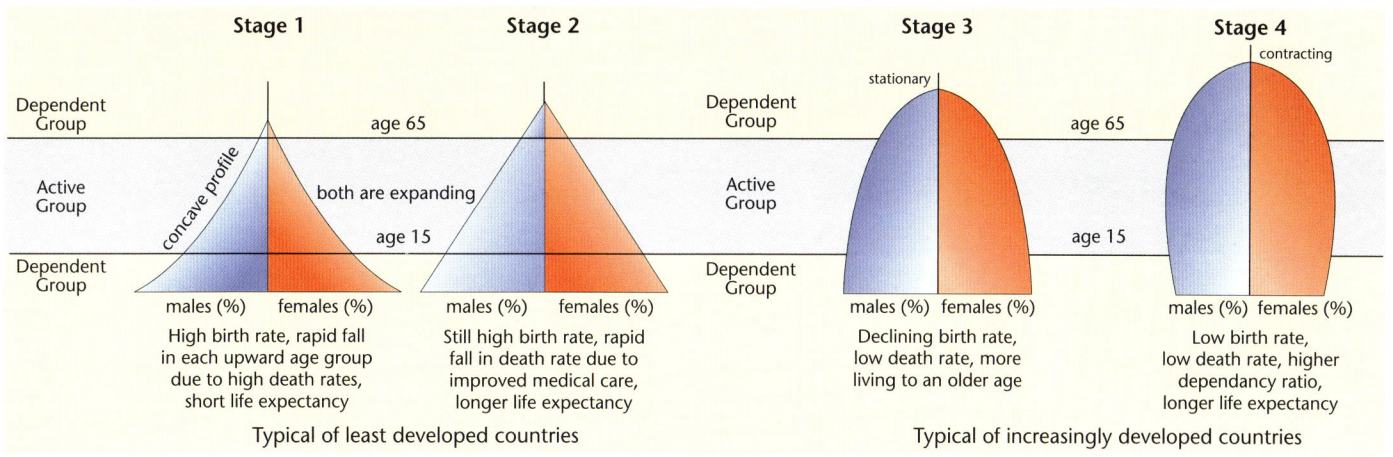

Fig. 42.2

Population pyramids can be reduced to four basic models. Each model represents a stage in the structure of a population as it changes from an undeveloped economy to a developed cconomy.

DEPENDENCY RATIO

One of the most important aspects of the age structure of a population is its dependency ratio.

- A **large young population** represents a vast potential market for consumer goods. In the developing world, 36 per cent of the population is under fifteen. The attraction for multinational companies lies in the prospective buying power of these new customers in countries such as China.

- A developing country generally has a large young population. Large families place a great **strain on family income**. Whatever income increase parents might achieve is rapidly used up in providing education, health care, clothing and food for their children.

- A **large old population** may have profound social implications. A disproportionate number of either old or young people, or both, in the population may put an intolerable burden on those who are at work and who must pay for services such as education, health care and pensions. An ageing population is not just a European problem. By 2006, India's population will include 86 million people aged sixty or over.

As people age, health and community services must be improved to cope with their needs.

The dependency ratio can be expressed as the following if figures are given in millions rather than as a percentage.

$$\frac{\text{children (0–14) and elderly (65 years and over)}}{\text{those of working age}} \times 100$$

For example, in a country the figures are

$$\frac{13{,}387 + 10{,}512}{31{,}616} \times 100 = 75.59$$

So for every **100 people** of **working age** there were **75.59** people **dependent** on them.

● *What evidence in this photograph suggests that Japan's economy is technically advanced?*

Case Study: Japan

The percentage of elderly people in Japan's population is getting larger, while the percentage of young people is getting smaller. This is creating a top-heavy population pyramid, which has serious implications for Japan's economy. Japanese people are the most long-lived in the world. In 2000, there were more than 10,500 Japanese people (83 per cent of them female) over 100 years of age, which was 1,700 (16 per cent) more than in 1999. By 2025, nearly 26 per cent of the Japanese people will be aged sixty-five years or more, compared to just 12 per cent in 1990.

Women are being encouraged to bear more children, even though Japan's population density is one of the highest in the world, at over 860 people per square kilometre; its physiologic population density, however, is 3,070 per square kilometre.

Case Study: Japan's Changing Population Structure

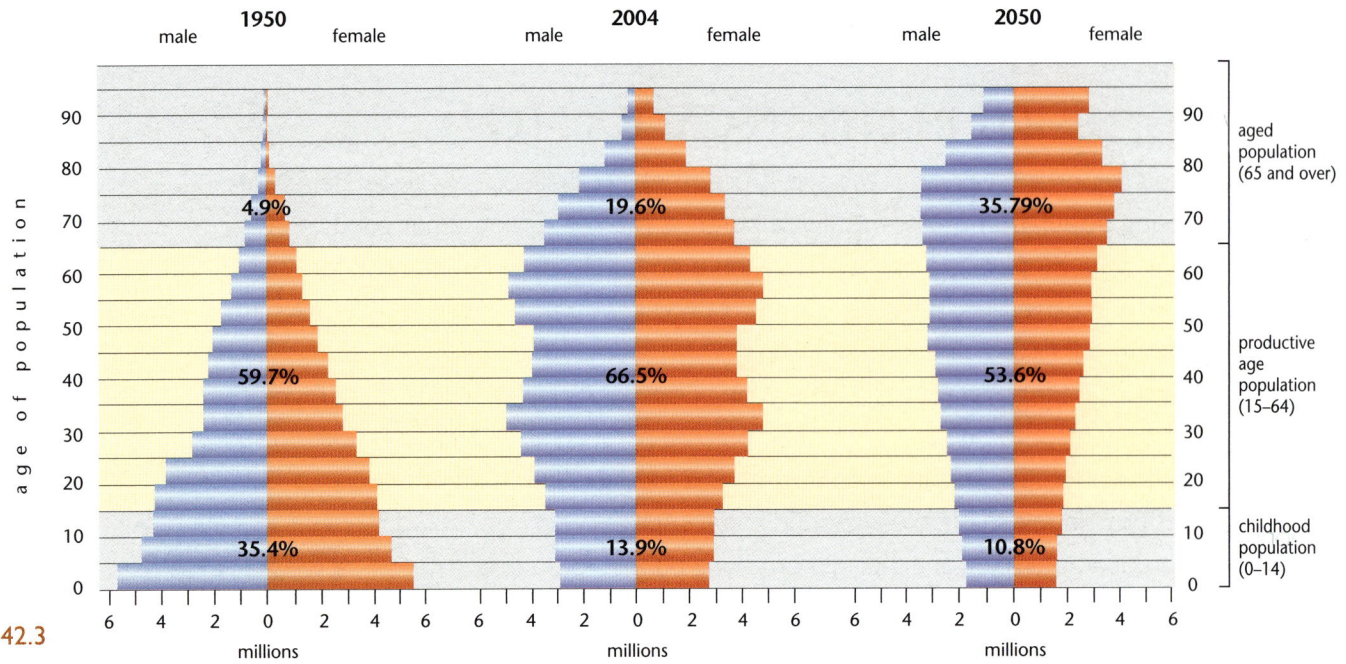

Fig. 42.3

Physiologic density refers to the number of people in a country relative to the amount of productive agricultural land.

Activity

Study the population pyramids of Japan in Fig. 42.3, then answer the following.

1. a. What percentage of the population was in the 15–64 age group in 1950?
   b. Which age group (0–14 or 15–64 or 65 and over) will have shown the greatest increase between 1950 and 2050?
   c. What percentage of population was classified as dependent in 2004? (Think of dependency ratio.)
   d. Identify one socio-economic problem that might arise from the high percentage of '65 and over' population in 2050.

2. a. Explain how Japan's projected structure for 2040 differs from that for 2006.
   b. Suggest some measures that Japan's government should undertake to satisfy its future social and economic needs in 2040.

3. Examine the shape and location of Japan's islands in the Pacific Ocean on your atlas, then explain the physical processes that led to their formation.

292

CHAPTER 43
PATTERNS OF POPULATION CHANGE IN IRELAND

Ireland's population declined from 1841 to 1961. It rose from 1961 to 2006.

Apart from Luxembourg, Ireland has the smallest population in western Europe. It also has the lowest population density: fifty-one people per square kilometre.

The Republic of Ireland's population **declined** from just **over 6.5 million people** in 1841 **to under 3.0 million** by 1926. At that time the majority of Irish people lived in rural areas. The West of Ireland had a high population density. Famine and emigration were the main reasons for this decline.

Between 1926 and 1961, Ireland's population remained stable at just under 3 million people between 1926 and 1951. During the 1950s it fell significantly, reaching its **lowest level of 2.8 million people in 1961.** This rapid fall was due to increased unemployment and emigration. Since then there has been a gradual increase in population to its present level (as of April 2006) of 4.23 million people, which is the highest on record in the twentieth and twenty-first centuries.

Ireland's young population is decreasing due to better education levels and higher living standards.

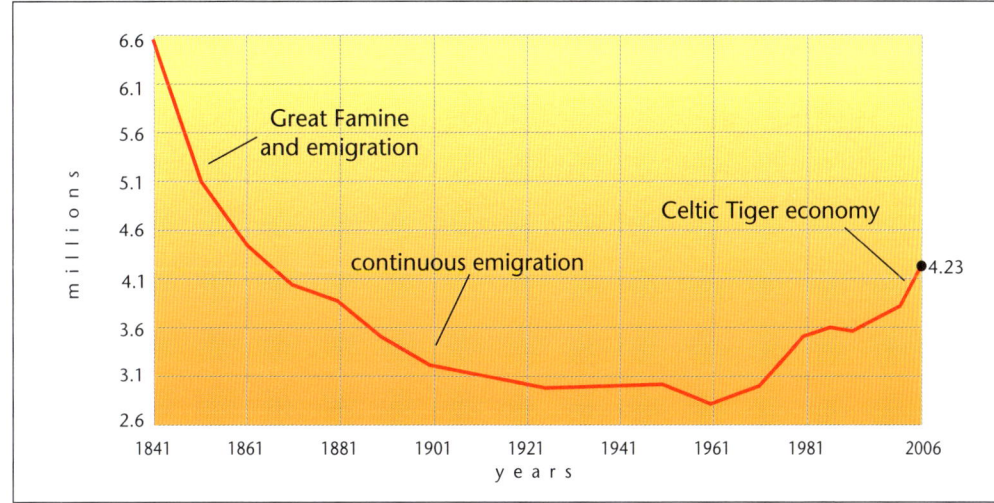
Fig. 43.1 Ireland's population for its twenty-six counties, 1841–2006.

Activity
Study the population graph for Ireland in Fig. 43.1 and answer the following.

1. What was the pattern of change in Ireland's population between 1841 and 1961?
2. What was the main cause of this trend? Explain fully.
3. What was the population trend between 1961 and 2006? Suggest some reasons for this trend.

Age Structure

There have been clear changes in the age structure of Ireland's population since 1961.

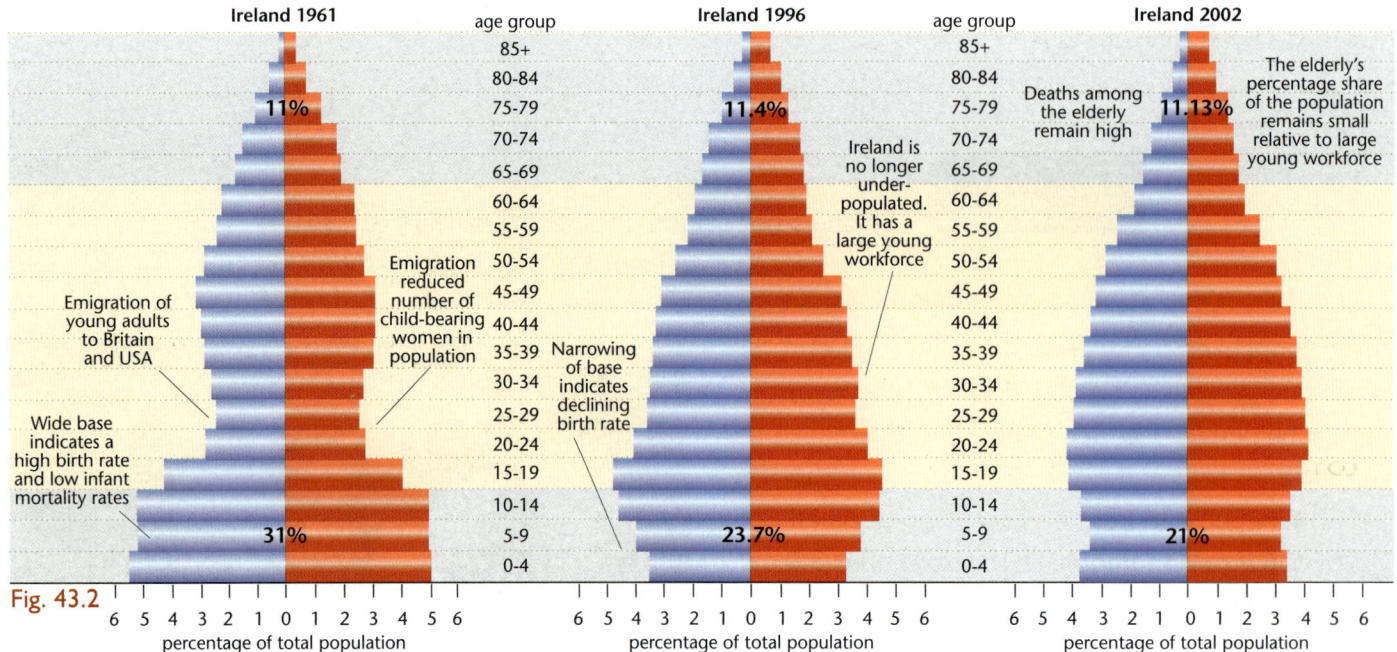

Fig. 43.2

Declining Fertility Rates

Annual births increased by 22 per cent between 1960 and 1980, declined by 35 per cent between 1980 and 1994 and then increased again by 27 per cent between 1994 and 2006. The situation is illustrated graphically in Fig. 43.3.

So, while **the number of women aged twenty to thirty-nine has doubled** between 1961 and 2006, **the average number of children per woman has halved** over the same period, leading to a similar number of births in both years (60,000 in 1961 compared with 61,684 in 2006).

> Ireland's population structure, fertility (birth) rates and mortality (death) rates have changed over time.

Fig. 43.3 Births 1960–2004.

Activity

Study the chart in Fig. 43.3.

1. Does the graph between 1961 and 1980 represent a rise or fall in the fertility rate? Explain.
2. Using evidence from the chart, describe the changes in the fertility rate for the years 1980–2006.

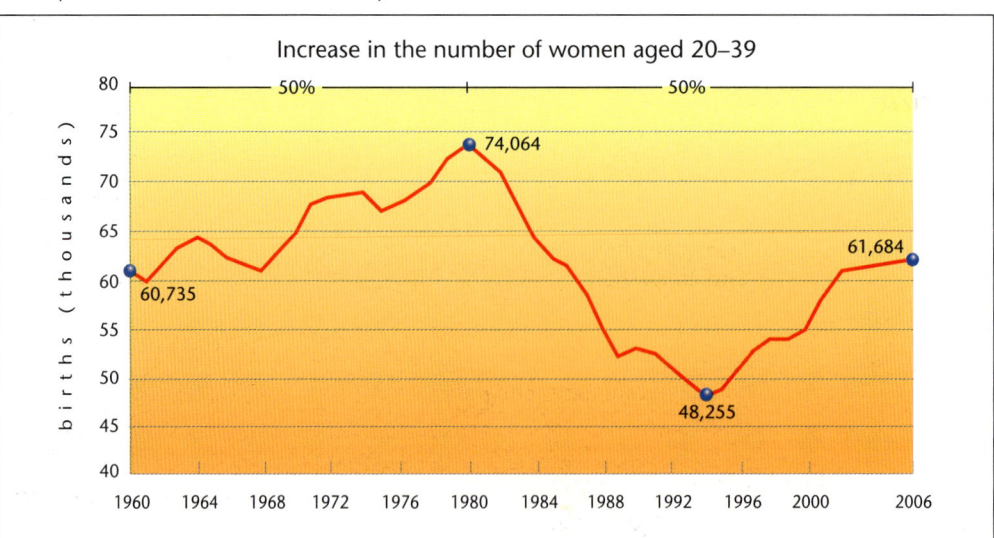

Fertility levels fell to their lowest rate of 1.85 births per woman in 1994. Since then this trend has been reversed and births rose to 1.98 per woman in 2006. This is still below the replacement level of 2.1 births per woman.

The decline in birth rates came about mainly because of changing attitudes to women in Irish society. These changes include:

- Changing attitudes to family planning: Irish women are having fewer children and are delaying child-bearing until their thirties.
- Increasing numbers of women (both married and single) in the workforce.
- Increased educational achievements.
- Increasing urbanisation in Ireland.
- The decline in the influence of the Catholic Church.

- *Do you agree that elderly people are increasingly enjoying an active retirement in Ireland today?*

Death Rates

- Life expectancy at birth increased for men from 57.4 years in 1926 to 75.1 in 2002. This represents a gain of 17.7 years over the seventy-six-year period. The corresponding female rates were 57.9 and 80.3 years, respectively – a gain of 22.4 years.
- The major gains in both male and female life expectancy were recorded in the immediate post-war period, 1946–61. These gains resulted from improved living conditions as well as from advances in maternity services and medical treatment. These included immunisation and the virtual elimination of tuberculosis (TB), which significantly increased survival rates. The reduction was most noticeable in the case of infant deaths.
- Despite the improvements that have occurred, life expectancy for both males and females in Ireland remains relatively low compared with many other EU countries (see Table 43.1). It is expected that in 2036, female life expectancy will be 86.9 years and male life expectancy 82.5 years. Life expectancy in all EU countries is expected to continue to rise.

Country	Males	Females
Austria	74.6	81.15
Belgium	74.6	81.4
Denmark	74.1	79.4
France	75.1	83.01
Germany	74.4	80.9
Greece	76.03	81.2
Iceland	77.3	81.9
Ireland	75.1	80.3
Italy	75.9	82.5
Luxembourg	74.02	80.8
Netherlands	75.5	81.4
Norway	75.8	81.9
Portugal	72.4	79.6
Spain	75.4	82.6
Sweden	77.07	82.5
Switzerland	76.8	82.7
United Kingdom	75.13	80.66

Table 43.1 Life expectancy in selected European countries.

Activity

Carefully study the figures for life expectancy in the European countries listed in Table 43.1.

1. Which country has the longest life expectancy for:
   a. females
   b. males?
2. Suggest why Ireland has such low life expectancies when compared with other countries.
3. Suggest reasons why life expectancy has improved in recent years.

Infant mortality rate refers to the number of children who die under the age of one year for every 1,000 children born in that year. **Child mortality rate** refers to the number of children who die under the age of five years for every 1,000 children born in that year.

Dependency Ratio

There has been a **constant decline in the dependency ratio since 1980.** This is due to a fall in birth rates during this time (a narrowing of the base caused by reducing birth rates/fertility rate). There has also been a slight decrease in the age groups over sixty-five years of age. These reductions have caused a **bulge** in the working age groups and so have reduced the overall dependency ratio.

As time moves on, some other factors will aid the dependency ratio:

- **Immigration** (in-migration): If inward migration continues as is expected, it will increase the percentage of people in working age groups and consequently will relieve some pressure on the ratio.
- **Working students:** The percentage of part-time working students is rising quickly. By 2011, the rate for fifteen-to nineteen-year-olds and twenty-to-twenty-four-year-olds is expected to reach 14 per cent and 25 per cent, respectively.
- **Married women:** The percentage of married women working outside the home in paid employment has risen dramatically in recent years. As Ireland still lags behind other EU states, some rise is expected to continue in the near future.

One factor that may slow down the falling ratio is the increasing number of people who seek early retirement. However, this increase may be softened by:

- Increased personal pension contributions as a consequence of recent increased taxation allowances.
- The creation of a new government pension fund to provide old-age pensions.

Activity

1. Explain what is meant by 'fertility rates'.
2. How do fertility rates affect the rate of population growth?
3. Explain what is meant by:
   a. mortality rate
   b. infant mortality rate
   c. child mortality rate.

Multi-part Questions

1. Study the population pyramids for 1991 and 2026 in Fig. 43.4.

   A. i. Does the chart indicate a future rise or fall in the birth rate? [15 marks]

      ii. Identify the future trend in the age groups 60 to 85+. What effect will this trend have on the dependency ratio? [20 marks]

   B. From your understanding of population pyramids so far, explain the quality of life one would expect to have in Ireland in 2026. Use evidence from the chart to support your answer. [30 marks]

   C. Into which category would you classify Ireland's population pyramid for 2026? Explain. (See the pyramid models on page 291.) [30 marks]

2. Carefully study the population pyramids for 1991 and 2026, then answer the following.

   A. i. Calculate the total population under the age of fifteen years for:

      a. 1991

      b. 2026.

      c. Which is greater?

      ii. Calculate the total population of 65+ years for:

      a. 1991

      b. 2026.

      c. Which is greater?

      iii. Into which stage of the population cycle would you place Ireland based on this population pyramid? Explain. [20 marks]

   B. Explain the effects that these changed dependency numbers may have on Ireland in 2026. [30 marks]

   C. State and explain the patterns of change in Ireland's population since 1900. [30 marks]

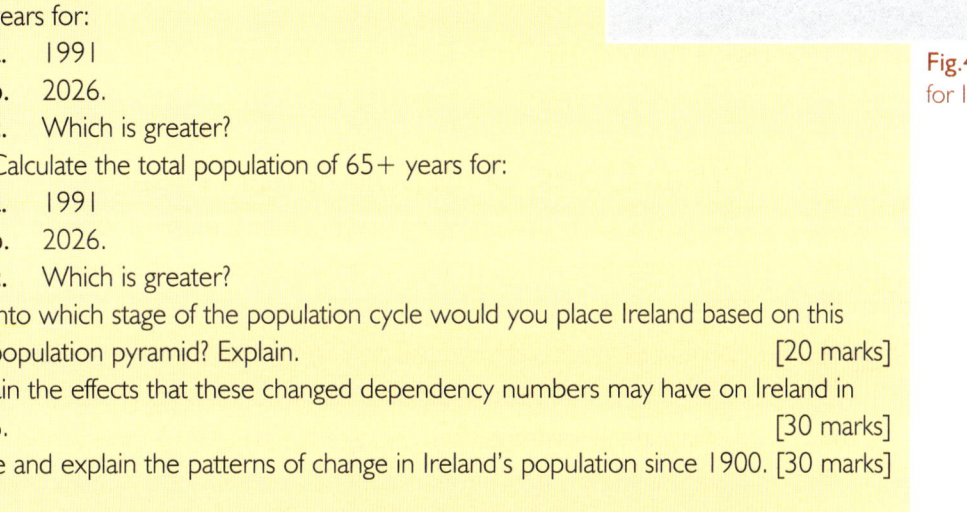

Fig.43.4 Population pyramids for Ireland, 1991 and 2026.

3.

Population Structure – Ireland – Census 2002		
Age (years)	Number	Percentage
65–85	436,001	11
15–64	2,653,774	68
0–14	827,428	21
Totals	3,917,203	100

   A. Examine this table. Calculate the dependency ratio for Ireland. [20 marks]

   B. Examine two of the major implications for Ireland of such a population structure. [30 marks]

   C. Comment on the need for the development of a common immigration policy by the countries of the European Union. [30 marks]

CHAPTER 44
CAUSES AND EFFECTS OF OVERPOPULATION

KEY IDEA!

Population characteristics have an impact on people's way of life, their families and their living standards.

The **optimum population** of an area is the number of people working with all the available resources of that area who will produce the highest standard of living and quality of life available to them. Theoretically there is an optimum population for every country. This optimum is not the same for every region, as the available resources will change from region to region. Thus some places have a high optimum population while others may have a lower optimum population. This concept of an optimum population is never static. It will change in every area over time because of many factors.

Three-child families   Two-child families

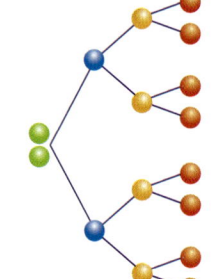

What Does Overpopulation Mean?

Overpopulation occurs when there are **too many people** in an area for the **resources** of that area to maintain an **adequate standard of living**. Overpopulation does not merely depend on the total population living in a country, or necessarily on the density of the population.

For example, **the Netherlands** has an average density of **420 people per square kilometre**. It is not overpopulated. On the other hand, the **Calabria region in southern Italy** has a population density of only **137 people per square kilometre** and is overpopulated.

Activity

In just three generations, three-child families produce more than treble the number of people generated by two-child families. How may some governments influence family size? Suggest some disadvantages of this.

Fig. 44.1

298

The Netherlands has a total population of 15.75 million people in an area the size of Munster in Ireland. It is one of the richest nations in the world. In 1990, the Irish Republic had a total population of just 3.5 million people. In that year over 70,000 people emigrated due to unemployment. **Ireland was therefore overpopulated**, even though it is 1.7 times larger and had only one-quarter of the population of the Netherlands. Between 1995 and 2001 Ireland was underpopulated and did not have sufficient workers. The government searched abroad for nurses, teachers and civil servants. Now, with a population of 4.23 million, Ireland's unemployment rate will hopefully remain low.

CAUSES AND EFFECTS OF OVERPOPULATION

The causes of overpopulation include:

- The unwise development of resources.
- The influence of society and culture.
- The impact of income levels.
- The impact of technology on population growth.

The Unwise Development of Resources
Case Study: The Aral Sea Region

The Aral Sea, once one of the world's largest lakes, has been shrinking for forty years. In the 1950s the Aral Sea supported mixed agricultural use around its shores and a flourishing fishing industry. The surrounding river deltas were fertile regions, fringed with forests and rich in animals and plants. Fish used to breed in the abundant delta lakes, and the reeds that surrounded them were harvested to make paper. **The Aral Sea has no outlet.** The rivers' **waters simply evaporated** in the summer heat and kept a local ecosystem and its dependent population of 30 million people in balance with the second largest inland body of water in Asia.

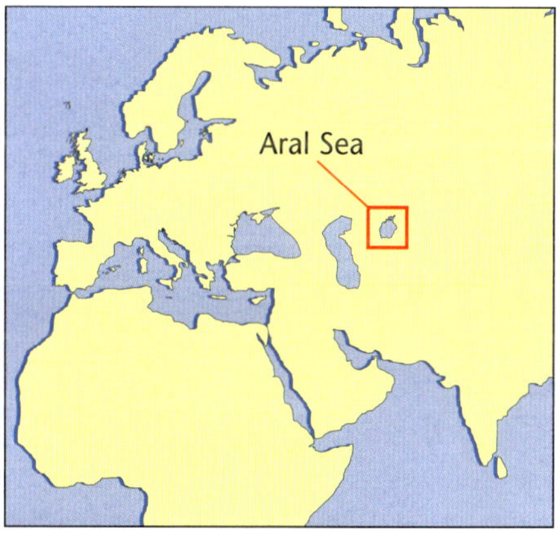

Fig. 44.2 The location of the Aral Sea in Asia.

Causes of Overpopulation: Human Interference

The former Soviet Union government constructed canals to divert the waters of the two largest rivers, the Amu and Syr, which flow through a desert region to feed the Aral Sea. This was done to **increase agricultural production** by irrigating 7 million hectares of cotton, rice and melons for their markets.

Consequently, between 1960 and 1987, only a tiny amount of fresh water reached the Aral Sea. Then **water levels** in the sea **dropped by 13 metres,** creating serious environmental problems.

Consequences

- As the sea shrank, salinity increased from 10 per cent to about 40 per cent due to the evaporation of seawater.
- Fishing communities have been economically devastated; fishermen are no longer needed and beached trawlers lie in dry ports.

Fig. 44.3 This sketch clearly shows a shrinking Aral Sea. The original coastline can be up to 80 km from the reduced shoreline.

- Some ports are up to 50 km from the seashore today.
- Most of the urban populations of the port towns have migrated from the region.
- Dust storms from exposed lake bed sediments increase dust and salt content in the air.
- Canals are leaking, creating waterlogging in some areas.
- Summers are hotter (up to 45°C). Winters are colder as the sea is much reduced.
- Many fish species have been wiped out and the area's fishing industry has been devastated.
- Cancer and other diseases, e.g. hepatitis A and typhoid, are five times the national average.

Thus the region is overpopulated.

Fishing trawlers that once fished the Aral Sea lie idle on the exposed sea bed.

Traditional Hindu marriages are especially colourful and ornate events.

The Influence of Society and Culture on Overpopulation

Some factors that influence overpopulation and people's quality of life include **religious** and **cultural** factors.

Religious Influence

Many of the major religions support family development and oppose artificial birth control and abortion. Consequently, strongly religious societies tend to experience high birth rates, e.g. India and Brazil. Muslim countries and predominantly Catholic countries have high birth rates. Irish birth rates were very high up to the 1970s. This led to overpopulation and subsequent emigration to Britain and the United States. Birth rates in many South American countries are still high due to religious and cultural factors.

Cultural Influence
Case Study: India

Half of India's people live on less than $1 per day, and 48 per cent of the adult population and 62 per cent of adult women are illiterate. Women are severely discriminated against, and 53 per cent of children under five years are malnourished.

Twenty per cent of the world's maternal deaths and 25 per cent of its child deaths occur in India. In the city of Mumbai (Bombay), over half of its 15 million people sleep on pavements or live in mud-and-tin huts. Much of this poverty is influenced by **high fertility rates** and the **status of women**.

High Fertility Rates

An important socio-cultural influence on the population of Kolkata (Calcutta) is the **high fertility rate of Indian women**. Generally women **marry early**, have **little choice** in their male-arranged marriage and enter a household with the prime task of producing male heirs for their husband's family name and genes to continue. Mindful of family honour, females are secluded from other males by not working outside the household and often by practising purdah (screening women from the sight of men).

Many Indian mothers are malnourished, as their families are poor.

Status of Women

A direct link was shown to exist between the status of women and chronic **persistence of hunger** in the lives of Indian women, especially rural Indian women. They, along with their children, are the most lacking in opportunities to end their own and their families' hunger.

India has exceptionally high rates of **child malnutrition**, because tradition in India requires that **women eat last and least** throughout their lives, even when pregnant and feeding their children. Malnourished women give birth to malnourished children, perpetuating the cycle. Fear of **violence also suppresses the aspirations** of most women.

The Impact of Income Levels
Level of Economic Development

Generally speaking, high birth rates and large families are characteristic of underdeveloped countries. This is attributed to the need to ensure adequate support for parents in their old age, to the general low level of education and limited expectations.

Many South-East Asian countries are reducing their birth rates due to an improvement in living standards.

In contrast, where people are well off and levels of education are more advanced, birth control is more feasible and families are often small so as not to interfere with material gain.

Fig. 44.4 Young women in Kerala state have a literacy rate of 92 per cent.

Effects of Rising Incomes

The population transition model (see page 284) suggests that as people of less developed countries raise their income, birth rates will automatically decline, as they have done in rich countries.

In regions such as South and South-East Asia, large families are seen as an economic advantage. **Birth rates only fall when, through education, parents realise that having more children decreases rather than increases their standard of living.**

A dramatic example of this effect occurred in Thailand, where, as soon as parents realised that future prosperity was linked to secondary schooling (which is expensive in Thailand), the fertility rate dropped from six to two in a decade.

India's last census in 2001 revealed a sharp social divide between poor northern states with a high population growth rate and the richer, quickly developing southern states with their sharp decrease in growth rates over the last decade.

The state of Kerala in southern India has the lowest birth rates in the country. Women's literacy rates in this state are among the highest at 92 per cent among young women.

● What evidence in this photograph suggests that people in this area of southern Italy have low incomes?

Low Income Leading to Out-Migration
Case Study: The Mezzogiorno in Southern Italy – An Industrially Underdeveloped Region

For most of the twentieth century, the southern part of Italy, called the Mezzogiorno, has been overpopulated. Incomes in the Mezzogiorno have traditionally been much lower than in other parts of the country. This southern region suffers from a number of physical and economic disadvantages that cause out-migration.

Because of its intense Mediterranean summer heat and the region's lack of water, its steep Apennine mountain slopes and limited mineral resources, the region has consistently been unable to provide a sufficient income for its population.

The region, which has traditionally had high birth rates, continues to suffer from out-migration. Most migrants move to the industrialised core region of northern Italy. Over 5 million people have left the region since 1951, including 1.1 million between 1983 and 1993.

The Impact of Technology on Overpopulation

Modern technology may affect local and global populations in many ways. For example, it may increase food production in some regions that suffer from severe food shortages or increase population numbers by substantially reducing death rates.

Case Study I: Genetically Modified (GM) Foods

The earth is finite and so has a limited ability to produce the food supply necessary to sustain the world's growing population, especially in regions such as China, India and other developing countries. One potential solution to address the problem of insufficient crop yields to support populations is the use of genetically modified (GM) foods. These GM foods are from crops that have been modified genetically to contain a desired trait, such as salt tolerance, disease resistance or increased nutritional value.

Genetically modified foods have the ability to reduce hunger in some world regions.

Genetically modified foods can:

- Increase plants' resistance to pesticides and herbicides, thus reducing the need for pollutant chemicals.
- Allow plants to manufacture their own pesticides to ward off insects.
- Increase the yields of many staple crops and so ward off starvation in many areas of the world.
- Allow plants to grow under adverse weather conditions or in poor soil, thus increasing the amount of arable land on the planet.

Case Study 2: Gene and Germ-line Therapy

Gene Therapy

Gene therapy techniques promise to end or curb much human suffering from painful, debilitating and sometimes fatal genetic diseases. This treatment, or genetic modification, would only have to be administered once – after that, the modification would become part of a person's genome.

Germ-line Therapy

This involves the removal or **replacement of faulty genes**. This technique, if applied to everyone born with a certain disease, would eliminate that disease from the population.

If both therapies were introduced it could in time lead to larger populations by substantially reducing death rates. This could increase dependency ratios and so affect levels of sustainability in some areas.

Many argue against both of these techniques: they claim that the premature use of such techniques could have results even worse than the diseases that the scientists are trying to cure.

THE IMPACT OF POPULATION GROWTH RATES ON DEVELOPMENT

Developed Countries

The theory that is generally accepted with regard to population growth rates and development is that as average family size falls, a country becomes wealthier. In its senile stage, when a country is urbanised, highly educated and well off, the birth rate falls below the replacement level of 2.1 children per woman. This applies to Germany, France and Italy today. This reduction seems to be maintained above all by the high direct, indirect and opportunity **costs of raising and educating children in cities**.

Studies have also shown, however, that:

- Some fluctuations do occur within this model. For example, marriages and births increase **following an improvement** of business conditions and decline when business falls away.
- The interaction of three key elements of **resources, tastes and opportunity costs** do affect family size. The standard of living aspired to by young couples in the 1960s was only modest because they were reared during an era of scarcity. Most mothers at this time were also housewives. Consequently, family size grew.
- In recent decades there are high **material aspirations** among young people. Also, participation in the labour force by women makes demands on time and energy at the expense of raising children. This desire to retain standards and occasional economic downturns combine to reduce birth rates.

Developing Countries

Effect of High Population Growth on Development

The **poorest nations** of the world generally have the **fast-growing populations**.

High dependency ratios result when rapid population growth produces large numbers of children and youth relative to the labour force. Governments and families spend far more on children than the children can quickly repay because they are not earning income. In addition, as modern schooling and health care replaces child labour, household savings decrease, government costs increase and this leads to a drop in a country's GDP (income), so increased education costs a lot in the short term.

- *Explain the advantages associated with small family sizes in developed countries.*

High Fertility and Poverty

Many people are convinced that there are **links** between **high fertility** and resulting population growth on the one hand and **persistent poverty** and **low wages** in developing countries on the other. Large families associated with high population growth appear to transmit poverty across generations. Because poor people in developing countries have large families, their incomes are consistently low. In addition, the availability of a large cheap workforce in some countries slows the introduction of newer, more efficient technology.

There is substantial evidence that having smaller families increases families' savings. A significant part of economic growth achieved among the newly industrialised countries of Asia results from the savings created by families.

At family level, the ability to plan the number and timing of child births can dramatically affect the quality of life through improved mother and child health, and more productive use of time, energy and income. Women stand to increase earnings the most, although their low status in some societies often limits this opportunity.

Adult education helps women to have greater control over their own lives.

The **rate of population growth** and the **size of a country's income** matter. Even in the case of countries that can adjust, it is recognised that it takes time and effort for government and other institutions to:

- Expand urban transport and communications.
- Provide new and better health and educational services.
- Successfully introduce new technology.
- Enforce environmental regulations and expand trade.

Developing countries where the population growth eases through a decline in the birth rate will be more likely to increase income and will have more time to create needed jobs.

- *What advantages and disadvantages are created by high population densities in places such as Bangladesh and India?*

305

CHAPTER 45
CHANGING MIGRATION PATTERNS

KEY IDEA!

Population movements have an impact on the donor and receiver regions.

Refugees displaced as a consequence of war.
- *Does this photograph show voluntary or forced migration?*

The term **migration** is normally used to describe **the movement of people to live in another place for more than a year**. This topic focuses on long-term or permanent changes in people's place of residence. Emigration (leaving a country) and immigration (settling in a new country) is usually what we think of in this regard. But permanent movement within national boundaries is probably more significant than either of these in today's world.

Voluntary or Forced Migration

It may be difficult to say whether a particular person's migration was forced or voluntary. In some cases, people are forced to flee for their lives. Others, however, choose to leave because they feel they would be able to live better lives elsewhere, maybe among people with similar cultures or beliefs. Nevertheless, we refer to all migrations that are not forced as voluntary migrations. This means that the migrants make a positive choice to move and weigh up the advantages and disadvantages of leaving what they know behind. This must be balanced against the difficulties of their new life ahead and the rewards that they hope it will bring.

Push and Pull Factors

The migrant's destination is said to have a 'pull' effect and one's homeland is seen as having a 'push' effect when one is thinking of moving. There may be conflicting forces; some may suggest that it would be better for the person to stay, others that the person would profit by leaving.

Each time someone emigrates, they have decided that the pull factor is in their favour. This may depend on their age, education and expectations in life, and all these factors will give different weights to the pros and cons of the move. This may depend on how flexible and adventurous the people are. Young people, for example, generally adapt to change more easily and rapidly than older people.

Access to information regularly plays an important part in voluntary migration. People who feel sure of their information are likely to weigh up the advantages of moving much more positively than others who are frightened of the unknown. In the case of Irish people in the twentieth century, letters, phone calls and regular comfortable transport all helped to promote migration even when push factors had declined.

Push factors include:
- Unemployment.
- Famine.
- War.
- Religious and political persecution.

Pull factors include:
- Prospect of jobs.
- Travel.
- Religious freedom.
- Higher living standard.
- Climate.

Migration in Ireland

The population distribution in Ireland has been dominated by two main factors since Famine times. These factors are:

- Migration from Ulster, Connacht and Munster to Leinster and abroad.
- Rural to urban migration.

The population distribution of Ireland today is very different from what it was in the nineteenth century. In 1841 the province of **Connacht** had over **1.4 million people**. Today it has just 503,083 people. This represents a 64 per cent fall in population. Leinster, on the other hand, had a population of 1,973,731 in 1841. Today, it has 2,292,939 people. With the exception of Leinster, the other three provinces have experienced massive depopulation since that time.

- *Study this photograph and the one on page 306, then discuss the differences in these people's reasons for migration.*

Migration from Ulster, Connacht and Munster to Leinster since 1926

Leinster has continued to increase its percentage share of the total population at each consecutive census since 1926. The remaining three provinces have increased their populations only since 2002.

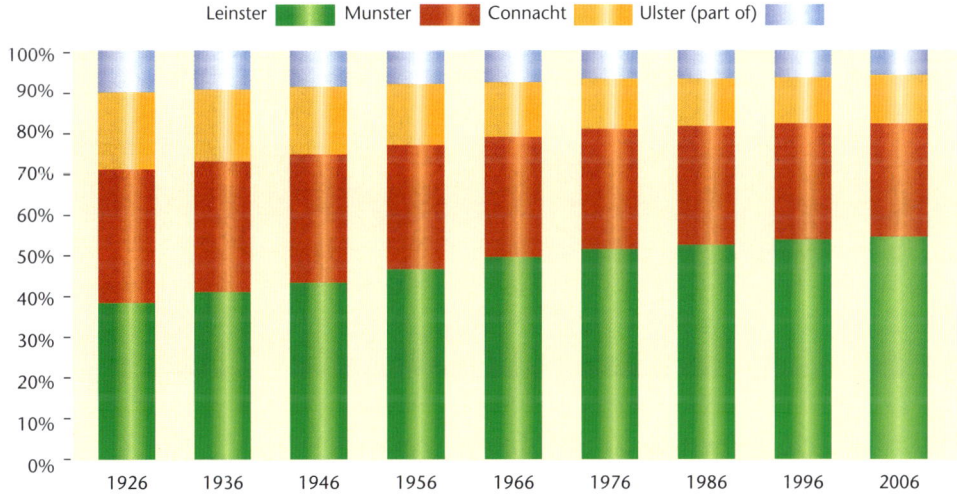

Legend: Leinster ■ Munster ■ Connacht ■ Ulster (part of) ■

X-axis: 1926, 1936, 1946, 1956, 1966, 1976, 1986, 1996, 2006

Fig.45.1 Provincial population shares, 1926–2006.

Activity

Carefully study Fig. 45.1 and answer the following.

1. How do the percentages for each province in 1926 compare to the present-day populations for these areas? (Have they increased or decreased and by how much?)
2. Give some reasons for this decrease (a) in Connacht and (b) in Munster.
3. When was the lowest population percentage reached for (a) Leinster (b) Ulster (c) Munster and (d) Connacht?
4. What patterns are evident from these figures for each region?
5. What overall pattern of change is evident from the percentage share of Ireland's population for each province?
6. What similarities, if any, exist between the patterns in your answer in questions 4 and 5?

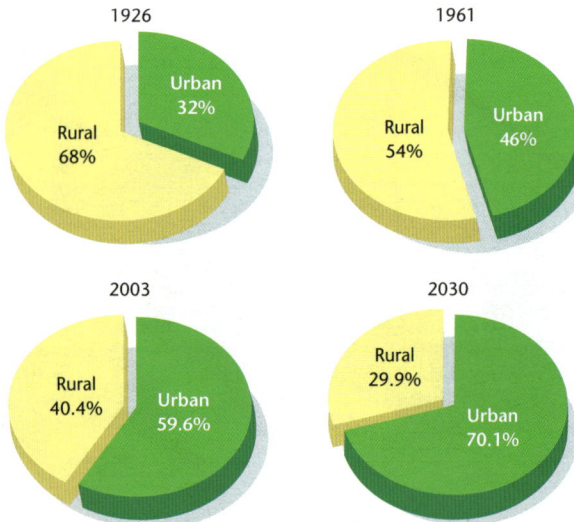

Fig. 45.2 Less than a third of the population lived in urban areas in 1926. The urban share has increased at each census since 1926, though the rate of increase has been tapering off in recent times. The 1971 census was the first in which the urban population exceeded the rural. By 2006 approximately 60 per cent of the Irish population was living in urban areas.

Rural to Urban Migration and Subsequent Growth of Irish Cities and Towns

The distribution of the population between urban and rural areas has undergone a major change over the last seventy years. Fig. 45.2 shows the percentage change of urban/rural population in 1926, 1961, 2003 and 2030.

The growth of urban areas in Ireland, especially over the past forty years, has been mainly due to:

- **Industrial estates**: Industrial estates provided increased employment, especially for young adults.
- **Services**: Commercial, financial and social services employed many in offices.
- **Accommodation**: Newly developed suburban housing estates since the 1960s provide comfortable accommodation near essential services, such as hospitals, universities and schools.

- *Use evidence from the photograph to explain why Irish towns and cities have expanded over recent decades.*

Post-1950 Migration Trends to and from Ireland

The population of the Irish Republic in 1951 was approximately 2.9 million people. This was a fall of over 3.5 million people since 1841, some four years before the Great Famine. Emigration was the main contributory factor in this decline, which continued into the twentieth century. The highest emigration rate occurred in 1958, when net migration figures reached 58,000 people. Throughout the 1950s there was a total net migration of 409,000 people. Emigration in this decade was responsible for the historically low population level of 2.8 million people recorded in 1961.

Post-1960 migration patterns created the following trends:

- Reduced emigration during the 1960s to as little as 5,000 in 1971.
- Net in-migration from 1972 to 1979.
- High emigration from 1980 to 1991.
- High in-migration from 1995 to 2006.

Why did so many people emigrate during the 1950s and previous decades?

Industrialisation

1962–79: Ireland experienced its own industrial revolution in the 1960s. Foreign multinational companies were attracted to Ireland by financial incentives, such as tax-free industrial exports, grants and modern industrial estates for footloose industries. Industrial emigration slowed and by the 1970s there was net in-migration for the first time in the twentieth century. This trend continued until 1979.

Recession

1980–95: An international recession caused a reversal of Ireland's migration trend of the 1960s and 1970s. Many factories were closed or scaled down. There was a net out-migration of 20,000 people in 1985. A revival in international financial markets in the 1990s created a change in Ireland's migration pattern once more and out-migration started to decline.

The Celtic Tiger economy has encouraged many EU citizens to live and work in Ireland.

Celtic Tiger

1996–2006: Ireland's industrial rise from the low of the 1980s was unprecedented. Its economy boomed and the demand for labour is such that non-Irish workers at one time were sought by semi-state companies and the civil service to fill job vacancies.

Net immigration (the balance between in- and out-migration) reached a historical high point in 2006. The number of immigrants increased at this time while the number of emigrants declined to a record low.

In 2005, 38 per cent of immigrants were nationals of the ten new EU accession states that joined the EU in 2004. Seventeen per cent of immigrants were from Poland and 9 per cent were from Lithuania.

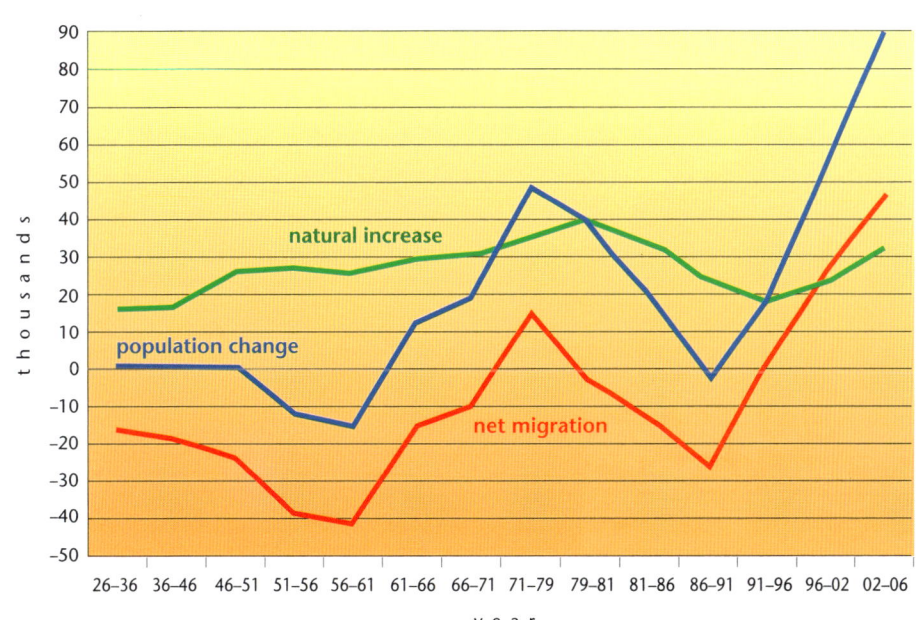

Fig. 45.3 Components of population changes, 1926–2006.

Activity

Examine the chart for migration in Ireland (Fig. 45.3), then answer the following.

1. What does 'net migration figures' mean?
2. Identify and explain the recent change in migration patterns.
3. In your view, explain the positive effects that this migration change has had on Ireland since 1931.

Effects of Migration
Some Positive Effects of Emigration

- **Safety valve:** Emigration provided Ireland with the solution to its oldest problem, a lack of jobs for its people. This was true until the mid-1990s, when the 'tiger' economy reversed this situation. Emigration provided successive Irish governments with a 'safety valve' that reduced total population numbers throughout the twentieth century, especially during the 1950s and 1980s. Had emigration not occurred then, a population with high birth rates and an increasing unemployment problem would have increased pressure on Ireland's resources, causing chronic overpopulation. Indeed, Ireland has experienced a unique situation in its population structure. While other national populations in the EU grew, Ireland's population was in decline even though it had the highest birth rate in the EU.

- **Political rivals:** Countries (populations) or governments or both can also benefit when politically unwanted people emigrate.

- **Remittances and tourism:** Throughout the twentieth century, and continuing today, many emigrant countries earned substantial income from 'remittances', money sent by emigrants or guest workers to their homeland. This was very much a reality in the case of Ireland. Many Irish emigrants, especially before the 1960s, sent home money to rear younger brothers and sisters.

Ireland was by no means unique in terms of emigration acting as a safety valve. There was a total of 750,000 emigrants from Norway and 1,100,000 from Sweden between 1840 and 1914, equivalent to 40 per cent and 25 per cent, respectively, of each country's natural increase during that period.

In 1990, annual worldwide remittances amounted to **US$71 billion**. During the 1990s, Egyptians working abroad sent home what amounted to almost a third of their country's foreign earnings. Remittances by Filipinos are estimated at US$8 billion annually, almost three times the amount of foreign aid received by the Philippines. The Philippine government publicly encourages this trend.

In the past, many ships that sailed from Ireland were packed with immigrants.

Many Irish emigrants were successful in the construction industry in Britain and America.

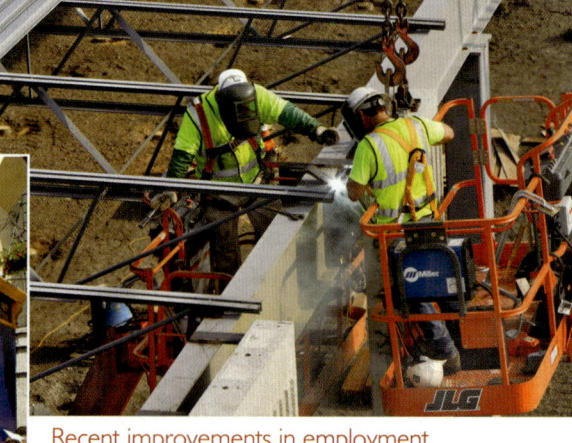

Recent improvements in employment opportunities offer a bright future for Ireland's young people.

Some Negative Effects of Emigration

Loss of skilled workforce: A careful examination of the population pyramid for 1961, Fig. 43.2 on page 294, shows that a large number of people between the ages of sixteen and forty were absent from the Irish workforce. These ages make up the most youthful and energetic groups in a population's workforce. The absence of such people limits a nation's ability to increase productivity and change, so income levels remain low. This is referred to as a 'brain drain'.

Over 17 per cent of all immigrants to Ireland in 2005 were Polish, most of whom were twenty-five years of age and over. This loss for Poland has a negative effect on the Polish economy.

- **Smaller home market:** A large number of young adults in a country increases the demand (a market) for products. They have disposable income and are among the largest spenders, which creates a demand for manufactured goods and services. If people emigrate, it reduces this home market.

- **Depopulation:** The West of Ireland suffers from a number of **environmental disadvantages**. Much of the West comprises **highland and extensive mountain areas**. Much of this is covered by **blanket bog** and much of the soil is too wet. Farms are small and uneconomic. In the past, mass emigration from these regions left the area without its young and able workers. Farms were left in charge of an **ageing, low-output** population. Market towns and villages, such as Ballina and Foxford in Co. Mayo, struggled for survival. As people left the region, there were fewer services. There was an insufficient number of local people to support them, which created a cycle of decline. The West still struggles to recover from this cycle.

Some Positive Effects of Immigration

- **Foreign migrants:** Ireland suffers a shortage of labour in certain areas, such as nursing and some civil service departments. Foreign skilled workers are sought after by government agencies and they have been somewhat successful in attracting some professionals, such as nurses from the Philippines. Many other migrant workers are in paid employment as construction workers, waitresses and shop assistants. This situation has helped Ireland to fill lower-paid employment not sought after by locals.

- **Cultural effects:** Migrants may enhance a culture by making it more outward-looking and cosmopolitan, especially in the case of a peripheral island nation such as Ireland. Because Ireland has for so long been a place of emigration rather than immigration, people from only a few different cultures have settled here. Most of these are associated with the food industry. These include Chinese, Indian and Thai people, and the medical profession, such as doctors and nurses from countries such as India, the Philippines and some African nations. Many migrants enter Ireland in increasing numbers.

Many migrants fill job vacancies in Ireland.
- *What positive effects can such migrants have on Irish society?*

311

- **New skills:** Migrants bring new skills to a country. These skills vary depending on the levels of economic development of the nations from which they come. Many of Ireland's university graduates and skilled tradespeople learned new skills and industrial work practices while working overseas. Many immigrants, such as the Polish community in Ireland, are highly educated and have been a positive influence on Ireland.

Children are often the ones who suffer most as a consequence of ethnic conflict and consequent migration. Their educational and social needs may not be met at a time when they are most vulnerable.

A **refugee** is someone who has left his or her own country or is unable to return to it owing to a well-founded fear of persecution for reasons of race, religion, nationality, membership of a particular group or political opinion.

Some Negative Effects of Immigration

- **Repatriation and racism:** When migrant workers are employed, it is generally on a fixed-contract basis. Their numbers are closely watched in relation to trends of demand and need. In Germany, such workers were called *Gasterbeiter* (guest workers). This suggests that after some time when they were no longer needed they could be sent home, even if they had a family who had adjusted to that society.

    The fall of communism and the unification of East and West Germany caused many financial and social difficulties, including unemployment within Germany. Right-wing groups in some cases blamed the guest workers for their unemployment difficulties. This led to racist attacks on the homes of guest workers.

- **Refugees:** Wars, ethnic hatred and different living standards have created a large percentage of African international migration since the Second World War. Independence from colonial rule in Africa led to civil wars within nations and to conflicts between nations. In the last two decades, millions of refugees have fled to neighbouring countries to escape civil wars. In 1999, Guinea, with a population of only 7.5 million people, cared for 700,000 refugees from civil wars in four neighbouring countries.

Activity

1. Explain three positive effects of immigration for Ireland in recent times.
2. Explain two negative effects of emigration for Ireland in the past.
3. a. Name three neighbouring Irish counties that have continuously suffered from out-migration during the twentieth century.
   b. Name one Irish province that has increased its population at every census since 1926.
   c. Explain the factors that were responsible for the continued population increase during this period.

CHAPTER 46
MIGRATION IN EUROPE

Recent migration trends affect migration policies in Ireland and the EU.

Early Migration to Europe

For over fifty years or more, thousands of poor economic migrants (migrants looking for work) migrated to the EU core regions. They came from the undeveloped regions of southern Europe, such as Spain and the Mezzogiorno region in southern Italy. Many also came from North Africa and Turkey. They were welcomed as they sought employment in services and poorly paid jobs that locals did not want.

Later, some of these migrants brought their families, and because of high birth rates their numbers increased substantially over time. The low birth rates of the EU core countries also created a need for their work. This was during a time of economic boom.

When oil prices soared in the mid to late 1970s, jobs were lost and unemployment rose. These economic migrants were then seen as a burden on the state and as taking jobs from locals. Some suffered racist attacks from right-wing groups.

Famine has struck many regions in Africa over the past forty years.

Migrants from Africa

The following push factors led many African people to migrate to Europe from the 1980s onwards:

- Famine struck many African regions such as the Sahel.
- Former colonies gained independence, and this created civil unrest in some countries, leading to prolonged civil wars.
- Political persecution, corruption and oppressive laws, especially on women.
- Poverty.
- The break-up of the former USSR created stresses between former African governments and their Western allies.

Migrants from Eastern Europe

The 1990s saw a new wave of economic migrants from eastern Europe. These came because in the 1990s the break-up of the Soviet Union led many migrants to seek a better living standard and the protection of democratic laws. Many of these migrants enter along the Ukrainian-Slovak border.

Child soldiers are exploited as a consequence of a conflict that leads to mass displacement of populations.

313

Some fled the **ethnic cleansing** policies of Serbia in the former Yugoslavia. Many of these migrants sought refuge in southern Italy, the nearest and least patrolled border region of southern Europe at that time.

Every year, thousands of refugees are fleeing to Europe for these reasons. Each year hundreds drown crossing the Mediterranean, especially on the way from Africa to Spain, the Canary Islands, Malta and Italy. Others suffocate in sealed containers, starve in locked trucks, are killed by landmines between Turkey and Greece, or freeze on their way across mountains. If they manage to arrive they are not safe at all. In some countries they are enclosed in 'refugee centres' that do not differ from normal prisons.

Fortress Europe

Xenophobia is a hatred or fear of foreigners. It is suggested that the EU now suffers from this condition, as it appears to have tightened or refined its immigration policies to reduce the number of economic migrants and refugees. The anxiety over migrants stems from the need to be flexible enough to compete effectively in the global market.

According to the European Commission, the EU needs about **20 million immigrants** in the next twenty-five years in order to be able to compete economically with other big world economies, so global migration management has emerged as a philosophy:

- Due to the threat of terrorism after 9/11.
- Due to social instability in response to the break-up of the Soviet bloc.
- Where skills shortages are addressed in the interest of business.
- Because of the intense demand for free markets in the second and third worlds as a consequence of globalisation.

Borders such as this at Ceuta, in North Africa, resemble the Iron Curtain that divided Europe into the East and West after World War II.

Activity

Look at Fig. 46.1, then answer the following.

1. What percentage of total uprooted people were asylum-seekers?
2. What percentage were refugees?
3. In your opinion, do people generally wish to leave their homeland? Explain.

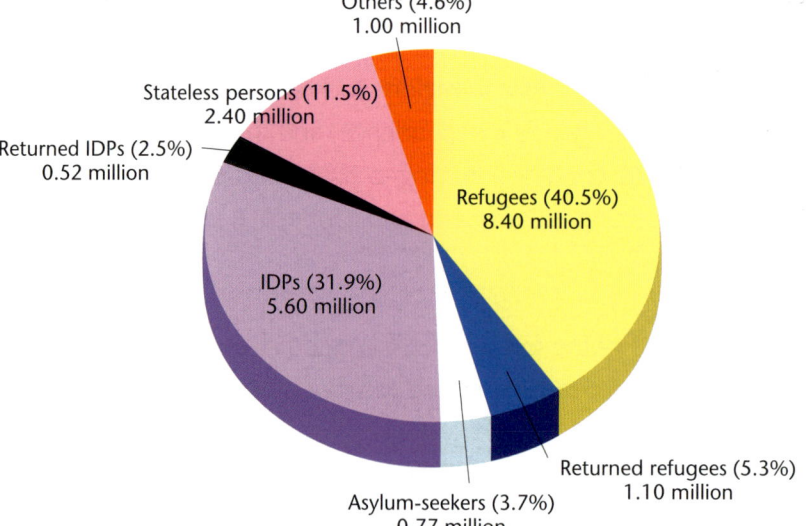

Others (4.6%)
1.00 million

Stateless persons (11.5%)
2.40 million

Returned IDPs (2.5%)
0.52 million

Refugees (40.5%)
8.40 million

IDPs (31.9%)
5.60 million

Returned refugees (5.3%)
1.10 million

Asylum-seekers (3.7%)
0.77 million

Fig. 46.1 UNHCR is the United Nations High Commission for Refugees. UNHCR's annual global count of uprooted people shows that the number of refugees fell from 9.5 million in 2004 to 8.4 million in 2005. But the overall number of concern for the agency rose by 1.3 million to 20.8 million during the same period because of UNHCR's expanded role in caring for the world's internally displaced people.

Consequences of Xenophobia

It is believed that a direct consequence of this managed migration programme is the division between good immigrants (who form an orderly queue and enter through legal routes) and bad immigrants (who jump the queue and live illegally). This leads the EU to:

- Militarise its borders.
- Create obstacles to asylum and migration.
- Set target-driven deportation programmes.
- Remove the problem of asylum by removing asylum-seekers altogether. There is a move towards offshore processing, with talk of immigration gateways in neighbouring countries to the EU, such as Libya. Here refugees can be warehoused until conflicts are resolved with a chosen few being selected for resettlement in Europe under a strict quota system.

Globalisation

Globalisation and international migration go hand in hand. **Globalisation** involves the **large-scale flows of goods and services**, **money**, **technology and people across international borders**.

Governments welcome economic flows but are nervous about people. Only about **3 per cent** of the world's population **are migrants**, but their concentration in certain regions often puts them at the front of social change. By 2000, **63 per cent** of the world's migrants were in developed countries, where they made up 8.7 per cent of the total population.

- *In your opinion, what opportunities does Ireland offer foreign migrant workers?*

How Globalisation Shapes Migration

Globalisation has increased the differences in income and human security between North and South due to:

- Global television that beams ideal images of lifestyles in the developed world into the poorest villages.
- Electronic communications that allow easy access to information on migration routes and work opportunities
- Long-distance travel that has become cheaper and more accessible.
- The lessening of the value of traditional modes of production that force people to move from rural areas to cities. When workers do not find enough work in the cities, overseas migration might be the next step.

Images of a better, richer world lead many people to leave their homes for a better life elsewhere.

Trafficking of Humans

The trafficking of human beings has been identified as a modern form of slavery. Human trafficking is a global phenomenon and affects virtually every country in the world whether as countries of origin, of transit or of destination. In a global context it is estimated that anywhere between 700,000 and 4 million women and children are moved across international borders each year. The profits to be made are similar to those in the illegal drugs and arms trade. The International Organisation of Migration (IOM) estimates that trafficking in humans is worth $8 billion annually. Ireland is not immune to international trends and should be proactive in addressing this relatively new phenomenon in Ireland.

Major container and ferry ports are regular routes through which people are moved illegally.

Migration Policies in the European Union

Ever since 1957, the treaty establishing the European Union has contained articles to ensure the free movement of workers within the community. This idea of the free movement of persons has gradually become established by means of treaties between EU members. This freedom guarantees that:

- All European citizens have the right to move and live anywhere within the EU. The reason for this policy is because **'the mobility of labour within the community must be one of the means by which the worker is guaranteed the possibility of improving his living and working conditions, and promoting his social advancement'.**

- The freedom to take up a job in another member state of the EU must not be put at risk and migrant workers are entitled to remain in the territory of a member state after working there.

Some member states have interpreted the meaning of this principle differently. For some, it applied only to community citizens, so border controls were still needed to check the identity of nationals of non-member countries. For others, it applied to everyone, so internal border controls were no longer necessary. After long discussion, only Ireland and the United Kingdom have not signed up to this agreement. In future, this principle will have to be adopted by all new member states.

Part of the difficulty of accepting some refugees is that some people from countries that were colonies of European powers have citizenship rights in these European countries. Other countries, such as Ireland, that were not colonial powers are reluctant to take responsibility for citizens of these colonies who seek refuge as a consequence of ethnic conflict at home. So far it appears that the EU members have agreed only on minimum standards and fears are that the agreed minimum standards may become the maximum to be achieved.

Migration policies allow EU citizens to travel freely within the Union, while others may or may not be allowed to enter or remain.

Common Immigration and Asylum Policy

A common EU immigration policy is needed and may include the following:

- The establishment of a **common border guard.** This body would implement agreed uniform measures towards asylum-seekers at all points of entry to the EU.
- The **quality and speed** of applications is to be improved so that genuine refugees fleeing religious and political persecution can be identified at an early stage.
- The use of a newly **established database**, Eurodac, designed to collect fingerprints of asylum-seekers and illegal immigrants to decide the country responsible for that individual. The country that will ultimately be responsible for awarding refugee status is the country in which the asylum-seeker first arrives.
- **Burden and responsibility-sharing** involves aid for less developed regions close to Africa (a major source of migrants), for example southern Spain and southern Italy, so effective protection can be provided to those who need it.
- The **rights of immigration detainees** under international human rights standards are respected and implemented.
- The fight against **illegal immigration and trafficking** in human beings, in particular women and children, must be strengthened.

Ireland's Immigration Policy

The main components of Ireland's immigration policy include:

- Nationals from the European Economic Area (EEA) do not need a visa to live and work in Ireland. The EEA consists of the EU states plus Norway, Iceland and Liechtenstein. For all others, a visa is essential.
- Those who need a visa must apply for a work permit before they enter the state.
- Persons who claim asylum do not have the right to work but they are given full-board accommodation while their claim is being processed, initially in Dublin and later at recognised centres throughout Ireland.

Since 1922, Irish citizenship has been based on **place of birth**, and all children born on the island of Ireland and the children and grandchildren of Irish immigrants could apply for citizenship. A **referendum** in 2004 changed the Constitution and under a new Article, only those born to **at least one Irish national parent** will acquire citizenship.

Those who do not require a visa include:

- People who have permission to remain in Ireland, such as people with special skills and foreign full-time students.
- People who have refugee status.
- People who have been granted permission to remain on humanitarian grounds.
- People who are claiming refugee status while their claim is being processed.

Support For Immigrants and Refugees

Ireland could take many steps to support its immigrants and refugees. These include:

- Improved government inter-departmental co-ordination to implement social inclusion policies.
- A government action plan against racism to reduce the number of victims of discrimination and racist attack, and to encourage a mindset that values diversity.
- Asylum-seekers need unhindered access to education, which is a basic human right. This is provided at varying degrees at primary and secondary levels, but access at third level is restricted. Education provides the key to social integration.
- The government should develop a specific policy statement on emigration that provides guidance to employers, unions and society in general.
- Increased funding for lifelong learning to help marginalised people gain access to the workplace.
- An action programme that allows the upward movement of professional people such as medical staff. At present, only indigenous Irish people are promoted.
- A need for translators for immigrants so that their medical needs can be met.
- The provision of social housing to long-term migrants, those who have skills to offer and can support themselves in the private sector, even while their claims are processed.
- Family reunification entitlements need to be specified, fair, transparent and non-discretionary.
- The encouragement of ethnic and cultural minorities in politics.
- Encouraging employers to play a key role in co-operative work practices to help integration. This has proven particularly helpful in Northern Ireland, even during the worst of the Troubles.

Activity
1. Describe the impact on and contribution made to local communities by immigrants.
2. Describe how the following might influence migration patterns in Ireland:
   a. changes to the economy
   b. foreign wars and famine.
3. Describe how Ireland's migration policy might meet the challenges in question 2.
4. Compare and contrast the experiences of Irish emigrants with the experiences of new immigrants to Ireland.
5. Critically analyse Ireland's immigration policy.
6. What is meant by xenophobia? Explain.

CHAPTER 47
ETHNIC, RACIAL AND RELIGIOUS ISSUES CREATED BY MIGRATION

KEY IDEA!

Some migration movements have led to tension and conflicts between migrants and their host populations.

The Meaning of Race

Race is a word that refers to **biological inheritance**. We are born with it. It refers to our **physical characteristics**, such as skin colour, height, physique, hair type, head shape and so on. They belong to our **DNA** characteristics that are passed on from generation to generation, from parents to offspring. But one thing is sure: there is no such thing as a pure race. We can see that some people have similar characteristics. For example, the people of Scandinavia are generally blue-eyed, fair-haired, fair-skinned people. This is probably because, historically, people have moved out of, rather than into, Scandinavia, so there has been less mixing of migrant groups in this region. The Aborigines in Australia were cut off on an isolated continent for so long that they are physically distinctive.

● *What evidence in this photograph indicates that Irish people have mixed genetic ancestry?*

If you look around your own classroom, how many students have similar characteristics? Probably none. Some are brown-haired, others red-haired, black-haired, fair-haired, blond-haired; fair-skinned, sallow-skinned; brown-eyed, blue-eyed, grey-eyed and so on. It is obvious, therefore, that through the generations we have inherited varied characteristics from migrant groups that have settled in Ireland. However, people regularly suffer discrimination based on skin colour alone or skin colour, eye shape and hair colour.

The Meaning of Ethnicity

'Ethnic' or 'ethnicity' generally refers to **a minority group with a collective self-identity within a larger host population.** Example of this are Italians in New York, Cubans in Miami or Chinese people in Ireland. Due to insecurity or because they have been forced, they may be found in 'ethnic islands' or 'ghettos'. The Irish are associated with the Bronx in New York and Camden Town in London. By living close to each other, the Irish helped each other – simple, uncomplicated, natural.

Members of an ethnic group generally claim a strong cultural identity over time. Race is rooted in the idea of biological classification, but the concept of ethnicity is rooted

Recent new laws in Ireland help to prevent discrimination on the grounds of race, colour, nationality or ethnic origin. The basic principle states that 'people should be judged on their merits as individuals rather than by reference to the group to which they belong'.

in the idea of **social groups that share nationality, genealogy, religious faith, shared language or cultural and traditional origins**.

Ethnic groups may be defined by:

- **Place of birth:** In many countries people may be classified on official records by their place of birth or that of their ancestors, such as Chinese, Puerto Rican, African-American or American-Irish.
- **Language and fertility rates:** Language may also be used to classify ethnic groups; for example, Hispanics in the USA (migrants from Spanish-speaking American countries, such as Mexico and Central America), who have been grouped by their common language and high fertility rates.
- **Religion:** Some ethnic groups, such as Muslims and Sikhs, prefer to be classified by their religion.

Ethnic Cleansing

This term was first used during the wars following the break-up of former Yugoslavia. It describes a policy where **ethnic groups are slaughtered** or **expelled by force, threat or terror** from a territory in which they live so that it can be exclusively occupied by the most powerful group. The deliberate elimination of the Muslim people from Bosnia-Herzegovina through forced out-migration or worse by the Serb army led to ethnic cleansing in many areas. The slaughter of entire Muslim populations of many valleys and towns, such as the massacre of Srebrenica, and the creation of enclaves (small pockets or areas occupied by certain ethnic groups) during these wars by the Serbs were a stark reminder of the Holocaust in World War II.

Mass graves were discovered in Bosnia after genocide by the Serbs.

Racial Division

Case Study: Apartheid in South Africa

Apartheid was **racial separation of blacks from whites as a principle of society enforced by law** and by government policy in South Africa. Centuries ago, Dutch and British settlers colonised and controlled this region. In 1931, Britain gave South Africa full independence. During this time and before 1948, racial segregation was widely practised. But in 1948 a policy of **racial discrimination became law** and was given the name 'apartheid'. Under this policy a minority of white people controlled a majority of black and coloured people. This racial discrimination by law ended only in the 1990s.

Apartheid imposed appallingly heavy burdens on the majority of South Africans. Non-whites could not buy land. They had to use shops, schools and other services that were separate from those for white people. The whites were well fed, well housed and well cared for, while the non-white majority suffered from widespread poverty, malnutrition and disease. Apartheid laws affected every aspect of life in South Africa.

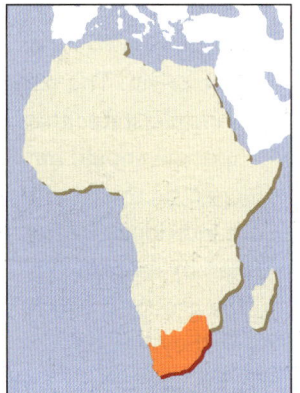

Fig. 47.1 South Africa is highlighted on the map of Africa.

Apartheid ended in 1994 after fifty years of racial inequality.

Civil Unrest and Social Segregation

Many countries of the EU were **colonial powers**. These countries include Britain, France, the Netherlands and Belgium. Some of their colonies were in Asia and Africa and these regions became the source areas for migrants to these former colonial powers.

Generally these migrants formed part of an **underprivileged group** that had limited access to jobs and houses and were forced to live in the poorest part of cities **near to the centre** or central business districts (CBDs). These urban regions are called **ghettos**. Many of these settled migrant communities and their various populations form **ethnic groups**. They have a vulnerable status owing to the inequalities of citizenship laws.

Social segregation also occurs in the urban regions of Belfast and Derry.

Consequently, **social and racial segregation** (against people with dark skin and/or African-sounding names) prevails. High unemployment rates develop, leading to social unrest. Riots may occur as a backlash against this injustice. The riots in Paris and other French cities in 2005 occurred for these reasons.

Right-wing groups blame the causes of poverty, unemployment and disadvantage within immigrant communities on the immigrants' culture, similar to views held in the USA before the civil rights movement emerged. In France, for example, an unemployment rate of 5 per cent for French university graduates can be compared to the unemployment rate of 26.5 per cent for university graduates of North African origin.

The 2005 civil unrest in France was a series of riots and violent clashes in which vehicles and public buildings were set on fire.

321

Nationalist and unionist groups clashed during the 'marching season'.

Religious Conflict
Case Study: Northern Ireland

Large numbers of **English and Scottish settlers** were brought to Northern Ireland as part of the **Ulster Plantation** of the seventeenth century. These settlers belonged to **Protestant** faiths, whereas the local population was Catholic. Many conflicts occurred over the centuries between these two cultures. The Protestant majority created a separate state, **Northern Ireland**, or 'the six counties', with close ties to Britain. The Catholics wanted independence from Britain.

During the 1970s, conflict occurred between these two religious groups. Catholics were discriminated against in jobs and housing and were denied basic civil rights. Civil unrest between both groups lasted until the 1990s. Many people died during these 'Troubles'.

Activity

1. Give two reasons why refugees can play a positive role in the development of Irish society in the twenty-first century.
2. Explain why the EU immigration policy may negatively influence people's interaction with foreign migrants.
3. State and explain two misconceptions that Irish people may have about asylum-seekers and refugees.
4. Explain how migration can lead to civil unrest and social segregation.
5. Define what you understand by the term 'Irish'.
6. What opposition or racism did Irish emigrants experience in some countries in the past?
7. Which groups of immigrants are more likely to suffer racial abuse in Ireland?
8. Why have Irish attitudes to some foreign immigrants changed in recent years?
9. What do you understand by the term 'economic migrant'?

CHAPTER 48
RURAL TO URBAN MIGRATION IN THE DEVELOPED AND DEVELOPING WORLD

 **KEY IDEA!** Migration has affected the rural areas that people leave behind and the cities where they arrive.

Urban Migration

Cities in **developed countries** are self-supporting areas that developed as a consequence of industrialisation. The growth of industry and industrial estates in urban areas attracted rural dwellers to take up employment in towns and cities. **Industrialisation came first and cities grew** due to industrialisation.

The urbanisation of **developing countries**, however, has been a consequence of population growth and the rural to urban migration that preceded industrialisation; the **cities came first and industry developed slowly** in these cities. This has happened because urban growth has been driven by 'rural push' forces rather than the 'urban pull' forces of prospective jobs in towns and cities as in urban areas of the developed world.

Rural poverty has forced millions of people in India into the cities in search of a better life.

In much of the developing world, rural populations, which grew quickly as a consequence of falling death rates with continuing high birth rates, face a difficult if not hopeless future of drudgery and poverty. In the past, emigration provided a safety valve, but most developed countries have prevented immigration by restricting migrants by various means and for as many reasons. The only hope for the growing numbers of impoverished rural dwellers has been to move to towns and cities relatively nearby. Here at least there is **hope of employment, the prospect of access to schools, health clinics, a safe water supply** and other kinds of **public facilities and services** that are often unavailable in rural areas.

Overall, the cities of the developing world have absorbed four out of five of the 1.2 billion city dwellers who have been added to the world's population since 1970.

Rural to urban migration creates Bustees (shanty towns) within Indian cities.

Rio de Janeiro is a megacity. There are expected to be twenty-six megacities (cities with populations of 10 million or more) by 2015.

Impacts of Rural to Urban Migration in Developing Countries

Rapid Urban Population Growth

Rural migrants have poured into cities out of desperation rather than being drawn by jobs and opportunities. Because these migrations have mostly been composed of teenagers and young adults, an important additional impact has been exceptionally **high rates of natural population increase** (high birth rates with low death rates). In most developing countries the rate of natural increase of urban populations exceeds the rate of net in-migration. On average, about 60 per cent of current urban population growth in developing countries is caused by natural increase within the cities.

Megacities

One striking result of the high rates of natural increase in urban populations has been the emergence of **megacities**, cities with populations of 10 million people or more. In 1960, New York and Tokyo were the only cities with 10 million or more inhabitants. Today, there are seventeen such megacities, for example Kolkata (Calcutta) and Mexico City. By 2015 there are expected to be twenty-six megacities: twenty-two in less developed regions, eighteen of them in Asia.

Shanty Towns

Another consequence of **urban population growth** in developing countries has been that many cities have grown **more rapidly than the jobs and housing they can provide.** This is called **overurbanisation** and it produces instant slums, called **shanties**. It is these slums and squatter settlements that must absorb the unprecedented rates of urban growth in the megacities of the developing world.

Squatter settlements are not necessarily slums, but most are. They have many names, such as *favelas* in Brazil and *bustees* in India.

Which countries are the cities mentioned in the text located in?

Overurbanisation occurs when migrants are driven from rural areas to large cities where slow economic growth does not provide sufficient jobs or shelter for them.

Child Workers

A 1995 UNICEF report blamed 'uncontrollable urbanisation' in less developed countries for the widespread creation of 'danger zones' where increasing numbers of children are forced to become beggars, prostitutes and labourers before they reach their teens. Pointing out that urban populations are growing at twice the general population growth rate, the report concluded that too many people are being squeezed into cities that do not have the jobs, housing or schools to accommodate them. As a consequence, the family and community structures that support children are being destroyed. The result is that more and more young children have to work to survive.

What is UNICEF and what does it do?

Male-Female Imbalance

In areas of out-migration in some less developed countries, it is generally the young males who migrate to cities, leaving the female family members, including wives, in the rural communities to tend the family's portion of land. The male migrants are urban dwellers loyal to a rural home and so are drawn back from time to time by community obligations.

Impacts of Rural to Urban Migration in Developed Countries

Urban Sprawl

Urban sprawl (**the spreading of cities out into the countryside**) was really a twentieth-century phenomenon in developed countries. It consists mainly of **large housing estate developments on the edges of cities**. The demand for spacious houses with front and rear gardens creates this urban growth problem. The quality of these houses is in stark contrast to the shanty developments on the outskirts of cities in less developed countries.

The suburb of Tolworth in the United Kingdom has spread out far into the countryside.

Growth Centres

One way to restrict urban sprawl is to create **growth boundaries**. This leads to the creation of growth centres such as the development of new towns some distance away from major cities, e.g. Leystad and Almere in the Netherlands.

Rural Depopulation

In the developed world the inability of large areas of land (even in excess of 40 hectares in Ireland) to support a family is causing a desire for rural people to migrate to cities to increase their income. This rural-urban movement has created large rural regions of low population density in developed countries. Examples of such areas in the EU are the West of Ireland and the Mezzogiorno in southern Italy.

Did you know that the world's cities take up just 2 per cent of the earth's land surface? Yet they account for 76 per cent of industrial wood use, 60 per cent of the water tapped for human use and 78 per cent of the carbon emissions from human activities, believed by most scientists to be the major cause of global warming.

Urban renewal has led to the development of many inner city areas such as Limerick city. Many other town developments, such as this one in Dublin, have created apartments in waterfront areas.

Almere was designed to accommodate overspill population from Amsterdam. It is a new town built on reclaimed land in the north-east polder. This photograph suggests that living in Almere would have many advantages.

From Rural Areas to Inner City

There is a conscious movement by two categories of people to inner city areas.

- Recent waves of immigration to **inner city** areas occur due to the low cost and easy availability of accommodation in large cities of, for example, the USA. The immigrants, e.g. Hispanics from Mexico, cluster within inner city zones and form **ethnic zones,** or **ghettos,** within these large cities. At present, large numbers of immigrants are finding accommodation in Dublin's north inner city. New shops have opened selling products, such as food, to suit the new cultural groups.

- There has been a spectacular growth of financial and business centres in some of the more prestigious cities, such as Dublin's International Financial Services Centre and London's Docklands. In such cities, many of the young middle class have turned their backs on the rural-urban movement to the suburbs, and purchase or rent accommodation in **urban renewal areas**. Such movement is generally by unmarried single people and divorced single people who find access to work, entertainment and friends easier.

Counter-urbanisation

The most recent pattern of internal migration has been an urban to rural movement in well-developed and urbanised countries. Since the 1960s this migration trend has occurred in some individual countries, such as Scotland, England and the Netherlands. But because it is now occurring throughout the developed Western world, it is being regarded as a new pattern.

Counter-urbanisation is an indirect impact of rural to urban migration, yet is also directly created by rural to urban movement.

Rural to urban migration has created large **conurbations.** These are large areas of urban environment created by the expansion of cities towards each other, such as the Randstad. In other words, conurbations are created by urban sprawl. Because of traffic jams, rush-hour traffic, limited open space, crime and a **deteriorating quality of life** in some cities, many people who lived in these urban environments have **moved to rural areas**. An additional factor driving this urban to rural movement is the high cost of housing in cities. These high city prices have allowed some people to sell their home in the city, buy or build a new home in a rural environment and have funds left over in their bank accounts for family security or other purposes.

Daily Rural to Urban Migration

Daily commuting to work from rural to urban areas is mainly associated with developed industrial societies. This occurs especially **into cities in the morning** and **out from cities in the evening**, as people go to and from work. This daily movement leads to **rush-hour traffic** and causes traffic jams throughout most urban regions of the developed world.

Three factors seem to have created this new trend:

- Widespread availability of **comfort services** provided by the state, such as electrification, piped water, well-surfaced and improved roads and network television. This can only be achieved in wealthy countries with sufficient funds to support populations in rural areas even though it is not economically viable to do so.
- **Improved private income** that allows people to choose where they want to live.
- The **trade-off** that people make between material things on the one hand and the **quality of life** and environmental considerations on the other. Quality of life is winning the battle, with people on higher incomes opting for a 'rural' location in peripheral areas.

The recent growth in the Irish economy has led to the building of many houses in rural towns throughout the country.

Rural to Urban Movement in Ireland

Renewal in Seaside Towns

The inclusion of seaside towns in urban renewal has led to a renewed interest in people making their homes by the sea and commuting to work each day. Seaside 'designated areas' policies have replaced dreary, damp old buildings with new ones that provide modern facilities, such as restaurants, fitness and swimming facilities, hotels and cafés. Some of these seaside towns, such as Cobh in Co. Cork and Malahide near Dublin, are near large towns and have become attractive to young families as the location for their family home. Many people commute to work each day from these places.

> Remember that rural to urban migration also continues as before during the process of counter-urbanisation.

Depopulation of the BMW Region

The geographical distribution of population in Ireland since the 1960s has become more uneven during this era of economic growth than in the past. The population of the **BMW Region declined**, while that of the **South and East Region increased**. This pattern is largely a reflection of the economic performance of the regions. This performance is based on two factors:

- **The decline in agricultural employment and share of GDP:** Agriculture employs only 93,000 people today compared to four times that number in 1961. The decline was greatest in the BMW Region, where farming was marginal and economic output low. Leitrim, Mayo and Roscommon were the most affected, losing over 80 per cent of their agricultural workforce. This encouraged a migration to towns and cities.
- **The urban structure of the regions:** Of crucial importance in population distribution has been the urban structure of the regions. The **north-west had few urban centres** that could attract the numbers leaving agriculture by offering alternative jobs in the service and

Daily commuting has increased in recent years as a consequence of high house prices in Dublin.

Many large, traditional family houses in seaside towns have been upgraded to modern standards.

manufacturing sectors. Relative to the area, the **number of towns** with over 5,000 population **in the west region is less than one-sixth that in the mid-east region.**

There has been a movement of people **into** rural regions in the vicinity of urban centres (particularly the cities), mostly fuelled by rapid house price inflation in the cities. This has created an explosive growth of villages and towns in urban hinterlands, especially in the east (see **Ireland's Urban Regions,** pages 167–9).

Multi-part Questions

1. 'Rural to urban migration impacts differently, both physically and socially, on urban regions in developed and developing countries.' Discuss. [20 marks]

2. Explain what is meant by counter-urbanisation. [20 marks]

3. A. Study Fig. 48.1, showing Irish migration patterns between 1987 and 2005.
   i. In which year did emigration peak?
   ii. When did immigration first exceed emigration?
   iii. Calculate the difference between emigration and immigration in 2005. [20 marks]

   B. Explain how Ireland's economic development affected migration patterns over time. [30 marks]

   C. Explain the consequences of rural to urban migration on donor and receiver regions in less developed countries. [30 marks]

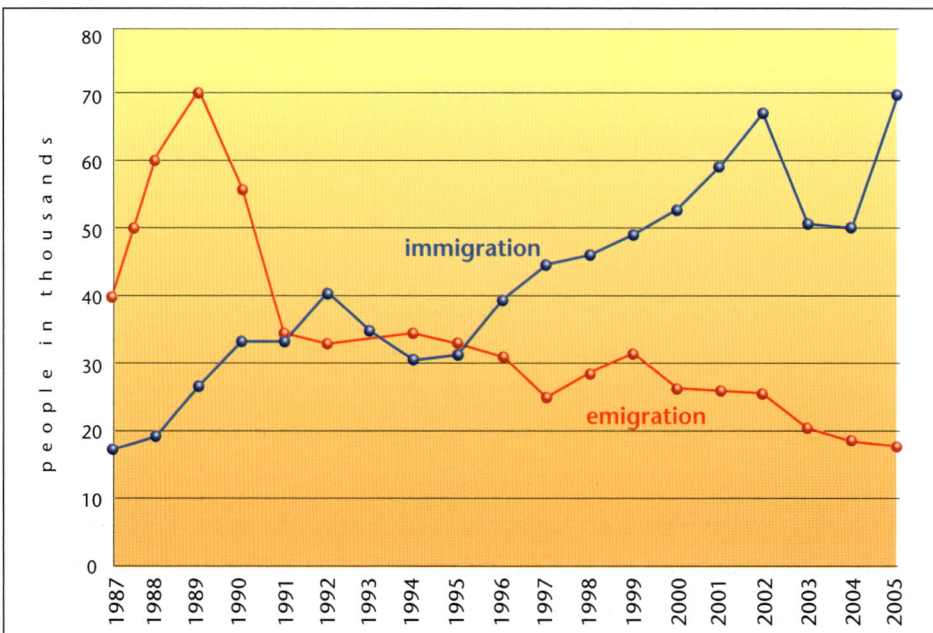

Fig 48.1 Ireland: Migration 1987–2005.

CHAPTER 49

SITE CHARACTERISTICS OF VILLAGES, TOWNS AND CITIES

 **KEY IDEA!**

Settlements can be identified in relation to site, situation and function.

Site and Situation of Settlements

Site refers to the characteristics of the ground or point at which the settlement is located. This was of major importance in the initial development and growth of the village or town. **Situation** refers to the location of the village or town relative to its surroundings, such as neighbouring settlements, rivers and uplands. The combined description of site and situation is called the **location** of a settlement. Situation, as well as human and political factors, determined whether or not a particular settlement remained small or grew into a larger town or city.

Function refers to the activities of a settlement, such as a seaside resort, market town or other commercial and industrial activities. As settlements grow, they add more and more functions. Some towns are classified by their main function, such as fishing port.

Early settlements in Ireland developed in a rural economy and aimed at being self-sufficient, mainly because transport was limited at that time. The most important factors that determined the site of a settlement are shown in Fig. 49.1 and are described below. It is important to note, however, that several of these factors would be combined when a choice was being made for siting of a settlement.

The most important factors are:

- **Water supply:** A nearby, constant clean water supply was essential for everyday needs. Water is heavy and difficult to carry. Until the 1950s, most rural villages and homes relied on a village pump or well for their water supply. In earlier times, rivers were sufficiently clean to provide clean drinking water. In hillside areas, many villages and farmhouses were located near a spring or well.
- **Avoidance of flooding:** By their very nature, many parts of river floodplains are covered by water during times of heavy rain. Because of this, only dry sites at selected fording (shallow) points of rivers were chosen for town development. Other, more low-lying areas were avoided for all settlement.
- **Food supply:** Towns and villages were generally built in level or gently sloping fertile areas where food could be produced from grazing of animals or tillage. Thus, all Irish urban settlements are in lowland areas.

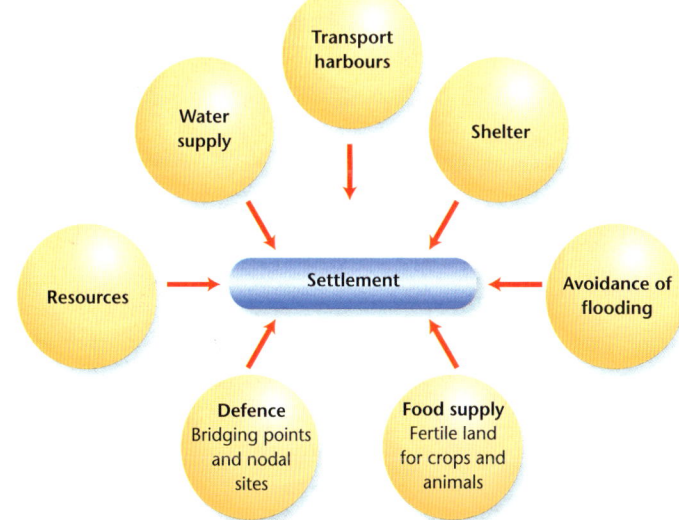

Fig. 49.1 Factors that determine the site of a settlement.

- **Defence, bridging points and nodal sites:** Some sites are of strategic importance, such as bridging points of rivers and harbour entrances. Routes focus on and meet at these places. In historic times, castles were built at such places to defend these sites.
- **Resources:** Settlements also grew in places where there were natural resources, such as minerals, e.g. Silvermines Village in Co. Tipperary, or at mineral springs, such as Lisdoonvarna in Co. Clare.
- **Harbours and seaside resorts:** Sheltered harbours and bays provided suitable sites for the development of settlements. As ships became larger, some ports lost their importance as they were not deep enough to accommodate these vessels.

Case Study: Location of Skibbereen – Sample Answer

Site

- Skibbereen is sited on the **left bank** (south side) of the Ilen River.
- The town is sited on **sloping land** between 5–40 m above sea level.
- The western side **slopes steeply** towards the river, while the eastern side is built on **more gently sloping** and **level** ground. It is sited on the left bank to **avoid** the **low-lying flat land** on the right bank.
- This flat area forms part of the **floodplain** of the River Ilen. The word 'marsh' suggests this is true.
- This site was chosen because of its elevated site and because it was a suitable **bridging point** of the river.

Situation

- Skibbereen is located in the **valley of the Ilen River**, which runs north-east to south-west across a low-lying hilly landscape.
- It is located at the **junction of major routes** across the lowland. The R593, R596, R631, R595 and the N71 and some third-class **roads all meet at Skibbereen**.
- Skibbereen is a bridging point of the Ilen River and so Skibbereen is a major **route focus**.

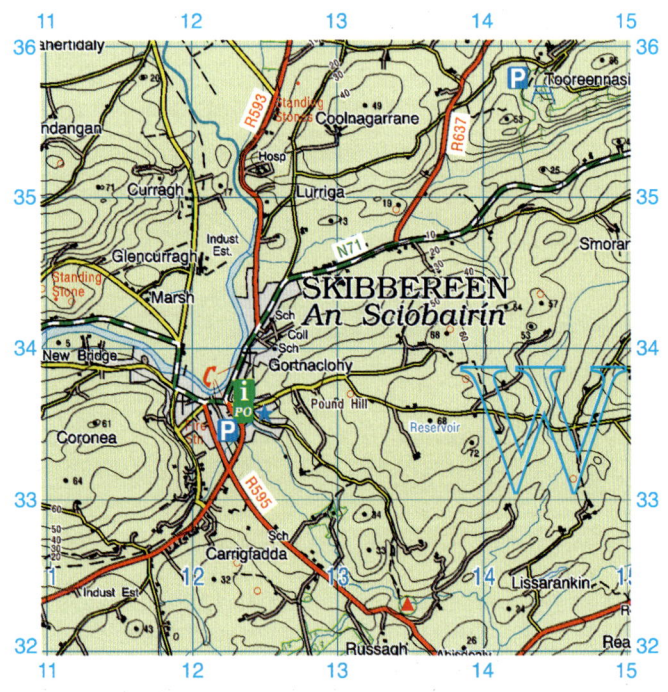

- *Which direction was the camera pointing when this photograph was taken?*

How to describe the location of a village or town

Site: The actual land on which the settlement is built.

1. What is the altitude of the land?
2. Is it flat or gently sloping?
3. Is it sited on a river? If so, which bank?
4. Is it a defensive site? (Is there a castle in the settlement nearby?)
5. Is it a bridging point of a river? If so, name the river.
6. Is it the lowest bridging point of the river?
7. Is it a confluence town? (Is it at or close to the confluence of two rivers?)
8. Does the place name suggest anything about the settlement?

Situation: The site in relation to the surrounding area.

1. Is it sited in a valley or on a lowland plain?
2. Is it near the coast? Is it at an estuary? Name the bay or inlet.
3. Where is the settlement in relation to some prominent relief feature?
4. Is it a focus of routes? Name the routes and classify them.

CHAPTER 50
LOCATIONAL CHARACTERISTICS OF IRELAND'S PREHISTORIC AND HISTORIC SETTLEMENTS

KEY IDEA! Settlements can be identified in relation to site, situation and function.

SITE CHARACTERISTICS OF VILLAGES, TOWNS AND CITIES

Settlement Characteristics

Period	Associated Structures
Pre-Christian farmers 4000 BC to 600 BC	Circular mounds of stones, dolmen, wedge tombs, megalithic tombs, fulacht fia, barrow, cairn, stone circle, passage grave, cairn, copper mines.
Celtic 6th century BC to 6th century AD	Circular earthen bank, circular stone wall, promontory fort, rath, cashel, lis, dun, doon, ogham stones, togher, stone fort.
Early Christian 6th to 11th centuries	Circular stone enclosure/bank, radial street pattern, round tower, small Irish monastery, high cross.
Viking 9th to 10th centuries	Irregular gable end of houses onto street. No surface features. Names such as Waterford and Wexford.
Norman 12th and 13th centuries	Castle, strong fortified stone walls, bridging point of river, tower house, town gate, town walls, motte.
Plantation 16th, 17th and 18th centuries	Large castles with ornamental gardens, diamond/fair green where streets meet. Town square, market house, towns with landlord's name, e.g. Mitchelstown, Charleville. Woods near castle.
Georgian 18th and 19th centuries	Geometric plan to streets, buildings often laid out around a crescent or green. Grain stores near canals/rivers. Square or rectangular town square.
Modern	Suburbs, housing estates, shopping centres, ring roads, multi-storey buildings, hospitals, car parks.

SITE, SITUATION AND FUNCTION OF IRELAND'S PREHISTORIC SETTLEMENTS

Ireland's First Settlements

The earliest settlers came to Ireland about 9,000 years ago (around 7000 BC). They were **hunters, fisherfolk** and **food-gatherers**. They were Mesolithic people, which means they belonged to the Middle Stone Age. The earliest evidence of these people – midden sites, called 'midden' on Ordnance Survey maps – dates from about 5,000 years ago. Midden sites are mounds of sand with bones of wild pig and deer as well as heaps of empty seashells. These midden sites are **sited near today's shoreline**, just **above high tide level**. Many of them are also **covered by sand dunes** that formed by wind and wave action after the sites were abandoned. Middens represent temporary settling places where people lived and hunted and gathered berries and shellfish.

Activity

Activity

1. Locate each midden site on the map extract using six-figure grid references.
2. Describe the general locational characteristics of these middens. (Where are they and why are they located here?)

What were the functions of middens? Why did their location suit their function?

Ireland's First Farming Settlements

Farming was first practised in Ireland about 7,000 years ago (5000 BC). These farming people belonged to the Neolithic, or New Stone Age, and they chose sites for their homes in places where cattle could be raised and some grain could be grown successfully. They chose **upland areas** and **raised, dry or hilly lowland** sites for their farms and tilled the surrounding land. Soils were rich in lime at that time, and the upland **soils** were lighter (grittier) and **easy to work** with **primitive** wooden farming tools.

Three regions were of particular importance:

- **The Burren:** Early farmers grazed cattle and grew crops in this region.
- **The lowland drumlin soils of Sligo to Dundalk** provided rich grazing.
- **West Cork**, where copper ore for smelting was available.

Neolithic people lived on their farmland and buried their dead in large stone tombs called **megaliths**. The site and situation of their tombs indicate the places where they lived and worked. Their tombs form a **dispersed pattern** across these regions, many of them in elevated areas. Later farming groups came during the Copper and Bronze Ages (2000–650 BC) and many of these groups also chose elevated sites to live on, worship and bury their dead. Descriptions such as **megalithic tombs, stone circle, barrow,**

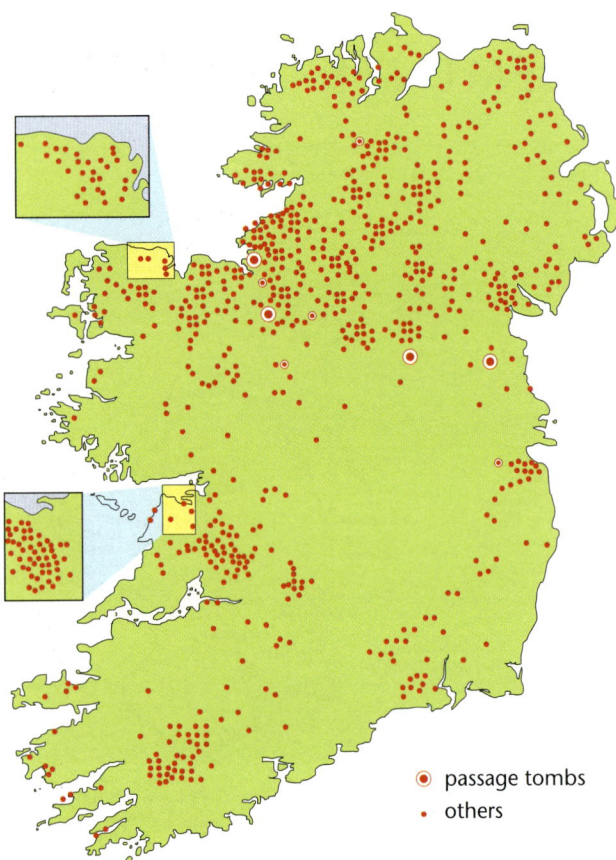

Fig. 50.1 Ireland's megalithic tombs.

• passage tombs
· others

cairns, cist, standing stones and fulachtai fiadh (all printed in red on Ordnance Survey maps) indicate the sites of all these early farming groups (see Fig. 50.1).

Celtic Settlements

From about 650 BC to AD 250, numerous groups of people who introduced a new culture migrated to Ireland. These newcomers were the Celts. The Celts had a structured society that included royal families, druids, judges, freemen and farmers. They lived in communities, some large and some small, **throughout farming lowland.** They also divided the country into divisions called **tuaths** (kingdoms).

Structures such as **hill forts, ring forts, crannogs, cashels** (circular stone forts) and **promontory forts** are associated with the Celts. Promontory forts were built on cliff edges for protection against attack. Forts were mostly circular in shape and their use varied from house enclosures to animal shelters, ceremonial sites and defence. **Elevated sites**, such as **hilltops** or **cliff edges**, were regularly chosen for the largest of these structures.

Celtic settlements may be identified by names such as **Rath** (Rathluirc), **Lios** (Lisdoonvarna), **Dun** (Dundalk), **Caher** (Cahir), **Cashel** (Cashel). Folklore referred to some of these settlements as fairy forts.

Stone circles were places of religious worship during the Stone Age in Ireland.

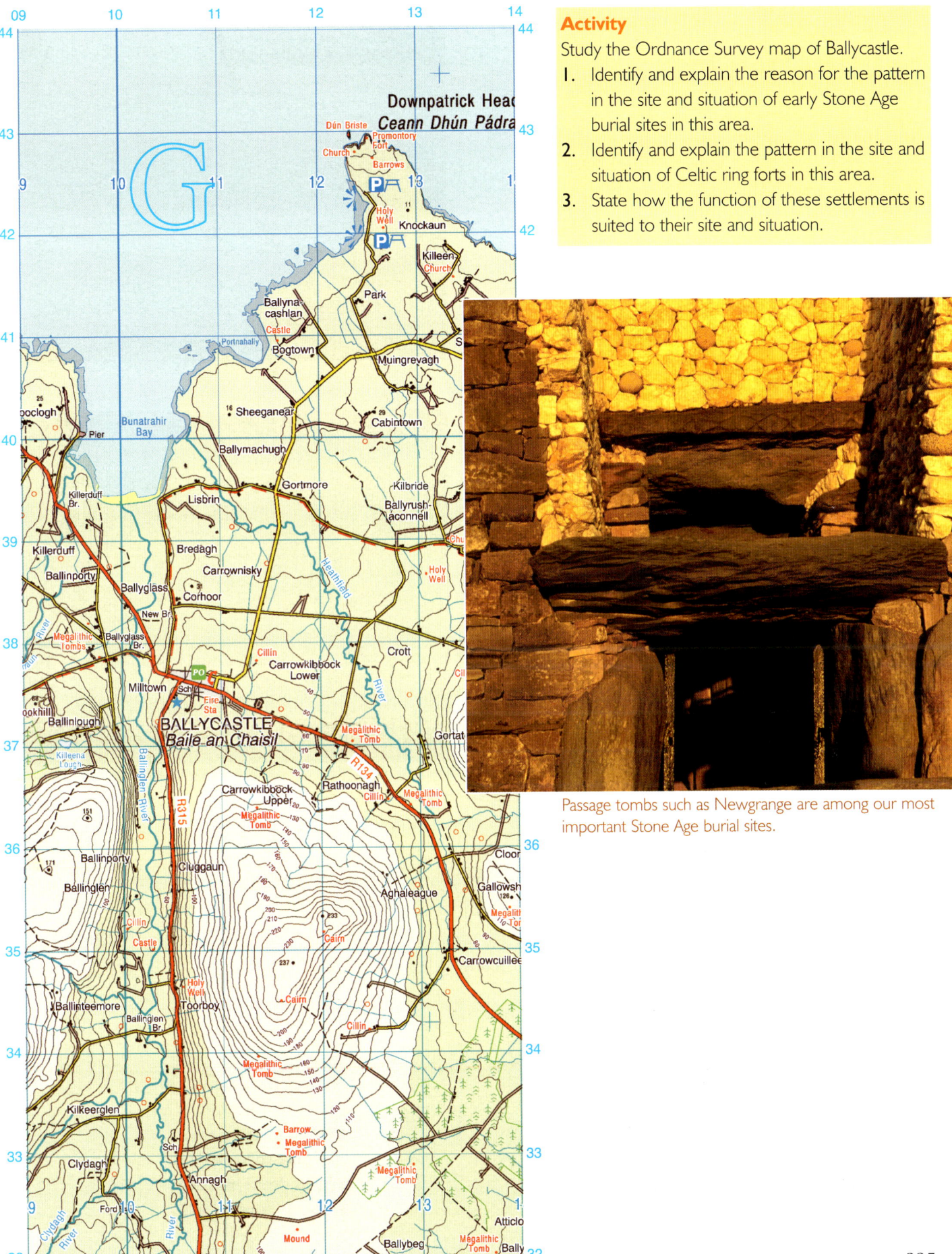

Activity
Study the Ordnance Survey map of Ballycastle.
1. Identify and explain the reason for the pattern in the site and situation of early Stone Age burial sites in this area.
2. Identify and explain the pattern in the site and situation of Celtic ring forts in this area.
3. State how the function of these settlements is suited to their site and situation.

Passage tombs such as Newgrange are among our most important Stone Age burial sites.

farming land with rich limestone soils

part of original lake (the lake has been drained and this is now dry land)

Iron Age stone forts on a hilltop

A royal ceremonial hill fort at the Hill of Tara.

Dun Aengus is a stone promontory fort on a cliff in the Aran Islands.

Activity

The Lough Gur area has had continuous settlement since early farming times. Using evidence from the map only, suggest why Knockadoon Hill was a suitable location for early settlement.

The Celts established a network of routeways throughout Ireland. In wet and marshy areas they built roads, called toghers, from planks of wood on brushwood.

Circular stone forts were called 'cashel' or 'caher'. Many cashels surrounded early Irish monasteries.

Small Hermit Monasteries

Sites chosen by early missionaries were in **scattered, isolated scenic areas**. Generally they were in **glaciated valleys**. The peace and rugged natural beauty of the surrounding land formed an integral part of early monastic life. It was a simple life **located away from people** where the monks could feel close to God. These monks were called **hermits**. Some of them lived in small 'beehive' huts built of stone. Most, however, lived in thatched timbered buildings that have since decayed. Nearby was their **church**, often a small stone building, where they worshipped.

A local stream, lake or spring provided an unpolluted supply of fresh water. At that time rivers had enormous quantities of trout and salmon throughout the year. Some food crops were grown nearby on fertile ground.

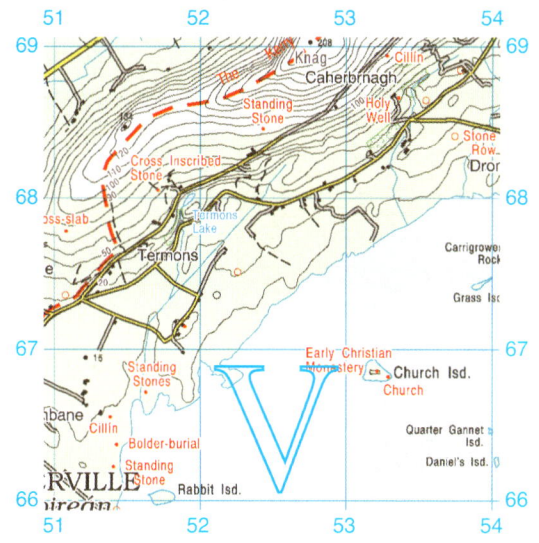

'Monastery', 'Cillín', 'Holy Well', 'Ch.' and 'Cross-inscribed Stone' indicate early Christian monastic settlements.

> Crannogs were generally used as cattle enclosures. They were man-made islands in lakes and were built for protection.

SITE, SITUATION AND FUNCTION IN THE HISTORIC DEVELOPMENT OF IRISH TOWNS

Large Monastery Settlements

Monasteries were built:

- **At route centres**, such as Clonmacnoise in Co. Offaly.
- **On fertile plains and river valleys**, such as Kells in Co. Meath, and Kilkenny city.

Some monasteries grew into substantial settlements that became centres of education for people in Ireland, Britain and the European continent at a time when such schools were not available elsewhere. At the centre was the monastery, with its church or churches, round tower, monks' dwellings and graveyard with high crosses, all of which were enclosed by a circular stone wall.

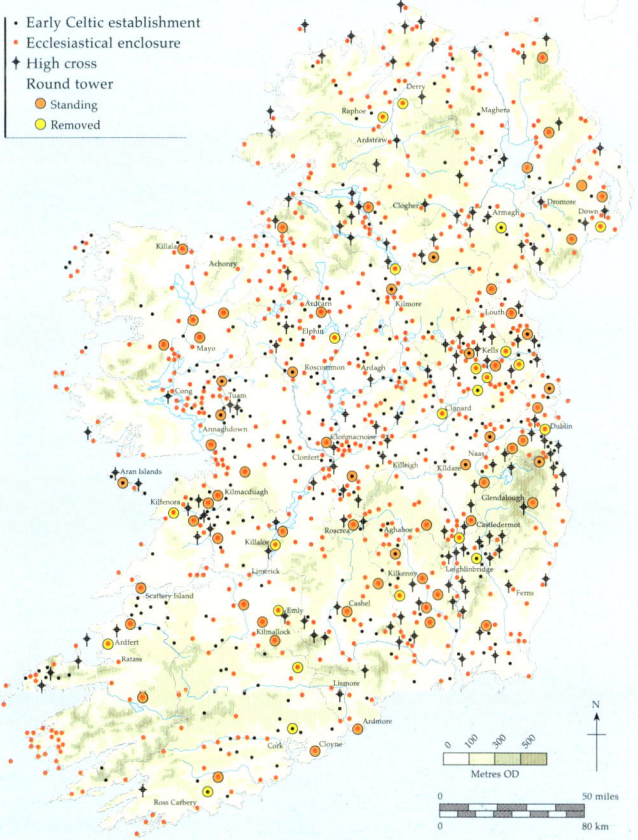

Fig. 50.2 The locations of early Irish monasteries.

● *Identify regions in Ireland where high densities of early monastic ruins exist.*

337

Place names can help to identify some early Christian monastic settlements. The words 'manistir', 'cill' or 'ceall' mean a church, so settlements with names beginning with any of these words may have monastic origins. Examples include Kilkenny, Kilbride and Monasterevin. As these towns grew, they developed functions other than religious and educational, such as metalworking and other trades.

Some early monasteries are identifiable from the air. They are small stone buildings with steep roofs or gables. A circular wall around the monastery may still be seen. Later monasteries had round towers. These were tall, circular, tapering stone towers built to protect their occupants against attack.

Activity

Describe the site, situation and function of this settlement. In your answer, refer to evidence on the map and photograph.

To recap, look at the ESB video on the Shannon Basin. Then focus on the part dealing with Clonmacnoise.

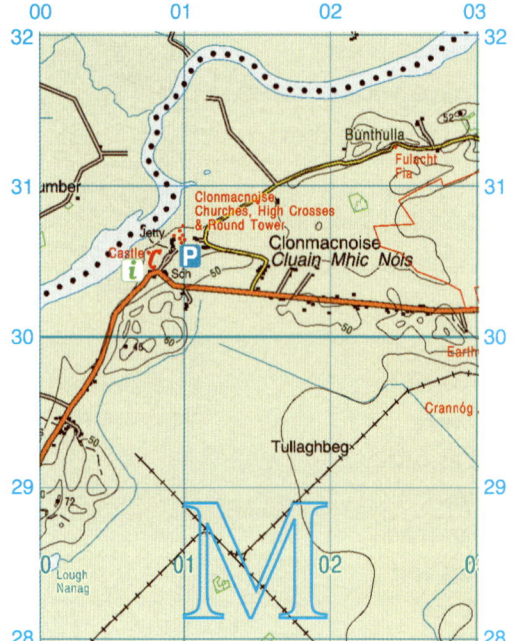

Clonmacnoise, Co. Offaly.

Viking Settlements

The Vikings first came to Ireland in the late eighth century and established our first formal towns on coastal estuaries. These settlements were built on defensive sites at waterside locations that also acted as **trading bases** or **ports for trade** between Ireland, Britain and continental Europe. These **sheltered river estuaries** provided safe anchorage for the Viking longboats.

Norman and Medieval Settlements

The Normans came to Ireland in 1169 and landed at Bannow Bay in Co. Wexford. From there they spread west and north, capturing the best farmland and setting up castles to defend their captured land.

The Normans were particularly good at choosing **defensive sites,** and most of their settlements have survived and developed into Ireland's most prosperous cities and towns. The Normans often chose sites for their mottes and castles where there were already thriving monastery settlements, such as Clonmacnoise, Roscrea and Kilkenny. In most cases, however, they chose new sites that were easily defended, such as **bridging points**, **river loops**, **elevated sites** or **islands** in rivers. For example, Cahir Castle, Co. Tipperary, is sited on an island in the River Suir. Sometimes the first building was a motte and bailey, while other times it was a stone castle.

Unplanned towns developed around these defensive buildings, which provided protection for the townsfolk and soldiers. These towns grew by **adding buildings and** functions, such as abbeys. The towns were surrounded by high walls and their guarded gateways were the only ways of entering or leaving the settlements. The larger the settlement, the more gateways it had.

Fig. 50.3

King John's Castle in Limerick city was built at a fording point of the River Shannon.

Other Functions of Norman Towns

The Normans, who were Christian, encouraged religious orders such as the Cistercians and Franciscans to establish monasteries here, so these religious buildings, called **abbeys**, are often found **near Norman castles** throughout the south and east, where most Norman towns are. As fish formed a large part of the monks' diet, these abbeys are generally sited **near rivers**. Monastic lands near the towns were called **granges**.

During the Middle Ages, these abbeys performed a number of functions. They frequently provided **alms** for the poor, **education** for the young, **accommodation** for travellers and **hospitals** for the ill.

The abbeys also created **urban growth** by increasing trade. They created markets within Ireland and abroad for cattle, horses and wool. These activities helped the Norman towns to grow into **market centres** where **fairs** and **markets** were held regularly. Industries such as **milling** and **tanning** leather associated with market towns also developed. Because of these developments, Norman towns thrived and survive as our main towns today.

Some towns, such as Ennis in Co. Clare, developed around abbeys. Can you identify the abbey in this photograph?

● *What functions would this abbey have offered the people of this early settlement?*

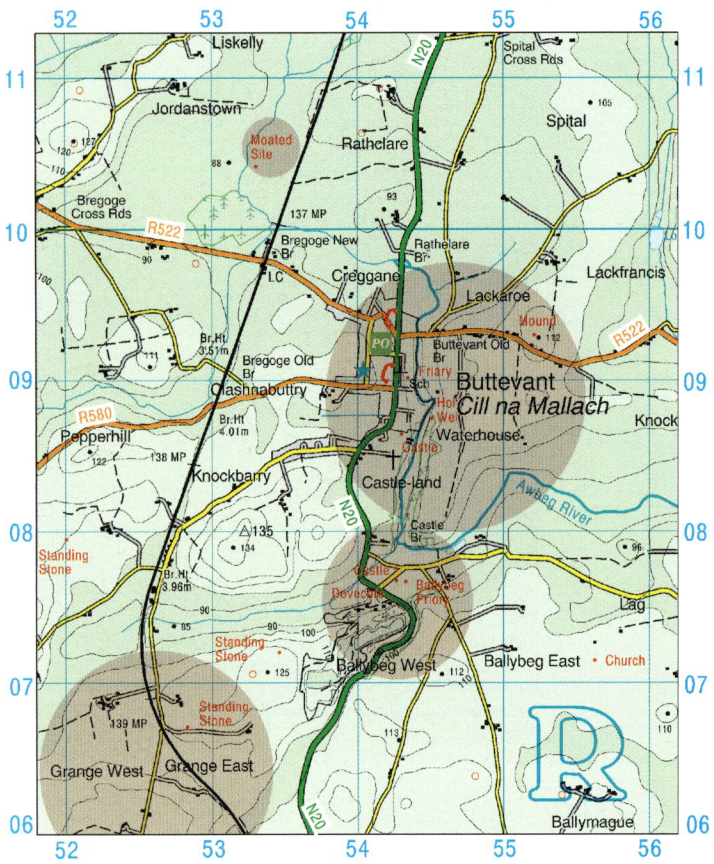

Recognising Castles and Abbeys in Aerial Photographs

Generally, today's dwellings, commercial offices and other buildings have either a brick or plaster finish. Some share similar characteristics. In Norman times, castles and abbeys also had common characteristics. They were built of stone and had tower-like features. Look for these structures on a map or photograph to identify a town's origins. Norman and medieval towns were unplanned settlements.

Gothic arch

living quarters

cloister

stone building

nave

castle-like tower top

bell tower

Tintern Abbey, a Cistercian abbey founded by the Normans in Wexford in 1200 AD.

The presence of an abbey tells us three things about a town:

- It was a Norman town.
- The abbey had many functions in the daily life of the settlement.
- Abbeys were closed down in the sixteenth century as towns lost some of their functions.

Abbeys had Gothic-style architecture, with pointed windows and doorways. Like castles, abbeys were built of stone. They also had bell towers that resembled castles.

Ross Castle, in Killarney, is a popular tourist attraction.

Jerpoint Abbey shows many structural features of Norman abbeys.

Activity

Identify the functions of the buildings in these photographs.

Planned Plantation Towns and Villages

Planned towns and villages were built as part of the plantations of the sixteenth and seventeenth centuries. Plantation towns and villages had a number of functions, including:

- Defending settlers against attack from dispossessed Irish farmers by enclosing the towns with defensive walls.
- Encouraging settlers to come to Ireland.
- Creating business and wealth by building market squares and fair greens to accommodate farm animals and market stalls on market and fair days.
- Introducing the Protestant faith by building new churches.
- Providing homes for businesspeople and other traders and workers.

Activity

Study the photograph of Moy village.

1. Describe the layout (plan) of this village.
2. Describe the site of the village and state why it was suited to the functions of the village.
3. Identify two modern functions of the village.
4. What evidence in the photograph shows that Moy village continues to add new functions to ensure survival?

Moy village in Co. Tyrone is a planned plantation settlement.

341

Kenmare is a planned plantation town.

These settlements were **planned** and some, such as Durrow in Co. Offaly, had a **square** or **green**. The **streets** were **wide** and well planned. They had fine and graceful buildings, some of which were shops, while others were erected as town dwellings for the country gentry, merchants and army officers. Many were two, three or four storeys in height.

Most of these planned towns were **located near a large estate, castle or demesne**, which was owned by the local landlord on whose land the town was built. He often took a special interest in the layout of the settlement, which gave it its own unique character.

Activity

Study the photograph of Kenmare in Co. Kerry.

1. What evidence in the photograph suggests that this town was a planned settlement?
2. What advantages does the planned layout of this town offer today's planners in helping to cope with traffic flow within the town?

Wexford still operates as a fishing port. Many coastal towns and villages developed port or recreational facilities.

Ireland's Coastal Cities and Towns

Ireland's largest coastal settlements are sited at the lowest bridging points of rivers before they enter the sea. As such they were defensive sites that could control our deepest sheltered harbours and were the **meeting points of inland and coastal routeways**. They were all either Viking, Norman or plantation defensive towns that served large fertile hinterlands, so they also had **market functions**.

Over the centuries they added new functions to provide services for each town and their trade areas. These functions included **port functions, milling, brewing, manufacturing, law, education (universities), recreation, cultural, religious** and **administrative**. Some large coastal cities and towns include Dublin, Cork, Limerick, Galway (cities), Wicklow, Wexford, Dingle and Sligo (towns).

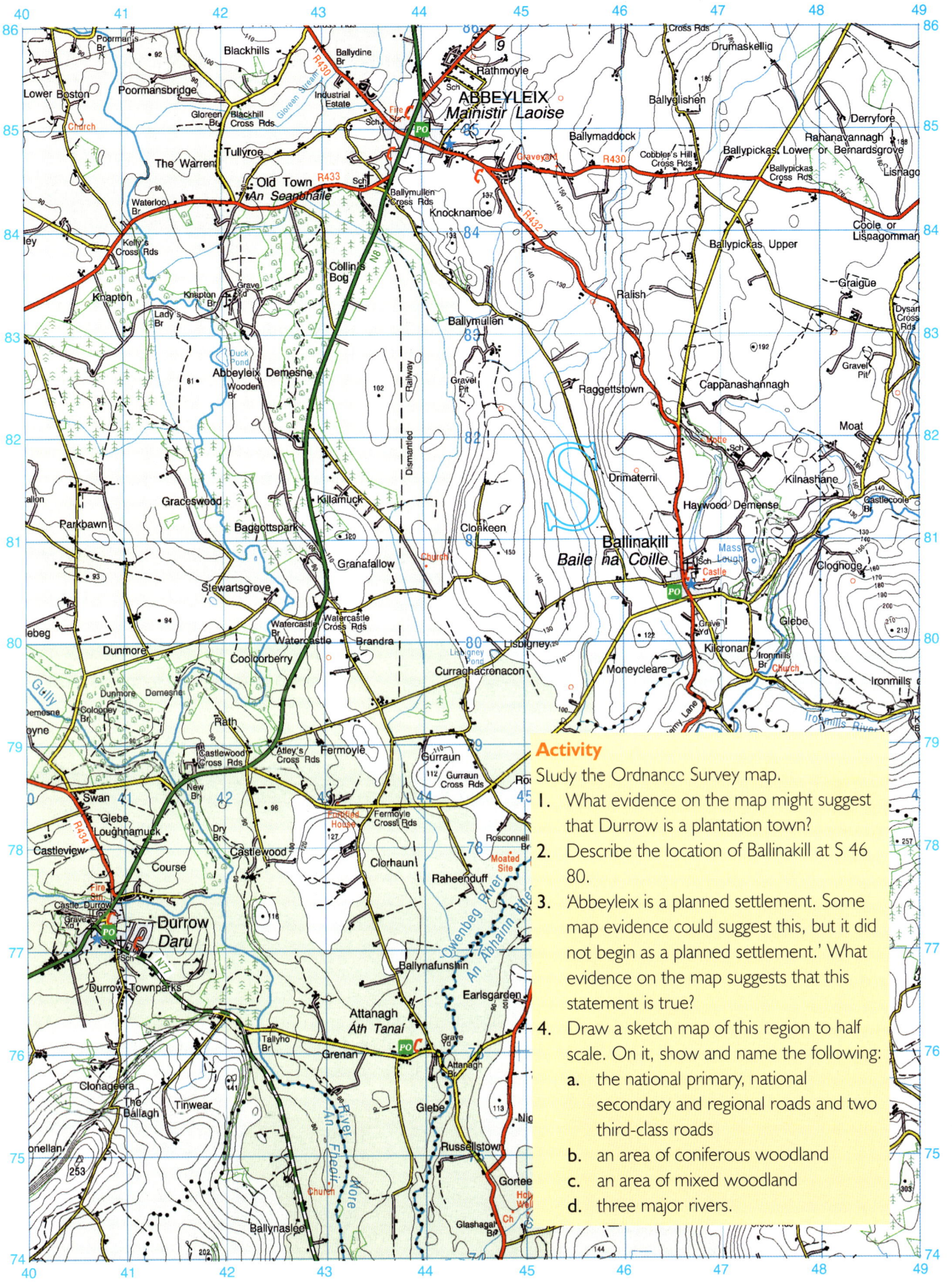

Industrial and Town Growth in the Eighteenth and Nineteenth Centuries

Canal Towns

Some of Ireland's largest rivers, such as the Shannon, the Liffey, the Erne and the Barrow, were deepened, widened and connected by canals during the eighteenth and nineteenth centuries. This allowed barges to carry **heavy and bulky goods** from our largest coastal ports to inland towns that were already sited on rivers. In addition, these towns now found themselves sited on **canals**. Inland towns, such as Athy, Carlow, Athlone and Carrick-on-Shannon, became river ports that catered for the transport of **people** and **goods**, including grain and timber brought from the hinterlands of inland canal towns to the coast for export. They also catered for the transport of goods, such as beer and coal, from coastal ports to inland areas.

All this cargo had to be loaded and unloaded by hand and stored on the canal side, so large **grain stores**, **mills**, **warehouses** and **hotels** were built on waterside sites in these canal towns. This increased trade, created employment and increased the prosperity of these settlements.

The quays at New Ross retain many of the grain stores and mills that encouraged trade along the Barrow and Nore.

Activity

Study the Ordnance Survey map and the photograph.
1. What evidence along the River Barrow suggests that this river was canalised?
2. Identify a building or buildings directly associated with canal transport. Explain fully.
3. What economic developments in the town would have been encouraged as a consequence of the canal?

Locks were built on rivers to allow the controlled raising and lowering of water levels to accommodate barge movement.

Ireland's Railway Towns

Inland Railway Towns

Some inland towns that were fortunate enough to be sited on railways achieved increased economic growth in the **nineteenth century**. These towns grew because of increased trade in goods and passenger services. **Hotels** were built **near railway stations** for overnight accommodation. Towns such as Thurles, Portarlington, Mullingar, Athlone and Mallow boomed as cattle were transported from fairs to processing factories, ports and cattle-rearing areas.

Today, the railway is regaining some lost business. Traffic congestion on roads leading into our main towns and cities and the high cost of suburban family homes encourage many people to travel by train again. This has led to a revival of some of our railway stations sited on main lines in towns leading to Dublin.

Seaside Towns

Some seaside towns grew as **railways** that **joined them to nearby cities** and towns were built. Weekend railway trips to the seaside boosted those coastal settlements that were planned with new streets and hotels to accommodate tourists. These tourist towns were **sited near beaches** and **developed around bays** with two- and three-storey buildings facing out over the beaches towards the sea. Bray in Co. Wicklow and Tramore in Co. Waterford grew at this time. The railways to some seaside towns have been dismantled since the 1950s due to the rise in car ownership.

Fig. 50.4 Many buildings in seaside towns have features like bay windows and plaster details. These houses were built at the end of the nineteenth century.

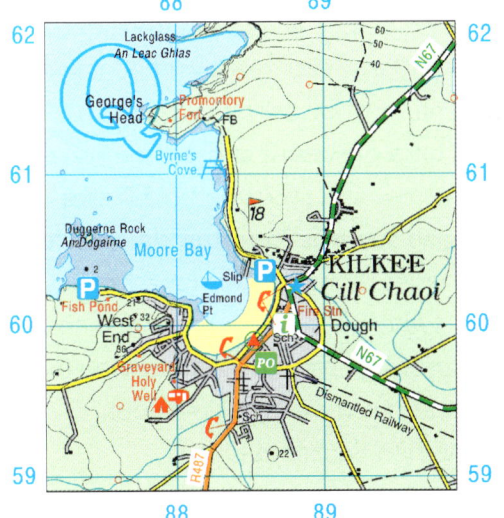

Activity

Study the Ordnance Survey map of Kilkee.

1. What evidence on the map suggests that the railway once played an active part in the development of the town?
2. What does this suggest about the historical development of Kilkee?

345

Activity
Study the Ordnance Survey map of Mullingar. Use evidence from this map to explain the historical development of Mullingar. In your answer, refer to canals, railway and roads and other modern developments.

A Georgian residence.

Expansion of Ireland's Large Cities and Towns

Most urban rebuilding and development took place during the **Georgian period** (1714–1830). The architectural style, Georgian, takes its name from the four Georges, the English kings who ruled during this period.

In Dublin, Cork, Limerick and Galway, suburbs were added to the cities. The older parts of the cities became run down and some developed into **slum areas.**

The new Georgian suburbs had **wide streets with blocks of buildings and squares or parks** for the wealthy property owners who lived in their large **four-storey, red-brick terraced** mansions. The streets were wide to cater for horse-drawn carriages and carts for delivering goods. These wide streets reflected **a time of wealth and prosperity** and they differed from the narrow and unplanned older areas of a city. Today, these **Georgian suburbs form the city centre areas of all our largest cities**. Many terraced mansions have been changed into flats. Others have been renovated and are used as offices for insurance companies, solicitors and private business. Some of these terraced mansions overlook Stephen's Green and Merrion Square in Dublin.

New Towns

New towns, such as **Shannon New Town** and **Tallaght**, were built since the 1960s. Shannon was built to meet the needs of people working in Shannon's industrial estate and airport. Tallaght and Blanchardstown in Dublin were built to cater for the surge in Dublin's population as a consequence of rural to urban migration and movement from Dublin's inner city to the suburbs. A ring of rapidly growing towns has now developed around the city to create the urban region known as Greater Dublin.

Large Gothic-style churches like this one in Cobh were built in the nineteenth century.

Traditional eighteenth- and nineteenth-century shop fronts can be seen in many of Ireland's cities and towns.

Classical (public) style for courthouses and banks reflected the power of law and finance in society.

CHAPTER 51
RURAL SETTLEMENT PATTERNS

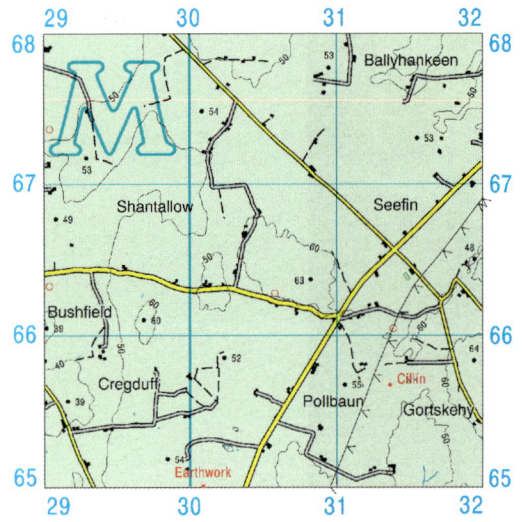

Dispersed (scattered) rural settlements.

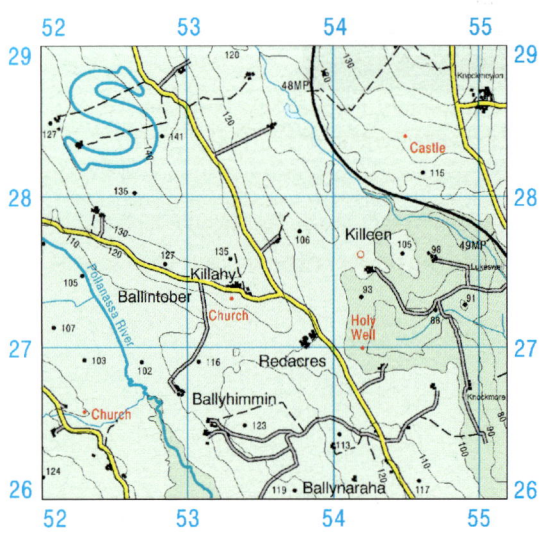

Clustered rural farm settlements.

Dispersed Settlement

Dispersed or scattered housing patterns initially developed when land was 'enclosed' and **farms were created** from commonage in the **eighteenth century**. Each farmer built a farmhouse on his own land. This gave rise to widely separated houses, especially in the east and south of Ireland, where farms were large. In the west and north-west of Ireland, where farms or plots of land were small, farmhouses were still dispersed but were more closely spaced. Many farmhouses throughout the country were located at **the end of long passageways** or on roadside sites.

Since the 1960s, many single-storey, two-storey and dormer-style houses have been built by non-farming people on scattered roadside sites. In such cases, the owners either availed of sites that farm owners willingly sold or gave to family members. Such **one-off housing** is regarded as unsustainable development by some county councils. They fear pollution of groundwater from septic tanks and an inability of services to cater for older people in isolated dwellings.

● Identify the settlement pattern in this part of the West of Ireland.

Clustered Settlement

Dwellings form a cluster where:

- Farmhouses were built in clusters. These dwellings may be remnants of the old *clochán* system where small landholders owned separate parcels of land that surrounded the farm village. This pattern was especially common in the west and north-west of Ireland.

- In parts of Co. Kilkenny and Co. Waterford, where farmhouses were built in clusters rather than on their own individual farms during the plantations.

- At road junctions in isolated rural areas where a shop, church or post office may have developed.

Ribbon Settlement

Ribbon settlement, or ribbon development, is relatively recent. It has mainly developed since the 1960s. Individual, one-off houses form a continuous (or almost continuous) line leading out from villages and small towns for a kilometre or more. Ireland's National Development Plan regards such development as unsustainable development that does not blend with the local landscape and is outside speed limit zones. Such development has occurred up to now because:

- Local planning authorities have granted planning permission in the past.

- Services, such as telephone cables, water supply pipes and electricity lines, were readily available nearby.

- Landowners could boost their income for essential needs such as education of their children or a child's inheritance. These roadside sites fetched high prices.

- New shops, filling stations and bed and breakfast accommodation wanted roadside sites on routes leading into and out of villages and towns with ready access to passing traffic so as to survive and prosper as businesses.

A linear pattern at Maghera in Co. Donegal.

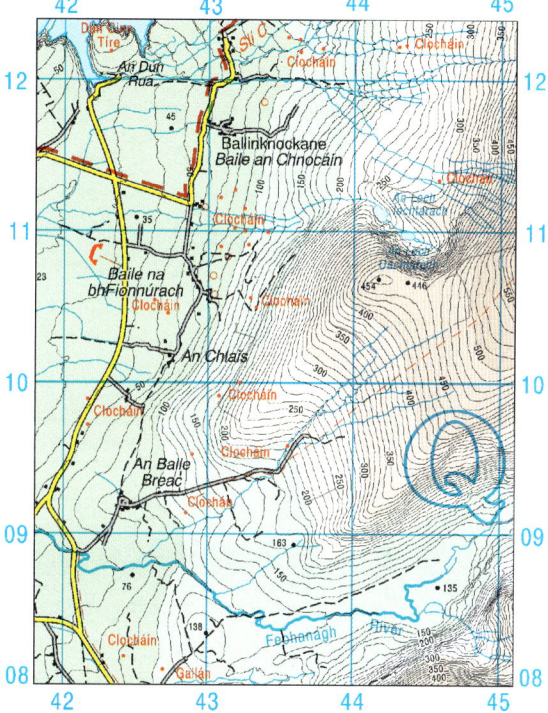

The Irish word *clochán* refers to rural farming settlements where farmhouses formed a cluster. Most of these houses have been abandoned by their owners.

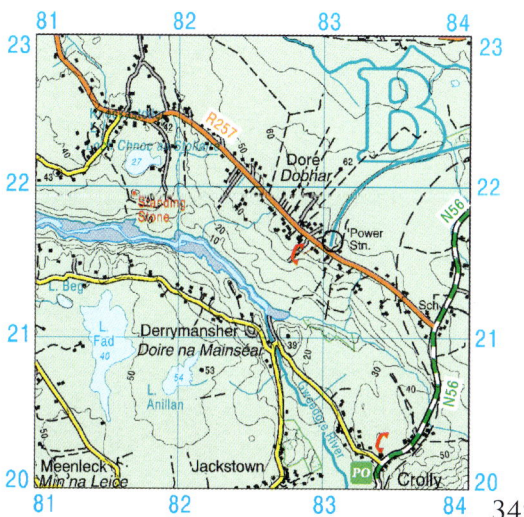

Activity

2006 Leaving Certificate Ordinary Level

Examine the 1:50,000 OS map of Abbeyleix on page 343 and answer the following.

1. Name and give locations for two patterns of rural settlement on the map.

2. Explain the development of one of these patterns in detail.

Ribbon settlement is an undesirable pattern and is in conflict with the desires of the National Development Plan.

Multi-part Questions

1. **A.** Study the Ordnance Survey map on page 343, then draw a sketch map and mark and name the following on it:
   i. two important rivers
   ii. one area of mixed woodland and one area of coniferous woodland
   iii. the highest point on the map
   iv. urban region
   v. two important routes. [20 marks]

   B. i. Locate and identify any two patterns of rural settlement.
   ii. Explain how these settlement patterns developed. [30 marks]

   C. Explain, using examples, how Ireland's urban regions developed over time. (30 marks)

2. Carefully study the Ordnance Survey map of Durrow on page 343.
   A. Describe the location of Durrow. [20 marks]

   B. Explain the social and economic development of any of the urban settlements on this Ordnance Survey map. [30 marks]

   C. Explain how changing fertility rates affect the economic development of a country or countries that you have studied. [30 marks]

3. **A.** Draw a sketch map to half scale of the Ordnance Survey map of Thurles region on page 359. On it, mark and name:
   i. the Suir River and the named tributary
   ii. a shaded region that represents the floodplain of the Suir River
   iii. one national primary road
   iv. one national secondary road
   v. two regional roads. [20 marks]

   B. List the causes and effects of overpopulation in any region that you have studied. [30 marks]

   C. Explain how the development of Ireland's transport system influences its urban development. [30 marks]

4. **A.** Draw a sketch map to half scale of the Ordnance Survey map of the Thurles region on page 359. On it, mark and name:
   i. the road network
   ii. the urban region of Thurles
   iii. a railway line and station. [20 marks]

   B. 'There is a long history of settlement throughout the region shown on the map.' Explain this statement. [30 marks]

   C. From your studies of landscape evolution on page 114, discuss how this region has developed its physical characteristics. [30 marks]

CHAPTER 52
PLANNING STRATEGIES IN RURAL AREAS

 **KEY IDEA!**

Planning strategies encourage sustainable development in rural regions.

COUNTY AND NATIONAL DEVELOPMENT PLANS

Sustainable development is that which seeks an acceptable quality of life for present and future generations. It also recognises that **the actions of the present affect the inheritance of future generations** and that natural environments must be supported to secure this aim. **Sustainable development** is the key to managing economic and **environmental interdependence**.

Those responsible for planning in both rural and urban areas **try to promote the orderly development of the landscape** to:

- Ensure the land is used for the common good (the good of everybody).
- Meet the needs of society for housing, food and materials, employment and leisure.
- Support policies concerned with regional development, social integration, urban renewal and the maintenance of strong rural communities.
- Balance competing needs and protect the environment as much as possible.

> Sustainable development is an approach in which the exploitation of resources, the direction of investments, new technological developments and institutional change are made to support future as well as present needs.

Careful planning can help to achieve these objectives in a number of ways:

- Controlling the development of transport, natural resources and the efficient use of energy.
- The careful location of industry, houses and business, shops and services.
- Controlling the shape, size and structure of settlements.
- Effectively using already developed areas.
- Protecting and supporting our natural environment and wildlife habitats, including areas and features of outstanding beauty.
- Accommodating new developments in an environmentally sustainable and sensitive manner.
- Strengthening villages and towns, both socially and economically, in order to improve their potential as growth centres.

Scattered one-off houses like these in the West of Ireland are not in keeping with the tradition of the region. Do you agree or disagree with this statement?

County development plans encourage housing in rural villages. Such development would reduce one-off housing along rural roads. It would also increase the efficiency and reduce the cost of social services, such as energy supplies, phone lines, post offices, day care centres and other community facilities.

But in order to achieve these aims, the councils should promote policies that provide appropriate serviced sites adjoining or in these villages or small towns. Councils should recognise that rural villages or small towns are a resource that needs to be carefully managed to meet the needs of their local communities. At this stage there is a need to define the difference between rural-generated housing and urban-generated housing.

Urban-Generated Housing

This is housing in rural locations sought by people living and working in towns and cities. This would include second homes and holiday homes. There are difficulties with such housing. Some **coastal** and **lakeside areas** are experiencing development pressures from this kind of house construction. This process is driven by the increasing affluence of Irish people, the needs of the tourist industry and the increasing amount of leisure time available.

There is also the problem that overdevelopment of holiday homes leads to off-season ghost towns where houses lie unoccupied for most of the year.

Rural-Generated Housing

Rural-generated housing is defined as housing needed in rural areas in already established communities by people working in rural areas or in nearby urban areas. Rural housing is a contentious issue.

Some people like to live in the countryside because it is more peaceful than urban areas. They may like to live there close to their parents or families in the area where they grew up. They may also like to live in a house that they have designed to suit their own needs or desires.

It is also cheaper to build than to buy. Some people may wish to build on land that their family already owns. One-off housing, however, raises a number of issues, including:

● Groundwater pollution from domestic septic tanks.
● Increased traffic hazards due to new entrances.
● Inappropriate house design for the region.
● Removal of wildlife habitat, such as ditches.
● Social isolation away from and stretching of social services as people get older.
● More traffic on minor roads.
● An increase in unsustainable car transport that uses large quantities of energy/fuel.
● The problem of building to sell on.
● Spoiling village and town boundaries by creating urban development.

Many argue that while new rural housing developments may have economic disadvantages, these considerations are outweighed by the social advantages of rural environments, such as:

- The need for rural communities to be sustained by energetic young people who wish to live and raise families in a rural environment as their parents did.
- A rural environment is cleaner and healthier for young children.
- Rural communities generally have lower crime and substance abuse rates.
- Lower rates of urban sprawl as a consequence of rural development.

Some attitudes within local authorities have softened in response to political pressure. Planning permissions for one-off houses have increased in some areas. This is contrary to the aims of the National Development Plan. Public debate has helped soften the rigid views of some planning authorities, but the policies still enforced have some defects.

- House styles are inconsistent. Traditional two-storey houses may be granted permission in some areas, while refused just a kilometre away.
- House designs that are completely out of character for a site may be constructed, while 'suitable' designs for other localities are rejected.
- Section 4 planning permissions that allow county councillors to intercede on behalf of a planning applicant have allowed some applications to be granted that would otherwise be refused.
- The inconsistencies create the feeling among the public that planning in some local authorities is still corrupt.

Department of the Environment guidelines stress the need to ensure a clear dividing line between urban and rural land use to help prevent urban sprawl and maintain the rural landscape. Do you feel this has been created by present planning departments?

Environmental Impact Assessment (EIA)

Compulsory environmental impact assessment for major individual developments, such as new roadways, forestry that exceeds 70 hectares and the location of waste material disposal areas (dumps), is now an integral and valuable part of development planning and land use management procedures. In addition, with few exceptions, county councils and urban councils have the power to require EIAs for projects that do not reach acceptable levels of agreement or standards if the authority considers that a development would be likely to have significant effects on the environment.

Strategic Environment Assessment (SEA)

In addition to EIAs, SEAs examine in a general way the policies, plans and programmes of environmental impact assessment.

Activity
Explain the difference between EIAs and SEAs.

CHAPTER 53
URBAN HIERARCHY, HINTERLAND AND CENTRAL PLACE THEORY

The nature of central place services and the areas they serve have an important bearing on the arrangement of towns.

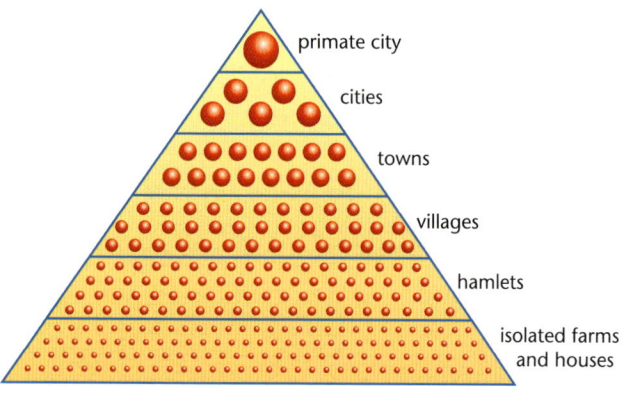

Fig. 53.1 The urban hierarchy of a country is arranged like a pyramid.

Cork city provides an ever-growing list of low- and medium-order services for its hinterland.

URBAN HIERARCHY

Urban settlements can be classified according to size, function and population density. They range in size from the smallest, called a **hamlet**, through **village**, small and large **towns**, to small and large **city**. The small places, such as hamlets and villages, provide for the everyday needs of their residents and those in their immediate vicinity (called hinterland). They have a very limited range of goods and services.

Towns have a larger range of services. Cities offer more sophisticated shopping and entertainment.

Centre	Services
City	**All low-order, medium-order and high-order services** Large industrial regions/estates, commercial downtown, department stores, regional hospital, private hospital, port, courthouse, financial institutions (e.g. banks), financial advisors, large jewellery stores, restaurants, fashion shops, dentists, universities.
Town	**Medium-order and all low-order services** Large supermarkets, car sales, hotel, jeweller, two or more banks, financial advisor, solicitors' offices, builders' providers, small industrial estate, small hospital, courthouse, dentist.
Village	**Many low-order services, one or more medium-order service** Grocery, supermarket, post office, garage(s), filling station, butcher, hair salon, café, bar(s), community hall, sports centre, school(s), doctor, chemist.
Hamlet	**Few low-order services** Post office, grocery store, bar, filling station.

Table 53.1

Central Place Theory

Central place theory is an attempt to explain the relationship between the **spacing** and the **size** of settlements. However, the idea is based on a flat plain with equal transport in every area and no competition between settlements or shops.

Three Basic Concepts of Central Place Theory

Range of Goods

There are low-, middle- and high-order goods and services.

- **Low-order** goods are those that are required frequently, such as bread, milk, newspapers and petrol. Customers are not prepared to travel very far to obtain these goods.
- **Middle-order** goods and services, such as large supermarkets, doctors' surgeries and chemists, do not exist in every hamlet or village since they are required less often. A customer is prepared to travel further for these services than for low-order goods.
- **High-order** goods are items or services such as furniture, jewellery, law offices, universities and dentists. These goods and services have a high value and are required only occasionally, so customers are willing to travel further for these goods and services than for either low- or middle-order goods and services.

Frequency of Demand

This refers to the level of demand for goods and services, i.e. whether they are required daily, weekly, monthly or yearly. Normally the frequency of demand declines from low- through medium- to high-order goods and services.

Threshold

Each shop or service has its own market area, and a certain **minimum population** or **threshold** population is required before it becomes a **viable** financial proposition. A low-order good has a very low threshold population due to its high frequency of demand, while a high-order good has a high threshold population due to its low frequency of demand. It has been suggested that in the United Kingdom, about 300 people are necessary for the success of a village shop; 500 for a primary school; 2,500 for a doctor; 25,000 for a shoe shop; 50,000 for a small department store; 60,000 for a large supermarket; 100,000 for a large department store; and over 1 million for a university. Services locate where they can maximise the distance from their nearest rival. Such analysis is used by planners for the creation of new towns.

Conurbation

A **conurbation** is an urban area larger than a city. It forms when two cities expand towards each other to create a large urban environment. When two or more conurbations expand and meet, they form a megalopolis. Los Angeles is a megalopolis, as it is an urban environment formed by the joining of many conurbations. Another megalopolis is in north-east USA where cities from Boston to Washington, DC create a very extensive urban environment.

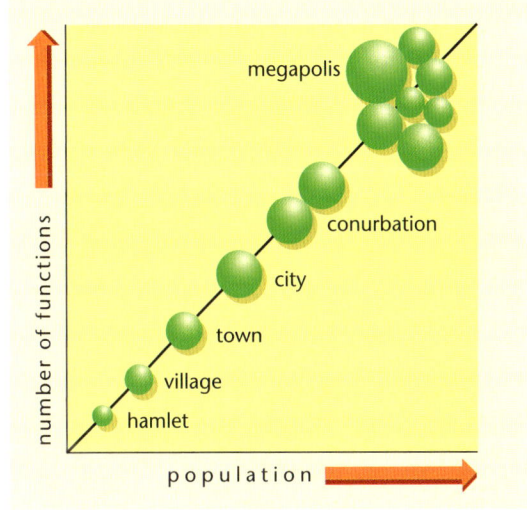

Fig. 53.2 As a settlement's size increases, so does its population and range of services and functions.

- *Are these products low-, medium- or high-order goods?*

355

Trade Area or Hinterland

The idea of the area around a town being linked economically and socially to the urban centre (city, town, village or hamlet) is fundamental to central place theory. The area served by a central place (settlement, e.g. city or town) may be called its trade area, but other names may be used, such as **hinterland**, market area or service area. One simple way to define a hinterland would be to ask shopkeepers and other businesses where their customers come from. Plotting these locations on a local map would then define the limits of the village's influence, i.e. its hinterland or its trade area.

Central place theory describes hinterlands as circular in shape and equal in size, but the real situation is not as simple as this. Hinterlands may resemble a circular form, but they are regularly distorted because of the physical landscape. Barriers, such as mountain ranges, unbridged rivers, the coast or a large lake, may cause distortion. Political boundaries may have the same effect. Alternatively, a good, **well-surfaced**, **wide roadway** may cause a hinterland to increase lengthways in that direction. This is because people can reach the town quicker and more easily than another settlement that may be closer to their home. Also, the road may connect with another nearby town and so add it to its hinterland.

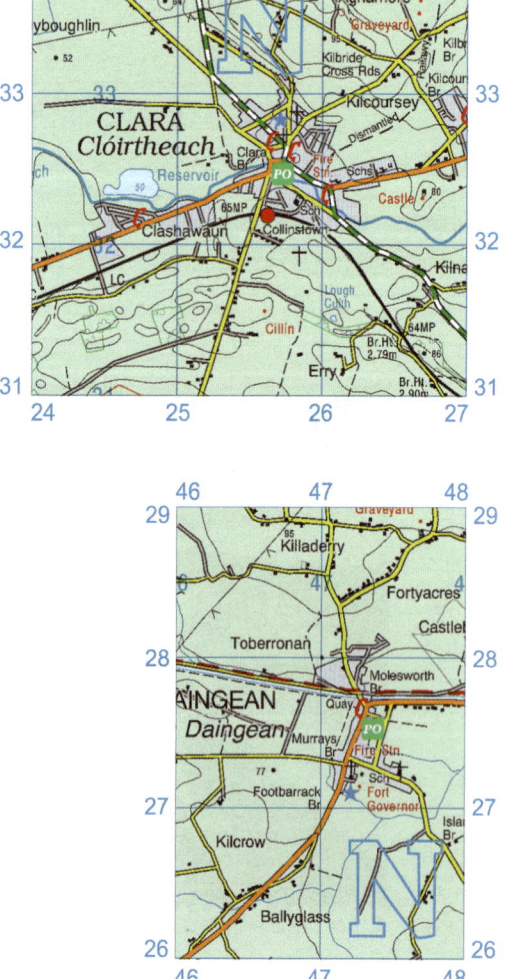

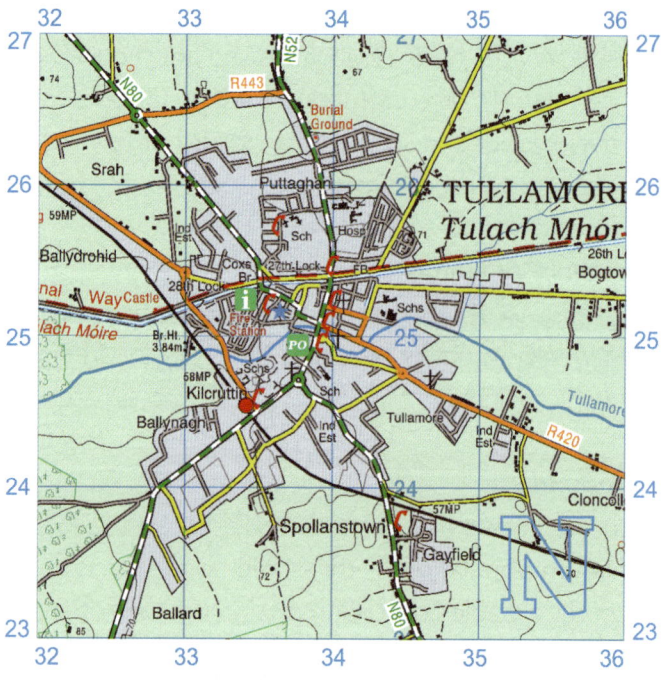

Activity

Study the three urban centres on the map extracts above.

1. List each in rank order.
2. Justify this rank order based on evidence from each map extract.

The size of a **hinterland** is **partly dependent** on the size and functions of its central place, i.e. settlement, village or town. For example, a seaside resort is likely to be smaller than a market town of similar population. This is because the functions of a successful market town are generally far greater than those of a seaside resort. Hinterland size is also affected by **population density**. Larger hinterlands are likely in areas of low population, and people are willing to travel (or have to travel) longer distances for their low-order services. Shops, on the other hand, need to draw people from a long distance in such areas to reach their threshold to survive economically. In recent years An Post attempted to close many of its rural post offices because they were not 'viable economic units'. In other words, they were not able to pay for themselves, but due to political pressure they remained open. In recent years small rural villages have lost many of their services because rural depopulation has forced schools, garda stations, Protestant churches, grocery shops and many more services and functions to close.

A city will have many surrounding towns, villages and townlands as part of its hinterland.

Changes in Population Size and Number of Functions

Over the last fifty years there has been a decrease in the number of services available in small settlements and an increase in the number of functions provided by large settlements. This may be due to many factors, for example:

- Small villages are no longer able to support their former functions (village shop) as the greater wealth and mobility (car ownership) of some rural populations enable them to travel further to larger centres where they can obtain, in a single visit, both high- and low-order goods.
- Domestic changes (deep freezers, convenience foods) mean that rural householders no longer need to make use of daily, low-order services previously available in their village.
- As larger settlements attract an increasingly larger threshold population, they can increase their variety and number of functions and, by reducing costs (supermarkets), are likely to attract even more customers.
- In areas experiencing rural depopulation, villages may no longer have a population large enough to maintain existing services.

Activity: Proposed Fieldwork
Why not use central place theory to identify the hinterland of your town or village?
- Locate a map of your local area that includes all surrounding villages.
- Identify the various services and functions of your settlement.
- Create a questionnaire that will identify the distances people are willing to travel for those services and functions.
- Plot these distances and directions on your local map to identify the hinterland.

Central Place Concepts

The three concepts of **range of goods**, **frequency of demand** and **threshold** control the size and spacing of central places. In theory, the maximum hinterland on a featureless plain will be a circle. But this would leave areas between adjoining circles unserved by a central place. To avoid this, a pattern of **hexagonals** is drawn to represent the hinterlands of local settlements. This pattern allows the maximum area to be served, minimises travelling distance for the consumers and maximises the number of retail outlets possible.

Fig. 53.3

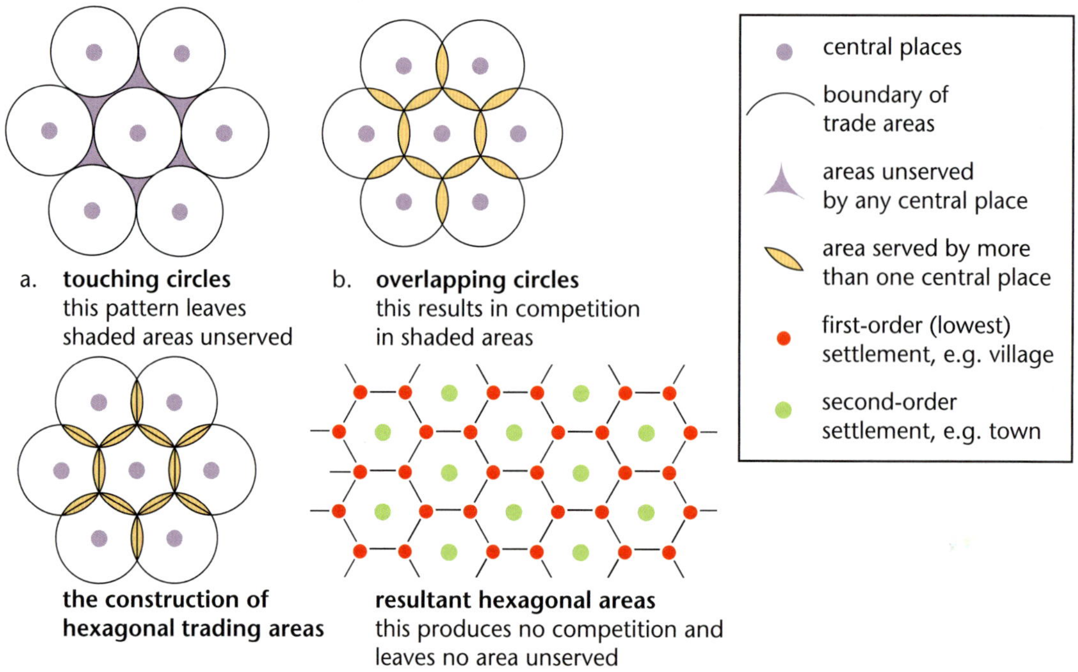

a. **touching circles**
this pattern leaves shaded areas unserved

b. **overlapping circles**
this results in competition in shaded areas

the construction of hexagonal trading areas

resultant hexagonal areas
this produces no competition and leaves no area unserved

Legend:
- central places
- boundary of trade areas
- areas unserved by any central place
- area served by more than one central place
- first-order (lowest) settlement, e.g. village
- second-order settlement, e.g. town

Criticisms of Central Place Theory

- Plains are not featureless or without factors of relief or drainage. Rivers and hills do upset roads.
- Modern transport systems reduce the costs of travel over certain distances, thus favouring some centres. These include motorways, tunnels, ferries and railways.
- Population distribution is rarely even and is influenced by transport routes and the location of resources.
- Modern settlements offer a wide range of goods and services, each with its own market. Settlements also compete with each others' neighbouring hinterlands.
- People do not always act rationally. People have preferences in relation to shopping areas. Similarly, traders do not always act on the basis of population statistics when setting up a shop or business.
- Like other models, central place theory is meant as a simplification of reality to help understand the spacing of settlements. It is not meant to be exact. It is useful in regional planning and in market analysis of the trade areas of different shops and their profitability.

Activity

Study the Ordnance Survey map of Thurles on the opposite page.

1. Identify the largest settlement on this map and state what category of settlement it is; for example, is it a city, a town, a village or another type of settlement?
2. Identify other settlements on the map and state their category/categories.
3. List these settlements in terms of their size (called rank size) and in order (called rank order), beginning with the largest.
4. Which of these settlements has the smallest hinterland (trade area) and which has the largest? Explain your answers using evidence from the map.
5. Which of these settlements would offer low-order services and functions only? Explain fully.
6. Which of these settlements would offer low-order and middle-order services? Explain fully.
7. At home, write out why Thurles is a successful urban centre. In your answer, use the concepts that you have learned in this chapter to explain your answer. To help you with the exercise, use the following headings: relief and drainage; population density; transport; hinterland (trade area); and services and functions.

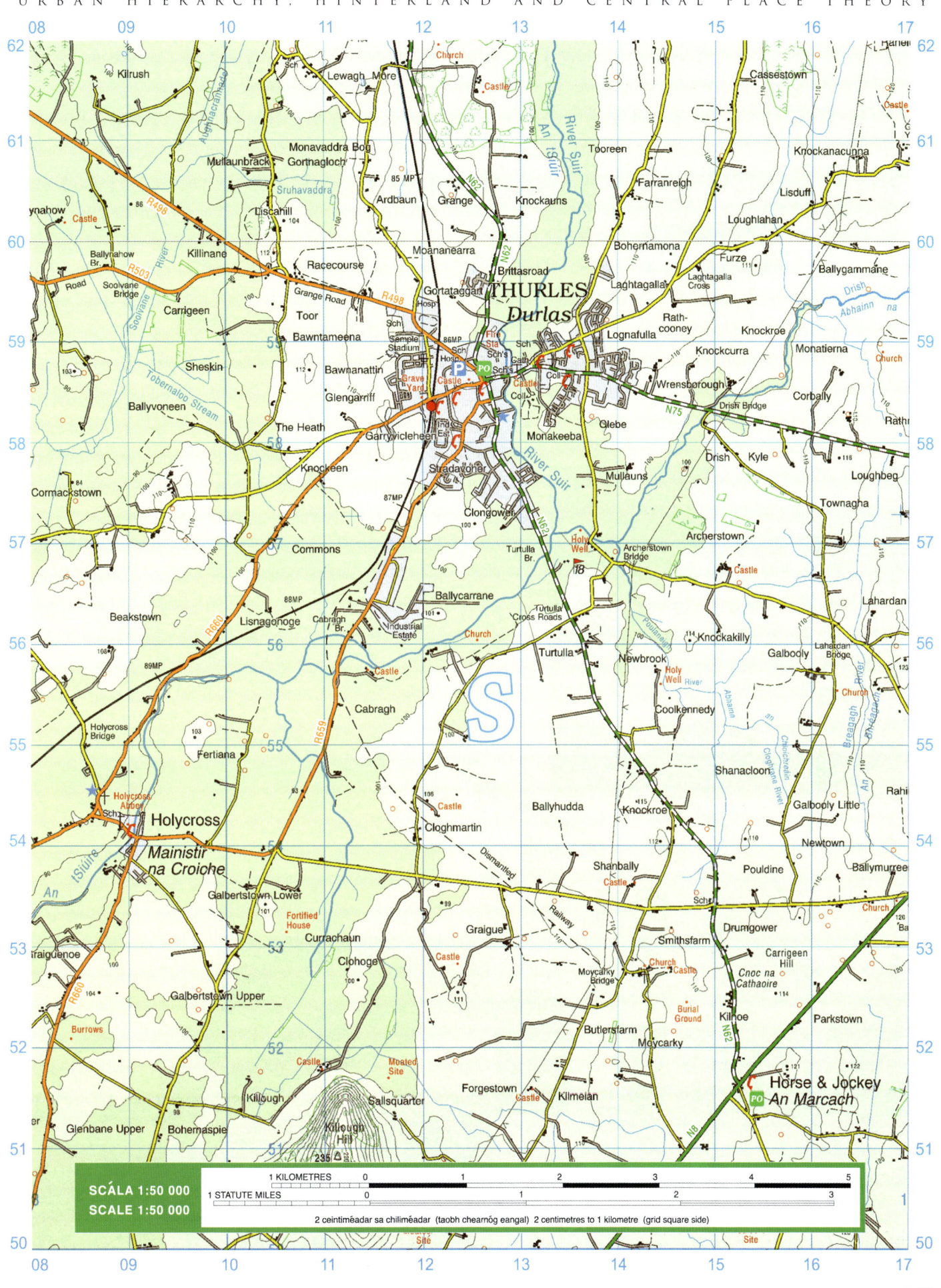

CHAPTER 54
THE FUNCTIONS AND SERVICES OF SETTLEMENTS CHANGE OVER TIME

KEY IDEA! Cities, towns and villages are dynamic. They are and need to be in a constant state of change in order to survive and prosper. Over time, the original functions may be overshadowed by newer functions.

Settlements, and especially cities and towns, never remain static; they are constantly changing their shape, size, plan, architecture and function. This becomes evident if you visit a settlement over several years. The amount of change and the kind of change vary, of course, between one settlement and another, but in time all undergo change of some sort. For example, the functions of Limerick have changed over time.

Limerick city was once an important defensive settlement and the lowest bridging point on the River Shannon. It was originally founded by the Vikings and later captured by the Normans in the twelfth century and by the English in 1691 after a long siege. Today it is a university city, a major industrial centre, a religious centre, a commercial centre and a market town.

Activity
Study the Ordnance Survey map of Thurles on page 359, then explain the historical change in its functions over time. Use evidence from the map to support your answer.

Activity
Identify the past or present functions of the buildings or structures shown in these photographs.

360

Case Study: Caher in Co. Tipperary – A Market Town

Caher originally had a defence function. The word 'caher' suggests the town began as a stone fort in Celtic times. In Norman times it developed into a large town that included such buildings as an abbey, a mill and a castle. The castle was built on an island in the River Suir. Later and over time, other functions were added that increased the prosperity of the town and helped it survive and develop into the busy town that it is today.

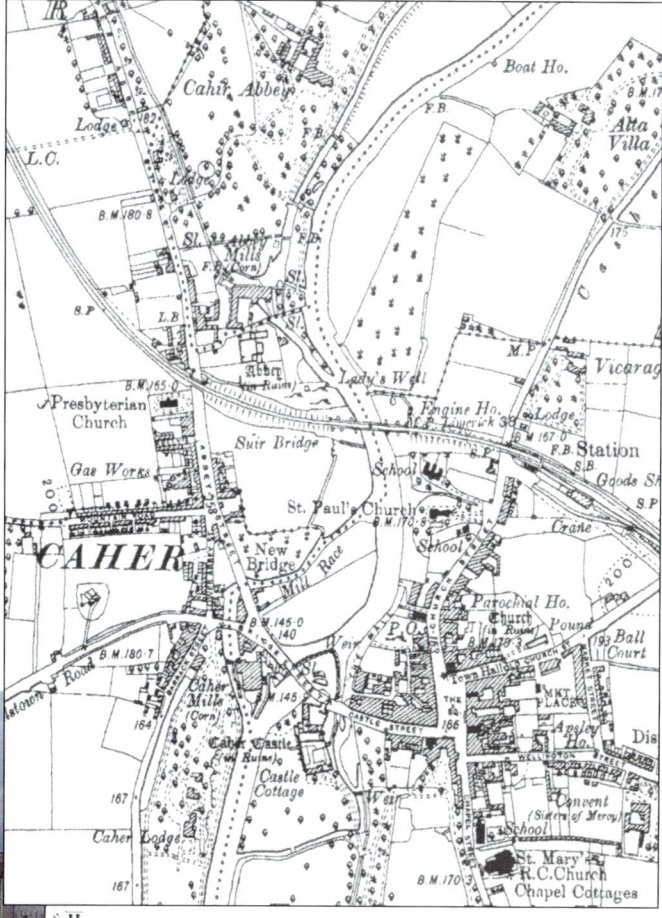

1905 edition of Ordnance Survey map of Caher.

Caher in Co. Tipperary is a busy market town.

The original functions of some settlements may no longer be active, but many towns still offer some old functions, such as a market function or port function.

Change over time could form the basis of a good field study: old town/new town.

Activity

1. Examine the map and the photograph on this page, then identify how the services and functions of Caher have changed over time.
2. List the functions that Caher still offers since its foundation in Celtic times.

CHAPTER 55
CHANGING URBAN LAND USE PATTERNS

KEY IDEA! Cities display an ever-changing land use pattern.

Activity

Study the land use map of Galway city.

1. Identify the land use of the area coloured dark blue.
2. Identify some city centre activities in this zone.
3. Which land uses in particular will preserve the city centre as the dominant commercial area of the city?

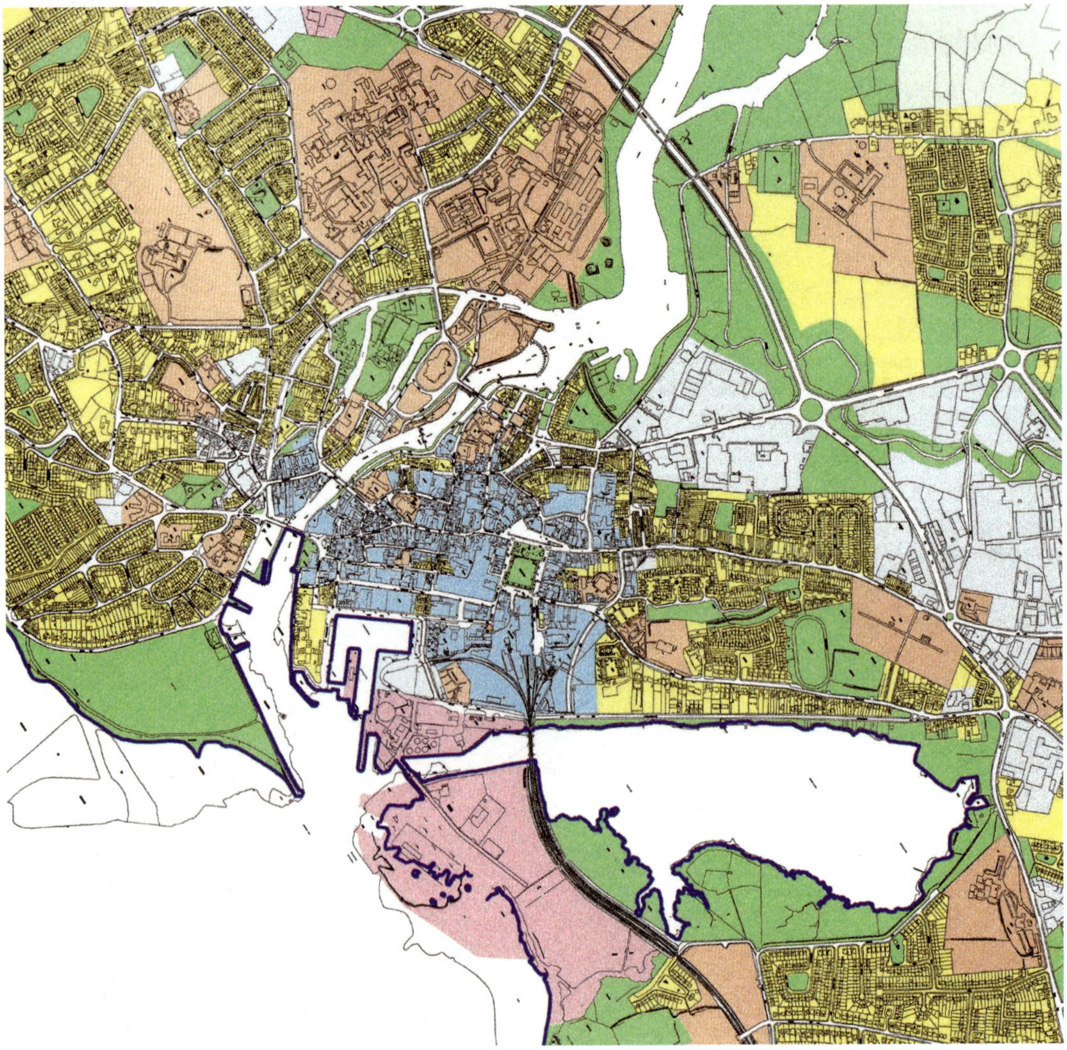

Zoning objective

- To protect residential amenities and to provide for limited associated uses
- To protect residential amenities and to provide for low-density residential development
- To provide for institutional and community facility use
- To provide for city centre activities, particularly those which preserve the city centre as the dominant commercial area of the city
- To provide for light industry and commercial uses other than those reserved in CC zone
- To provide for industrial and related uses
- To provide for recreational and amenity uses
- To provide for the development of agriculture and protect areas of visual importance and/or areas of high amenity
- To provide for the development of agriculture and to protect rural character.

MODERN CITIES OF THE DEVELOPED WORLD

The creation of different land use zones is essential in the planning and development of modern cities.

Case Study: Land Use Zones in Galway City

Fig. 55.1 Land use map of Galway city.

LAND USE ZONES

Over time, cities have grown in size and population. Their edges are extending out into rural areas far from their oldest parts where they originally began. During their existence, the patterns in land use of these settlements have changed over time. These patterns may show differences and similarities in land use or social groupings (high- and low-income areas) within a city. They reflect how various cities have grown economically and socially (culturally) in response to changing conditions over many centuries. American geographers and sociologists have proposed models in an attempt to explain how this has happened. However, their theories did not include how European or other world cities developed.

The Concentric Zone Theory by Burgess

Burgess made some assumptions as a basis for his theory in 1924. These were:

- The oldest buildings were in or close to the city centre.
- Buildings became progressively newer towards the city boundary.
- Cities contained a variety of well-defined ethnic and income-level residential areas.
- The poorer groups had to live close to the city centre and places of work, as they could not afford transport or expensive housing.
- There were no areas of heavy industry.

Burgess's Model: Concentric Circles

- The oldest part is now the **central business district** (CBD). It contains the major shops and offices. It is the centre for commerce and entertainment, and the focus for transport routes. Today, some very old buildings may exist but have been renovated and their land use changed as part of urban renewal schemes.

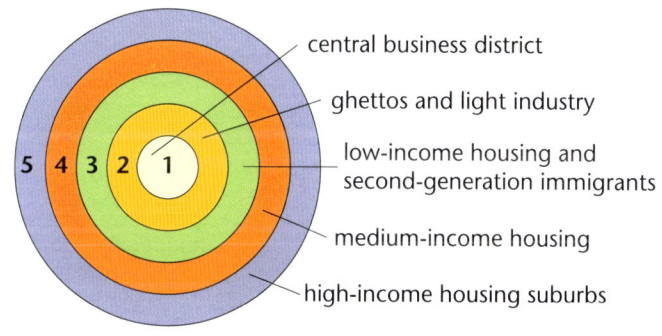

central business district

ghettos and light industry

low-income housing and second-generation immigrants

medium-income housing

high-income housing suburbs

Fig. 55.2 The concentric zone theory – Burgess Theory (1924).

- The **transition zone** is where the oldest **housing** is either **deteriorating** into **slum** or being invaded by light industry. The inhabitants tend to belong to ghetto communities of **poorer social groups** and first-generation immigrants.
- Zone 3 includes areas of **low-income housing** that are occupied by those who have slightly improved their position financially and moved from zone 2. Other residents include second-generation immigrants who work in nearby factories to reduce transport costs. This zone still holds true of American cities that experience high rates of immigration (see **Invasion and Succession**, page 377).
- **Medium-income housing** of good quality. This includes private terraced and semi-detached houses and council estates. Most of these would belong to the period 1918–39 (inter-war years).
- **High-income housing** occupied by people who can afford the expensive properties and the high cost of commuting. This zone includes some villages close to the city boundary.

363

Today's Criticism of Burgess

- Zones are never as clear-cut as shown on the model.
- This model was based on Chicago in the 1920s. Urban development has changed greatly since them.
- North American cities received many African-American immigrants from the southern states at that time, which created ghetto communities. The wealth of white communities tended to increase relative to the length of time they had lived in the city.
- New shopping centres, industrial estates and business parks did not exist at that time.

The Sector Theory by Hoyt

In 1939, Hoyt made similar assumptions to Burgess, with a few additional ones:

- **Wealthy people,** who could afford the highest rates, chose the best sites. Competition based on 'ability to pay' resolved land use conflicts.
- Wealthy residents could afford **private cars** or **public transport** and so lived **further from industry** and closer to main roads.
- **Similar land uses** attracted other similar land uses. This created a concentration of like functions that repelled others. This created the concept of **sector development**.

Hoyt's Model – Sectors/Wedges

- The sector theory suggests that **land uses** near the central business district **grew outwards as sectors** or wedges along main routes.
- The low-income housing of Burgess should be called oldest housing and not based on social issues.
- As **land uses attract similar land uses**, it concentrates a function in a particular area that repels other functions. This land use will form a wedge shape over time as the city expands.
- This suggests that if an area in the nineteenth century was one of low-income housing, then a wedge of low-income housing would develop at that side of the city over time. If another area had light industry, then a wedge of industry would develop a similar wedge or sector.

Today's Criticisms of Hoyt

- Zones are never as clear-cut as shown on the model.
- Each zone generally contains more than one land use or function.
- No consideration of European cities was included.
- Renovation and renewal schemes are not included.

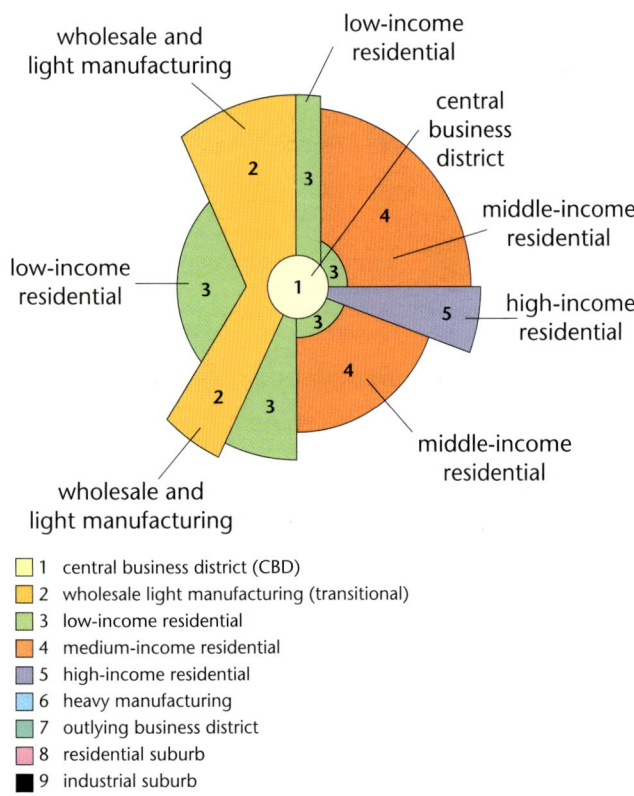

1 central business district (CBD)
2 wholesale light manufacturing (transitional)
3 low-income residential
4 medium-income residential
5 high-income residential
6 heavy manufacturing
7 outlying business district
8 residential suburb
9 industrial suburb

Fig. 55.3 Hoyt's sector theory.

The Multiple Nuclei Theory by Ullman and Harris (1945)

Basic Assumptions

- Modern cities have a more **complex structure** than that suggested by Burgess or Hoyt.

- Cities do not grow from one CBD, but from several independent centres.

- Each nucleus acts as a growth point and probably has a function different from other nuclei in that city; it may be financial, medical, retail or administrative.

- Growth occurs outward from each nucleus until they all merge into one large urban region.

The Relevance of the Models to Modern Cities

- No two cities are alike, and some aspects of each of the models may have relevance to every city.

- Inner city low-income communities do exist close to the CBD, but so do high-income residential areas.

- Urban renewal schemes have demolished or renovated old buildings. The central business districts of some cities, e.g. Limerick, have many newly constructed city blocks.

- Modern cities have expanded dramatically. Suburban housing estates, business parks, industrial estates and shopping centres create urban sprawl.

- Shopping centres and regional hospitals have formed **growth centres**, as suggested by Ullman and Harris, around which large residential and other compatible land uses have developed. Dublin, Galway, Limerick and Cork have developed in this way since the 1960s.

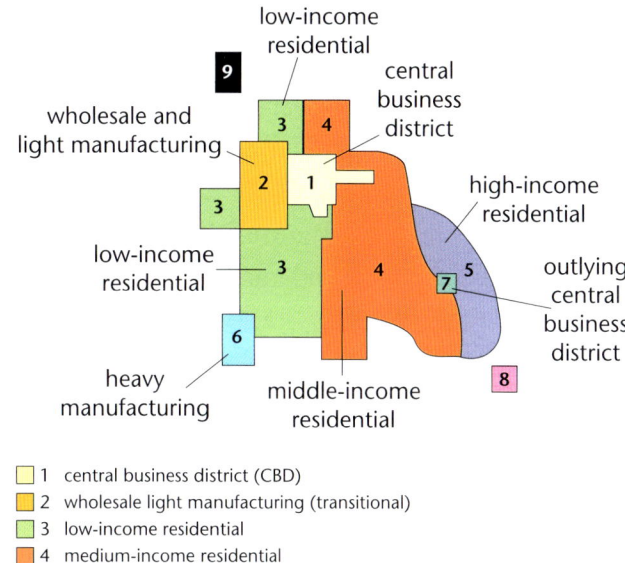

1 central business district (CBD)
2 wholesale light manufacturing (transitional)
3 low-income residential
4 medium-income residential
5 high-income residential
6 heavy manufacturing
7 outlying business district
8 residential suburb
9 industrial suburb

Fig 55.4 The multiple nuclei theory.

LAND VALUES

Models of urban land values are based on the assumption that in a free market the highest bidder will obtain the use of the land. The **highest bidder** is likely to be the one who can **obtain the maximum profit** from that site and so can pay the highest rent.

The **most expensive**, or 'prime', sites in most cities are in the CBD, mainly because space is scarce and there is also easy access. High prices can be offset by building upwards. This increases floor area and makes more intensive use of land.

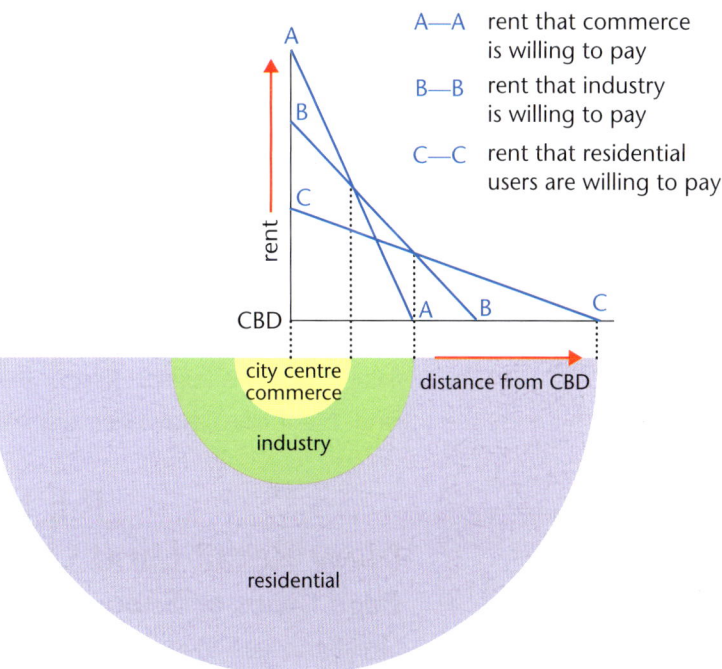

A—A rent that commerce is willing to pay

B—B rent that industry is willing to pay

C—C rent that residential users are willing to pay

Fig. 55.5 The cost of sites and rent decreases with distance from the centre.

365

Department stores, such as Brown Thomas and Marks & Spencer, can afford to pay premium prices due to their large customer base. Offices also compete for these expensive properties.

Central Business District (CBD)

The CBD is the heart of the city. It is a city's main commercial, financial, administrative and transport centre. Some of its characteristics are:

- It has the highest land values in the city.
- It contains the major department stores and specialist shops.
- It is constantly undergoing structural change to keep shops and offices at the highest modern standards.
- It contains the tallest buildings in the city.
- It has the greatest concentration of pedestrians and shoppers, e.g. Grafton Street in Dublin.
- It is the focus of all major routes.

Fig. 55.6

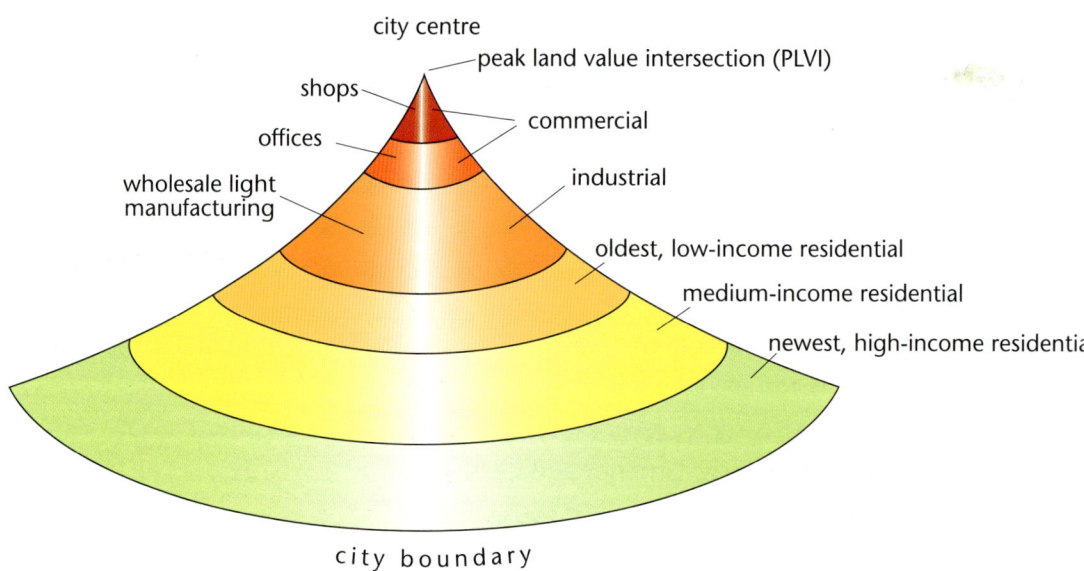

Activity
1. Which is the oldest part of most cities?
2. Which is the youngest part?
3. Why do most people prefer to do their Christmas shopping in the CBD?
4. What other shopping areas are attractive for shopping?

Land values drop substantially with distance from the CBD. This is because land use, such as industry, needs more space and uses it less intensively. Residential land, the flattest curve, is located further from the city centre where there is less competition for land. Most cities, however, display some aspects of each theory.

RETAIL LAND USE

New Retail Land Use Centres

Edge Cities or Suburban Downtowns

Great changes have occurred in the shopping behaviour of customers and the location and character of the shopping environment. In Britain, the USA and other industrialised countries of the developed world, new edge cities are developing as a consequence of out-of-town shopping centres. These shopping centres are developing on **cheaper land**

● *Identify the various land uses visible on this photograph of Galway city.*

The desire for accessibility to customers affects the spacing and siting of shopping centres and shops. The spacing of these centres corresponds to the influence of central place theory, range and threshold (see page 355). In **small towns**, the **central area** is the only shopping district. Next are the **regional shopping centres that serve large parts of the suburbs and their hinterlands**. Some cater for low-income groups, while other centres cater for middle- and higher-income shoppers.

beyond the edge of existing cities. There are two types: those that include food outlets and those that comprise only non-food outlets. **Their aim is to capture wealthy mobile customers**, and sites near major motorway interchanges (where motorways meet) are chosen for their development. Some of these out-of-town developments have **attracted offices, hotels, numerous department stores, industrial parks, entertainment facilities such as sports stadiums, and vast parking for up to 90,000 cars** with additional space for hundreds of buses. Some are becoming so large that they are termed **suburban downtowns** or **edge cities**. One example is Tyson's Corner in Virginia, USA.

Out-of-town shopping centres often form the hub of new edge cities. This is a view of Tyson's Corner in Virginia, USA, an edge city.

Fig. 55.7

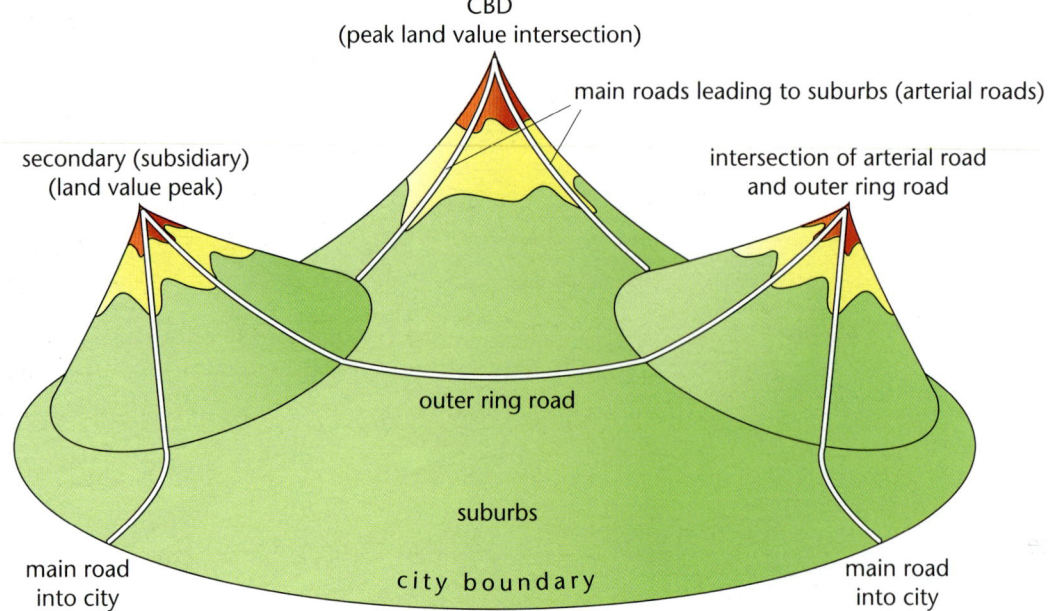

The creation of a multi-centred urban model reduces potential traffic from the central city area. It also creates separate, distinct, economic, social and politically independent urban districts.

In Britain in 2000, up to 40 per cent of retail sales were from out-of-town locations, compared with 5 per cent in 1980. In some areas planners are considering a change of attitude for new developments that are likely to make a serious impact on the vitality of the CBDs of the nearby cities or towns.

As these suburban downtowns flourish, they attract tens of thousands of local residents who organise their lives around them. They offer workplaces, shopping, leisure activities and all other elements of a complete urban environment. The traditional **CBD is becoming less important** for goods and services. It increasingly serves the less affluent residents of inner city areas and those working downtown in offices and factories. The rise of these outer cities, suburban downtowns or edge cities has produced a new multi-centred urban land use zoning pattern. This consists of the traditional CBD, as well as a set of increasingly equally important suburban downtowns, with each servicing a different and self-sufficient surrounding hinterland.

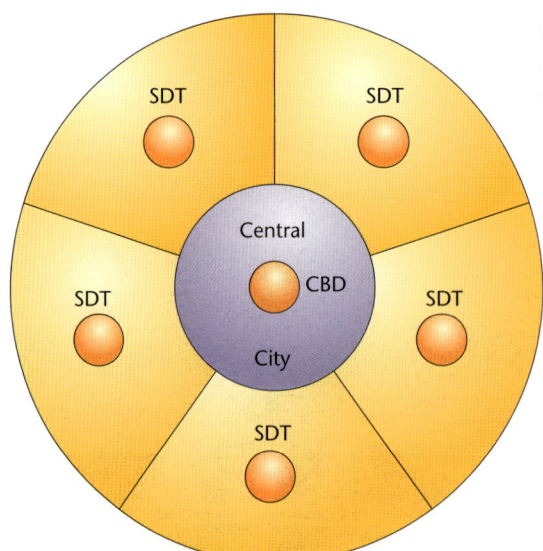

Fig. 55.8 The ideal form of a multi-centred urban region model.

Suburban shopping centres in Ireland offer many attractions for shoppers. List the advantages of suburban shopping centres. List the disadvantages of shopping in CBD areas.

Activity
1. What are edge cities or suburban downtowns?
2. Are there any suburban downtowns in Ireland? Explain.
3. Explain the advantages of the urban model, Fig. 55.8. Use the following headings to develop your answer: (a) traffic flow (b) shopping pattern, (c) employment centres.

Case Study: Tokyo City

Tokyo developed around the castle of the Edo-era shoguns, near the present Imperial Palace. Later, religious, cultural and financial districts developed to the north and east. Over many centuries the mainly wooden-built city was destroyed many times by earthquakes and by bombing in World War II. Because of this, old land use zones were lost when the city was rebuilt. The modern city has no single CBD. Instead it has many individual centres, each with its own specialised land use, such as government offices, finance, shopping, entertainment, transport and education. Most of these land use areas are linked by a network of railways that form a circle within the city.

INDUSTRIAL ZONES

There has been considerable movement in the location of industry in urban areas over time. Industry in the early nineteenth century was located in what are now parts of the inner city.

Since the 1950s many of these inner city zones have suffered from industrial decline due to the closure of some factories and the movement of others to edge-of-city sites, such as Long Mile Road and Park West in Dublin. Entire communities in many industrial cities of the English Midlands were supported by coal mining. When these collieries closed, new enterprise zones (EZs) were created in inner city regions, where new small industries could operate successfully.

Manufacturing industry that relies on **bulk transport**, such as large ships, for the movement of bulky raw materials or finished products is attracted to **port areas within coastal cities** and towns. Deep-water facilities such as at Ringaskiddy in Cork Harbour encourage industry to cluster around these areas. Such industries include chemicals, oil refining, heavy metal and engineering, power stations and fish processing.

Industrial Estates

From the 1960s new industrial estates were developed for the specialised use of light industries. They located in suburban regions, on national primary or national secondary routes.

Most **modern industry** is 'light', footloose and clean when compared to older, heavy industry. Such modern industry is located in industrial estates close to present city boundaries.

Business Parks

Warehousing estates, business and science parks are generally located on large areas of less expensive land with new buildings and modern technology, and with access to ring roads and motorways.

Tokyo is a modern multi-centred urban region.

New business parks encourage some industries and services to locate in suburban areas.

● *Identify the dominant land use in this photo.*

369

MODERN CITIES OF THE DEVELOPING WORLD

The cities of the developing world have varied origins. They have a different structure from those of the developed world. There are some similarities between these developing world cities. Their rapid expansion since 1950 has created sprawling expanses of shanty dwellings that extend from 40–100 km from their CBD.

Functional Zones in Third World Cities

● **The CBD** is similar, with offices and shops, and competition for space is even greater than in developed world cities.

● **Inner zone:** During colonial times, the wealthy landowners and merchants built large mansions around the CBD. The quality of some of these may have deteriorated, but the well-off continue to live in these homes or in new modern high-rise apartments in this inner zone close to the CBD.

● **Middle zone** consists of poorer-quality housing. Many are self-built homes that are gradually improved over time. Some basic services such as running water, sewage systems and electricity may have been provided by local authorities.

● **Outer zone** is the reverse of developed cities. The quality of homes deteriorates with distance from the city centre. This is where migrants from rural regions live in shanties, or *bustees,* that lack basic services.

● **Industry** has either been planned or has grown spontaneously along main roads that lead out of the city.

Fig. 55.9

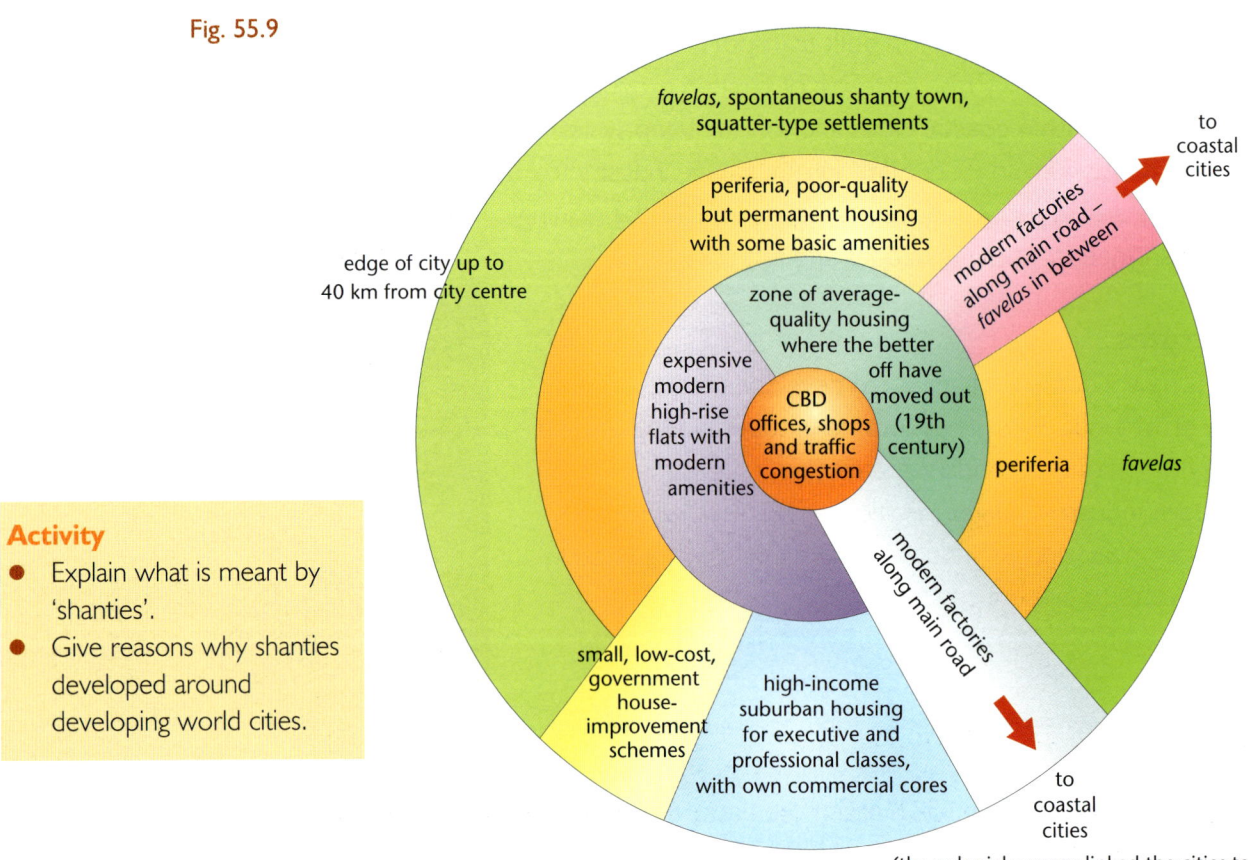

Activity
● Explain what is meant by 'shanties'.
● Give reasons why shanties developed around developing world cities.

Shanty housing and industry develop along routeways from Nairobi in Kenya.

Multi-part Questions

1. **A.** Draw a sketch map of Carlow town centre on page 383. On it, mark and name:
   i. the main street pattern
   ii. five different land use zones. [20 marks]

   B. Different activities compete for space in urban areas. As a result, different land use zones develop. Referring to examples you have studied, examine how these land use zones change as urban centres grow. [30 marks]

   C. Explain the basis of urban hierarchy and hinterland. [30 marks]

2. **A.** Draw a sketch map of the photograph on page 277. On it, mark and identify:
   i. the street pattern
   ii. four different land use zones. [20 marks]

   B. Describe one theoretical model that attempts to explain the development of land use zones in a developed world city. [30 marks]

   C. Explain how county and national development strategic plans influence planning strategies in rural areas. [30 marks]

3. **A.** Draw a sketch map of the Thurles region on page 359 to half-scale. On it, mark and name:
   i. the urban region of Thurles
   ii. one national secondary route
   iii. two regional routes
   iv. a lake region
   v. one major river. [20 marks]

   B. Explain the concept of central place theory. [30 marks]

   C. Describe one theoretical model that attempts to explain the development of land use zones in a developing world city. [30 marks]

CHAPTER 56
THE EXPANSION OF CITIES AND PRESSURE ON RURAL LAND USE

KEY IDEA!

As cities expand, green belts within cities or rural environments on the edge of cities come under increasing pressure to change their use.

Parks, no matter how small, offer recreational areas within cities.

Urban expansion is a worldwide problem. Some regions, such as the United States, display such urban expansion that the term **megalopolis** has been applied to the way cities cluster to form vast urban environments.

Today, with 71 per cent of its population living in towns and cities, Europe ranks among the world's most highly urbanised areas. This is especially true in northern and western Europe, where 84 and 79 per cent of the population, respectively, live in urban areas. This percentage rises even higher in certain places: in Belgium, 97 per cent; in the United Kingdom, 90 per cent.

GREEN BELTS AND NATURAL AREAS WITHIN CITIES

Green belts are open spaces of agricultural land, parks or areas of woodland within large towns and cities. They are specifically designed to break up the monotony of urban development such as housing estates and industrial zones. They are designed by urban planners and become permanent features when legislated by local government.

Green belts in urban areas have many purposes:
- They prevent continuous development in large towns and cities, which improves the quality of urban environments.
- They provide sports fields, areas for leisure walks, runs and golf courses.
- Urban recreation areas such as Central Park in New York City and St Stephen's Green in Dublin provide a welcome relief from an office environment at lunch hour and a pleasant place for local residents.

As cities and conurbations grow, more and more pressure is put on existing green belts and farmland for urban expansion.

Large cities such as London continue to expand at the expense of the countryside. There are plans for twenty new towns for the Greater London Area. This proposal is facing opposition from environmentalists, who argue that this kind of development will counteract urban renewal schemes within the city and have a severe impact on existing green belt areas.

Sustainable Development

Urban development should include the **maintenance of natural areas** and the protection of their wildlife populations so that people can have **contact with nature close to their homes**.

Experience shows that vandalism and damage are greatly reduced where there is **a sense of involvement in a local project** and when **local people** feel they have a stake in an urban green space. Such issues might include rezoning, access and visitor pressure in regions of high population densities. Management must combine **ecological awareness** with **understanding of the needs of the urban population**.

The use of small parks and decorative trees help to create a more appealing environment for urban dwellers.

Children who have been exposed to natural areas are more inclined to be better aware of the advantages of keeping close to nature and being responsible citizens.

Water as a resource has many people-friendly uses in an urban environment.

Green belts may be used for many recreational activities, such as cycling, jogging or walking.

373

Traditional Landscapes

Hedgerows and Wildlife

The desire for individual family homes in suburban areas has increased the demand for housing at city fringes. This leads to the clearance of hedgerows and unique wetlands that host varied flora and fauna populations. The loss of this heritage close to cities:

- Alienates urban children from contact with nature.
- Weakens wildlife populations or loses them forever.
- Replaces local rural place names with urban ones.

Activity: Brainstorming Session
1. Study the photographs in this chapter, then discuss the advantages of green spaces like those in the photographs in urban areas. Refer to two aspects and in each case give a well-developed explanation.
2. Identify two types of land use development that cause Irish cities to expand into the countryside.

CHAPTER 57
RESIDENTIAL AREAS AND SEGREGATION WITHIN CITIES

KEY IDEA!

People with different incomes, cultural or racial backgrounds tend to cluster in separate parts of a city.

Residential land use occupies between 72 and 80 per cent of most cities and towns. The characteristics of citizens and the areas where they live vary greatly between different parts of the city. Dwellings differ according to their age, arrangement, style, building material, condition and size. They may be classed, however, into two groups: single family homes and multi-family homes.

Single family homes range from scraps of metal and wood in shanty towns to small nineteenth-century terraced redbrick houses in inner city areas to luxury villas set in large gardens in wealthy residential districts.

Multi-family homes include three- or four-storey tenements housing two or three families and modern high-rise apartment blocks accommodating hundreds of families. These are most often found in inner city areas. The principal factors for choosing a home include the type of house, price, location and neighbourhood environment.

● *Does this dwelling belong to a low-, middle- or high-income family?*

Many old neighbourhoods have been refurbished and are thriving residential areas once again.

Some housing estates built in the 1970s are poorly maintained. Burnt-out cars are a common sight in some low-income estates.

SOCIAL STRATIFICATION

The factors that influence the choice and purchase of individual homes lead to the segregation of people into separate areas of a city. A particular location and environment in a city will attract a certain type of dwelling and a certain income group. For example, local authorities provide subsidised housing for the poorer section of the population. Some developments may be for those with large families, and others for older citizens. Such local government developments may contribute to segregation because of the high density of homes in some estates, such as South Hill and Moyross in Limerick.

Other multi-storey council flats in Dublin's inner city have created zones of low-income residents, many of whom are long-term unemployed people. These neighbourhoods contrast greatly with wealthier areas of Dublin, such as around Ballsbridge and Donnybrook in Dublin 4.

Dublin City Council has housed many low-income families in inner city apartment blocks.

High-quality, high-cost housing forms distinct zones in parts of Dublin's urban area.

Some residential groups interact with developers and planners to produce areas with compatible neighbours with whom they have most in common. They may act to exclude some people and land uses from their neighbourhoods in order to preserve the 'atmosphere' of their area and the value of their property. This discrimination has been highlighted in some Irish cities and towns in relation to the settling in housing estates of some people from the Travelling community.

Ghettos

A ghetto is a section of a city settled by a minority racial, religious or national group. The majority of the inhabitants have particular socio-economic characteristics that distinguish them from the urban population as a whole. The term '**ghetto**' was originally used for the areas in European cities where Jews settled or were forced to live. Today, the term is applied to slum areas where black people and other **minority groups**, such as Puerto Ricans in New York, Chinese in San Francisco, Roman Catholics in Belfast, North Africans in Paris and lower castes in Kolkata (Calcutta), have particular characteristics in common (See **Civil Unrest and Social Segregation**, page 321).

The ghetto is usually a product of **discrimination by society** against the group concerned, but it can also be created by **forces of security** or **bonding** within the group. An **underprivileged group** that has limited access to jobs and houses is often forced by circumstances to live in the poorest part of the city close to the centre or central business district (CBD). Unity within a group is reflected in the desire of many minority groups to maintain their identity as a people with a separate history and culture. This can be more readily achieved by living together in one area.

The ghetto offers common interests and friendships, even if living conditions are poor. Uniting forces are particularly strong amongst recent immigrant groups, who may cluster together for support in a new society.

A ghetto community offers support and security for members of minority ethnic or economic groups.

Activity

1. Explain the advantages of local authority housing to some urban dwellers.
2. What is a ghetto? Explain.
3. Explain the terms:
   a. invasion and succession
   b. congestion.
   Explain why these can be positive forces within residential areas.

Invasion and Succession

Cities that experience high rates of in-migration, such as American cities, have tended to become structured into a series of concentric zones of neighbourhoods of different ethnic groups, income levels and social status through processes of **invasion and succession** and **congregation**. Invasion **and succession** is a process of **neighbourhood change** whereby **one social or ethnic group succeeds another** by increasing their numbers and becoming the dominant group.

Congregation is the **clustering of neighbourhoods** of specific groups of people, which over time develop into one large community with certain criteria in common. This occurs when similar kinds of households go through similar search patterns, make similar decisions about where to live and eventually settle in areas where there are people with whom they can readily identify.

Social segregation is clearly visible today in many American cities. New York, for example, has many areas where ethnic groups form clearly defined residential zones. These include Harlem for black people, Chinatown for Chinese and Little Italy for Italians.

Individuals from many European countries lived within 'ethnic areas' by choice rather than by force. As they prospered, they became more secure and moved to middle-class American suburbs.

Shanty-town dwellings are built from galvanised iron, timber sheets, plastic and any other materials available.

Shanty Towns (see page 400)

Shanty town development is associated with cities of the developing world.

CHAPTER 58
URBAN PROBLEMS IN THE DEVELOPED WORLD

KEY IDEA! Problems can develop from the growth of towns and cities (Chapters 58–63).

TRAFFIC MOVEMENT AND CONGESTION IN TOWNS AND CITIES

Traffic movement and congestion in towns and cities are two of the most consistent and pressing problems in urban areas of the developed world. Roads provide the most flexible and cost-effective means of transport because they enable a door-to-door transfer of people and goods at reasonable cost. Because of its efficiency, however, road transport has become the most desirable and also most overused form of travel within towns and cities.

Vehicles use roads for a number of purposes, such as:

- The transfer of people to and from work, shopping and leisure.
- The transfer of raw materials and manufactured products.

Roads and streets influence the **land use zoning** of urban areas and directly affect the **shape** and direction of **urban expansion**. In many instances they add to an individual city or town's character.

Three main factors influence traffic movement and congestion in cities and towns:

- Street patterns.
- Problems of traffic movement.
- Traffic control.

The Influence of Street Patterns on Traffic

Unplanned Streets

With the exception of new towns, most urban areas developed over a long period of time, which creates problems for traffic.

Most of our coastal cities were founded by the Vikings, and most of Ireland's other cities and towns began either in Norman or Plantation times. The oldest parts of these settlements are located in their central business districts

Unplanned streets in old cities create congestion and poor traffic flow, but trams or light rail systems reduce the need for car transport.

(CBDs), **and some streets are narrow, winding and unplanned.** Street patterns may vary from one part of a town to another, indicating development over a long time. Many unplanned streets meet at irregular angles where markets were once held.

On-street Parking

Traffic movement is generally confined to a **one-way system** in these narrow and winding streets. If on-street parking is allowed, it is usually **confined to one side** of the street only. In such cases **single** and **double yellow lines** along the street edge prevent daytime parking to avoid congestion. Parking may be **allowed within white rectangular boxes**. Traffic movement is easily regulated on wide, planned streets where one-way traffic systems work well in association with on-street parking.

Off-street Parking

Off-street parking is **in multi-storey car parks** or in areas where buildings have been demolished. This reduces traffic congestion in these places.

Planned Street Patterns

Roman towns were laid out in **rectangular blocks**, and their streets formed a **grid plan**. Many towns in Croatia, Italy, France and England are of Roman origin. The defensive town walls usually formed a square or rectangle. There were four main gates and the two connecting main streets intersected at right angles. This pattern was extensively used during **colonial times** throughout America.

In some of Ireland's largest cities, such as Limerick, Dublin and Derry, buildings form **rectangular blocks** with parallel main streets and others intersecting at right angles. This pattern evolved mainly because land was sold in regular blocks rather than because of any formal urban planning. Traffic movement is easily regulated in these cities because streets are wide, on-street parking is allowed and one-way traffic systems work well. It is the increased volume of urban traffic since the 1990s in Ireland, however, which has caused extensive congestion within CBDs and on roads approaching Irish urban settlements.

Many of Wexford's streets are narrow.

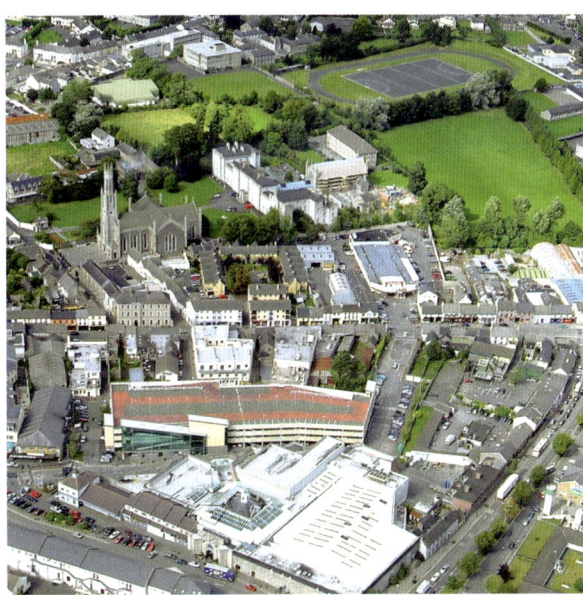
Urban renewal has helped relieve traffic congestion in Carlow.

This grid plan in Washington, DC is typical of American planned cities.

Problems of Traffic Movement

Problems associated with traffic movement may be divided into three main categories:

- Rush hour.
- Traffic within and between suburbs.
- Traffic through rural towns on routes leading to Dublin.

Rush Hour

Traffic into and within city and suburban downtown centres is usually to work or school and occurs in the morning between 7 a.m. and 9:30 a.m. and is called the **morning rush hour**. In the late afternoon between 3:30 p.m. and 6:30 p.m. the return journey from school and shopping is followed by the journey from work. This peak time is called **evening rush hour**. It is during these peak times that traffic congestion is at its most extreme. It is at present the greatest problem that cities have to overcome. Traffic jams many kilometres long and up to three lanes wide are a regular occurrence during the rush hour in major cities of the developed world.

The expansion of towns and cities in the developed world out into the countryside has created **urban sprawl** on a massive scale. A substantial number of car owners from these suburban areas use their vehicles during rush hours. This movement clogs main arterial roads, motorways and suburban streets. On some occasions it may be quicker to gain access to the motorway or freeway to shop in a regional suburban downtown area some distance away than to go to the nearest local shops.

Traffic Within and Between Suburbs

This is of two main types:

- Movement from home to 'suburban downtowns'.
- Movement from home to leisure/shopping centres and schools.

Weekend and late evening patterns are different from those in the working week. Weekend movements are often from the cities to suburban shopping centres and to rural areas for leisure and sporting activities.

> The increased volume of urban traffic in recent decades causes constant congestion within cities of the developed world.

Activity

1. Explain three ways that street patterns influence traffic flow in Irish towns.
2. Explain why towns of colonial origin differ in their street plan to other older towns.
3. Explain the main causes of traffic congestion in Irish towns today.

Some recent developments, such as the **widening of the M50 motorway**, **improvements to the N7** and the **M1 to Belfast**, have improved traffic flow. The **DART commuter railway** provides an efficient north-south service linking suburban coastal towns such as Howth and Bray to Dublin. The **LUAS system** and the **Port Tunnel** are successful improvements that ease traffic congestion in the Greater Dublin region.

Traffic Control Solutions

Traffic must be monitored and controlled to deal with present traffic problems. There are four general approaches to reduce the problem:

- Provide more road space and off-street parking areas to ease the problem of increasing numbers of cars. This can be achieved by urban renewal schemes. These schemes allow planners and architects in inner city areas to:
  - Construct new **multi-storey car parks**.
  - Create **new streets** by demolishing old buildings.
  - Create **one-way streets**, restricted turns (no left or right turn) at street junctions, clearways (single and double yellow lines), parking metres, disc parking, multi-storey car parks and video camera monitoring.

Dual carriageways in cities such as Dublin are choked with traffic.

- Develop **ring roads** to keep as much traffic as possible away from urban downtowns. Also, the creation of raised motorways through inner city areas is a possibility, but this has been opposed in many places for environmental reasons. It has already been used in multi-centred cities, such as Los Angeles. Brussels and Stockholm also have raised motorways through their CBDs.
- Develop **bypasses** to allow long-distance traffic to avoid town centres on our national primary routes.
- **Develop an efficient public transport system**, either above or below ground, or both, with frequent and fast services. London, New York and Paris have these services and they are very effective. Dublin's LUAS system has been a dramatic success. This company has become profitable after just one year. This encourages further development of the LUAS, Metro and DART rail systems.

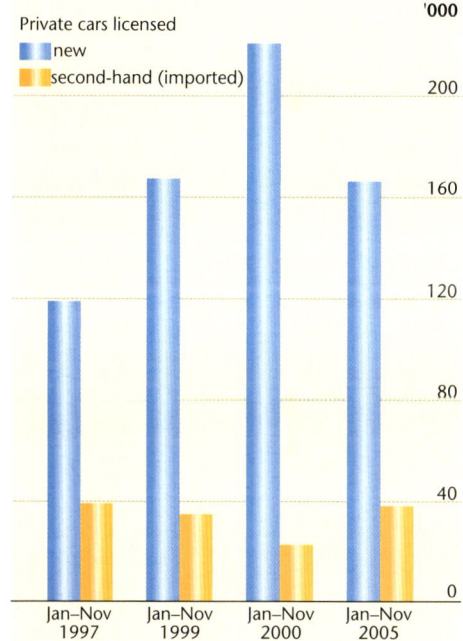

Fig. 58.1 Private car licensed figures for Ireland.

Activity

Examine Fig. 58.1 and answer the following.

1. What trends are evident from the chart?
2. How many vehicles were licensed in 1997?
3. What problems have these trends created for Irish cities and towns? Explain fully.
4. Explain reasons for this trend in car ownership.
5. Explain ways to reduce traffic congestion within urban regions.

Case Study: New York

Manhattan Island forms the central business district (CBD) of New York City and is the core of a vast urban region of over 250 square kilometres that contains 20 million people. It has many distinctive land use areas, including Central Park, midtown and downtown Manhattan. Harlem is a low-income residential zone. Chinatown and Little Italy are cultural or ethnic communities that have formed around the city's core.

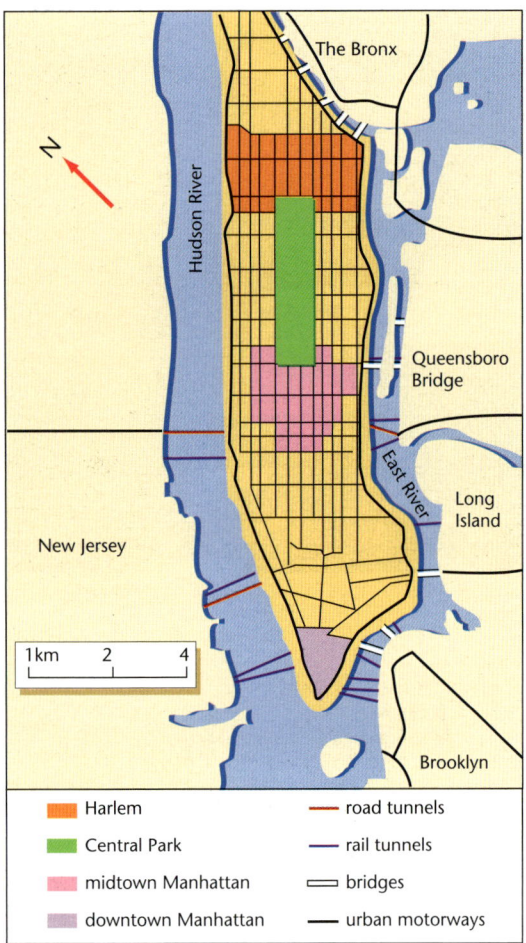

Fig. 58.2 Manhattan Island.

Harlem — road tunnels
Central Park — rail tunnels
midtown Manhattan — bridges
downtown Manhattan — urban motorways

Activity

Study Fig. 58.2 and, with the aid of your atlas, answer the following.

1. Identify some city regions that form part of New York's metropolitan area.
2. a. Describe New York's street pattern.
   b. Explain how this pattern helps in the flow of traffic within the city.
3. How does the site of New York City influence traffic flow into and out of the city?
4. Explain how the public transport system within New York City reduces potential street traffic.

Because it is located on an island, entrance to Manhattan is gained either by bridges or tunnels across the Hudson and East Rivers. Morning rush hour consists of continuous traffic jams as out-of-town traffic is confined to these access points leading into Manhattan. Public transport helps reduce traffic overcrowding by keeping an estimated half a million cars out of Manhattan's CBD each day.

New York's **subway** is an efficient underground rail network that reduces the need for cars on the city's streets.

Activity

Use a PC to identify other land use zones in Manhattan Island. These should include ethnic or cultural areas, high- and low-income residential areas, industrial areas and shopping areas.

● *Identify the land uses of the following areas in New York City: Wall Street, Park Avenue, Madison Avenue, Fifth Avenue and Broadway.*

Carlow town.

A *Rules of the Road* booklet would help you to identify the various road markings.

Activity

Study the aerial photograph of Carlow, then, using the evidence from the photo:

1. Identify the various ways in which Carlow controls its traffic flow. In your answer, refer to (a) road markings (b) public and private parking and (c) urban planning.

2. Identify one way in which towns such as Carlow have radically reduced their traffic flow to eliminate congestion on its main street.

3. Explain how the services and functions of Carlow visible on the photograph indicate that this town has a large hinterland.

4. Explain how the twentieth- and twenty-first-century expansion of Carlow can be explained through your studies of changing land use patterns of developed world urban regions.

CHAPTER 59

URBAN DECAY, URBAN SPRAWL AND THE ABSENCE OF COMMUNITY

KEY IDEA!

Rapid change within cities has resulted in a number of problems for urban residents and urban planners. These problems include zones of urban decay and urban sprawl and the absence of community.

Zones of Urban Decay and Urban Sprawl

Rapid urban growth in cities has resulted in the mass movement of people from inner city communities to new homes in the suburbs. This movement has created zones of decline in some inner city areas and zones of urban sprawl at the edges of these cities.

Reasons for Urban Decay

Derelict buildings, poor-quality housing and the closure or movement of old industries from inner city areas has led to large-scale movement of people away from these areas. Inner city areas had many disadvantages, including the following.

Urban decay occurs in all towns, such as in this area in Cobh.

- Inner city areas are the oldest parts of cities. Because of this, inner cities contained a large number of old buildings and poor-quality housing. The density of buildings was also high and there was little, if any, space for recreation as part of these dwellings (see **Urban Renewal and Redevelopment**, page 395).
- Large numbers of young couples abandoned inner city areas for homes in the suburbs. Many of the people who remain are elderly, single, on low incomes or unemployed.
- Some city councils rehoused some inner city communities in the 1970s in poorly designed multi-storey buildings. Many of these high-rise buildings lacked basic facilities, such as lifts, and so presented difficulties, especially for the very young and older people. In other instances entire inner city communities were rehoused in the suburbs (see page 394).
- Many inner city communities have a high percentage of residents dependent on social welfare. This leads to high crime rates and substance abuse and creates an environment that is not attractive for investment. This in turn creates a cycle that increases social problems.

● Constant traffic congestion, the high cost of land and ageing buildings pushed old industries from inner city areas. Most industrial parks are now located in the suburbs as modern factories prefer greenfield sites in industrial estates where all facilities are provided for industry only.

Reasons for Urban Sprawl

The growth of towns and cities has transformed urban living patterns. As a country develops from an agriculture-based society to an industrial economy, large-scale movement of people from rural areas to towns and cities takes place. Some 29 per cent of the world's population was living in urban areas in 1950. Today the figure is 50 per cent, and it is predicted that this figure will increase to **60 per cent by 2030**. The vast majority of these people will live either in suburbs of the developed world or in shanty towns in the developing world. As all cities increase in size, more and more **agricultural land** will fall **victim to urban sprawl**.

Bear in mind that not all inner city areas suffer high crime rates, nor are they all decaying communities. Many inner city communities are thriving and take an active part in promoting innovative practices, such as adult learning and land use planning.

Car Ownership

As a society gets wealthier, more cars are purchased. The efficiency of the motor car and the improvement in roads allow more and more people to live in suburban areas and get to work, school or to leisure facilities by car. Increased wealth has created **rapid housing growth** on the edges of cities and a corresponding **increase in car ownership**. Just over 11 per cent of the Irish population walk to work and only 2 per cent cycle.

Access to Work

The concentration of office employment and major department stores in city centre areas creates a daily routine of travel to and from work in the morning and evening, so people travel from suburban housing, dormitory towns and individual homes into the city centre during rush hour. The expansion of suburbs has caused the edges of these settlements and that of the city to merge, creating a vast urban environment.

Industry

Increased traffic congestion in cities has forced all new large-scale industries to set up along the edges of cities, either in industrial parks or in land zoned for industrial development. Industries use up large amounts of land because expansion and easy access by large trucks to individual industries is vital to their continued success.

Urban sprawl in Los Angeles has caused this urban region to spread out into the surrounding area.

Many family members of working age own their own cars and commute to work daily.

New urban roads help to reduce traffic congestion.

Consequences of Absence of Community

Because of overcrowding and poor-quality homes, entire inner city communities were rehoused by Dublin's councils in suburban housing estates. These inner city communities were well established with many three-generation families living near each other. Once these families were moved, they were separated into different suburban areas. Family support that was so important within their inner city communities was no longer present. This created insecurity and a loss of identity that could not be restored in the short term.

When young people move from inner city communities, they leave behind their parents, who form a high percentage of inner city residents. When this occurs, services such as youth clubs and community facilities such as schools close for lack of numbers. This removes the vitality of these areas and creates a cycle of decay in inner city regions.

Case Study: Ballymun in Dublin

Many parts of Dublin's inner city were slum regions in the 1960s. The buildings were damp, overcrowded and lacked basic services. The residents were rehoused in tower blocks on Dublin's northside by Dublin Corporation, the city's local authority at that time.

The effects of resettlement were as follows:

- Inner city communities that had developed over many generations were broken up.
- Social support of family members and neighbours was shattered.
- The tower blocks were not suited to young families. Space was limited and lifts often did not work.
- The concept of 'urban neighbourhood' did not develop.

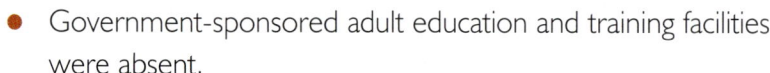

- Government-sponsored adult education and training facilities were absent.
- High unemployment, a high school drop-out rate, crime and drug abuse quickly took over the lives of Ballymun's community. This created a cycle of poverty that made Ballymun one of Ireland's most impoverished urban regions.

Ballymun's New Planning Strategy

A master plan, drawn up by Dublin City Council and local residents, was launched in 1998. This plan is now in action and when completed will provide for:

- Demolition of the tower blocks.
- New residential houses and units to a maximum of four storeys tall to house a community of 30,000 people.
- The construction of a town centre and main street for commercial activities.

Ballymun's regeneration is offering hope to the local residents who have campaigned for this change over the past twenty years.

- The creation of neighbourhood centres with shops and community facilities.
- The development of new routes linking Ballymun to surrounding communities.
- The development of a business and technology park.

Inner city areas like Dame Street in Dublin suffer from traffic congestion.

O'Connell Street in Dublin has a constant heavy traffic flow.

Activity

Identify the various problems that arise as a consequence of traffic congestion in Dublin. In your answer, make reference to: (a) the cost of congestion to transport providers such as truck companies (b) the environment and (c) the quality of life for commuters.

Case Study: Paris

Paris, often described as the nicest city in the world, is a large sprawling primate city that has over 10 million people. It also welcomes over 30 million tourists each year. Lying at the heart of the Paris Basin, Paris is France's core area.

Transport

Paris has an efficient underground rail service, the **Metro**, which has recently been extended. The city has recently built an additional 900 km of motorway to cope with the projected growth of the city. The Arc de Triomphe is the centre of the city's main avenues. Because Paris was a planned city, its streets are wide and capable of carrying large numbers.

Urban Decay and Redevelopment

Paris has many ageing industrial areas within the city where poor, overcrowded communities live. It has many ghettos where Muslim immigrants and people of various nationalities from former colonies in Africa and South-East Asia reside (see page 321). Urban planners have tried to solve some of these inner city problems in the following ways:

- Renewal of inner city residential areas. Over the past twenty years, some 200,000 units of social housing have been built. However, **affordable housing remains a problem** for many Parisians and migrant workers.

Some historic buildings in Paris include:
- Arc de Triomphe.
- Louvre.
- Eiffel Tower.
- Sacré-Coeur Basilica.

387

Remember the Paris Basin in Chapter 28.

What is meant by social housing?

- Creating a new financial centre, La Défense, was an effort to revitalise the inner city. In 1960, La Défense was an underdeveloped site not far from the city centre. By the mid-1980s it housed over 200,000 residents and 100,000 workers in newly built high-rise offices. Since 1990, over 77,000 jobs have been created in other developments around La Défense. This development has been one of the most successful schemes of urban renewal in the world.
- Eight new suburban downtowns were developed around the city to create new housing and employment and to reduce commuter traffic to the city centre.
- Five new towns were developed outside the city. These are now well-established settlements with more than 100,000 inhabitants each.
- Eight growth centres were selected to reduce the dominance of Paris as a primate city. Roads and rail links were improved and new industries were attracted to each of these centres.

Fig 59.1
- *Use this map to identify two advantages of Paris's public transport network.*

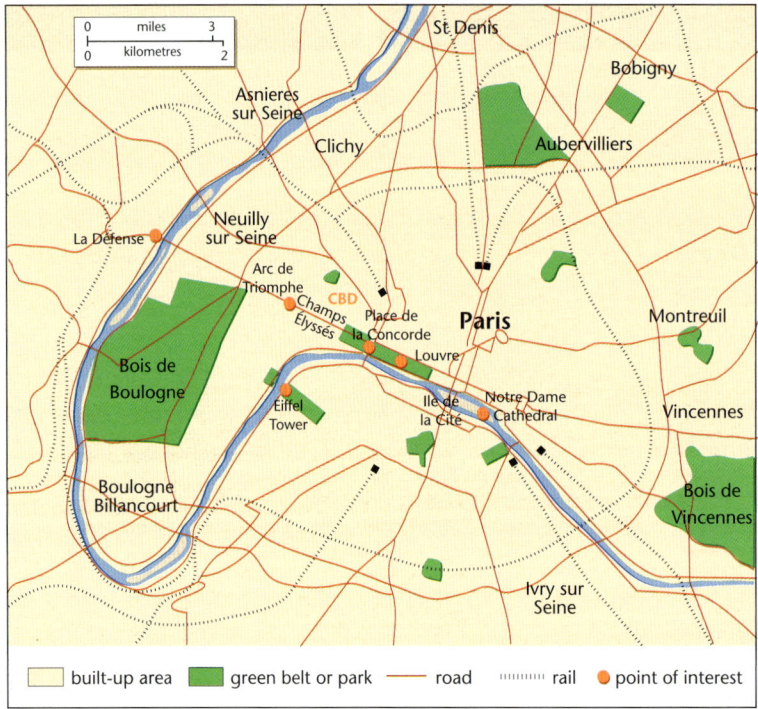

| | built-up area | | green belt or park | — road | rail | point of interest |

Activity

1. **a.** Explain how street patterns affect the functioning of urban areas on a daily basis.
   b. Explain how income and ethnic issues create residential segregation in urban areas.
   c. Explain how rapid change within cities results in a number of problems for urban residents and urban planners.
2. What is a ghetto? Explain.
3. Explain why Paris has large populations of many ethnic groups.
4. Explain why some of these ethnic communities feel alienated from the urban majority in Paris.
5. Explain how French planners have attempted to solve urban decay within the Paris region.
6. What is a suburban downtown? Explain fully.

CHAPTER 60
CONSERVATION OF THE BUILT ENVIRONMENT

KEY IDEA!

Areas and buildings of historic importance should be preserved in Irish towns and cities.

As with the natural environment, there is now much greater awareness of the value of conserving our built environment. The repair and retention of older buildings with important architectural details revitalises cities and towns and adds to their aesthetic value and identity. New measures to protect our heritage include:

- An obligation on local authorities to maintain a record of protected buildings as part of their development plans.
- Ensuring that where a building is protected, the whole of the building, including interior and courtyard, is protected.
- An active role for local authorities in ensuring that protected buildings are not endangered by neglect.
- Special streetscapes and other features of interest, such as ornamental doorways and signs, need to be protected.
- Designers will have some freedom to adopt more sympathetic and appropriate approaches when adapting architecturally valuable buildings for new uses. In addition, the Programme for Local Urban and Rural Development provides financial support of up to 50 per cent to local authorities and conservation groups to promote conservation measures in towns and cities.
- In cases where historic buildings or sites cannot be protected for some reason, these areas should be excavated and recorded.

As part of Limerick's Strategic Plan, specific buildings were listed for conservation. These include King John's Castle, St Mary's Cathedral and Villiers Almshouses.

> Identify some historic buildings or streets with particular charm in your town that should be preserved as part of our heritage. List the historic characteristics of each of your choices.

Activity

1. List the characteristics of each of the buildings in the photographs that identify them as suitable for preservation.
2. What advantages do such buildings offer as part of our built environment and why should they be preserved?

389

CHAPTER 61
URBAN GROWTH AND THE ENVIRONMENT

KEY IDEA!

Environmental problems can develop from the growth of towns and cities.

As world population grows, more and more people are living in towns and cities. Urban growth on a large scale began with the Industrial Revolution in 1750 when coal was first burned in engines to produce steam for power. Today, the combustion of fossil fuels, peat, coal, oil and natural gas in cities for heating, transport, industry and power is releasing huge amounts of carbon dioxide, chlorine and nitrous and sulphur oxides into the atmosphere. These gases create major environmental problems for urban and rural areas.

The Greenhouse Effect and Global Warming

Industry and people's homes and their cars produce vast quantities of greenhouse gases. These greenhouse gases will allow the sun's rays through but will not allow heat radiated from the earth's surface into outer space. As these gases increase in the atmosphere, so too does the amount of heat from the earth. This build-up of heat is causing the earth's atmosphere to overheat, leading to **global warming**. In time, this is expected to lead to the melting of ice cap regions and to a corresponding rise in sea levels and submergence of some coastal areas.

The United States, an urbanised society, contains just 5 per cent of the world's population but produces 25 per cent of the gases that cause global warming. Approximately 7 tonnes of greenhouse gases are emitted per person every year in the USA. About 82 per cent are from burning fossil fuels to generate electricity and to power cars. As an individual, you can affect 32 per cent of the total emissions per person by choices you make in three areas of your life. These areas are the **amount of electricity** we use in our homes, the **waste** we produce and the **type of personal transport** we use.

Global warming projections

Average fluctuations, degrees centigrade

Temperature rises projected by computer models (arrow) roughly match historical trends

Development of iron and steel industries

1.5
1.0
0.5
0

1850 1875 1900 1925 1950 1975 2000 2025 2050

Sources: IPCC, US National Climatic Data Center, Reuter, Associated Press

Fig. 61.1

● *How have global temperatures been affected by the iron and steel industries? Use evidence from the chart to support your answer.*

Activity

Study the chart in Fig. 61.2 showing the per capita (per person) production of greenhouse gases by the world's most developed countries.

1. Which country has the greatest per capita production of greenhouse gases?
2. How does Ireland rank in this table?
3. How does Ireland's per capita production compare with all other European countries?
4. What changes in our lifestyle should we make to reduce this production level?

Fig. 61.2 Greenhouse gas emissions per capita, MMTCE (million metric tonnes of carbon equivalent)/million people.

Smog

Smog is a combination of smoke and fog. The word accurately describes the canopy of air pollution that hangs over a densely built-up area in winter under calm atmospheric conditions. This is when there is an **air inversion,** with cooler, still air near ground level trapped by warmer air above. Because there is no wind to blow it away, the smoke belching out of chimneys and car exhausts builds up in the air.

Smoke is the most visible pollutant, but it may conceal a range of dangerous chemicals, such as sulphur dioxide and nitrous oxides as well as a variety of gases from industrial plants. Above a certain level of concentration, smog causes a deterioration in health, especially among those already suffering from respiratory complaints, such as asthma or bronchitis. Old people, young children and those who already have lung disease are the most vulnerable.

Fig. 61.3 Air inversion.

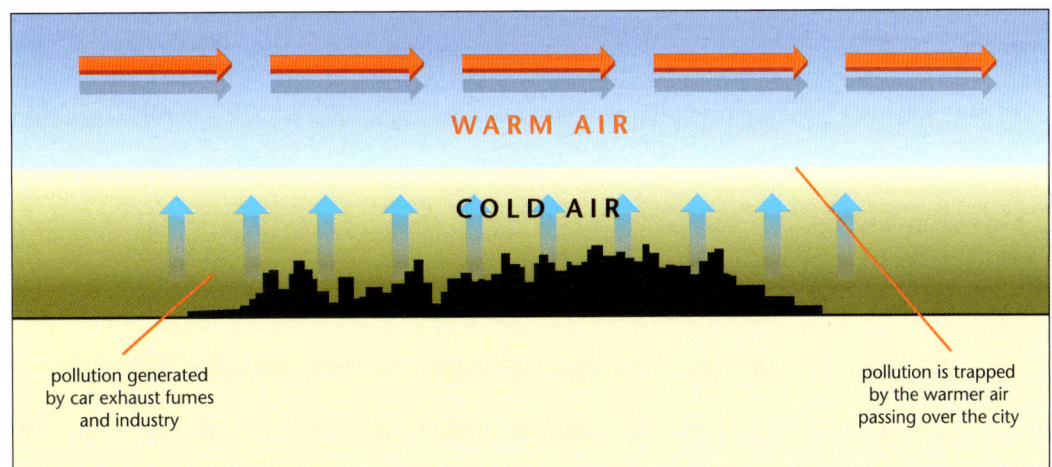

pollution generated by car exhaust fumes and industry

pollution is trapped by the warmer air passing over the city

Most Irish cities today are smoke-free zones. Irish sources of natural gas have provided a clean smokeless fuel that is environment-friendly. Bituminous coal is banned and this has improved air quality in our major urban cities of Dublin, Cork, Limerick and Galway.

Activity

1. What is smog?
2. How does smog affect the urban environment?
3. How does smog affect people's health?

Case Study: Dublin and Ireland

Ireland's Greenhouse Gas Emissions

- Ireland's target under the Kyoto Protocol limits the growth of greenhouse gas (GHG) emission to a **maximum of 13 per cent above 1990** levels for the 2008–12 period. In 2004, actual national emissions were 23.1 per cent above 1990 levels.
- The transport sector, the fastest-growing contributor to national GHG emission levels, has shown a growth rate of 144 per cent in the period 1990–2004.
- Transport accounts for 18.4 per cent of total national greenhouse gas emissions, with road transport accounting for an estimated 93 per cent of the GHGs in Ireland in 2004.
- The highest pollution levels occur along the main traffic routes and areas of greatest traffic congestion. The times of greatest pollution coincide with rush hour in the morning and evening. In places where traffic congestion has been improved, a noticeable drop in pollution levels has also occurred.

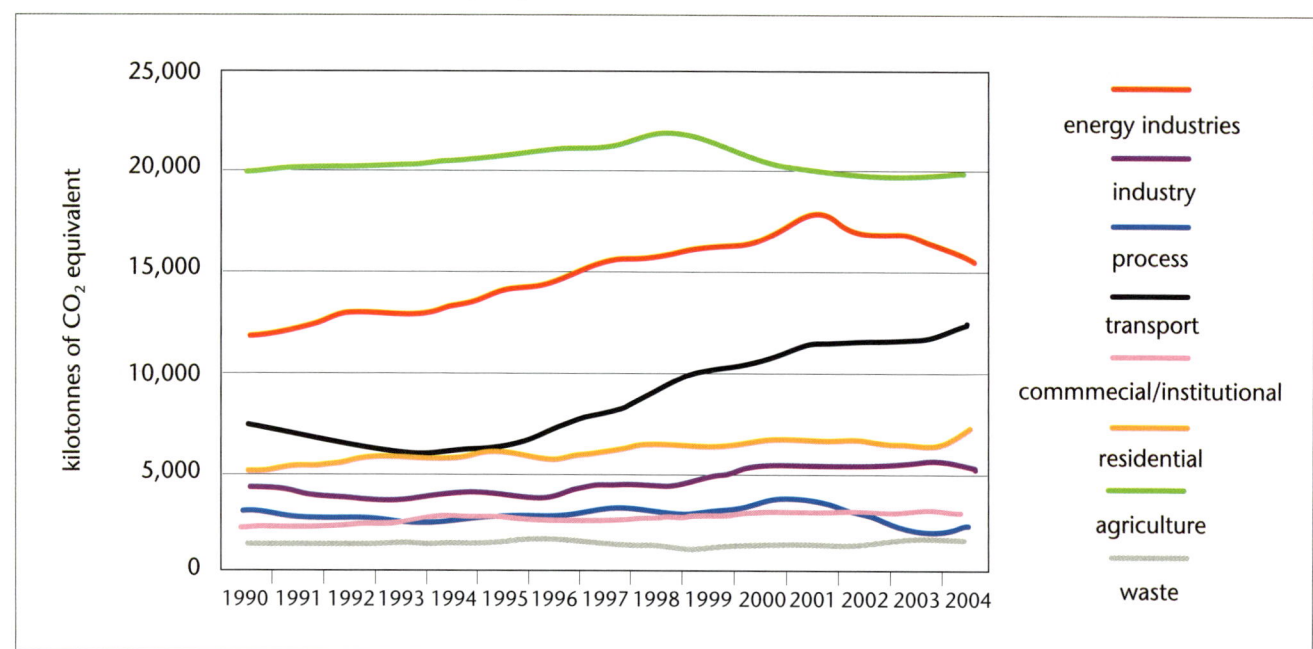

Fig. 61.4 Trends of greenhouse gas emissions per sector, 1990–2004.
(CO₂ = carbon dioxide)

Activity

Carefully study Fig. 61.4, indicating sources of greenhouse gas emissions in Ireland.
1. a. Identify the sector that has produced the most CO_2 equivalent kilotonnes since 1990.
   b. What percentage change increase does this figure represent?
2. Name two other sectors that have increased their greenhouse gas emissions.
3. Name one sector that produces fewer emissions now than it did in 1990.
4. Name one sector that has remained unchanged in its emissions tonnage.
5. Explain why the two sectors with the highest emissions have failed to limit their emissions.

Ireland has signed various international agreements, called protocols, to reduce emissions of greenhouse gases and ozone-damaging chlorine over the period 2008–12. For many years, Ireland has generated one of the highest per capita emissions of some gases, such as sulphur dioxide. The outlook in relation to greenhouse gases is of much more concern, as **emissions in 2010 will be at least 30 per cent higher than in 1990** if present trends continue. This projected increase is more than twice that allowed by Ireland's legally binding commitments under the **Kyoto Protocol** of 1997. One of the reasons for this difficulty is that the Irish economy is fossil fuel intensive.

Urban Waste

Today, 12 per cent of urban waste water in Ireland goes untreated into inland rivers and lakes and into coastal waters, compared to 29 per cent in 2000. €1 billion was invested under the National Development Plan 2000–06 for all waste water treatment.

The Environmental Protection Agency's report in 2000 found that local authorities had implemented few new management systems to reduce effluent discharge. Now new environmental regulations are the driving forces of change so that local governments and private companies must comply with our new laws. Audits are now carried out regularly to monitor all agencies and enforce the laws.

> The ESB coal-fired power station at Moneypoint in Co. Clare has introduced new methods to reduce sulphur emissions.

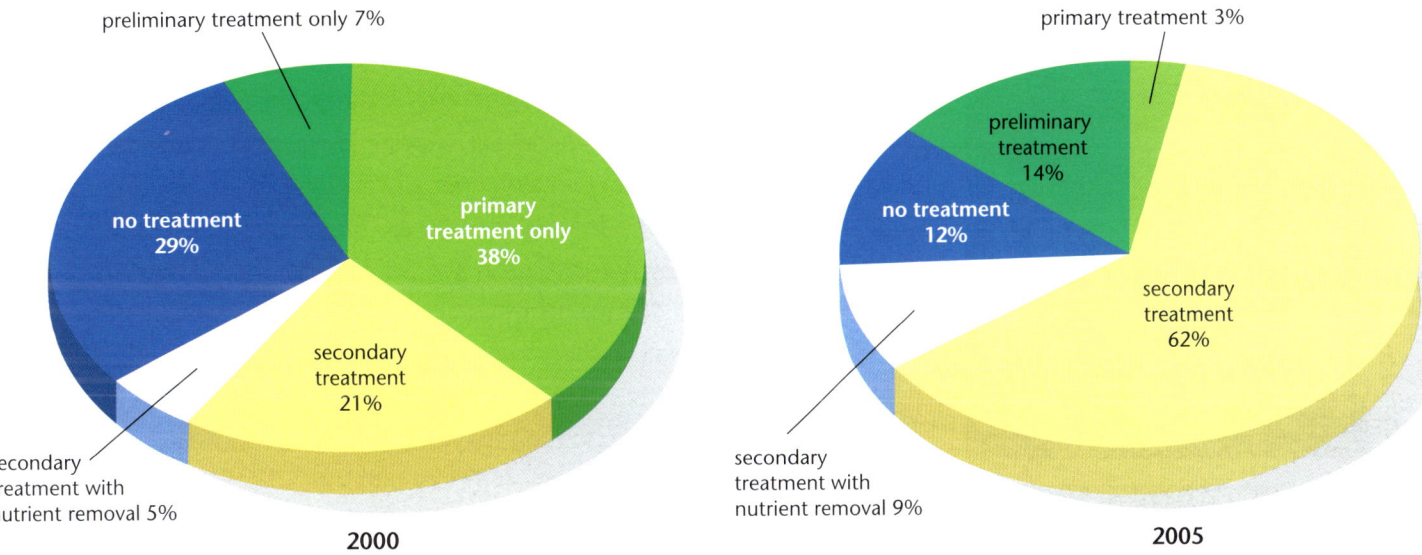

2000

2005

Fig. 61.5 Discharge treatment facilities for urban areas in 2000 and 2005.

Activity
1. What are international protocols?
2. Find out which industrialised nations withdrew from the Kyoto Protocol.
3. Explain:
    a. the political reasons for this withdrawal
    b. the effects on world pollution levels.
4. Study the charts of urban water discharge for 2000 and 2005 in Fig. 61.5.
    a. Explain the main improvements in discharge treatment.
    b. State the effects this change should make to water quality throughout Ireland's
       (a) coastal waters (b) inland waters.

CHAPTER 62
URBAN PLANNING AND URBAN RENEWAL IN IRISH CITIES

Urban planning should involve:
- The replacement of regions of urban decay.
- The introduction of sustainable development programmes.

PROBLEMS IN IRISH CITIES AND TOWNS IN THE 1970S AND 1980S

Urban areas faced many economic and social problems. The first problem that was dealt with related to the **provision of better housing**. Residential 'working-class' houses and flat accommodation in many inner city areas were damp, unhealthy slums. The residents of these areas were rehoused in suburbs such as Ballymun in Dublin and South Hill and Moyross in Limerick. Little thought was given, however, to the provision of social facilities in these new developments. No input in these developments was encouraged from the relocated communities, so in time they became crime-ridden ghettos.

The economic recession of the 1980s led to mass emigration from Ireland. As a means to improve employment opportunities and increase commercial activities, a new drive to improve urban regions was undertaken. Our central business districts (CBDs) were in decay. Many city centre buildings were old and suffered from the following drawbacks:

- Georgian town houses were converted over time into flats and offices. Their facades were crumbling and their lintels and windowsills had sagged.
- Five-storey grain stores and mills lay unused for many decades.
- Factories, such as bakeries, hide, bacon factories and food-processing industries, operated from city centre sites.
- Traditional shop fronts were replaced with tiles and neon signs that led to deterioration in the quality of streetscapes.

By the 1980s, the buildings in inner city regions of Irish towns were greatly in need of attention.

- Offices and hotels were outdated and lacked parking facilities.
- Young couples migrated from downtown areas, causing depopulation of towns and cities.

Urban Renewal and Redevelopment

Faced with such difficulties, city and town planners set about changing this situation. **Urban renewal and redevelopment schemes** were encouraged in the following ways:

- Tax incentives were offered to those who invested in rebuilding or renovating derelict structures.
- Rates relief applied to businesses that operated from these new or renovated shops.
- New streets were created in some places where buildings were demolished.
- Pedestrian-only streets were introduced for the first time.
- Ring roads were constructed to relieve congestion in city centre regions.
- The M50 was built around Dublin to divert traffic from the city centre.
- A new public transport network was developed in Dublin that, when completed, would involve the DART line, LUAS, Metro, park and ride facilities, quality cycling routes and quality bus corridors.

These urban planning strategies and renewal schemes were generally successful.

- **More shoppers** were drawn to city centre areas and business improved.
- The **construction industry boomed** and many were employed in the construction of the city developments.
- **Apartment blocks** provided accommodation for workers in the offices and shops.
- New **shopping malls** were developed in suburban regions and they served local and distant communities.

Ballymun's community was neglected and the area suffered many social disadvantages in tower blocks like these.

Urban renewal led to the redevelopment of many inner city areas.
- *What advantages did these renewal developments bring to inner city regions?*

395

Increased urban traffic comes from a rise in commuting from new residential developments within Dublin's hinterland.

- *Would you agree that community input is an essential part of any successful urban renewal programme? Explain.*

Small natural regions should form an integral part of any urban renewal scheme. This allows access for children and adults to wildlife and tranquillity within an urban setting.

The urban centres, however, continued to lose their populations. As the economy improved, so did **the cost of housing**. The soaring prices, especially in Dublin, drove most **young couples** to **distant suburbs** where they could find affordable housing.

The improvement in employment in Ireland's tiger economy and the need for access to jobs led to increased urban and suburban traffic. This has caused **deterioration in the quality of life** for commuters and urban dwellers in the following ways:

- Increasing separation between home, work and town centre has caused increased growth in private car traffic.
- Increased air pollution from traffic.
- Increased traffic congestion that leads to increased stress and a longer working day.

Recently, increased immigration since 1995 has caused a rise in urban dwellers in all our administrative urban regions except in Limerick and Cork.

SUSTAINABILITY AND URBAN REGIONS
Recent Developments

The most recent urban renewal schemes are designed to support sustainability of these urban environments. As an essential part of their programmes, these plans include **input from local communities** in order that they feel part of the developments. The Tallaght Redevelopment Plan, for example, involved ideas from the local community and grant-aided a **volunteer programme** to help with social and community issues.

The European Commission has published '**Sustainable Urban Development in the European Union**: A Framework for Action'. This is aimed at better co-ordinated and targeted community action for urban problems and has four interdependent policy aims:

- **Strengthening** economic prosperity and employment in towns and cities.
- **Promoting** equality, social inclusion and regeneration in urban areas.
- **Protecting** and improving the urban environment towards local and global sustainability.
- **Contributing** to good urban governance and local empowerment.

Recommendations for New Urban Strategic Plans

- Renewal and redevelopment should no longer be inextricably linked to or led by tax incentives. They must include not just the economic, but also the **social** and **environmental** implications of developments for local areas and communities.
- Urban regeneration must be linked to an area-based **integrated** strategic plan or integrated area plan (IAP).
- Aspects such as community development, education and training, employment, economic development, urban design, conservation and transport and telecommunications networks must be integrated for a successful outcome.
- Redevelopment plans must be **area-focused** to reflect the specific needs of the area. They must also address the positive and negative attributes of the area (such as offering sustainable job creation).
- They must **involve the local community** and representative groups in order to source at first hand local needs and strengths and ensure integration of these issues.
- They must set **measurable targets** and objectives.
- They must be **realistic**.

An additional recommendation was that the external space associated with individual units should not be dominated by parking spaces for residents, as it has been in the past. These spaces offer little in the way of safe areas for play or recreation by different age groups. They also offer a poor visual environment when viewed from inside the residential units.

Shopping centres were initially developed in Ireland's cities in the 1970s.

Retailing and Employment in the City Centre

Retailing is a matter of utmost importance to the growth and development of all cities. In terms of floor area it is a major land user, and gives rise to demands on traffic flow and parking facilities. Retailing is also a major employer, accounting for up to 20 per cent or more of the total employment in a city. The principal attraction of **city centre shopping** is generally the **non-food category**, such as clothing, sports goods and household appliances. The viability of a city centre, therefore, is dependent to a great degree on traditional shopping patterns. **For city centres in Ireland to continue to thrive, the number and size of suburban shopping centres must be restricted and the number of non-food outlets be encouraged to locate in city centre areas only.**

We have already studied the effect of suburban downtowns on large cities such as New York and Los Angeles. Large suburban shopping centres in Ireland act in a similar way to suburban downtowns in America and attract more and more business as they grow larger. The restriction on non-food outlets in these areas would encourage people to continue to shop in city centres.

The Square in Tallaght provided a focal point for this urban community.

397

Urban Renewal Programmes

Urban renewal programmes are essential for the revitalisation of inner city areas. These programmes have identified **obsolete** and **derelict sites** in all Irish large towns and cities. To achieve the goals of strategic urban plans, the government introduced new schemes to encourage the development of these sites for industrial, commercial and residential uses.

Sustainable development encourages the use and reuse of existing buildings that have been in use for many decades, or even centuries. Their continued use for years to come, not as museum pieces but as buildings that adapt and change as society and life itself adapts and changes, will help preserve the character of our cities and towns as well as our architectural heritage.

The redevelopment in inner city areas has brought **new life to city centre shopping areas**. The new modern shopping facilities, streetscapes and restaurants encourage people to visit city centre districts during the day and at night.

Some areas in Ireland's cities that have benefited from urban renewal programmes include Cruises Street in Limerick, Broad Street in Waterford, Merchants Quay in Cork and Temple Bar in Dublin.

Urban renewal schemes have transformed inner city areas (such as inner city Waterford) into vibrant and dynamic residential and commercial districts.

Activity

1. **a.** Explain some problems experienced by Irish cities in the 1970s and 1980s.
   b. Describe some measures that were taken by local governments to overcome or solve these problems.
   c. Critically analyse these local government solutions in light of sustainable urban growth in Ireland.
2. Explain ways that local governments encourage sustainable urban renewal schemes.
3. Explain some advantages of urban renewal schemes in some Irish cities.
4. Examine the aerial photograph of Waterford city on page 398.
   a. Explain from evidence in the photograph how this city continues to implement urban renewal schemes.
   b. Explain the likely outcomes of these schemes.

Programme Reviews for Strategic Plans

Planning reviews are important because they may:

- Identify deficiencies in earlier planning developments.
- Identify new trends, such as shopping trends, which develop as society changes.
- Advise on new planning criteria to be followed to:
  - Encourage private investment into town centres.
  - Protect the proper functioning and viability of town centre trading.
  - Protect the range of activities and services of town centres.
- Reverse damaging trends such as the closure of inner city community services, such as sports clubs.
- Assess and advise on new types of development schemes to ensure they support sustainable urban growth. Some new schemes, such as **large-scale regional shopping centres**, can have adverse effects on the viability of town centres and on

The revival of inner city regions such as Spanish Arch in Galway has brought new life to these areas.

traffic patterns. For example, regional shopping centres are generally located at new route foci, such as roundabouts on ring roads or bypass route junctions. These locations have the ability to **draw traffic across town** for shopping purposes and so lead to congestion, although their original function was to divert traffic away from the urban environment and reduce congestion. Such large-scale shopping centres are no longer a viable option and not necessary in Ireland, as our cities are small. (Only Dublin exceeds a population of 1 million people.) They also have a negative effect on town centres by offering a similar range of services and activities. Neither do they have the support of public transport systems that help to reduce traffic movements.

CHAPTER 63
EXPANSION AND PROBLEMS IN DEVELOPING WORLD CITIES

KEY IDEA!

Problems include:

- Housing.
- Unemployment.
- Basic services.
- Transport.

The pull factors that draw people to cities have led to the rapid growth of urban areas and urban populations, leading to serious problems in providing housing, basic services and jobs.

HOUSING PROBLEMS

The flood of rural migrants to cities of the developing world is causing a housing crisis in those cities. Most authorities have failed to provide adequate shelter for their rapidly growing urban populations and most of the poor must survive by their own efforts and skills. Estimates suggest that one-third of urban dwellers of the developing world cannot find or afford accommodation that meets basic health and safety standards. Consequently, they have three options:

- To sleep rough on pavements or other public places.
- To rent a single room if they have some money.
- To build their own shelter on land they do not own and have no legal right to build on.

SHANTY TOWNS

Self-built shelters, or 'squatter settlements', are called shanty towns. They are generally located on the **outskirts of cities**, on small **inner city sites** or on **hillside sites**, many of which are unstable and prone to landslides. Shanty dwellers face the constant **threat of eviction** or the bulldozing of their homes. Nobody knows how many people live in any one shanty. Most figures are estimates. It is estimated that 30 per cent of Rio de Janeiro's total population live in shanties. The equivalent figures are 25 per cent in Sao Paulo, 45 per cent in Mexico City, 40 per cent in Mumbai (Bombay) and 60 per cent in Kolkata (Calcutta).

Homes in shanty towns are generally of a poor standard. Walls may be made from galvanised iron, plastic or cardboard boxes, while the main frame of the dwelling is often of poles nailed together. Roofs are of similar materials, often stabilised with

- *What conditions evident in this photograph indicate serious housing problems?*

weights such as old tyres. In some parts of Kolkata, large concrete pipes are used as shelters. Many shanties are built on **land that is liable to flooding**. In Guayaquil in Ecuador, shanties extend out into the tidal bay. Homes are connected by raised wooden pathways over the water.

In **Kolkata**, permanent slums, or *bustees*, **are well protected in law**. Residents cannot be ejected and are entitled to basic services, such as water and light. Pavement dwellers – those who literally live on the city's pavements or in traditional squatter havens, such as under bridges, along canals, on land destined for roads or other public use – are not protected and don't receive services. They can be moved by the government without any rights to relocation or compensation. Still, some pavement dweller families have lived on the same spot for three generations.

Over time, shanty families renovate and improve their homes. However, some shanty 'houses' are leased to families, and *bustee* families who cannot pay the rent are evicted. Many of these 'houses' have just one room no bigger than a standard-sized bathroom. A family of eight may occupy this tiny space that serves as both a kitchen and bedroom. Houses are generally clean and tidy. **One in three people in Kolkata lives in** *bustees*, and over 500,000 homeless people live and sleep on the streets.

> Squatter settlements are not necessarily slums, but many of them are. In Chile, squatter settlements are called *callampas*, meaning 'mushroom cities'; in Turkey they are called *gecekondu*, meaning they were built after dusk and before dawn. In India they are called *bustees*; in Peru *barriadas*; in Brazil *favelas* and in Argentina simply *villas miserias* ('villages of misery').

BASIC SERVICES

Basic services, such as clean water supplies, rubbish removal and mains sewage disposal, are available only in parts of some shanty areas. Open sewers are common and the stench of human waste is ever present. The smell increases when temperatures are high in summer. In South-East Asia, monsoon rain causes sewers and canals to overflow. This contaminated 'warm' water creates an ideal breeding ground for malaria, cholera and typhoid and other waterborne bacteria. Immunisation programmes are inadequate or non-existent and many people die unnecessarily.

Over 11 million children under the age of five died in 2000, most from preventable causes.

The absence of electricity supplies in relatively new shanties severely hinders the improvement of hygiene standards.

In developing countries, **one child in three does not complete five years of schooling**. Providing primary education for everyone remains a great challenge. Success in this area will give millions more the skills to rise out of poverty. Enrolment rates are up in most regions, but the quality of education

Many children attend makeshift schools in shanties.

has been suffering. Far too many children remain out of school. To increase enrolments and provide better education, resources (money) must be invested in training teachers and improving facilities. Governments must also **increase family and community participation, and eliminate the gender bias** that limits educational opportunities for girls.

UNEMPLOYMENT

The right to work is a basic human need. Without work there is no money for countless millions of shanty dwellers. They do not have access to social welfare benefits. Many shanty dwellers belong to the **informal sector**; that is, they have to find their own form of employment. They may provide services such as driving rickshaws or work as street traders (for example, selling drinks or food), shining shoes or making saleable goods out of waste products. They live at **subsistence level** – making just enough to get by. As a consequence, their children suffer from malnutrition because their diet lacks fresh vegetables, protein, calories and vitamins. This has other implications. **Malnutrition is a symptom of poverty.** There are over 150 million underweight children in developing countries, a large percentage of whom live in shanties. Malnutrition inhibits mental and physical development. In addition, malnourished mothers are more likely to have low-weight babies, so the cycle continues.

Great numbers of unemployed poor people on the street pavements of Kolkata.

Often new arrivals to the shanties far outnumber the available jobs, so unemployment is high.

TRANSPORT

Governments in wealthy countries direct vast amounts of money towards reducing traffic congestion in cities. In many cases they are making only slight improvements. In Ireland, for instance, billions of euros are being invested in improving urban traffic, yet many feel that in Dublin we are losing the battle. The roads and streets are clogged with traffic, especially during rush hour. That this situation has deteriorated so rapidly in recent years in a city with a little over 1 million people has surprised even the planners.

It is not difficult, therefore, to understand that congestion occurs in developing world cities where **populations exceed 10, 15 or 20 million people**, and most of these figures are only estimates. The type of traffic congestion can vary. In India, for example, **local traditional forms of transport**, such as rickshaws, oxcarts, donkeys and, in some cases, elephants, compete with other road users. Even though the thought of owning a motor car is beyond the wildest dreams of most Indian people, some Indian cities, such as Delhi, are clogged with cars, buses and trucks.

The speed of expansion of cities in developing countries has had a direct effect on traffic flow. This rapid growth is unprecedented anywhere else in the world. Karachi in Pakistan, a city of 1.1 million people in 1950, now has a population of 11 million and it is estimated to reach 20.6 million in 2015. It took

Traffic congestion is an everyday experience on streets in cities of the developing world.

London 190 years to grow from half a million to 10 million. By contrast, Kolkata took less than seventy-five years to grow from half a million to 10 million inhabitants.

Activity

1. Explain three major social problems affecting urban regions in developing world countries.
2. Explain how the lack of one basic social service prevents many shanty dwellers from reaching higher levels of employment.
3. Explain how social unrest can lead to low educational standards.

India is not, as yet, a highly urbanised society, but we should not lose sight of the numbers involved. Only 26 per cent of its population lived in cities in 2000, but that 26 per cent represented more than 260 million people – nearly as many as the entire population of the United States.

India's rate of urbanisation is on the rise. People are arriving by the hundreds of thousands in the already teeming cities, swelling urban India by about 5 per cent annually, almost three times as fast as the overall population growth.

Case Study: Kolkata, Eastern India

Kolkata (Calcutta) has a population of 127 million people and **a natural increase of 2 per cent**. The city has 500,000 homeless people and over 4 million of Kolkata's population live in slums, called *bustees*.

Kolkata was the political capital of Britain's Indian Empire until Delhi was chosen instead in 1911. Kolkata remained India's largest trading, financial and industrial centre until well into the 1950s, when Mumbai (Bombay) became more important. Now there are fewer factories in Kolkata and fewer jobs in manufacturing. The city's economic decline is indicated by the fact that of all Asian megacities, Kolkata alone has a minus net migration; more people move out than in.

Some of Kolkata's problems stem from the political division that created Pakistan and East Pakistan (now Bangladesh) and cut off a large part of Kolkata's hinterland and filled the city with 500,000 refugees. The Indian part of the city had risen virtually without any urban planning, and the migrants created almost unimaginable conditions.

Housing

Kolkata is notorious for its **slums** and its **pavement dwellers**, even though other cities may be as badly off in this regard. For over twenty years international agencies and the government have tried to improve living conditions in the city by supplying water taps and toilets. Maintenance is usually so bad, however, that the end results are little better than at the beginning.

Industry and Roads

No new industry has been established in the city for years. As industrial production has declined, so has the real income of workers.

Mountains, deserts and coastlines combine to make the Indian sub-continent one of the world's most vividly defined geographic regions. To the north, the Himalayas create a natural 'wall'. To the east, mountains and dense forests divide the region from South-East Asia. To the west, rugged highlands, the Sulaiman Range, and large deserts separate it from neighbouring countries Iran and Afghanistan.

Draw a map of the Indian sub-continent. On the map, mark and name the main cities, rivers, deserts and elevated areas.

Fig. 63.1

● *What physical characteristics define the Indian sub-continent as a natural region?*

Remember the ethnic, racial and cultural difficulties that face the Indian sub-continent at present.

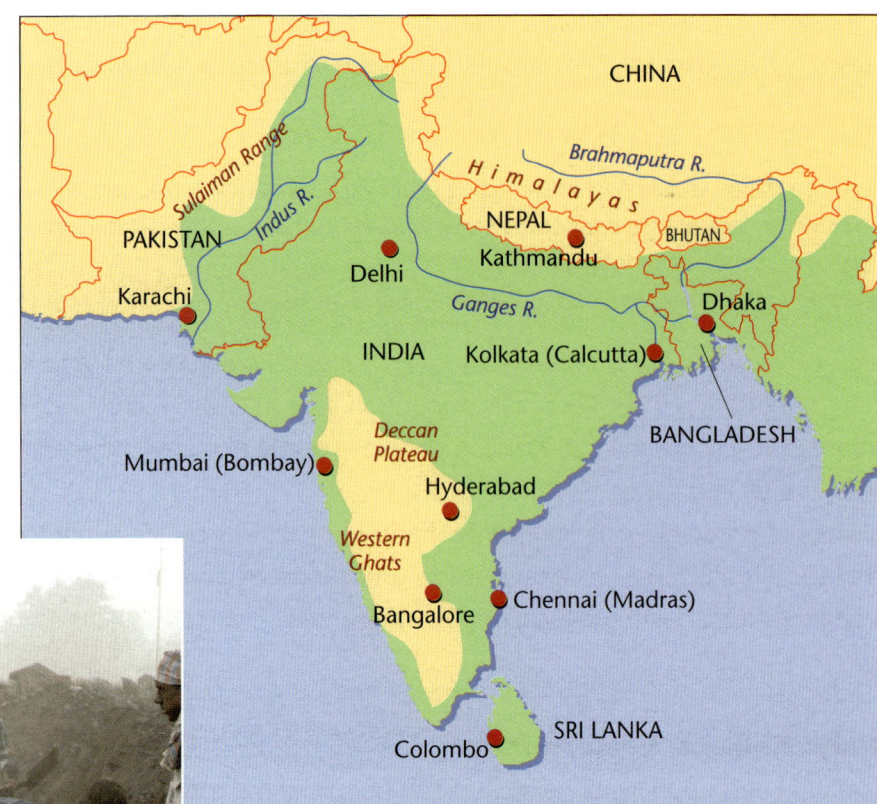

Many women and children work in unsafe environments in Kolkata in order to earn meagre incomes to enable them to survive.

Mumbai is one of India's rapidly expanding cities. It attracts many back-office service industries for multinational companies.

There have been several development problems for Kolkata and its satellite cities. Nearly all development initiatives have tried to disperse population by developing industry throughout the metropolitan area.

It has not worked, however, because the necessary roads and bridges were not finished in time to support the changes. In addition, the city lacked the energy and drive to develop smaller growth centres that could take root and thrive on their own.

The Indian government supports many of Kolkata's industries, but at a high cost. Old industries, such as carpet making and cotton weaving, continue to use child labour to enable them to compete in foreign markets. The hinterland of Kolkata – Bihar – is sometimes called **India's Rustbelt** and it is the poorest of India's twenty-five states. Part of this decline is due to the poverty of the neighbouring countries, such as Bangladesh, around the Bay of Bengal.

CHAPTER 64
THE FUTURE OF URBANISM

 **KEY IDEA!**

Successful future urban development needs to be inclusive of all social groupings.

ISSUES RELATING TO CITIES OF THE FUTURE

Cities are complex spaces where **webs of technologies**, such as water supplies, energy, transport and communication networks, **bind spaces together**, while social, recreational and employment activities **keep its various communities apart**. Cities of today (and of tomorrow) are places:

- Composed of different parts, culturally mixed and multi-centred urban areas.
- Where stark contradictions and huge tensions co-exist.
- Where highly planned and expensive developments that took planners and skilled consultants many years to put together exist in some areas, while other parts of the same city appear to be uncared for.

Modern cities often display great contrasts in people's income and living conditions.

The Dual City

The term 'dual city' relates to **social division within urban areas**. This is based on evidence of increasing social division (**rich versus poor**) where a large proportion of a city's population **are cut off from the wealth-creating activities**, such as services and manufacturing industries, which we normally associate with improving people's quality of life. This group forms what is termed an '**underclass**' and is surplus to the needs of a 'modern' society. This group of poor people is composed of a very high proportion of **ethnic minorities, sick, elderly, disabled people and single parents** who have become socially isolated from many areas of city life. Inner city areas and council estates have become identified with these minority groups. In addition, within these 'underclass urban areas', **many make a living on an informal basis** (paid in cash, tax free) or illegally, independent from the taxable income of society in general.

The policy of including the urban poor in a city's development, as was the case in the twentieth century, is being undermined. This new policy, encouraged by recent economic trends such as the Celtic Tiger economy and by government policy, **leads to exclusion** from the chance or ability to improve one's living standards, and to alienation from the general population.

This '**age of extremes**' is becoming an **acceptable social policy**, as if it were the inevitable evolution of life within cities of the future everywhere, especially as urban populations increase across the world. This results in a growing sense of despair **among**

Activity

1. Explain what is meant by 'the dual city'.
2. Explain, using examples, what is meant by the statement 'this age of extremes is becoming an acceptable social policy'.
3. Explain why increased international migration could lead to increased social division within cities.

the poor and an increasing sense of insecurity or racism **among the rich**. This fear among the rich is reinforced by trends in international migration and the mixing of a wide range of ethnic and racial groups and leads to a severe separation of rich from poor.

This increasing separation or alienation will eventually lead to a situation where the **rich or affluent will live and interact only with each other**, while **the poor will live and interact only with poor people**. This trend is encouraged when many people are forced out of the housing market by higher pricing and when social or local government housing is reduced or withdrawn completely.

Urban Renewal, Mega-projects and Flagship Developments

Social improvement of cities is too often related to the physical and economic structure and appearance of cities rather than to the quality of life of its existing citizens.

Urban Renewal

Urban renewal projects generally affect local housing in two ways:

- The physical removal of poor residents may occur when existing dwellings are demolished to make way for newer developments. The demolished buildings are generally cheaper, low-value dwellings that serve low-income and vulnerable members of society.
- Forced out-migration through house price increases. Rundown hotels and rooming accommodation that provided a valuable source of cheap accommodation are demolished.

Derelict urban areas are often cleared to make way for modern flagship developments.

Mega-projects

Urban mega-projects represent a new, specialised form of the urban living environment that is being rapidly introduced throughout cities across the globe by a combination of design consultants, investment groups and planning authorities. Such mega-projects include casinos, parks, multi-storey cinemas, hotels, offices, expensive high-security housing (gated communities) and sometimes golf courses with security personnel to ensure safety. The United States has many such developments, for example in Florida. They are also becoming popular in the cities of India, China and South-East Asia but to a lesser degree than in the developed world.

Many mega-projects may be funded through tax incentives and zoning, giving rise to dispersed settlements throughout some cities with no clear planning strategy for their locations.

Flagship Developments

Flagship developments include office developments such as Canada Tower at Canary Wharf in London's Docklands. (The proposed development for Dublin's dockland area was rejected by planning authorities in 2001 as it was believed to be too large a development for a medium-sized city. They favoured a scaled-down version of the same proposal.) These developments are generally financed through some form of public-private partnership between government and private individuals or companies. Dublin's financial centre (IFSC) is a huge success that has created many jobs and investment companies.

Most cities will try to promote themselves as a good place to live and work. The cities promote their business opportunities as well as their lifestyle activities. Now, as always, cities are desperate to create the impression that they lie at the centre of something exciting. Dublin's image abroad as a young, vibrant city with good nightlife and a yuppie culture may be attributed in part to our numerous rock groups, such as U2.

New apartment blocks have been built in many Irish cities.

Canary Wharf was a flagship development in London's Docklands.

Activity

1. Explain what is meant by:
   a. mega-projects
   b. flagship developments.
2. Explain why Dublin has become a major tourist centre in recent years.

Industry

The image of industry within a city is changing. It is no longer associated with the factory, the smokestack chimney and the storage yard of the nineteenth and twentieth centuries. Now it promotes itself within well-designed landscaped lawns and gardens, lakes and sculptures, such as in Park West in Dublin. Industrial buildings are ultra-modern, futuristic buildings of mirrored glass and high technology. Their industrial activities are no longer the heavy, dirty and dangerous work of the past, but associated with technology, skill and cleanliness.

Mega-projects, flagship developments and new business parks act as economic stimulants or magnets that are intended to attract people, spending and jobs that create a cycle of consumption, products and employment. They may act as stimulants to other economic developments by local authorities or others that aim to spread the effects of development across the city.

Dublin's cafés, nightclubs and street furniture create the image of a city confident in itself and its future.

407

Use of Public Space and Social Control

The streets and pedestrian public spaces where people had more or less free and open access are beginning to be used more and more only by **'those who belong'**. The poorer citizens 'stand out' and homeless people are moved on. Urban public space has never been truly public in many countries. Some cities, such as London and Dublin, still have their public spaces, such as Hyde Park and St Stephen's Green.

Surveillance within Cities

In many cities, the activities of many people or groups are constantly monitored by **CCTV cameras**. The cameras are sometimes used to exclude poor groups from some areas, such as from high-priced shopping centres in Sao Paulo in Brazil. Thirty 'danger zones' have been identified in Berlin, giving police extensive new powers of search and eviction.

'Undesirables' are excluded from redeveloped areas in many US cities. Some geographers question whether 'public space' still exists in some Western cities. Have shopping malls become the controlled public spaces of future cities as middle-income people flock to these centres on Sundays and at festive seasons?

When CCTV was first introduced, it was expected that it would lead to:

● A significant reduction in crime within CBD areas, creating a 'feel-good factor' among shoppers and residents.

● A revitalisation of town and city centres through increased consumer use and spending.

There has been no properly conducted survey, however, to prove whether or not CCTV leads to crime reduction. Indeed, there is the suggestion that the presence of CCTV has led to the feeling that responsibility for security lies elsewhere or that somehow cameras by their very presence enforce security, leading to 'bystander indifference' to crime and disturbances in city centre areas. The use of CCTV won widespread support in Britain and it is now an accepted feature of many towns and cities today.

Development of Neighbourhoods and Sustainability

It has been argued that long-term successful development of cities in the future lies in encouraging development at neighbourhood level. So instead of planners and consultants dictating massive structural change to cities so that they will prosper, the more practical and realistic way forward is **for a neighbourhood to deliver solutions to a neighbourhood's own problems** with its own resources or with government aid. The key to sustainable neighbourhood success seems to lie in **rejecting blueprints from outside in favour of those generated locally**, which build on local expertise and knowledge, respect local conditions and have social and environmental aims. This is called **'organic planning'**. It is based on the principle that what works in one neighbourhood may not necessarily work in another.

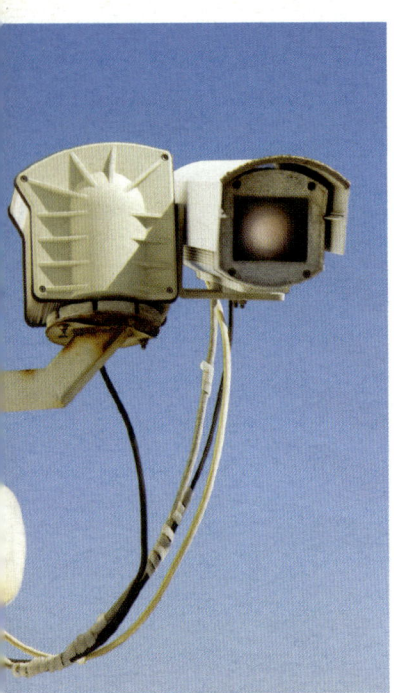

CCTV cameras often help in regulating traffic and identifying thieves.

Activity

1. Explain two ways that CCTV cameras have helped improve social order in Irish urban areas.
2. Explain one way that CCTV cameras may be viewed as a negative development within urban areas.
3. Explain what is meant by the following statement: 'The success of an urban region depends on development at neighbourhood level.'

CHAPTER 65
RACIAL GROUPS

KEY IDEA!

Race is biological inheritance.

THE MEANING OF RACE

Many people associate race with factors such as language, religion and nationality. These are cultural factors and can be changed by anyone if they so wish. Racial character, on the other hand, cannot be changed. We are born with it.

In other words, race is simply **biological inheritance**. Race refers to **physical characteristics**, such as skin colour, height, hair type, physique and shape of head. Scientists call these characteristics **physical traits**; they are passed on through genes from parent to offspring.

Is There Such a Thing as a Pure Race?

Simply, there is no such thing as a pure race. Widespread migration and intermingling of people leading to interbreeding between people of different continents has blurred all racial boundaries. For this reason, many scientists use the term 'ethnic group', which relates to race, in order to describe large groups of people having certain physical characteristics in common.

- The people of Scandinavia form an especially distinctive group: fair-haired, fair-skinned, tall and blue-eyed. This may be explained by a combination of the area's relatively isolated position and its northern latitude. Also, historically, people have moved out of rather than into Scandinavia.
- The Aborigines of Australia were cut off on this once isolated continent for so long that as a group they remain physically and genetically distinctive.
- The Kalahari bush people were similarly isolated in the semi-arid region of south-west Africa.

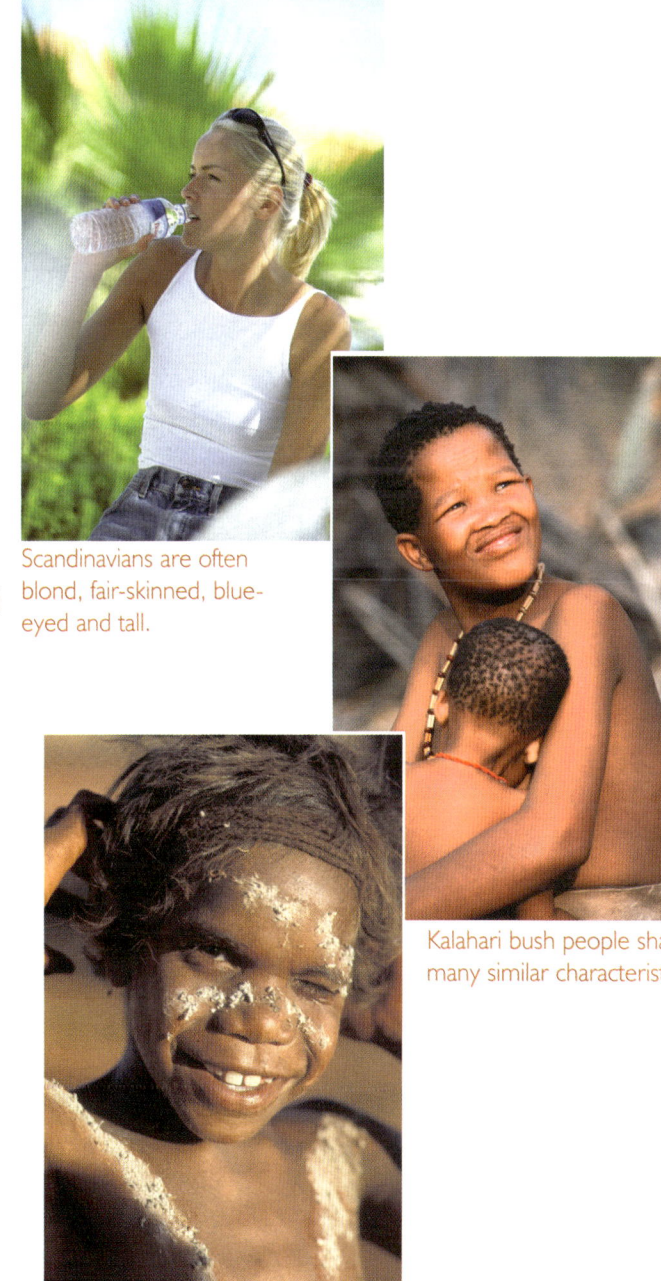

Scandinavians are often blond, fair-skinned, blue-eyed and tall.

Kalahari bush people share many similar characteristics.

Australian Aborigines lived on an isolated continent and so are racially distinctive.

SKIN COLOUR AND RACE

Can you explain the difference between 'culture' and 'race'?

Initially, the human race was divided according to skin colour, the most obvious physical characteristic. Five groups were recognised: white, yellow, red, brown and black. Even though this was an easy way to do things, it was neither satisfactory nor scientific. For instance, both the sub-Saharan Africans and the Aborigines have very dark skin, but they belong to two distinct ethnic groups.

Skin colour has been an excuse for inhumanity for thousands of years. Today's scientists believe that, initially, dark-coloured and light-coloured skin evolved because of humans **adapting to environments**, such as hot, sunny climates and cooler, cloudier climates. **Because** humans adapted, **they survived** and their offspring **passed** on these **traits** through their **genes**.

The development of dark skin was essential to survival in tropical latitudes.

The development of vitamin D3 was more essential to the survival of northern Europeans than the risk of cancer.

It is believed that skin colour is a result of the presence of a molecule called **melanin. We all have the same number of melanin-producing cells**, but more melanin per cell is produced in darker-coloured people. In dark-skinned people these cells produce forty-three times more melanin per cell than light-skinned people. Because it is 'an amount thing', **interbreeding between races results in a wide range of shades of colour.**

When humans lost their covering of body hair, they would have been vulnerable to the effects of **ultraviolet light. Melanin** is necessary to combat the effects of ultraviolet (UV) light by absorbing these dangerous rays and so protects against cancer. The greater the intensity of light, the greater the need for melanin. Groups near the tropics needed greater amounts of this substance than groups who later lived at higher latitudes, and so became dark-skinned. In addition, dark skin was essential to combat the effects of light on the production of **folic acid,** which is essential if people are **to remain fertile** and to produce healthy offspring.

Humans need some **UV light to create vitamin D3**.

More genetic differences may exist between different Irish teenagers than between this Indian girl and these Irish youngsters.

Because there is less UV light available at higher latitudes than lower latitudes, **some humans developed genes for** creating **lighter-coloured skin**.

Activity

1. Explain why there is no such thing as a pure race. In your answer, refer to:
   a. migration
   b. skin colour
   c. genetic make-up.
2. Explain how the need to survive led to the variations in human skin colour.

SKIN COLOUR AND GENETIC MAKE-UP

Anthropologists differ amongst themselves as to how many distinct ethnic groups there are, but most recognise five or six groups.

1. Caucasoid (white, Caucasian): Europeans and people of European ancestry, brown-skinned peoples such as Arabs and people of the Indian subcontinent.

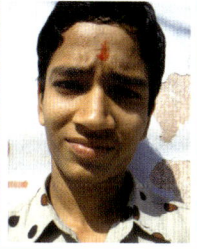

2. Northern, Central and East Asian: Chinese, Inuit, Samis and American Indians (Amerindians).

3. Africans and black people of African descent (Afro-Americans).

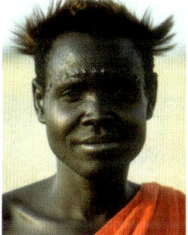

4. Black Australian Aborigines.

5. The Bush people of the Kalahari Desert.

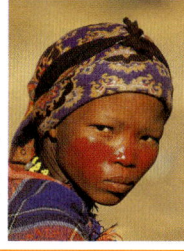

Identify the physical characteristics of the people in each of these photographs.

411

CHAPTER 66
RACIAL LOCATION PATTERNS AND RACIAL CHARACTERISTICS

 **KEY IDEA!**

Three major racial groups occupy most of the world's regions.

Fig. 66.1 This is a generalised map of racial distribution. The fact that many black people live all along the Brazilian east coast and many whites of Spanish descent live all along the west coast of South America is not shown here.

Caucasians are found scattered throughout the world because Europeans colonised many regions.

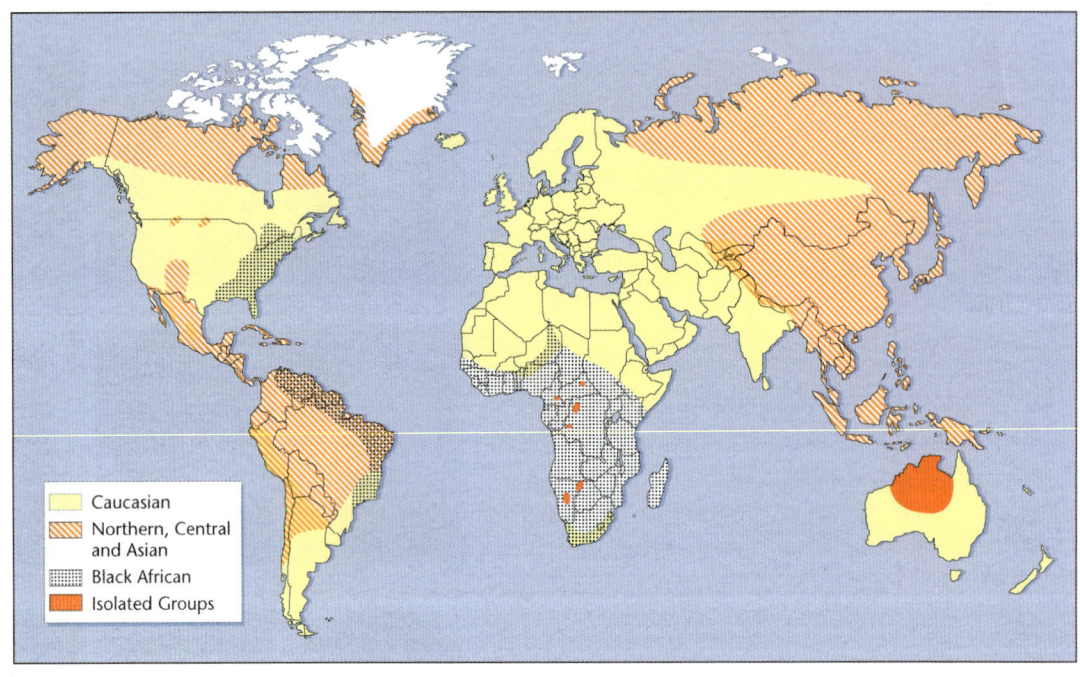

Caucasian
Northern, Central and Asian
Black African
Isolated Groups

CAUCASIANS

Caucasians are the most widespread racial group. This group occupies a broad zone across America and from the Atlantic coasts of Europe and North Africa to the Indian Ocean and the Bay of Bengal and filters up into central Asia. Other Caucasians are found from eastern Brazil south to Argentina and Chile, Australia, New Zealand and South Africa.

General Racial Characteristics

The general racial characteristics include: fair to brown skin, light to brown hair which is straight to wavy, light blue to brown eyes, and medium to tall in height. The group is thought to have evolved in the general area of the Caucasus Mountains between the Caspian Sea and the Black Sea. The Caucasian group may be subdivided into three sub-groups: the Nordic group, the Alpine group and the Mediterranean group. The Nordic group are mainly the people of Scandinavia, who are especially distinctive: fair hair, blue eyes, high cheekbones and tall.

● *Identify the characteristics of these Scandinavian people.*

412

NORTH, CENTRAL AND EAST ASIAN

People from central, east, south-east and north Asia mainly have light brown skin, darkening southwards in Malaysia and Indonesia, which may reflect the effect of increased sun. Inuit belong to this group. After Asian people crossed the Bering Strait from Siberia to Alaska, they moved south through North and South America. Their descendants, the American Indians (Amerindians), belong to this ethnic group.

General Racial Characteristics

The general racial characteristics include: light brown or reddish-brown skin, a broad head with a flat face and nose, straight and coarse black to brown hair, brown eyes and short to medium height.

● *Identify the characteristics of these Chinese children.*

BLACK AFRICAN

Most of the black African people live south of the Sahara. Other regions include the United States, the Caribbean Islands, Brazil and Britain.

Some people from East Africa have a more mixed set of characteristics, as contact with Arab and Indian traders indicates racial mixing.

A young Zulu female.

An African-American family.

An Inuit family.

Identify the physical characteristics of the people in each of these photos.

General Racial Characteristics

The general racial characteristics include black to brown skin, long head with projecting jaw, black to dark brown hair of a coarse texture and dark eyes. The most distinctive black features occur amongst the people of West Africa. These features become less distinctive as distance increases from this core region.

413

CHAPTER 67
MULTIRACIAL SOCIETIES

KEY IDEA!

Migration, both forced and voluntary, created multiracial societies.

Many European countries, such as Britain, the Netherlands, Spain and France, were once colonial powers. Consequently, many former citizens of these colonies now live in these countries.

BRITAIN – A MULTIRACIAL SOCIETY

Britain had many colonies. Fig. 67.1 shows the extent of the British Empire across the world.

Activity
1. Identify, in rank order, the various ethnic groups in Britain.
2. Explain why South Asians form the largest ethnic group in Britain.

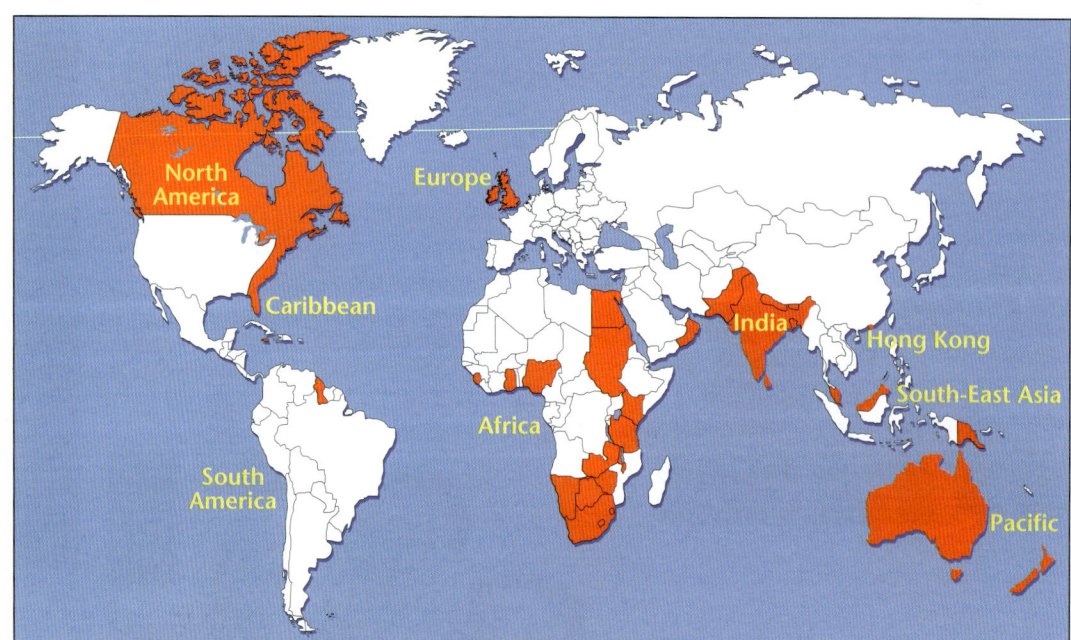

Fig. 67.1 The former colonies of the British Empire.
● *Identify the various racial or ethnic groups that live within these colonial regions.*

Ethnic or ethnicity refers to a minority group with a collective self-identity within a larger host nation.

The ethnic or multiracial population in Great Britain has evolved from mass immigration of people from former British colonies in the Caribbean and South Asian subcontinent during the 1950s and 1960s. Ethnic minorities make up 8.8 per cent of the population of Great Britain and accounted for 7.2 per cent of all people of working age in 2000. South Asian people, consisting of Indians, Bangladeshis and Pakistanis, are the largest ethnic minority group. They make up 4.4 per cent of the population, followed by black people from the Caribbean and Africans, who make up 2.2 per cent. The Chinese make up 0.4

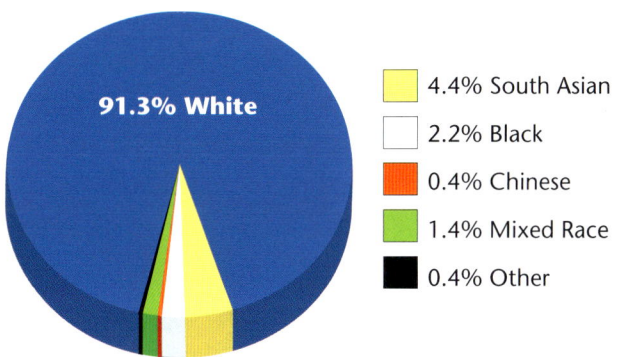

Fig. 67.2 Great Britain's multiracial poulation.

4.4% South Asian
2.2% Black
0.4% Chinese
1.4% Mixed Race
0.4% Other

91.3% White

per cent of the population. People from ethnic minorities remain concentrated in the larger urban areas, especially in Greater London, and in some cases form a majority of the local population in certain districts, such as Notting Hill and Southall.

At the peak of immigration in 1961, before the **Commonwealth Immigrants Act** came into effect in 1962, some 50,000 people arrived from the West Indies in one year. The migration was in fact encouraged from the Caribbean by the offer of employment from London Transport and the National Health Service.

Britain was the centre of the **triangular traffic** whereby British ships took **goods to Africa**. These goods were exchanged for **slaves**. The same British ships then transported the slaves to the Caribbean and North America before returning home with **industrial raw materials** such as cotton. The majority of these slaves worked in the plantations of the Caribbean and North America, but some came to Britain to be personal household servants. Over time, they intermarried with native-born Britons.

FRANCE – A MULTIRACIAL SOCIETY

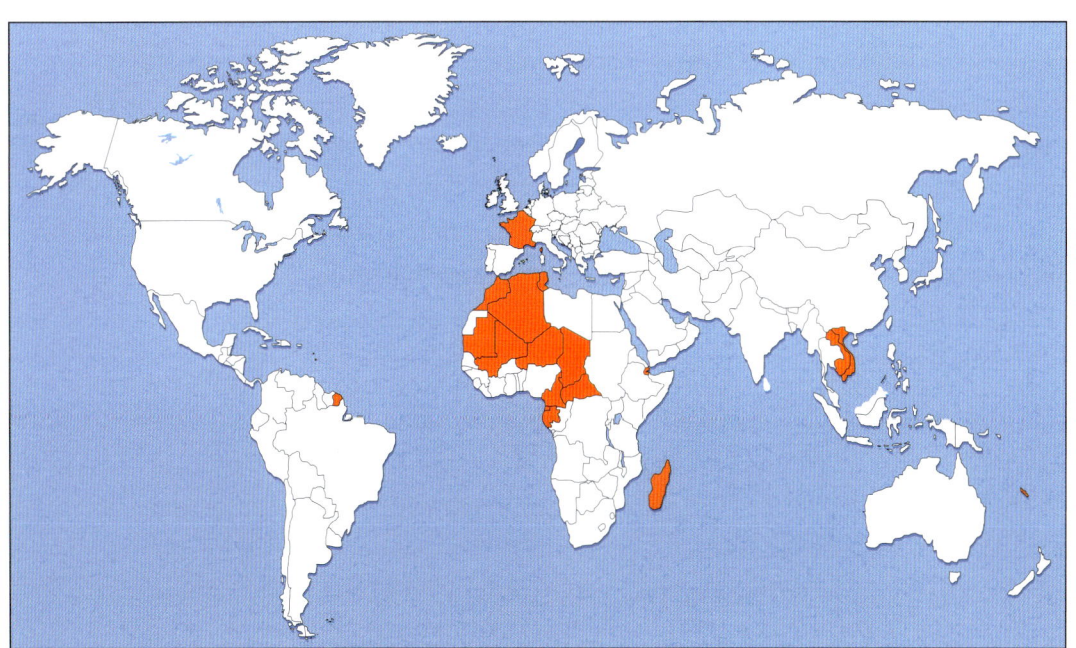

Fig. 67.3 This map shows the extent of the former French Empire.

Activity
1. Study the map of the former French Empire in Fig. 67.3, then identify the highlighted countries that formed part of this region.
2. Which of these countries form part of sub-Saharan Africa?

415

French citizens include many people from France's former colonies.

Some ethnic groups prefer to live in cultural areas or ghettos of French cities.

Like Great Britain, France was a former colonial power. The French state keeps few immigration statistics beyond the numbers of foreign-born migrants legally resident in France or those who have become French citizens (about 4 million). There is no official figure for the total number of French residents of foreign background, nor any breakdown of where they come from, but it is estimated that about 14 million French citizens – nearly one-quarter of the total population – have at least one immigrant parent or grandparent.

A large share of the post-war immigrants and their offspring come from former French colonies in North Africa, such as Algeria; from countries in sub-Saharan Africa, such as Senegal; and from countries in South-East Asia, such as Vietnam. Much of this population is concentrated in suburbs and urban centres such as Marseilles and Lyons. Most immigrants live in ghetto-like communities. In addition, large past migrations and high birth rates among immigrants have made Islam France's second-largest religion.

Many immigrants, especially those from Algeria and Morocco, came to France as 'guest workers' in the 1960s and 1970s. Migrants were seen as an asset for economic development within the core countries of the EU, including France and Germany. Migrant workers performed jobs not wanted by the French, because the jobs were poorly paid, unpleasant, dirty or involved heavy manual work. The migrants were glad of employment and sent home much of their earnings to help their families' incomes. France was also pleased that such jobs were being done while French citizens could accept better-paid and higher-quality jobs.

In France, all citizens are deemed equal and indistinguishable in relation to the state. 'In France, once you are French, you are French and that's it.'

CHAPTER 68
RACIAL MIXING

KEY IDEA!

Brazil's multiracial society lives in relative harmony.

Case Study: Brazil – A Cultural Melting Pot

Brazil's population of 167 million people is as diverse as that of the United States. Its native Amerindian people were drastically reduced following European colonisation. No more than 275,000 Amerindians now survive deep in the Amazon region.

There are about 80 million black people in Brazil. These are the descendants of the slaves brought by the Portuguese to work the sugar and cotton plantations along the north-east coast. Significantly, however, there has been much racial mixing, and 67 million Brazilians have combined European, African and some Amerindian ancestry. The remaining 91 million, now barely in the majority at 55 per cent, are mainly of European origin, the descendants of immigrants from Portugal, Italy, Germany and Eastern Europe. This complex society also has large numbers of Lebanese and Syrians as well as the largest community of ethnic Japanese outside Japan. The Japanese now number 1.3 million and have filtered right to the top of Brazilian society.

Brazil stands apart from all other nations by its progress in dealing with its racial divisions. Black people are still the least advantaged, but ethnic mixing is so common that hardly any group is unaffected and official statistics about 'blacks' and 'whites' are almost meaningless.

In the hunger for land, many Amerindians (native Americans) have been forced off their lands and into reservations by the Brazilian government. This has occurred because the government does not recognise the ownership rights of the Amazonian Indians to their traditional tribal lands, rather than because of racial bias towards them.

Brazil has one of the most racially diverse populations in the world. It is called 'a melting pot' of races.

● *What evidence in this picture of the Brazilian World Cup team indicates Brazil is a cultural melting pot?*

Fig. 68.1

● *Identify the African countries where slaves were captured and subsequently transported to the Americas during the slave trade.*

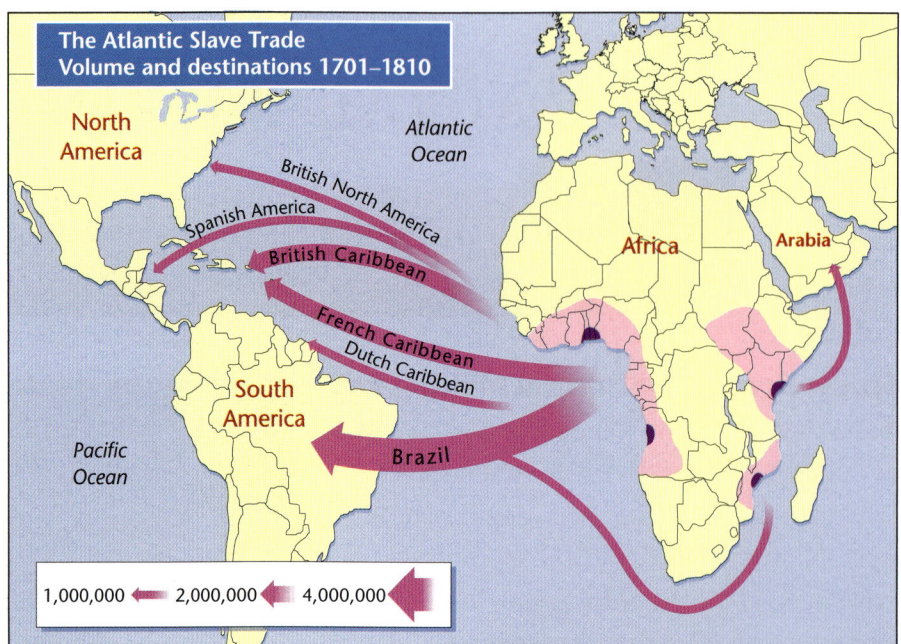

The Atlantic Slave Trade
Volume and destinations 1701–1810

North America

Atlantic Ocean

British North America

Spanish America

British Caribbean

French Caribbean

Dutch Caribbean

South America

Pacific Ocean

Brazil

Africa

Arabia

1,000,000 ← 2,000,000 ← 4,000,000 ←

Activity

Use the scale of the flow chart in Fig. 68.1 to identify the numbers of West Africans that were transported to:

● Brazil
● the Caribbean
● North America.

Activity

Study this extract, then answer the following.

1. Explain why Brazil has such a mixed racial population.

2. Explain some advantages of living in a multicultural society such as Brazil.

3. Explain the advantages and disadvantages for black people who live in Brazil.

4. Is racial discrimination active in Brazil? Explain.

5. Use the web to research Brazil's music and dance.

No other country outside Africa has such a large black population – about half of the total of 160 million people – yet blacks are almost totally absent from positions of power – from all levels of government, from congress, senate, the judiciary, the higher ranks of the civil service and the armed forces. Even in Salvador, the major slave port for nearly 300 years, where blacks make up more than 80 per cent of the population, very few are found in its local government.

A rights group reported in 2000 that racial discrimination is active in Brazil. Black and mixed-race Brazilians still have higher infant mortality rates, fewer years of schooling, higher rates of unemployment and earn less for the same work. Black men are more likely to be shot or arrested as crime suspects, and when found guilty, get longer sentences than white men. Yet there is no black movement in Brazil, no open racial conflict and no apparent racial tension.

Black Americans who live in Salvador say they feel much more at ease there than in the racially divided USA. One of the reasons for this huge difference between the USA and Brazil is that while in America race is defined by your ancestors – one drop of black blood makes you black – in Brazil what counts is your appearance. If you look white, or whitish, then you are white. For black Brazilians it is this very blurring of racial lines that makes it so difficult to fight racism. Paradoxically, it also offers the chance for Brazil to become a real racial democracy, once it faces up to and takes steps to combat racism.

by Jan Rocha

Racial Mixing in the United States of America

The African-American group is the only group to have involuntarily immigrated to the United States. A recent survey indicated that while nearly two-thirds of whites thought that race relations would eventually improve, only 44 per cent of blacks agreed.

One way by which the 'American melting pot' works is through the intermarriages of different racial, ethnic and national groups. Only one-quarter of non-Hispanic (not of Spanish blood) whites were married to someone with an undivided ethnic heritage identical to his or her own.

However, the melting pot has not welded that many unions across racial lines. Roughly 99 per cent of African-American women and 97 per cent of African-American men marry one of their ethnic group. This is not to take away from the fact that for every 100,000 married couples in the United States in 2000, there were over 400 black-white unions compared to 126 in 1960.

America is a multiracial society where racial mixing has been slow to occur.

Research some information on the civil rights movement in the United States and some active racist groups such as the Ku Klux Klan (KKK).

Consider that it was only in November 2000 that, after a state election, Alabama became the last state to overturn a law that prohibited blacks and whites from marrying.

How has music been influenced by migration patterns to the New World?

See **Ghettos**, page 376.

Large numbers of Hispanics live in ghetto communities such as Spanish Harlem in New York City, where they share a common culture with other residents.

CHAPTER 69
RACIAL CONFLICT

 **KEY IDEA!**

Migration has led to conflict between racial groups.

Case Study: Racial Conflict in the United States

At the end of World War II, Americans showed increasing concern over racial discrimination. In the South, segregation laws separated the ethnic groups in public schools and prevented blacks from entering restaurants, theatres and other public places reserved only for whites. In the North, where no segregation laws existed, blacks still faced discrimination in buying homes and seeking jobs. Many national leaders, both black and white, emphasised the need to end racial discrimination and to guarantee blacks their civil rights.

In the South, especially in the states of Alabama and Mississippi, violence against blacks by whites was rarely fully investigated. Blacks felt they were not protected by the law and were sometimes subjected to brutal beatings. Many were murdered by racist groups such as the Ku Klux Klan (KKK).

Watch the film *Mississippi Burning*. This will give you some idea of the racial conflict that existed in the United States.

Civil rights marches created tension that often led to violence by police.

The Ku Klux Klan is a racist group in the southern US.

The Black Panther movement sought civil liberties for African-Americans during the 1960s and 1970s.

Violence and racial tension occurred. Most civil rights demonstrations stressed non-violence, but the demonstrations sometimes caused tension that resulted in violence. Violence increased as the civil rights campaign intensified. Martin Luther King, the leader of the civil rights movement and a Nobel Peace Prize winner, was assassinated.

City ghettos bred unrest. Because of discrimination in the selling and renting of housing, many blacks were denied the right to live where they chose. Such unrest led to the Black Panther movement.

Search the web for information on the **Black Panther Movement**.

RACIAL CONFLICT IN INDIA

Racial conflict in India may be looked at under two headings:

- The caste system in India.
- Northern and southern Indians.

The Caste System

The caste system refers to the way people in India are divided by religious laws into groups in society. It is a **hereditary division** of society into classes **on the basis of occupation, colour, wealth or religion**.

India has four castes. The highest-ranking group are the Brahmans. **All the people who do not belong** to any of the four groups become outcasts, or **untouchables**. Due to the work of some leaders, such as Mahatma Gandhi, new laws passed in 1955 granted full social standing to untouchables and any discrimination against them became a punishable crime.

The concern of a true Hindu is not his ranking in terms of wealth within society, but rather his ability to be reborn into a higher existence during each successive life. Simply, a Hindu believes 'everything lies in the hand of God. We hope to go to the top, but our karma (action) binds us to this level.' This refers to the concept of reincarnation.

With the **introduction** of European and particularly **British systems** to India, the caste system began to change. It was a natural reaction of Indians attempting to adjust to the new regime and to make the most of whatever opportunities may have been presented to them. **The castes became rigid social divisions**. No one could rise to a higher caste than the one into which they were born. Consequently, no marriages took place between castes. The Hindu legal code, called the **code of Manu**, said that a person would be born again into a higher caste if he lived righteously and followed the code rigidly.

A sacred cow wanders a street next to two members of the untouchables caste working as street cleaners.

Recent advances in education are reducing the impact of the caste system, especially in the cities.

Why do you think discrimination is more common in rural areas than urban areas?

India today has become more flexible in the way the caste system works. In general, urban people are less strict about the caste system than rural people. In cities, people of different castes marry and mingle with each other. In some rural areas there is still **discrimination based on castes** and on people being considered **untouchables**.

Sometimes in villages and cities there are violent clashes associated with caste tensions. Although laws have changed, most of the communities that were low in the caste hierarchy remain low in the social order, even though the economic status of some may have changed. Communities that were high in social ranking remain high today. Most of the dirty or unpleasant manual jobs are still done by the Dalits (untouchables), while the Brahmans remain at the top of the hierarchy as doctors, engineers and lawyers.

A light-skinned couple in northern India.

Northern and Southern Indians

The British ruled India, as they did other lands, by adopting a strategy of divide and conquer. They promoted religious, ethnic and cultural divisions among the people they colonised to keep them under their control. One cultural division the British promoted was that India is a land of two races – the lighter-skinned Aryans, speaking a language of European origin (see **Indo-European Family**, page 432) in the northern half of the country and the darker-skinned Dravidians, who speak a different language, in the southern half. The Dravidians were the original inhabitants of India whom the invading Aryans supposedly conquered, dominated and drove to the south. This idea turned the people of southern India against the people of northern India, as if the darker-skinned southerners were a different race. European thinkers of that time believed in a racial theory of man that was based on colour alone. They saw themselves as belonging to a superior 'white' or Caucasian race.

Racial Conflict in Spain

See **Basques**, pages 428, 469–70, 473.

A darker-skinned woman in southern India.

CHAPTER 70
THE IMPACT OF COLONISATION AND MIGRATION ON RACIAL PATTERNS

Colonisation and migration affected racial patterns in many ways, such as population numbers, racial distribution, racial assimilation and segregation.

COLONISATION
Imported Diseases Affected Native Populations

The conquest of the Aztec, Mayan and Incan civilisations by Spanish conquerors like Cortes and Pizarro and subsequent Spanish armies led to quick and efficient defeat of the native Amerindians. Only some communities protected by their isolated location deep in the forests or high in the mountains survived the onslaught for a time. Eventually they too fell victim to the soldiers and also to the **diseases brought by the Spanish**. This clash of cultures spelled disaster for the native populations. The native people in the Americas had **no immunity to the diseases** from Europe: smallpox, typhoid fever, measles, influenza and mumps. Nor did they have any immunity against the tropical diseases that were later introduced when the Europeans brought African slaves to the Americas.

These diseases took enormous tolls on human life in the hot, humid lowlands of Middle America. Many of the dispossessed natives were relocated in newly built towns in overcrowded conditions. Here, disease spread rapidly. Middle America had between **15–25 million Native Americans** in this region when the Spaniards arrived. Only a century later, just **2.5 million** survived.

Colonisation by the Spaniards led to the destruction of existing cultures. Ancient cities were replaced with new coastal ports for exporting raw materials.

This photo of Machu Picchu shows the obsolete terraces that once produced an abundant food supply for the Incas.

FORCED MIGRATION – PUSH FACTORS
Forced Migration of African Slaves to the Americas

The forced migration of African slaves to the Americas expanded the distribution of the black African racial group. This occurred because the rapid decline of the Native American population **along coastal lowlands of Middle America and Caribbean islands** created a population that was too small to provide a sufficient labour force to work the cotton, tobacco and sugar plantations. The labour shortage generated the **transatlantic slave trade from Africa** that transported millions of black African people to the coastal rim of Middle America and to Brazil's east and northern coastlines. There are approximately **80 million black people in Brazil** today, forming half of Brazil's total population.

Slaves were also introduced to the **colonies in the American South**, which today includes the states of Virginia, Georgia, Alabama, Mississippi and the Carolinas. The descendents of these African slaves continue to live on the **Gulf Coast and eastern states of the USA** close to where their ancestors came from originally. They form about 13 per cent of the US total population today.

Fig. 70.1 The distribution of black Africans in the Americas.

424

Asylum-Seekers and Refugees

Many countries of the EU were colonial powers. These countries include Britain, France, the Netherlands and Belgium. Some of their colonies were in **Africa,** and these regions in particular have become the source regions for migrants to these former colonial powers and to other EU countries, such as Ireland.

Former colonies gained **independence after World War II** and others in more **recent times**. After independence, there was sometimes **civil unrest** leading to prolonged civil wars. **Political persecution** and **oppressive laws** forced many others to leave their native regions.

Every year, of these thousands of refugees, many hundreds drown **crossing the Mediterranean** to Europe. Others **suffocate** in sealed containers or **starve** in locked trucks. Many have been granted refugee status and this leads to the development of new mixed racial societies, such as in Ireland.

Recent refugees to Europe have increased the distribution of black African nationals to countries such as Ireland.

COLONISATION AND MIGRATION – PULL FACTORS

Voluntary Migration of Europeans to the Five Continents

The voluntary migration of Europeans to Northern Asia, South Asia, North Africa, Australia, North America and South America has created a **worldwide distribution** of the **Caucasian race**.

Initial migrations to North and South Asia were probably by **nomadic tribes** that carried their **Indo-European languages** with them across Russia and south to Iraq and India.

Later migrations by **Islamic Caucasian groups** from the Middle East carried their religion across **North Africa** and colonised the desert lands of the Sahara region.

The migration of the **Spanish colonists** has led to a distribution of Hispanic Caucasians from **western USA to the southern tip of South America**. The migration of **Europeans**, especially British, French, Dutch and Italian settlers to **North America,** led to the conquest of the North American continent. The first permanent colonies were set up in the early 1600s.

This was a westward migration across the continent by many who sought religious freedom or to escape poverty and famine, or simply hoped for a better life. These migrations **doomed the Native American tribes;** they were evicted from their traditional hunting grounds, slaughtered in battle and eventually the survivors were pushed into reservations at the foothills of the Rocky Mountains.

The transportation of convicts and settlers to Australia in the nineteenth century helped colonise that continent. Asian migrants and the almost pure race of the indigenous black Australian Aborigines make up the remainder of the population. Later, in the 1960s, incentives were offered to British residents to travel to Australia to help build up its economy.

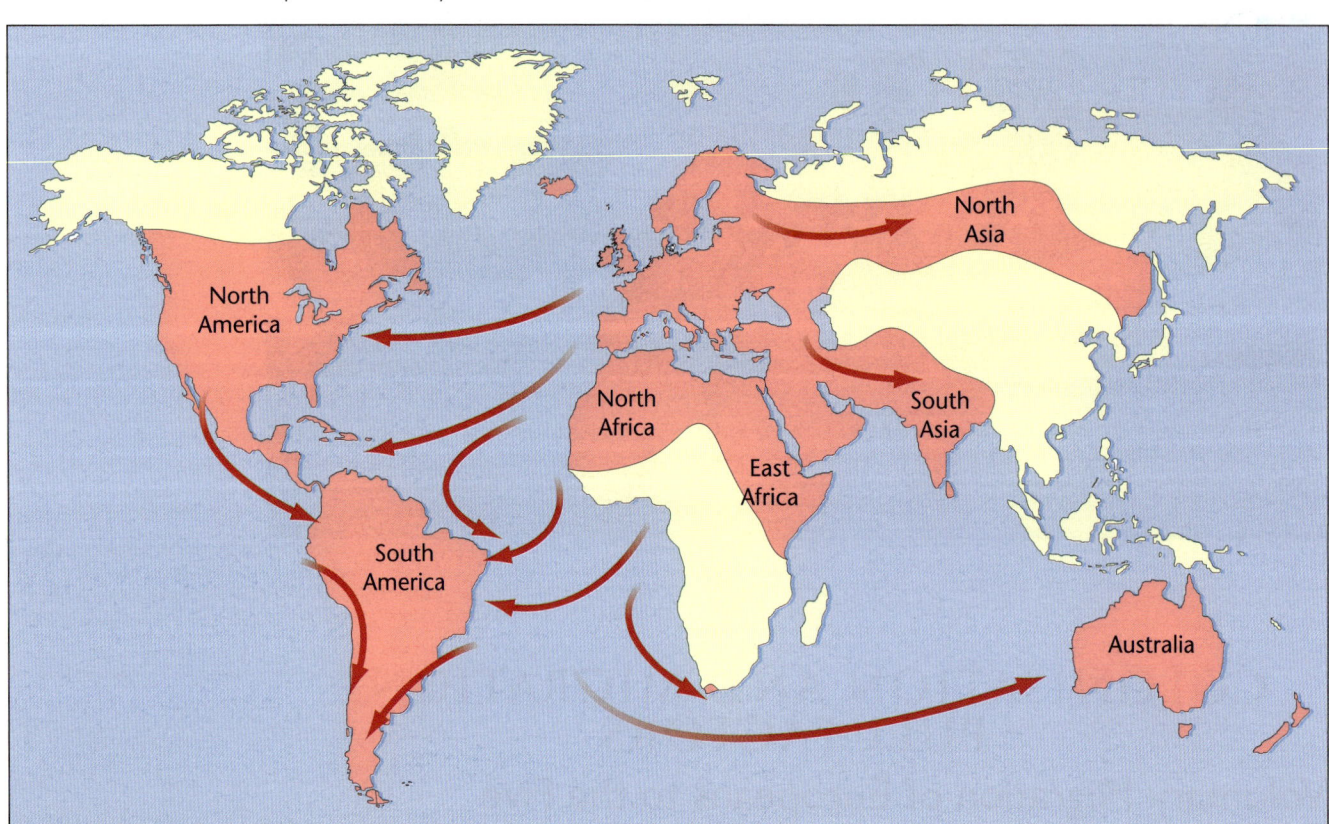

Fig. 70.2 European colonisation and migration patterns.

Racial Segregation in Cities
See **Civil Unrest and Social Segregation,** page 321.

Racial Patterns in the United States
Americans are choosing to live in distinct regions with others exactly like themselves. This is causing a regionalisation of distinct groups within the United States.

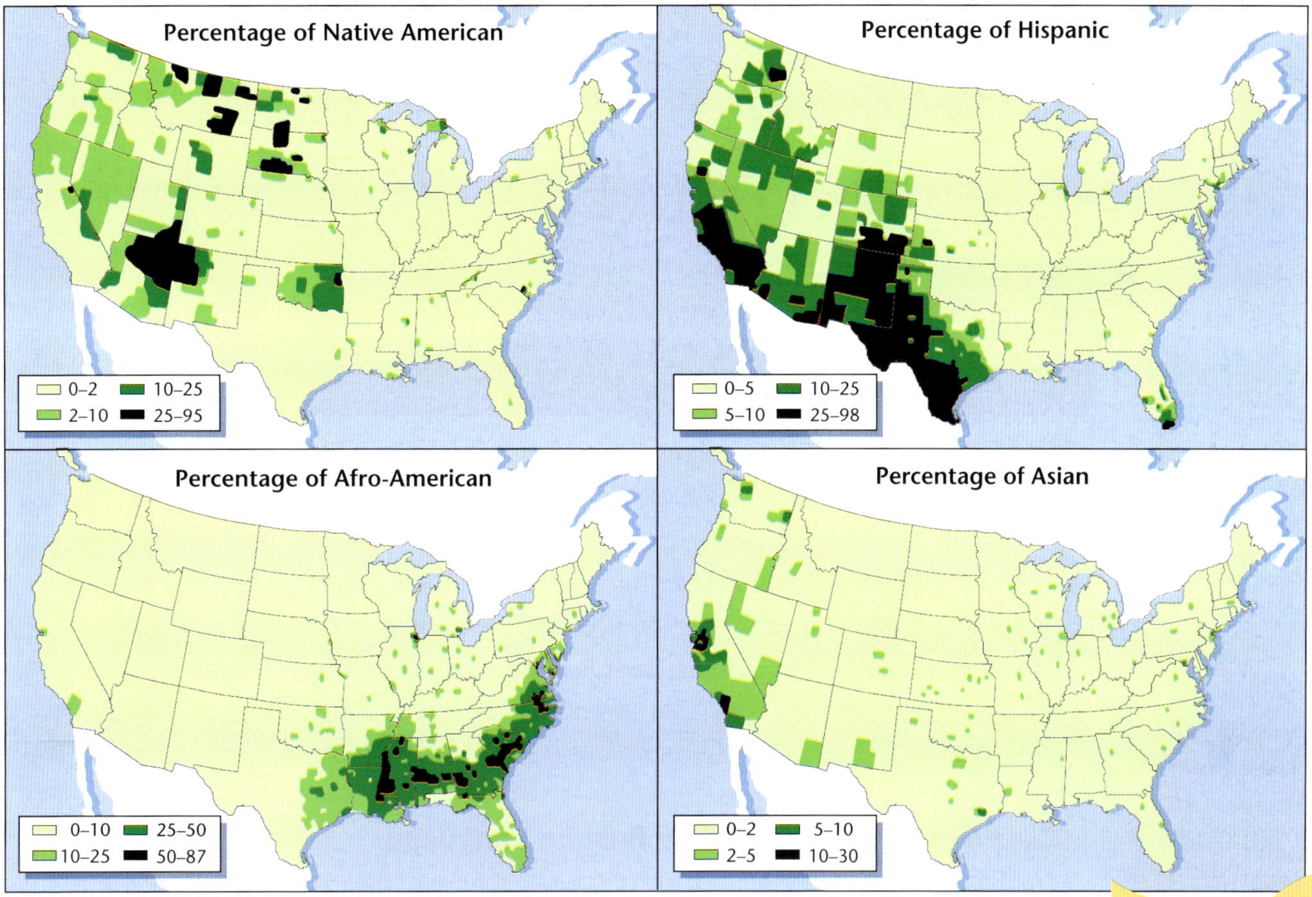

Percentage of Native American

Legend:
- 0–2
- 2–10
- 10–25
- 25–95

Percentage of Hispanic

Legend:
- 0–5
- 5–10
- 10–25
- 25–98

Percentage of Afro-American

Legend:
- 0–10
- 10–25
- 25–50
- 50–87

Percentage of Asian

Legend:
- 0–2
- 2–5
- 5–10
- 10–30

Fig. 70.3 Distribution of ethnic groups in the United States.

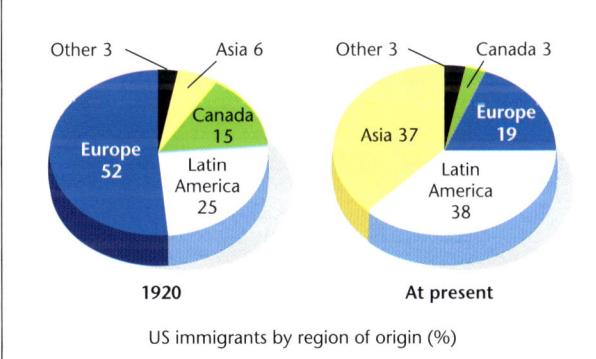

1920
- Other 3
- Asia 6
- Canada 15
- Europe 52
- Latin America 25

At present
- Other 3
- Canada 3
- Europe 19
- Asia 37
- Latin America 38

US immigrants by region of origin (%)

Fig. 70.4 Perceived economic opportunity, war and immigration policy all contribute to fluctuating levels in the flow of migrants.

Activity

1. Examine Fig. 70.5, then explain why:
   a. most Native Americans live in upland areas of the west
   b. most Hispanics live in the south-west
   c. most Afro-Americans live in the south-east and east
   d. most Asians live in the west.

2. What conclusions in terms of racial origin can be drawn from Fig. 70.4?

Remember the key ideas from your Junior Certificate that most migrants settle in those regions closest to where they came from originally.

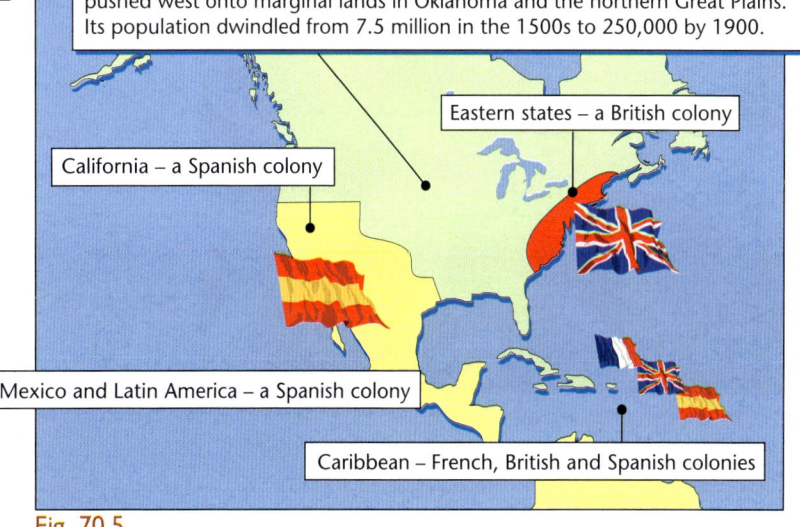

The Native American population, decimated by wars and European diseases, was pushed west onto marginal lands in Oklahoma and the northern Great Plains. Its population dwindled from 7.5 million in the 1500s to 250,000 by 1900.

Eastern states – a British colony

California – a Spanish colony

Mexico and Latin America – a Spanish colony

Caribbean – French, British and Spanish colonies

Fig. 70.5

427

CHAPTER 71
LANGUAGE AS A CULTURAL INDICATOR

KEY IDEA!

Language is a cultural bonding agent.

The development of speech and language has been one of the most fundamental developments of human cultural evolution. It is the means by which people can express themselves and communicate with others. It is also the chief means by which heritage is passed on from one generation to the next. **A common language acts as a powerful cementing factor in a social group. It welds the people into a community and develops mutual understanding, so it is important in creating nationality.** Conversely, the existence of different languages, whether between or within states, such as within India, may be an obstacle to understanding, co-operation and unity within that country.

The Flemings and Walloons in Belgium have created two distinct cultures/identities. See Chapter 22, page 148.

Case Study: Euskera – The Basque Language

The Basque people are very proud of their culture, and their language forms a crucial part of their unique identity. The history of their language has played its part in creating a **Basque culture**. The language of the Basques is called **Euskera**. It is spoken by about 520,000 people – about 25 per cent of the Basque people in Spain. One of the **oldest living languages,** it is not known to be related to any other language, so it is not Indo-European. It is believed that Euskera was spoken in the Basque region in Neolithic, or Stone Age, times. The first written texts in Basque date from the tenth century.

Things have not been easy for the Basque language. Besides competing with Spanish and French, Basque was a **forbidden language** after the Spanish Civil War in the **1930s** during the reign of the dictator **General Franco**. Children had to study in unfamiliar Spanish in school and were punished if they spoke Basque, their native tongue. During that time, in defiance of this policy Basque schools called *iskastolas* were started. This helped the Basque language to be taught in state schools.

Because there were many dialects of Basque, steps were taken in 1964 to create a unified Basque language. Their history of isolation, reflected in their gene pool (see page 470), may be the reason their language has survived while surrounding languages have been swamped by Indo-European influences.

Language and communication is the key to understanding cultures and to creating peace and harmony in a society.

Cultural Groups and Cultural Regions

The importance of language as a cultural identifier involves **language issues** in numerous political conflicts, ranging from **regional self-government** (such as in the Catalan region in north-east Spain and the Basque region of northern Spain) to the selection of languages in which school classes should be taught.

In many Western European countries such as Ireland, schools are under increasing pressure to find strategies to address the special needs of students whose home language is not the language used in school.

As a symbol of their culture, members of an ethnic group may seek to protect their language from being overwhelmed by the language of the dominant society. For example, in **Chinatowns** in cities, Chinese is the favoured language as it forms part of the identity of the majority of people within that ghetto area. The street signs and shop fronts all add to the area's character as a **cultural region**.

Bilingual signposts along the Mexican border with the USA reflect the huge Hispanic population in this area.

In some urban regions, cultural groups retain their traditional language for dialogue among people of their own culture.

Foreign students in Ireland use English because it is the most dominant language here.

'**Cultural regions**' is the general term for areas where some portion of the population shares some degree of cultural identity. Language is clearly evident in such regions through place names. The choice of language on signs is another visible symbol of culture on the landscape.

Criteria to define such regions must be chosen carefully. In some cases it may be convenient to use a single factor, such as language, to define regions such as Gaeltacht areas. In this instance, both the physical and cultural landscapes of the widely separated Gaeltacht regions mostly lie in the West of Ireland. They have a rugged terrain with small farms, scattered villages and few public services available locally. A majority of people within these areas identify with the same language and religion.

Activity
Explain how language can lead to cultural regions within cities.

The case of the **English language as a factor in determining culture is useful** only in **its broadest scale,** however, because of the numerous peoples whose primary language is English. The English, Irish, Canadians, Americans, Scots, Nigerians, Jamaicans and Indians all speak the English language as their primary tongue, but they differ greatly in their cultures. Americans and Canadians, for example, are often thought by some (including Americans) to share a single culture. Canadians, however, have their own specific values, heroes and traditions despite sharing language, religion, technology and other cultural traits with the United States.

The West of Ireland has a distinctive cultural character.
● *Describe the physical characteristics of Gaeltacht regions.*

In the 1990s a number of cities in India were renamed in the local regional language in response to a Hindu cultural revival. Bombay, for example, is now Mumbai.

See Chapter 22, Cultural Regions.

French colonies in Africa have French as their primary tongue.

Activity
1. Is language alone always an exact cultural indicator?
2. Discuss how language acts as an indicator of culture and identity. In your answer, refer to:
   a. the Basques (page 428)
   b. the Flemings and Walloons (page 148)
   c. ethnic regions in cities (page 429; see also **Civil Unrest and Social Segregation**, and **Ghettoes**, pages 321 and 376)
   d. Gaeltacht regions (pages 436–7).

CHAPTER 72
THE MAJOR LANGUAGE GROUPS

The complexity of human language and speech is dependent on a number of brain and body mechanisms found only in our species, *Homo sapiens*. These include a vocal tract (voice box) that permits a wide **range of speech sounds**, areas of the brain that control and **interpret these sounds** and an **efficient memory** that can use past experiences as a guide to the future.

Even though thousands of languages are spoken in the world today, populations that share similar cultures and live only a short distance apart may still speak languages that are quite distinct and not readily understood by neighbouring populations.

The first languages were dispersed in a number of ways:

- The most obvious dispersal was migration. As the early peoples spread out across the globe, they carried their languages into uninhabited territory.

- Languages would also have spread as a result of **contact between different peoples**. For example, the invention and adoption of food production (called the Neolithic Spread) would have encouraged agricultural peoples to migrate into territories occupied by hunter-gatherers, who may then have **adopted** both the cultivation techniques and language of the immigrants.

- A third form of language dispersal involves the **replacement of an existing language** by one spoken by a dominant group. The development of complex societies allowed incoming minorities with some form of centralised organisation to dominate larger populations which in many cases later adopted the language of the elite. For example, Ireland adopted English as a consequence of the military expansion of the British Empire.

Tourism, migration and business transactions across Europe have led to the introduction of languages such as Italian, French and German into Irish schools.

THE MAJOR LANGUAGE FAMILIES

Fig. 72.1 The major languages of the world.

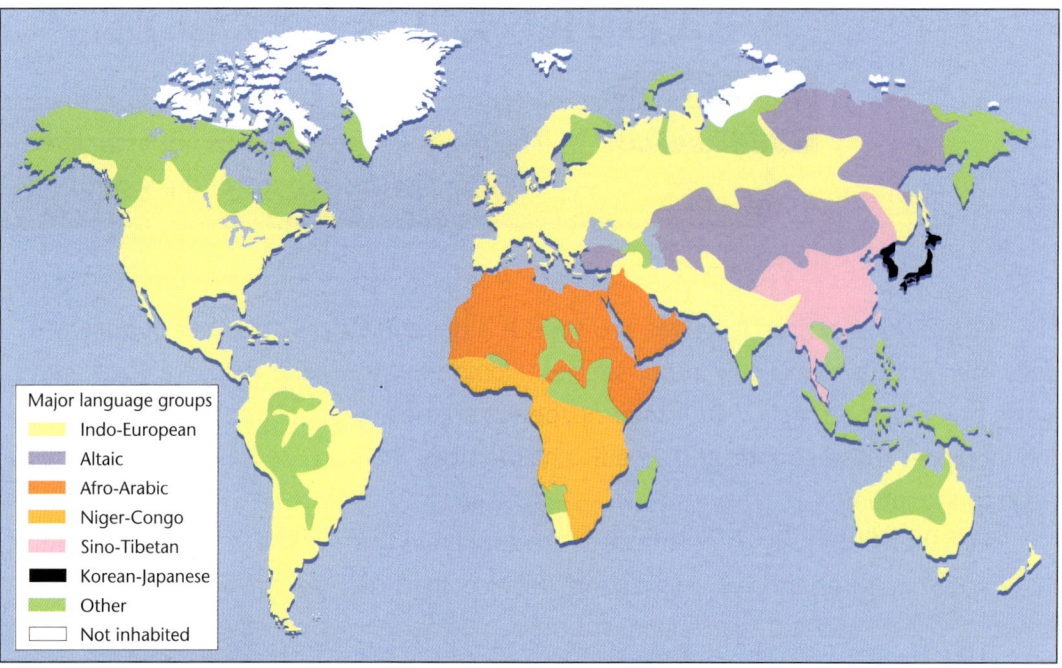

Major language groups
- Indo-European
- Altaic
- Afro-Arabic
- Niger-Congo
- Sino-Tibetan
- Korean-Japanese
- Other
- Not inhabited

Italian migration into the United States led to large Italian-speaking communities in many US cities.

Most Indian people in southern Asia speak a language that is related to the Indo-European language family.

Indo-European Family

The **Indo-European** family is the most important language family. About **half the world's population** speaks languages originating from this family. Most of the nations that gave rise to Western civilisation speak Indo-European languages. No one knows where the parent Indo-European language was first spoken. It probably began in the area south of the Baltic Sea.

Its speakers migrated to various regions and the language changed along the way. They now live in other regions, such as North and South America, across Russia to the Pacific Ocean and southern Asia, including Iran, Iraq, Pakistan and northern India as well as Malaysia and Australia. This language **spread** mainly through **conquest and colonisation**.

In North America, Britain and France took control of the land, while in Central and South America the Spanish and Portuguese introduced the Portuguese language (Brazil) and the Spanish language from Mexico southwards to Argentina and Chile. It is important to note that the **northern** half of **India speaks languages of Indo-European origin,** while the **southern** half **speaks Dravidian ones**. Indo-European was brought to northern India by groups of migrants that wandered eastwards from central Europe. The Indo-European language family has eight living branches. It includes:

- **Germanic:** This includes English, German, Dutch Flemish and the Scandinavian tongues – Danish, Icelandic, Norwegian and Swedish.
- **Romance, or Latin-Romance:** This includes French, Spanish, Portuguese Italian and Romanian.

- **Balto-Slavic:** This includes Russian, Ukrainian, Polish, Czech, Slovak, Serbo-Croatian, Slovenian, Bulgarian, Lithuanian and Latvian.
- **Indo-Iranian:** This includes Hindustani, Bengali, Persian and Pashto.
- **Greek**.
- **Celtic:** This includes Irish, Scots Gaelic, Welsh and Breton.
- **Albanian**.
- **Armenian**.

Many simple, basic words are similar in Indo-European languages. For example, the English word 'mother' is *meter* in Greek, *mater* in Latin, *madre* in Spanish, *Mutter* in German and *mat* in Russian.

Many words in German and English originate from a common tongue.

Sino-Tibetan Family

The Sino-Tibetan language family is second in importance, with over 1 billion speakers. This family includes **Chinese,** with its many dialects, as well as **Thai**, **Burmese** and **Tibetan**. These languages are the leading languages of East Asia.

The Sino-Tibetan or Chinese languages consist of **one-syllable words**. Speakers show the different meanings of otherwise identical words by changing their tone of voice. This language is one of the oldest living languages and has been spoken since about 2000 BC. The many dialects are different enough in pronunciation to be considered foreign languages.

China has suffered **many invasions** in the past and has seen many empires come and go. Each of these has had an effect on **language and dialect**. The country has also always been heavily populated and during some of the historical dynasties many Chinese migrated southwards in search of better land and living conditions. Mountain ranges run north to south down to South-East Asia and so **valleys provided corridors of migration** for many hundreds of thousands of people. These migrations influenced language in agricultural regions to the south, such as Thailand and Myanmar (Burma).

See Languages in Chapter 29, India. This is a link to your case studies.

Punjabi is the language spoken by the Sikhs, who are the majority cultural group in the Punjab, a state in northern India.

Arabic-Semitic Family

The Arabic-Semitic language family, which includes **Hebrew** and **Arabic**, is concentrated in north and north-east Africa, the Middle East and the Arabian Peninsula. It includes countries such as Morocco, Algeria, Tunisia and Egypt. The spread of the Muslim faith across North Africa brought the Arabic language to this region and it is the official language of these countries. In addition, the gold and salt trades that used the

The Chinatown sections of Western cities have a distinctive character, with their bright neon language signs and oriental-style building designs. (See **Ghettos**, page 376.)

The Arabic language and Islamic faith unite people across North Africa and in Arabian countries, creating a distinctive cultural region.

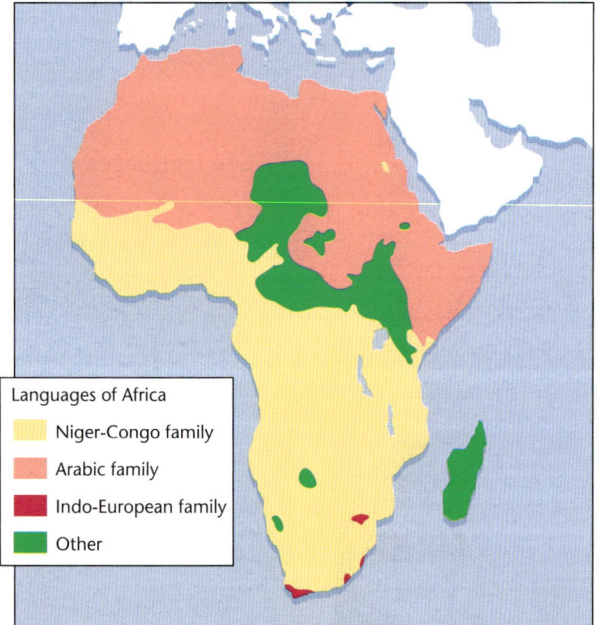

Fig. 72.2 Africa has many languages, especially in the areas south of the Sahara Desert.

Languages of Africa
- Niger-Congo family
- Arabic family
- Indo-European family
- Other

caravan routes crossing the Sahara created dialogue and helped the spread of Arabic (see **Islam,** page 443).

Ural and Altaic Family

The Ural and Altaic language family includes Finnish, Hungarian, Turkish, Mongol, Manchu and most of the languages spoken in the Asian part of Russia.

Niger-Congo Family

The Niger-Congo language family group is also called **Bantu**. The language is used in an area stretching from the Sudan in the north to South Africa in the south, and extending across the entire width of Africa to include the Democratic Republic of Congo, Somalia, Mozambique and Tanzania. It includes many tribal languages, including **Swahili**, which developed as a **pidgin** language for trading purposes between Arab and African traders. This language group probably originated in what is now Cameroon.

Swahili developed as a 'pidgin' language due to contact between African and Arab traders along the East African coast.

Japanese and Korean Family

The Japanese and Korean language family is largely limited to Japan, North Korea and South Korea.

Dravidian Family

The Dravidian language family is located in **southern India** and **Sri Lanka**. It consists of Tamil, Telugu and other regional languages.

Activity
1. Explain why skin colour and language provided useful tools in the origin of ethnic conflict and discrimination in India (see page 422).
2. Explain how a language of the Sino-Tibetan family helps create cultural regions within American and some European cities.
3. Explain how the recent spread of new languages to Ireland is helping to create cultural areas in Dublin. (Think of the Liberties area.)

CHAPTER 73
LANGUAGE AND MASS MEDIA

Mass media have been influential in the spread of European languages.

Some languages spread faster than others. In the past this may have been due to colonisation and migration. Some languages, such as English, however, are promoted indirectly but with increasing success by the influence of television and the internet. News is one of the foundation stones of broadcasting and quality news programmes have major viewing appeal.

TV programme providers such as Sky (English) and Canal (French) and the internet, with their ability to transmit images and news information as it happens, have increased the influence of mass media on language throughout the world. Such satellite world news coverage enters people's homes every day, thus increasing the influence of English or French in ex-colonial regions.

Hollywood in Los Angeles is the world centre of the film industry. English-language television programmes, such as *Friends*, also encourage the spread of the language. Hollywood stars and major films now have a worldwide audience. Music groups and individual singers, such as the Beatles and U2, Elvis and Eminem, and their music entertain audiences around the world.

In Kibera, one of the biggest slums in Kenya, a notice advertises an English football game.

This photo shows how well foreign regions and their languages can invade even isolated communities, such as this hill tribe in Laos in South-East Asia.

● *How can this negatively affect some languages? Explain.*

Activity

1. Suggest two other ways in which English has become a threatening influence on other languages. In one instance, refer to the influence of film as a threat.
2. Has TG4 helped in the promotion of the Irish language? Explain.

CHAPTER 74
POLICIES FOR SURVIVAL OF MINORITY LANGUAGES

KEY IDEA!

Government action helps in protecting minority languages.

It is believed that **diversity is the cornerstone of innovative development within the European Union (EU)**. It is argued that language plays a central role in this diversity, so attention must be given to maintaining this existing pool of variety in the EU. It is estimated that as many as 40 million citizens of the EU regularly use a regional or minority language that has been passed on from generation to generation, generally in addition to the official language or languages of that state. These languages are not those of immigrants or dialects of official languages but are recognised by the **European Charter for Regional or Minority Languages.**

This definition covers a wide variety of languages and an equally wide variety of social, political and language situations. Catalan, for example, is spoken by some 7 million people in north-east Spain, south-west France and the town of Alghero in Sardinia. Most Catalan speakers live in the **self-governing communities** of north-east Spain, where Catalan is spoken by the majority of the population and has official status alongside Spanish.

Additional examples include **Irish** and **Luxembourgish**, which despite their official status as national languages in their own countries bear many of the characteristics of regional and minority languages. In total, over sixty indigenous regional and minority language communities can be identified. All of these minority language groups, however, share a deep interest in the survival and continued development of their languages and cultures and the importance of their contribution towards the diversity of cultures within the EU.

Language plays a very important role in creating cultural identity. The *sardana*, Catalunya's national dance, is performed every week in the Plaça de la Seu, in Barcelona.

GAELTACHT REGIONS

In *Regional Geography* you studied the Gaeltacht areas that are scattered along the western and southern coasts of Ireland from Donegal to Waterford. You also learned that their total populations amounted to 86,000 people, and of these over 61,000 of them over the age of three years spoke Irish. The **Gaeltacht regions** are the **heartland of Gaelic language and culture**. However, there have been great changes in the boundaries of the Gaeltacht since it was first established. The present Gaeltacht, where Irish is the majority language, is much reduced in area and is today confined to relatively small isolated pockets, mainly in the peninsulas of the west coast of Ireland. Yet their presence forms an **integral part of Ireland as a nation,** and their special importance is supported by government grants, pay allowances and other financial incentives.

Initially, there were two categories of Gaeltacht regions:

(a)   In **Fior Gaeltacht** districts over 80 per cent of the population spoke Irish in their everyday life.

(b)   In a **Breac Gaeltacht** district between 25 and 79 per cent of the population spoke Irish.

Using these criteria, the commission that was established in 1925 was able to identify and create distinctive cultural regions based on the Irish language. Today in the Republic of Ireland there are 1.5 million people who claim to have some ability to speak and understand Irish. This totals over 41 per cent of the population of the state and it is over three times the number of people who claimed this ability in 1926. This increase reflects the continued efforts of government and voluntary bodies that promote the Irish language.

The Irish language is promoted through radio and TV programmes.
● *Would you consider this to be a successful way of promoting Irish?*

Initiatives for the Survival of the Irish Language

Some initiatives are government-sponsored, while others are voluntary. Some of these initiatives include:

● Festivals that promote the language through art exhibitions and music.

● An audio-visual industry that promotes Irish culture within the Gaeltacht and throughout Ireland. These influences include:

    –   Radio na Gaeltachta.

    –   The TV station TG4.

● Local radio stations such as Leirithe Lunasa Teo in Corca Dhuibhne and Nemeton Teo in An Rinn.

● Irish language schools, na Gaelscoilanna.

Annual Feiseanna, such as Fleadh Cheoil na hÉireann, promote Irish culture and traditions.

Find out the names of some of the festivals that promote the Irish language and culture and write a brief note about these activities and events.

Activity

1.   Do you think that Gaeltacht areas are distinctive cultural regions? Why? In your answer, refer to:
    ● language
    ● location
    ● landscape.

2.   Write as much as you can on any two initiatives for the survival of the Irish language. Say how successful you think each has been.

- Summer colleges in the Gaeltacht areas: These are also a welcome and vital source of income for families who provide accommodation and food for the students, as well as bringing the students in direct contact with Gaeltacht families.

Supports for Survival

Some county development plans support the Gaeltacht areas by demanding that place names are written in both Gaelic and English.

- Respect for linguistic and cultural diversity is one of the cornerstones of the EU. This ideal is now enshrined in **Article 22 of the European Charter of Fundamental Rights**, which states, '**The Union respects cultural, religious and linguistic diversity.**'
- The **European Bureau of Lesser-Used Languages** (EBLUL) is an organisation at the European Commission in Brussels. It works on behalf of people in the EU who speak minority languages by creating and promoting policies that support these languages under threat of extinction. For example, there are small Italian-speaking communities in Slovenia and Croatia and Polish-speaking communities in the Czech Republic. All these minority languages are in danger of being swallowed up by the majority language in those countries.
- The EU gives **financial support** to the **EBLUL** and its information network.
- The EU also offers funding for practical initiatives aimed at protecting and promoting regional and minority languages.
- International conferences are held at regular intervals to identify ways to improve the situations of minority languages under threat. These are organised by the Foundation for Endangered Languages (FEL).

Signposts are an indication of the spoken language in a region.
- *Is it important that some signposts should be bilingual?*

Ladin is a minority language spoken in some valley regions in Austrian mountain areas.

Activity
1. Explain the importance of the EBLUL in helping minority languages within the EU.
2. Explain how the survival of the Basque minority language plays its part in creating a cultural region within northern Spain. (See pages 428 and 469–70.)

CHAPTER 75
RELIGION AS A CULTURAL INDICATOR

Religion is a cultural bonding agent.

Religion, like language, can be a defining component of a **cultural identity** and one that provides the basis for the choice of clothing, food, tools and occupation.

As a social system based on the concept of a divine being, or god, and involving beliefs, values and behaviours, religion organises many aspects of culture.

Religion changes landscapes through the construction of **religious buildings**, such as churches. Mosques, with their minarets (towers), are visibly different from churches and contribute to the difference between Muslim and Christian landscapes. The absence of particular types of building, such as bars and pig farms, from Muslim communities occurs because alcohol and pork are taboo in Islam.

The **choice of clothing**, such as the concealing chador worn by Muslim women, and headwear, such as the turbans worn by Sikh men, who also have long beards, are personal signs of those religions. Shared beliefs and values establish strong group identification, and because groups can also be linked to specific areas, certain patterns of different religions result.

Attitudes to women, birth control and materialism can also be associated with patterns relating to certain religions.

While most religions involve the worship of some god, or gods, supreme beings play a minor role in some faiths, such as Buddhism. Nor do all religions have practices, core doctrines or moral codes that are common to every follower.

The great majority of the world's religions evolved among particular peoples who had no interest in attracting converts. Few tribal peoples, for example, would attempt to persuade their neighbours to adopt their religious beliefs and practices. Similarly, some prominent religions, such as Hinduism and Judaism, make no effort to seek converts.

However, this is not always the case. Religion is often the **cause** of great **social conflict**, particularly when two proselytising religions are in competition. Even within religions that have a core doctrine, comparatively minor differences of faith or practice can cause bitter divisions, such as between Catholic and Protestant communities in Northern Ireland. Frequently, religious conflicts are aggravated by **historical factors** and by the extent to which religious divisions are influenced by other divisions, such as language, ethnicity and class.

Sikh clothing is culturally distinctive.

Muslim women wear a chador as part of their culture.

Jewish people regard Jerusalem as their holy city.

Activity

1. Explain how religion plays its part in creating different cultural groups in Northern Ireland.
2. Explain the part played by religion in creating the Islamic cultural region throughout North Africa and the Middle East (see Chapter 76).

CHAPTER 76
THE DISTRIBUTION OF THE WORLD'S MAJOR RELIGIONS

KEY IDEA! The distribution of the world's major religions contributes to cultural identities as a consequence of past migration.

PATTERNS OF RELIGIOUS GROUPS

Religious groups tend to be concentrated in regions. The global distribution of these regions reflects past migrations of peoples and the spread of the religions. Religions began in localised areas, such as Christianity in the Holy Land and Islam in Mecca and Saudi Arabia, and then expanded outwards through the influence of missionaries and migrations.

Many cathedrals have Gothic-style architecture with pointed arches in windows and doors.

Activity
Examine Fig. 76.1 showing the distribution of the major religions of the world and Fig. 72.1, page 432, of the major languages of the world, then answer the following.
1. Identify three regions where similarities exist between the distribution of religions and languages.
2. Briefly account for these similarities.

Judaism

Judaism was originally the tribal religion of a people who traced their past back to **Abraham**. Following a command of God, Abraham is said to have migrated with his followers from the city of Ur in Mesopotamia (now modern-day Iraq) to Canaan in Palestine in the eastern Mediterranean. The Bible tells us that God promised the land to Abraham and his heirs. Moses led many Jews from Egypt back to Palestine in about 1200 BC.

Jews, who later migrated throughout the world, thought of Palestine (now Israel) as their spiritual birthplace because their religion developed there. Although Judaism has a comparatively small number of believers (around 14 million), it is important both for its role in the origins of Christianity and Islam and for its continuing influence on cultural and political events in the Middle East.

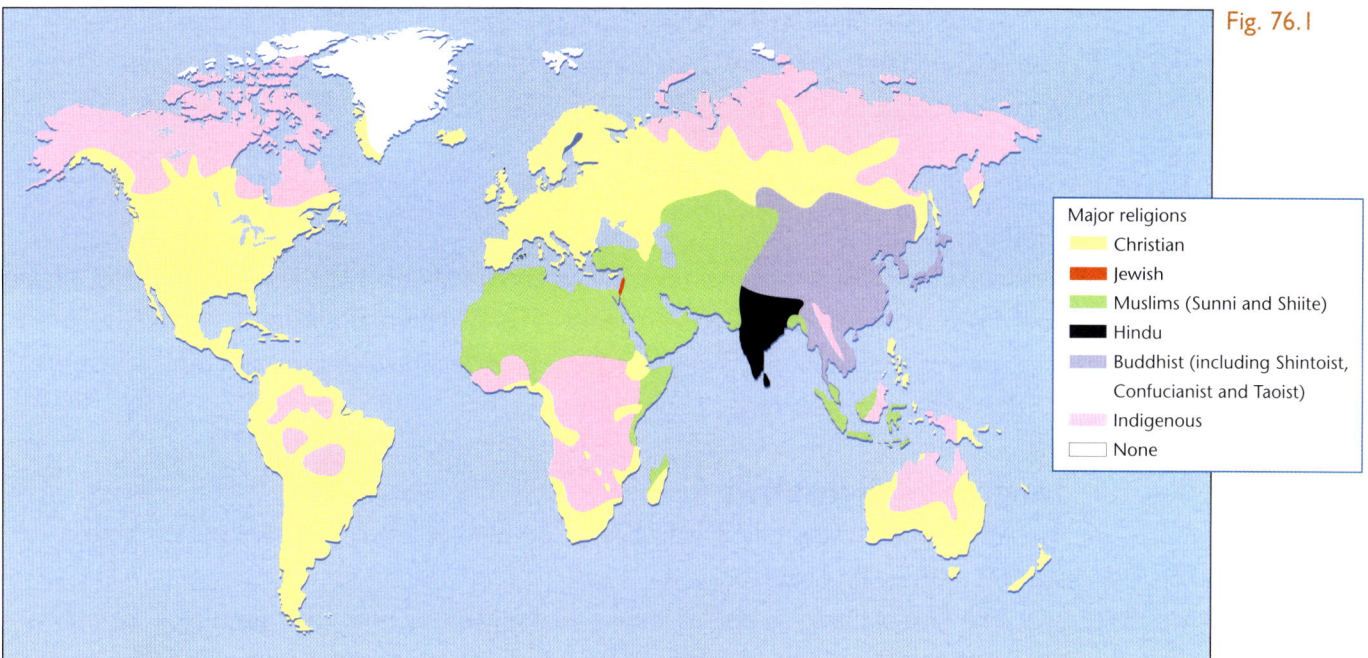

Fig. 76.1

Major religions
- Christian
- Jewish
- Muslims (Sunni and Shiite)
- Hindu
- Buddhist (including Shintoist, Confucianist and Taoist)
- Indigenous
- None

Which religions cover:

- The largest area?
- The second largest area?
- Why are some regions listed as having no religion (none) (see Fig. 76.1)?

Israel was founded to provide a **secure homeland for the world's Jews**. Since 1948, Jews have travelled from other countries to Israel. Many fled their own lands because of persecution. Israeli law provides that any Jew from anywhere in the world has the right to settle in Israel. In 1970, the law was amended to grant Israeli nationality to the wife of any immigrant Jew, to his descendants for two generations and to the wives of those descendants, whether or not they are Jewish. According to Judaism, a Jew is a person who has a Jewish mother or who has converted to Judaism.

Fig. 76.2 Israel was created to provide a homeland for the Jewish people in 1948.

Cultural Ties

Diet

Orthodox Jews follow dietary rules that come from biblical laws. They do not eat pork or pork products. They eat the meat of only those animals that chew the cud and have cloven hooves, such as cattle and sheep. They eat only those fish that have scales and fins, so they do not eat shellfish.

441

Some Jews observe the dietary laws as a sign of their faith, as a means of keeping their Jewish identity or as a way of bringing holiness into the simple act of eating. The word 'kosher', meaning 'fit' or 'proper', is used to describe food that complies with these laws.

Clothing

Orthodox Jews strictly observe Jewish laws and traditions. Male Jews usually wear a head covering out of respect to God's presence. This is known as a kippa or yarmulka. Some wear beards and sideburns. They also wear a prayer shawl known as a tallit. These are public representations of their Jewish faith.

Language and Symbols

Modern Hebrew is the official language of the state of Israel. Nearly 4 million Israelis speak it as their first language.

The Star of David symbol is known as the Magen David. First used as a decorative feature during Roman times, it now appears on the Israeli national flag. This became a very public symbol during the Holocaust when all Jews had to wear it as a symbol of their ethnicity or risk being shot.

St Peter's Basilica in Rome is the centre of the Christian world.

Christianity

Christianity is the largest religious group, with over 33 per cent of the world's population as believers. Christianity originated as a movement within Judaism. Fundamental to its doctrine is the belief that **Jesus Christ** was the Messiah prophesied in the Old Testament. Jesus began his career in Palestine and travelled around the country with a group of twelve chosen disciples.

Christianity spread rapidly. The Romans persecuted the Christians for many years until Emperor Constantine granted them freedom of religion. Through the Edict of Milan in AD 313, Christianity became the official religion of the Roman Empire. Christianity continued to spread after the fall of the Roman Empire in the fifth century, reaching most of Europe by AD 1000.

During medieval times, the Church strongly influenced political and intellectual life in Europe. It developed great wealth and power and Christianity bound almost all of Europe in a single faith. Europe was then known as Christendom. **The rulers of Spain and Portugal were Christians** and were the main cause of spreading the Christian faith to the **Americas**. During the fifteenth and sixteenth centuries in particular, the Christian faith was spread to North and South America following Christopher Columbus's exploration and later the actions of the Spanish conquistadors, such as Cortes and Pizarro.

Canada was colonised by the French and the British, while the USA was mainly British up to the eighteenth century. During the nineteenth century, mass migration from

Europe took place. In the nineteenth and twentieth centuries the British colonised Australia, while the **Jesuits** were influential in carrying Christianity to **China**. Christianity had spread throughout Russia before the Russian Revolution against Czar Nicholas.

Cultural Ties

Rome is the centre of the Roman Catholic faith and St Peter's Basilica is a centre of pilgrimage. Christians pray in public at times of trouble or before performing an important task, for example, athletes who bless themselves before they compete.

Tall cathedrals and statues form part of Christian landscapes. A statue of Christ on a hill overlooking Rio de Janeiro in Brazil is 30 m tall and looms over the city. The statue has become known the world over as the symbol of Rio. Individuals wear a cross and chain as a symbol of their Christianity.

Arts

Many religious paintings were created by Renaissance artists. Music has been part of Christian worship for centuries and many composers in the Middle Ages were monks who spent their lives writing and singing church music. Later, in 1741, German-born composer Handel wrote his oratorio 'Messiah' and it is still performed today. Many famous films and plays, e.g. the Passion play, are based on religious themes.

Islam

Islam sprang from the same roots as Judaism and Christianity. Islam is the name given to the religion preached by the **Prophet Mohammed** in the seventh century. Mohammed was an Arab who was born in Mecca about AD 570. He believed he had been sent to warn and guide his people and to call them to worship God, Allah. Mohammed preached that there is only one god and that he, Mohammed, was God's messenger. Those who believe in this faith are called Muslims.

> Can you identify some cultural symbols from the everyday life of people of the Christian faith?

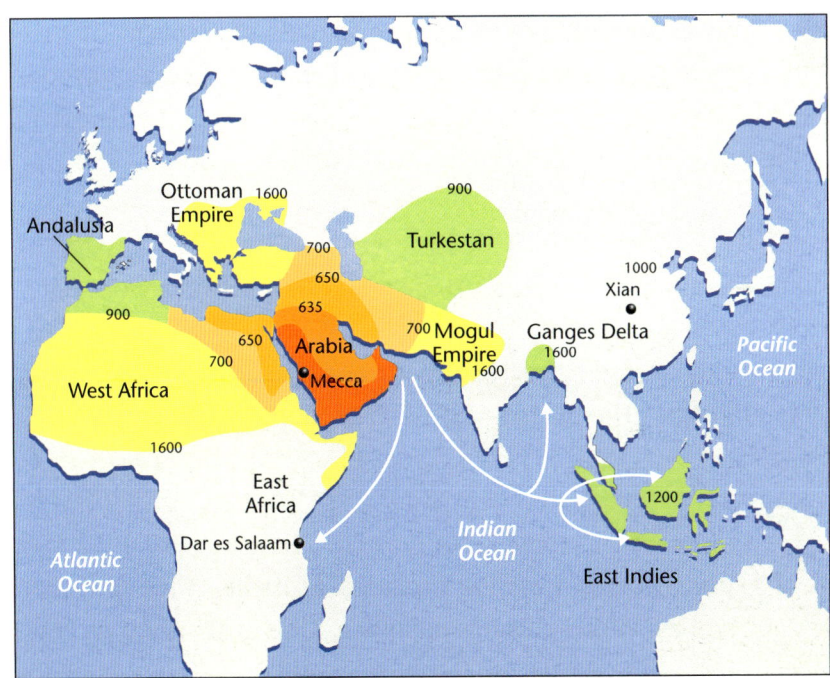

Fig. **76.3** The spread of Islam, AD 630–1600.

Activity

Examine the map showing the spread of Islam, then answer the following.
1. Which European countries were affected by the spread of Islam?
2. Identify two ways this migration affected the culture and life of people in any two of these European countries.

Some men in hot desert lands wear white cotton shirts, baggy dark trousers or long cotton coats. Most city dwellers wear Western-style clothing.

Muslims face east towards Mecca to pray.

After Mohammed died in AD 632, the new caliph (Muslim ruler) and his successors waged holy war, called *jihad*. Within a hundred years they had built an empire across the **hot desert lands that stretched from northern Spain and north-west Africa to India**. The Muslims threatened Western Europe until Charles Martel, the leader of the Franks, defeated them at the Battle of Tours in 732. A consequence of this colonisation process can be seen in the influence of the Moors in Spain and by the presence of large numbers of Muslim people in countries that make up former Yugoslavia.

The Arab conquerors taught the inhabitants of their captured lands their Arabic language and their Islamic faith. The **Arabic language eventually replaced the native languages** in most of these regions, and Arabic became the language of the Muslim culture. However, in countries east of the Arabian peninsula, such as in Iran and in Iraq, Indo-European languages are spoken even though they practise Islam.

Islam has **two major branches**, Sunni and Shiite. This separation occurred during the seventh century over leadership of the religion. Sunnis make up about 84 per cent of all Muslims and dominate the Arabian peninsula, northern Africa and most Muslim countries around the world. Shiites are the majority of the population in Iran, which is about 90 per cent Shiite, and in Iraq, which is some 60 to 65 per cent Shiite. Indo-European-speaking Shiites mainly live east of Arabia, while the Arabic-speaking Sunnis live west of the Arabian peninsula.

Cultural Ties

Mecca is the centre of the Muslim faith. All Muslims aim to make a pilgrimage (the *hadj*) to Mecca once in their lifetime. Mosques and their minaret towers form part of Muslim landscapes. Five times each day the *adhan*, or call to prayer, from the minarets is heard in Muslim communities.

Education

The science of astronomy is important to Muslims because it can be used to work out the direction of Mecca. It also helped them to determine the correct times to pray. The astrolabe and quadrant, instruments used in astronomy and navigation, were developed and made accurate by the Muslims. The Islamic world also produced the first skilled, specially trained pharmacists.

'Moors' is the name given to Arabs who invaded Spain from North Africa.

Clothing

Muslims wear all sorts of different clothes, from the traditional garments of the Arabian desert to modern Western clothes. In some Islamic countries, it is traditional for women to veil their faces. The veil may cover the lower part of the face up to the eyes, or may cover the whole face. Women and men do not mix socially.

Food

Some dietary rules restrict what a Muslim may eat. Islam forbids the drinking of alcohol and Muslims do not eat pork. Other animals may be eaten provided they are slaughtered following certain rules – *halal* – so pigs and pubs are absent from Islamic countries.

Hinduism

Hinduism is mostly confined to the Indian subcontinent and parts of South-East Asia, such as Malaysia and Indonesia, mainly because of its non-missionary nature. Hinduism has its roots in the religion of Indo-European peoples who migrated into India thousands of years ago.

The sacred texts of Hinduism are the Vedas, which explore the place of human beings and the roles played by various gods in the functioning of the universe. Hindus are monotheists. They believe in one high god, Brahma, the Absolute.

Hinduism may be divided into three branches, or sects, each with its own view of the nature and name of the high god, Vishnu, Shiva or Shakti. Families, by long tradition, support one branch or another. All branches are to be found in every part of India. The three sects continue together more or less in harmony. Educated Hindus believe that the three gods are merely different ways of looking at the same high god.

Cultural Ties

Hindus build ornate temples to worship in. The River Ganges plays a central role in the Hindu faith. Hindus believe that the river can cleanse the spirit of an individual of all sin and of those of countless previous generations. People give offerings to the Ganges in the form of fruit, money, candles or flowers. Many festivals are held each year to honour deities.

At Varanasi, Hinduism's holiest city, and other cities and towns along the Ganges, the river banks are lined with Hindu temples and dozens of wide stone staircases called *ghats*. These steps allow bathers in search of spiritual healing to enter the river's waters to bathe.

Activity

1. From which city and state did Islam spread?
2. When did Islam reach India and Pakistan?
3. When did Islam reach north-west Africa?
4. Which was the conquering group that brought Islam to south-eastern Europe? When did this occur?
5. Give an example of conflict in the twentieth century that arose as a result of migration or religious influence.

Hinduism

India

Indian Ocean

Fig. 76.4

Millions of Hindus gather on the steps at Varanasi to wash in the sacred River Ganges. They believe that touching the water can wash away a believer's sins.

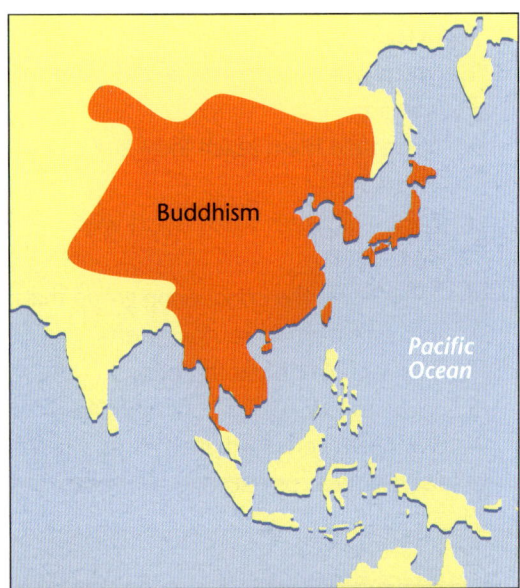

Fig. 76.5

Buddhism

Buddhism is one of the major religions of the world. It was founded in India as an offshoot of Hinduism and is based on the teachings of **Siddhartha Gautama**. He was born a member of the Hindu priestly caste about 563 BC. Buddhism started near the border of what are now India and Nepal, where Siddhartha was **born, reached enlightenment and died**. Lumbini, now in Nepal, and Bodh Gaya and Kusinagara in India are sacred places in this religious region linked to these three events.

Missionaries carried Buddhism to regions of eastern Asia such as China and Japan. Different branches of the religion developed and Buddhism also merged with other religions. The number of Buddhists worldwide is uncertain because individuals often practise Buddhism along with cultural Chinese and Japanese religions. Buddhism is dominant in Tibet, now part of China. It is also common in China, Korea, Japan and in parts of South-East Asia, such as Vietnam.

Buddhism is mostly confined to east and South-East Asia. Here, crowds offer alms to Buddhist monks in Thailand.

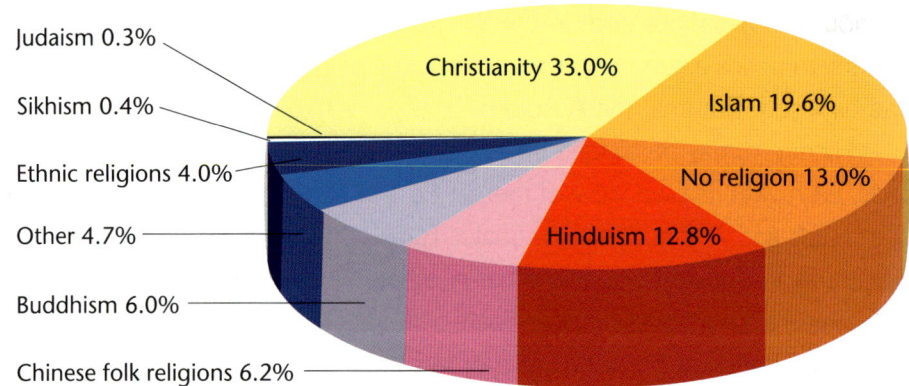

Judaism 0.3%
Sikhism 0.4%
Ethnic religions 4.0%
Other 4.7%
Buddhism 6.0%
Chinese folk religions 6.2%
Christianity 33.0%
Islam 19.6%
No religion 13.0%
Hinduism 12.8%

Fig. 76.6

Activity

1. The pie chart in Fig. 76.6 shows the percentages of the world's population belonging to the major religions. Despite their small number, the Jews (0.3 per cent) have had a major influence on history, culture and other religions.
   a. List the world's religious groups in rank order.
   b. To which language group do most of the world's largest religious group belong? Explain fully.
   c. Explain why this religion has spread over such a large number of regions.
   d. In which region of the world is Hinduism practised?
   e. Which language groups do people practising Hinduism belong to? Explain fully.
   f. Why is it that the Chinese folk religious group makes up only 6.2 per cent of the world's population, even though the Chinese number 1.2 billion people?
   g. In which cultural region or area of the world is Islam the dominant religion?
   h. Explain why Islam dominates in this area.
2. The success of the spread of Islam and the present-day distribution pattern of the Islamic faith may have been due in part to climatic factors. Discuss.
3. Explain why the Christian faith is practised in areas in Africa that are widely separated from each other.

CHAPTER 77
THE RELATIONSHIP BETWEEN CHURCH AND STATE

KEY IDEA!

The Irish nation was greatly influenced by the Catholic Church during the twentieth century.

The Irish Constitution

The Irish Constitution of 1937, introduced by Eamon de Valera, recognised the **'special position of the Catholic Church'** as the 'religion of the great majority of citizens' (Article 44). At the same time, the Constitution guaranteed 'freedom of conscience and the free profession and practise of religion' to a list of other religious groups, including the Jewish community.

At the beginning of the eighteenth century, a series of harsh laws called **'The Penal Laws'** were introduced into Ireland to penalise the vast majority of the Irish people just because they were **Roman Catholics**. These Penal Laws stated that a Catholic could not hold any office of state, nor stand for parliament, vote, join the army or navy, practise law or buy land. Thus the association of the **Catholic religion** with **politics**, **law** and **land** was **firmly established** in the minds and hearts of the Irish people; it was to dominate Irish society until recent times. Daniel O'Connell's campaign to repeal these laws encouraged this association and he successfully channelled the influence, or in other words, the power, of the Catholic Church's bond with the Irish people into politics. He linked them together so firmly that succeeding generations found it difficult to separate them.

Up until the 1970s Irish society was mainly a rural one. The ownership of land played an important part in Eamon de Valera's image of Ireland and the rural farming communities provided large numbers of young men for the priesthood and religious life. Farming communities and businesspeople could afford, more than others, to send their sons to university (often with state grants) or campaign for political office. This created a religious, farming, professional and political circle of power that continued until recent times.

Eamon de Valera recognised the 'special position of the Catholic Church' as an influencing factor in Irish political affairs.

Up to the 1970s, many young people in Ireland entered religious orders.

Research the 'Mother and Child' scheme under Dr Noel Browne.

447

Regular Orange Order marches displayed the dominance and political power of the Protestant community in Northern Ireland.

Northern Ireland

In 1911, on the island of Ireland, 62 per cent of the members of the Church of Ireland and almost all of the 444,000 **Presbyterians** lived in the same nine Ulster counties. Political controlling influence was predominantly Presbyterian, **industry** being a major influence, since it was mostly the Presbyterians who built the docks, **the shipyards** (the largest in the world at that time) and **linen mills**. Ulster Presbyterianism and the spread of **Calvinism** from Scotland had its roots in the seventeenth-century **Plantation of Ulster**. The rise of the **Orange Order** in the nineteenth century among the wealthy landowners and industrialists made this the representative body of the Protestant community.

The Orange Order fostered a sense of community amongst Protestants and institutionalised the instinct of **racial superiority** over the conquered Catholics. This led to **social segregation**, especially noticeable **in the cities**, which led to the **ghettos** in Belfast and Derry, where Catholics were housed in certain housing estates in one part of a city while Protestants were housed in others. It also led to **gerrymandering**.

Gerrymandering

After the partition of Ireland, a proportional representation (PR) system of local elections was introduced by the British government to give minorities a fairer say in the electoral system. However, this was seen as a threat to the Ulster state by the unionist government in Northern Ireland and it was abolished in 1922. All local government electoral boundaries were redrawn in such a way that unionist majorities were guaranteed, despite the fact that Catholics formed a majority of the population in many counties. The **right to vote** for local councils was limited to those **who held property** and people with several properties had several votes. Since Protestants generally had more property than Catholics, it strengthened Protestant control of Northern Ireland. This system led to **widespread corruption and discrimination against Catholics** in jobs, housing and other local services; this continued until the 1970s. **Civil rights marches**, encouraged by successful marches by the black community in the United States, indirectly led to gradual change in Northern Ireland.

Catholic nationalists were forced to march in the 1960s and 1970s to gain civil rights.

Activity
1. Explain how the influence of the Catholic Church in political affairs evolved over time.
2. Who was Dr Noel Browne? Explain how conflict arose between him and the Church in Ireland during the 1950s.
3. Explain the origin of the Presbyterian faith in Ulster and its influence on politics.

CHAPTER 78
RELIGIOUS CONFLICT

KEY IDEA!

Social unrest can arise when different religious communities come into contact.

Members of different religions live side by side without problems in many areas of the world, but religious conflict can arise when different religious communities come into contact. Some conflicts arise over political and economic opportunities while others may occur over beliefs and values.

The following case studies look at some disputes that have arisen as a consequence of religious differences.

Case Study 1: India
The Kashmir Dispute in the Indian Subcontinent

India and Pakistan are two countries united by history and divided by destiny. Their rivalries over five decades have prevented both countries from realising their full economic and political potential.

The two countries have fought three wars, two of them over the disputed region of Kashmir. This region is small, but because it is located in the foothills of the Himalayas, its strategic importance and beauty make it a prized possession.

The Punjab state in India is a rich farming region where the Sikh faith dominates. See pages 467–8.

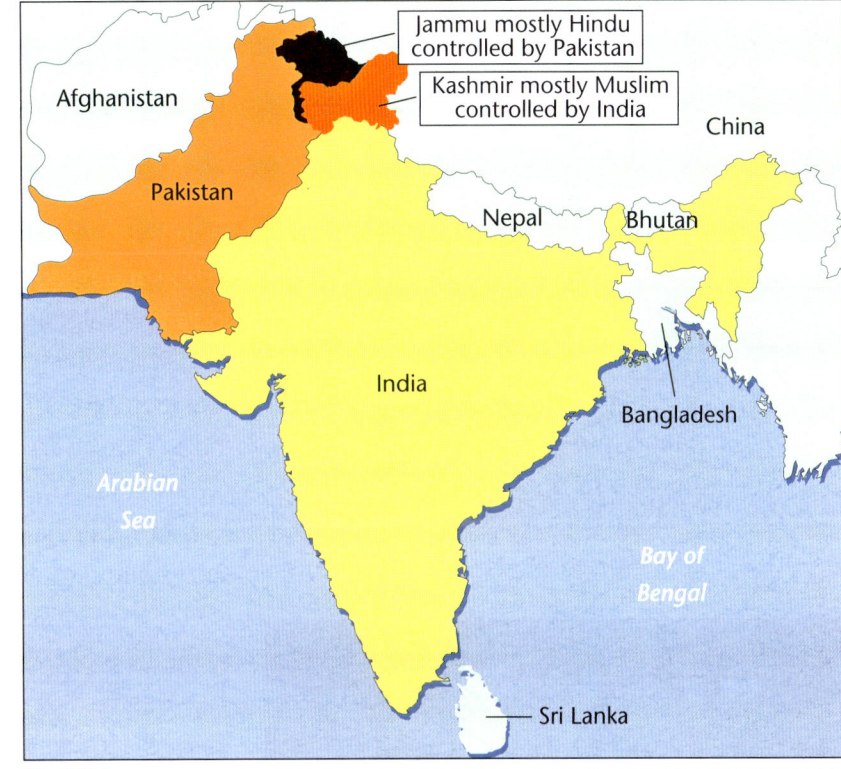

Jammu mostly Hindu controlled by Pakistan

Kashmir mostly Muslim controlled by India

Afghanistan

Pakistan

China

Nepal

Bhutan

India

Bangladesh

Arabian Sea

Bay of Bengal

Sri Lanka

Fig. 78.1

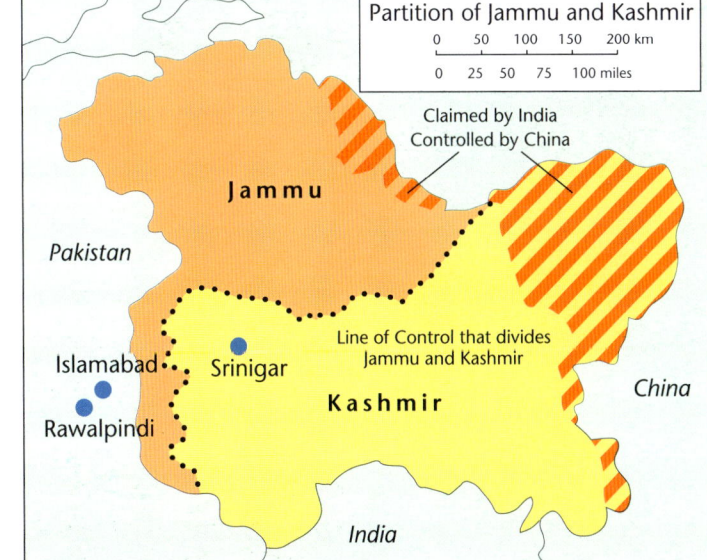

Partition of Jammu and Kashmir

0   50   100   150   200 km

0   25   50   75   100 miles

Claimed by India Controlled by China

Jammu

Pakistan

Islamabad · Srinigar

Rawalpindi

Line of Control that divides Jammu and Kashmir

Kashmir

China

India

Fig. 78.2

449

Kashmir is a mountainous region in the Himalayan range. The Vale of Kashmir is a rich agricultural region within the mountains that has a cooler and more temperate climate than the scorched land of much of India. In this picture, women are separating chaff from straw in Kashmir.

The Indian subcontinent was a colony of Britain until its partition in 1947.

Access to fresh water supplies is a major concern in India, especially in areas of political conflict.

The Kashmir Dispute

See also Chapter 36, pages 252–3.

The region called Kashmir is really two states:

- **Jammu**, which is **controlled by Muslim Pakistan** and has a **Hindu majority** population.
- **Kashmir**, which is **controlled by Hindu India** and has a **Muslim majority** population.

These two states are divided by a ceasefire line called the 'Line of Control' drawn up by the United Nations in 1949, two years after the first war.

In 1947 the subcontinent was **divided into two nations based on religious grounds**: **Pakistan,** a Muslim state, and **India,** a Hindu state. The leaders of each state in the subcontinent decided whether the state would join with Pakistan or India. But the division of the subcontinent did not include Jammu and Kashmir because the Maharaja, who was a Hindu and ruled both states, had signed agreements with both India and Pakistan to remain neutral.

A revolt within Kashmir by the Muslim group against Hindu rule led to the Maharaja joining the states he controlled with India. This led to war and a dispute that even today has remained unsolved.

In 1996 the Indian and Pakistani prime ministers agreed to settle their dispute peacefully. A threat of war occurred again in 2002 when Pakistan and India amassed troops along both sides of the Line of Control. Today the conflict continues as before.

Besides the political divide that separates both nations, there is another issue that is of great importance to both countries.

Because much of Pakistan is desert, Pakistan is concerned that the **River Indus** has several of its main **head-streams** rising in Indian-controlled Kashmir. The waters of the River Indus and its tributaries are Pakistan's lifelines because they provide large volumes of clean water for **irrigation** and for industrial and domestic uses. Not having control of these head-streams puts Pakistan in a sensitive position.

Case Study 2: Religious Conflict in Northern Ireland

For more than thirty years the words 'Northern Ireland' have created images of violence and bitter sectarian division as Catholics and Protestants have fought each other. Between 1966 and 2000, over 3,600 people were killed and 36,000 injured as the conflict spread beyond Northern Ireland's borders into Britain and the Irish Republic.

The Roots of the Conflict

Since the **reign of Henry VIII (1509–49)**, when Catholic Ireland was brought under Protestant England, tension has existed between the two faiths. During the reign of **James I (1603–25)**, large numbers of Protestants were settled in Northern Ireland as part of the **Ulster Plantation**, creating a Protestant majority in the region that exists to this day. Following the defeat of the Catholic James II by the Protestant William of Orange at the Battle of the Boyne in 1690, most of the land in Ireland was handed over to Protestant control.

Civil unrest in Northern Ireland generally reaches a peak during the marching season.

The **Treaty of 1921** after the War of Independence recognised this religious division by dividing the country into two separate political units, a predominantly **Catholic south**, the Republic of Ireland, and a predominantly **Protestant north**, Northern Ireland. Most of Northern Ireland's minority Catholic population do not trust the Protestant majority and would prefer to belong to a single united Ireland. Most of the Protestants, on the other hand, are determined to remain part of the United Kingdom. The result has been an ongoing cycle of protest and violence as paramilitary groups from both sides have sought to press home their point with bombs and guns.

The **Good Friday Agreement** in 1998 has transformed the politics of Northern Ireland. It created a 108-member assembly and a fourteen-member executive body in which both Catholic and Protestant political representatives sit together in government, only the second time such power sharing has occurred since 1920. The main paramilitary groups are either disbanded or inactive, the British military presence is being scaled down and the IRA has decommissioned its weapons. Foreign money has poured into the region as international companies are encouraged by the continuing peace within the North.

Activity

1. When did religious division first take root in Ireland?
2. Which events in the twentieth century created distrust between religious groups in Northern Ireland?
3. What efforts are being made to strengthen trust between both communities today?

However, while some paramilitary groups have laid aside their weapons, splinter factions such as the Republican Real IRA and the Loyalist Red Hand Commandos have failed to call a ceasefire. A much smaller percentage of Protestants – 52 per cent – fully backed the Good Friday Agreement, compared to 96 per cent of Catholics. Hopefully sectarian violence in Northern Ireland is all in the past.

Dialogue between the various political groups has led to a ceasefire and peace within Northern Ireland.
● *Can you identify each of these three politicians?*

Trying to find a compromise between the police and opposing religious and political groups is often difficult.

Activity

1. Explain the origins of the religious conflict that continues in Ulster today.
2. What political differences today have resulted from this dispute?

452

CHAPTER 79
EVERYDAY EXPRESSIONS OF CULTURE AND IDENTITY

 **KEY IDEA!**

People's everyday lives provide indicators of their cultural origin and identity.

Nations and cultural groups express their unique identity through social activities such as sports, traditions, dress code, food, music, art and festivals.

FESTIVALS AND SPORTS IN IRELAND

More than any other activities, Irish sports, music and art express our unique identity.

Sport

The **Gaelic Athletic Association** (GAA) has promoted Gaelic hurling and football as their most important sports. Almost every parish throughout the island of Ireland has its own GAA club, based on an open membership policy. The most important events in the GAA are the All-Ireland Finals in Croke Park in Dublin in September each year. GAA sports are played in many countries where Irish emigrants and their descendants live.

New traditions also evolve over time. Successful Irish **soccer** and **rugby** teams in recent decades have added another dimension to Irish sport. Because these sports are played internationally, it allows Irish sportspeople to express their national feelings on an **international stage**. The outward expression of enjoyment of the game and respect for opposing teams has endeared many to our unique identity.

Music and Dance

Traditional Irish music and dance is a popular expression of Irish culture. *Lord of the Dance* and *Riverdance* companies have enhanced this image on a worldwide stage. **Feis Ceoil** competitions are held each year and these festivals encourage

GAA sports are an expression of Irish culture and identity.

Irish soccer and rugby have offered new opportunities to express our feelings of Irishness.

Traditional Irish music and dance have led to the creation of many festivals throughout Ireland.

this custom. Special costumes are worn for the participants in these festivals. The designs on female costumes are based on ancient Celtic patterns. Such music and dance competitions are held in cities throughout the world where Irish emigrants and their descendants live today.

Festivals

There are numerous festivals held in Ireland throughout the year, but the most important ones are held on St Patrick's Day. These festivals give the opportunity for various **Irish groups**, **emigrant groups and cultural groups** within Ireland to express themselves and their identity on St Patrick's Day in parades throughout Irish towns and cities. The most famous **St Patrick's Day Parade** is held on Fifth Avenue in New York and represents the influence of a large Irish-American emigrant population.

The **Twelfth of July** festival expresses the culture and identity of the unionist community in Northern Ireland. It has a British identity. This festival is, however, regularly associated with outbreaks of violence between the nationalist and the unionist communities in the North and represents the serious divisions that exist between these different cultural groups.

St Patrick's Day parades are held in many cities throughout Ireland and in America.

The Twelfth of July festival expresses a unionist identity in Ireland.

FESTIVALS AND SPORTS IN EUROPE

Basque Festival

In **Pamplona**, a city in the Basque region of Spain, an event is held that has made the city famous. Every year, six bulls are allowed to run freely though the city's streets before being killed later that day by matadors in bullfights. Many people run ahead of the bulls and sometimes they get hurt by the bulls.

Sport

The Finnish people like outdoor sports. In winter they enjoy ice hockey, ice skating, ski jumping and cross-country skiing. Popular summer sports include *pesapallo* (a Finnish form of baseball), swimming, boating and hiking.

In summer, thousands of city families flock to their cottages and saunas on lakes, the coast or the offshore islands.

Some people risk their life during the bull running in Pamplona in the Basque region.

Ice skating is a popular pastime in Finland.

CHAPTER 80
THE NATION-STATE

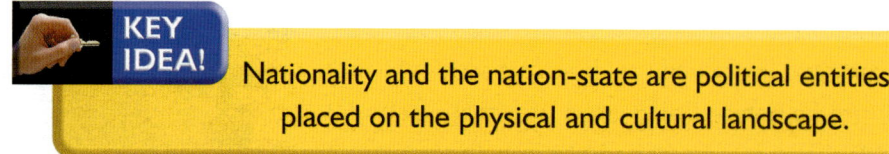

KEY IDEA!

Nationality and the nation-state are political entities placed on the physical and cultural landscape.

The term 'nation-state' implies not only that a country occupies a specific area of land, but that this area is occupied by a national group that shares a common culture. In France, for example, the nation (the people who share a French culture) and the territory of France are virtually the same. This condition applies generally to most of the countries of Europe today. The notable exception here is Belgium, which is composed of two distinct national groups: Flemings and Walloons.

Fig. 80.1
- *Identify the countries on the map that became nation-states after the break-up of the former Soviet Union.*

Fig. 80.2 Some newly-formed nation states of the mid- to late-twentieth century in the Middle East, south and south-east Asia.

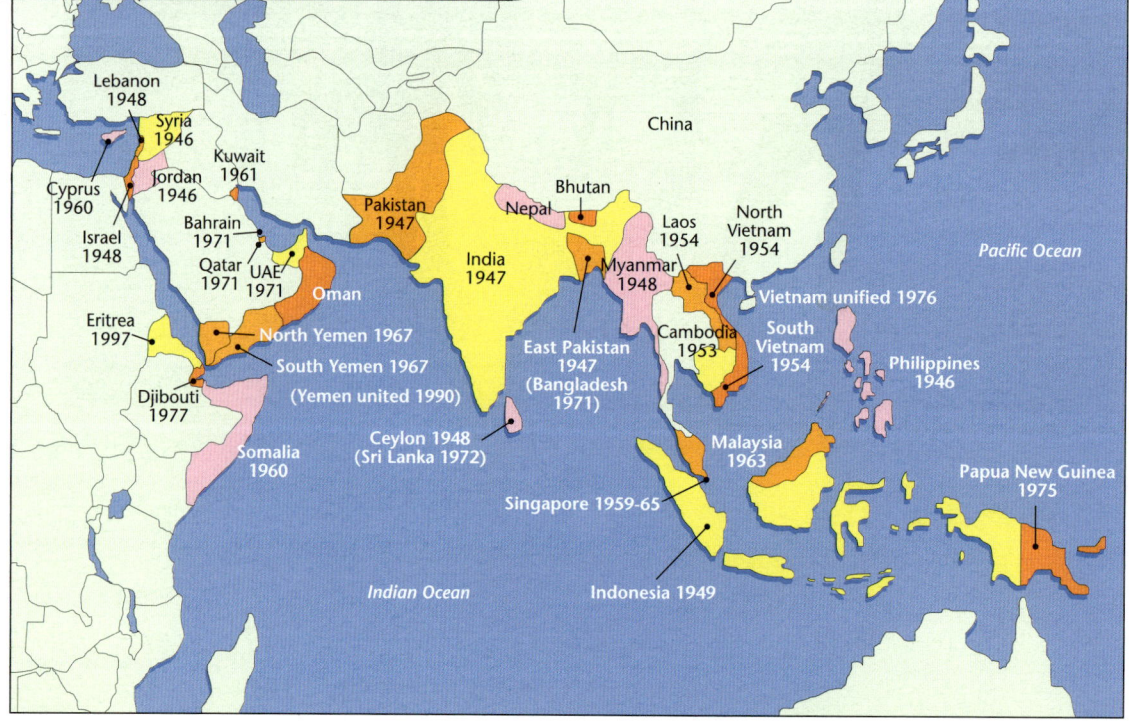

What Do We Mean by the Term 'Nation-State'?

It is useful to think of a nation-state as a combination of three elements:

- Nation (ethnicity).
- State (the institution or regime of power).
- Territory (the area enclosed and defined by a political boundary on a map).

A NATION OR NATIONALITY

The idea of nationality emerged shortly after the American and French Revolutions, and since then nationalism has become a powerful force in world politics. **A nation** is a group of people who believe that they are **an ethnic community** with deep **historical roots** and the right to own their own sovereign state.

Nationalism is the cause through which such groups claim their right to be a sovereign power within a particular area of land or territory. The invention of the printing press and the creation and standardising of some language dialects, such as Italian, played a leading role in forming national identities.

Although ethnic identity was an important factor in the formation of many nation-states, nations rarely consisted of a single ethnic group. Indeed, such states are very rare, Iceland being one of very few such states. Most countries, or nation-states, include more than three ethnic groups within their nations. A major role within mass education has been to integrate diverse ethnic groups and regional minorities into a single community.

A nation can be defined as a group of people who feel bound together through personal ties and who possess a unity and solidarity that has grown through the following influences:

- By following a common way of life.
- By sharing common experiences.
- By possessing common cultural traits.
- By inheriting a common tradition.

Some individual sports may unite various cultural groups.

Activity

1. Do you think that the images of Ireland are representative of Irish people as a nation today? Explain.
2. What other images of Ireland could you suggest that would give a more balanced representation of Irish people as a nation?

The Criteria for Nationality

Many reasons may be suggested for the creation and maintenance of national feeling, such as race, language, religion and a common enemy.

Race

Belonging to a particular race may produce national feeling, but as we have already discussed, there is no such thing as a pure race. Due to widespread migrations over countless centuries, the peoples of the world have intermingled so that genetically we are incredibly similar. When race is used as criteria, it is usually in the context of superiority. The Nazis, for example, spoke of the superiority of the 'German race' when in fact no German race or even ethnic group existed. The Germans are mostly a mixture of Alpine and Nordic peoples, subgroups of the Caucasian family. (See **Caucasians**, page 412.)

Language

Language is an important element unifying national groups. It acts as a bonding agent that cements common feelings and the traditions that go to make up a grouping such as a nation. Language contributes to cultural unity by facilitating the expression of common experience and achievement. It helps people to understand each other and removes barriers to taboos that interfere with the communication process.

Religion

Historically, religion was important as a moulding influence in politics. The Protestant challenge to the Roman Catholic Church in the sixteenth century helped nationalism, since it involved a rejection of foreign influences. In the Protestant countries, the churches became largely nationalised. For example, the Anglican Church in England became the official church of the state. In the Republic of Ireland, during most of the twentieth century, the Roman Catholic Church had a close association with the state and its institutions.

Today, religion plays a less significant role in politics, although it is still important in places such as India and Pakistan, where religious conflict between Hindus and Muslims continues. This is also true of Israel, where Palestinian Muslims and Jewish Israelis are in conflict.

Activity

Explain how the following factors fostered the concept of an Irish nation:

- language
- religion
- history
- sport.

Language is an important element associated with nationality.

Common Enemy

Rivalry, dislike and hatred between two groups will stimulate national feeling. The **security of the group** will weld its people together and create a **united national feeling**. This is easily demonstrated by the historical dislike between the French and the Germans, the Dutch and the Germans, the Finns and the Russians, the Muslims and Hindus, and the Arabs and Jews.

Hindus and Muslims have clashed regularly in the past over religious and political issues.

Activity

1. What is meant by the term 'nation-state'?
2. Explain three factors that help to foster the feeling of nationality.

STATES, THEIR BOUNDARIES AND FRONTIERS

At a glance, the political map of the world shows that it is divided into political units called states or countries, each of which is defined by (enclosed by) a boundary. Some of these states are very large, while others are tiny.

States are political regions ruled by regimes of power, such as democracies, monarchs or military regimes. Their boundaries sometimes conform to natural physical barriers such as rivers, mountain ridges and oceans. Sometimes, however, they do not and, although on a map the boundaries may appear as specific lines, in reality boundaries are sometimes just undefined, imaginary lines across deserts, plains, farms, lakes and seas.

A **frontier**, on the other hand, is a zone or belt of territory, a no man's land, which separates one group of people from another. It is sometimes referred to as a border, such as the border between Northern Ireland and the Irish Republic, or the Scottish border between Scotland and England.

Fig. 80.3

Activity

Examine the map of Europe in Fig. 80.3, then answer the following.

● Identify the countries 1–9 and the physical barriers 10–16 that form political boundaries in whole, or in part, between these neighbouring nation-states.

The Principality of Monaco is a tiny state on the Mediterranean coast. Its capital is Monte Carlo.

National Territory

For any state to exist, it is essential that it has a certain area of land and a certain minimum population. A state exists when a feeling is born of collective security. This happens only when groups of people occupying a certain region and using its resources to meet their needs feel that they have a common bond or inheritance to defend. The presence of other groups of people occupying adjoining territories, who are likely to be rivals or enemies, have historically been an important factor in helping to cement such groups to form a nation.

GEOGRAPHICAL SETTING
Shape, Size and Location of a Nation-State
Shape

The shape of a country can be an advantage or a disadvantage; for example, the more compact the country, the better. A circular shape is best, as a circle encloses a large area with a minimum of boundary. Others, however, are long and narrow, such as Italy. This has the disadvantage of a core north and a peripheral south. There is some social division between the rich northerners and the poorer southerners from the Mezzogiorno.

Greece and Indonesia are nations made up of many islands. A long shape may create climatic differences leading to isolated peripheral regions, such as the cold Norrland region in Sweden.

Activity
Explain the factors that help to define Italy as a nation-state. In your answer, refer to:
- language
- history
- religion
- physical boundaries.

Size

Size is important for two reasons.
- Size may create a better sense of national security. During a number of wars, Russia, for example, was able to let its armies retreat and manoeuvre during invasion to defeat its enemy. This happened during the Napoleonic Wars and again during World War II. Small countries are vulnerable to attack; an example is Kuwait, which was easily overrun by Iraqi forces during the reign of Saddam Hussein.
- Large regions usually contain a larger supply of natural resources than small regions do. Russia, because of its large size, has almost every possible natural resource. This has made it a powerful state. The United States also has a large area with many climates and resources at its disposal.

Fig. 80.4 Russia's size creates a certain security against attack from a foreign power. It also provides it with a wide range of essential natural resources.

Would you identify yourself as European? Explain.

Location

Location involves two factors: **absolute location** and **relative location**.

- Absolute location refers to the country's position on the globe, which is defined by lines of latitude and longitude. This cannot change.
- Relative location may change over time depending on certain factors. In the past, places were isolated because they were inaccessible. This may have been because they were remote islands far from mainland areas, such as Australia, or because they were in a mountainous region. Today, due to the development of air transport, high-speed rail systems and modern ferries, they may no longer be isolated.

European identity includes many diverse ethnic groups.

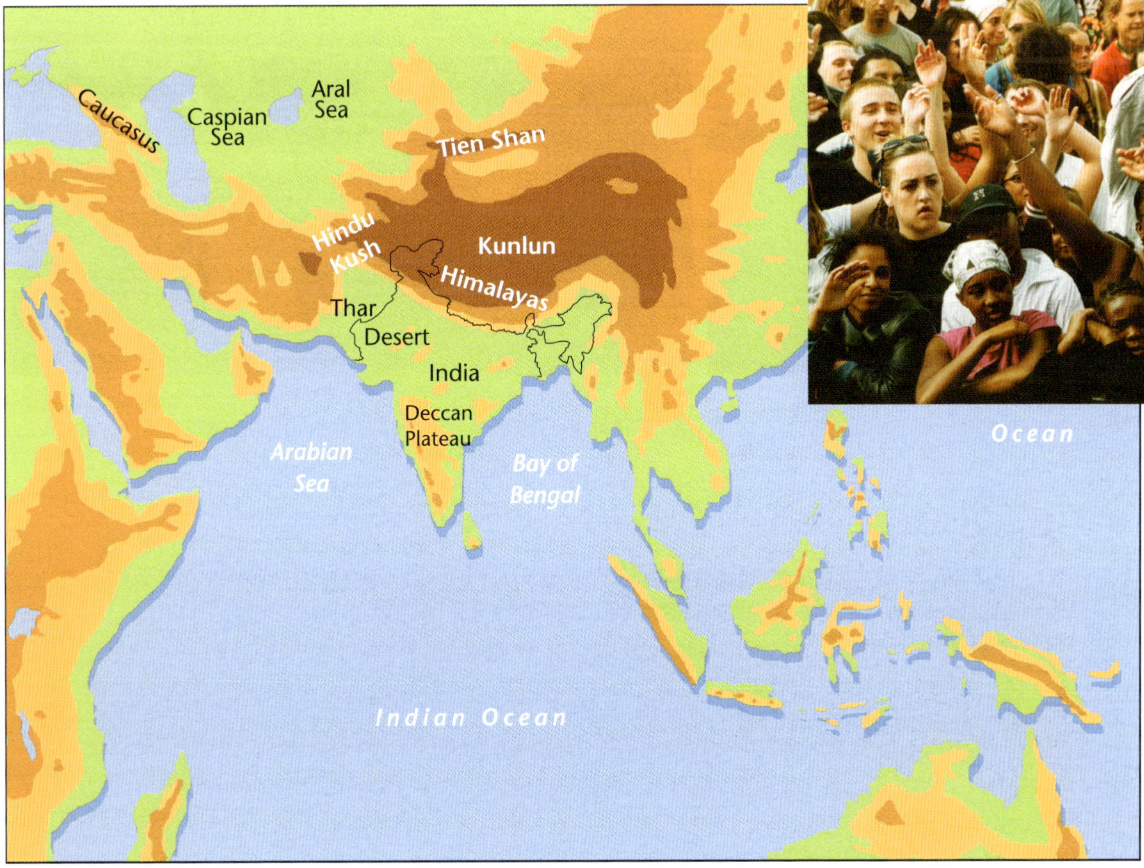

Fig. 80.5
- Explain, with the aid of this map and your atlas, how the relative location of India has changed over the past century.

A New Concept of Nationalism

In Europe, where the nation-state first began, the European Union, a supra-national regional state, continues to change the European landscape. Most of Western Europe has been combined within the European Union, while a number of other European states have applied for admission and await entry. Some political analysts see the European Union as the beginning of the end of the territorial nation-state as we have known it. It has undoubtedly led to debate on long-held ideas on what makes a nation.

Widespread migration of people from Africa and Asian nations to countries that were not colonial powers is a new phenomenon. The speed at which this is happening may create culture shock and the host nations **feel threatened by 'different others'**. This new and changing sense of nationalism is one of resistance to new forces of change. Instead of trying to include immigrants, recent trends across the European Union suggest that methods of **excluding those who are 'different'** are preferred and that a new division of 'self' and 'other' is gaining ground. The tie between nationality and citizenship may be entering a crisis.

Underlying every **welfare nation-state** is the principle of supporting those citizens who are poor and on the fringe of society. Western democracies support this principle. However, recent immigration trends to Europe have created fears that Western democracies may be unable to cope with the demand on welfare. Immigrants are viewed as liabilities rather than as intelligent people with the same hopes and desires that European emigrants had when they emigrated to the New World.

Some people fear that mass migration may create a strain on national government as well as social conflict.

Many in Ireland view new migrants as refugees who deserve a new life with all the rights laid down by the UN charter.

Activity

1. Explain the meaning of nationalism.
2. Explain how a sense of nationalism can lead to a fear of 'different others'.
3. Explain how the location, shape and size of Ireland has helped create:
    a. a nation-state
    b. a sense of nationalism.

CHAPTER 81
ISSUES RELATING TO PHYSICAL AND POLITICAL BOUNDARIES

KEY IDEA!

Territorial land, natural resources or nationality are just some of the issues associated with plotting a nation's boundary on a map.

PHYSICAL AND OFFSHORE BOUNDARIES

National Territory

Physical boundaries follow natural features in the physical environment, such as rivers, mountain ridges, lakes and seas. Rivers are easily recognised as boundaries, but river channels may change location due to meandering. The United States and Mexico have negotiated the boundary along the Rio Grande (called Rio Bravo in Mexico) numerous times in the twentieth century to reflect changes in the location of the river's channel.

Water Supplies

One of the issues most likely to lead to conflict between neighbouring countries will concern the management of fresh water supplies. The importance of international rules that govern the allocation of these waters cannot be overemphasised. Worldwide, there are more than 300 major river basins, covering about 50 per cent of the world's total land area. Many of these basins straddle country borders, even more so today due to the break-up of the former Soviet Union and Eastern Europe. Examples of river basins straddling more than one state include the Nile River, with nine countries sharing the basin, and the Danube River in Europe, shared by seventeen countries.

Low river water levels in Pakistan regularly lead to disputes with its neighbour, India, over irrigation schemes.

The potential for water conflicts over trans-boundary waters is clear, especially in times of water scarcity. Is the upstream state entitled to use all of the water that originates in its territory? Are the existing developments, such as irrigation schemes, of downstream states protected against later use of their upstream neighbours?

Look at a map of South Asia, then focus on the River Indus. Find its head-streams, see where they rise and follow their courses until they meet the River Indus. Now explain why the use of these waters is of concern to India and Pakistan.

Case Study: River Indus (India/Pakistan)

The River Indus begins in Tibet in China, with India and Pakistan being the downstream users. The partition of India and Pakistan by the British disrupted an irrigation system that had been in place for over 5,000 years. This led to conflict between India and Pakistan when India withheld water flows to canals in Pakistan. It was only through the intervention of the World Bank that the countries could reach agreement. Since then the countries have tried to settle their disputes through peaceful means.

Mineral and Fish Resources

Boundaries between states are understood to extend above surface, beneath it, and for those with coastlines, offshore. The water, seabed and their resources, such as oil and gas, **within 200 nautical miles** of the seashore belong exclusively to that country. This area is called a country's **Exclusive Economic Zone (EEZ)**. Territorial seas, over which states have virtually the same authority as over land, extend 12 nautical miles offshore. States must, however, allow 'innocent passage' of foreign ships through these waters.

Problems with locating political boundaries are common because many coastal states, such as Denmark, Germany and Sweden, are not separated by 400 nautical miles of ocean. So, lines halfway between the nearest shorelines of adjoining states must be defined. Such formal boundaries must go through a series of stages for agreement before they become legal. Beyond EEZs lie the high seas, open to all states for transport and resource development.

Coastal waters are a major natural resource. Many foreign ships fish illegally in Ireland's EEZ. This trawler is one of many ships apprehended by the Irish Navy each year.

Mineral rights on continental shelves provide vast sources of oil and gas for nations such as Norway and Britain.

Activity

Explain why the passage of some vessels through territorial waters would be of concern to every nation with a coastal location. In your explanation, refer to:

● military vessels
● fishing vessels
● transport ships.

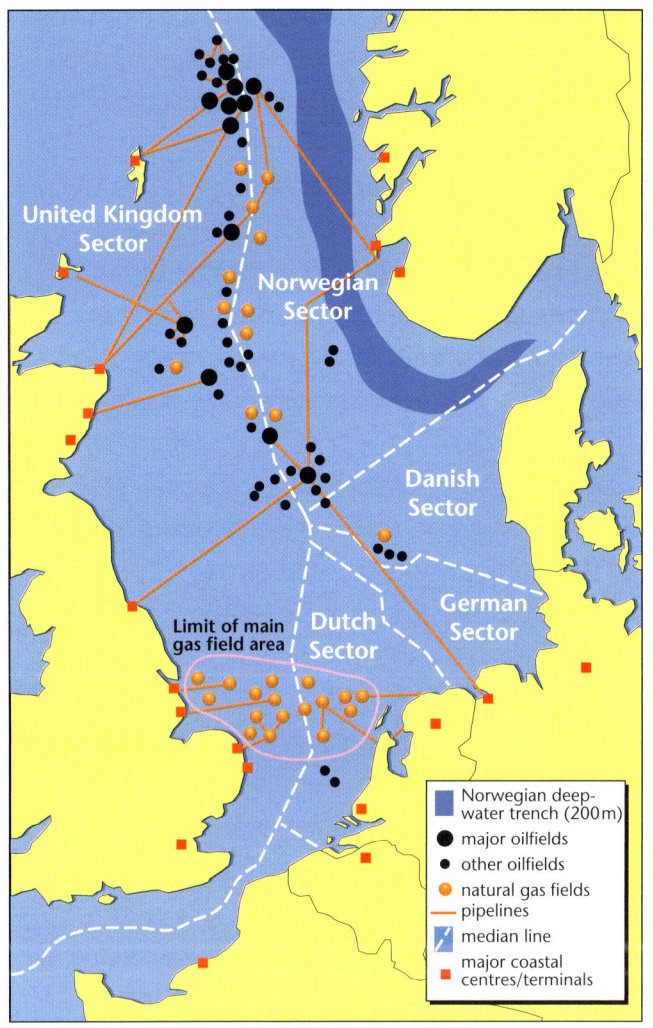

Fig. 81.1

Political Boundaries

The boundaries of a state define its ability to enforce its laws. Laws, whether on taxation or criminal activities, can be enforced only within the area defined by its political boundaries. As a result, individuals may place their money in a bank in another state where tax laws are less costly, such as in Switzerland, the Cayman Islands or elsewhere. Agreements between states have made hiding 'hot' money less secure and extradition treaties between countries have made the return of criminals and their assets less troublesome.

Governments use borders (boundaries between countries) to control the flow of goods, people, money and communications both into and out of the state. Relationships with bordering states are managed according to international guidelines, but political decisions on how they function may change from government to government.

Effects of Political Boundaries on Cultural Groups

The boundaries of most modern African states are the result of European colonial powers, such as France, Portugal, the United Kingdom and Spain, dividing up Africa at the Berlin Conference in 1884–85 to benefit themselves. This was done without concerns for the homelands of the hundreds of African ethnic groups. A continuing legacy of these 'artificial' boundaries has been ethnic conflict.

In Rwanda and Burundi, for example, the rivalry between Hutus and Tutsis resulted in hundreds of thousands of deaths in 1994. In Nigeria in the late 1960s, over 1 million people died when the Ibo ethnic group attempted to create a separate state of their own.

Case Study 2: Partition on the Island of Ireland

The 'border' between Northern Ireland and the Republic of Ireland has its origins in the creation of the **Irish Free State in 1921**, after the War of Independence. A **Boundary Commission** was set up to decide where the frontier should be drawn between the British statelet of Northern Ireland and the newly independent Irish Free State, which went on to become the Irish Republic in 1948.

Northern Protestants, called unionists because of their support for wishing to remain in the Union with Britain, had a clear majority over Catholics in only four northern counties – Antrim, Down, Derry and Armagh. This was deemed too small a territory to form a viable unionist state, so the predominantly Catholic counties of Fermanagh and Tyrone were added to the province of Northern Ireland.

Fig. 81.2

Revise the section on the dispute over the political boundary of Jammu and Kashmir, pages 449–50.

- Three of Ulster's counties – Donegal, Cavan and Monaghan – were now in the Irish Free State. The remainder were in British-controlled Northern Ireland.
- Countless farms were divided between the Irish Free State and Northern Ireland.
- The city of Derry, now in Northern Ireland, was cut off from its natural hinterland of Donegal.
- Many people were unhappy with this division. Both Protestant unionists stranded on the Irish Republic side of the border and Catholic nationalists trapped on the Northern Ireland side felt betrayed by this political boundary. The **Boundary Commission** surveyed residents of the border areas to gauge their wishes, but concluded in 1925 that any changes would not be compatible with economic and physical considerations.
- The division led to the violence of the IRA, the UDA and other paramilitary groups in Northern Ireland.

- *Explain why military posts such as this were built along the border that separates Northern Ireland from the Irish Republic.*

The border created divisions within the island of Ireland.
- *Give two examples of this division.*

CHAPTER 82

CULTURAL GROUPS WITHIN NATION-STATES

KEY IDEA!

Almost every nation-state contains at least one minority or cultural group.

Case Study 1: Turks in Germany

There are 1.8 million Turks in Germany, 139,000 of them in Berlin alone, making them the largest group of foreign workers. In your elective you studied these *Gastarbeiter*, or **guest workers**. They were recruited to do low-paid jobs in Germany that German workers would not do from 1961 onwards. The migrants dreamed of earning money and retiring to a small business and a secure life back in Turkey. Many of their **families joined them** in Germany. In 1973 after the oil crisis, recruitment stopped and many did go home. But the population of Turks in Germany has been kept high because many remained, family members continued to come from Turkey and there is a high birth rate among this ethnic group.

Many Turks came to Germany to work as *Gastarbeiter*, or guest workers.

Many Turks of the second and third generations born or raised in Germany have little knowledge of Turkey. Turkey has a similar status to what Ireland had for Irish-Americans, kept alive by a myth of final return, particularly among the first generation who came to Germany as adults. They plan for a retirement that will take them back to Turkey for good, but more and more older German Turks are retiring in Germany. They want to be close to their children and grandchildren. The second and third generations show little sign of wanting to 'return' to a place and a culture with which they are increasingly unfamiliar.

There is a high percentage of school-going German youths of Turkish origin. This increases educational costs for the state, as their home language is Turkish.

Case Study 2: Sikhs

The Sikhs are a cultural group who belong to a religion founded by **Guru Nanak** about 500 years ago to unite Muslims and Hindus of all castes into a single faith. This faith gained millions of followers in the **Punjab region**. Guru Nanak taught there was one, universal god. The holiest Sikh shrine is the Golden Temple in Amritsar. During colonial rule, many Sikhs won the respect and trust of the British and many thousands were employed as policemen and soldiers. As a result, a large Sikh middle class developed in the rich agricultural region called the Punjab.

● *Identify the traditional dress code of these Sikh girls.*

● *Name the characteristics that identify these people as Sikhs.*

Some Muslim women wear burqas, an all-enveloping attire that cloaks a woman from head to toe.

The culture of the Sikhs is strongly influenced by their **religious beliefs** and every important Sikh ceremony is performed in the presence of the Holy Granth (Sikh Bible). In order to unite Hindus and Muslims, the Sikh faith asked its followers to throw off all divisions of caste, colour and race. As members of the same cultural group, all Sikh men resemble each other by wearing five symbols, called the 'K' symbols. They are:

● 'Kesh' (uncut hair).
● 'Kangha' (wooden comb).
● 'Karra' (steel bracelet).
● 'Kachha' (short breeches).
● 'Kirpaan' (blade 6" to 9") to symbolise self-respect.

Sikh male adults wear a **dastar**, or turban, to show their commitment to Sikhism. Turbans are made from a piece of material five metres long and one metre wide that is turned clockwise around the head six times. Sikh women are also required to cover their heads, usually with a long scarf called a **chunni**. Sikhs who follow all of these conditions are called **Khalsa**. People who follow only some of these requirements are called **Sahajdharis**.

Sikhs are clearly different from other Indians in their appearance and dress code. This symbol of distinct identity is called **bana**. Many Sikhs seek independence from India. In order to satisfy this demand, the Indian government made Punjab a separate Punjabi-speaking state where the Sikhs are the majority rulers. However, many Sikhs want full independence in a newly renamed state they call **Khalistan**.

Activity
1. Explain the economic and social factors that led to the creation of a Turkish cultural group within Germany.
2. Explain why Sikhs form a cultural group within India. In your answer, refer to:
   ● religion
   ● dress
   ● language.

CHAPTER 83
CULTURAL GROUPS WITHOUT NATIONALITY

KEY IDEA!

The factors that create cultural identity lead to a recognition of cultural groups within nation-states.

Many cultural groups do not have a nation-state of their own. They live as a **minority group** within a nation-state. Examples of such groups include the Basques in Spain and nationalists in Northern Ireland.

Refer back to **Cultural Groups and Political Regions**, Chapter 31, page 232.

Case Study 1: The Basques

The Basque Country is a region that covers an area of 20,644 square kilometres at the western end of the Pyrenees, the mountains that divide France from Spain. It is made up of seven districts, four of which are in Spain and form the largest section, while the other three are in France. Three of these historic Basque territories, Araba, Bizkaia and Gipuzkoa in the north of Spain, are grouped together to form a political unit, known as **Euskadi**, or the Autonomous Community of the Basque Country. **Euskadi** has a population of 2 million people with an average population density of 300 people per square kilometre, higher than the EU average. They have their own president and parliament but are represented internationally by Spain.

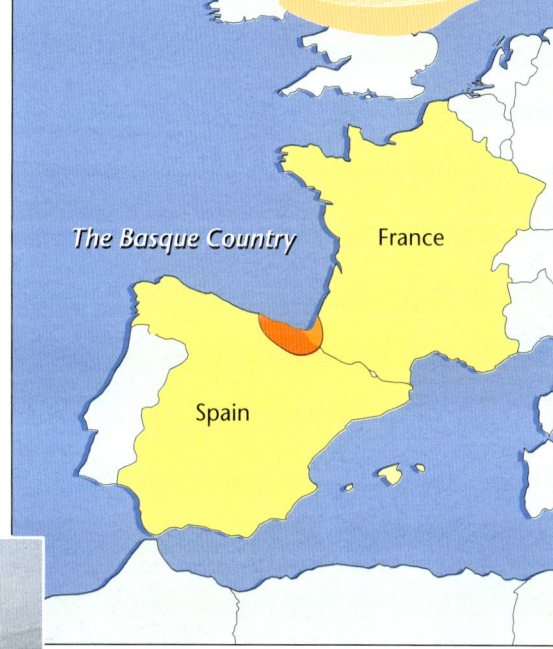
Fig. 83.1 Part of the Basque region lies in Spain, with the other part in France.

The scenic landscape of the Basque region adds to its attraction for tourists.

Activity
1. Define the absolute location of the Basque region.
2. Identify the territories that form Euskadi.
3. What is meant by the Autonomous Community of the Basques?
4. How does the Basque region of Navarra differ from Euskadi?

Spain's other Basque district, Navarra, is another region separate from Euskadi and is less troubled politically. The people, about 200,000 of them in the Basque districts in France, are culturally distinct but completely a part of France.

Who Are the Basques and Why Are They Different?

The Basques are a very old cultural group. They were living in the Pyrenees over **4,000 years ago**, long before the Celtic tribes of central Europe moved west to Britain and Ireland. They speak Basque, which they call Euskera, a language unrelated to any other human tongue (so it is **not Indo-European**).

Basques are dark in complexion, though not as dark as most French people or Spaniards of this region. Their melanin cells produce less melanin than those of the majority French or Spanish population. **Their genes are different** from their neighbours. The Basques have the highest proportion of Rh-negative blood (rhesus-negative blood) in Europe. They also have one of the highest percentages of type O blood (55 per cent). The Basques have virtually no B blood type, nor the related AB group.

The genes of the Irish, Welsh and also to some extent the English and Scottish are closely related to the genes of the Basques due to past migrations from the Basque region.

What Do They Do?

Traditionally, the Basques were herders. Today, Spain's Basque region has many businesses. Bilbao, the region's largest city, is known for its steel plants and shipbuilding yards based on its coal and iron ore supplies. The region has a positive science and technology plan to strengthen this type of business and industry. Most people live in the larger urban areas. France's Basque region is more rural.

Cultural Diet

Basque cuisine is based on seafood, especially cod and hake, a type of whitefish, and squid cooked in its own ink sauce. Basque dishes are very popular throughout Spain and most major cities have Basque restaurants.

Pamplona is a major tourist town and is associated with the running of the bulls in a summer festival.

Shipbuilding is one of the Basques' most traditional employers. Its local coal and iron ore deposits led to the development of this industrial activity.

The Basque region in Spain is fast becoming an important tourist destination within Spain.

NATIONALISTS IN NORTHERN IRELAND

People who live in Northern Ireland and wish to be part of a united Ireland are called nationalists. Since partition, nationalists have lived under British rule and until recent times have suffered discrimination on many fronts. They are **Irish in their traditions** and **customs** and feel a strong sense of being Irish, rather than being British, as unionists do. Most nationalists are **Catholics** and are represented by political organisations such as the SDLP or Sinn Féin.

Some nationalists show their identity by displaying Irish symbols on their houses.

The nationalist population developed their sense of Irishness, just as the majority of the people of the Irish Republic did, as a consequence of the British occupation of the island of Ireland and the treatment at the hands of the British Forces and Royal Ulster Constabulary (Northern Ireland's police force). The events of 1916–21 and the oppressive treatment of the Catholic minority for over seventy years have cemented nationalist feelings that created an Irish identity.

The demand for civil rights and equal treatment with Protestant citizens led to **civil rights marches** in the 1960s and 1970s. These marches led to clashes between police and marchers that reached a peak in the shooting dead of thirteen unarmed civilians in the city of Derry by the British forces on what is now called Bloody Sunday. Over 20,000 people gathered in Derry in 2002 to mark the thirtieth anniversary of this atrocity.

A minority of extreme nationalists support the IRA, an illegal armed organisation. At present, a cessation of military activities is part of the peace process that continues to dominate Northern politics today.

The distribution patterns of the urban population of Catholics and Protestants have led to ghettos in cities such as Derry and Belfast. Ethnic clashes between Catholic and Protestant ghetto communities regularly continue to occur.

Nationalists are generally Catholics who often campaign for civil liberties on the streets of towns in Northern Ireland.

Activity

1. Explain how British rule in Ireland helped create the Irish nation.
2. Explain the factors that led to civil rights marches in Northern Ireland in the 1960s and 1970s.
3. Explain how gerrymandering affected nationalists' civil rights in Northern Ireland. (See page 448.)

CHAPTER 84
CONFLICTS BETWEEN NATIONAL GOVERNMENTS AND CULTURAL GROUPS

 **KEY IDEA!** Many cultural groups within nation-states want a separate nation-state of their own. This regularly leads to conflict.

Violence breaks out regularly between cultural groups and the governments of their nation-states. This violence generally occurs because of injustice, lack of civil liberties, religious persecution or a demand for independence. In many cases it is a mixture of some or all of these factors.

THE IRA AND THE BRITISH GOVERNMENT IN NORTHERN IRELAND

Since Ireland was partitioned, a minority group called **the IRA** has waged a **guerrilla war** to unite the whole island of Ireland into a single state. For many years, and for as many reasons, the activities of the IRA were on a small scale. Conflict between them and the British government was confined to occasional clashes and raids on arms supplies. Then, due to the indifference on the part of the British government for equality and civil rights for Catholics in Northern Ireland, the IRA renewed its campaign in the 1960s. The demand for basic rights – jobs, housing, voting – threw the six counties into a state of crisis.

The bombing of Omagh by the Real IRA created public outrage from all sections of society in Northern Ireland and the Irish Republic.

The **peaceful demand for civil rights** was met with violence from the British forces and the police. This violence reached its peak during a peace rally in January 1972, later known as **Bloody Sunday**. Thirteen people were shot dead and many others injured when the British Army fired on the marchers.

Consequently, the IRA intensified its campaign and focused its attention on a bombing campaign in British cities and army barracks in Northern Ireland and along the border region. The introduction of **internment**, imprisonment without trial, intensified the campaign. This led to the deaths of ten IRA volunteers who went on hunger strike to highlight their claim for political status rather than criminal status within Northern jails.

Sectarian violence between Catholics and Protestants also led to IRA activity. Eventually both the IRA and the British Army admitted that military victory for either side was not possible.

Finally, the ending of 'military operations' in 1994 by the IRA was a result of the Irish Peace Initiative led by SDLP leader John Hume and Sinn Féin leader Gerry Adams, and supported by the Irish, British and American governments. Peace talks continue.

Activity

1. Who are Sinn Féin?
2. Who do they represent?
3. What is internment?

THE SPANISH GOVERNMENT AND THE BASQUES

As mentioned on page 469, the Basques are a cultural group who live at the western end of the Pyrenees in Spain and France.

A small number of violent extremists are represented by **ETA**. ETA (in Basque it means 'Basque Homeland and Freedom') is an **armed nationalist group** which believes that complete independence from Spain and France can only be achieved by **military means**, similar to what the IRA believed about the reunification of Ireland. Initially, ETA was founded in 1958 because the Basque people were oppressed during the reign of the fascist dictator Franco in Spain. Because they were 'different', Franco saw them as a threat and tried to eliminate all political opposition to his rule. ETA was set up as a **non-violent group,** but their every move for independence was put down by force. This made them opt for armed resistance.

The influence of ETA on Basque society is not measured only by the impact of its armed struggle. A key concept of ETA is the 'renationalisation of the Basque country' – to restore the Basque region to its full cultural personality. This has had a great impact on the social, political and cultural life of the Basque region. However, ETA is not represented in power sharing in government like their role model in Ireland, the IRA, so ETA has returned to the very methods it discarded as hopeless in 1998, after years when terrorist violence proved unsuccessful in achieving greater economic and political independence from Spain's central government.

In addition, Basque nationalism has risen in France, an area that was originally stable. Policy changes on social conditions and welfare and the loss of influence by trade unions have led to discontent. Remember that ETA seeks complete independence from Spain by military means.

The majority of Basques seek more autonomy within their region by peaceful means.

ETA seeks complete independence from Spain by military means.

Activity

1. Who are ETA? Explain why ETA intensified its campaign of violence in Spain.
2. What similarities, if any, exist between the campaigns of violence waged by ETA and the IRA?
3. Culture and identity are tied to ideas of ethnicity, which includes race, language, nationality and religion. Discuss this in relation to the Basques.

CHAPTER 85
CASE STUDY: GERMANY

 **KEY IDEA!**

Identity involves a variety of cultural factors, such as nationality, language, race and religion.

GERMANY'S PHYSICAL AND POLITICAL BOUNDARIES

This region was studied in *Regional Geography* on pages 253–6.

Germany has a number of well-defined natural boundaries. Only on the western edge is the boundary less well defined. Northern Germany forms part of the North European Plain, which is a natural region in Western Europe. Southern Germany forms part of an upland region that was uplifted due to earth movements at the same time the Alps were formed. The crushing movement created by the collision of the African and Eurasian Plates was less severe in Germany than it was in Italy and Switzerland, and so its uplands are not as high as the Alps that define its southern borders.

Germany's political borders used natural features where possible, such as the River Rhine that separates France from Germany, the River Oder that separates it from Poland, the Bohemian Forest uplands that divide it from the Czech Republic, and the Alps that divide it from Austria and Switzerland. The Baltic and North Seas separate Germany from its northern neighbours, with the exception of Denmark, to which it is connected by a narrow stretch of lowland.

Fig. 85.1

Activity
Draw a sketch map of Germany. On it, mark and name:
- two seas
- four major rivers
- three upland regions
- four cities.

OLD AND NEW POLITICAL BOUNDARIES OF GERMANY

Old Boundaries

The present German nation has its beginnings in the German Empire in 1871. It ended with World War I in 1914. It was a federal state where each state ruled itself, except in certain matters reserved for the government in Berlin. Its area was larger than that of today's Germany. It included Alsace-Lorraine, a region of present-day France and all north-western and western regions of present-day Poland.

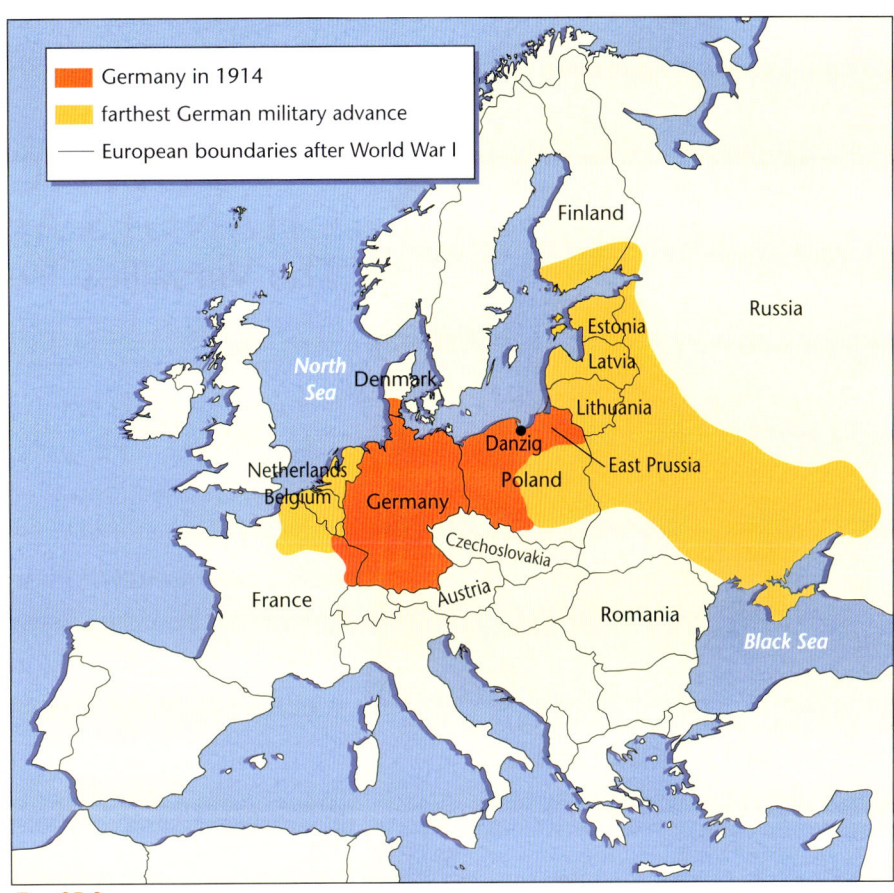

Fig. 85.2
● *Identify the nation-states on the map that were captured by Germany during World War I.*

RELIGIOUS CONFLICT WITHIN THE GERMAN EMPIRE

About one-third of the people of the new German Empire were Catholic; the rest of the people were Protestant. Protestantism was a faith begun by the teachings of **Martin Luther in 1517**. To protect their interests, German Catholics organised themselves into a new party, called the Centre Party. They opposed the creation of the German Empire and demanded a firm guarantee of the freedom of the Catholic Church in the new Germany. At the same time, Pope Pius IX proclaimed **papal infallibility** to be a doctrine of faith. This meant that when ruling on matters of faith or morals, the Pope was inspired by God and could not make a mistake. Bismarck felt this 'infallibility' issue would lead to interference by the Church in state matters.

Some of the Catholics believed in this rule while others did not. This division among the Catholics, called *Kulturkampf*, was used by **Bismarck** to crush all opposition to his rule. He introduced **the May Laws,** which restricted the influence of the Church in the running of the German state. The powers of the clergy were restricted and priests were not allowed to raise political topics in their sermons. Civil marriages were made compulsory. By 1876 all bishops were either in prison or in exile and over one-third of the 4,600 Catholic parishes were without a priest. Many of these laws were withdrawn after 1879 when a new Pope was elected and new agreements were signed.

POLITICAL BOUNDARY CHANGES AFTER WORLD WAR I
The Versailles Treaty

When Archduke Franz Ferdinand of Austria was assassinated in Sarajevo, Germany, under the leadership of Kaiser William II, was brought into World War I in support of Austria. Austria and Germany were opposed in the war by Russia, Britain and France. After the war, the German Empire had fallen and Germany had lost all of its lands in Poland and Alsace-Lorraine in France. New boundary lines were drawn to reflect these changes and the River Rhine now formed the boundary between France and Germany. Under the Treaty of Versailles to ensure a secure border for France in this region, no German troops were allowed to enter the 'Rhineland'.

Bavarian houses set in upland areas have verandas and potted plants typical of this region.

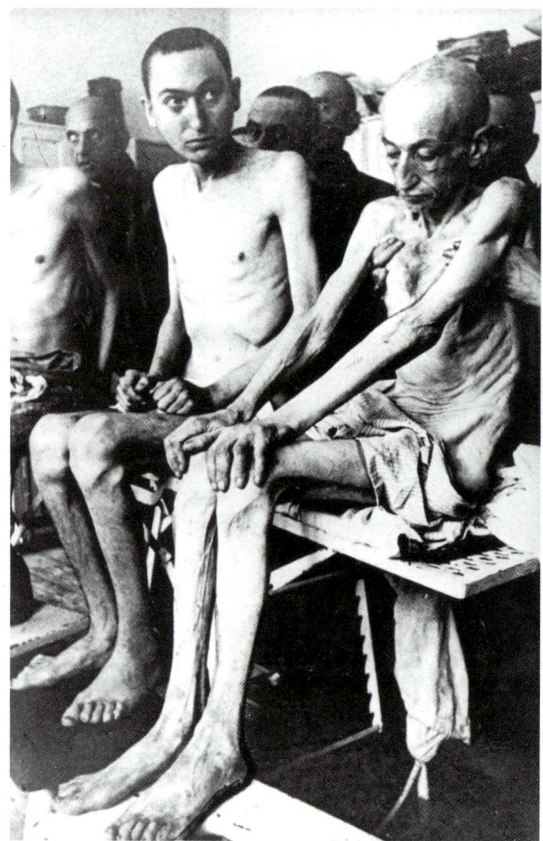
Millions of Jews were killed during the Holocaust. Concentration camps were set up to separate Jews from society at large.

Fig. 85.3
● Identify the countries occupied by Germany during World War II.

476

Changing Boundaries under Hitler

Adolf Hitler was a violent and ambitious man. He wanted to make Germany the most powerful country in Europe. In order to do this, he invaded neighbouring countries and took them over by force. Hitler had three main aims.

The Influence of Language

Hitler wanted to unite all German-speaking people into one single nation-state. There were many German-speaking people in parts of Poland, Czechoslovakia and Austria. Hitler wanted to bring these people under the control of Germany.

Racial Policy

Hitler regarded Germans as a **master race** of people, superior to all others. He wanted to rid a greater Germany of all others who were inferior and could dilute this breed by intermarriage. Thus marriage between ethnic groups, such as Jews and Germans, was forbidden.

More Living Space

Hitler wanted to create **more living space** for Germans. He believed the Treaty of Versailles had robbed Germany of much of its territory, so he wanted Germany to have parts of Czechoslovakia, Austria, Poland and Russia to give the German people more farmland for growing foodstuffs and raw materials for vital industries.

As a result of Hitler's policies, Germany invaded Austria in 1938. Later, in 1939, the Germans invaded Czechoslovakia and in September 1939, they invaded Poland. The invasion of Poland led to the outbreak of World War II. These invasions increased the area of Germany and changed its political boundaries again. They lasted until the end of the war in 1945.

NEW BOUNDARIES

From 1949 to 1990 new political boundaries were drawn in Germany. At the end of World War II Germany was divided by the Allied Powers. Three zones occupied by Western powers were united to form the country of West Germany, which was called the Federal Republic of Germany. From the German zone that the USSR controlled, it created the new state of East Germany, which was called the German Democratic Republic.

Berlin, the historic capital of Germany, was also divided. East Berlin became the capital of East Germany. West Berlin was an outpost of West Germany deep within the East German state. In 1961, the East Germans built the Berlin Wall to divide the city and set up military checkpoints to control the

Activity

1. Explain the historical factors that led to the Versailles Treaty.
2. Explain how national feeling in Germany was affected by the Versailles Treaty.
3. What part did Adolf Hitler play in changing national feeling during the 1930s?

See Chapter 69, **Racial Conflict**, page 420.

The Iron Curtain:
A political boundary that separated Eastern communist-controlled countries from Western European countries, and West Germany from East Germany.

Fig. 85.4

477

The removal of the Berlin Wall was followed by the reunification of Germany.

Many German cities and industrial areas suffered great damage during World War II.

movements of people from East to West Berlin. This wall symbolised the division between East and West during the Cold War, which you studied in your Junior Certificate History course.

In 1990 East and West Germany were reunited, the Berlin Wall was removed and the German people felt they were a nation once more.

Consequences of Changing Political Boundaries
Changing Citizenship

Germany's current eastern boundary roughly corresponds to the one of the Holy Roman Empire in the tenth century, because many areas of Europe that were formerly German-speaking now lie behind political boundaries outside of Germany. For example, Alsace-Lorraine is now a part of France. In earlier centuries, Austria and South Tyrol, Switzerland, Liechtenstein and Luxembourg, parts of Russia and the Balkan countries were within the boundaries of Germany. Until recent times, people from these regions could claim immediate German citizenship once they were inside Germany's political boundaries. These people are referred to as **ethnic Germans**.

ETHNICITY AND RACE

Hitler believed that German people were of a superior race to all other humans. He wrote that they would stay 'pure' by avoiding marriage to Jews and Slavs. However, as you have studied in your elective, there is no such thing as a pure race. Hitler's view of 'others' as different led to racial persecution and the death of over 6 million Jews during the Holocaust.

Ethnic Groups within Germany – Role of Migration
Who Are Ethnic Germans?

Ethnic Germans are descendants of Germans who lived in lands in Eastern Europe and Russia that had at one time been German territory. These ethnic Germans had the right to German citizenship according to Germany's constitution. Because they became citizens immediately upon arrival in Germany, ethnic Germans received financial and social assistance to ease their integration into German society. Because they came from many different countries, they did not speak German and so even language training was provided. Generally they were readily accepted into German society.

With the fall of communism and the removal of the Iron Curtain, however, the number of ethnic Germans swelled. In the mid-1980s about 40,000 came each year. In the period 1991–93, about 400,000 ethnic Germans settled in Germany. Since January 1993, immigration of ethnic Germans has been limited to 220,000 per year.

Under the new restrictions, once in Germany, ethnic Germans must live in certain areas. If they leave these areas, they lose many of their benefits and are treated as if they are foreigners.

Although officially German, ethnic Germans are poor, have little or no knowledge of the German language and prefer to remain in their own social group. They form a cultural group within Germany.

Much rebuilding and renewal has taken place in Berlin since reunification, although reunification has created some difficulties for the German people.
● *Identify two problems resulting from reunification.*

Ossies and Wessies

After reunification in Germany in 1990, many industries in the former East Germany were exposed to competition from more efficient industries in the West. Many were forced to close, creating mass unemployment. Because they were now living in a democracy, East Germans had the choice of migrating to West Germany, where there are better employment prospects. Within three years of reunification, over 3 million people had migrated to West Germany, but they were not so welcome when they arrived. Many felt they were treated as second-class citizens in their own country. This discrimination led to the terms Ossies, meaning East Germans, and Wessies, referring to West Germans.

Ossies resented the superior attitude of the wealthier West Germans and also felt that the Wessies had not done enough to secure them employment in their own eastern region.

Wessies, on the other hand, resented the fact that their taxes were increased to support the unemployed Ossies. Increased migration from eastern Germany put pressure on housing and employment supplies in western Germany. A belief that Ossies were lazy and ungrateful was also common among the wealthier Wessies.

Turks in Germany

See page 467.

Some Germans fear that eastern Germans may become a major strain on Germany's finances and lower living standards throughout the western part of Germany.

Activity

1. Explain how the reunification of Germany has led to social division in Germany.
2. Explain why some foreign nationals in Ireland should be granted citizenship based on social justice.

RELIGIONS IN GERMANY

The Reformation began in Germany when Martin Luther published his teachings in 1517. This religious challenge gave rise to Protestantism. By 1600, most people in northern and central Germany had become Protestants, mostly Lutherans. Those in the west and south remained Catholic.

In the 1970s the distribution of the Christian faiths was similar to above. About 50 per cent of West Germans were Protestants and about 80 per cent of East Germans were Protestants. The East German government tried to discourage religious practice. It tried to replace confirmation and other religious ceremonies for young people with ceremonies in which they dedicated themselves to communism. Nevertheless, only 7 per cent of the East Germans at that time claimed to be non-religious.

In Germany today, the percentages are different. In the former GDR (East Germany), less than 25 per cent of the population belongs to a religious community. In the West, the figure is 90 per cent. Germany's present population of over 80 million people may be divided into four religious groups.

Basic law in Germany guarantees full religious freedom and it provides protection against discrimination on religious grounds. A special feature of German law allows religious groups the possibility of collecting a church tax through public tax offices. In other words, it

Cologne's Gothic cathedral contains many art treasures. On the high altar are relics that are said to be those of the Magi, brought from Rome to Cologne in 1164.

| Roman Catholic 30% | Protestant 30% | Non-religious group 30% | 10% |

Muslims, Orthodox Christians, Hindus, Buddhists and Jews in Germany

Fig. 85.5

may be deducted from someone's salary by the state and paid directly into church funds. For this to occur, German law states that there must be a church structure with an associated teaching body.

This is not so with Islam. Muslims do not have such a church structure in Germany and so Islam does not have a public-body status and Islamic religious education is not yet permitted in state schools.

Lutheran churches follow the teachings of Martin Luther. He opposed the sale of indulgences and his beliefs led him to question many of the rules of the Christian church at that time.

MUSIC IN GERMANY

Music plays a major role in German culture. Classical as well as traditional music are important.

Classical Music

Four of the most famous German classical composers include the following:

- **Johann Sebastian Bach** spent most of his life in Leipzig working in the Lutheran church of St Thomas as a cantor, organist and composer.

- **Georg Friedrich Handel** started his career as a child performer on the piano. He worked as a musician and composer for the Hamburg opera house.

- **Felix Mendelssohn** was another very successful musician, teacher and composer.

- **Richard Wagner** is mostly known for his opera music, which is moving and powerful in its effects.

Traditional Music

The Munich Oktoberfest – known locally as the *Wiesen* – is the biggest public festival in the world and was first held in 1810. Each year it attracts about 6 million visitors, who drink a total of about 5 million litres of beer and consume about 200,000 pairs of pork sausages, mostly in 'beer tents' put up by the traditional Munich breweries. People often listen to traditional brass band music during the Oktoberfest.

This famous festival attracts visitors from all over the world, who spend about €1 billion during the sixteen days of the festival. About 12,000 people are employed to stage this festival.

The Oktoberfest festival in Munich has continued for nearly 200 years.

Activity
Explain how music is an important bonding influence within the German nation.

481

SPORT IN GERMANY

An Active Sporting Nation?

In 2001, the number of Germans who were members of the country's 87,000 sports clubs was estimated at 26.8 million – or one in three German citizens – an increase of 3 million people on the 1990 figure. The actual figure may be closer to 18 million German club members. However, some sportsmen and sportswomen belong to more than one club, whereas others are merely passive or social members.

This figure is even more impressive if you consider the fact that only 29 per cent of German sportsmen and sportswomen play their sports 'primarily in a club'. Fifty-eight per cent of people regularly participating in sport do not belong to any organisation, i.e. they may cycle or jog. Another 12 per cent use a commercial facility such as a fitness centre or a dance studio. In fact, the number of fitness centres has more than doubled since 1985, rising from 2,800 to 6,500.

According to a report commissioned by the Institut für Demoskopie in Allensbach in March 2001, 63 per cent of Germans claim to take part in sporting activities, and 34 per cent do so at least once a week. The German government is becoming increasingly concerned about the health of the 37 per cent of Germans who do not take part in any sporting activity, not least for financial reasons. Medical research has shown lack of exercise and physical work to be one of the reasons for the increase in cardiovascular diseases, and about 30 per cent of medical costs incurred in Germany result from heart, circulatory or metabolic disorders.

This is a major problem in an ageing population, as 52 per cent of German adults who don't exercise are aged fifty or over, and only one in ten German adults between the age of thirty-five and sixty does two hours or more of moderate sporting activity per week.

Soccer is a major sport in Germany. Every major town has a soccer club. The most famous German soccer club is Bayern-Munich.

Athletics is a popular sport. Many of Germany's athletes are Olympic champions.

Skiing is a favourite sport in the Bavarian region of southern Germany. Its cold winters and heavy snowfalls make this mountainous region attractive as a location for ski resorts.

Germany has many professional football clubs, such as Bayern-Munich.

GEOECOLOGY

CHAPTER 86
SOIL MAKE-UP AND CHARACTERISTICS

KEY IDEA!

Soil is made up of a mixture of various ingredients and has many characteristics.

THE COMPOSITION OF SOIL

A mixture of **mineral matter**, **organic matter**, **air** and **water** make up soil. These all combine together to make soil a fertile **natural resource**. The proportions are approximately as shown in Fig. 86.1, although they may vary from one soil type to another and even according to changes in weather.

Mineral Particles

Mineral particles are the largest ingredient and usually make up about 45 per cent of the soil. Most minerals exist in the form of tiny particles. These particles were weathered or eroded from the soil's **parent rock** over a long period of time. The parent rock might be local or might have been broken up and carried from other regions by agents of erosion, such as moving ice.

Mineral particles contain **compounds**, which help to make the soil fertile. These compounds largely depend on the nature of the parent rock. Limestone, for example, provides particles with plenty of **calcium**, which helps the bone development of grazing animals.

Mineral **particles vary in size**. Those derived from sandstone may, for example, be large and coarse. Particles derived from clay, on the other hand, are very small and tightly packed.

Some minerals are **soluble**. They can dissolve in water and so take a liquid form. Soluble minerals are very important. They nourish plants because plant roots can absorb them.

Organic Matter

Organic matter includes the remains of plants and animals. Although it makes up only about 5 per cent of the soil, organic matter plays a vital role in soil fertility.

- Many **living creatures** live in the soil. Some of these, such as earthworms, are visible to the naked eye. They help to keep soil fertile while they live (see the photo on page 484) and contribute to organic matter when they die. But the vast majority of animals are too small to be seen without the aid of a microscope. These include

organic matter

air

mineral particles

water

Fig. 86.1

Activity

1. Rank the components (ingredients) of soil according to their proportions shown in Fig. 86.1.
2. How might each of the following processes alter the proportions of the soil components shown:
   a. a period of drought
   b. the laying of water-drainage pipes
   c. the addition of animal manure.

483

bacteria and fungi and are called **micro-organisms**. They play a vital role in the production of organic matter.

- When plant litter (leaves or twigs) falls on the ground or when animals die, they are broken down by micro-organisms. This causes the plant and animal remains to decay into a dark, jelly-like substance called **humus**. Humus is found mainly near the surface of the soil, where it gives the soil a dark appearance. It is also helps to make the soil fertile (see the box on this page).

When earthworms burrow through the soil:
- They help air and water to pass through.
- They loosen the soil, which helps plant roots to penetrate it.
- They mix the soil.
- When earthworms die, their bodies decay into humus.

Soil micro-organisms under a microscope. These creatures are so tiny that millions of them can live in a teaspoonful of soil.

Air

Air is found in the spaces between soil particles. It usually makes up about 25 per cent of the soil's volume, though it is more plentiful in loosely grained, sandy soil than it is in tightly grained, clay soils. Air is essential for soil fertility. It supplies the **oxygen and nitrogen** that plants and micro-organisms need in order to live.

Water

Water typically makes up about 25 per cent of soil volume, though this would depend on climate. In desert areas, the amounts of water in soil can be so small that almost no vegetation can grow. In very wet areas, some soils can become waterlogged or filled with water.

A moderate amount of rainwater is usually good for soil fertility. As water moves slowly through the soil, it **dissolves soluble minerals**. It then distributes these minerals to plants that can absorb them in liquid form through their roots. The water and the dissolved minerals nourish the plants.

SOIL CHARACTERISTICS

Texture

Texture refers to the coarseness or smoothness of soil. It depends on the size of the particles that make up the soil.

Sandy Soils

Sandy soils have large particles and a **loose, coarse texture**. Large spaces between particles allow plenty of air and water to pass through sandy soils. This helps fertility. The loose texture makes sandy soils easy to cultivate.

On the other hand, water passing easily through sandy soils can leach nutrients out of the soils. This reduces fertility. There may also be a shortage of water in the soil during long spells of dry weather. That is why farmers may irrigate and frequently fertilize sandy soils.

Clay

Clay soils have very tiny particles that fit together very tightly. These **tight-fitting particles** prevent air and water from passing through them, and the soil can become waterlogged. Clay soils are heavy and sticky when wet and hard and cracked when dry. They are therefore difficult to plough and are more suited to grass. Farmers may add lime and use land drainage schemes to make clay soils more fertile.

Loam

Loam soils contain fairly even amounts of sand and clay particles. They contain sufficient air and allow enough drainage to make them **ideal for agriculture**.

Structure

The cementing action of water or humus causes individual particles of soil to cling together in small groups called **peds**. The structure of soil depends on **the shape of these peds**, which can vary from one soil type to another.

- **Crumb structure:** Soil is said to have a crumb structure if the peds form **rounded** shapes, looking something like breadcrumbs. Water and air can move through this kind of soil, which therefore tends to be fertile.
- **Platy structure:** The peds in platy soil tend to be **flat and overlapping**. This stops water from moving through the soil. This kind of soil is generally infertile and waterlogged.

The main characteristics of soil include:
1. Texture
2. Structure
3. Colour
4. Organic content
5. Water retention
6. Water content
7. pH value

A typical clay particle is about one-fivehundreth part of a millimetre in diameter!

Experiment to Test Soil Texture
- Take a screw-topped jar and fill three-quarters of it with soil.
- Pour water into the jar so that it is almost full.
- Shake the jar well for about 60 seconds.
- Leave to settle overnight.

Layers of different-sized particles will collect in the jar. The largest sandy particles will be at the bottom and the finest clay particles will be on top. Use the sizes of each layer to try to determine if your soil sample is sand, clay or loam.

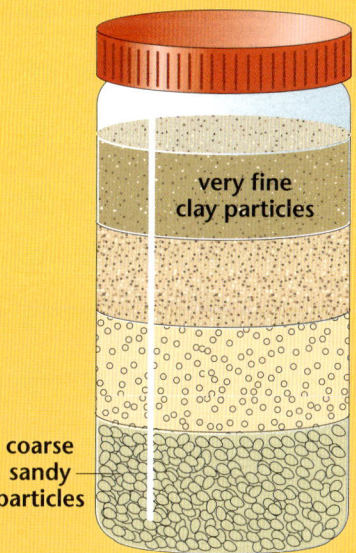

very fine clay particles

coarse sandy particles

Fig. 86.2

Colour

Soil types can vary in colour, which in turn can be a sign of the soil's level of fertility.

- **Black or brown soils are usually very fertile for the following reasons:**
  - They are dark because they contain a lot of **humus**, which makes the soil fertile.
  - Dark soils tend to be **warm**, because they absorb more sunlight than light-coloured soils. Warm conditions help organic material to break down into humus and help seeds to germinate (grow) more quickly.
- **Grey soils** are normally **infertile**. Their surface layers are grey because heavy rain has washed (**leached**) dark humus and other minerals down through the soils and often out of reach of plant roots.
- **Red soils** are common in regions of tropical or equatorial climates close to the Equator. A combination of high temperatures and plentiful rainfall creates intense chemical weathering, which causes iron in the rocks to break down into **iron oxide, or rust**. This is what gives **tropical red soil** its rusty, red colour.

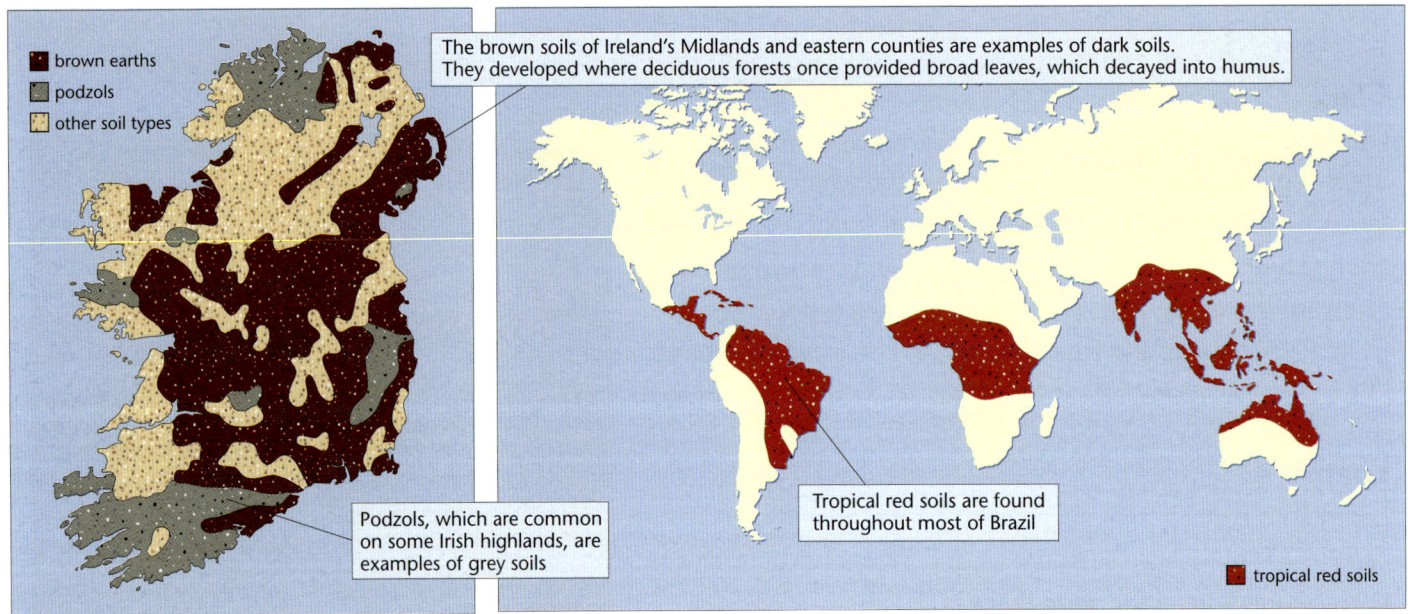

brown earths
podzols
other soil types

The brown soils of Ireland's Midlands and eastern counties are examples of dark soils. They developed where deciduous forests once provided broad leaves, which decayed into humus.

Podzols, which are common on some Irish highlands, are examples of grey soils

Tropical red soils are found throughout most of Brazil

tropical red soils

Fig. 86.3   Fig. 86.4

Organic Content

Revise **organic matter** on pages 483–4.

You have learned that the organic content of soil comes from **the remains of plants and of animals** such as earthworms, slugs and insects. Plant litter or dead animals are broken down into humus by micro-organisms, such as bacteria. Humus plays a vital role in making soil fertile. It follows, therefore, that the more plant litter, animals and micro-organisms there are in soil, the more fertile that soil is likely to be.

Water-Retention Properties

The degree to which soils hold water largely depends on their **structure** and **texture**.

- **Structure:** Soils with **crumb structures** allow water to move easily through them and so tend to be relatively dry. Soils with **platy structures** do not easily let water through and so tend to have a high water content.
- **Texture:** The photographs below show that soils of varying textures have different water-retention properties.

Loam soils have a texture between that of sand and clay. The loam soils tend to be well drained, while retaining enough moisture to maintain high levels of fertility.

Coarse **sandy soils** have such large spaces between their particles that they retain little water. While these soils often favour the growing of vegetables, they may suffer from water shortages in times or places of little rainfall.

Smooth **clay soils** hold so much water that they may be poorly drained and even waterlogged. They often provide good grasslands for cattle, but are usually too heavy for tillage farming.

- **Relief:** The shape of the land surface can also affect water retention in soils (see Fig. 86.5).

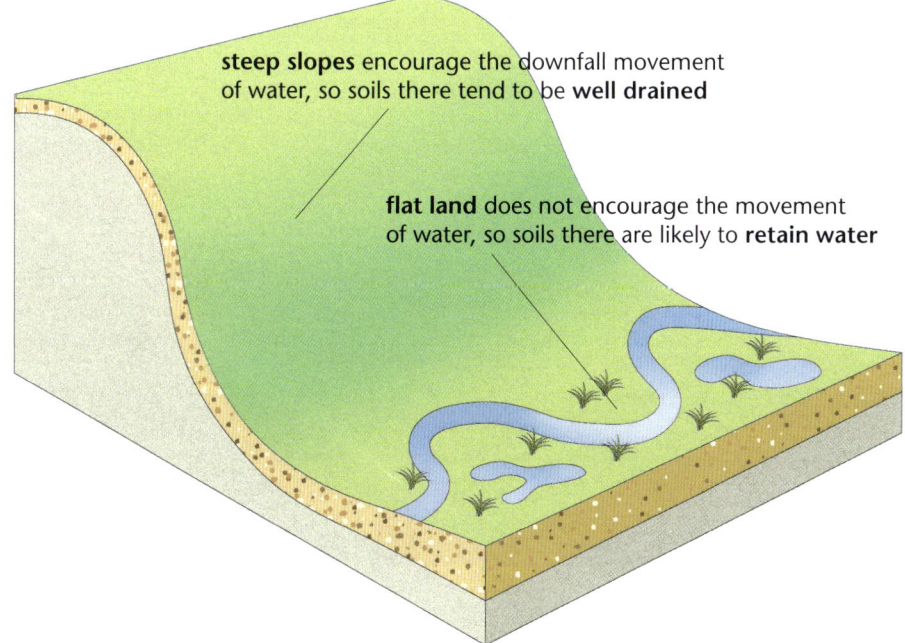

steep slopes encourage the downfall movement of water, so soils there tend to be **well drained**

flat land does not encourage the movement of water, so soils there are likely to **retain water**

Fig. 86.5 How relief affects water retention in soil.

487

Water Content

The amount of water in soil is influenced by the following factors:

- Water content in soil is affected by that soil's **water-retention properties**, as described previously.
- **Precipitation:** Soils in areas of **high rainfall**, such as in the mountains of Kerry or Connemara, tend to contain more water than soils in the relatively dry south-east of Ireland.
- **The nature of the underlying rock:** Soils overlying permeable rock tend to hold more water than soils on impermeable rock. Permeable rock, such as limestone, allows water to pass through it and so to escape more easily from the soil above. Impermeable rock, such as slate, blocks the downward movement of water and so tends to increase the water content in the overlying soil.
- **The presence of a hard pan:** Soils that are heavily leached sometimes contain an impermeable hard pan, which blocks the downward movement of water. The surface layers of this kind of soil often become saturated with water. (Leaching is explained fully on page 490.)

The pH Value of Soil

A soil's pH value measures its level of **acidity** or **alkalinity**. Soils with low pH values are said to be acid, while those with high pH readings are alkaline. Soils with a pH reading of about 7 are described as neutral. (See Fig. 86.6.)

- **Alkaline soils** contain a lot of calcium. They develop mainly on limestone or chalk landscapes.
- **Neutral or slightly acidic soils** encourage the growth of bacteria that break down organic matter into humus. These soils are best suited to farming.
- **Acid soils** often occur in areas of heavy rainfall, where rainwater leaches calcium (which is alkaline) out of the soil. Too much acidity discourages micro-organisms. This means that plant remains will not break down, so the soil is usually infertile. Lime may be added to reduce acidity.

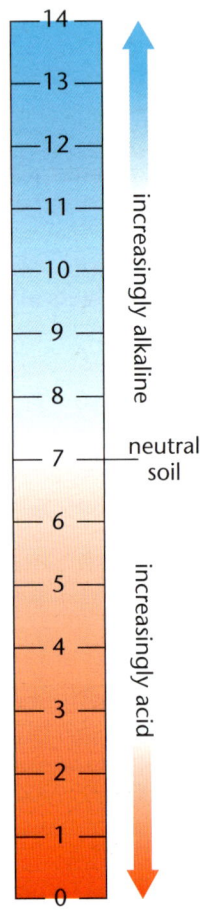

Fig. **86.6** The pH values of soil.

See questions 1 and 2 on page 526.

Infertile acid soils cover this mountain in the West of Ireland. Peat develops because plant remains have not broken down.

488

CHAPTER 87

PROCESSES THAT AFFECT SOILS

KEY IDEA!
A variety of physical processes (happenings) may affect soil. No two soils are exactly the same.

We have already examined the general characteristics of soil, but soils vary and no two soils are exactly alike. This is partly because a variety of physical processes may affect any particular soil (see box on right). These processes may operate together, but not all processes will operate in any one soil.

Weathering

Weathering helps to break down parent rock into small particles, which are the main ingredient of soil.

- **Physical weathering** causes parent rock to shatter. It is carried out by agents such as frost action and temperature changes. **Frost action** is common on Irish mountainsides in winter. **Temperature changes** are very effective in hot deserts, where daytime temperatures are very high and night-time temperatures are often below freezing.

- **Chemical weathering** causes rock to decompose. This happens, for example, when carbonic acid in **rainwater** reacts with the calcium carbonate in **limestone**. Rainwater can also slowly dissolve **granite,** resulting in the formation of clay soil.

> **Physical processes that affect soil:**
> - Weathering
> - Soil erosion
> - Leaching
>   – Podzolisation
>   – Laterisation
> - Calcification
> - Humification

Soil Erosion

The agents of erosion not only break down parent rock, they also transport the resulting mineral particles and soil over great distances and deposit them in other areas.

Rivers, for example, grind down rock into fertile **alluvial soil,** which is deposited in the lower sections of **river valleys** such as those of the Shannon and the Liffey. **Wind** has deposited fertile **loess** soils in the Paris Basin of France. **Boulder clay** has been deposited in many parts of Ireland by **glacial ice** during the last Ice Age.

Existing soil is subject to attack by the agents of erosion. **Gully erosion,** caused by heavy rain, severely damages soil in those parts of the Amazon rainforest that have been cleared for agriculture. **Wind erosion** blows away topsoil from those areas of Africa's Sahel region that have been cleared of vegetation cover.

● *Describe this soil erosion in the Amazon Basin, Brazil.*

Leaching

In countries such as Ireland, rainfall exceeds evaporation. In such areas, rainwater will percolate (soak) down through the soil. This downward movement might be quite rapid in permeable, large-grained, loosely packed soils, such as sandy soils.

Water often dissolves minerals, humus and other plant nutrients on the upper horizons (layers) of the soil. **As the water seeps downwards, it carries these nutrients with it.** This process is called **leaching**. Severe leaching reduces soil fertility because it washes plant nutrients down beyond the reach of many plant roots.

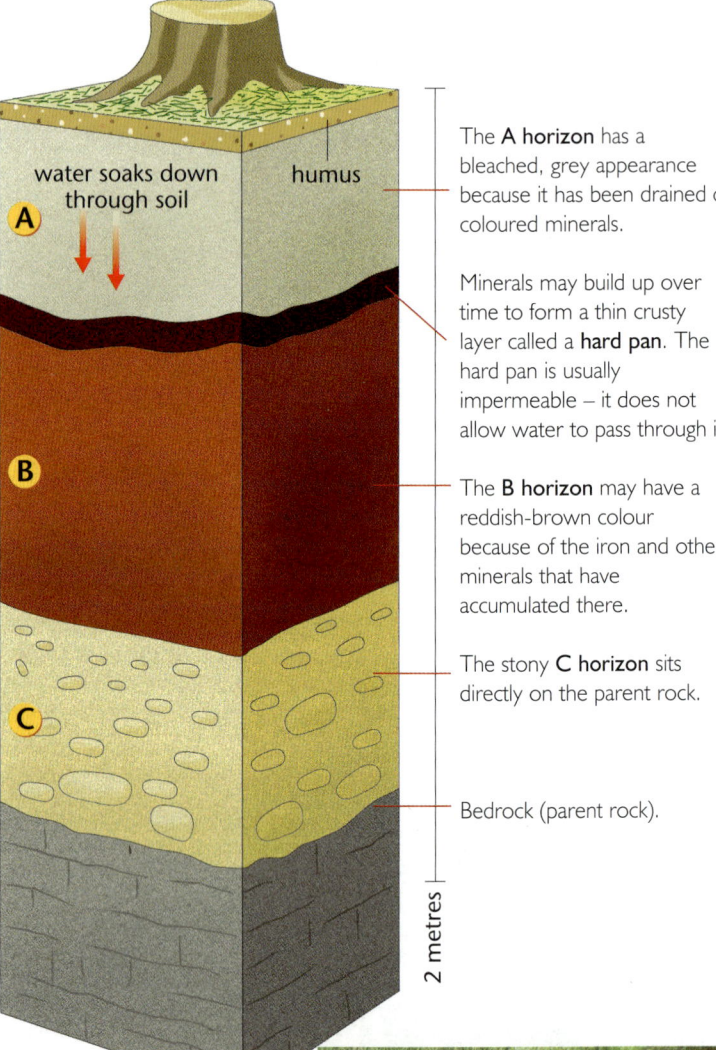

water soaks down through soil

humus

A

B

C

The **A horizon** has a bleached, grey appearance because it has been drained of coloured minerals.

Minerals may build up over time to form a thin crusty layer called a **hard pan**. The hard pan is usually impermeable – it does not allow water to pass through it.

The **B horizon** may have a reddish-brown colour because of the iron and other minerals that have accumulated there.

The stony **C horizon** sits directly on the parent rock.

Bedrock (parent rock).

2 metres

Fig. 87.1 Soil profile of podzols. A soil profile is a vertical section of the soil from surface to bedrock. It contains horizontal layers called horizons.

Podzolisation

Podzolisation is an **intense form of leaching**. It can occur in **cool areas of heavy rainfall**, such as on many of Ireland's highlands. It also occurs in areas of coniferous forest or moorland vegetation. This vegetation causes the rainwater seeping through it to become so acidic that it would dissolve most soil nutrients.

Podzols (the soils associated with podzolisation) have very distinct **soil profiles** (see Fig. 87.1).

Lateralisation

Lateralisation is a form of **extreme leaching** that happens in **tropical and equatorial regions**. **Heavy rainfall** is the main cause of this leaching. **High temperatures** also contribute by speeding up the chemical reactions of water on rock. High temperatures also break down iron in the rock into **iron oxide** or rust. The presence of iron oxide gives the soil a red, rusty appearance. That is why some soils in these regions are called **tropical red soils**.

Activity

1. With the help of an atlas and the map on page 493, name three countries where you would find:
   - podzols
   - tropical red soils.

A podzol soil horizon.
- *Identify the A horizon, the hard pan and the B horizon.*

Calcification

Calcification happens in places with dry climates, where evaporation exceeds precipitation. **Water seeps up through the soil by capillary action**, which is the opposite of leaching described on page 490.

Calcification results in calcium being built up close to the surface of the soil. This helps to make the soil very fertile, as in the **chernozem**, or the 'black earth' soils, of the **steppes** (grasslands) of Russia and the Ukraine. Chernozems are also found in the **prairies** of the United States.

Humification

Most soil contains **organic matter**, which consists of dead animal remains and plant litter. **Micro-organisms**, such as bacteria and fungi, work on the organic matter. They cause it to decay slowly into a black, jelly-like substance called **humus**.

Oxygen is also needed to assist the breakdown of organic matter into humus. Air in the soil therefore plays an important role in the process of **humification**. Humus makes the soil fertile. It converts nitrogen, calcium and other nutrients into soluble forms so that they can be easily absorbed by plant roots.

Rich black earth soils being ploughed in the Ukraine.
- *Why, in your opinion, is this soil so dark in colour?*
- *Describe two processes that you think help to make this soil fertile.*
- *For what type of farming is this soil being used?*

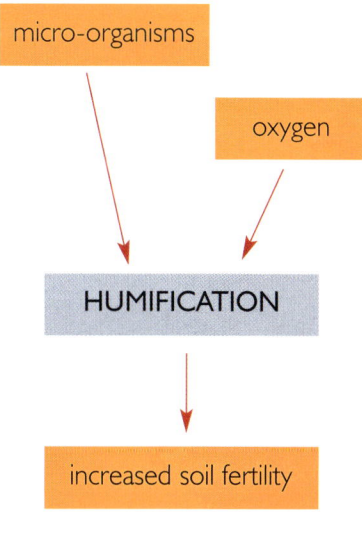

Ukraine

How Capillary Action Works

After rain, gravity causes water to sink through the soil. But following long periods of dry weather, the water is absorbed upwards through the dry soil. This acts something like water does on a wet surface when a dry towel is put over the water to soak it up.

Activity
1. Locate the chernozem soils of the steppes and prairies on the map on page 493.

micro-organisms

oxygen

HUMIFICATION

increased soil fertility

See question 3 on page 526.

CHAPTER 88
THE GLOBAL PATTERN OF SOILS

KEY IDEA!

Major soil types form global patterns owing to climatic and other factors.

Brown earth is Ireland's zonal (and most common) soil type.

Peaty, intrazonal soils are found in some poorly drained areas of Ireland.

Sand dunes provide an example of immature (not fully formed) azonal soil.

Learn any three of the examples given below.

HOW SOILS ARE CLASSIFIED

Zonal Soils

Climate is the most important factor affecting soil formation. Soils are therefore usually classified **according to the climate types** that help to form them. They are called zonal soils because they occupy large climatic zones or regions of the earth's surface. **Brown earth**, for example, is the zonal soil type in Ireland and other regions of cool temperate oceanic climate.

Zonal soils develop over long periods of time. They therefore have well-formed soil profiles with clear horizons.

Intrazonal Soils

Within zonal soil belts, strong **local factors** can sometimes create different types of soil in certain areas. These are called intrazonal soils. Poor drainage, for example, creates **peaty soils** in parts of Connemara.

Azonal Soils

Azonal soils are soils that are **not yet fully developed**. They do not have clear soil profiles. Recent deposits of **sand** – as in sand dunes – is an example of azonal soil.

How Zonal Soils are Related to Climate and Vegetation Zones		
Zonal soil	**Climate zone**	**Vegetation zone**
Tundra soil	Tundra	Tundra
Podzols	Cold Temperate Continental	Coniferous forest (taiga)
Brown earths	Cool Temperate Oceanic	Deciduous forest
Chernozems/grassland soils	Warm Temperate Rainy and Steppe	Grasslands
Desert and semi-desert soils	Desert	Desert
Terra rossa	Mainly Warm Temperate Oceanic	Mainly Mediterranean
Latosols/tropical red soils	Equatorial/Tropical	Rainforest
Mountain soils	Mountain climate	Mountain vegetation

The global pattern of soils is shown on the map in Fig. 88.1. This map shows only the **general locations** of the world's most common *zonal soils*. It does not show the many intrazonal and azonal soils that exist within each zone.

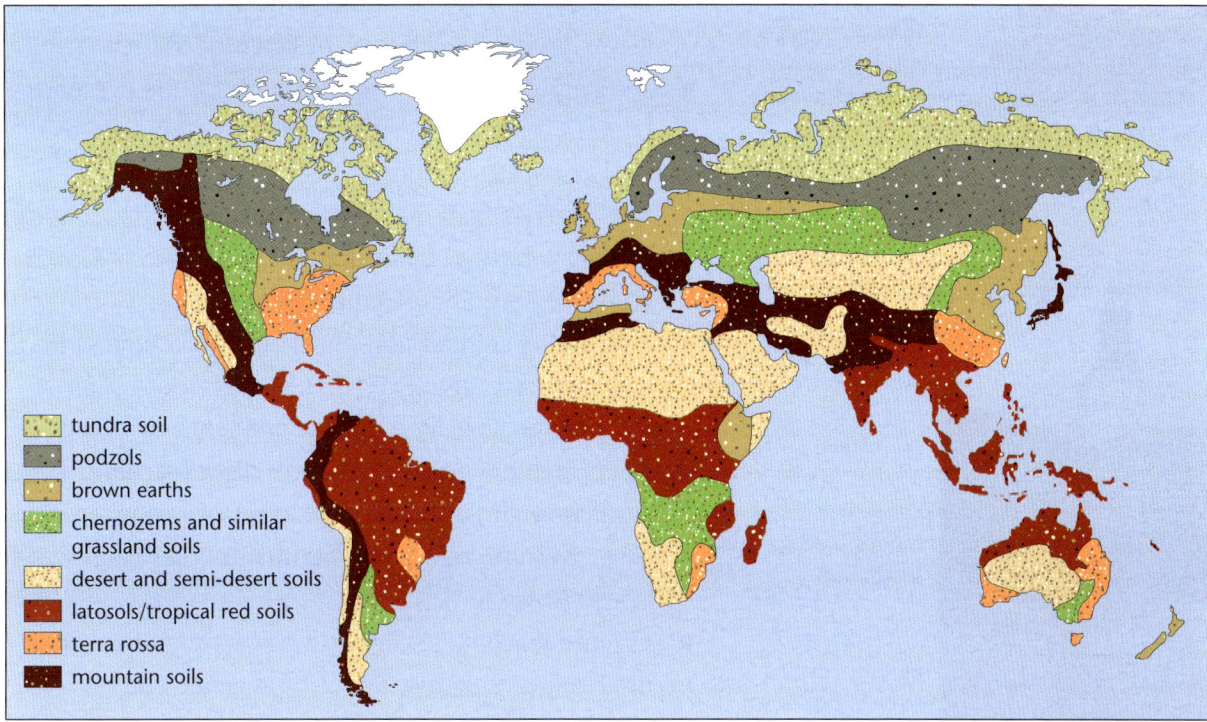

tundra soil
podzols
brown earths
chernozems and similar grassland soils
desert and semi-desert soils
latosols/tropical red soils
terra rossa
mountain soils

Fig. 88.1 The global pattern of zonal soils.

BROWN EARTHS
Sample Study of a Major Soil Type

You will see from Fig. 88.1 that brown earths are common in temperate latitudes (40° to 60° North) within the continent of Europe. They occur mostly in areas of Cool Temperate climate. They stretch from Ireland in the west to Russia in the east and from Scotland in the north to Portugal in the south.

Most brown earths:

- Have a **crumb texture** and are **well drained**.
- Are **slightly acidic**.
- Have a **dark brown colour** throughout their profile.
- Are usually very **fertile**.

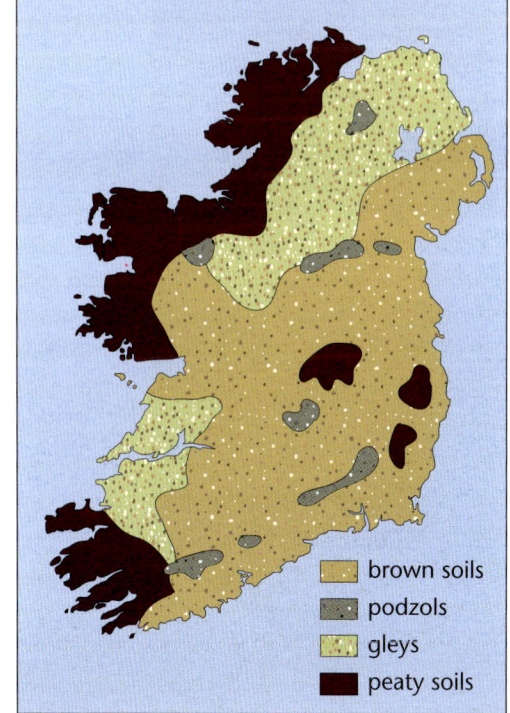

brown soils
podzols
gleys
peaty soils

Fig. 88.2 Ireland's principal soils.

493

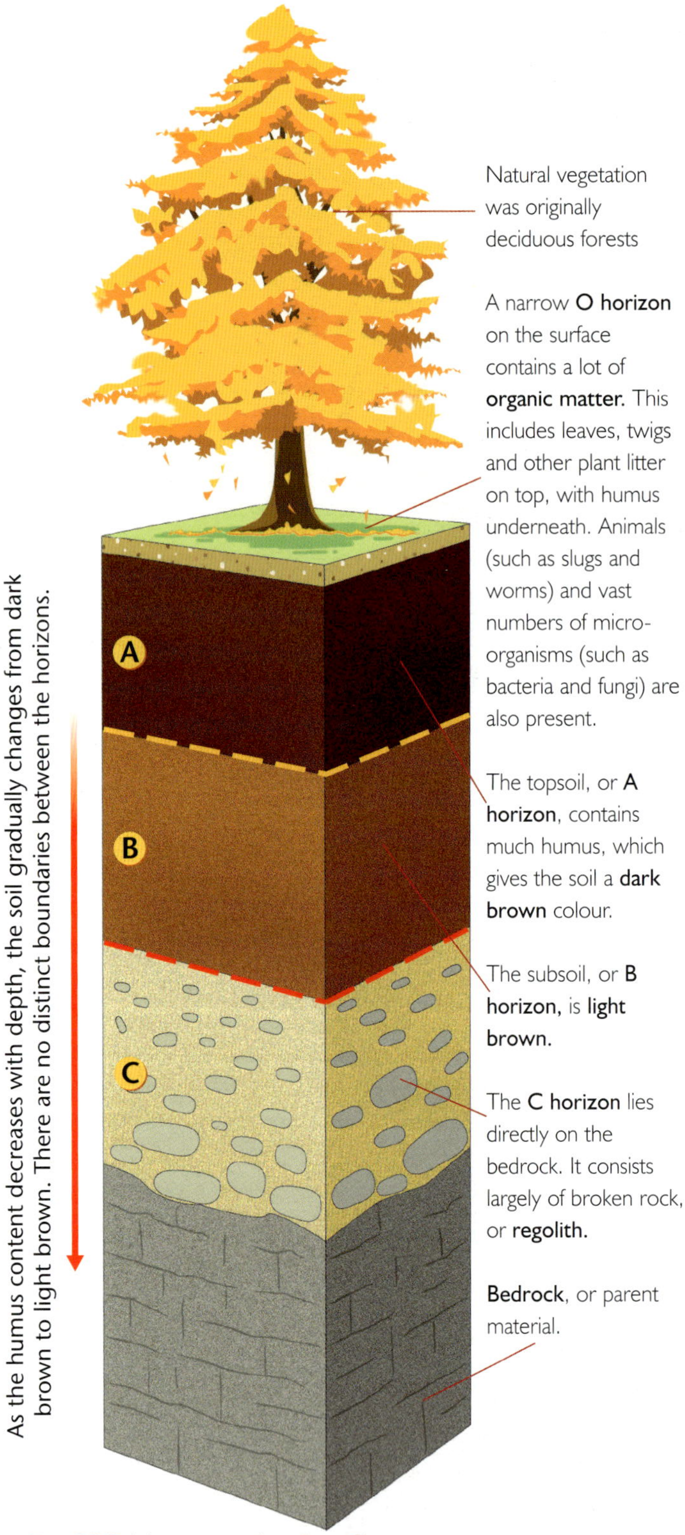

The causes of these characteristics are as follows:

- Brown earths developed in areas that were once covered in dense **deciduous forests**, with heavy undergrowth. These forests provided an abundance of leaves, twigs and other **plant litter** for the soil.
- Temperate climate is warm enough for the presence of vast numbers of animals such as earthworms as well as **micro-organisms**, such as bacteria and fungi. The micro-organisms break down plant litter to form **humus**, which gives the soil its dark brown colour, its crumb texture and much of its fertility.
- **Burrowing animals** and the **crumb structure** of the soil assist **drainage** and help the movement of **air** through the soil. This in turn contributes to fertility.
- There is enough rain to provide **slight leaching**. This, together with the burrowing action of worms and other **animals**, **mixes the humus** through the soil and increases soil fertility.
- **Limited leaching** also gives the soil a **slightly acidic** pH reading of usually 5 to 7. This is because rainwater absorbs carbon dioxide in the atmosphere and so becomes a very weak carbonic acid.
- **There is not enough leaching to create impermeable hard pans**, which would hinder drainage. Brown earths are therefore **well drained**.

You will see from Fig. 88.2 that brown earth is the principal but not the only soil type in countries such as Ireland. It is also worth noting that, even within a small country such as Ireland, there are different varieties of brown earths:

- **Acid brown soils** have formed on bedrocks such as granite or sandstone, which are low in lime.
- **Brown podzolic soils** have formed in areas where leaching is relatively high. The A horizons of these soils have a pale ashy rather than a brown colour.

Brown earths have been cultivated for centuries and now contain very few of the deciduous forests which once nourished them. Farmers now nourish the soils with artificial fertilizers, manure and lime. When properly maintained, these soils are very suitable for a wide range of agriculture, ranging from tillage to pasture to forestry.

As the humus content decreases with depth, the soil gradually changes from dark brown to light brown. There are no distinct boundaries between the horizons.

Natural vegetation was originally deciduous forests

A narrow **O horizon** on the surface contains a lot of **organic matter**. This includes leaves, twigs and other plant litter on top, with humus underneath. Animals (such as slugs and worms) and vast numbers of micro-organisms (such as bacteria and fungi) are also present.

The topsoil, or **A horizon**, contains much humus, which gives the soil a **dark brown** colour.

The subsoil, or **B horizon**, is **light brown**.

The **C horizon** lies directly on the bedrock. It consists largely of broken rock, or **regolith**.

Bedrock, or parent material.

Fig. 88.3 A brown earth soil profile.

See questions 4 and 5 on page 526.

494

CHAPTER 89

PEOPLE AND SOILS

 **KEY IDEA!**

People impact on soils.

PEOPLE AND SOIL EROSION

Soil is a renewable resource that can be used again and again. But it depends on vegetation cover for its fertility and health and sometimes even for its survival. People sometimes destroy or remove this vegetation cover. The soil can then be swept away by landslides or become exposed to **agents of erosion**, such as wind and running water.

- **Wind erosion** happens when wind removes dry, exposed topsoil from the land.
- **Sheet erosion** is the removal of a uniform layer of topsoil by rainwater washing evenly down a slope.
- **Gully erosion** happens when rainwater concentrates into small streamlets and carves gashes into the land's surface. It forms numerous grooves or gullies in the ground.

How Vegetation Protects Soil

- Plant leaves and other vegetation **intercept** raindrops. They stop heavy rain from pounding off the soil and loosening it. Some rain will evaporate off the plants without ever reaching the ground. This reduces the possibility of sheet or gully erosion in wet climates.
- Plant roots **absorb** water from the soil. This helps to prevent mudflows in wet climates.
- Plant roots **bind** the soil together. This helps to prevent it from being washed or blown away.
- Dead plant roots leave channels that help water to **percolate** through the soil. This assists soil drainage.
- Tree trunks help to **block** landslides and avalanches (snow slides) in mountain areas.
- Plant litter provides humus that **fertilizes** the soil. This allows more vegetation to grow and continue to protect the soil.

Activity
1. What kind of soil erosion can you identify in this photograph?
2. How might people help to cause this erosion?

How People Destroy Vegetation Cover

Human activities can destroy vegetation cover and help to cause soil erosion.

- **Overgrazing** happens when too many farm animals are allowed to graze the land. The animals can strip the soil of so much of its vegetation cover that the soil becomes exposed to landslides, mudflows or to the agents of erosion. Animals can also expose the soil by trampling vegetation with their hooves.
- **Overcultivation** happens when people grow crops year after year on the same patch of land without fertilizing the soil, resting it or practising crop rotation. This causes the soil to become deficient in minerals, so that crops eventually fail to grow. The soil is then left without protective cover and is exposed to erosion.
- **Deforestation** happens when people cut or destroy forests that protect the soil from landslides, mudflows, avalanches or the agents of erosion.

Case Study 1: The Burren

The Burren is a karst area of largely exposed limestone in north Co. Clare. There are places where its almost bare rock surface supports very little farming or human habitation. Yet there is evidence that, from the Stone Age to Celtic times, this area was farmed successfully and was quite heavily populated (see Fig. 89.1 and the photograph below). The Burren then must have had sufficient soil and grass cover for agriculture.

Scientists believe that overgrazing by Ireland's cattle farmers of old might have exposed the Burren's soil to the elements. Rain may then have stripped the land of its soil, leaving the underlying limestone exposed.

> You have already learned about the Burren on page 58.

The Burren
Co. Clare

Fig. 89.1

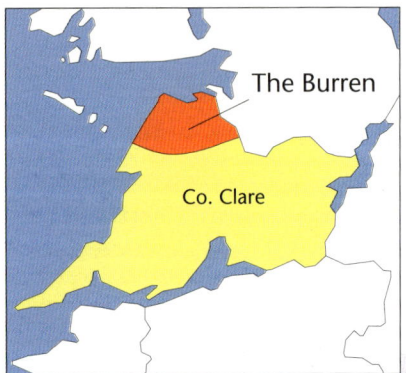

Parts of the Burren, Co Clare.

Activity

1. How many square kilometres does the map fragment represent?
2. Count the number of antiquities (ancient buildings, etc.) on the map and calculate their density per square kilometre.
3. Count the number of present-day buildings on the map and calculate their density. (Note: Do not confuse buildings with spot heights on the map.)
4. Try to account for (explain) the contrast between the densities calculated in questions 1 and 2.

Case Study 2: Duncarton Hill

The night of 19 September 2003 produced a nightmare experience for the residents of Pollathomas in north-western Co. Mayo. With a terrifying roar, thousands of tonnes of mud, rock and earth swept down nearby Duncarton Hill. Roads and bridges were torn up. Holiday homes were destroyed. Parts of a graveyard were swept into the sea. An elderly woman was trapped in her home while mud ripped through her house. Miraculously, no one died in the terrible mudslide.

Prolonged heavy rain, which had saturated the soil, was the immediate cause of the mudflow, but human activities might also have contributed. Some locals believe that sheep had been allowed to overgraze Duncarton Hill. Others fear that rock-breaking work near the foot of the hill might have loosened peat and soil. More say that a road built to service an aviation tower at the top of the hill might have undermined topsoil and blocked the free drainage of water downhill.

Activity

In what way might the human activities shown here contribute to desertification?

Case Study 3: Desertification in the Sahel

Desertification is the spread of desert conditions, usually following the erosion of exposed topsoil. The world's worst instance of desertification is happening in the Sahel region of Africa. The Sahel is on the southern borders of the Sahara desert (see Fig. 89.2). Desertification is so bad there that desert conditions are spreading southwards into the Sahel at the rate of 5 to 10 km each year. You will see from this case study that human activities help to cause desertification in the Sahel.

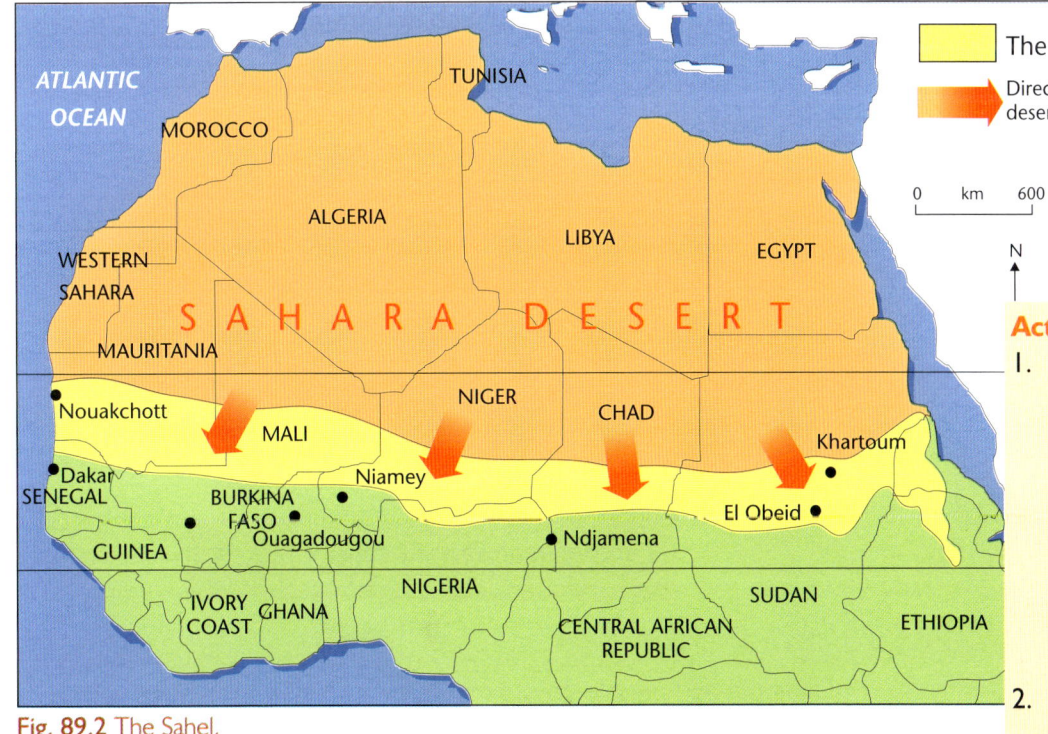

Fig. 89.2 The Sahel.

Activity

1. Use this map to describe the location and extent of the Sahel. Refer to the approximate length, width and area of the region. Refer to its latitude, its orientation (the direction in which its long axis points) and the countries which it partly occupies.

2. Sahel is an Arabic word for 'shore'. Why do you think the Sahel is so called?

Causes of Desertification

Climate Change

The excessive burning of fossil fuels, especially in rich First World countries, has contributed to global warming and other climate changes that affect the Sahel.

- Rising temperatures have caused **more evaporation** and less condensation. This has reduced rainfall levels.
- Over the past twenty years, **rainfall has decreased** by one-third.
- There have been several long and serious **droughts**, for example from 1968 to 1973.

Some **vegetation** that is not drought resistant **dies** as a result of these changes.

Population Growth

High birth rates have led to an annual population increase of nearly 2 per cent. Because of this:

- **More cattle** are needed. They overgraze the land and trample vegetation.
- **More food crops** are needed. The land is overcultivated.
- **More firewood** is needed. Trees and shrubs are cleared for firewood.

Local Customs

Peoples such as the **Masai** measure their wealth by the number of cattle they own. They keep so many cattle that the land is **overgrazed**.

Wells

Wells are sunk to provide water. The wells **use up groundwater** that took centuries to accumulate. This causes the water table to fall. Cattle herders come to live near wells, so that the areas surrounding the wells become **overgrazed and trampled**.

Cash Crops

Governments encourage the growing of cash crops to raise money and to pay international debts. The Niger government, for example, encouraged the growth of groundnuts.

The growth of a single crop in the same place year after year (**monoculture**) takes many nutrients from the soil. The soil becomes infertile and eventually the **crop fails**.

The Sahel is also referred to on page 515.

Activity

Explain how the sinking of wells such as the one shown in the photograph might contribute to desertification in the Sahel.

The Sahel.

There is less vegetation cover, so the soil becomes exposed to wind erosion.

↓

DESERTIFICATION TAKES PLACE

↓

Cattle die and people go hungry. Famines occur. Millions of people migrate from the Sahel into the savannah grasslands further south. The overpopulation of the grasslands causes desertification there.

Case Study 4: The American Dust Bowl

In the 1930s, overcropping led to serious soil erosion in that part of the Midwest of the United States known as the Dust Bowl (see Fig. 89.3).

The Great Plains of the Midwest are windy, semi-arid (dry) areas of **natural grassland**. Throughout the 1920s, farmers **ploughed** the plains to plant wheat, which could be sold at a high price. In the early years, there was sufficient rainfall and the plains were golden with wheat.

Then, throughout the 1930s, the **rains failed**. The farmers continued to plough and plant, but nothing would grow. With no vegetation to protect it, the soil became dry, loose and dusty. Winds whipped across the barren fields, carrying away the soil in great clouds of dust. With their farms ruined by **wind erosion**, many farmers abandoned their homes. Like refugees, they headed west to California in search of work and survival.

You have already learned about the Dust Bowl on page 116.

The dust was everywhere. It piled up against walls, clogged machinery and even crept into houses where people struggled to breathe. Children wore dust masks going to and coming from school. Farmers watched helplessly as their farms blew away.

Fig. 89.3
The Dust Bowl.

Activity

1. Which six states of the USA were part of the Dust Bowl?
2. What enabled the wind to create the dust storm shown in the photo?

CONSERVING SOIL

Throughout the world, people employ different methods of preventing or reducing soil erosion. Some of these methods of **soil conservation** are as follows.

Improving Vegetation Cover

You have learned that the removal of vegetation cover is a major cause of soil erosion. It follows that one of the best ways of combating soil erosion is to increase or improve vegetation cover. There are many ways of doing this.

Crop Rotation

Different crops remove and replace various minerals in the soil. Crop rotation is the planned growing of **different crops in the same place from one year to another** so that the soil does not become deficient in any particular mineral. This helps to keep the soil healthy and fertile so that it will always produce enough vegetation cover to protect it from erosion.

Regrassing

Wind erosion in regions such as the Sahel can be reduced by replanting tough drought-resistant grasses in places threatened by erosion. The grasses will trap wind-blown soil, while their roots will help to bind the surviving soil together.

A similar method of soil conservation is practised on Irish coastal sand dunes, where **marram grass** is used as a means of 'anchoring' dunes against wind erosion.

Afforestation

The planting of trees also combats erosion. Trees are even more effective than grass at trapping wind-borne soil. The shallow roots of conifers bind the soil together very effectively. Trees also intercept heavy rainfall and reduce surface run-off that might result in gully erosion. Tree roots absorb moisture from the soil and so reduce the possibility of mudflows in wet, hilly regions, such as in the West of Ireland. Fruit-producing trees are of added benefit in Third World regions such as the Sahel, because they produce nutritious food for local people.

Shelter Belts

Well-separated lines of trees or shrubs break the force of the wind over the land between them. They can therefore act as shelter belts or protective barriers against wind erosion in places such as the Sahel or the Great Plains of the United States.

Revise How Vegetation Protects Soil on page 495.

Activity
Identify and describe the method of soil conservation shown in this photograph.

500

Reducing Surface Run-off

The surface run-off of water can result in gully erosion on hilly or even gently sloping areas. There are different methods of reducing surface run-off.

Stone Lines

Burkina Faso is a country that partly lies in the Sahel. This area suffers from very infrequent falls of heavy rain. People there place **lines of small stones across slopes** in order to reduce surface run-off. Rainwater gets trapped behind the stones, so it has a chance to soak into the ground. The stone lines also trap waterborne soil and prevent it from being removed from the area. Stone lines therefore replenish groundwater and reduce soil erosion. They work best on very gentle slopes, where they can result in a 50 per cent increase in crop yields.

See question 5 and 6 on page 526.

lines of stones built across slopes reduce run-off

water trapped behind the stones can infiltrate into the ground

Fig. 89.4 Stone lines in Burkina Faso.

Contour Ploughing

In contour ploughing, **ridges run across rather than up and down a slope**. These ridges act like little dams that hold rainwater and give it time to infiltrate the ground. They therefore prevent gully erosion by stopping water from rushing down the freshly ploughed soil. Contour ploughing can reduce soil erosion by up to 50 per cent. It is practised in those parts of the **Midwest of the United States** where large scale tillage farming is practised.

Terraces in China.

Terracing

Terracing prevents soil erosion in slopes that are too steep for contour ploughing. A series of **walls are built one above the other across a hillside**. Behind each retaining wall, a 'step', or terrace of land, is flattened and farmed. The tops of the retaining walls trap water that would otherwise flow rapidly downslope. Soil erosion is thus prevented. Terracing is common in **South-East Asia**, where water trapped behind terrace walls supports the growing of rice.

Activity
Describe how the use of terraces supports rice farming.

New Animals
Efforts have been made to reduce the large numbers of poor-quality cattle that overgraze much of the Sahel.

- **New breeds** of smaller, better-quality cattle are being introduced. They eat less, but produce more milk and meat than existing breeds.
- Limited numbers of **sheep and goats** are being introduced into areas where the only vegetation is poor-quality scrub. Sheep and goats can survive on such scrub.

501

CHAPTER 90
BIOMES

KEY IDEA!

Biomes are large world regions in which climate, soils, natural vegetation and animal life are all interrelated. The desert biome is an example.

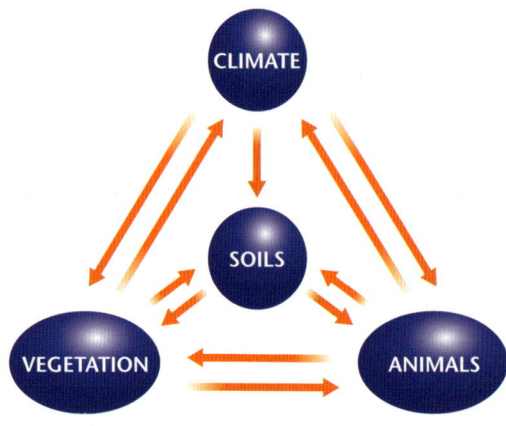

Fig. 90.1 Some interrelationships within a biome.

Biomes are large world regions in which climate, soils, natural vegetation and animal life are all interrelated (see Fig. 90.1). Vegetation and animals, for example, are adapted to the climate and soils of the biome in which they exist.

Biomes are usually named after the types of natural vegetation that occupy them. Ireland, for example, is within the **temperate deciduous forest biome**. This biome is so called because, under natural conditions, it was once covered with deciduous trees.

Geographers usually identify nine different biomes in the world. The map in Fig. 90.2 shows these biomes. It is, of course, a very simplified map, which gives only a very generalised idea of the location of biomes.

Fig. 90.2 World biomes.

Activity

Try to briefly explain each of the connections referred to in Fig. 90.1.

- tundra
- taiga (coniferous forest)
- temperate deciduous forest
- temperate grassland
- chaparral and/or evergreen hardwood (Mediterranean)
- desert
- tropical rainforest
- savannah grassland
- other biomes (ice, mountains, semi-arid)

Equator

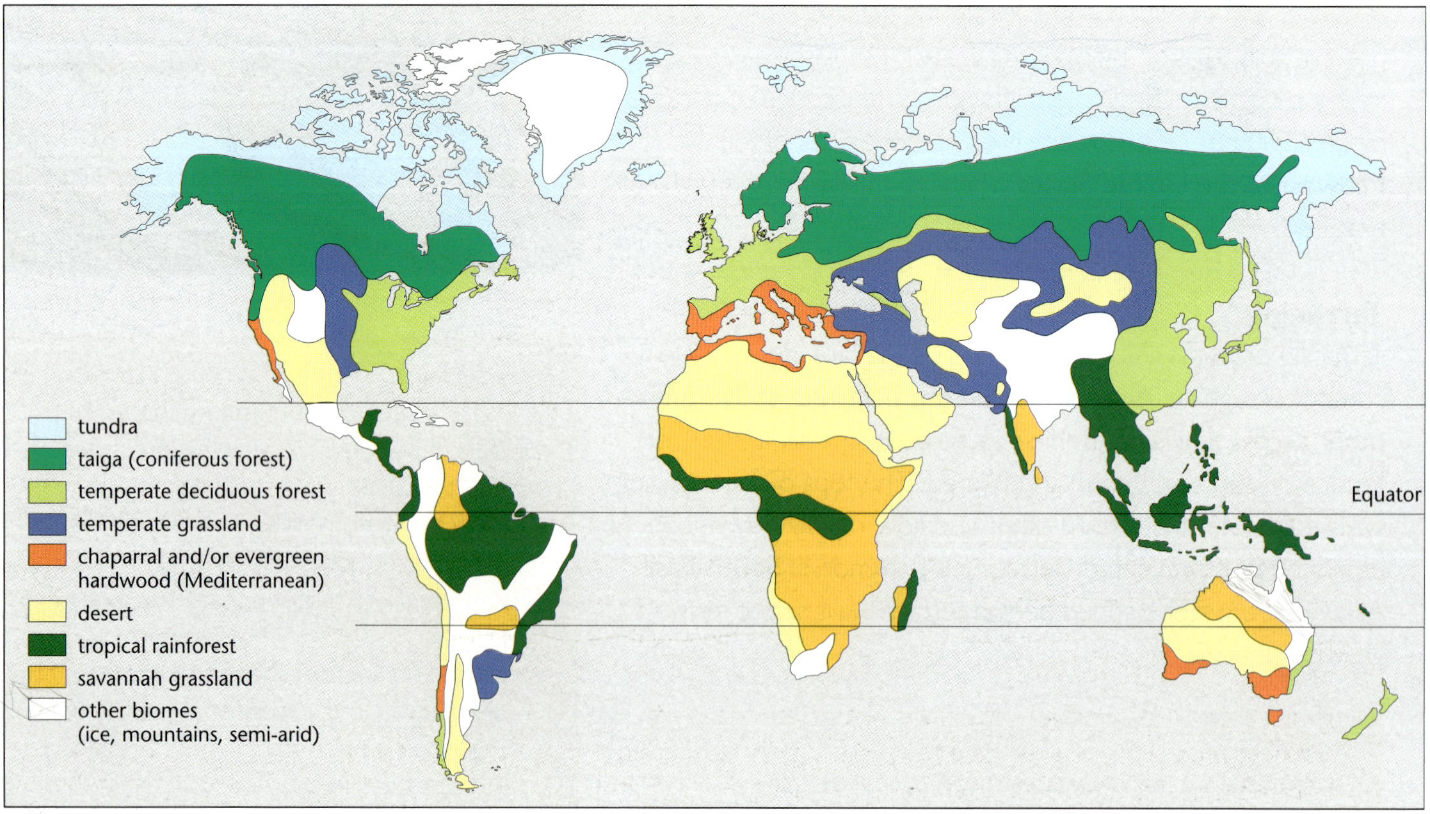

THE DESERT BIOME

The term 'desert biome' refers to the world's hot and mid-latitude deserts. This chapter will focus on the **hot deserts**, which are the most well-known and characteristic desert regions in the world.

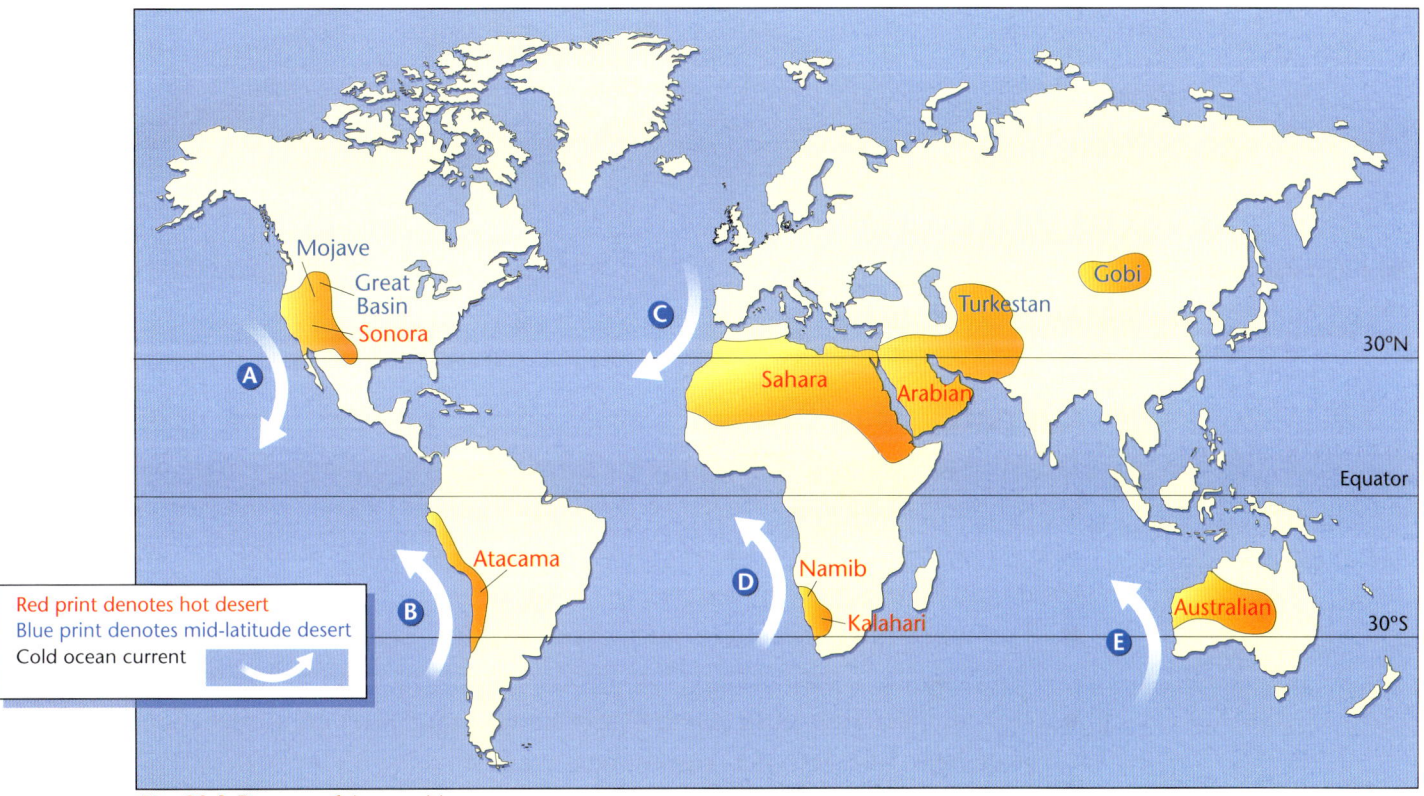

Fig. 90.3 Deserts of the world.

THE DESERT BIOME

Where Are the Hot Deserts?

Fig. 90.3 reveals that hot deserts are generally situated in tropical and sub-tropical zones **between 15° and 30°** north and south of the Equator. Much of this zone is in the path of the **trade winds** and some of it lies on the **high pressure belt** that exists over landmasses about 30° from the Equator.

Most hot deserts lie on the **western side of great continents**, near **cold ocean currents**.

Some desert areas, for example in North America, lie on the **leeward side of mountains**, where a rain shadow effect results in very little rainfall (see Fig. 90.4).

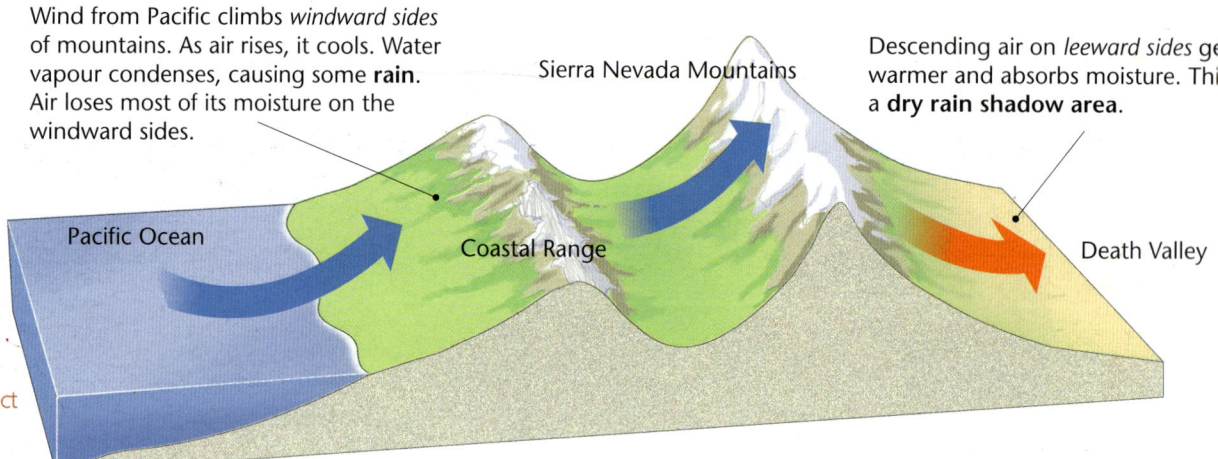

Wind from Pacific climbs *windward sides* of mountains. As air rises, it cools. Water vapour condenses, causing some **rain**. Air loses most of its moisture on the windward sides.

Sierra Nevada Mountains

Descending air on *leeward sides* ge warmer and absorbs moisture. Th a **dry rain shadow area**.

Pacific Ocean

Coastal Range

Death Valley

Fig. 90.4 Rain shadow effect on Death Valley, a desert area in California, USA.

Climate

Desert climate is **very dry**, with a yearly rainfall of between 0 and 250 mm. Rainfall is as unpredictable as it is rare. When rain does occur, it usually comes in the form of short, heavy downpours, which may affect small areas. These **'desert storms'** are usually of limited use for plant growth because:

- The heavy rains do not have much opportunity to infiltrate the soil. Rainwater runs rapidly on the surface, causing flash floods and eroding deep gullies.
- High temperatures cause rain to evaporate very quickly off the surface. Some rain evaporates even before it reaches the ground.

Very limited precipitation can also occur in the forms of dew or fog. Sudden drops in temperature can cause night **dews** in parts of the Sahara. **Fog** sometimes brings limited moisture to narrow coastal areas where cold ocean currents flow offshore. Such fogs occur regularly on the coastal sand dunes of the Namib Desert in Africa.

Deserts have **hot** climates, especially in summer, when daytime temperatures can reach higher than 45° C. But temperatures can drop by up to 30° C within an hour of sunset and night temperatures can fall below freezing point in winter. This **diurnal** (day/night) **temperature range** is greater than the average summer/winter temperature range of between 20° C and 25° C. That is why some geographers say that 'night is the winter of the desert'.

Why Deserts Are So Dry

- Some hot desert areas lie on the 'horse latitudes', **high pressure** belts that run across much of the earth at about 30° north and south of the Equator (see Fig. 90.3). Air descends towards the earth along these high-pressure belts. As it does so, the air becomes warmer. Warm air holds more water vapour than cooler air, so the descending air absorbs moisture. That is why high pressure brings prolonged dry conditions.

- Most hot desert regions are in the path of the **trade winds** that blow over much of the earth from 30° latitude towards the Equator (see Fig. 90.5). As these winds blow towards the Equator, they become warmer. Warm air holds more water vapour than cold air can. The trade winds therefore absorb rather than emit moisture, and they are therefore dry winds.

- Occasionally, moisture-laden winds can blow in from the western seas towards the deserts, but these winds must pass over cold **ocean currents**. As they do so, they are cooled and lose almost all of their moisture – usually in the form of fog – before they reach the land.

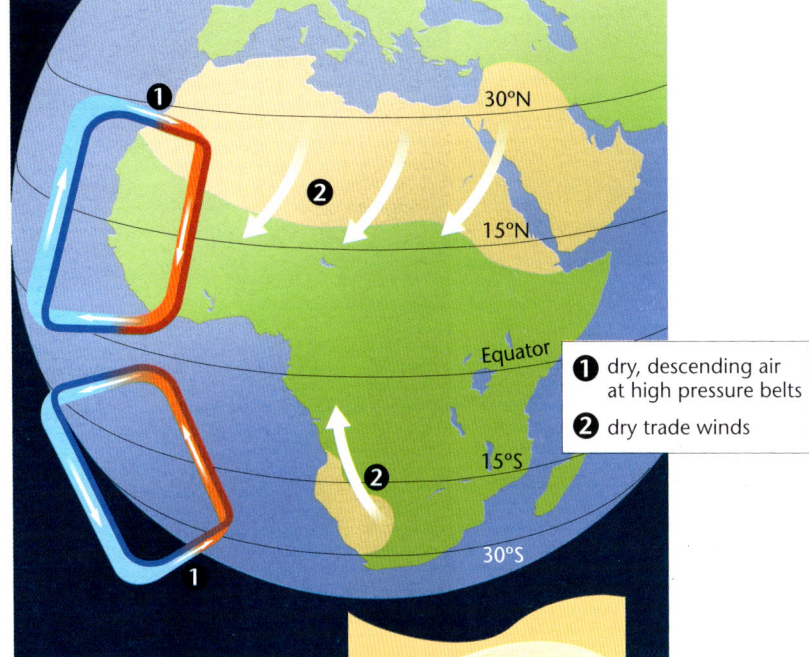

Fig. 90.5

❶ dry, descending air at high pressure belts

❷ dry trade winds

Although deserts are dry regions, very few desert areas are completely dry. Parts of the Atacama Desert in Chile are said to be the driest places on earth. They receive an average of less than 15 mm of rain per annum and sometimes receive no rain for years on end.

Why Deserts Are Hot by Day…

- Hot deserts are **within the tropics**, where the sun shines from almost vertically overhead in the summertime. These sunrays reach the earth's surface at almost right angles. They are therefore concentrated over small areas of ground and so give great heat.

- Another reason for high daytime temperatures is that the desert atmosphere contains little or **no cloud or humidity**, which would help to block sunrays. This, together with a general absence of vegetation or water bodies, allows sunrays to be absorbed rapidly into the desert surface. The surface then returns great heat to the atmosphere, giving rise to high atmospheric temperatures.

…And Cold by Night

- **Cloudless skies** allow daytime temperatures to rise rapidly. But with no clouds and little humidity to blanket it, the heat escapes quickly after nightfall.

A weather satellite photograph of Africa.

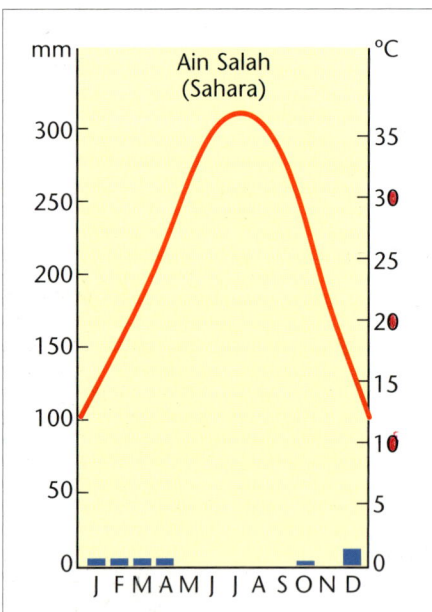

Fig. 90.6 Temperature and precipitation at Ain Salah, Algeria, in the Sahara Desert.

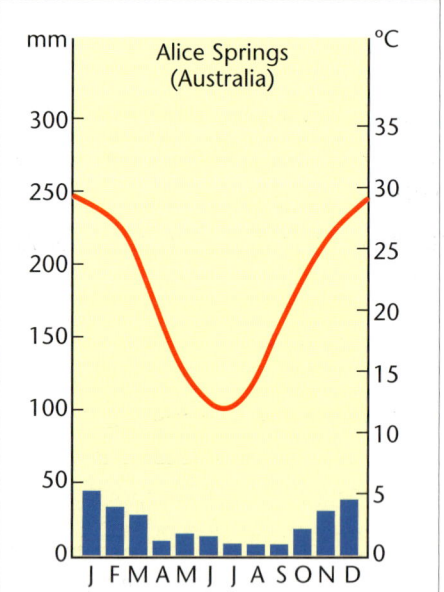

Fig. 90.7 Temperature and precipitation figures for Alice Springs in the Australian Desert.

Soils

Some hot desert areas have potentially fertile soils, which need only water to produce luxuriant plant life. Irrigation schemes, for example, have made deserts bloom in places such as southern California and parts of Libya. But soils in many desert areas **do not favour the growth** of a wide variety of plants. Some reasons for this are outlined below.

Little Soil Cover

Some desert areas have very deep soils. These limited areas are usually low-lying basins. Their soils were eroded from surrounding mountains and washed into the basins over tens of thousands of years by flash floods from occasional, torrential rainstorms. But most hot desert areas are rocky or stony, with very little soil cover.

Coarse Texture

Many regions have coarse-textured, gravelly soils. These occur where winds have blown away the finer dust and sand particles, leaving only heavier particles behind. Such soils are unable to retain moisture and so tend to be infertile.

Lack of Water and Humus

Very low precipitation results in desert soils being so dry (arid) that they are referred to as **aridisols**. Dry conditions cause vegetation to be very sparse and, in some areas, non-existent. Sparse vegetation leads to a shortage of plant litter, which in turn leads to a scarcity of humus. A scarcity of humus contributes to soil infertility. It can also result in soils being **grey** in colour.

Poor Development

Low precipitation also leads to a shortage of chemical weathering, which would contribute to the formation of soil. This, together with a shortage of humus, means that desert soils are often **poorly developed** and lack the clear horizons or the varied components that exist in most Irish soils. Soils in some desert areas consist of little more than a collection of broken-down mineral particles.

Fig. 90.8 The soil profile of a typical aridisol.

Activity
Contrast this profile with that of brown earth soil (Fig. 88.3) on page 494.

● Describe this Sahara Desert scene.

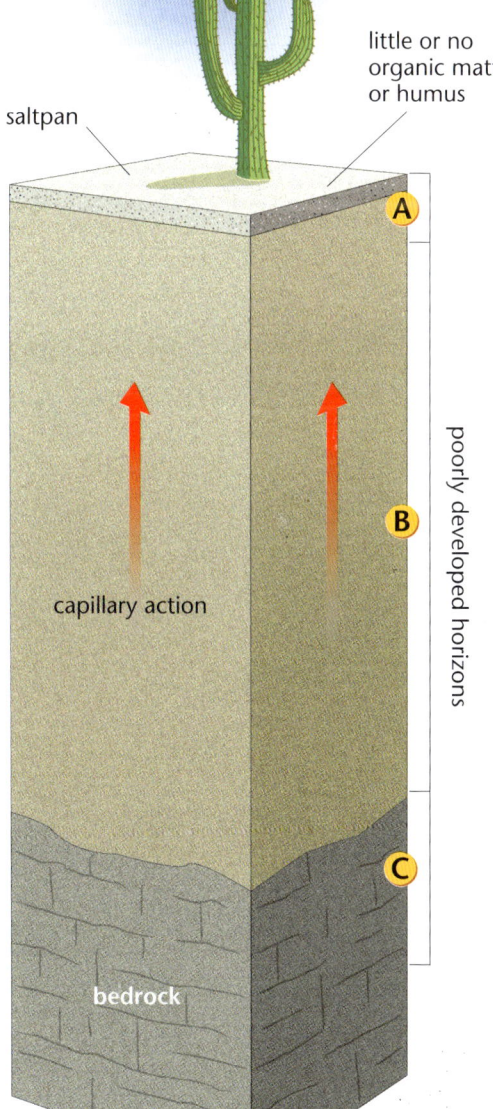

little or no organic matter or humus

saltpan

capillary action

poorly developed horizons

bedrock

A

B

C

Death Valley, a desert area in California, is one of the most barren places on earth, yet it contains more than 600 different plant species.

Salinisation

Hot, dry conditions cause moisture to move up through the soil by **capillary action** (see page 491). This causes large quantities of dissolved salts, such as chloride and sodium, to move up close to the surface in a process called **salinisation**. These salts are poisonous to most varieties of plants. They also form an impermeable crust, or **saltpan**, on or near the surface. The saltpan impedes the development of plant roots.

Vegetation

Vegetation is **scant** in hot deserts, mainly because of **a shortage of water** and of **high rates of evaporation** owing to elevated daytime temperatures. Yet many plant species survive. They have different ways of adapting to desert conditions.

- Many desert plants use large **root systems** to find water.
  - Some plants have *taproots* that reach deep into the ground in search of water. The most famous of these is the *mesquite bush*. Its roots are up to 50 m long.
  - Some cacti and other plants have *shallow roots*, which spread outwards (rather than downwards) for great distances, so that they create a large moisture-collecting area in times of rainfall.

The desert in bloom: these ephemerals bloomed suddenly following a rare desert downpour. Their life cycles will span only a few weeks.

- Some plants adapt to short and very infrequent desert downpours by growing very quickly. These plants are called **ephemerals**. The seeds of many ephemerals have waxy surfaces, which allow them to retain moisture for long periods of time. These seeds remain dormant, sometimes for years, awaiting desert rain. When rain does fall, the seeds develop into mature plants, burst into flower and produce a new generation of seeds, all within a few weeks. The old plants then die, while the new seeds become dormant and wait for the next period of rain. *Desert poppies* and the *creosote bush* of North America are examples of ephemerals.
- Many plants are **succulents**. They store water for long periods in their impermeable, waxy stems, in their roots or even in underground bulbs. The *barrel cactus* and the *giant saguaro* (see page 509) are examples of succulents.
- Some plants produce **juicy fruits**, which are eagerly devoured and digested by birds. The digested fruit seeds are then spread in bird droppings over large areas.
- The leaves and barks of some shrubs contain **poisonous or unpleasant substances**, which protect them from most hungry animals. The *Sodom apple*, for example, cannot be eaten by goats or camels.

- Plants such as the cereus, or 'desert dandelion', **bloom only at night**, when evaporation rates are lowest. The flowers of the cereus remain closed during the day to escape the drying effect of the hot sun.
- Some plants adapt in several different ways to their hot desert environments. The giant cactus, or *saguaro*, of North America is an example of such a plant (see Fig. 90.9).

Despite its thorny skin, some animals manage to burrow holes in the saguaro. This hole was made by a woodpecker. It is now the home of the elf owl, which is the world's smallest owl.

Oases

An oasis is an area of desert that has been made fertile by the presence of surface water. The water and the sun's heat usually contribute to the lush growth of vegetables, cereals, fig trees and other types of vegetation. The date palm is popular among oasis dwellers because it provides welcome shade as well as fruit.

Pleats (grooves) in its stem allow the saguaro to expand greatly. This allows the plant to store large quantities of water in its spongy inside during times of rainfall. The vertical grooves also help to direct **rainwater** to the base of the plant, where the plant's roots can absorb it.

Thorns (which are actually the plant's leaves) protect the saguaro from most species of **hungry animals**. The thorns also create areas of **still air** around the plant, protecting it from the drying effect of desert winds.

Waxy, impermeable skin acts like a plastic wrapper around the plant. It helps to prevent moisture within the plant from escaping.

Fig. 90.9 The giant cactus and how it adapts to desert conditions.

People and Hot Desert Vegetation

- People with large herds of cattle or sheep have **overgrazed** semi-desert areas, such as parts of the Sahel in Africa. This destruction of natural vegetation has contributed to desertification (the spread of desert conditions).
- People in areas such as southern California have used **irrigation** to produce high crop yields in hot deserts. But the rapid evaporation of irrigation water can result in **salinisation**, or the build-up of salt, near the surface of the land. Too much salt makes the soil toxic to plants.

Activity

Why is this rattlesnake relatively seldom seen in the desert?

The fennec fox.

Activity

1. How does the fennec fox obtain enough liquid to survive?
2. Suggest some advantages of the fennec fox's very large ears.

Fauna (Animals)

Hot deserts can support numerous animal species, but only if these animals adapt to prolonged very hot and dry conditions. Desert animals have different ways of adapting to these conditions.

The Hiders

Many animals survive by avoiding the scorching heat of the sun.

- Some creatures are **nocturnal**. They hide away in cool places during the day and come out at night to hunt and to eat. Animals such as the *rattlesnake* and *kangaroo rat* (which live in underground holes and burrows) and the *elf owl* (which lives in holes burrowed out of cacti) are examples of nocturnal animals.
- Some animals survive long, dry conditions by **hibernating** for extended periods. They remain very still and underground during these long periods and emerge only when rain finally arrives to frantically eat, mate and breed. An example of this are the *toads* of the Arizona Desert in the United States. They hibernate, often for more than a year, to await a desert rainstorm. They then emerge quickly to the surface and immediately enter flood pools to mate. Within 24 hours of mating, the females' eggs will be fertilized and hatched. Within two days, the pools will be full of tadpoles. Within two weeks (if the flood waters have not evaporated) a new generation of toads will emerge from the pools.
- Some animals avoid the heat by simply *staying in the shadow* of plants. The *jackrabbit* of North America uses cacti for shade, while many desert *insects* avoid the sun's rays by staying on the shaded sides of twigs or plant stems.

The Non-drinkers

Some animals do not need to drink water, because they get all the liquid they need from the food they eat.

- Carnivorous (meat-eating) animals, such as the *fennec fox*, get much of the liquid they need from the blood of their prey.
- The *desert gazelle* gets all the liquid it needs from the vegetation it eats. It conserves moisture by never urinating. Instead, it passes uric acid in the form of small, dry pellets.

Big-eared Animals

Animals lose heat through their ears, which contain many veins and blood vessels. The *fennec fox*, the *jackrabbit* and the *desert hedgehog* all have very large ears. This helps to keep them cool in the heat of the day.

The Birds

Most birds need regular water supplies, so few bird species live in deserts. Those that do have novel ways of adapting to their environment. The **roadrunner** of the North American deserts runs from place to place because it can use less energy by running than by flying. The roadrunner also has a very large tail, which it often spreads over itself like a parasol during the heat of the day.

The Marvellous Camel

Few large animals can withstand excessive heat or can retain moisture well enough to survive in hot, dry desert conditions. The camel is a notable exception. Known for centuries as 'the ship of the desert', the camel is perfectly adapted to the desert environment.

The roadrunner.
● *Explain how this bird adapts to hot desert conditions.*

During sandstorms, the camel can close its nostrils and lower its inner **eyelids** to protect its eyes.

A tough-skinned **mouth** enables the camel to chew thorny desert plants.

Fat in the **hump** acts as a food reserve. Because fat is concentrated in one area, the rest of the camel's body can cool more easily.

Coarse hair protects the camel's **back** from the sun

The camel can drink more than 100 litres of water at a time. By not sweating, it conserves body fluids. It can thus survive for up to several months **without water**.

Tough belly and kneepads enable the camel to lie on hot sand.

Wide, padded **feet** allow the camel to travel easily over soft sand.

See questions 7, 8 and 9 on page 526.

How the camel is adapted to desert conditions.

511

CHAPTER 91
HOW HUMAN ACTIVITIES HAVE ALTERED BIOMES

In many places, natural biomes have been altered by human activities or have been replaced completely by 'created' rather than natural environments. In this chapter we will study the impacts of the following human activities on biomes:

1. Early settlement and the clearing of forests.
2. The felling of tropical rainforests.
3. Intensive agricultural practices.
4. Industrial development.

Limestone pavement in the Burren.

Case Study 1: Early Settlement and the Clearing of Forests

From very early in human history, people have altered biomes by clearing forests to make homes. Since the invention of farming about 10,000 years ago, forests have also been cleared for agricultural purposes.

Ireland

Farmers first reached Ireland about 7,000 years ago, during **Neolithic** (New Stone Age) times. They mostly farmed upland areas because they could till the lighter, grittier soils of the uplands more easily than heavier lowland soils. Stone Age people could not, however, clear much of the existing deciduous forests with their stone tools. When the **Celts** arrived in Ireland around 500 BC, they brought iron tools with them. These allowed the Celts to clear more of Ireland's ancient forests of oak, ash and other broadleaved species.

Stone Age and Celtic farmers did, however, have considerable impact on the biome in particular parts of Ireland. Archaeological evidence suggests, for example, that **the Burren** in Co. Clare was heavily populated during Stone Age and Celtic times (see Fig. 89.1 on page 496). Farmers at this time appear to have cut down existing trees in order to graze their farm animals. They probably exceeded the **carrying capacity** of the land by grazing too many animals on it. This resulted in **overgrazing**,

512

which caused the grass cover to be almost all eaten and soils to be exposed to the weather. Rain and coastal winds then **denuded** (stripped) the land of its soil, leaving the underlying limestone exposed as it is today.

From the sixteenth century, as **English and Scottish planters** took over large parts of Ireland, the clearing of forests increased greatly. Tilled and other agricultural land replaced more and more of the old deciduous woodlands. Towns and roads also demanded more land. By 1921, at the end of English rule, less than 1 per cent of Ireland was covered in forest. Populations of forest animals, such as deer and foxes, had decreased greatly, while some species, such as the wolf, had become extinct. Today, only tiny fragments of our ancient Irish forest biome remain. These can be found near Killarney and Kenmare in Co. Kerry and near Lough Gill in Co. Sligo.

California

Before the mid nineteenth century, California in the United States was very lightly populated by Native Americans and by the descendants of earlier Spanish settlers. These people did little to modify California's **Mediterranean forest biome**. Then, the discovery of gold and the resulting gold rush caused hundreds of thousands of people to flood into California.

The forest biome was altered as settlers cut down oak, pine and other native trees to provide fuel and to make houses and pit props for gold mines. But it was the coming of **the railway** that really heralded a massive modification of California's natural biome. As the population of the state soared, forests were cleared for farmland, roads and railway lines, as well as for rapidly growing cities, such as San Francisco. Timber was carried away by rail to be sold in other parts of the United States. Over time, California's natural forest biome came to be replaced in some areas by **chaparral** (scrubland) and in most areas by 'created' environments of farmland or towns.

Meanwhile, California's most famous tree species – **the giant redwood** – was cleared almost to extinction. With less than 5 per cent of the old redwood forests now remaining, some redwood areas have been placed under state ownership so that they can be preserved. They include trees 100 m tall and more than 2,000 years old. The preservation of the remaining redwoods also preserves the habitats of several species of endangered flora (plants) and fauna (animals). In this way, fragments of California's original biome have been preserved from the interference of settlers.

These majestic redwoods once formed part of the natural biome of California.

Activity

How and why did settlers alter the Californian biome since 1850?

Revise **How Vegetation Protects Soil** on page 495.

Original Mediterranean vegetation (above) and secondary growth (below).

Italy

The natural biome of the Italian peninsula is one of **Mediterranean forests** of pine, cypress and cork oak trees as well as myrtle, laurel and other shrubs. These trees and shrubs played vital roles in the survival and protection of this biome. They provided suitable habitats for Mediterranean fauna. The trees soaked up water from the ground during occasional heavy rainstorms and their roots helped to bind the soil together on steep hillsides. Tree trunks helped to block landslides on steep slopes.

For thousands of years, people have modified the natural biome of Mediterranean Italy. From before the time of ancient Rome, settlers have cleared forests for firewood and farming. Where forests were cleared, **secondary growth** usually replaced the original trees. In some areas, this secondary growth consists of what is called *macchia* in Italy. *Macchia* contains shrubs such as myrtle, together with sweet-smelling smaller plants such as rosemary and lavender. *Garrigue*, a secondary growth of thorny bushes and plants, often developed on poorer soils.

From early times, people damaged the Mediterranean forest biome by **overgrazing** land with sheep and goats. This resulted in the occurrence of deadly **landslides and mudflows** on some hill slopes. With the removal of tree roots, water built up in the soil following rainstorms. When the soil became heavy and saturated, mudflows or landslides occurred, especially in the absence of tree roots and tree trunks that would help bind the soil together and prevent the downward movement of mud or regolith (loose rock).

Mudflows happen to this day on Italian hillsides. In 1998, following a period of heavy rain, a sea of mud ripped downhill through overgrazed slopes into the town of **Sarno** near Naples in Southern Italy. That mudflow left 135 people dead and 1,500 homeless.

Activity
Compare the remaining fragment of Mediterranean forest (top photo) with the *macchia* vegetation (bottom photo).

The Sahel

In parts of the Sahel region of Africa, a savannah grassland biome has been replaced largely by a hot desert biome. This process is called **desertification** and it has been caused partly by human intervention in the region.

For more on the Sahel, revise pages 497–8.

Population increase, together with many years of wetter than usual weather, encouraged many people to move into the Sahel between the 1930s and the 1970s. The people, whose numbers increased by a third in that period, cut down more and more trees and shrubs for **firewood**. They also burned trees and shrubs so that they could graze cattle more easily on the land. The number of cattle in the Sahel doubled during this period, so that serious **overgrazing** took place. All this caused the gradual deterioration of the existing biome.

From the 1960s onwards, the rains began to fail. Decades of wetter than usual conditions were replaced by many years of **drought**. The overgrazed vegetation failed to reproduce itself. Soils became dry, dusty and exposed to the weather. **Winds** began to blow away the topsoil, leaving much of the land barren, like that of the Sahara Desert to the north. Human activities, together with climatic variations, had resulted in desertification.

See question 10 on page 526.

Activity

What effects did the human activities shown in these photos have on vegetation cover and on desertification in the Sahel?

Case Study 2: The Felling of Tropical Forests

This study will focus on the effects of felling the world's **equatorial forests**.

Fig. 91.1 Equatorial forests are located close to the Equator. They cover vast areas in places such as the Amazon Basin, the Congo Basin and Indonesia.

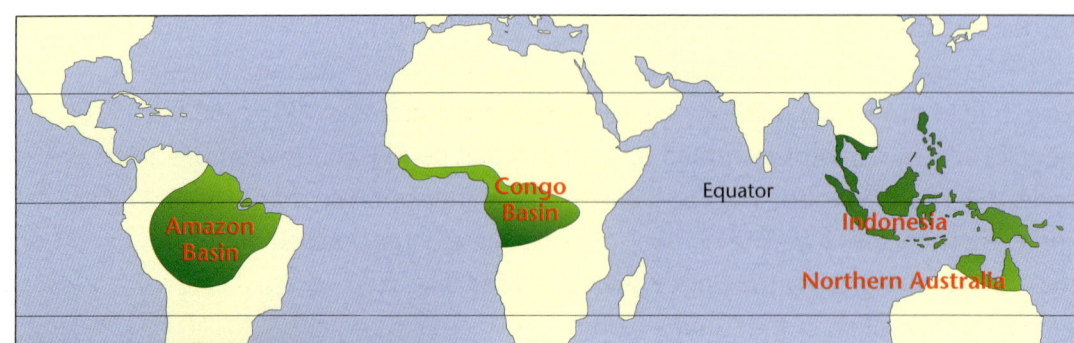

Dense forest in an equatorial region.

Equatorial climate provides high temperatures and plentiful rainfall all through the year. **The forest** is dense and luxuriant and its trees form an almost continuous canopy over the land. Beneath this canopy, a huge variety of smaller plants flourish. Millions of species of animals, ranging from tiny microbes to colourful birds, inhabit the forest. In their natural state, the equatorial forests contain the world's richest and most diverse biome.

The Impacts of Deforestation
Early and Later Forest Users

The original inhabitants of the equatorial forests include peoples such as the **pygmies** of the Congo Basin and the **Yanomani** and other 'Indian' tribes of the Amazon. Living in small groups, some of these tribes have for centuries slashed and burned tiny patches of forest in order to grow food crops such as manioc. In the absence of plant litter from trees, the cleared areas become infertile within a few years. When this happens, the people clear other patches of forest, leaving forest vegetation to reclaim the originally cleared areas. The small-scale activities of these indigenous (native) peoples left no permanent, damaging mark on the forest biome. Their activities are examples, therefore, of the **sustainable** use of forests.

Since the middle of the twentieth century, **large-scale clearances** of equatorial forests have taken place, especially in the Amazon Basin in Brazil. These clearances are carried out by a variety of people who come from outside the forest. They include rich cattle ranchers, logging companies, mining corporations and road builders. Using bulldozers and other heavy machinery, they clear such vast areas that they cause a hectare of forest to be destroyed every 1.5 seconds. Such clearances are clearly **unsustainable** and cause immense damage to the rainforest biome.

The Amazon Basin alone contains 40,000 different varieties of flowering plants. It is said that one square kilometre of the Basin contains as many plant and animal varieties as the whole of Europe.

Effects on Water and Soils

When the canopy of trees is cleared away, there is nothing to intercept (stop) heavy equatorial rains from hitting the ground directly. More rain then falls on the exposed ground and flows quickly into the rivers as surface run-off. This makes rivers bigger and more likely to **flood** nearby plains. Surface run-off also carries soil into rivers and some of this soil is deposited on riverbeds. This process causes river levels to rise and so contributes to flooding. Some floods have damaged the rainforest biome by destroying vegetation and animal habitats and by drowning countless animals. New settlements in the Amazon have also damaged the biome by **polluting** river water with everything from household waste to deadly mercury used in the process of gold mining.

When trees are cut, **soils** become exposed to the full force of equatorial rain. The rain sometimes erodes soil by **sheet erosion**, which is the even washing away of the soil's upper layers. More commonly, **gully erosion** takes place, as deep grooves are cut into the land surface. Without trees to soak up groundwater, **leaching** greatly increases, so that a great deal of soil nutrients are washed down below the reach of plant roots. The absence of trees also deprives soil of the plant litter that it needs to maintain fertility. **Infertility** develops rapidly, especially in the absence of artificial fertilizers being used by those who work the cleared land.

Destruction of Habitats

The habitats (homes) of forest peoples and of countless plants and animals are changed or destroyed by 'developers' who clear equatorial forests.

Forest peoples face cultural destruction and sometimes even human extinction at the hands of 'developers' in regions such as the Amazon Basin. The **Yanomani**, who live near the border between Brazil and Venezuela (see Fig. 91.2), are an example of such a people. For centuries the Yanomani lived off the forest in a sustainable way. They hunted, fished and practised subsistence* farming in a way that did not damage or upset the delicate balance of the tropical forest biome. Since the 1970s the Yanomani have seen their world disappear as rich cattle ranchers, miners and other 'developers' invade and deforest their territory. The Yanomani have little natural resistance against some of the **diseases** brought by outsiders. Illnesses such as measles have killed up to 90 per cent of the populations of some Yanomani villages. Those who survive are denied the human right to live undisturbed in their own environment. Their culture is diluted or destroyed by Western influences. Their traditional social life is shattered. Many are reduced to living miserable roadside existences as beggars or prostitutes.

Activity
Explain and describe the human impact on tropical forests shown in this photo.

*Subsistence farmers use most of the crops they grow and the animals they rear to feed themselves and their families.

The Amazonian rainforest is home to peoples like the Yanomani.

The world's rainforests contain up to 2 million species of plants and animals. One-quarter of all pharmaceutical drugs already owe their origins to rainforest species, despite the fact that up to now only about one-tenth of those species have been studied by people from outside the forests. But rainforest plants and animals survive in a finely balanced biome. When the biome is upset by deforestation, a multitude of **plant and animal species become extinct**. It is calculated that in the Amazon alone, one or more plant or animal species now becomes extinct every day.

Fig. 91.2

Worldwide Impacts

The much-feared process of **global warming** is caused by the gradual build-up in our atmosphere of carbon dioxide and other 'greenhouse gases'. The burning of fossil fuels is the main cause of this build-up. But trees use up carbon dioxide and convert it into oxygen, which is why equatorial forests have been described as 'carbon sinks' and 'the lungs of the world'. Deforestation in places such as the Congo and the Amazon Basin therefore decreases the amount of oxygen and increases the amount of carbon dioxide in the atmosphere. The burning of trees during deforestation further adds to the build-up of carbon dioxide. All this plays a role in global warming and in associated climate change. One result of global warming might be a rise in sea level by up to 6 m during this century. Such a rise would flood many low-lying parts of the world, such as Bangladesh and the south-east coast of the USA.

Another global impact of tropical deforestation is **desertification**, or the spread of deserts. We have seen how deforestation is exposing land to the elements and how heavy rain then removes topsoil from the land. This leaves the land barren and open to the spread of desert conditions. Desertification is already widespread in the Sahel region to the south of the Sahara Desert in Africa. Early signs of desertification now also exist at the edge of the Amazon Basin in north-east Brazil.

See question 11 on page 526.

The polar bear is an endangered species.

Case Study 3: Intensive Agricultural Practices

Intensive agriculture seeks to get the highest yield possible from the land. In doing so it sometimes leads to soil erosion, which alters and damages biomes.

Activity

How can the clearing of rainforests threaten the habitats of species such as the polar bear?

Clearing Natural Vegetation

Intensive farming can lead to soil erosion when it involves **removing natural vegetation** from the land surface. A cover of natural vegetation usually protects soil from erosion. When farmers remove this protection, the soil is exposed to the elements and can be eroded by wind or surface water. There are many examples of this happening throughout the world:

1. **The Burren** in Co. Clare is now a karst area of mostly bare, exposed limestone. It is thought that this area enjoyed a covering of soil and natural vegetation during Neolithic (New Stone Age) times. Scientists believe that overgrazing by cattle farmers of old might have removed so much natural vegetation that the soil was exposed to the elements. Surface water following rain may then have stripped away the soil, leaving the underlying rock exposed.

2. In the 1930s, overcropping led to serious soil erosion in that part of the Midwest of the United States known as **the Dust Bowl**. Natural grasslands were ploughed to plant wheat. When the rains failed, the wheat failed to grow. The dry, exposed soil was then blown away by the wind.

3. Overgrazing has led to massive wind erosion of soil in parts of **the Sahel**, which lies just south of the Sahara Desert in Africa. The removal of soil has led to desertification – the spread of desert conditions – over vast areas of the Sahel. Plant and animal life have been greatly reduced and the local biome has been seriously altered.

Revise pages 496–9.

Cash Crops in the Third World

The intensive growth of cash crops in Third World countries has damaged biomes. An example of this has been the cultivation of **groundnuts (peanuts) in the African state of Niger**.

Niger was once a colony of France. In the 1960s, the French government encouraged the growth of massive quantities of groundnuts in Niger. These nuts would be exported to France as a source of cooking oil. The growth of these nuts was an example of **monoculture**, which means that no other crop was grown on the land. The monocultural growth of groundnuts exhausts soil so much that, after they have been grown for three years, the land needs to be left fallow (rested) for a six-year period in order to recover its fertility. Because most African farmers could not afford to rest their land for such long periods, the soil gradually became infertile. As the infertile soil produced smaller crops, the farmers tried to expand groundnut production to other areas in order to maintain their incomes. This in turn caused cattle rearing and millet cultivation to be pushed into 'marginal' semi-desert areas, which were not suited to agriculture. During particularly dry years, this cultivated marginal land produced little or no crops or grass, leaving the soil bare and exposed to wind storms. As the wind carried the dusty topsoil away, some land became part of the Sahara Desert. Intensive farming had thus caused desertification to take place and had altered the biome.

Exhausted soil as a result of the monocultural growth of groundnuts in Niger.

The Use of Fertilizers and Insecticides

Fertilizers are widely used to provide plentiful crop yields in modern intensive farming. But the overuse of fertilizers sometimes results in too many **nitrates and phosphates** entering the soil. These nutrients can then combine with groundwater and seep into our rivers and lakes. Too high concentrations of nitrates and phosphates cause the rapid growth of weed-like **algae** in rivers and lakes. The algae can use up so much of the water's oxygen supply that fish and other water creatures die. Some rivers and lakes in Ireland become so polluted in this way that their surfaces become completely covered with green algae.

Pesticides are chemicals that are sprayed on the land and are used often in intensive farms. They are designed to kill insects that eat crops or that spread disease among animals. Many pesticides are dangerous poisons that can cause serious pollution where they are not used properly. A pesticide once commonly used in Third World countries was DDT, a chemical that destroys mosquitoes and so helps to prevent malaria. The problem with DDT is that it is **cumulative**. It builds up to harmful levels in animals other than mosquitoes. When DDT was sprayed on land, some of it was washed into rivers and lakes, where it was absorbed by water plants. When fish ate the water plants, they too became contaminated with DDT. People or other animals that ate the fish then also became contaminated. In this way, the pesticide poisoned an entire food chain and so damaged the biome.

Disappearing Hedgerows

Hedgerows that separate fields have been a traditional and pleasant feature of the Irish countryside. These hedgerows can be described as 'uneconomic' because they may occupy a lot of land, especially where they separate small fields. But they also provide natural habitats (homes) for numerous species of birds, animals and insects.

Over the past fifty years, farmers have bulldozed many hedgerows. They do so in order to reduce 'non-profitable' space on their farms and to create bigger fields that are better suited to the use of harvesters and other modern farm machinery. The destruction of hedgerows has increased the amount of farmland available and has led to farms being used more intensively. But it has also resulted in the destruction of habitat for many birds, mammals, insects and traditional trees and plants. By damaging local ecosystems, hedgerow clearances alter our biome.

Hedgerow clearances may also ultimately contribute to a reduction, rather than an increase, in crop yields. Damage to soil and crops may occur in the absence of hedges that once protected them from the force of the wind.

Activity
Describe the cause and the consequences of the algae shown here.

Activity
Contrast photo A with photo B under the headings of intensity of land use and biodiversity (the richness and variety of plant and animal life).

See question 12 on page 526.

Case Study 4: Industrial Development

Manufacturing industry can damage biomes in a number of ways. These range from the creation of **greenhouse gases** and **acid rain** to an increase in **air and water pollution**.

Global Warming

See **Worldwide Impacts** on page 518.

Global warming is one of the most serious threats to biomes throughout the world. The main cause of global warming is the increased use of **fossil fuels**, especially in the world's more economically developed countries. Factories are major users of fossil fuels, such as oil and gas. When fossil fuels are burned, carbon dioxide (CO_2) is released into the atmosphere. Carbon dioxide is a greenhouse gas, which traps solar energy. As it increases, it causes the atmosphere to gradually become warmer.

Scientists believe that severe **droughts** being experienced in African countries such as Sudan and Ethiopia may be a result of increased evaporation caused by global warming. These droughts are resulting in the desertification of much of Africa's Sahel region. They are causing the biome of much of this region to change from one of savannah grassland to one of hot desert.

Global warming is causing **polar ice caps to melt** and this could have devastating effects on the world's biomes. Ice cap and tundra regions near the poles could be so altered that polar bears, Arctic foxes and other inhabitants of these regions might become extinct. The melting of ice caps would also cause sea levels to rise so that vast, low-lying areas in all parts of the world would be submerged. This would result in the widespread destruction of biomes in places ranging from Bangladesh to the Netherlands to the Shannon Estuary.

The little egret.

Global warming may already be altering **Ireland's biome**. Recent winters have been among the mildest recorded and birds of warmer climates, such as little egrets, are beginning to colonise our shores. If global warming causes Ireland's climate to become warmer, we might yet produce fruits like oranges, but catch tropical diseases like malaria. Global warming could also disrupt the flow of the North Atlantic Drift. If this happens, Ireland might become so cold that our harbours could freeze in winter.

Activity

Outline the connection between industrial activity and the increase in Ireland's little egret population.

Acid Rain

Industrial development has contributed greatly to acid rain, which has a major effect on biomes. As stated earlier, factories burn huge amounts of oil and gas. The burning of these fossil fuels causes **sulphur dioxide and nitrogen oxides** to be released into the air. These gases combine with moisture to form weak **sulphuric and nitric acids**, which fall as acid rain.

Acid rain causes soils to become gradually more acidic and to experience more leaching. This in turn alters plant life. **Coniferous trees** suffer so much that acid rain is sometimes called 'forest death' in Sweden. The roots of conifers are poisoned, so many trees stop growing or die. It is estimated that half of Germany's trees have been damaged by acid rain. Acid rain also causes sulphur to build up in soils. This kills some plants, such as certain types of mushrooms. It causes other plants, such as nettles, to spread at an alarming rate.

When forests, water supplies and soils are altered by acid rain, so is **animal life**. Woodland animals in Europe, for example, have died in their millions as a result of acid rain.

Acid rain can also damage **lakes**, many to the point that they no longer support fish life. An estimated 15,000 lakes have been damaged in Norway, which receives acid rain in south-westerly winds blowing from countries such as Britain.

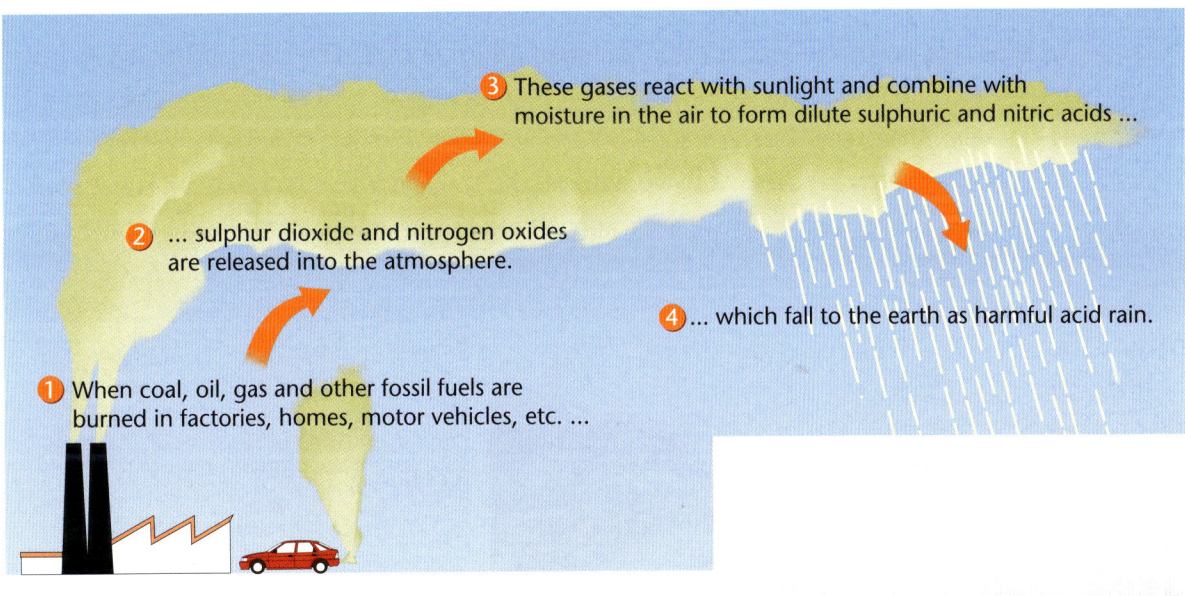

Fig. 91.3 How acid rain is caused.

3 These gases react with sunlight and combine with moisture in the air to form dilute sulphuric and nitric acids ...

2 ... sulphur dioxide and nitrogen oxides are released into the atmosphere.

4 ... which fall to the earth as harmful acid rain.

1 When coal, oil, gas and other fossil fuels are burned in factories, homes, motor vehicles, etc. ...

Activity
Describe the effects shown here of acid rain in the Black Forest, in Germany.

Death in Bhopal

This is an account of what happened after the gas leak in Bhopal.

'People simply started dying in the most hideous ways. The gases burned the tissues of their eyes and lungs and attacked their nervous systems. People lost control of their bodies. Urine and faeces ran down their legs. Women lost their unborn children as they ran. Some (people) vomited uncontrollably, went into convulsions and fell dead. Others choked to death, drowning in their own body fluids.'

Air Pollution

Some industries, such as smelters, steel mills and certain chemical plants, cause air pollution which harms animals and plants and so damages biomes. While industrial air pollution happens in all parts of the world, most of the worst examples happen in Third World countries, where governments are too weak or too poor to insist on high standards of environmental protection.

One of the world's worst examples of industrial air pollution happened in **Bhopal** in India (see Fig. 91.4). Union Carbide, an American-owned multinational company, operated a pesticide factory at Bhopal. The factory failed to make profit and was closed, but huge quantities of deadly chemicals continued to be stored in the abandoned plant.

On the morning of 3 December 1984, an explosion in the Union Carbide plant released a mixture of heavy, poisonous gases into the air. All the safety systems in the factory failed and the gases spread out across the ground, attacking the lungs, eyes and almost every other organ of the human body. Nobody knows how many people died of gas inhalation. Union Carbide estimated 3,800, while local people say that at least 15,000 perished. More people died slowly from poisoning, while up to 50,000 have not worked since then as a result of their injuries. The site of this accident has never been cleaned up properly. The remains of toxins from the explosion are now reported to have entered the soil and water in the area. These toxins kill plants and fish, poison animal and human food chains and so damage the biome.

Victims of Bhopal explosion.

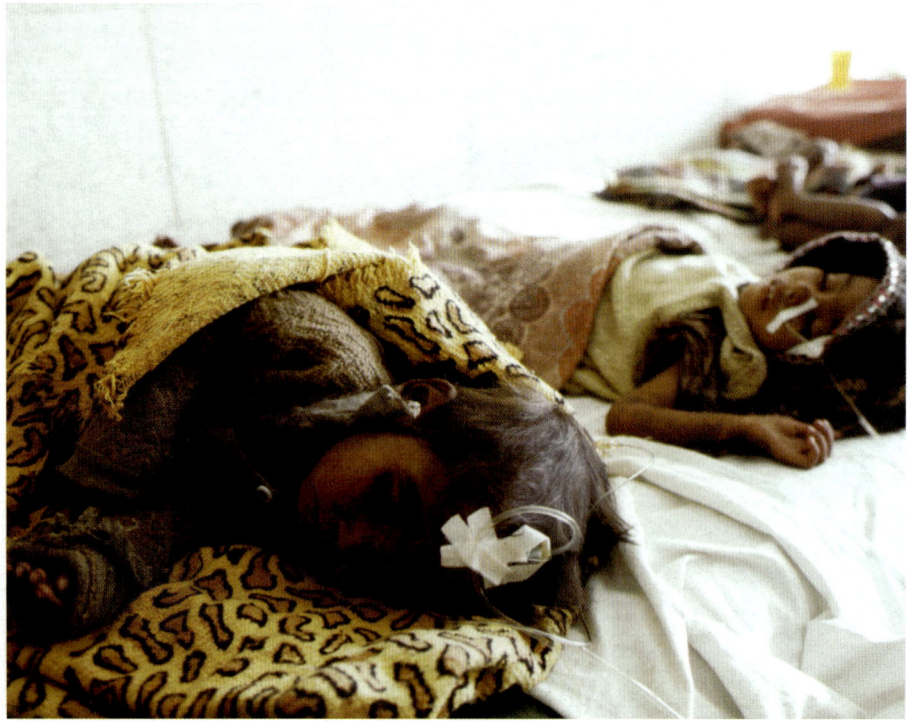

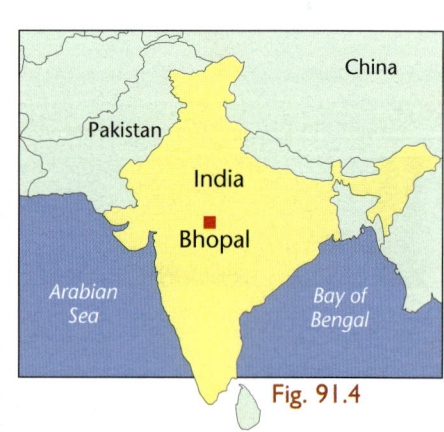

Fig. 91.4

Activity

1. How might an industrial accident like this effect a biome?
2. Why might disasters like this be more likely to happen in Third World countries than in economically developed countries?

Water Pollution

Water bodies, such as rivers and lakes, are important parts of our biomes. The water itself provides habitats for fish and other animals, while nearby land supports waterside creatures such as kingfishers, otters and water-loving plants. Industrial pollution may pollute water and so damage biomes in a number of ways.

Some industrial plants, such as thermal (heat-generating) power stations, use water for cooling purposes. This water becomes heated in the process and may then be released back into the rivers or lakes from which it was taken. **Warm water** does not contain as much oxygen as cool water. Heated water is therefore a pollutant in that it may result in the suffocation of fish or other water creatures.

Poisonous **chemicals**, such as lead, zinc and cyanide, are used in some manufacturing industries and may sometimes seep into rivers, lakes or groundwater. These chemicals are cumulative poisons. They build up gradually in animals until there is enough to kill the animals. Lake Erie in North America (see Fig. 91.5) once became so polluted that it had no animal or plant life at all. The River Cuyahoga, which flows into the lake through the old industrial city of Cleveland, once became so polluted with chemicals that experts feared it might catch fire!

Stricter anti-pollution laws have resulted in reduced industrial pollution of water in developing countries. But some industries still try to cut the costs of dealing safely with waste by illegally **dumping** chemicals when or where they think they will not be caught.

Fig. 91.5 Lake Erie and Cleveland.

See questions 13 and 14 on page 526.

Activity
How could the emission of warm water from this power station affect the biome of the area?

Examination Questions

1. Examine the factors that influence soil characteristics.

2. 'Soils can vary greatly in their make-up and characteristics.' Comment on this statement with reference to some soils that you have studied.

3. With reference to soils that you have studied, discuss the view that soils are affected by a combination of different processes.

4. 'Different soil types predominate in different parts of the world by adapting to local biomes.' Comment on this statement, with particular reference to Ireland's most common soil type.

5. *Examine how human activities can accelerate soil erosion.

6. Examine, with reference to European and non-European examples, the statement that people can conserve as well as destroy soils.

7. *Examine the main characteristics of a biome that you have studied.

8. *Illustrate the development of biomes, with reference to a specific example.

9. Explain how vegetation and animals are related to the physical geography of any biome that you have studied.

10. To what extent has early settlement and the clearing of forests altered biomes in European and non-European regions which you have studied?

11. *Assess the global implications of the continued felling of tropical rainforests.

12. Evaluate the view that intensive agricultural practices have had an impact on biomes in many parts of the world.

13. Describe some worldwide effects of industrial development on biomes.

14. *Assess the impact of human activity on a biome that you have studied.

* Denotes a question that has appeared in a Leaving Certificate examination or sample paper.

CHAPTER 92
FIELDWORK INVESTIGATION

Students should carefully read the guidelines set out in the syllabus for the geographical investigation.

THE GEOGRAPHICAL INVESTIGATION

The geographical investigation is a core area of study, and all students must carry out a fieldwork exercise and write a report on it. Field studies and investigations using primary and secondary sources are a very important part of studying geography. These practical investigations allow you to apply the core geographical skills you have studied and practised through all units of the syllabus. The investigation also encourages you to **experience and question relationships and issues in your own surroundings**.

To carry out the geographical investigation, you have to:

- Devise a strategy for it and **identify aims** and **objectives** to allow an effective investigation of the topic.
- **Select methods of gathering information** that are appropriate to the investigation topic.
- **Use suitable methods for gathering and recording information.**
- Write a report.
- Analyse and interpret results and draw valid conclusions.

Structuring and Organising the Investigation

You choose your investigation topic from a list put together by the Department of Education and Science. You have to complete your investigation by 1 December of Leaving Certificate year two. Although you may work in class groups, for assessment purposes each student must present their own full and complete report. No group projects are accepted.

Higher Level students are expected to write a report of 1,000 words or less. The investigation report must be presented in a reporting booklet provided by the State Examination Commission.

For your investigation you must use at least 60 per cent primary and up to 40 per cent secondary sources of information.

Primary sources give information that comes directly from the time or place that is being studied. These include original photographs, newspaper reports and maps of the time, and old buildings. Secondary sources are ones that may be written after the time period being studied but indirectly give us information about a time or place. These could include parish journals, historical accounts or interviews.

For further examples/information, refer to *Geographical Exploration, Investigating Ireland's Heritage* produced by the Heritage Council and edited by Tony Dunne. Copies have been issued to every school by CDVEC Curriculum Development Unit.

The **geography teacher** and **school principal** will **verify** that the investigation has been carried out by each Leaving Certificate candidate. The Geographical Investigation and Skills core unit allocates 20 per cent of marks at both Higher and Ordinary Level.

The table below shows the different steps of the geographical investigation and how many marks are allocated to each part. The different approaches to geographical skills for Ordinary and Higher Level students are shown in the way marks are allocated for each part of the investigation.

Stage	Activities	Proposed Assessment Weighting	
		Ordinary Level	Higher Level
Introduction: Posing the problems and devising a strategy	• Selecting a topic for investigation • Clear statement of the aim • An outline of the objectives • Identifying the types of information required	5%	5%
Planning and preparing the work to be carried out	• Selecting methods for collecting and gathering information • Designing a questionnaire or recording sheets • Deciding on locations for the investigation	5%	5%
Collecting data	• Using instruments to make measurements • Records of observations made in the field • Using questionnaires and surveys, as appropriate • Using a variety of secondary sources, e.g. documentary sources • Discussing the problems encountered	30%	30%
Preparing the report: Presenting results	• Organising data • Using illustrations, graphs, maps and tables • Using ICT, where appropriate, to prepare and present results and conclusions	40%	40%
Conclusion and evaluation for the report	• Analysis and interpretation of results • Drawing valid conclusions • Comparison of findings with established theory • Evaluation of the hypothesis • Examining the validity of the investigation and suggestions for improvements	20%	20%

FIELDWORK NO. 1

To Examine the Geomorphic Processes of Transportation and Deposition in a Coastal Environment

Use OSi Trailmaster to research and view your fieldwork locations.

The **first** task is to **choose a location** where coastal transportation and deposition is occurring. This location should be easily accessible to the students (access from a road) and it should be a place where activities can be carried out safely. This location should be within a reasonable distance of the school so that all the necessary activities can be carried out while students are fresh and enthusiastic.

The **second** task is to **prepare for this fieldwork** activity so that students understand what exactly they are expected to **observe**, **measure** and **record**. This would include some or all of the following:

- Identifying the objectives of the fieldwork.
- Recap on all coastal processes of transportation and deposition.
- Recap on all features/landforms of coastal deposition.
- Learn and practise all methods of measuring and recording coastal processes of transportation and deposition.
- Recap on all remedial work/interference by people in coastal environments.
- Create simple clinometers from large wooden protractors.
- Gather other instruments from other school departments, such as quadrats, ranging poles, measuring tapes, callipers, stopwatch for timing tasks.
- Creating a fieldwork worksheet for recording.

The **third task** is the fieldwork activity. This should involve the following activities so that the objectives of the fieldwork can be achieved:

- Observing coastal features and processes.
- Drawing sketch maps to identify and label the features/landforms of the coastal environment.
- Carrying out various measurements/calculations/tasks – these tasks should include:
  - finding the slope of the beach
  - measuring longshore drift
  - measuring the sizes of beach material.
- Recording the information from these tasks on a worksheet.

Some Instruments and Tasks to Find Height of Dunes

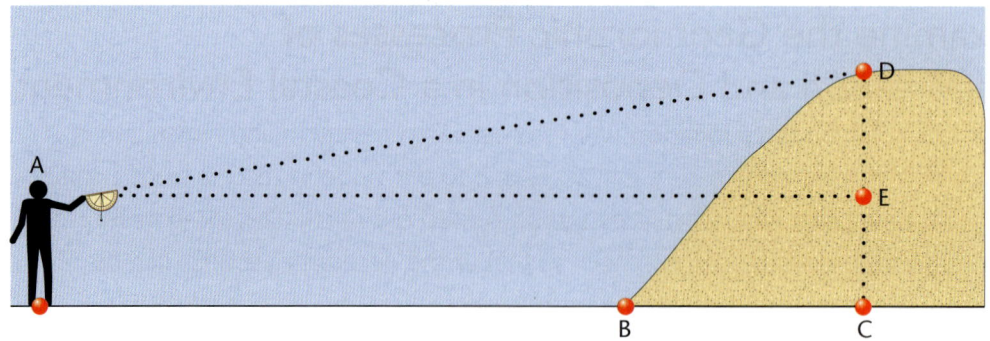

Task: To find height of sand dune

1. Find angle to top of dune.
2. Find length to base of dune. — Combined answers give horizontal distance
3. Estimate length of BC. — to base of sand dune = AC
4. Height of DE = AE x tan DAE
5. Height of dune = DE + height of student (EC)

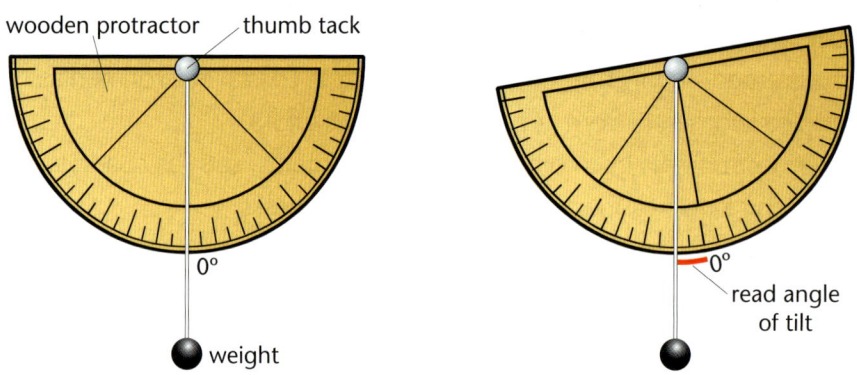

To find beach profile

- Use a clinometer to measure the beach profile.
- Get backsight and foresight for an average reading.

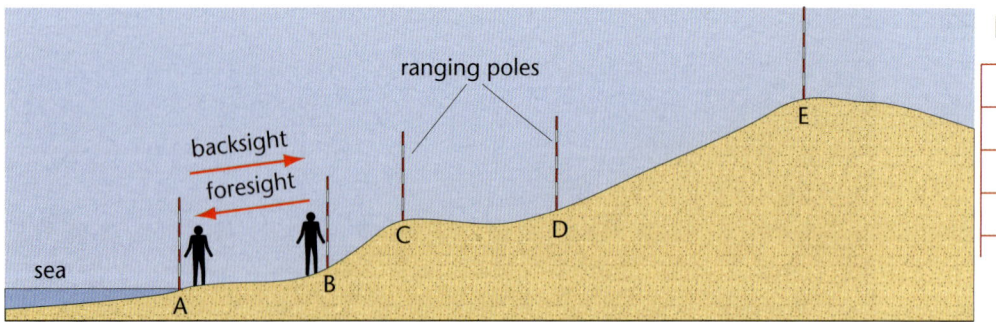

Recording Sheet

	A–B	B–C	
Dist.			
Angle			
Angle	B–A	C–B	

To find rate of longshore drift

This involves two measurements, i.e. time and distance.

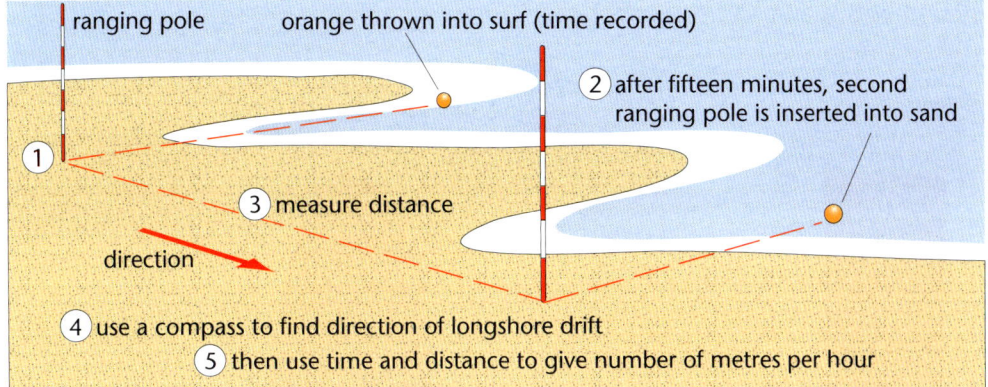

To find size of beach sediment up the beach

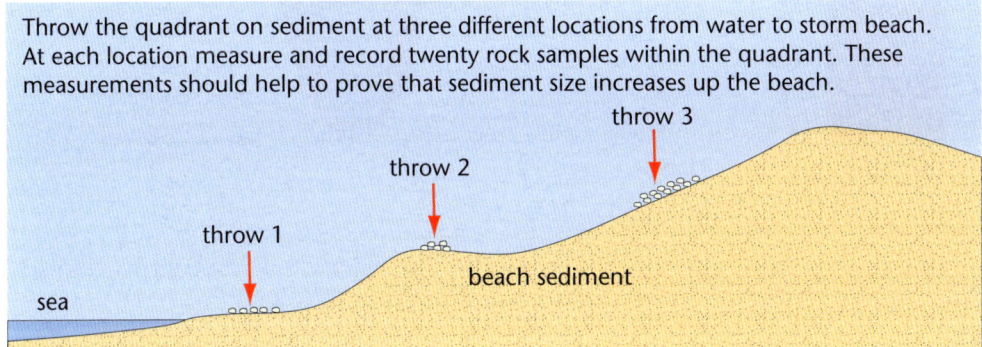

Throw the quadrant on sediment at three different locations from water to storm beach. At each location measure and record twenty rock samples within the quadrant. These measurements should help to prove that sediment size increases up the beach.

Beach Material Analysis
Presenting the Results

- Using graph paper, draw a bar chart to show the average size of the material at the three locations.
- The results can also be presented as a series of coloured circles drawn to a suitable scale.
- Get the average of all pebbles/stones found and draw a graph or chart or both to show these results.

If the type of rock is analysed, a percentage breakdown of rock type can be shown in chart form, e.g. a pie chart. This type of analysis may be justified in the case of proving transportation begins at a particular cliff face.

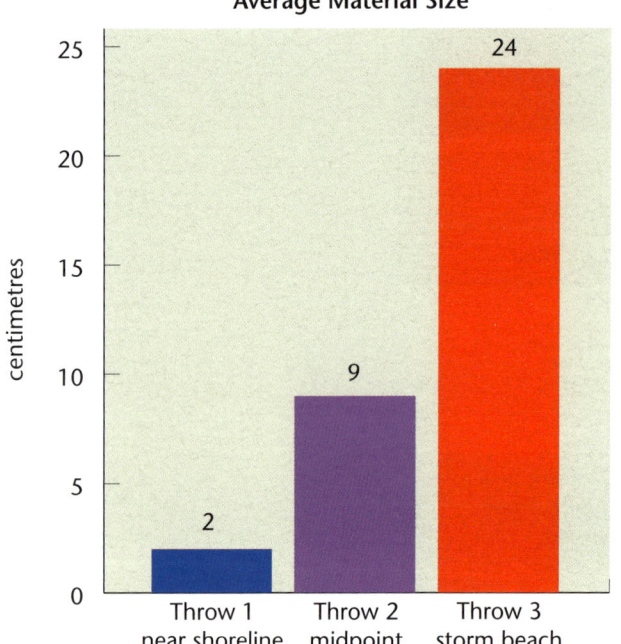

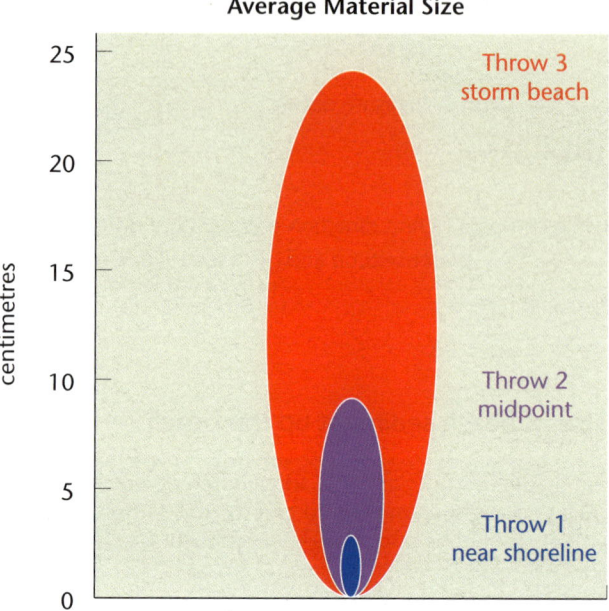

The fourth task is to write a report of the fieldwork. The report should be structured so that each task, result and conclusion should relate to each objective.

You should write up this report in a **booklet** similar to that presented by the Examinations Board. On it, sketch the various instruments and activities/worksheets you used during your fieldwork. This should be corrected and redone again until it is your best effort.

FIELDWORK NO. 2

Tips for a Fieldwork Exercise on River Study

A field study may include either erosion or deposition or both processes. Whichever is the case, a correct approach to the task must be carefully planned.

Aims and Objectives

- To understand the energy of running water and the factors that affect this energy.
- To identify landforms that result from variations in the energy of a river.
- To prove there is a relationship between sediment size, depth and speed of river.
- To prove that sediment shape is affected by transportation.
- To prove that certain features are associated with a particular stage in the course of a river.

When you do a fieldwork exercise, certain information must be gathered and recorded. There are four important points to remember:

- What information is needed and why.
- Where the information will be collected and why.
- How the information will be collected and why.
- When the information will be collected and why.

Make sure that you clearly identify the areas or activities of fieldwork that you take part in or contribute to.

Planning and Preparing for the Fieldwork

1. In class, review information on rivers, river features and river processes.
2. Choose a short section (about 200 m), or sections, of a shallow river suitable for the fieldwork. A shallow stretch of the river **with at least one bend** is usually the best choice for river study. This kind of river allows you to cross from one bank to the opposite side and makes precise measurement of depth, cross-section and pebble size easier.
3. Make copies of a map of the river section 1:2,500.
4. The class should work in groups. Initially:
   - Group A focuses on river bend(s).
   - Group B focuses on transportation by the river.
   - Group C focuses on the speed of river flow.
   - Group D focuses on the volume of river flow.

Remember, each group should carry out all tasks during the day.

With your teacher, make sure that the preparation is followed by co-ordinated activities to check that the fieldwork exercise goes according to plan.

Collecting Data

Group A

This group makes a cross-section of the river. You can practise this by making a simple cross-section of a slope in a grassy area or a slope in a field near the school buildings or schoolyard.

- Use measuring poles, line-levels, tape and cord to carry out this exercise.
- Indicate fast, medium and slow areas of the river by marking wide, medium and thin arrows on 'section line/tape'.
- Choose two points at A and B where there are significant bends in the river and follow through with skills learned in class or in a preliminary activity.

Group B

This group examines the material that the river carries. Bring to school samples of pebbles and stones taken from a riverbed near your home. Examine each sample and explain why they are rounded.

- Focus on cross-section skills and measuring poles, and find the depth of water at various points on the river at the location chosen. (This could be done in parallel to the cross-section line for Group A.)
- Measure and find the average diameter of stones and their minimum and maximum sizes. Use a quadrat to choose random samples.
- Create a chart with the following headings:
  - Section.
  - Depth.
  - Pebble Diameter.
- Create a graph using pebble size and depth to see if there is a relationship between the water depth and pebble size.

Group C

This group aims to identify factors that influence the speed of the river. The exercise can be done in the river at various points in a particular location. This could be a few yards upstream or downstream from the cross-section area of Group A or at a bend or another point.

- Research ways of measuring the speed of flow where the river is:
  - fast
  - slow
  - still.

This can be done using a drain in the schoolyard, a gallon or bucket of water, a cork, a stopwatch and a tape.

- Observe the size of pebbles at various speed locations and see if there is any relationship between speed and pebble size, or the width, speed and pebble size.
- Observe and debate factors, such as riverbed roughness, which might affect the speed of river flow.

Group D

This group aims to measure the cubic flow of water in a river. This can be done by:
- Finding the average depth and width across the river at the three crossing points chosen.
- Choosing the crossing points. Each crossing point should be about 5 m across.

To calculate the cubic flow of water of the river along each section chosen, use the formula:

volume = speed (metres/second) x depth x width.

All Groups

All groups should make photocopies of a map of the river from a 1:2,500 OS sheet.

- Mark each area being studied on the core map. (Your teacher may explain and practise map orientation with you.)
- Draw a sketch map of the river section. Use a viewfinder (with nine dimensions, as on a photograph).
- Note the direction of flow.
- Take photographs of the sections of the river needed for each group.
- Use a school video recorder, if available, to record the activities.

Results

- Each group should record their findings carefully on charts. A student can give a brief description of each fieldwork activity on site once each group has completed its work. This is to make sure that each group is aware of each other's work and its relevance for the fieldwork activity.
- Each group records and presents its findings so that results and conclusions can be drawn from the information gathered.

Conclusion and Evaluation

Each student should write a report that includes:

- Relevant and logical conclusions from the material gathered.
- Identify reasons for any changes in surveying methods.
- Identify skills you have learned.
- Identify areas that could be improved when carrying out a similar survey and fieldwork.

INDEX

PICTURE CREDITS

For permission to reproduce photographs the author and publisher gratefully acknowledge the following:

ALAMY: 13, 16B, 21T, 37, 48, 49, 57T, 58T, 59, 61B, 62T, 62B, 63, 70B, 71CB, 73, 75, 76, 81, 85B, 88, 99T, 100, 101, 102, 103, 104, 105, 107, 126B, 124T, 124B, 125, 127, 134R, 136, 141T, 156, 157, 160, 169, 174R, 176, 183, 188, 189, 190R, 191, 200, 201T, 206B, 222B, 226C, 231, 236T, 254T, 279B, 288T, 289, 292, 300L, 302, 304T, 307, 309, 310R, 310C, 311T, 311B, 313T, 323, 324B, 325, 326B, 328B, 336B, 339L, 340R, 341L, 346, 347TR, 347B, 348, 349, 351, 354, 355, 360C, 360T, 360B, 361, 367B, 372, 373BR, 375T, 376R, 378, 379B, 384, 385T, 387L, 389L, 389TR, 389BR, 394T, 394B, 396B, 402B, 407TR, 407L, 409T, 409C, 410BL, 411a, 411c, 411d, 411e, 411f, 411g, 411j, 411k, 411l, 411m, 411n, 411o, 412, 413T, 413BR, 413BC, 416B, 417TC, 417BC, 418, 419, 422T, 422B, 430T, 431, 432, 433T, 434B, 436, 438L, 439C, 444B, 450T, 454T, 454BL, 455B, 461, 462L, 469, 470C, 470B, 473B, 480T, 481R, 484L, 484R, 487R, 498, 509, 511B, 517, 518, 521T, 521B; BALLYMUN REGENERATION 386B; CORBIS: 19 © Karen Kasmauski, 20C © epa/Proteccion Civil de Colima, 20T © Roger Ressmeyer, 27T © Michael St Maur Sheil, 33 © Reuters, 34 © epa, 35T © David Smith/Sygma, 35B © Reuters/Yannis Behrakis, 43C © Bill Ross, 43B © M. Angelo, 44T © Patrick Durand/Sygma, 67R, 116T © Corbis, 68B © Vince Streano, 71T © Corbis Sygma, 80 © Wolfgang Kaehler, 83 © Tom Bean, 121T © Les Stone/Sygma, 138, 197, 234B, 371, 423T, 423B © Yann Arthus-Bertrand, 145 © Adam Woolfitt, 171 © George McCarthy, 193T © Sandro Vannini, 199 © Ted Spiegel, 202 © Patrice Latron, 234T © Abel Alonso/epa, 236C © Bogdan Croitoru/epa, 314 © Reuters/Anton Meres, 321TC © Robert Patrick/Sygma, 321TR © epa/Jon Hrusa, 321B © Jean-Michel Turpin, 338 © Bob Krist, 344 © felix Zaska, 377T © David Turnley, 430B © Dung Vo Trung/Sygma, 468T © Anthony Cassidy/JAI, 478T © Regis Bossu/Sygma, 478B © Hulton-Deutsch Collection, 479T © Svenja-Foto/zefa; DERFK SPEIRS 180T; DEPT OF COMMUNICATIONS, MARINE & NATURAL RESOURCES/ECOPRO CODE OF PRACTICE 126T; DEPT OF THE ENVIRONMENT, HERITAGE AND LOCAL GOVERNMENT 340L; DIGITAL PHOTO LIBRARY OF THE REGIONAL POLICY DIRECTORATE-GENERAL OF THE EUROPEAN COMMISSION 158; EC/ECHO SOUTH ASIA OFFICE 36; ECOSCENE: 490 © Peter Hulme, 514B © Andrew Brown, 521C © Frank Blackburn; EMPICS: 20B, 21C, 60, 147, 316B, 321TL, 420TL, 420R, 451, 452L, 464L, 470T, 473T; FINBARR O'CONNELL: 163, 164, 179, 373T; FLPA: 487C © Bob Gibbons, 492C © David Hosking, 492B © Terry Whittaker; GEOLOGICAL SURVEY OF IRELAND 69; GETTY: 524 © Getty, 447T © Hulton; HARALD FINSTER 161; IMAGEFILE: 16C, 26T, 28, 43T, 43B, 44C, 44B, 45, 53, 55T, 55B, 57C, 61T, 74, 78B, 85T, 85C, 89, 99C, 99B, 121B, 123, 126C, 130B, 146C, 146R, 150C, 152, 153, 165, 166, 167R, 177, 190L, 193B, 195, 203, 204, 206T, 212, 216R, 222T, 226B, 227T, 238, 254B, 287, 296, 319, 336T, 336C, 352, 369T, 369C, 382, 399, 401, 406, 407BR, 408, 410BR, 410TR, 411b, 411h, 411p, 128, 429T, 433B, 438R, 440, 445, 460, 464R, 476T, 479B, 480B, 481L, 481CL, 481CR, 482C, 487L, 488, 491, 496, 501, 507, 508, 510T, 512, 513, 514T, 516, 519, 522R, 522L, 523, 525; INPHO: 141B, 417B, 453T, 453B, 457; IRISH EXAMINER 239; IRISH IMAGE COLLECTION: 134L, 146L, 174L, 182; IRISH PICTURE LIBRARY: 310L, 447B © Fr Browne SJ Collection; IRISH TIMES: 151, 328T, 373BL, 375BL, 375BR, 376L, 395B, 397B, 458, 462R; KEVIN DWYER: 268R, 269, 330; LENSMEN 395T; LIMERICK CITY COUNCIL 142; LONELY PLANET IMAGES: 58B, 335 © Eoin Clarke, 326T, 347TL © Richard Cummins, 334 © Oliver Strewe, 341R © Denis O'Byrne,